chinese politics

The Sino-American-German Documentary
Project on Mainland China

<u>General Editors</u>

Jürgen Domes

Bih-jaw Lin

James T. Myers

With the Support of

Institute of International Relations, Taipei
Institute of International Studies, University of South Carolina
Research Unit on Chinese and East Asian Politics,
The Saar University

Volume One: Cultural Revolution to the Ninth Party Congress (1969)

Volume Two: Ninth Party Congress (1969) to the Death of Mao (1976)

Volume Three: Death of Mao (1976) to the Fall of Hua Kuo-feng (1980)

Volume Four: Fall of Hua Kuo-feng (1980) to the Twelfth Party Congress (1982)

chinese politics

Documents and Analysis

VOLUME FOUR:

Fall of Hua Kuo-Feng (1980)
to the Twelfth Party Congress (1982)

EDITED BY

James T. Myers

Jürgen Domes

Milton D. Yeh

With the Assistance of
Hung-yi Jan

UNIVERSITY OF SOUTH CAROLINA PRESS

Copyright © University of South Carolina Press 1995

Published in Columbia, South Carolina, by the
University of South Carolina Press

Manufactured in the United States of America

Library of Congress Cataloging-in-Publication Data
(revised for vol. 3)

Chinese politics : documents and analysis.

  (Sino-American-German Documentary Project on
Mainland China)
  Vol. 2 edited by James T. Myers, Jürgen Domes,
Milton D. Yeh, with a contribution by Eberhard
Sandschneider; vol. 3 edited by James T. Myers, Jürgen
Domes, Milton D. Yeh, with assistance of Linjun Wu.
  Includes bibliographies and indexes.
  Contents: v. 1 Cultural revolution to
1969 — v. 2. Ninth Party Congress (1969) to the death
of Mao (1976) — v. 3. The death of Mao (1976) to the
fall of Hua Kuo-Feng (1980)
  1. China—Politics and government—1949-Sources.

I. Myers, James T. II. Domes, Jürgen. III. Groeling,
Erik von. IV. Series : Sino-American-German Documentary
Project on Mainland China.
DS777.547.C47 1986   951.05   85–22466
ISBN 0–87249–475–6 (v. 1)
ISBN 0–87249–601–5 (v. 2)
ISBN 1–57003–062–6 (v. 3)
ISBN 1–57003–063–4 (v. 4)

FOREWORD

Two historic events have recently taken place that radically changed the status of communism in the world. One was the reunification of Germany in 1990, and the other was the disintegration of the Soviet Union the following year. These two events horrified the leaders of the People's Republic of China and made the Peking regime a focus of attention on the international stage. In these circumstances, a work like *Chinese Politics: Documents and Analysis*, which is a veritable treasure-trove of research material, takes on a new significance.

Volume 4, like its predecessors, is the result of a joint effort by scholars attached to three distinguished research institutions in three different countries--the United States, the Federal Republic of Germany, and the Republic of China on Taiwan. Professor James T. Myers and Jürgen Domes, and Dr. Milton Yeh have done a splendid job in editing this volume, as have the research teams at the three institutions concerned who shared the work of selecting and translating the material. Almost all the editing and final manuscript preparation were carried out at the University of South Carolina in close collaboration with the USC Press.

As director of the Institute of International Relations in Taipei, I am delighted to have an opportunity to introduce this four volume to emerge from the Sino-American-German Documentary Project on Mainland China. The Project has made an immense contribution to research on contemporary mainland China, and it has been a privilege for me to have been associated with such a distinguished team of scholars.

Bih-jaw Lin
Director
The Institute of International Relations
Taipei

EDITOR'S PREFACE

Volumes Three and Four of the Sino-American-German Documentary Project on Mainland China continue the cooperative effort between the University of South Carolina, the Institute of International Relations in Taipei, and the Saar University in Germany.

These two volumes were originally intended to be published as Volume Three of the series. During the course of the collection, analysis and editing of the documents, however, the size of the manuscript grew to such a size that the editors together with the University of South Carolina Press decided to publish the work in two volumes. The original "General Introduction" for Volume Three is thus reproduced as the introduction to both Volumes Three and Four.

As with the previous volumes, the romanization of Chinese names continues to present a problem. My two co-editors and their home institutions, along with many other scholars in the field, prefer the Wade-Giles system of romanization. On the other hand, documents in English issuing from the People's Republic of China during the period covered by these volumes have used the *Pinyin* system of romanization almost exclusively.

We have not solved the difficulties of mixing these two systems of romanizing Chinese sounds, but we have decided to handle the problem in the same manner as in previous volumes. We will maintain the Wade-Giles system of romanization as our preferred system. Everything in the present volume generated by the editors themselves whether by way of analysis or translation from the original Chinese, will rely on Wade-Giles. In those cases where an English translation of a document comes from another source such as the *New China News Agency* or the *Foreign Broadcast Information Service*, we will use the form of romanization contained in the translation. All major *pinyin* entries in the index are cross-listed in Wade-Giles.

As before, many people have given their time and talents to the preparation of these volumes. I owe my usual deep debt of gratitude to my co-editors Professor Jürgen Domes and Dr. Milton D. Yeh for their support, cooperation and wise counsel over the years. We have received substantial support from the Institute of International Relations in Taipei and I am personally indebted to former Director Bih-jaw Lin for many kindnesses large and small. We continue to receive support from the Institute of International Studies at the University of South Carolina and from the University administration for which I wish to express my thanks.

This project could not have been completed without the dedicated assistance of Dr. Linjun Wu who was my faithful graduate assistant for several years and who has now returned to her post at the Institute of International Relations in Taipei. A similar acknowledgement and expression of thanks is due to Mr. Hung-yi Jan who printed all of the many version of these two volumes and whose name appears on the title page of Volume Four.

Finally, I want to take the opportunity as preface writer once again to acknowledge the loving support of my dear wife Christina. She is ever and always my joy and my blessing.

James T. Myers
Director
The Center for Asian Studies
University of South Carolina

CONTENTS

DOCUMENTS

CHAPTER THREE

DOCUMENTS

CHAPTER FOUR

DOCUMENTS

CHAPTER FIVE

DOCUMENTS

chinese politics

GENERAL INTRODUCTION

by

Jürgen Domes and James T. Myers

The Coup d'Etat of October 6, 1976

The anti-Maoist mass movement of the spring and summer of 1976, the second purge of Teng Hsiao-p'ing [see *Volume Two*] and the death of five of the ten leading members of the inner core of the Chinese Communist Party (CCP), created the conditions for a critical struggle within the elite, which emerged almost immediately after the death of Mao Tse-tung in October 1976. Seven more or less distinct groups or factions could be identified in the course of this struggle:

1. Veteran civilian cadres who had survived the Cultural Revolution in office, the so-called "survival cadres";

2. Veteran civilian cadres who had been rehabilitated after being purged during the Cultural Revolution, the so-called "rehabilitated cadres";

3. The Cultural Revolutionary Left as the hard core of the left wing of the CCP;

4. The Mass Organization Left, consisting of a group of cadres, mostly "model peasants," "labour heroes," or staff from the party's basic

organizations who owed their rise in position to the Cultural Revolution;

5. The Secret Police Left composed of cadres of the Cultural Revolution who in the early Seventies had come to the top of the security establishment;

6. The central military apparatus;

7. The regional military leaders, a strongly fluctuating group whose political preferences were not easy to distinguish.

Even in the last three years before Mao's death, the coalitions and confrontations among these groups tended to focus on the question of succession to the office of the party leader.

Some urged that Chou En-lai should seize leadership or, in the case of Chou's illness and death, leadership might be assumed by Teng Hsiao-p'ing, who had become Premier Chou's closest assistant. Others advocated that the succession should be assumed by a leader of the Maoist Left.

Between the Cultural Revolutionary Left and the Mass Organization Left on the one hand, and the two military groups on the other, further political-power disagreements had developed about the question whether the newly formed urban militia should be an independent force or should be supervised by the People's Liberation Army (PLA).

In addition to these political-power conflicts, policy disputes emerged which intensified the intra-elite fragmentation.

Major policy disputes had emerged in five broad areas:

1. **Science and technology policy** - The Left emphasized that China should "rely on its own power." Civilian cadres and a great number of military leaders, on the other hand, urged the comprehensive importation of western technology.

2. **Educational policy** - The Left fought for the priority of political indoctrination over the teaching of factual knowledge. The Left further argued for combined work-study curricula as well as for open admission of politically reliable applicants to secondary and high schools. In opposition to this policy there were the rehabilitated cadres who stressed the teaching of factual

knowledge, strictly regularized instruction and the re-introduction of entrance examinations.

3. **Cultural policy** - The Left attempted to uphold the monopoly "revolutionary romanticism" which had been promoted by Mao's wife Chiang Ch'ing during the Cultural Revolution.

Both groups of veteran cadres, supported by some though not all of the regional military leaders, tended to favor a widening of the parameters of competition between different cultural styles. Above all, they favored a more positive attitude towards China's cultural heritage.

4. **Industrial wage policy** - The Left demanded the replacement of material incentives by equal wages for all workers. The veteran cadres, in particular, wanted to continue and, if possible, to expand, a highly differentiated, incentive-oriented wage system.

5. **Rural social policy** - The Left once again wanted to raise the level of agricultural collectivization by giving more power to the brigades and communes at the expenses of the smaller production teams, to reduce the size of private plots, and to restrict the peasants' private sideline occupations. Most of the regional military leaders, supported by the rehabilitated civilian cadres, wanted to preserve or even to expand the private plots, private animal breeding, and other individual activities of the peasants.

In the end, all of these power and policy disagreements came down to the same fundamental question which had dominated the crisis of the Cultural Revolution: should class struggle, development through mobilization and "permanent revolution" dominate, or should organizational stability, growth-oriented development, and modernization through technology have priority in the future of the People's Republic of China (PRC)? In other words, should the country follow Mao's prescripts of the Great Leap and the Cultural Revolution, or should development be pursued through the types of policies devised by Liu Shao-ch'i and Teng Hsiao-p'ing during the period of readjustment after the failure of the Great Leap and resumed by Chou En-lai after the fall of Lin Piao in 1971.

During the course of the intra-elite discussions which had begun around autumn 1975, two coalitions developed among the groupings within the elite which quickly formed themselves into factions. On the one hand, there were the Cultural Revolutionary Left, the Mass Organization Left and the Secret Police Left which merged together. Let us call them the United Left. This faction was opposed by the two groups of the civilian veteran cadres together with the representatives of the central military machine and the majority of the regional military leaders. We may call this faction the Military-Bureaucratic Complex. Immediately after Mao's death, the contrasts between these two factions intensified.

In the Politburo of the CCP, the Military-Bureaucratic Complex was represented by six full members and one candidate or alternate member. Eight full members of the Politburo and two candidate members stood for the United Left, while the positions of one or two full members and one candidate remained uncertain. In mid September, however, the United Left broke apart. Hua Kuo-feng and the other two representatives of the Secret Police Left changed sides thus giving the Military-Bureaucratic Complex a majority in a new coalition.

Hua Kuo-feng, who had risen rapidly from the lower and middle levels of the civil party machine and the security system, had long since proved himself to be an opportunist with a sober sense for the gravitation of power and a considerable degree of flexibility in questions of principle. The reluctance of most of the provincial party leaders and regional military leaders towards Chiang Chi'ing's new "Anti-Right Campaign" in the summer of 1976 apparently convinced Hua that the climate for a policy of development through mass mobililization was not at all favorable. Very soon after the earthquake disaster at T'angshan on July 28, 1976, Hua began to break away from the Maoists of the United Left by demonstratively seeking the company of military and veteran cadres and by avoiding the Cultural Revolutionary Left.[1]

It seems that, some time in the second half of September 1976, Hua made an agreement with the Military-Bureaucratic Complex: he would approve a purging of the cultural-revolutionary Left and a gradual retreat from the cultural-revolutionary program of late Maoism if the Complex would support his candidacy as Mao's successor. In the last days of September 1976 the communication between the members of the inner leading circle broke down. Chiang Ch'ing and her associates of the Cultural Revolutionary Left stridently called for a new purge of "capitalist-roaders," and for "all supporters of Chairman Mao's proletarian revolutionary line" to "heighten their vigilance".[2] This, however, was to be the last public statement made by the Cultural Revolutionary Left.

On the evening of October 6th, 1976, soldiers under the leadership of Marshal Yeh Chien-ying and General Wang Tung-hsing arrested the whole leadership core of the Cultural Revolutionary Left: Chiang Ch'ing, Wang Hung-wen, Chang Ch'un-ch'iao, and Yao Wen-Yuan, henceforth to be known as the "Gang of Four." The Peking Workers' Militia did nothing to help Chiang Ch'ing's group with the exception of a few skirmishes on the part of some of its units with PLA troops. The leader of the Workers' Militia, Politburo alternate Ni Chih-fu, had changed sides at the last moment and joined the Military-Bureaucratic Complex. In the city of Shenyang, Mao's nephew, Mao Yuan-hsin, was arrested and thus his attempt of a local coup failed.

In the two days following the Peking coup d'etat, a critical situation developed in Shanghai, the most important leftist stronghold. A short time before, in the first days of October, General Hsu Shih-yu had come from Canton to Nanking and had temporarily taken over the command over the Nanking military district, a position he had previously held from 1954 to 1973.

During the night of October 6 - 7, General Hsu's troops entered the city of Shanghai. During the following days, they disarmed the Shanghai workers' militia with considerable bloodshed. Most of the members of the Shanghai Municipal Committee of the CCP were arrested. The leaders of the coup d'etat had thus won a swift and complete victory, but it was still more than two weeks until the results of the victory would be officially announced to the Chinese people.

At a mass rally on T'ienanmen Square in Peking on October 23, Hua Kuo-feng was proclaimed Chairman of the Central Committee of the CCP and of the Central Committee's Military Commission. More than half of the rally participants were soldiers. Hua himself appeared in military uniform, indicating that the PLA had been the decisive factor in the crisis.

The major address at the rally was given by Wu Te, First Secretary of the Peking Municipal Committee of the CCP. Wu's fierce attacks on the Cultural Revolutionary Left were combined with the promise: "We shall continue to criticize Teng."[3] Only two of the ten members of the Politburo's Standing Committee now remained in office: Hua Kuo-feng and Yeh Chien-ying.

Apart from these two, a civilian cadre, Li Hsien-nien, the long-time Minister of Finance who had survived the Cultural Revolution in office, was gaining influence. Including these three party leaders, only twelve out of the twenty-two full members of the Politburo remained in their positions. Seven of them could be considered representatives of the Military-Bureaucratic Complex, while five others were representatives of the Secret Police and Mass

Organization Left who had previously belonged to the United Left, but who had changed sides during the crisis.

The Cultural Revolutionary Left was now removed from the political scene of the PRC. Also temporarily removed from this scene was Teng Hsiao-p'ing. In a spa near Canton, he was waiting for further developments.

Maoism without Mao

Due to its quick and efficient action on October 6, 1976, the new leadership eliminated the inner core of the Cultural Revolutionary Left and destroyed its organizational strongholds. However, the new leaders could not yet be sure of their undisputed control over the entire country. While the ruling elite was involved in power and policy conflicts, the party was losing its influence on China. This trend had been increasingly evident since the April crisis of 1976 which had been marked by the mass demonstrations in T'iananmen Square and the second ouster of Teng Hsiao-p'ing [see *Volume Two*].

Work discipline slackened and a growing number of citizens refused to obey the orders given by the cadres. The cadres themselves, in fact, were no longer sure about the course of policy that the leadership was going to take. They therefore tried to "please the masses" by sluggishly executing orders from the upper levels. Strikes, workers unrest and sabotage of railroad traffic continued and in some cases increased. In some regions the factional struggle escalated to armed struggle.

Between November 1976 and June 1977 the media reported open attacks on CCP offices and PLA barracks, as well as street fights and organized resistance in seventeen administrative units. In 1980 a leading CCP cadre estimated the number of deaths attributable to the unrest in the winter of 1976-77 at 45,000 to 50.000.[4]

In order to consolidate its power, the new leadership turned to restrictive measures supported by the PLA and the security system. More and more "criminal elements" and saboteurs were reported to have been publicly executed. In August 1978, for example, a report released by Amnesty International documented thirty-eight executions of "counterrevolutionary and bad elements" between November 1976 and February 1978.[5] Such an uncompromising repression of unrest soon began to show the desired effects. During the first half of 1977 the unrest was dramatically reduced, and by early summer order was restored again in most of the country.

The efforts taken toward consolidation were supported by changes within the leadership personnel as well. Between October 1976 and July 1977 the leading core appointed new provincial party leaders in thirteen of the 29 administrative units. Nine of those leaders were rehabilitated cadres who had been purged during the Cultural Revolution and four had survived the Cultural Revolution in office. A number of new appointments strengthened the group of rehabilitated cadres also in the central PLA organs. However, significant changes in national policy introduced by the Hua - Yeh - Li - triumvirate [Hua Kuo-feng, Yeh Chien-ying, Li Hsien-nien] were still quite limited.

In the area of wage policies, the highly differentiated pay scale was definitely reconfirmed, and the egalitarian attempts of late Maoism disappeared. In education, final examinations were re-introduced to colleges and secondary schools, and access to universities was restricted through strict entrance examinations. In the field of culture, Chiang Ch'ing's revolutionary model operas and "revolutionary romantic" piano concerts were no longer performed. They were replaced by similar works, some of which particularly praised the memory of Chou En-lai. Others honored Hua Kuo-feng, who was now called "the wise leader." Traditional puppet theaters and ballet operas started to be performed again in December 1976, whereas the classical Peking court opera did not reappear until 1978. In February 1977 Beethoven, Mozart and Bach were rehabilitated and by the summer of that year, translations of nineteenth century Russian and Western literature - considered decadent only a year before - could again be bought in bookstores. Thus, the parameters of cultural activities were gradually widening.

Hua Kuo-feng and his supporters of the Secret Police and the Mass Organization Left, however, were determined to save as much as possible of Mao Tse-tung's heritage. In this attempt, they were partially supported by Yeh Chien-ying and Li Hsien-nien, who feared that a fundamental revision of Maoist policy could destabilize the political system. For Hua himself, a continuation of Maoism was necessary since he claimed to have received his legitimization as Mao's successor through Mao himself.

Hua's attempt to preserve as much as possible of Mao's concepts began in the area of agricultural and rural societal policies, where the new party leader could claim a certain expertise. In December 1976 the Second National Conference on Learning from Tachai in Agriculture convened in Peking. In his final address to the conference Hua called for an increase in the level of collectivization in the communes. At the expense of the smaller production teams, Hua advocated that the powers of the communes and production brigades should be gradually increased in order to "prepare, step by step, the transition to communism."[6]

On March 1, 1977, the fifth volume of the *Selected Works of Mao Tse-tung* was published. On the occasion of its publication the CCP media again celebrated Mao's "Great Theory of Continuing The Revolution Under The Leadership of The Proletariat." Three weeks earlier, on February 7, the group around Hua had already stated their program of continuing Maoism without Mao. In a joint editorial of the three central publications of the Party and Army they proclaimed: "Whatever policy Chairman Mao formulated we shall all resolutely defend, whatever instructions Chairman Mao gave we shall all steadfastly abide by".[7] In the intra-elite conflict that began to unfold one year later this statement was to provide the pejorative name for the group around Hua. By its opponents the group was referred to as the "whatever faction." With Teng Hsiao-p'ing's second comeback to national political life, a new intra-elite conflict was inevitable.

During the first six weeks after Hua's proclamation as party leader on October 23, 1976, the media occasionally repeated Wu Te's promise to continue the criticism of Teng. Soon, however, the promise was forgotten. On January 4, 1977, a commentary of the provincial radio in Hunan asked for a criticism of Teng for the last time.[8] In January and February, wall posters calling for Teng's rehabilitation appeared in Peking. In a joint letter to the Party center, General Hsu Shih-yu and General Wei Kuo-ch'ing, First Secretary of the Kuangtung Provincial Committee of the CCP, also demanded the rehabilitation of Teng Hsiao-p'ing. Otherwise, the writers threatened, Hua's legitimacy as party leader would be called into question.[9]

Apparently the venture was also joined by seven or eight provincial party leaders.[10] Thus the central leadership of the party had to face the possibility of an open conflict if nothing was done to rehabilitate Teng. The pressure exposed on Hua at an enlarged meeting of the Politburo from March 10 to 23, finally drove him to agree to Teng's rehabilitation. A short time later, Teng left his hideaway in Canton and returned to Peking.

One problem, however, still remained to be solved: Hua and his close associates insisted that Teng had to write a statement of self-criticism before he could be admitted to leadership again. Teng, however, refused to write such a statement. At a Politburo meeting in May a compromise was finally reached: Teng agreed to write a letter to the Central Committee which would not mention any self-criticism but which would fully recognize Hua as party leader. The statement was to be followed by Teng's rehabilitation. The

Third Plenum of the 10 CCP Central Committee, meeting from July 16 - 21, 1977, affirmed the arrangement by putting Teng third in the hierarchy of the party leadership behind Hua and Yeh Chien-ying but ahead of Li Hsien-nien.[11]

Teng's rehabilitation now gave way to the Eleventh Party Congress of the CCP, whose 1510 delegates met in Peking from August 12 - 18, 1977.[12] The Party Congress was clearly dominated by Teng, Marshal Yeh Chien-ying and Hua Kuo-feng, whose opening address lasted for seven hours. In his speech Hua honored Mao in hymn-like praise, mentioning him 178 times. Hua then declared: "With the smashing of the Gang of Four" our country's first Great Proletarian Revolution, which lasted for eleven years, is herewith pronounced as victoriously completed!"[13] Thus, ironically, the Cultural Revolution had gained its "victory" through the arrest of its initiators and with the triumphant return of one of its main opponents: Teng Hsiao-p'ing.

In fact, what Hua's proclamation really indicated was that the Military-Bureaucratic Complex of veteran cadres, military leaders and the security establishment had asserted itself in the aftermath of Mao's death. The triumph of the Military-Bureaucratic Complex was confirmed by the composition of the CCP Eleventh Central Committee (CC). A total of 35.4 percent of the members of the Tenth CC did not re-appear in the Eleventh CC. Broken down, this figure represented 17.8 percent of the civilian cadres, 29.6 percent of the military, and a huge 76.5 per cent of the mass-organization representatives. 19.1 per cent of those members of the Tenth CC who had joined the Party before 1935 did not reappear in the Eleventh CC as opposed to 71.9 percent of those who had become party members after 1949. The share of mass organization representatives among the full members of the CC decreased from 17.9 to 11.2 per cent. Hence, the purge of the cultural revolutionary Left mainly affected the CC members with low Party seniority and those who had come from the mass organizations. That the new CC was more cadre-oriented, was also indicated by the fact that the share of seats going to PLA representatives decreased from 37.5 to 32.4 percent.

Above all, the leadership group had become older than its predecessor: at the time of its appointment the eleventh CC showed an average age of 64.6 years in contrast to the average of 62.1 years for the tenth CC. Five politicians were appointed to the Standing Committee of the Politburo:

> **Hua Kuo-feng** (fifty-six), representing those cadres who had supported Mao during the Cultural Revolution;

Marshal Yeh Chien-ying (eighty), representing the central military machine;

Teng Hsiao-p'ing (seventy-three), representing the rehabilitated cadres;

Li Hsien-nien (seventy-two), representing those cadres who had survived the Cultural Revolution in office;

General Wang Tung-hsing (sixty-one), representing the Secret Police Left.

Of twenty-three full members and three alternates of the new Politburo, twelve full members and two alternates had survived the Cultural Revolution in office. Six full members had advanced in their careers as a result of the Cultural Revolution, and five members and one alternate belonged to the group which had been purged.

Teng Hsiao-p'ing could firmly rely on only nine votes of the Politburo (including his own), while Hua Kuo-feng had the support of seven votes. The balance was thus held by the seven Politburo members who tended to follow the lead of Yeh Chien-ying and Li Hsien-nien. As long as Yeh and Li supported Hua, he would be able to maintain his leadership of the CCP. Teng was not yet ready to assert himself against Mao's successor.

With the conclusion of the Eleventh Party Congress, the leadership of the CCP was once again restored. Now the leading positions of the state administrative machine had to be filled. This process was undertaken at the first session of the Fifth National People's Congress (NPC), meeting in Peking from February 26 to March 5, 1978. The Congress ratified the decisions made on the Second Plenum of the Eleventh CC, which had met the previous month from February 18 to 23. As Chairman of the Standing Committee of the NPC, Marshal Yeh Chien-ying, the previous Minister of Defence, had now become ceremonial chief of state. Out of the 196 members of the NPC Standing Committee 154 or 78.6 percent were members of the CCP; 25 belonged to the non-Communist united front parties; 17 were regarded as independent. Hua Kuo-feng was confirmed as Prime Minister of the State Council. Teng Hsiao-p'ing remained in his position as first Vice-Premier. The fourteen members of the inner cabinet - Prime Minister and thirteen Vice-Premiers - included three whose career had been advanced by the Cultural Revolution, seven who had survived it in office and four who had been purged.

The situation among all of the 45 members of the State Council, however, was different from that in the inner cabinet. That group consisted of 23 members who had been purged and of 18 members who had survived the Cultural Revolution in office. There were only four members of the State Council whose careers had been advanced by the Cultural Revolution. With 22 to 24 members aligned with Teng Hsiao-p'ing, he could count on the support of nearly half of the 45 members of the State Council. Yeh Chien-ying and Li Hsien-nien could rely on the support of 17 to 19 members, while Hua Kuo-feng could rely on the support of only four.

Apart from passing the third Constitution of the PRC to be promulgated within a period of 24 years (a constitution which retained its validity for only five years)[14] the Congress was characterized by fundamental decisions concerning China's political development. In a six-hour speech on February 26, 1978, Hua Kuo-feng presented these decisions as a report of the State Council with the title: "Unite and fight for the building of a modern, powerful socialist country."[15] Under the heading of the "Four Modernizations" he called for extensive efforts in order to transform the PRC into a "modern, socialist, industrial superpower" by the year 2000. In order to achieve this aim, Hua presented a ten-year plan for the years from 1976 to 1985. During this period agriculture was to become mechanized up to 85 percent. The average annual output of the agricultural sector was expected to increase by four to five per cent, and the industrial output to increase by ten percent.

As an example for the intended push of modernization, Hua held up the old Maoist model of the agricultural production brigade at Tachai and, as an industrial model to be emulated, the oil fields of Tach'ing [see *Volume Two*]. Hua expressed his hope that by 1980 a third of all industrial companies and administrative districts in China would have become Tach'ing-type districts. Thus Mao's successor had basically called for a new "Great Leap Forward," which this time, however, was intended to be supported by the extensive importation of technology from Japan, the United States and Western Europe. In principle, the new policy line of the Hua Kuo-feng group was intended to follow Mao's old concepts with, however, the allowance for several revisions. One type of revision followed the example given by the USSR under Stalin in the 1930s, while another relied on the developmental strategies that had already been on the Chinese policy in the early and mid-1950s.

Teng Hsiao-p'ing and his supporters, however, insisted on further and more extensive corrections in Chinese domestic policy. They were aiming at a new, critical review of Mao's person and doctrine, at a drastic lowering of the level of collectivization in the countryside and at an extension of the cultural parameters. With the help of this revisionist program Teng prepared his offensive for the intra-elite conflict which would begin in the spring of 1978.

Teng Hsiao-P'ing's Offensive

From April 27 to June 6, 1978, a National Army Political Work Conference was held in Peking.[16] At first the conference seemed to be a demonstration of leadership consensus along the lines set by the Eleventh Party Congress. In the course of the meeting, however, Teng Hsiao-p'ing and his associates used the conference to give the signal for an all-out offensive against the forces around Hua Kuo-feng.

On May 11, Teng's assistants published an article introducing the central slogan of the offensive: "Practice is the only norm of truth." They argued that all ideological guidelines always had to stand the test of whether they corresponded to political, economic and social realities.[17] At the conference itself, the contrasts within the leading elite became evident through the speeches given by Hua, by Yeh Chien-ying, and by Teng. Hua and Yeh called upon the army to "keep **steadfast** and **unfold** the good tradition of political work." Teng, on the other hand, demanded that the army should "**restore** and **unfold** the good tradition of political work".[18] The terminological divergence indicated that parts of the elite were striving for a fundamental and critical reappraisal of the Cultural Revolution in particular, and of the whole period of late Maoism since 1958 in general.

From June to October 1978, the political scene in China was dominated by the discussion about the "norm of truth." At the outset, the central and provincial media still published coded attacks on Teng and his associates, accusing them (without naming them) of trying to "cut down the banner of the Thought of Mao Tse-tung."[19] On June 24, the Party's central organ, the Peking *Jen-min Jih-pao (People's Daily)*, took Teng's side by declaring that in fact "revising the Thought of Mao Tse-tung according to reality" and the "only norm of truth" were by no means "revisionism" but a "correct Marxist procedure."[20] On August 1, this statement was also adopted by the newspaper of the PLA. By mid-September the declaration was generally accepted in ten provinces. By early October, it dominated the whole country. Even Hua, who had obviously lost the first battle, now began to talk about restoring the Party's good, traditional work.

By aiming his thrust at Mao's doctrines, Teng had eroded the legitimacy of Hua and his supporters. The debate on the "norm of truth" was by no means a scholastic exercise; it rather established the future of the PRC. The thrust of Teng Hsiao-p'ing's attack on Hua Kuo-feng and his "whatever" faction insisted that Mao Tse-tung's doctrines, and Maoism without Mao, must give way to a more flexible application of Marxism-Leninism and must also allow an all-out revision of the political concepts of the late Chairman.

In the second advance of their offensive from October 1978 onwards, Teng and his supporters started to make use of oppositional forces within the society. During the summer of early autumn 1978, the anti-Maoist societal coalition of 1976 had come up again in China's cities and in a number of villages.

Young intellectuals, illegally returning from their countryside exile (*hsia-fang*) to their hometowns, workers, and great parts of the urban youth began to call for a liberalization of the methods of leadership. A central demand of these groups asked the leading elite to recognize the anti-Maoist mass demonstrations on T'ienanmen Square in the centre of Peking on April 5th, 1976, as a positive action. Up to that time it had been judged a "counter-revolutionary incident."

In early October, We Te, party leader in Peking, and General Ch'en Hsi-lien, commander of the army forces in the capital, were removed from their posts. Both, however, kept their seats in the Politburo. The two had been in charge for the violent suppression of the demonstrations in April 1976. On November 15, 1978, a resolution of the CCP Peking Municipal Committee was published which solemnly proclaimed the manifestations of April 5, 1976, as "entirely revolutionary activities"; all those who had been persecuted and sentenced in connection with the demonstration were now declared rehabilitated .[21]

During the second half of November, the CCP media were busily rewriting the story of the demonstrations of April 1976. What had been "a sinister counterrevolutionary plot of freaks and monsters" now became "a great people's movement." Parts of the population of Peking perceived these developments as a signal to show publicly their opposition to the policy of the leading elite. From November 18, the number of wallposters appearing in the capital increased steadily, especially on a wall along Ch'angan Boulevard which was soon called the "Democracy Wall." During the following days, the police and the security forces stopped interfering with the placement of wallposters, and in talks with foreign correspondents Teng Hsiao-p'ing himself gave cautious praise for the wallposters and their criticism. From late November, the wave of criticism, known as "the Peking spring in winter," spread to other cities and soon became a Democracy and Human Rights Movement. Meetings were held, and organizations and circles were formed. During December a number of unofficial publications appeared, some as individual copies, some as journals, finally numbering as many as thirty.[22]

The movement began with criticizing Wu Te and other party leaders, who were accused of suppressing the demonstrations of April 1976. From mid-December, however, the scope of the argumentation widened. The movement now comprised quite different political beliefs, from reform oriented Communists to democratic socialists and radicals, and even to a growing group of liberals. In Shanghai a leaflet directly addressed Hua Kuo-feng:

> (Y)ou won the respect of Mao by murdering the martyrs of
> T'ienanmen Square. With such a "fighting experience" you
> then advanced with express speed.[23]

Soon, fundamental political criticism began. One of the major leaders of the movement, Wei Ching-sheng, called for the democratization of the PRC's political system as a necessary "fifth modernization," without which the other four could not be achieved.[24] Finally, one of the most radical groups of the movement, the "Thaw-Society," founded in Kueiyang, K'unming and Peking, demanded a guarantee of civil rights, free discussion of conflicting ideologies, freedom of assembly, information and association and an open electoral competition between the CCP and Kuo Min Tang (KMT) [Nationalist Party] throughout China.[25]

The societal pressure deriving from the Democracy and Human Rights Movement strengthened Teng Hsiao-p'ing and his associates. From November 11 to December 15, 1978, a Central Work Conference of the CCP met in Peking. Its decisions were ratified by the Third Plenum of the Eleventh CCP Central Committee which met from December 18 - 22. The leading party elite decided on a thoroughgoing revision of the rural societal policy, distinctly differing from that proposed by Hua.[26] The level of collectivization was lowered; the Central Committee prohibited any interference in to the "sovereignty of the production groups" in favor of the brigades and communes. The party leadership guaranteed the peasants their private plots, allowed a wider range of free family sideline occupations and legalized free markets in the villages. In addition to these changes, production groups could now be split into "working groups" of three to five families, who would now be able, based on contracts made with the government, to plan and carry out the agricultural production. Important changes were thus introduced into the villages, a point to which we shall return below.

In addition, the Third Plenum declared that Mao Tse-tung had been a "great Marxist" - not the "greatest" Marxist as before - but that it would not be "really Marxist" to expect "that a revolutionary leader was without faults and mistakes."[27] P'eng Te-huai and T'ao Chu were posthumously rehabilitated, and nine other cadres who had recently been rehabilitated were readmitted to the Central Committee. Ch'en Yun, Madam Teng Ying-ch'ao (the widow of Chou En-lai), Hu Yao-pang (Teng's close associate) and General Wang Chen were appointed members of the Politburo. Ch'en-Yun, concurrently vice-chairman of the Central Committee, was also elevated to the Standing Committee of the Politburo.

Teng Hsiao-p'ing could now rely on at least twelve of the 27 members in the Politburo; Hua was supported by seven, while eight members, including Yeh Chien-ying and Li Hsien-nien, took a neutral position. In the Standing Committee, the intra-party groupings were well balanced. They included two members whose career had been advanced by the Cultural Revolution, two cadres who had survived the Cultural Revolution in office and two rehabilitated cadres. What is more, supporters of Teng took over the leadership of the General Office as well as of the Organization, the Propaganda, and the United Front Work Departments of the Central Committee. Hu Yao-pang was charged with rebuilding the Central Committee Secretariat which had been abolished during the Cultural Revolution. While a compromise had forced Teng to agree to the continuation of General Wang Tung-hsing and Wu Te in the Politburo, he had succeeded in consolidating his influence in the leading organs of the CCP.

In the first months of 1979, however, Teng's offensive faced another crisis. The crisis was caused by the growth of the Democracy and Human Rights Movement, which was now entering the state of mass-demonstrations. In early January 1979, more than 10,000 peasants from four provinces demonstrated in Peking against the CCP rural societal policy. They were led by Fu Yueh-hua, a young intellectual, who was working in a factory. On February 5 and 6, approximately 25,000 young intellectuals, who had illegally returned from their rural exile, came together in Shanghai. In their efforts to dramatize their demand for legalization and the distribution of permissions to work they blocked the central station and the traffic for twelve hours until security forces drove them away.[28]

As had already been the case in the "Hundred Flowers" Movement of 1957, the leading elite was again losing control over the activities of the opposition. And like 1957 the elite prepared to retaliate.

The dramatic worsening of the Democratic and Human Rights Movement coincided with Organizational and factional difficulties encountered by the PLA in the Vietnam War, which had been principally initiated by Teng Hsiao-p'ing. Both developments supported Teng's opponents in their arguments of March that year for a drastic reduction of Teng's influence. In an extended meeting of the Politburo on March 16, 1979, however, Teng succeeded in dismissing these attacks by counterattacking his opponents.[29] On March 30 he finally proclaimed the "Four Cardinal Principles" (*ssu hsiang chi-pen yuan-tse*) as a limit to political activities. These principles, which have since become the core of the CCP doctrine are: 1) adherence to the Socialist road, 2) the dictatorship of the proletariat, 3) leadership of the Communist Party, 4) "Marxism-Leninism, Mao Tse-tung Thought as a compulsory guideline for all political, economic and social work."[30] In this way the party had begun its retaliation.

After Fu Yueh-hua's early arrest on January 18, a number of leading opponents were arrested in Peking in the first days of April, among them Wei Ching-sheng and Jen Wan-ting. Hundreds of arrests and several executions in other cities followed, and by the fall of 1979 the movement had been totally suppressed. In October Wei Ching-sheng was sentenced to fifteen years in prison.[31] In late November the "Democracy Wall" was cleared of all wallposters, and in December, Fu Yueh-hua was sentenced to two years of imprisonment.[32] Once again, an attempt to introduce civil rights, freedom and pluralistic forms of debate to the PRC had failed. The critics of 1978 had now become dissidents and many of them went underground.

There was a widespread feeling that the democracy activists had been betrayed by Teng Hsiao-p'ing who had first used them and then discarded them, just as the Red Guards of the Cultural Revolution had felt betrayed by Mao Tse-tung in 1967-68. Teng Hsiao-p'ing, however, had not merely used the movement as means of strengthening his position in the autumn of 1978; by opposing the movement in March 1979 he also averted a crisis from which his power political and policy offensive were suffering. With the offensive against the democracy advocates, he now continued to prepare for Hua Kuo-feng's final fall from power, and to push forward his policy of a controlled revision of the Party's doctrine together with the introduction of economic reforms.

At the Fourth Plenum of the Eleventh Central Committee, meeting in Peking from September 25 to 28, 1979, Teng Hsiao-p'ing succeeded in consolidating his position. Twelve new members joined the Central Committee, all of whom had only recently been rehabilitated. Among them was P'eng Chen, the first victim of the Cultural Revolution and former mayor of Peking. He was also appointed full member of the Politburo, as was Chao Tzu-yang, formerly a Politburo alternate member and one of Teng's closest assistants. Teng could now rely on thirteen or fourteen of the twenty-eight members of the Politburo (one member had died). Hua Kuo-feng was still supported by seven members and seven or eight members could be counted in the middle group around Yeh Chien-ying and Li Hsien-nien.

The shift in the intra-elite balance of power became also evident with the beginning of the re-evaluation of the Cultural Revolution. In an address on the eve of the thirtieth anniversary of the foundation of the PRC, Marshall Yeh Chien-ying, the ceremonial Chief of State, declared: "what we call the Thought of Mao Tse-tung... is indeed the crystallization of the collective wisdom of the party." Moreover, he condemned the Cultural Revolution as an event which "brought to the country a whole decade of suppression, tyranny and bloodshed."[33] In the last two months of 1979, the CCP media scathingly criticized the "atrocities" and "crimes" committed during the Cultural Revolution. These attacks were to prepare for the ultimate posthumous rehabilitation, that of Liu Shao-ch'i, who had died in prison in 1969. His rehabilitation, however, was not only encountered opposition from Hua Kuo-feng's "Whatever Faction," but also met with the resistance of some older generals, most importantly, perhaps, Yeh Chien-ying.

Yet when the Fifth Plenum of the Eleventh CCP Central Committee convened for a six-day meeting in Peking on February 23, 1980, Teng and his supporters had overcome this resistance. The Plenum ratified their second victory. Liu Shao-ch'i, China's former "Khrushchev," the party's greatest "capitalist roader, renegade and traitor," was rehabilitated as a "great Marxist" and a "valiant revolutionary fighter."[34] Moreover, the revisionist forces around Teng and Ch'en Yun now secured the majority within the party leadership for themselves. Four of Hua's supporters, General Wang Tung-hsing, General Ch'en Hsi-lien, Wu Te and Chi Teng-k'uei were expelled from the Politburo. Wang Tung-hsing thus also left the Standing Committee of the Politburo, to which two of the then closest friends of Teng were newly admitted: Hu Yao-pang and Chao Tzu-yang.

Thirteen or fourteen of the now twenty-four members of the Politburo belonged to Teng Hsiao-p'ing - Ch'en Yun group, seven or eight supported the middle group around Yeh Chien-ying and Li Hsien-nien, while Hua Kuo-feng could depend on only three members. Considering the fact that Ch'en Yung-kuei, the representative of the "Tachai model" in agriculture, was no longer invited to the sessions of the Politburo, Hua could in fact only count on two votes. From 1977, the revisionists had almost doubled their strength; the late Maoists around Hua, however, had lost more than half of their former strength. In the Politburo Standing Committee there were now four rehabilitated cadres, two survivors and Hua, who was isolated as the only remaining cadre whose career had been advanced in the Cultural Revolution.

During the spring and summer of 1980, Teng and Ch'en fashioned further far-reaching political changes, mainly concerning the rural societal policy. During the course of 1979, they succeeded in giving the responsibility for planning and production to the small work teams. They also extended the peasants' private plots of land from three and five percent to ten and fifteen percent of the productive land, and abolished all restrictions concerning family sideline occupations including private breeding and free markets.

With this, they introduced the decollectivization of agricultural production. Within a system of contracts, first concluded for three years but soon for up to fifteen years, the individual peasant got, on regular payment and on an agreed quota of delivered goods, the productive land, which he could farm on a private basis but which remained collective property. By the end of 1982 this *de facto* rent system would include 95 percent of the productive land which was still formally held as collective property. Between 1983 and 1985, the People's communes and production brigades finally were abolished and in many places the production groups, which had by and large lost their function, also disappeared.

After Teng and his supporters had succeeded in isolating Hua Kuo-feng in the inner leading core they could now turn to the last phase of their offensive, aiming at the fall of Mao's successor as party leader. In early September 1980, under the pretext of a "division of the functions of party and state," Teng Hsiao-p'ing and Ch'en Yun as well as four other members of the Politburo declared their resignation as Vice-Premiers. Following this same principle, they caused Hua Kuo-feng to resign as Prime Minister on September 10. His place was taken by Chao Tzu-yang, a dedicated follower of Teng Hsiao-p'ing.[35]

Yet, Hua still held the position as Chairman of the Central Committee and of its Military Commission. His removal from these posts came after a series of meetings of the Politburo which lasted from November 10 to December 5, 1980. In the course of these sessions the pressure placed on Hua finally made him agree to self-criticism. He admitted that he had followed a "leftist style of leadership," tried to avoid or at least to delay the rehabilitation of Teng Hsiao-p'ing and Ch'en-Yun, and attempted to introduced a "leftist style of a new 'great Leap'." On December 5, the Politburo, presumably in an unanimous vote, passed a resolution which announced Hua's final fall from power:

> During the last four years, comrade Hua Kuo-feng has also done some successful work, but it is extremely clear that he lacks the political and organizational ability to be the chairman of the party. That he should have never been appointed chairman of the Military Commission, everybody knows.[36]

Moreover, the Politburo decided to suggest to the Sixth Plenum of the Eleventh Central Committee that Hu Yao-pang should be appointed Chairman of the Central Committee and Teng Hsiao-p'ing Chairman of the Military Commission. The two were to assume the powers of these positions immediately, while Hua was still permitted to keep these posts officially and continue to "receive foreign guests in the capacity of the Center's Chairman."[37] As expected, the Sixth Plenum, meeting in Peking from June 27 - 29, 1981, confirmed these personnel decisions of the Politburo.

With this offensive, the revisionist forces around Teng Hsiao-p'ing had achieved their aims: the forces of late Maoism were excluded from further participation in the political decision-making process of the PRC.

Compromise Politics

The discussions within the leading elite, however, did not end with the victory over Maoism. Differentiations among the revisionist forces became evident by spring 1981. The winners of the conflict from 1978 to 1980 agreed on resolving any difference of opinion through majority decisions in the Politburo and its Standing Committee, and on avoiding any public factional discussions. They jointly took the view that the agricultural production should be decollectivized, that light and consumer goods industries should take priority over raw material and heavy industries, that the policy of deficit spending as promoted by Hua, should be replaced by a strict budgetary policy. They also agreed on allowing elements of private initiatives and free enterprise within the socialist planned economy. However, Teng and Ch'en soon disagreed about the scope and speed of the economic reforms.

During the first half of 1981 three opinion groups could be distinguished within the leading elite:

1. A revisionist group around Teng Hsiao-P'ing, Hu Yao-pang and Chao Tzu-yang, which could rely on eight votes in the Politburo.

2. A New middle group under the leadership of Ch'en Yun and P'eng Chen, which could rely on six votes in the Politburo and which represented an enlightened neo-Stalinism.

3. The previous middle group of orthodox Stalinists around Yeh Chien-ying and Li Hsien-nien which, supported by the two remaining Late-Maoists, Hua Kuo-feng and Ni Chih-fu, could rely on nine votes in the Politburo.

In the Standing Committee of the Politburo Ch'en Yun, the neo-Stalinist, held the decisive vote between three revisionist and three orthodox members, the latter group including Hua. It was in particular the older generals of the PLA, whose majority had supported Teng's offensive against Hua in 1978-1979, who in late 1980 gradually developed doubts about a too-rapid progress towards a revisionist policy of economic, organizational and cultural reforms.

The criticism of these generals was mainly directed against both a far-reaching reevaluation of Mao's person and policy as well as a quick and fundamental expansion of the parameters of competition for different styles and approaches in the realm of cultural policy. The revisionists were pushed toward a first compromise when in late June 1981 the Sixth Plenum of the Eleventh Central Committee passed a "Resolution on some problems of the party history since the foundation of the PRC."[38] At the time of its adoption, the resolution was regarded as a final judgement of Mao and his policy.

In a first draft of the resolution produced in August 1980, it was stated that Mao had displayed great merit during the struggle of the CCP for the power in China until 1949 and also during the first seven years of PRC history, but it was also stated that he had committed "mistakes" in 1958-1959 as well as in the early period of the Cultural Revolution, and even some "crimes" during the last years of his life. A second draft of October 1980 did not mention the accusation of "crimes" anymore and "severe mistakes" were now confined to the Cultural Revolution. In the final version of the

Resolution, Mao's "mistakes" were restricted to some decisions made during the Great Leap Forward and to the Cultural Revolution. The document admitted that the main cause of the Cultural Revolution lay in Mao's "erroneous leadership," but declared that his errors were those of a "great proletarian revolutionary." In a final assessment, the resolution stated:

> While committing serious mistakes, he still thought that his theory and practice were Marxist and herein lies his tragedy.

This compromise resolution of the Sixth Plenum, however, would not be the revisionists' only concession towards the orthodox and Neo-Stalinists. At the Twelfth Party Congress, planned for the end of 1981 but finally convened in September 1982, Teng and his supporters tried to force a fundamental restructuring of the party and to reduce the orthodox representatives in the leading committees drastically. In a series of successive drafts concerning a new party constitution,[39] they developed a program which they hoped would be adopted by the Party Congress:

> 1. A thoroughgoing rejuvenation of the leading group. For this purpose the drafts of the revisionists provided for age limits and limits on the period of office in the leading organs of the Party.

> 2. As an incentive for elderly Party leaders to leave the Central Committee and the Politburo, they proposed the establishment of a Central Advisory Committee (CAC) of the CCP. It was supposed to work as a sort of "upper house" with limited authority on the level of the Central Committee.

> 3. The abolition of the Politburo Standing Committee and the takeover of all daily decisions by the Secretariat of the Central Committee.[40]

> 4. The official declaration in the Party statute that "large-scale class struggle in the form of turbulent mass movement are already a thing of the past." This was in order to emphasize the transition to a stabilized period of institutionalized and orderly Party rule.

However, at the seven-day Central Work Conference which began on July 30, 1982, convened to prepare for the Party Congress, the revisionists could only push through parts of their program. Again a compromise was forced upon them by the stiff resistance from the orthodox Stalinists and at least parts of the neo-Stalinists.

The final draft of the Party Constitution no longer mentioned any age limits or limits on the period of office-holding in the leading organs of the Party. The Standing Committee of the Politburo remained in existence and became, with the abolition of the position of Chairman of the Central Committee, the new collective leadership of the CCP. The Central Secretariat was to be responsible for the daily work of the Party Center, while the General Secretary was given the responsibility for convening meetings of the Politburo and its Standing Committee and overseeing the work of the Secretariat. The revisionists only succeeded in achieving the establishment of the CAC; they failed in their attempt to have included in the Party Constitution the declaration that the time of "large-scale class struggle" was over. After the Seventh Plenum of the Eleventh Central Committee had ratified the decisions of the Work Conference on August 6, the 1545 delegates met for the Twelfth Party Congress from September 1 - 11, 1982.[41]

The congress was opened with a report of the Central Committee read by Hu Yao-pang. He confirmed the compromise decisions on the reevaluation of Mao Tse-tung and his policies as well as the policy of a controlled and restricted relaxation of socialist economy an planning as followed since 1978.[42]

Concerning the personnel decisions of the congress, the appointment of the Twelfth Central Committee and the CAC on September 10 and 11, and the appointment of the Politburo and its Standing Committee at the First Plenum of the Twelfth Central Committee on September 12 and 13, the revisionists were more successful, though they could not reach a definite majority within the leading elite.[43] Of the 210 full members of the Twelfth Central Committee, 46.7 per cent were entirely new, 46.2 per cent were accepted from the Eleventh Central Committee and 7.1 per cent advanced from candidates to full members.

The average age of the full members of the Twelfth Central Committee, 64.4 years, was only slightly lower than that of the Eleventh Central Committee at the time of its appointment in 1977, when the average age was 64.6 years. A significant rejuvenation of the leading group had obviously not been achieved. The percentage of civilian cadres rose from 55.4 to 66.3, while the percentage of the PLA decreased from 32.4 to 25.2, and the representatives of the mass organizations saw their percentage decrease from 11.2 to 7.1. For the first time since the Cultural Revolution, the rehabilitated cadres achieved a majority of 52.9 per cent in the Central Committee, an increase of 36.3 per cent over 1977. The membership of those who had advanced during the Cultural Revolution shrank from 52.2 percent to only 7.6 percent.

Hua Kuo-feng was removed from the Politburo as was Ch'en Yung-kuei, who had not been invited to the sessions of the Politburo since 1980. General Hsu Shih-yu, P'eng Ch'ung and Keng Piao were transferred from the Politburo to the Standing Committee of the Central Advisory Committee. The ailing Marshall Liu Po-ch'eng retired from all his Party positions. Seven new members joined the Politburo. Four of them, Hsi Chung-hsun, Liao Ch'eng-chih, Wan Li and General Yang Te-chih, belonged to the group of revisionists. Sung Jen-ch'iung and Hu Ch'iao-mu represented the Neo-Stalinists while General Yang Shang-k'un in political respect counted as a neo-Stalinist but in personal respect showed solidarity with Teng. The revisionists among the six members of the Standing Committee of the Politburo were represented by Teng Hsiao-p'ing, Hu Yao-pang and Chao Tzu-yang; Yeh Chien-ying and Li Hsien-nien represented the orthodox and Ch'en Yun the neo-Stalinists. Such a lineup in the Standing Committee made further compromises necessary.

Moreover, Teng strengthened his position by becoming Chairman of the CAC and keeping his position as a Chairman of the Military Commission. Ch'en Yun was confirmed as First Secretary of the Central Commission for Discipline Inspection (CCDI). During the first year after the Twelfth Party Congress, General Yang Yung, member of the Secretariat, and Liao Ch'eng-chih, member of the Politburo, died. After the death of these politicians the distribution of intra-elite forces within the central leading Party committees could be estimated as follows:

> The revisionists were represented in the Politburo by ten out twenty-four full members, in the Secretariat by five of nine members and in the Central Military Commission by three of nine members.

> The Neo-Stalinists were represented by six members of the Politburo, by three members of the Secretariat and by two members of the Central Military Commission.

> The orthodox Stalinists were represented by eight members of the Politburo and by for members of the Central Military Commission, but only by one member of the Secretariat.

Thus, after the twelfth Party Congress, there still was no definite revisionist majority within the leading committees of the CCP. It was therefore still necessary for political decisions to be made by compromises. With regard to the distribution of forces within the decision making bodies, these compromises inevitably led to a policy of enlightened Stalinism in the following years. Five elements distinguished the element of enlightenment :

1. The new rural societal policy of decollectivization of agricultural production while the formal policy of collective property in productive agricultural land.

2. The beginning de-centralization of industrial management and the introduction of free markets in the cities.

3. The limited and controlled widening of the parameters for private initiative and smaller private enterprise.

4. The attempts to establish a system of socialist legality by introducing civil and criminal codes as well as regulations of civil and criminal court procedures.

5. The stress on factual knowledge and performance in education, which led to a noticeable improvement of the social position of intellectuals, in particular of the technological and scientific intelligentsia.

These elements of enlightenment, however, were limited by five elements of Stalinism:

1. The primary role of planning in economic policies, expounded in the often-repeated statement that "the planned economy is the main factor, and the market economy an auxiliary."

2. Definite limitations on private economic initiatives and the stress on the "socialist sector" as the main factor in the economic system.

3. The continued persecution of political and intellectual dissent.

4. The clear stress on party discipline and on the indoctrination of the Party members as well as the "masses" with the ideas of "Marxism-Leninism and the Thought of Mao Tse-tung."

5. The permanent insistence on the Four Cardinal Principles as a basis and framework for all political and social activities.

The combination of these elements of enlightenment and Stalinism as well as the conflicts between them became, after the Twelfth Party Congress, the determining factors for the political development of the PRC in the years ahead.

NOTES

1. **Jen Min Jih Pao** (People's Daily) [hereafter **JMJP**], Peking, October 1, 1976.

2. **Kuang Ming Jih Pao** [hereafter **KMJP**], Peking, October 4, 1976.

3. **JMJP**, October 25, 1976.

4. Information provided to Prof. Jürgen Domes by a vice-chairman of the Chinese People's Association for Friendship with Foreign Countries in Peking, September 1980.

5. Amnesty International, *Political Imprisonment in the People's Republic of China* (London: Amnesty International, 1978), pp. 26f., 65-69.

6. **JMJP**, December 28, 1976.

7. **JMJP**, February 7, 1977.

8. Hunan People's Broadcasting Station, January 4, 1977.

9. A copy of this letter--an internal document of the CCP's Kuangtung Provincial Party Committee--is available in the archives in T'aiwan, although it was not published there. A German translation can be found in **Der Spiegel** (Hamburg) 31:17 (April 1977), pp. 161-164.

10. Statement by a member of the Chinese Academy of Social Sciences in an interview with Prof. Jürgen Domes, Peking, September 1980.

11. **JMJP**, July 23, 1977.

12. Hua Kuo-feng, "Political Report at the Eleventh Congress of the CCP," in *Chung-kuo Kung-ch'an-tang ti-shih-i-tz'u ch'uan-kuo tai-piao ta-hui wen-chien hui-pien* [Collection of Documents of the Eleventh CCP Party Congress] (Peking: People's Publishing House, 1977), pp. 4f.

13. *Ibid.*, p. 30.

14. "Constitution of the PRC," March 5, 1978, in *Chung-hua jen-min Kung-he-kuo ti-wu-chieh ch'uan-kuo jen-min tai-piao ta-hui ti-i-tz'u hui-yi wen-chien* [Documents of The First Session of The Fifth NPC of The PRC] (Hong Kong: San Lien Bookstore, 1978), pp. 76-104.

15. Hua Kuo-feng, "Unite and Strive to Build a Modern, Powerful Socialist Country!: Report on the Work of the Government Delivered at the First Session of the Fifth NPC," February 26, 1978, *Documents Fifth NPC*, pp. 3-70.

16. **JMJP**, May 30, 1978.

17. **JMJP**, May 11, 1978.

18. **JMJP**, June 6 1978 [emphasis added]. The speech can also be found, in a slightly edited version, in *Teng Hsiao-p'ing wen-hsuan* [Selected Writings of Teng Hsiao-p'ing] (Peking: People's Publishing House, 1983), pp. 108-120.

19. Hu Chi-wei, "The Struggle in the Higher Circles of the Party," **Cheng-ming** [Debate], Hong Kong, No. 34 (August 1980), p. 51. This is a reprint of a speech by the then-editor of **JMJP**, at the Central Party School on September 13, 1979, which was not published inside the PRC.

20. **JMJP**, June 24, 1978. See also **China News Analysis** (Hong Kong, No. 1134 September 22, 1978).

21. **KMJP**, Peking, November 16, 1978.

22. A very lively account of the early days of the Human Rights and Democracy movement by a Canadian correspondent in Peking can be found in John Fraser, *The Chinese: Portrait of People* (New York: Summit Books, 1980), pp. 199-271. See also Fox Butterfield, *China: Alive in the Bitter Sea* (New York: Times Books, 1982), pp. 206-434. The most comprehensive collection of journals and other materials of the movement is Institute for the Study of Chinese Communist Problems, T'aipei, ed., *Ta-lu ti-hsia k'an-wu hui-pien* [Collection of Mainland Underground Publications], 15 vols. to date (Taipei: CKYC Publishers, 1980). Of a considerable number of materials from that period in English translation, the three most useful are Lin Yi-tang, ed., *What They Say: A Collection of*

Current Chinese Underground Publications (Taipei: Institute of Current China Studies, 1980); James D. Seymour, ed., *The Fifth Modernization: China's Human Rights Movement, 1978-1979* (Standfordville, N.Y.: Coleman, 1980); and David S. G. Goodman, *Beijing Street Voices: The Poetry and Politics of China's Democracy Movement* (London: Marion Boyars, 1981).

23. **Kuan Ch'a Chia** [The Observer], Hong Kong, February 1979, pp. 37f.

24. Chin Sheng (Wei Ching-sheng), "Human Rights, Equality, and Democracy," **T'an-suo** [Exploration], March 1979, as cited in James D. Seymour, *The Fifth Modernization*, p. 141.

25. "Manifesto of the Thaw Society," March 8, 1979; wall poster in Peking. Photograph in the possession of Prof Jürgen Domes.

26. Communique of the Third Plenum of the CCP Eleventh Central Committee, **JMJP**, December 23, 1978.

27. *Ibid.*

28. Peking Central People's Broadcasting Station, Feb. 8 and 12, 1979; **Wen Hui Pao**, Shanghai, Feb. 9, 1979; Shanghai People's Broadcasting Station, Feb. 12, 1979.

29. **Chieh Fang Chun Pao** (Liberation Army Daily), March 1979.

30. **JMJP**, May 22, 1979

31. **New China News Agency (NCNA)**, Peking, Oct. 16, 1979.

32. **JMJP**, December 26, 1979.

33. **NCNA**, Peking, September 30, 1979.

34. **JMJP**, March 1, 1980.

35. **JMJP**, September 11, 1980.

36. "Notice of the Meeting of the Politburo of the CCP Central Committee," December 5, 1980, Internal Party Document, **Chung Kung**

Yen Chiu (Studies in Chinese Communism), Taipei, 17:4, April 1983, pp. 82f.

37. *Ibid.*

38. "Resolution on Several Problems of Party History Since the Establishment of the PRC, Unanimously Approved by the Sixth Plenum of the Eleventh CCP Central Committee," June 27, 1981, **Hung C'hi** (Red Flag), Peking, No. 13 (July 1981), pp. 3-27.

39. Document *Chung-fa* (1980) No. 29, April 4, 1980; reprinted in **Fei-ch'ing yueh-pao** [Rebel Situation Monthly], T'aipei, no. 9 (1980), pp.74-83 and 97. A very concise description of the debates on the Party statute that preceded the Twelfth Party Congress is given by Peter Schier, "Die Vorgeschichte des XII. Parteitages" [Antecedents of the Twelfth Party Congress], **China Aktuell** (Hamburg), December 1982, pp. 724-732.

40. This suggestion was made by Hu Yao-pang in an interview with the director of AFP, Henri Pigeat (**AFP**, Peking, August 23, 1982; Chinese in **Ta Kung Pao**, Hong kong, August 26, 1982).

41. **JMJP**, September 2, 1982.

42. *Ibid.*

43. **NCNA**, Peking, September 10, 11 and 12, 1982.

CHAPTER ONE

THE FALL OF HUA KUO-FENG

Documents in this chapter recount the process by which Teng Hsiao-p'ing dismissed Hua Kuo-feng from the Party. Because Hua Kuo-feng legitimized his leadership by adhering to strict Maoism, in order to remove the base of Hua's power, Teng attacked Hua's relationship with Mao Tse-tung.

Document No. 1 is an example of one of the editorials solicited by Teng that appeared in the mass media arguing that the power of the Party should not be based on a single person. Such opinions undermined the position of Hua Kuo-feng, who was then the Chairman of the Party. Documents Nos. 2 and 3 record that Hua Kuo-feng resigned his post as Chairman of the Party, and that both Hu Yao-pang and Chao Tzu-yang were promoted to take over the decision-making power of the Party. Meanwhile, the Party adopted a resolution in which three charges were brought against Hua Kuo-feng (Document No. 4). The trumped-up charges manufactured by Teng and his followers appeared in the official media -- the People's Daily (Document No. 5). The first of these charges is that Hua had followed inflexibly whatever instructions Mao had given before. From this charge, Teng's attack on Hua would have been interpreted as an attack on Mao. For the Party as a whole, the repudiating campaign against Hua Kuo-feng would be equal to actively rejecting Maoism. That is why the Party, headed by Teng Hsiao-p'ing, published a resolution, shown in Document No. 4, to differentiate in a subtle way Mao from Maoism, the latter of which was defined as the honorable revolutionary experience gained and shared by all senior communists, including Mao himself. Document No. 6 endorses this symbolic motion to secure the legitimacy of the CCP.

DOCUMENTS

1. **Hongqi** Special Commentator, "Power Should Not Be Concentrated in the Hands of Individuals," **Beijing Review**, No. 44, November 3, 1980.

2. "Notification of the Central Committee Politburo Meeting," Issued by the Politburo of the Central Committee, December 5, 1980.

3. "Communique of the Sixth Plenary Session of the Eleventh Central Committee of the CPC," Adopted on June 27, 1981, **Beijing Review**, No. 27, July 6, 1981.

4. "Resolution on Certain Questions in the History of Our Party since the Founding of the People's Republic of China," Adopted by the Sixth Plenary Session of the Eleventh Central Committee of the Communist Party of China on June 27, 1981, **Beijing Review**, No. 27, July 6, 1981.

5. "Material For Studying the 'Resolution On Certain Questions in the History of Our Party since the Founding of the State,'" **Jenmin Jihpao (People's Daily)**, Beijing, July 21, 1981; **FBIS - CHI**, July 22, 1981.

6. Wu Lu, "Differentiate Mao from Mao Zedong Thought: Understanding the Documents of the Sixth Plenary Session of the CCP Central Committee," **Jenmin Jihpao (People's Daily)**, Beijing, July 24, 1981; **FBIS - CHI**, July 27, 1981.

*****

DOCUMENT NO. 1

POWER SHOULD NOT BE CONCENTRATED IN THE

HANDS OF INDIVIDUALS

by

Hongqi Special Commentator

(**Beijing Review**, No. 44, November 3, 1980)

The "cultural revolution" has taught the Chinese Communist Party and the Chinese people many lessons. An important one is that serious consequences result when the power of the Party is concentrated in the hands of individuals for a considerable period of time.

Manifestations and Damage

Concentration of power in individuals' hands has the following manifestations:

--The power to make final decision in the Party is assumed by individuals;

--Individuals can cancel presumptuously the resolutions of the Party and decisions of the collective;

--The personal will of the leaders substitutes for collective leadership in the Party's leading bodies at various levels and only what the first secretary says goes;

--One man holds too many posts concurrently. In some places, a number of leading posts are often given to a single person.

Under certain circumstances, concentration of power in the hands of individuals will inevitably lead to a distortion of power: The power of the Party turns into the power of individuals; and the power which should be used in the interests of the Party is changed into a power which runs counter to the Party's will and interests, or even a power which is used by individuals to dominate the Party.

The following problems spring up whenever a distortion of power occurs after the Party's power has been concentrated in individuals' hands for a long time.

--Inner-Party democratic life is smothered. Those who hold power can wield it as they wish while others cannot and dare not raise different opinions. The power-holders are always extolled and eulogized merely because of their power and they cannot see their weaknesses or mistakes. They do not like to carry out self-criticism. But in our political life, if people cannot speak out freely or make criticism and self-criticism, there will be no real democracy.

--The unhealthy trend of leading members holding life-long posts, which exists in the Party, is strengthened. To allow one person to arrogate to himself complete power will inevitably lead to the situation of an individual holding on to that power for a long time.

--Factionalism is abetted and the Party's unity weakened. Those who have too much power in their hands are liable to be infatuated with it. Those who submit to the power-holders will prosper and those who resist will suffer. Under this situation, opportunists flourish while people who hold on to principles are discriminated against and excluded.

--Individuals are deified. Once a leaders is deified, he will be followed blindly and eulogized feverishly; irrational actions become prevalent.

In the history of our Party, calamities occurred when too much power was wielded by one person so that he alone decided everything. This over-concentration of power did not exist from the Zunyi Meeting in 1935 -- especially from the Yanan Rectification Campaign in 1942 -- to the Eighth Party Congress in 1956. Under the leadership of Comrade Mao Zedong, democratic life in the Party was normal during this period. The tendency to over-concentrate power grew gradually because of the tremendous growth of prestige of the Party's leaders after the victory in the revolution, the great achievements in the early years of socialist construction and the continuance of imperfections in the socialist democratic system. It became increasingly conspicuous after the struggle against what was called Right deviation in 1959. Though socialist democracy and democratic centralism were repeatedly emphasized afterwards, there was hardly any effect. Thus what was done was far removed from theory.

Causes

Apart from purely personal factors, the concentration of power in the hands of individuals has its deep social, historical and ideological roots.

China experienced a long period of feudal rule and the present socialist society emerged directly from the womb of a semi-feudal and semi-colonial society. Therefore, feudalistic ideology is so prevalent that it has permeated every corner of the society, affecting the habits of people. For instance, the concepts of respectability and inferiority, the hierarchical system and patriarchal behavior manifest themselves everywhere. At the same time, we are swamped by the mentality and habitual force of small producers, especially of the peasants. The ideology of the agricultural small producers is characterized by the belief that they cannot take their destiny into their own hands, but rather entrust it to some "saviour." They sincerely sing the "saviour's" praises and hope he will be a wise emperor. They also embrace the concept of returning kindness with loyalty. All this provides an extensive social basis for individuals to arrogate to themselves complete power. We can be sure that, so long as the ideological remnants of feudalism have not been totally eradicated and the small producer mentality has not been reformed, there will always be the possibility that power can be distorted.

Secondly, the problem arises from a lack of proper understanding of the truth. Our Party is an entity made up of its leading organ (its Central Committee), its organizations at various level and its members. The Party's line and policies are laid down by its leaders, that is, the leading cadres in the Central Committee, on the basis of pooling the wisdom of the masses. All its goals and tasks are fulfilled by the Party members and masses through organizational work of its leading members. Therefore, people naturally link the victory of the revolution and the successes in work with the leaders of the Party and easily attribute the achievements to some individuals. Many people, including some comrades holding very high posts, cannot see this. They often think highly of themselves and underestimate the strength of the Party and the collective. All this reflects the one-sidedness and superficiality of thinking which provides one important reasons why the Party's power is concentrated in a few people's hands and is abusively exercised.

Thirdly, the wielding of power by a few individuals in the Party is connected with the practice during the period of the Communist International when the power of Communist Parties of all countries was highly concentrated. The practical needs of the revolutionary struggle and situation made it necessary at that time to concentrate power to a certain degree in the hands of a few people. But, when the situation changed, especially when the Party seized state power, we failed to introduce corresponding changes. This tradition of centralizing power in a few people's hands, as was reflected in theory, overemphasized centralism in respect to the Party's principle and system of democratic centralism. In the history of our Party, there were times when struggles against decentralism and assertion of independence were unduly emphasized, but there was no occasion when decentralization and giving more power to the localities were overemphasized. Moreover, the concentration of power in individuals' hands has never been opposed. This history has made people believe mistakenly that it is natural for power in the Party to be concentrated in the hands of a few individuals. Serious consequences will ensue if we do not conscientiously restrict the over-concentration of power, which took shape in the Party's history, but, rather, turn what was a one-time necessity into a common practice or even institutionalize it.

The Party Leads, Not Individuals

The goal of our political life is to facilitate the smooth progress of our socialist modernization by creating a political situation of stability, unity and liveliness, in which there are both centralism and democracy, both discipline and freedom and both unity of will and personal ease of mind. Therefore, it is necessary to constantly improve democratic centralism and socialist democracy. We must pay full attention to those actions which are detrimental to the development of such a situation and to the carrying out of democratic centralism, including those which foster the concentration of power by any individual. Practical measures must be taken to overcome these trends step by step in a planned way.

Of course, our opposition to power being centralized in the hands of a few individuals does not mean that we deny the necessity of centralization, the strength of authority or the role of an individual. The personal authority we talk about does not denote that an individual alone exercises authority. Nor does it mean all powers of the Party must be given to one man. The Party of the Chinese proletariat has needed and will need its own outstanding leadership which enjoys high prestige among the people. But this leadership can only be collective. It cannot be realized through any single individual.

The Party needs its outstanding and authoritative leadership. It asks its leaders to perform their roles well within the limits of their functions and powers.

This is totally different from concentrating the Party's power in the hands of individuals. While the former is a necessary part of democratic centralism, the latter is in opposition to and undermines democratic centralism. The cause of the proletariat is a cause of hundreds of millions of people. It is the Party, not any single individual, that forms the vanguard of the proletariat to give leadership to the cause. In the fight for the proletarian cause, no man, however talented, experienced and competent, can do everything well, because there is a limit to what he can hope to accomplish. What is more, everyone is fettered by his inherent weaknesses and shortcomings. This is why man is always a man, and not a deity.

*****

DOCUMENT NO. 2

NOTIFICATION OF THE CENTRAL COMMITTEE POLITBURO MEETINGS

Issued by the Politburo of the Central Committee

December 5, 1980

(Source: Institute of International Relations, Taipei)

There were nine continuous meetings held in Central Committee Political Bureau on November 10, 11, 13, 14, 17, 18, 19, 29 and December 5 of 1980. In these meetings Liu Bocheng and Nie Rongzhen were absent due to illness (Nie Rongzhen wrote a letter to approve the resolutions of the meetings). Chen Yongqui and Sai Fuding were not notified to attend the meetings. The attendants included twenty two committee members of Central Committee Political Bureau and one reserve committee member as well as seven secretaries of Central Secretariat.

The topic of conference was the new nomination list which would be submitted to the Sixth Plenary Session of the CCP Eleventh Central Committee. All the twenty-nine attendants expressed their own opinions in the conference.

After the extended conference of Central Committee Political Bureau from August 18 to 23 of 1980, many party members having attended that conference suggested that Hua Guofeng is no longer fit to hold his present positions as the Chairman of Central Committee and the Chairman of Central Military Committee. While discussing "Resolutions on Certain Questions in the History Of Our Party Since the Founding of the People's Republic of China, quite a few party members from central governmental agencies or central national agencies or army system thought that we should settle questions about events in the fourth period of our history. They indicated that Hua Guofeng made some blunders during the four years, from 1977 to 1980, of smashing "the Gang of Four" especially in the first two years. They asked for him to be removed from his present positions. After completely reviewing the inquiry, the Central Standing Committee thinks it is necessary to change Hua's position.

In the first meeting of the conference, Mr. Hua handed in his resignation and explanatory report of his actions on smashing the Gang of Four. Those in attendance gave their own opinions about Hua's errors in the past and his explanatory report.

In general, Hua did contribute his part in smashing the Gang of Four, but he should go through the historical analysis thoroughly instead of giving all credit to Hua himself.

For a long time, Hua Guofeng had insisted on a principle called "two whatevers " which violated Marxism. The purpose of Hua raising the "two whatevers" was to continue the leftist policies advocated by Chairman Mao in his later years. Hua has changed some of his thoughts after the Third Plenary Sessions; however, his basic ideology has not changed at all.

The series of political slogans advanced by Hua around the Eleventh National Party Congress were inherently the slogans of Great Proletarian Cultural Revolution. Thought there was a certain historical background, Hua did not take his personal responsibility. Hua only condemned things related to the Gang of Four and never initially raised any resolution to redress errors of Great Proletariat Cultural Revolution. His stand on rehabilitating many old party cadres and of reversing many unjust verdicts, false accusations and wrongdoing, and his attitude toward top leaders of central government obviously disappointed most party members' expectations.

Hua was enthusiastic in creating and accepting new personal cult. He enjoyed being called the Wise Leader, being appreciated in the extreme and his picture being hung by Chairman Mao's. Such things were not stopped until not long ago. To misplace the relationships of individual vs. party and individual vs. people is a crucial ideological error and a serious error in party style.

In 1977 and 1978, Hua advocated some leftist slogans in the economy. The abrupt economic advances in these two years caused a great loss and much difficulty in the national economy. Though the primary reason was lack of experience, Hua should bear part of responsibility for the economic failure.

Hua carried out some achievements in the past four years. Unfortunately, his achievements did not show that he is competent to be a central leader in politics and organizations. His lack of competence as Chairman of the Military Committee was much in evidence.

For these reasons, the Central Committee Political Bureau deems that Hua is not an appropriate person to hold his present positions.

Many party members suggested the selection of Deng Xiaoping as the Party Chairman and Chairman of Military Committee because of the popular confidence which he enjoys. But Deng Xiaoping believes that a younger leader with persistence on correct political direction is more proper. Hu Yaobang, in his sixties, is a fit candidate. Deng would like to hold the position as the Chairman of Military Committee temporarily till a suitable candidate appears. The final decision will be made by the Sixth Plenary Sessions; meanwhile, the Central Committee Political Bureau agrees with Deng's suggestions.

In addition to expressing his appreciation to the attendants' criticism and rehanding in his resignation, on the last day of the conference, Hua Guofeng asked to be released from the Central Committee Political Bureau and Central Military Committee before the Sixth Plenary Sessions, thus enabling him to concentrate on his own problems. The Central Committee Political Bureau accepts Hua's plea with a provision that Hu Yaobang shall receive foreign guests as a Chairman before the formal decision of the Sixth Plenary Sessions. The Central Committee Political Bureau hopes that Hu could be selected as a standing member of Central Committee Political Bureau and Vice Chairman of the Party by the Sixth Plenary Session of the 11th Central Committee.

The Central Committee Political Bureau indicates that Hua made some leftist mistakes and other mistakes instead of "line" mistakes. Those terms without precise scientific definition such as "lines," "line mistakes," and "line struggles" shall be mentioned as little as possible since they have made bad impact on the Communist Party. The Central Committee Political Bureau also points out that each organization shall not blame those cadres who were inevitably affected by Hua.

Central Committee Political Bureau passed several resolutions in the conference: (1) Raising suggestion to the Sixth Plenary Sessions for releasing Hua Guofeng from his positions as Chairman of the Party and Chairman of Central Military Committee, (2) Raising suggestion to the Six Plenary Sessions for selecting Hu Yaobang Chairman and Deng Xiaoping Chairman of Central Military, and (3) Before the Six Plenary Sessions, Hu Yaobang will be in charge of Central Committee Political Bureau and Central Standing Committee and Deng Xiaoping is in charge of Central Military Committee without formal titles. The Central Committee Political Bureau emphasizes that (1) and (2) are only suggestions without any compulsion as to the decision of the Sixth Plenary Session. The Sixth Plenary Session shall follow the normal procedure to discuss, vote and select before their final determination.

Since it is a significant change, the Central Committee Political Bureau has decided to release the contents of this conference to all cadres above "Jun" rank of every province in order to let them prepare for the change and convey this message to the 4000 comrades who are attending the Party History Seminar. To assure the stability and unity of whole party, whole nation and whole military force, the Central Committee Political Bureau requires the twenty nine persons attending the meeting keep it as supreme secrete leaking the contents to none.

Those attending this conference have decided to revise the "Resolution on Certain Questions in the History Of Our Party Since the Founding of the P.R.C." according to the suggestions which were raised. The suggestions discussed and passed by the Central Committee Political Bureau shall be discussed and revised in the Party History Seminar of 4000 comrades, then raised to the Sixth Plenary Session of the 11th Central Committee for discussion and passage. The Central Committee Political Bureau thinks it is an opportune moment to pass the resolution without any delay.

*****

DOCUMENT NO. 3

COMMUNIQUE OF THE SIXTH PLENARY SESSION
OF THE ELEVENTH CENTRAL COMMITTEE OF THE CPC

Adopted on June 29, 1981

(**Beijing Review**, No. 27, July 6, 1981)

The Eleventh Central Committee of the Communist Party of China held its Sixth Plenary Session in Beijing from June 27 to 29, 1981. It was attended by 195 Members and 114 Alternate Members of the Central Committee and 53 non-voting participants. Members of the Standing Committee of the Political Bureau of the Central Committee, Comrades Hu Yaobang, Ye Jianying, Deng Xiaoping, Zhao Ziyang, Li Xiannian, Chen Yun and Hua Guofeng, presided at the session.

Items on the agenda of the Plenary Session were: 1) Discussion and approval of the Resolution on Certain Questions in the History of Our Party Since the Founding of the People's Republic of China; 2) Re-election of principal leading members of the Central Committee and election of new ones. The above-mentioned agenda was thoroughly deliberated and conscientiously discussed at a preparatory meeting held before the Plenary Session. This session is another meeting of great significance in the history of our Party following the Third Plenary Session of the Eleventh Central Committee, a meeting for summing up experience and closing the ranks to press forward. This session will go down in history for fulfilling the historic mission of setting to rights things which have been thrown into disorder in the guiding ideology of the Party.

Applying Marxist dialectical materialism and historical materialism, the Resolution on Certain Questions in the History of Our Party Since the Founding of the People's Republic of China unanimously adopted by the Plenary Session correctly sums up the major historical events of the Party in the thirty-two years since the founding of the People's Republic of China, particularly the "great cultural revolution." The resolution scientifically analyses the rights and wrongs in the Party's guiding ideology using these events, analyses the subjective factors and social causes that gave rise to mistakes, realistically evaluates the historical role played by Comrade Mao Zedong, the great leader and teacher, in the Chinese revolution and fully elaborates the great significance of Mao Zedong Thought as the guiding ideology of the Party. The resolution affirms the correct path for building a modern and powerful socialist country, a path which has been gradually established since the Third Plenary Session and which conforms to the realities in China, and further points out the orientation for the continued advance of our country's socialist cause and the work of our Party. The Plenary Session believes that the adoption and publication of the resolution will exert a great and far-reaching influence on unifying the thinking and understanding of the whole party, the whole army, and of the people of all nationalities throughout the country so that they may strive with one heart and one mind to carry out our new, historical task.

The Plenary Session unanimously approved Comrade Hua Guofeng's request to resign his post as Chairman of the Party Central Committee and Chairman of its Military Commission. The Plenary Session re-elected the principal leading members of the Central Committee and elected new ones by secret ballot. The results of the elections are:

1)   Comrade Hu Yaobang -- Chairman of the Central Committee;

2)   Comrade Zhao Ziyang -- Vice-Chairman of the Central Committee;

3)   Comrade Hua Guofeng -- Vice-Chairman of the Central Committee;

4)   Comrade Deng Xiaoping -- Chairman of the Military Commission of the Central Committee;

5)   The Standing Committee of the Political Bureau of the Central Committee made up of the Chairman and Vice-Chairmen of the Central Committee. They are Hu Yaobang, Ye Jianying, Deng Xiaoping, Zhao Ziyang, Li Xiannian, Chen Yun and Hua Guofeng.

6)   Comrade Xi Zhongxun -- Member of the Secretariat of the Central Committee.

The Plenary Session holds that the election and re-election of the principal leading members of the Central Committee will play an important part in strengthening the Central Committee's collective leadership and unity on the basis of Marxism and ensuring the full implementation of the Party's correct line and policies formulated since the Third Plenary Session.

The Plenary Session gave full play to democracy. All comrades present spoke out freely, adopted the scientific approach of seeking truth from facts and displayed the spirit of criticism and self-criticism in summing up historical experience and discussing and deciding the choice of persons as leading members of the Central Committee. This restored and carried forward the fine tradition formed by our Party during the Yanan rectification period. The session vividly demonstrates our Party's strong unity and fully reflects the growth and flourishing of our cause.

The Plenary Session believes that, just as the Party's correct summing up of historical experience in the period of the democratic revolution brought great revolutionary victories, the correct summing up of the Party's historical experience since the founding of the People's Republic of China will help bring about new great victories in our future socialist construction. The Plenary Session calls the whole Party, the whole army and the people of all nationalities throughout the country to hold high the banner of Marxism-Leninism and Mao Zedong Thought, rally more closely around the Party Central Committee, carry forward the spirit of "the Foolish Old Man who removed the mountain," be resolute, surmount all difficulties and work hard to turn China step by step into a modern and powerful socialist country with a high degree of democracy and civilization.

*****

DOCUMENT NO. 4

RESOLUTION ON CERTAIN QUESTIONS IN THE
HISTORY OF OUR PARTY SINCE THE FOUNDING OF
THE PEOPLE'S REPUBLIC OF CHINA

Adopted by the Sixty Plenary Session of
the Eleventh Central Committee of the
Communist Party of China on June 27, 1981

(**Beijing Review**, No. 27, July 6, 1981)

Review of the History of the 28 Years before
the Founding of the People's Republic

1. The Communist Party of China has traversed sixty years of glorious struggle since its founding in 1921. In order to sum up its experience in the thirty-two years since the founding of the People's Republic, we must briefly review the previous twenty-eight years in which the Party led the people in waging the revolutionary struggle for new democracy.

2. The Communist Party of China was the product of the integration of Marxism-Leninism with the Chinese workers' movement and was founded under the influence of the October Revolution in Russia and the May 4 Movement in China and with the help of the Communist International led by Lenin. The Revolution of 1911 led by Dr. Sun Yat-sen, the great revolutionary forerunner, overthrew the Qing Dynasty, thus bringing to an end over 2,000 years of feudal monarchical rule. However, the semi-colonial and semi-feudal nature of Chinese society remained unchanged. Neither the Kuomintang nor any of the bourgeois or petty-bourgeois political groupings and factions found any way out for the country and the nation, nor was it possible for them to do so. The Communist Party of China and the Communist Party of China alone was able to show the people that China's salvation lay in overthrowing once and for all the reactionary rule of imperialism and feudalism and then switching over to socialism. When the Communist Party of China was founded, it had less than sixty members. But it initiated the vigorous workers' movement and the people's anti-imperialist and

anti-feudal struggle and grew rapidly and soon became a leading force such as the Chinese people had never before known.

3. In the course of leading the struggle of the Chinese people with its various nationalities for new democracy, the Communist Party of China went through four stages: the Northern Expedition (1924-27) conducted with the cooperation of the Kuomintang, the Agrarian Revolutionary War (1927-37), the War of Resistance Against Japan (1937-45) and the nationwide War of Liberation (1946-49). Twice, first in 1927 and then in 1934, it endured major setbacks. It was not until 1949 that it finally triumphed in the revolution, thanks to the long years of armed struggle in conjunction with other forms of struggle in other fields closely coordinated with it.

In 1927, regardless of the resolute opposition of the Left wing of the Kuomintang with Soong Ching Ling as its outstanding representative, the Kuomintang controlled by Chiang Kai-shek and Wang Jingwei betrayed the policies of Kuomintang-Communist co-operation and of anti-imperialism and anti-feudalism decided on by Dr. Sun Yat-sen and, in collusion with the imperialists, massacred Communists and other revolutionaries. The Party was still quite inexperienced and, moreover, was dominated by Chen Duxiu's Right capitulationism so that the revolution suffered a disastrous defeat under the surprise attack of a powerful enemy. The total membership of the Party which had grown to more than 60,000, fell to a little over 10,000.

However, our Party continued to fight tenaciously. Launched under the leadership of Zhou Enlai and several other comrades, the Nanchang Uprising of 1927 fired the opening shot for armed resistance against the Kuomintang reactionaries. The meeting of the Central Committee of the Party held on August 7, 1927 decided on the policy of carrying out agrarian revolution and organizing armed uprisings. Shortly afterwards, the Autumn Harvest and Guangzhou Uprisings and uprisings in many other areas were organized. Led by Comrade Mao Zedong, the Autumn Harvest Uprising in the Hunan-Jiangxi border area gave birth to the First Division of the Chinese Workers' and Peasants' Revolutionary Army and to the first rural revolutionary base area in the Jinggang Mountains. Before long, the insurgents led by Comrade Zhu De arrived at the Jinggang Mountains and joined forces with it. With the progress of the struggle, the Party set up the Jiangxi central revolutionary base area and the Western Hunan-Hubei, the Haifeng-Lufeng, the Hubei-Hunan-Anhui, the Quongya, the Fujian-Zhejiang-Jiangxi, the Hunan-Hubei-Jiangxi, the Hunan-Jiangxi, the Zuojiang-Youjiang, the Sichuan-Shaanxi, the Shaanxi-Gansu and the Hunan-Hubei-Sichuan-Guizhou and other base areas. The first, Second and Fourth Front armies of the Workers' and Peasants' Red Army were also born, as were many other Red Army units. In addition, Party organizations and other revolutionary organizations were established and revolutionary mass struggles unfolded under difficult conditions in the Kuomintang areas. In the Agrarian Revolutionary War, the First Front Army of the Red Army and the central revolutionary base area under the direct leadership of Comrades Mao Zedong and Zhu De played the most important role. The front armies of the Red Army defeated in turn a number of "encirclement and suppression" campaigns launched by the Kuomintang troops. But because of Wang Ming's "Left" adventurist leadership, the struggle against the Kuomintang's fifth "encirclement and suppression" campaign ended in failure. The First Front Army was forced to embark on the 25,000-li Long March and made its way to northern Shaanxi to join forces with units of the Red Army which had been persevering in struggles there and with its 25th Army which had arrived earlier. The Second and Fourth Front Armies also went on their long march, first one and then the other arriving in northern Shaanxi. Guerrilla warfare was carried on under difficult conditions in the base areas in south China from which the main forces of the Red Army had withdrawn. As a result of the defeat caused by Wang Ming's "Left" errors, the revolutionary base areas and the revolutionary forces in the Kuomintang areas sustained enormous losses. The Red Army of 300,000 men was reduced to about 30,000 and the Communist Party of 300,000 members to about 40,000.

In January 1935, the Political Bureau of the Central Committee of the Party convened a meeting in Zunyi during the Long March, which established the leading position of Comrade Mao Zedong in the Red Army and the Central Committee of the Party. This saved the Red Army and the Central Committee of the Party which were then in critical danger and subsequently made it possible to defeat Zhang Guotao's splittism, bring the Long March to a triumphant conclusion and open up new vistas for the Chinese revolution. It was a vital turning point in the history of the Party.

At a time of national crisis of unparalleled gravity when the Japanese imperialists were intensifying their aggression against China, the Central Committee of the Party headed by Comrade Mao Zedong decided on and carried out the correct policy of forming an anti-Japanese national united front. Our Party led the students' movement of December 9, 1935 and organized the powerful mass struggle to demand an end to the civil war and resistance against Japan so as to save the nation. The Xian Incident organized by Generals Zhang Xueliang and Yang Hucheng on December 12, 1936 and its peaceful settlement which our Party promoted played a crucial historical role in bringing about renewed co-operation between the Kuomintang and the Communist Party and in achieving national unity for resistance against Japanese aggression. During the war of resistance, the ruling clique of the Kuomintang continued to oppose the Communist Party and the people and was passive in resisting Japan. As a result, the Kuomintang suffered defeat after defeat in front operations against the Japanese invaders. Our Party persevered in the policy of maintaining its independence and initiative within the united front, closely relied on the masses of the people, conducted guerrilla warfare behind enemy lines and set up many anti Japanese base areas. The Eighth Route Army and the New Fourth Army--the reorganized Red Army--grew rapidly and became the mainstay in the war of resistance. The Northeast Anti-Japanese United Army sustained its operations amid formidable difficulties. Diverse forms of anti-Japanese struggle were unfolded on a broad scale in areas occupied by Japan or controlled by the Kuomintang. Consequently, the Chinese people were able to hold out in the war for eight long years and win final victory, in co-operation with the people of the Soviet Union and other countries in the anti-fascist war.

During the anti-Japanese war, the Party conducted a rectification movement, a movement of Marxist education. Launched in 1942, it was a tremendous success. It was on this basis that the Enlarged Seventh Plenary Session of the Sixth Central Committee of the Party in 1945 adopted the Resolution on Certain Questions in the History of Our Party and soon afterwards the Party's Seventh National Congress was convened. These meetings summed up our historical experience and laid down our correct line, principles and policies for building a new-democratic New China, enabling the Party to attain an unprecedented ideological, political and organizational unity and solidarity. After the conclusion of the War of Resistance Against Japan, the Chiang Kai-shek government, with the aid of US imperialism, flagrantly launched an all-out civil war, disregarding the just demand of our Party and the people of the whole country for peace and democracy. With the wholehearted support of the people in all the liberated areas, with the powerful backing of the students' and workers' movements and the struggles of the people of various strata in the Kuomintang areas and with the active co-operation of the democratic parties and non-party democrats, our Party led the People's Liberation Army in fighting the three-year War of Liberation and, after the Liaoxi-Shenyang, Beiping-Tianjin and Huai-Hai campaigns and the successful crossing of the Changjiang (Yang-tze) Rive, in wiping out a total of 8 million Chiang Kai-shek troops. The end result was the overthrow of the reactionary Kuomintang government and the establishment of the great People's Republic of China. The Chinese people had stood up.

4. The victories gained in the twenty-eight years of struggle fully show that:

1) Victory in the Chinese revolution was won under the guidance of Marxism-Leninism. Our Party had creatively applied the basic tenets of

Marxism-Leninism and integrated them with the concrete practice of the Chinese revolution. In this way, the great system of Mao Zedong Thought came into being and the correct path to victory for the Chinese revolution was charted. This is a major contribution to the development of Marxism-Leninism.

2) As the vanguard of the Chinese proletariat, the Communist Party of China is a party serving the people wholeheartedly, with no selfish aim of its own. It is a party with both the courage and the ability to lead the people in their indomitable struggle against any enemy. Convinced of all this through their own experience, the Chinese people of whatever nationality came to rally around the Party and form a broad united front, thus forging a strong political unity unparalleled in Chinese history.

3) The Chinese revolution was victorious mainly because we relied on a people's army led by the Party, an army of a completely new type and enjoying flesh-and-blood ties with the people, to defeat a formidable enemy through protracted people's war. Without such an army, it would have been impossible to achieve the liberation of our people and the independence of our country.

4) The Chinese revolution had the support of the revolutionary forces in other countries at every stage, a fact which the Chinese people will never forget. Yet it must be said that, fundamentally, victory in the Chinese revolution was won because the Chinese Communist Party adhered to the principle of independence and self-reliance and depended on the efforts of the whole Chinese people, whatever their nationality, after they underwent untold hardships and surmounted innumerable difficulties and obstacles together.

5) The victorious Chinese revolution put an end to the rule of a handful of exploiters over the masses of the working people and to the enslavement of the Chinese people of all nationalities by the imperialists and colonialists. The working people have become the masters of the new state and the new society. While changing the balance of forces in world politics, the people's victory in so large a country having nearly on-quarter of the world's population has inspired the people in countries similarly subjected to imperialist and colonialist exploitation and oppression with heightened confidence in their forward march. The triumph of the Chinese revolution is the most important political event since World War II and has exerted a profound and far-reaching impact on the international situation and the development of the people's struggle throughout the world.

5. Victory in the new-democratic revolution was won through long years of struggle and sacrifice by countless martyrs, Party members and people of all nationalities. We should by no means give all the credit to the leaders of the revolution, but at the same time we should not underrate the significant role these leaders have played. Among the many outstanding leaders of the Party, Comrade Mao Zedong was the most prominent. Prior to the failure of the revolution in 1927, he had clearly pointed out the paramount importance of the leadership of the proletariat over the peasants' struggle and the danger of a Right deviation in this regard. After its failure, he was the chief representative of those who succeeded in shifting the emphasis in the Party's work from the city to the countryside and in preserving, restoring and promoting the revolutionary forces in the countryside. In the twenty-two years from 1927 to 1949, Comrade Mao Zedong and other Party Comrades managed to overcome innumerable difficulties and gradually worked out an overall strategy and specific policies and directed their implementation, so that the revolution was able to switch from staggering defeats to great victory. Our Party and people would have had to grope in the dark much longer had it not been for Comrade Mao Zedong, who more than once rescued the Chinese revolution from grave danger, and for the Central Committee of the Party which was headed by him and which started the firm, correct political course for the whole Party, the whole people and the people's army. Just as the Communist Party of China is recognized as the central force leading the entire people forward, so Comrade Mao Zedong was recognized as the great leader of the Chinese Communist Party and the whole Chinese people, and Mao Zedong Thought, which came into being through the collective struggle of the Party and the people, is recognized as the guiding ideology of the Party. This is the inevitable outcome of the twenty-eight years of historical development preceding the founding of the People's Republic of China.

Basic Appraisal of the History of the thirty-two Years Since the Founding of the People's Republic

6. Generally speaking, the years since the founding of the People's Republic of China are years in which tthe Chinese Communist Party, guided by Marxism-Leninism and Mao Zedong Thought, has very successfully led the whole people in carrying out socialist revolution and socialist construction. The establishment of the socialist system represents the greatest and most profound social change in Chinese history and is the foundation for the country's future progress and development.

7. Our major achievements in the thirty-two years since the founding of the People's Republic are the following.

1) We have established and consolidated the people's democratic dictatorship led by the working class and based on the worker-peasant alliance, namely, the dictatorship of the proletariat. It is a new type of state power, unknown in Chinese history, in which the people are the masters of their own house. It constitutes the fundamental guarantee for the building of a modern socialist country, prosperous and powerful, democratic and culturally advanced.

2) We have achieved and consolidated nationwide unification of the country, with the exception of Taiwan and other islands, and have thus put an end to the state of disunity characteristic of old China. We have achieved and consolidated the great unity of the people of all nationalities and have forged and expanded a socialist relationship of equality and mutual help among the more than fifty nationalities. And we have achieved and consolidated the great unity of the workers, peasants, intellectuals and people of other strata and have strengthened and expanded the broad united front which is led by the Chinese Communist Party in full co-operation with the patriotic democratic parties and people's organizations, and comprises all socialist working people and all patriots who support socialism and patriots who stand for the unification of the motherland, including our compatriots in Taiwan, Xianggang (Hongkong) and Aomen (Macao) and Chinese citizens overseas.

3) We have defeated aggression, sabotage and armed provocations by the imperialists and hegemonists, safeguarded our country's security and independence and fought successfully in defence of our border regions.

4) We have built and developed a socialist economy and have in the main completed the socialist transformation of the private ownership of the means of production into public ownership and put into practice the principle of "to each according to his work." The system of exploitation of man by man has been eliminated, and exploiters no longer exist as classes since the overwhelming majority have been remolded and now live by their own labor.

5) We have scored signal successes in industrial construction and have gradually set up an independent and fairly comprehensive industrial base and economic system. Compared with 1952 when economic rehabilitation was completed, fixed industrial assets, calculated on the basis of their original price, were more than 27 times greater in 1980, exceeding 410,000 million yuan; the output of cotton yarn was 4.5 times greater, reaching 2,930,000 tons; that of coal 9.4 times, reaching 620 million tons; that of

electricity 41 times, exceeding 300,000 million kwh; and the output of crude oil exceeded 105 million tons and that of steel 37 million tons; the output value of the engineering industry was 54 times greater, exceeding 127,000 million yuan. A number of new industrial bases have been built in our vast hinterland and the regions inhabited by our minority nationalities. National defense industry started from scratch and is being gradually built up. Much has been done in the prospecting of natural resources. There has been a tremendous growth in railway, highway, water and air transport and post and telecommunications.

6) The conditions prevailing in agricultural production have experienced a remarkable change, giving rise to big increases in production. The amount of land under irrigation has grown from 300 million mu in 1952 to over 670 million mu. Flooding by big rivers such as the Changjiang, Huanghe (Yellow River), Huai-he, Haihe, Zhujiang (Pearl River), Liaohe and Songhuajiang has been brought under initial control. In our rural areas, where farm machinery, chemical fertilizers and electricity were practically non-existent before liberation, there is now a big increase in the number of agriculture-related tractors and irrigation and drainage equipment and in the quantity of chemical fertilizers applied, and the amount of electricity consumed in 7.5 times that generated in the whole country in the early years of liberation. In 1980, the total output of grain was nearly double that in 1952 and that of cotton more than double. Despite the excessive rate of growth in our population, which is now nearly a billion, we have succeeded in basically meeting the needs of our people in food and clothing by our own efforts.

7) There has been a substantial growth in urban and rural commerce and in foreign trade. The total value of commodities purchased by enterprises owned by the whole people rose from 17.5 billion yuan in 1952 to 226.3 billion yuan in 1980, registering an increase nearly 13-fold; retail sales rose from 27.7 billion yuan to 214 billion yuan, an increase of 7.7 times. The total value of the state's foreign trade in 1980 was 8.7 times that of 1952. With the growth in industry, agriculture and commerce, the people's livelihood has improved very markedly, as compared with pre-liberation days. In 1980, average consumption per capita in both town and country was nearly twice as much as in 1952, allowing for price changes.

8) Considerable progress has been made in education, science, culture, public health and physical culture. In 1980, enrollment in the various kinds of full-time schools totalled 204 million, 3.7 times the number in 1952. In the past thirty-two years, the institutions of higher education and

vocational schools have turned out nearly 9 million graduates with specialized knowledge or skills. Our achievements in nuclear technology, man-made satellites, rocketry, etc., represent substantial advances in the field of science and technology. In literature and art large numbers of fine works have appeared to cater for the needs of the people and socialism. With the participation of the masses, sports have developed vigorously, and records have been chalked up in quite a few events. Epidemic diseases with their high mortality rates have been eliminated or largely eliminated, the health of the rural and urban populations has greatly improved, and average life expectancy is now much higher.

9) Under the new historical conditions, the People's Liberation Army has grown in strength and in quality. No longer composed only of ground forces, it has become a composite army, including the naval and air forces and various technical branches. Our armed forces, which are a combination of the field armies, the regional forces and the militia, have been strengthened. Their quality is now much higher and their technical equipment much better. The PLA is serving as the solid pillar of the people's democratic dictatorship in defending and participating in the socialist revolution and socialist construction.

10) Internationally, we have steadfastly pursued an independent socialist foreign policy, advocated and upheld the Five Principles of Peaceful Coexistence, entered into diplomatic relations with 124 countries and promoted trade and economic and cultural exchanges with still more countries and regions. Our country's place in the United Nations and the Security Council has been restored to us. Adhering to proletarian internationalism, we are playing an increasingly influential and active role in international affairs by enhancing our friendship with the people of other countries, by supporting and assisting the oppressed nations in their cause of liberation, the newly independent countries in their national construction and the people of various countries in their just struggles and by staunchly opposing imperialism, hegemonism, colonialism and racism in defence of world peace. All of which has served to create favorable international conditions for our socialist construction and contributes to the development of a world situation favorable to the people everywhere.

8. New China has not been in existence for very long, and our successes are still preliminary. Our Party has made mistakes owing to its meager experience in leading the cause of socialism and subjective errors in the Party leadership's analysis of the situation and its understanding of Chinese conditions. Before the "cultural revolution" there were mistakes of enlarging the scope of class struggle

and of impetuosity and rashness in economic construction. Later, there was the comprehensive, long-drawn out and grave blunder of the "cultural revolution." All these errors prevented us from ignoring the greater achievements of which we should have been capable. It is impermissible to overlook or whitewash mistakes, which in itself would be a mistake and would give rise to more and worse mistakes. But after all our achievements in the past thirty-two years are the main thing. It would be a no less serious error to overlook or deny our achievements or our successful experiences in scoring these achievements. These achievements and successful experiences of ours are the product of the creative application of Marxism-Leninism by our Party and people, the manifestation of the superiority of the socialist system and the base from which the entire Party and people will continue to advance. "Uphold truth and rectify error" -- this is the basic stand of dialectical materialism the Party must take. It was by taking this and stand that we saved our cause from danger and defeat and won victory in the past. By taking the same stand, we will certainly win still greater victories in the future.

The Seven Years of Basic Completion of The Socialist Transformation

9. From the inception of the People's Republic of China in October 1949 to 1956, our Party led the whole people in gradually realizing the transition from new democracy to socialism, rapidly rehabilitating the country's economy, undertaking planned economic construction and in the main accomplishing the socialist transformation of the private ownership of the means of production in most of the country. The guidelines and basic policies defined by the Party in this historical period were correct and led to brilliant successes.

10. In the first three years of the People's Republic, we cleared the mainland of bandits and the remnant armed forces of the Kuomintang reactionaries, peacefully liberated Tibet, established people's governments at all levels throughout the country, confiscated bureaucrat-capitalist enterprises and transformed them into state-owned socialist enterprises, unified the country's financial and economic work, stabilized commodity prices, carried out agrarian reform in the new liberated areas, suppressed counter-revolutionaries, and unfolded the movements against the "three evils" of corruption, waste and bureaucracy and against the "five evils" of bribery, tax evasion, theft of state property, cheating on government contracts and stealing of economic information, the latter being a movement to beat back the attack mounted by the bourgeoisie. We effectively transformed the educational, scientific and cultural institutions of old China. While successfully carrying out the complex and difficult task of social reform and simultaneously undertaking the great war to resist U.S. aggression and aid Korea, protect our homes and defend the country, we rapidly rehabilitated the country's

economy which had been devastated in old China. By the end of 1952, the country's industrial and agricultural production had attained record levels.

11. On the proposal of Comrade Mao Zedong in 1952, the Central Committee of the Party advanced the general line for the transition period, which was to realize the country's socialist industrialization and socialist transformation of agriculture, handicrafts and capitalist industry and commerce step by step over a fairly long period of time. This general line was a reflection of historical necessity.

1) Socialist industrialization is an indispensable prerequisite to the country's independence and prosperity.

2) With nationwide victory in the new-democratic revolution and completion of the agrarian reform, the contradiction between the working class and the bourgeoisie and between the socialist road and the capitalist road became the principle internal contradiction. The country needed a certain expansion of capitalist industry and commerce which were beneficial to its economy and to the people's livelihood. But in the course of their expansion, things detrimental to the national economy and the people's livelihood were bound to emerge. Consequently, a struggle between restriction and opposition to restriction was inevitable. The conflict of interests became increasingly apparent between capitalist enterprises on the one hand and the economic policies of the state, the socialist state-owned economy, the workers and staff in these capitalist enterprises and the people as a whole on the other. An integrated series of necessary measures and steps, such as the fight against speculation and profiteering, the readjustment and restructuring of industry and commerce, the movement against the "five evils," workers, supervision of production and state monopoly of the purchase and marketing of grain and cotton, were bound to gradually bring backward, anarchic, lop-sided and profit-oriented capitalist industry and commerce into the orbit of socialist transformation.

3) Among the individual peasants, and particularly the poor and lower-middle peasants who had just acquired land in the agrarian reform but lacked other means of production, there was a genuine desire for mutual aid and co-operation in order to avoid borrowing at usurious rates and even mortgaging or selling their land again with consequent polarization, and in order to expand production, undertake water conservancy projects, ward off natural calamities and make use of farm machinery and new techniques. The progress of industrialization, while demanding agricultural products in

ever increasing quantities, would provide stronger and stronger support for the technical transformation of agriculture, and this also constituted a motive force behind the transformation of individual into co-operative farming.

As is borne out by history, the general line for the transition period set forth by our Party was entirely correct.

12. During the period of transition, our Party creatively charted a course for socialist transformation that suited China's specific conditions. In dealing with capitalist industry and commerce, we devised a whole series of transitional forms of state capitalism from lower to higher levels, such as the placing of state orders with private enterprises for the processing of materials or the manufacture of goods, state monopoly of the purchase and marketing of the products of private enterprise, the marketing of products of state-owned enterprises by private shops, and joint state-private ownership of individual enterprises or enterprises of a whole trade, and we eventually realized the peaceful redemption of the bourgeoisie, a possibility envisaged by Marx and Lenin. In dealing with individual farming, we devised transitional forms of co-operation, proceeding from temporary or all-the-year-round mutual-aid teams, to elementary agricultural producers' co-operatives of a semi-socialist nature and then to advanced agricultural producers' co-operatives of a fully socialist nature, always adhering to the principles of voluntariness and mutual benefit, demonstration through advanced examples, and extension of state help. Similar methods were used in transforming individual handicraft industries. In the course of such transformation, the state-capitalist and co-operative economies displayed their unmistakable superiority. By 1956, the socialist transformation of the private ownership of the means of production had been largely completed in most regions. But there had been shortcomings and errors. From the summer of 1955 onwards, we were over-hasty in pressing on with agricultural co-operation and the transformation of private handicraft and commercial establishments; we were far from meticulous, the changes were too fast, and we did our work in a somewhat summary, stereotyped manner, leaving open a number of questions for a long time. Following the basic completion of the transformation of capitalist industry and commerce in 1956, we failed to do a proper job in employing and handling some of the former industrialists and businessmen. But on the whole, it was definitely a historic victory for us to have effected, and to have effected fairly smoothly, so difficult, complex and profound a social change in so vast a country with its several hundred million people, a change, moreover, which promoted the growth of industry, agriculture and the economy as a whole.

13.   In economic construction under the First Five-Year Plan (1953-57), we likewise scored major successes through our own efforts and with the assistance of the Soviet Union and other friendly countries. A number of basic industries, essential for the country's industrialization and yet very weak in the past, were built up. Between 1953 and 1956, the average annual increases in the total value of industrial and agricultural output were 19.6 and 4.8 percent respectively. Economic growth was quite fast, with satisfactory economic results, and the key economic sectors were well-balanced. The market prospered, prices were stable. The people's livelihood improved perceptibly. In April 1956, Comrade Mao Zedong made his speech *On the Ten Major Relationships*, in which he initially summed up our experiences in socialist construction and set forth the task of exploring a way of building socialism suited to the specific conditions of our country.

14.   The First National People's Congress was convened in September 1954, and it enacted the Constitution of the People's Republic of China. In March 1955, a national conference of the Party reviewed the major struggle against the plots of the careerists Gao Gang and Rao Shushi to split the Party and usurp supreme power in the Party and the state; in this way it strengthened Party unity. In January 1956, the Central Committee of the Party called a conference on the question of the intellectuals. Subsequently, the policy of "letting a hundred flowers blossom and a hundred schools of thought contend" was advanced. These measures spelled out the correct policy regarding intellectuals and the work in education, science and culture and thus brought about a significant advance in these fields. Owing to the Party's correct policies, fine style of work and the consequent high prestige it enjoyed among the people, the vast numbers of cadres, masses, youth and intellectuals earnestly studied Marxism-Leninism and Mao Zedong Thought and participated enthusiastically in revolutionary and construction activities under the leadership of the Party, so that a healthy and virile revolutionary morality prevailed throughout the country.

15.   The Eighth National Congress of the Party held in September 1956 was very successful. The congress declared that the socialist system had been basically established in China; that while we must strive to liberate Taiwan, thoroughly complete socialist transformation, ultimately eliminate the system of exploitation and continue to wipe out the remnant forces of counter-revolution, the principal contradiction within the country was no longer the contradiction between the working class and the bourgeoisie but between the demand of the people for rapid economic and cultural development and the existing state of our economy and culture which fell short of the needs of the people; that the chief task confronting the whole nation was to concentrate all efforts on developing the productive forces, industrializing the country and gradually meeting the people's

incessantly growing material and cultural needs; and that although class struggle still existed and the people's democratic dictatorship had to be further strengthened, the basic task of the dictatorship was now to protect and develop the productive forces in the context of the new relations of production. The congress adhered to the principle put forward by the Central Committee of the Party in May 1956, the principle of opposing both conservatism and rash advance in economic construction, that is, of making steady progress by striking an overall balance. It emphasized the problem of the building of the Party in office and the need to uphold democratic centralism and collective leadership, oppose the personality cult, promote democracy within the Party and among the people and strengthen the Party's ties with the masses. The line laid down by the Eighth National Congress of the Party was correct and it charted the path for the development of the cause of socialism and for Party building in the new period.

The Ten Years of Initially Building Socialism in All Spheres

16. After the basic completion of socialist transformation, our Party led the entire people in shifting our work to all-round, large-scale socialist construction. In the ten years preceding the "cultural revolution" we achieved very big successes despite serious setbacks. By 1966, the value of fixed industrial assets, calculated on the basis of their original price, was four times greater than in 1956. The output of such major industrial products as cotton yarn, coal, electricity, crude oil, steel and mechanical equipment all recorded impressive increases. Beginning in 1965, China became self-sufficient in petroleum. New industries such as the electronic and petrochemical industries were established one after another. The distribution of industry over the country became better balanced. Capital construction in agriculture and its technical transformation began on a massive scale and yielded better and better results. Both the number of tractors for farming and the quantity of chemical fertilizers applied increased over 7 times and rural consumption of electricity 71 times. The number of graduates from institutions of higher education was 4.9 times that of the previous seven years. Educational work was improved markedly through consolidation. Scientific research and technological work, too, produced notable results.

In the ten years from 1956 to 1966, the Party accumulated precious experience in leading socialist construction. In the spring of 1957, Comrade Mao Zedong stressed the necessity of correctly handling and distinguishing between the two types of social contradictions differing in nature in a socialist society, and made the correct handling of contradictions among the people the main content of the country's political life. Later, he called for the creation of "a political situation in which we have both centralism and democracy, both discipline and freedom, both unity of will and personal ease of mind and liveliness." In 1958, he proposed that the focus of Party and government work be shifted to technical revolution and socialist construction. All this was the continuation and development of the line adopted by the Eighth National Congress of the Party and was to go on serving as a valuable guide. While leading the work of correcting the errors in the great leap forward and the movement to organize people's communes, Comrade Mao Zedong pointed out that there must be no expropriation of the peasants; that a given stage of social development should not be skipped; that egalitarianism must be opposed; that we must stress commodity production, observe the law of value and strike an overall balance in economic planning; and that economic plans must be arranged with the priority proceeding from agriculture to light industry and then to heavy industry. Comrade Liu Shaoqi said that a variety of means of production could be put into circulation as commodities and that there should be a double-track system for labor as well as for education[1] in socialist society. Comrade Zhou Enlai said, among other things, that the overwhelming majority of Chinese intellectuals had become intellectuals belonging to the working people and that science and technology would play a key role in China's modernization. Comrade Chen Yun held that plan targets should be realistic, that the scale of construction should correspond to national capability, considerations should be given to both the people's livelihood and the needs of state construction, and that the material, financial and credit balances should be maintained in drawing up plans. Comrade Deng Xiaoping held that industrial enterprises should be consolidated and their management improved and strengthened, and that the system of workers' conferences should be introduced. Comrade Zhu De stressed the need to pay attention to the development of handicrafts and of diverse undertakings in agriculture. Deng Zihui and other comrades pointed out that a system of production responsibility should be introduced in agriculture. All these views were not only a vital significance then, but have remained so ever since. In the course of economic readjustment, the Central Committee drew up draft rules governing the work of the rural people's communes and work in industry, commerce, education, science and literature and art. These rules which were a more or less systematic summation of our experience in socialist construction and embodied specific policies suited to the prevailing conditions remain important as a source of reference for us to this very day.

In short, the material and technical basis for modernizing our country was largely established during that period. It was also largely in the same period that the core personnel for our work in the economic, cultural and other spheres were trained and that they gained their experience. This was the principal aspect of the Party's work in that period.

17. In the course of this decade, there were serious faults and errors in the guidelines of the Party's work, which developed through twists and turns.

Nineteen fifty-seven was one of the years that saw the best results in economic work since the founding of the People's Republic owing to the conscientious implementation of the correct line formulated at the Eighth National Congress of the Party. To start a rectification campaign throughout the Party in that year and urge the masses to offer criticisms and suggestions were normal steps in developing socialist democracy. In the rectification campaign a handful of bourgeois Rightists seized the opportunity to advocate what they called "speaking out and airing news in a big way" and to mount a wild attack against the Party and the nascent socialist system in an attempt to replace the leadership of the Communist Party. It was therefore entirely correct and necessary to launch a resolute counterattack. But the scope of this struggle was made far too broad and a number of intellectuals, patriotic people and Party cadres were unjustifiably labelled "Rightists," with unfortunate consequences.

In 1958, the Second Plenum of the Eighth National Congress of the Party adopted the general line for socialist construction. The line and its fundamental aspects were correct in that it reflected the masses' pressing demand for a change in the economic and cultural backwardness of our country. Its shortcoming was that it overlooked the objective economic laws. Both before and after the plenum, all comrades in the Party and people of all nationalities displayed high enthusiasm and initiative for socialism and achieved certain results in production and construction. However, "Left" errors, characterized by excessive targets, the issuing of arbitrary directions, boastfulness and the stirring up of a "communist wind," spread unchecked throughout the country. This was due to our lack of experience in socialist construction and inadequate understanding of the laws of economic development and of the basic economic conditions in China. More important, it was due to the fact that Comrade Mao Zedong and many leading comrades, both at the centre and in the localities, had become smug about their successes, were impatient for quick results and overestimated the role of man's subjective will and efforts. After the general line was formulated, the great leap forward and the movement for rural people's communes were initiated without careful investigation and study and without prior experimentation. From the end of 1958 to the early stage of the Lushan Meeting of the Political Bureau of the Party's Central Committee in July 1959, Comrade Mao Zedong and the Central Committee led the whole Party in energetically rectifying the errors which had already been recognized. However, in the later part of the meeting, he erred in initiating criticism of Comrade Peng Dehuai and then in launching a Party-wide struggle against "Right opportunism." The resolution passed by the Eighth Plenary Session of the Eighth Central Committee of the Party concerning the so-called anti-Party group of Peng Dehuai, Huang Kecheng, Zhang Wentian and Zhou Xiaozhou was entirely wrong. Politically, this struggle gravely undermined inner-Party democracy from the central level down to the grass roots; economically, it cut short the process of the rectification of "Left" errors, thus prolonging their influence. It was mainly due to the errors of the great leap forward and of the struggle against "Right opportunism" together with a succession of natural calamities and the perfidious scrapping of contracts by the Soviet Government that our economy encountered serious difficulties between 1959 and 1961, which caused serious losses to our country and people.

In the winter of 1960, the Central Committee of the Party and Comrade Mao Zedong set about rectifying the "Left" errors in rural work and decided on the principle of "readjustment, consolidation, filling out and raising standards" for the economy as a whole. A number of correct policies and resolute measures were worked out and put into effect with Comrades Liu Shaoqi, Zhou Enlai, Chen Yun and Deng Xiaoping in charge. All this constituted a crucial turning point in that historical phase. In January 1962, the enlarged Central Work Conference attended by 7,000 people made a preliminary summing-up of the positive and negative experience of the great leap forward and unfolded criticism and self-criticism. A majority of the comrades who had been unjustifiably criticized during the campaign against "Right opportunism" were rehabilitated before or after the conference. In addition, most of the "Rightists" had their label removed. Thanks to these economic and political measures, the national economy recovered and developed fairly smoothly between 1962 and 1966.

Nevertheless, "Left" errors in the principles guiding economic work were not only not eradicated, but actually grew in the spheres of politics, ideology and culture. At the Tenth Plenary Session of the Party's Eighth Central Committee in September 1962, Comrade Mao Zedong widened and absolutized the class struggle, which exists only within certain limits in socialist society, and carried forward the viewpoint he had advanced after the anti-Rightist struggle in 1957 that the contradiction between the proletariat and the bourgeoisie remained the principal contradiction in our society. He went a step further and asserted that, throughout the historical period of socialism, the bourgeoisie would continue to exist and would attempt a comeback and become the source of revisionism inside the Party. The socialist education movement unfolded between 1963 and 1965 in some rural areas and at the grass-roots level in a small number of cities did help to some extent to improve the cadres' style of work and economic management. But, in the course of the movement, problems differing in nature were all treated as forms of class struggle or its reflections inside the Party. As a result, quite a number of the cadres at the grass-roots level were unjustly dealt with in the latter half of 1964, and early in 1965 the erroneous thesis was advanced that the main target of the movement should be "those Party persons in power taking the capitalist road." In the ideological sphere, a number of literary and art works and schools of thought and a number of representative personages in artistic, literary and academic circles were subjected to unwarranted, inordinate political criticism. And there was an increasingly serious "Left" deviation on the question of intellectuals and on the question of education, science and culture. These errors eventually culminated in the "cultural revolution," but they had not yet become dominant.

Thanks to the fact that the whole Party and people had concentrated on carrying out the correct principle of economic readjustment since the winter of 1960, socialist construction gradually flourished again. The Party and the people were united in sharing weal and woe. They overcame difficulties at home, stood up to the pressure of the Soviet leading clique and repaid all the debts owed to the Soviet Union, which were chiefly incurred through purchasing Soviet arms during the movement to resist U.S. aggression and aid Korea. In addition, they did what they could to support the revolutionary struggles of the people of many countries and assist them in their economic construction. The Third National People's Congress, which met between the end of 1964 and the first days of 1965, announced that the task of national economic readjustment had in the main been accomplished and that the economy as a whole would soon enter a new stage of development. It called for energetic efforts to build China step by step into a socialist power with modern agriculture, industry, national defence and science and technology. This call was not fulfilled owing to the "cultural revolution."

18. All the successes in these ten years were achieved under the collective leadership of the Central Committee of the Party headed by Comrade Mao Zedong. Likewise, responsibility for the errors committed in the work of this period rested with the same collective leadership. Although Comrade Mao Zedong must be held chiefly responsible, we cannot lay the blame on him alone for all those errors. During this period, his theoretical and practical mistakes concerning class struggle in a socialist society became increasingly serious, his personal arbitrariness gradually undermined democratic centralism in Party life and the personality cult grew graver and graver. The Central Committee of the Party failed to rectify these mistakes in good time. Careerists like Lin Biao, Jiang Qing and Kang Sheng, harboring ulterior motives, made use of these errors and inflated them. This led to the inauguration of the "cultural revolution."

The Decade of the "Cultural Revolution"

19. The "cultural revolution," which lasted from May 1966 to October 1976, was responsible for the most severe setback and the heaviest losses suffered

by the Party, the state and the people since the founding of the People's Republic. It was initiated and led by Comrade Mao Zedong. His principal theses were that many representatives of the bourgeoisie and counter-revolutionary revisionists had sneaked into the Party, the government, the army and cultural circles, and leadership in a fairly large majority of organizations and departments was no longer in the hands of Marxists and the people; that Party persons in power taking the capitalist road had formed a bourgeois headquarters inside the Central Committee which pursued a revisionist political and organizational line and had agents in all provinces, municipalities and autonomous regions, as well as in all central departments; that since the forms of struggle adopted in the past had not been able to solve this problem, the power usurped by the capitalist-roaders could be recaptured only by carrying out a great cultural revolution, by openly and fully mobilizing the broad masses from the bottom up to expose these sinister phenomena; and that cultural revolution was in fact a great political revolution in which one class would overthrow another, a revolution that would have to be waged time and again. These theses appeared mainly in the May 16 Circular, which served as the programmatic document of the "cultural revolution," and in the political report to the Ninth National Congress of the Party in April 1969. They were incorporated into a general theory -- the "theory of continued revolution under the dictatorship of the proletariat" -- which then took on a specific meaning. These erroneous "Left" these, upon which Comrade Mao Zedong based himself in initiating the "cultural revolution," were obviously inconsistent with the system of Mao Zedong Thought, which is the integration of the universal principles of Marxism-Leninism with the concrete practice of the Chinese revolution. These theses must be thoroughly distinguished from Mao Zedong Thought. As for Lin Biao, Jiang Qing and others, who were placed in important positions by Comrade Mao Zedong, the matter is of an entirely different nature. They rigged up two counter-revolutionary cliques in an attempt to seize supreme power and, taking advantage of Comrade Mao Zedong's errors, committed many crimes behind his back, bringing disaster to the country and the people. As their counter-revolutionary crimes have been fully exposed, this resolution will not go into them at any length.

20. The history of the "cultural revolution" has proved that Comrade Mao Zedong's principal theses for initiating this revolution conformed neither to Marxism-Leninism nor to Chinese reality. They represent an entirely erroneous appraisal of the prevailing class relations and political situation in the Party and state.

> 1) The "cultural revolution" was defined as a struggle against the revisionist line or the capitalist road. There were no grounds at all for this definition. It led to the confusing of right and wrong on a series of

important theories and policies. Many things denounced as revisionist or capitalist during the "cultural revolution" were actually Marxist and socialist principles, many of which had been set forth or supported by Comrade Mao Zedong himself. The "cultural revolution" negated many of the correct principles, policies and achievements of the seventeen years after the founding of the People's Republic. In fact, it negated much of the work of the Central Committee of the Party and the People's Government, including Comrade Mao Zedong's own contribution. It negated the arduous struggles the entire people had conducted in socialist construction.

2) The confusing of right and wrong inevitably led to confusing the people with the enemy. The "capitalist-roaders" overthrown in the "cultural revolution" were leading cadres of party and government organizations at all levels, who formed the core force of the socialist cause. The so-called bourgeois headquarters inside the Party headed by Liu Shaoqi and Deng Xiaoping simply did not exist. Irrefutable facts have proved that labelling Comrade Liu Shaoqi a "renegade, hidden traitor and scab" was nothing but a frame-up by Lin Biao, Jiang Qing and their followers. The political conclusion concerning Comrade Liu Shaoqi drawn by the Twelfth Plenary Session of the Eighth Central Committee of the Party and the disciplinary measure it meted out to him were both utterly wrong. The criticism of the so-called reactionary academic authorities in the "cultural revolution" during which many capable and accomplished intellectuals were attacked and persecuted also badly muddled up the distinction between the people and the enemy.

3) Nominally, the "cultural revolution" was conducted by directly relying on the masses. In fact, it was divorced both from the Party organizations and from the masses. After the movement started, Party organizations at different levels were attacked and became partially or wholly paralysed, the Party's leading cadres at various levels were subjected to criticism and struggle, inner-Party life came to a stand still, and many activists and large numbers of the basic masses whom the Party has long relied on were rejected. At the beginning of the "cultural revolution," the vast majority of participants in the movement acted out of their faith in Comrade Mao Zedong and the Party. Except for a handful of extremists, however, they did not approve of launching ruthless struggles against leading Party cadres at all levels. With the lapse of time, following their own circuitous paths, they eventually attained a heightened political consciousness and consequently began to adopt a skeptical or wait-and-see attitude towards the "cultural revolution," or even resisted and opposed it. Many people

were assailed either more or less severely for this very reason. Such a state of affairs could not but provide openings to be exploited by opportunists, careerists and conspirators, not a few of whom were escalated to high or even key positions.

4) Practice has shown that the "cultural revolution" did not in fact constitute a revolution or social progress in any sense, nor could it possibly have done so. It was we and not the enemy at all who were thrown into disorder by the "cultural revolution." Therefore, from beginning to end, it did not turn "great disorder under heaven" into "great order under heaven," nor could it conceivably have done so. After the state power in the form of the people's democratic dictatorship was established in China, and especially after socialist transformation was basically completed and the exploiters were eliminated as classes, the socialist revolution represented a fundamental break with the past in both content and method, though its tasks remained to be completed. Of course, it was essential to take proper account of certain undesirable phenomena that undoubtedly existed in Party and state organisms and to remove them by correct measures in conformity with the Constitution, the laws and the Party Constitution. But on no account should the theories and methods of the "cultural revolution" have been applied. Under socialist conditions, there is no economic or political basis for carrying out a great political revolution in which "one class overthrows another." It decidedly could not come up with any constructive programme, but could only bring grave disorder, damage and retrogression in its train. History has shown that the "cultural revolution," initiated by a leader laboring under a misapprehension and capitalized on by counter-revolutionary cliques, led to domestic turmoil and brought catastrophe to the Party, the state and the whole people.

21. The "cultural revolution" can be divided into three stages.

1) From the initiation of the "cultural revolution" to the Ninth National Congress of the Party in April 1969. The convening of the enlarged Political Bureau meeting of the Central Committee of the Party in May 1966 and the Eleventh Plenary Session of the Eighth Central Committee in August of that year marked the launching of the "cultural revolution" on a full scale. These two meetings adopted the May 16 Circular and the Decision of the Central Committee of the Communist Party of China Concerning the Great Proletarian Cultural Revolution respectively. They launched an erroneous struggle against the so-called anti-Party clique of Peng Zhen, Luo Ruiqing, Lu Dingyi and Yang Shangkun and the so-called

headquarters of Liu Shaoqi and Deng Xiaoping. They wrongly re-organized the central leading organs, set up the "Cultural Revolution Group Under the Central Committee of the Chinese Communist Party" and gave it a major part of the power of the Central Committee. In fact, Comrade Mao Zedong's personal leadership characterized by "Left" errors took the place of the collective leadership of the Central Committee, and the cult of Comrade Mao Zedong was frenziedly pushed to an extreme. Lin Biao, Jiang Qing, Kang Sheng, Zhang Chunqiao and others, acting chiefly in the name of the "Cultural Revolution Group," exploited the situation to incite people to "overthrow everything and wage full scale civil war." Around February 1967, at various meetings, Tan Zhenlin, Chen Yi, Ye Jianying, Li Fuchun, Li Xiannian, Xu Xiangqian, Nie Rongzhen and other Political Bureau Members and leading comrades of the Military Commission of the Central Committee sharply criticized the mistakes of the "cultural revolution." This was labelled the "February adverse current," and they were attacked and repressed. Comrades Zhu De and Chen Yun were also wrongly criticized. Almost all leading Party and government departments in the different spheres and localities were stripped of their power or re-organized. The chaos was such that it was necessary to send in the People's Liberation Army to support the Left, the workers and the peasants and to institute military control and military training. It played a positive role in stabilizing the situation, but it also produced some negative consequences. The Ninth Congress of the Party legitimatized the erroneous theories and practices of the "cultural revolution," and so reinforced the positions of Lin Biao, Jiang Qing, Kang Sheng and others in the Central Committee of the Party. The guidelines of the Ninth Congress were wrong, ideologically, politically and organizationally.

2) From the Ninth National Congress of the Party to its Tenth National Congress in August 1973. In 1970-71 the counter-revolutionary Lin Biao clique plotted to capture supreme power and attempted an armed counter-revolutionary coup d'etat. Such was the outcome of the "cultural revolution" which overturned a series of fundamental Party principles. Objectively, it announced the failure of the theories and practices of the "cultural revolution." Comrades Mao Zedong, and Zhou Enlai ingeniously thwarted the plotted coup. Supported by Comrade Mao Zedong, Comrade Zhou Enlai took charge of the day-to-day work of the Central Committee and things began to improve in all fields. During the criticism and repudiation of Lin Biao in 1972, he correctly proposed criticism of the ultra-Left trend of thought. In fact, this was an extension of the correct proposals put forward around February 1967 by many leading comrades of the Central Committee who had called for the correction of the errors

of the "cultural revolution." Comrade Mao Zedong, however, erroneously held that the task was still to oppose the "ultra-Right." The 10th Congress of the Party perpetuated the "Left" errors of the Ninth Congress and made Wang Hongwen a vice-chairman of the Party. Jiang Qing, Zhang Chunqiao, Yao Wenyuan and Wang Hongwen formed a gang of four inside the Political Bureau of the Central Committee, thus strengthening the influence of the counter-revolutionary Jiang Qinq clique.

3) From the Tenth Congress of the Party to October 1976. Early in 1974 Jiang Qing, Wang Hongwen and others launched a campaign to "criticize Lin Biao and Confucius." Jiang Qing and the others directed the spearhead at Comrade Zhou Enlai, which was different in nature from the campaign conducted in some localities and organizations where individuals involved in incidents connected with the conspiracies of the counter-revolutionary Lin Biao clique were investigated. Comrade Mao Zedong approved the launching of the movement to "criticize Lin Biao and Confucius." Then he found that Jiang Qing and the others were turning it to their advantage in order to seize power, he severely criticized them. He declared that they had formed a gang of four and pointed out that Jiang Qing harbored the wild ambition of making herself chairman of the Central Committee and "forming a cabinet" by political manipulation. In 1975, when Comrade Zhou Enlai was seriously ill, Comrade Deng Xiaoping, with the support of Comrade Mao Zedong, took charge of the day-to-day work of the Central Committee. He convened an enlarged meeting of the Military Commission of the Central Committee and several other important meetings with a view to solving problems in industry, agriculture, transport and science and technology, and began to straighten out work in many fields so that the situation took an obvious turn for the better. However, Comrade Mao Zedong could not bear to accept systematic correction of the errors of the "cultural revolution" by Comrade Deng Xiaoping and triggered the movement to "criticize Deng and counter the Right deviationist trend to reverse correct verdicts," once again plunging the nation into turmoil. In January of that year, Comrade Zhou Enlai passed away. Comrade Zhou Enlai was utterly devoted to the Party and the people and stuck to his post till his dying day. He found himself in an extremely difficult situation throughout the "cultural revolution." He always kept the general interest in mind, bore the heavy burden of office without complaint, racking his brains and untiringly endeavouring to keep the normal work of the Party and the state going, to minimize the damage caused by the "cultural revolution" and to protect many Party and non-Party cadres. He waged all forms of struggle to counter sabotage by the counter-revolutionary Lin Biao and Jiang Qing cliques. His death left the whole Party and people in

the most profound grief. In April of the same year, a powerful movement of protest signalled by the Tian An Men Incident swept the whole country, a movement to mourn for the late Premier Zhou Enlai and oppose the gang of four. In essence, the movement was a demonstration of support for the Party's correct leadership as represented by Comrade Deng Xiaoping. It laid the ground for massive popular support for the subsequent overthrow of the counter-revolutionary Jiang Qing clique. The Political Bureau of the Central Committee and Comrade Mao Zedong wrongly assessed the nature of the Tian An Men Incident and dismissed Comrade Deng Xiaoping from all his posts inside and outside the Party. As soon as Comrade Mao Zedong passed away in September 1976, the counter-revolutionary Jiang Qing clique stepped up its plot to seize supreme Party and state leadership. Early in October of the same year, the Political Bureau of the Central Committee, executing the will of the Party and the people, resolutely smashed the clique and brought the catastrophic "cultural revolution" to an end. This was a great victory won by the entire Party, army and people after prolonged struggle. Hua Guofeng, Ye Jianying, Li Xiannian and other comrades played a vital part in the struggle to crush the clique.

22.   Chief responsibility for the grave "Left" error of the "cultural revolution," an error comprehensive in magnitude and protracted in duration, does indeed lie with Comrade Mao Zedong. But after all it was the error of a great proletarian revolutionary. Comrade Mao Zedong paid constant attention to overcoming shortcomings in the life of the Party and state. In his later years, however, far from making a correct analysis of many problems, he confused right and wrong and the people with the enemy during the "cultural revolution." While making serious mistakes, he repeatedly urged the whole Party to study the works of Marx, Engels and Lenin conscientiously and imagined that his theory and practice were Marxist and that they were essential for the consolidation of the dictatorship of the proletariat. Herein lies his tragedy. While persisting in the comprehensive error of the "cultural revolution," he checked and rectified some of its specific mistakes, protected some leading Party cadres and non-Party public figures and enabled some leading cadres to return to important leading posts. He led the struggle to smash the counter-revolutionary Lin Biao clique. He made major criticisms and exposures of Jiang Qing, Zhang Chunqiao and others, frustrating their sinister ambition to seize supreme leadership. All this was crucial to the subsequent and relatively painless overthrow of the gang of four by our Party. In his later years, he still remained alert to safeguarding the security of our country, stood up to the pressure of the social-imperialists, pursued a correct foreign policy, firmly supported the just struggles of all peoples, outlined the correct strategy of the three worlds and advanced the important principle that China would never seek hegemony. During the "cultural revolution" our Party

was not destroyed, but maintained its unity. The State Council and the People's Liberation Army were still able to do much of their essential work. The Fourth National People's Congress which was attended by deputies from all nationalities and all walks of life was convened and it determined the composition of the State Council with Comrades Zhou Enlai and Deng Xiaoping as the core of its leadership. The foundation of China's socialist system remained intact and it was possible to continue socialist economic construction. Our country remained united and exerted a significant influence on international affairs. All these important facts are inseparable from the great role played by Comrade Mao Zedong. For these reasons, and particularly for his vital contributions to the cause of the revolution over the years, the Chinese people have always regarded Comrade Mao Zedong as their respected and beloved great leader and teacher.

23. The struggle waged by the Party and the people against "Left" errors and against the counter-revolutionary Lin Biao and Jiang Qing cliques during the "cultural revolution" was arduous and full of twists and turns, and it never ceased. Rigorous tests throughout the "cultural revolution" have proved that standing on the correct side in the struggle were the overwhelming majority of Members of the Eighth Central Committee of the Party and the Members it elected to its Political Bureau, Standing Committee and Secretariat. Most of our Party cadres, whether they were wrongly dismissed or remained at their posts, whether they were rehabilitated early or late, are loyal to the Party and people and steadfast in their belief in the cause of socialism and communism. Most of the intellectuals, model workers, patriotic democrats, patriotic overseas Chinese and cadres and masses of all strata and all nationalities who had been wronged and persecuted did not waver in their love for the motherland and in their support for the Party and socialism. Party and state leaders such as Comrades Liu Shaoqi, Peng Dehuai, He Long and Tao Zhu and all other Party and non-Party comrades who were persecuted to death in the "cultural revolution" will live for ever in the memories of the Chinese people. It was through the joint struggles waged by the entire Party and the masses of workers, peasants, PLA officers and men, intellectuals, educated youth and cadres that the havoc wrought by the "cultural revolution" was somewhat mitigated. Some progress was made in our economy despite tremendous losses. Grain output increased relatively steadily. Significant achievements were scored in industry, communications and capital construction and in science and technology. New railways were built and the Changjiang River Bridge at Nanjing was completed; a number of large enterprises using advanced technology went into operation; hydrogen bomb tests were successfully undertaken and man-made satellites successfully launched and retrieved; and new hybrid strains of long-grained rice were developed and popularized. Despite the domestic turmoil, the People's Liberation Army bravely defended the security of the motherland. And new prospects were opened up in the sphere of foreign affairs. Needless to say,

none of these successes can be attributed in any way to the "cultural revolution," without which we would have scored far greater achievements for our cause. Although we suffered from sabotage by the counter-revolutionary Lin Biao and Jiang Qing cliques during the "cultural revolution," we won out over them in the end. The Party, the people's political power, the people's army and Chinese society on the whole remained unchanged in nature. Once again history has proved that our people are a great people and that our Party and socialist system have enormous vitality.

24. In addition to the above-mentioned immediate cause of Comrade Mao Zedong's mistake in leadership, there are complex social and historical causes underlying the "cultural revolution" which dragged on for as long as a decade. The main causes are as follows:

1) The history of the socialist movement is not long and that of the socialist countries even shorter. Some of the laws governing the development of socialist society are relatively clear, but many more remain to be explored. Our Party had long existed in circumstances of war and fierce class struggle. It was not fully prepared, either ideologically or in terms of scientific study, for the swift advent of the newborn socialist society and for socialist construction on a national scale. The scientific works of Marx, Engels, Lenin and Stalin are our guide to action, but can in no way provide ready-made answers to the problems we may encounter in our socialist cause. Even after the basic completion of socialist transformation, given the guiding ideology, we were liable, owing to the historical circumstances in which our Party grew, to continue to regard issues unrelated to class struggle as its manifestations when observing and handling new contradictions and problems which cropped up in the political, economic, cultural and other spheres in the course of the development of socialist society. And when confronted with actual class struggle under the new conditions, we habitually fell back on the familiar methods and experiences of the large-scale, turbulent mass struggle of the past, which should no longer have been mechanically followed. As a result, we substantially broadened the scope of class struggle. Moreover, this subjective thinking and practice divorced from reality seemed to have a "theoretical basis" in the writings of Marx, Engels, Lenin and Stalin because certain ideas and arguments set forth in them were misunderstood or dogmatically interpreted. For instance, it was thought that equal right, which reflects the exchange of equal amounts of labor and is applicable to the distribution of the means of consumption in socialist society, or "bourgeois right" as it was designated by Marx, should be restricted and criticized, and so the principle of "to each according to his work" and that

of material interest should be restricted and criticized; that small production would continue to engender capitalism and the bourgeoisie daily and hourly on a large scale even after the basic completion of socialist transformation, and so a series of "Left" economic policies and policies on class struggle in urban and rural areas were formulated; and that all ideological differences inside the Party were reflections of class struggle in society, and so frequent and acute inner-Party struggles were conducted. All this led us to regard the error in magnifying class struggle as an act in defence of the purity of Marxism. Furthermore, Soviet leaders started a polemic between China and the Soviet Union, and turned the arguments between the two Parties on matters of principle into a conflict between the two nations, bringing enormous pressure to bear upon China politically, economically and militarily. So we were forced to wage a just struggle against the big-nation chauvinism of the Soviet Union. In these circumstances, a campaign to prevent and combat revisionism inside the country was launched, which spread the error of broadening the scope of class struggle in the Party, so that normal differences among comrades inside the Party came to be regarded as manifestations of the revisionist line or of the struggle between the two lines. This resulted in growing tension in inner-Party relations. Thus it became difficult for the Party to resist certain "Left" views put forward by Comrade Mao Zedong and others, and the development of these views led to the outbreak of the protracted "cultural revolution."

2) Comrade Mao Zedong's prestige reached a peak and he began to get arrogant at the very time when the Party was confronted with the new task of shifting the focus of its work to socialist construction, a task for which the utmost caution was required. He gradually divorced himself from practice and from the masses, acted more and more arbitrarily and subjectively, and increasingly put himself above the Central Committee of the Party. The result was a steady weakening and even undermining of the principle of collective leadership and democratic centralism in the political life of the Party and the country. This state of affairs took shape only gradually and the Central Committee of the Party should be held partly responsible. From the Marxist viewpoint, this complex phenomenon was the product of given historical conditions. Blaming this on only one person or on only a handful of people will not provide a deep lesson for the whole Party or enable it to find practical ways to change the situation. In the communist movement, leaders play quite an important role. This has been borne out by history time and again and leaves no room for doubt. However, certain grievous deviations, which occurred in the history of the international communist movement owing to the failure to handle

the relationship between the Party and its leader correctly, had an adverse effect on our Party, too. Feudalism in China has had a very long history. Our Party fought in the firmest and most thoroughgoing way against it, and particularly against the feudal system of land ownership and the landlords and local tyrants, and fostered a fine tradition of democracy in the anti-feudal struggle. But it remains difficult to eliminate the evil ideological and political influence of centuries of feudal autocracy. And for various historical reasons, we failed to institutionalize and legalize inner-Party democracy and democracy in the political and social life of the country, or we drew up the relevant laws but they lacked due authority. This meant that conditions were present for the overconcentration of Party power in individuals and for the development of arbitrary individual rule and the personality cult in the Party. Thus, it was hard for the Party and state to prevent the initiation of the "cultural revolution" or check its development.

A Great Turning Point in History

25. The victory won in overthrowing the counter-revolutionary Jiang Qinq clique in October 1976 saved the Party and the revolution from disaster and enable our country to enter a new historical period of development. In the two years from October 1976 to December 1978 when the Third Plenary Session of the Eleventh Central Committee of the Party was convened, large numbers of cadres and other people most enthusiastically devoted themselves to all kinds of revolutionary work and the task of construction. Notable results were achieved in exposing and repudiating the crimes of the counter-revolutionary Jiang Qing clique and uncovering their factional setup. The consolidation of Party and state organizations and the redress of wrongs suffered by those who were unjustly, falsely and wrongly charged began in some places. Industrial and agricultural production was fairly swiftly restored. Work in education, science and culture began to return to normal. Comrads inside and outside the Party demanded more and more strongly that the errors of the "cultural revolution" be corrected, but such demands met with serious resistance. This, of course, was partly due to the fact that the political and ideological confusion created in the decade-long "cultural revolution" could not be eliminated overnight, but it was also due to the "Left" errors in the guiding ideology that Comrade Hua Guofeng continued to commit in his capacity as Chairman of the Central Committee of the Chinese Communist Party. On the proposal of Comrade Mao Zedong, Comrade Hua Guofeng had become First Vice-Chairman of the Central Committee of the Party and concurrently Premier of the State Council during the "movement to criticize Deng Xiaoping" in 1976. He contributed to the struggle to overthrow the counter-revolutionary Jiang Qing clique and did useful work after that. But he promoted

the erroneous "two-whatever's" policy, that is, "we firmly uphold whatever policy decisions Chairman Mao made, and we unswervingly adhere to whatever instructions Chairman Mao gave," and he took a long time to rectify the error. He tried to suppress the discussions on the criterion of truth unfolded in the country in 1978, which were very significant in setting things right. He procrastinated and obstructed the work of reinstating veteran cadres in their posts and redressing the injustices left over from the past (including the case of the "Tien An Men Incident" of 1976). He accepted and fostered the personality cult around himself while continuing the personality cult of the past. The Eleventh National Congress of the Chinese Communist Party convened in August 1977 played a positive role in exposing and repudiating the Gang of Four and mobilizing the whole Party for building China into a powerful modern socialist state. However, owning to the limitations imposed by the historical conditions then and the influence of Comrade Hua Guofeng's mistakes, it reaffirmed the erroneous theories, policies and slogans of the "cultural revolution" instead of correcting them. He also had his share of responsibility for impetuously seeking quick results in economic work and for continuing certain other "Left" policies. Obviously, under his leadership it is impossible to correct "Left" errors within the Party, and all the more impossible to restore the Party's fine traditions.

26. The Third Plenary Session of the Eleventh Central Committee in December 1978 marked a crucial turning point of far-reaching significance in the history of our Party since the birth of the People's Republic. It put an end to the situation in which the Party had been advancing haltingly in its work since October 1976 and began to correct conscientiously and comprehensively the "Left" errors of the "cultural revolution" and earlier. The plenary session resolutely criticized the erroneous "two-whatever's" policy and fully affirmed the need to grasp Mao Zedong Thought comprehensively and accurately as a scientific system. It highly evaluated the forum on the criterion of truth and decided on the guiding principle of emancipating the mind, using our brains, seeking truth from facts and uniting as one in looking forward to the future. It firmly discarded the slogan "Take class struggle as the key link," which had become unsuitable in a socialist society, and made the strategic decision to shift the focus of work to socialist modernization. It declared that attention should be paid to solving the problem of serious imbalances between the major branches of economy and drafted decisions on the acceleration of agricultural development. It stressed the task of strengthening socialist democracy and the socialist legal system. It determined and redressed a number of major unjust, false and wrong cases in the history of the Party and settled the controversy on the merits and demerits, the rights and wrongs, of the prominent leaders. The plenary session also elected additional members to the Party's central leading organs. These momentous changes in the work of leadership signified that the Party re-established the correct line of

Marxism ideologically, politically and organizationally. Since then, it has gained the initiative setting things right and has been able to solve step by step many problems left over since the founding of the People's Republic and the new problems cropping up in the course of practice and carry out the heavy tasks of construction and reform, so that things are going very well in both the economic and political sphere.

1) In response to the call of the Third Plenary Session of the Eleventh Central Committee of the Party for emancipating the mind and seeking truth from facts, large numbers of parties and other people have freed themselves from the spiritual shackles of the personality cult and the dogmatism that prevailed in the past. This has stimulated thinking inside and outside the Party, giving rise to a lively situation where people try their best to study new things and seek solutions to new problems. To carry out the principle of emancipating the mind properly, the Party reiterated in good time the four fundamental principles of upholding the socialist road, the people's democratic dictatorship (i.e., the dictatorship of the proletariat), the leadership of the Communist Party, and Marxism-Leninism and Mao Zedong Thought. It reaffirmed the principle that neither democracy nor centralism can be practised at each other's expense and pointed out the basic fact that, although the exploiters had been eliminated as classes, class struggle continues to exist within certain limits. In his speech at the meeting in celebration of the thirtieth anniversary of the founding of the People's Republic of China, which was approved by the Fourth Plenary Session of the Eleventh Central Committee of the Party, Comrade Ye Jianying fully affirmed the gigantic achievements of the Party and people since the inauguration of the People's Republic while making self-criticism on behalf of the Party for errors in its work and outlined our country's bright prospects. This helped to unify the thinking of the whole Party and people. At its meeting in August 1980, the Political Bureau of the Central Committee set the historic task of combating corrosion by bourgeois ideology and eradicating the evil influence of feudalism in the political and ideological fields which is still present. A work conference convened by the Central Committee in December of the same year resolved to strengthen the Party's ideological and political work, make greater efforts to build a socialist civilization, criticize the erroneous ideological trends running counter to the four fundamental principles and strike at the counter-revolutionary activities disrupting the cause of socialism. This exerted a most salutary countrywide influence in fostering a political situation characterized by stability, unity and liveliness.

2) At a work conference called by the Central Committee in April 1979, the Party formulated the principle of "readjusting, restructuring, consolidating and improving," the economy as a whole in a decisive effort to correct the shortcomings and mistakes of the previous two years in our economic work and eliminate the influence of "Left" errors that had persisted in this field. The Party indicated that economic construction must be carried out in the light of China's conditions and in conformity with economic and natural laws; that it must be carried out within the limits of our own resources, step by step, after due deliberation and with emphasis on practical results, so that the development of production will be closely connected with the improvement of the people's livelihood; and that active efforts must be made to promote economic and technical co-operation with other countries on the basis of independence and self-reliance. Guided by these principles, light industry has quickened its rate of growth and the structure of industry is becoming more rational and better coordinated. Reforms in the system of economic management, including extension of the decision-making powers of enterprises, restoration of the workers' congresses, strengthening of democratic management of enterprises and transference of financial management responsibilities to the various levels, have gradually been carried out in conjunction with economic readjustment. The Party has worked conscientiously to remedy the errors in rural work since the later stage of the movement for agricultural co-operation, with the result that the purchase prices of farm and sideline products have been raised, various forms of production responsibility introduced whereby remuneration is determined by farm output, family plots have been restored and appropriately extended, village fairs have been revived, and sideline occupations and diverse undertakings have been developed. All these have greatly enhanced the peasants' enthusiasm. Grain output in the last two years reached an all-time high, and at the same time industrial crops and other farm and sideline products registered a big increase. Thanks to the development of agriculture and the economy as a whole, the living standards of the people have improved.

3) After detailed and careful investigation and study, measures were taken to clear the name of Comrade Liu Shaoqi, former Vice-Chairman of the Central Committee of the Communist Party of China and Chairman of the People's Republic of China, those of other Party and state leaders, national minority leaders and leading figures in different circles who had been wronged, and to affirm their historical contributions to the Party and the people in protracted revolutionary struggle.

4) Large numbers of unjust, false and wrong cases were re-examined and their verdicts reversed. Cases in which people had been wrongly labelled bourgeois Rightists were also corrected. Announcements were made to the effect that former businessmen and industrialists, having undergone remoulding, are now working people; that small trades people, peddlers and handicraftsmen, who were originally laborers, have been differentiated from businessmen and industrialists who were members of the bourgeoisie; and that the status of the vast majority of former landlords and rich peasants, who have become working people through remoulding, has been redefined. These measures have appropriately resolved many contradictions inside the Party and among the people.

5) People's congresses at all levels are doing their work better and those at the provincial and county levels have set up permanent organs of their own. The system according to which deputies to the people's congresses at and below the county level are directly elected by the voters is now universally practiced. Collective leadership and democratic centralism are being perfected in the Party and state organizations. The powers of local and primary organizations are steadily being extended. The so-called right to "speak out, air views and hold debates in a big way and write big-character posters," which actually obstructs the promotion of socialists democracy, was deleted from the Constitution. A number of important laws, decrees and regulations have been reinstated, enacted or enforced, including the Criminal Law and the Law of Criminal Procedure which had never been drawn up since the founding of the People's Republic. The work of the judicial, procuratorial and public security departments has improved and telling blows have been deal at all types of criminals guilty of serious offenses. The ten principal members of the counter-revolutionary Lin Biao and Jiang Qing cliques were publicly tried according to law.

6) The Party has striven to readjust and strengthen the leading bodies at all levels. The Fifth Plenary Session of the Eleventh Central Committee of the Party, held in February 1980, elected additional members to the Standing Committee of its Political Bureau and re-established the Secretariat of the Central Committee, greatly strengthening the central leadership. Party militancy has been enhanced as a result of the establishment of the Central Commission for Inspecting Discipline and of discipline inspection commissions at the lower levels, the formulation of the Guiding Principles for Inner-Party Political Life and other related inner-Party regulations, and the effort made by leading Party organizations and discipline inspection bodies at the different levels to rectify unhealthy

practices. The Party's mass media have also contributed immensely in this respect. The Party has decided to put an end to the virtually life-long tenure of leading cadres, change the overconcentration of power and, on the basis of revolutionization, gradually reduce the average age of the leading cadres at all levels and raise their level of education and professional competence, and has initiated this process. With the reshuffling of the leading personnel of the State Council and the division of labor between Party and government organizations, the work of the central and local governments has improved.

In addition, there have been significant successes in the Party's efforts to implement our policies in education, science, culture, public health, physical culture, nationality affairs, united front work, overseas Chinese affairs and military and foreign affairs.

In short, the scientific principles of Mao Zedong Thought and the correct policies of the Party have been revived and developed under new conditions and all aspects of Party and government work have been flourishing again since the Third Plenary Session of the Eleventh Central Committee. Our work still suffers from shortcomings and mistakes, and we are still confronted with numerous difficulties. Nevertheless, the road of victorious advance is open, and the Party's prestige among the people is rising day by day.

Comrade Mao Zedong's Historical Role and Mao Zedong Thought

27. Comrade Mao Zedong was a great Marxist and a great proletarian revolutionary, strategist and theorist. It is true that he made gross mistakes during the "cultural revolution," but, if we judge his activities as a whole, his contributions to the Chinese revolution far outweigh weigh his mistakes. His merits are primary and his errors secondary. He rendered indelible meritorious service in founding and building up our Party and the Chinese People's Liberation Army, in winning victory for the cause of liberation of the Chinese people, in founding the People's Republic of China and in advancing our socialist cause. He made major contributions to the liberation of the oppressed nations of the world and to the progress of mankind.

28. The Chinese Communists, with Comrade Mao Zedong as their chief representative, made a theoretical synthesis of China's unique experience in its protracted revolution in accordance with the basic principles of Marxism-Leninism. This synthesis constituted a scientific system of guidelines befitting China's conditions, and it is this synthesis which is Mao Zedong Thought, the product of the integration of the universal principles of Marxism-Leninism with the concrete

practice of the Chinese revolution. Making revolution in a large Eastern semi-colonial, semi-feudal country is bound to meet with many special, complicated problems, which cannot be solved by reciting the general principal of Marxism-Leninism or by copying foreign experience in every detail. The erroneous tendency of making Marxism a dogma and deifying Comintern resolutions and the experience of the Soviet Union prevailed in the international communist movement and in our Party mainly in the late 1920s and early 1930s, and this tendency pushed the Chinese revolution to the brink of total failure. It was in the course of combating this wrong tendency and making a profound summary of our historical experience in this respect that Mao Zedong Thought took shape and developed. It was systematized and extended in a variety of fields and reached maturity in the latter part of the Agrarian Revolutionary War and the War of Resistance Against Japan, and it was further developed during the War of Liberation and after the founding of the People's Republic of China. Mao Zedong Thought is Marxism-Leninism applied and developed in China; it constitutes a correct theory, a body of correct principles and a summary of the experiences that have been confirmed in the practice of the Chinese revolution, a crystallization of the collective wisdom of the Chinese Communist Party. Many outstanding leaders of our Party made important contributions to the formation and development of Mao Zedong Thought, and they are synthesized in the scientific works of Comrade Mao Zedong.

29. Mao Zedong Thought is wide-ranging in content. It is an original theory which has enriched and developed Marxism-Leninism in the following respects:

1) On the new-democratic revolution. Proceeding from China's historical and social conditions, Comrade Mao Zedong made a profound study of the characteristics and laws of the Chinese revolution, applied and developed the Marxist-Leninist thesis of the leadership of the proletariat in the democratic revolution, and established the theory of new-democratic revolution--a revolution against imperialism, feudalism and bureaucrat-capitalism waged by the masses of the people on the basis of the worker-peasant alliance under the leadership of the proletariat. His main works on this subject include: *Analysis of the Classes in Chinese Society, Report on an Investigation of the Peasant Movement in Human, A Single Spark Can Start a Prairie Fire, Introducing "The Communist," On New Democracy, On Coalition Government and The Present Situation and Our Tasks.* The basic points of this theory are:

I) China's bourgeoisie consisted of two sections, the big bourgeoisie (that is, the comprador bourgeoisie, or the bureaucrat-bourgeoisie) which was dependent on imperialism, and the national bourgeoisie which had revolutionary leanings but wavered. The proletariat should endeavour to get the national bourgeoisie to join in the united front under its leadership and in special circumstances to include even part of the big bourgeoisie in the united front, so as to isolate the main enemy to the greatest possible extent. When forming a united front with the bourgeoisie, the proletariat must preserve its own independence and pursue the policy of "unity, struggle, unity through struggle;" when forced to split with the bourgeoisie, chiefly the big bourgeoisie, it should have the courage and ability to wage a resolute armed struggle against the big bourgeoisie, while continuing to win the sympathy of the national bourgeoisie or keep it neutral.

II) Since there was no bourgeois democracy in China and the reactionary ruling classes enforced their terroristic dictatorship over the people by armed force, the revolution could not but essentially take the form of protracted armed struggle. China's armed struggle was a revolutionary war led by the proletariat with the peasants as the principal force. The peasantry was the most reliable ally of the proletariat. Through its vanguard, it was possible and necessary for the proletariat, with its progressive ideology and its sense of organization and discipline, to raise the political consciousness of the peasant masses, establish rural base areas, wage a protracted revolutionary war and build up and expand the revolutionary forces.

Comrade Mao Zedong pointed out that "the united front and armed struggle are the two basic weapons for defeating the enemy." Together with Party building, they constituted the "three magic weapons" of the revolution. They were the essential basis which enabled the Chinese Communist Party to become the core of leadership of the whole nation and to chart the course of encircling the cities from the countryside and finally winning countrywide victory.

2) On the socialist revolution and socialist construction. On the basis of the economic and political conditions for the transition to socialism ensuing on victory in the new-democratic revolution, Comrade Mao Zedong and the Chinese Communist Party followed the path of effecting socialist industrialization simultaneously with socialist transformation and adopted concrete policies for the gradual transformation of the private ownership of the means of production, thereby providing a theoretical as well as

practical solution of the difficult task of building socialism in a large country such as China, a country which was economically and culturally backward, with a population accounting for nearly one-fourth of the world's total. By putting forward the thesis that the combination of democracy for the people and dictatorship over the reactionaries constitutes the people's democratic dictatorship, Comrade Mao Zedong enriched the Marxist-Leninist theory of the dictatorship of the proletariat. After the establishment of the socialist system, Comrade Mao Zedong pointed out that, under socialism, the people had the same fundamental interests, but that all kinds of contradictions still existed among them, and that contradictions between the enemy and the people and contradictions among the people should be strictly distinguished from each other and correctly handled. He proposed that among the people we should follow a set of correct policies. We should follow the policy of "unity--criticism--unity" in political matters, the policy of "long-term coexistence and mutual supervision" in the Party's relations with the democratic parties, the policy of "let a hundred flowers blossom, let a hundred schools of thought contend" in science and culture, and, in the economic sphere the policy of overall arrangement with regard to the different strata in town and country and of consideration for the interests of the state, the collective and the individual, all three. He repeatedly stressed that we should not mechanically transplant the experience of foreign countries, but should find our own way to industrialization, a way suited to China's condition, by proceeding from the fact that China is a large agricultural country, taking agriculture as the foundation of the economy, correctly handling the relationship between heavy industry on the one hand and agriculture and light industry on the other and attaching due important to the development of the latter. He stressed that in socialist construction we should properly handle the relationships between economic construction and building up defence, between large-scale enterprises and small and medium-scale enterprises, between the Han nationality and the minority nationalities, between the coastal regions and the interior, between the central and the local authorities, and between self-reliance and learning from foreign countries, and that we should properly handle the relationship between accumulation and consumption and pay attention to overall balance. Moreover, he stressed that the workers were the masters of their enterprises and that cadres must take part in physical labor and workers in management, that irrational rules and regulations must be reformed and that the three-in-one combination of technical personnel, workers and cadres must be effected. And he formulated the strategic idea of bringing all positive factors into play and turning negative factors into positive ones so as to unite the whole Chinese people and build a powerful socialist country. The important ideas of Comrade Mao Zedong concerning the socialist revolution and socialist construction are mainly contained in such major works as *Report to the Second Plenary Session of the Seventh Central Committee of the Communist Party of China, On the People's Democratic Dictatorship, On the Ten Major Relationships, In the Correct Handling of Contradictions Among the People and Talk at an Enlarged Work Conference Convened by the Central Committee of the Communist Party of China.*

3) On the building of the revolutionary army and military strategy. Comrade Mao Zedong methodically solved the problem of how to turn a revolutionary army chiefly made up by peasants into a new type of people's army which is proletarian in character, observes strict discipline and forms close ties with the masses. He laid it down that the sole purpose of the people's army is to serve the people wholeheartedly, he put forward the principle that the Party commands the gun and not the other way round, he advanced the Three Main Rules of Discipline and the Eight Points for attention and stressed the practice of political, economic and military democracy and the principles of the unity of officers and soldiers, the unity of army and people and the disintegration of the enemy forces, thus formulating by way of summation a set of policies and methods concerning political work in the army. In his military writings such as *On Correcting Mistaken Idea in the Party, Problems of Strategy in China's Revolutionary War, Problems of Strategy in Guerrilla War Against Japan, On Protracted War and Problems of War and Strategy*, Comrade Mao Zedong summed up the experience of China's protracted revolutionary war and advanced the comprehensive concept of building a people's army and of building rural base areas and waging people's war by employing the people's army as the main force and relying on the masses. Raising guerrilla war to the strategic plane, he maintained that guerrilla warfare and mobile warfare of a guerrilla character would a long time be the main forms of operation in China's revolutionary war. He explained that it would be necessary to effect an appropriate change in military strategy simultaneously with the changing balance of forcee between the enemy and ourselves and with the progress of the war. He worked out a set of strategies and tactics for the revolutionary army to wage people's war in conditions when the enemy was strong and we were weak. These strategies and tactics include fighting a protracted war strategically and campaigns and battles of quick decision, turning strategic inferiority into superiority in campaigns and battles and concentrating a superior force to destroy the enemy forces one by one. During the War of Liberation, he formulated the celebrated ten major principles of operation. All these ideas

constitute Comrade Mao Zedong's outstanding contribution to the military theory of Marxism-Leninism. After the founding of the People's Republic, he put forward the important guideline that we must strengthen our national defence and build modern revolutionary armed forces (including the navy, the air force and technical branches) and develop modern defence technology (including the making of nuclear weapons for self-defence).

4) On policy and tactics. Comrade Mao Zedong penetratingly elucidated the vital importance of policy and tactics in revolutionary struggles. He pointed out that policy and tactics were the life of the Party, that they were both the starting-point and the end-result of all the practical activities of a revolutionary party and that the Party must formulate its policies in the light of the existing political situation, class relations, actual circumstances and the changes in them, combining principle and flexibility. He made many valuable suggestions concerning policy and tactics in the struggle against the enemy, in the united front and other questions. He pointed out among other things:

that, under changing subjective and objective conditions, a weak revolutionary force could ultimately defeat a strong reactionary force;

that we should despise the enemy strategically and take the enemy seriously tactically;

that we should keep our eyes on the main target of struggle and not hit out in all directions;

that we should differentiate between and disintegrate our enemies, and adopt the tactic of making use of contradictions, winning over the many, opposing the few and crushing our enemies one by one;

that, in areas under reactionary rule, we should combine legal and illegal struggle and, organizationally, adopt the policy of assigning picked cadres to work underground;

that, as for members of the defeated reactionary classes and reactionary elements, we should give them a chance to earn a living and to become working people living by their own labor, so long as they did not rebel or create trouble; and

that the proletariat and its party must fulfil two conditions in order to exercise leadership over their allies: (a) Lead their followers in waging resolute struggles against the common enemy and achieving victories; (b) Bring material benefits to their followers or at least avoid damaging their interests and at the same time give them political education.

These ideas of Comrade Mao Zedong's concerning policy and tactics are embodied in many of his writings, particularly in such works as *Current Problems of Tactics in the Anti-Japanese United Front, On Policy, Conclusions on the Repulse of the Second Anti-Communist Onslaught, On Some Important Problems of the Party's Present Policy, Don't Hit Out in All Directions* and *On the Question of Whether Imperialism and All Reactionaries Are Real Tigers.*

5) On ideological and political work and cultural work. In his *On New Democracy*, Comrade Mao Zedong stated:

Any given culture (as an ideological form) is a reflection of the politics and economics of a given society, and the former in turn has a tremendous influence and effect upon the latter; economics is the base and politics the concentrated expression of economics.

In accordance with this basic view, he put forward many important ideas of far-reaching and long-term significance. For instance, the theses that ideological and political work is the life-blood of economic and all other work and that it is necessary to unite politics and economics and to unite politics and professional skills, and to be both red and expert; the policy of developing a national, scientific and mass culture and of letting a hundred flowers blossom, weeding through the old to bring forth the new, and making the past serve the present and foreign things serve China; and the thesis that intellectuals have an important role to play in revolution and construction, that intellectuals should identify themselves with the workers and peasants and that they should acquire the proletarian world outlook by studying Marxism-Leninism, by studying society and through practical work. He pointed out that "this question of 'for whom?' is fundamental; it is a question of principle" and stressed that we should serve the people wholeheartedly, be highly responsible in revolutionary work, wage arduous struggle and fear no sacrifice. Many notable works written by Comrade Mao Zedong on ideology, politics and culture, such as *The Orientation of the Youth Movement, Recruit Large Numbers of Intellectuals, Talks at the Yanan Forum of Literature and Art, In Memory of Norman Bethune, Serve the People* and *The Foolish Old Man Who Removed the Mountains*, are of tremendous significance even today.

6) On Party building. It was a most difficult task to build a Marxist, proletarian Party of a mass character in a country where the peasantry and other sections of the petty bourgeoisie constituted the majority of the population, while the proletariat was small in number yet strong in combat effectiveness. Comrade Mao Zedong's theory on Party building provided a successful solution to this question. His main works in this area include *Combat Liberalism, The Role of the Chinese Communist Party in the National War, Reform Our Study, Rectify the Party's Style of Work, Oppose Stereotyped Party Writing, Our Study and the Current Situation, On Strengthening the Party Committee System and Methods of Work of Party Committees*. He laid particular stress on building the Party ideologically, saying that a Party member should join the Party not only organizationally but also ideologically and should constantly try to reform his non-proletarian ideas and replace them with proletarian ideas. He indicated that the style of work which entailed integrating theory with practice, forging close links with the masses and practicing self-criticism was the hallmark distinguishing the Chinese Communist Party from all other political parties in China. To counter the erroneous "Left" policy of "ruthless struggle and merciless blows" once followed in inner-Party struggle, he proposed the correct policy of "learning from past mistakes to avoid future ones and curing the sickness to save the patient," emphasizing the need to achieve the objective of clarity in ideology and unity among comrades in inner-Party struggle. He initiated the rectification campaign as a form of ideological education in Marxism-Leninism throughout the Party, which applied the method of criticism and self-criticism. In view of the fact that our Party was about to become and then became a party in power leading the whole country, Comrade Mao Zedong urged time and again, first on the eve of the founding of the People's Republic and then later, that we should remain modest and prudent, guard against arrogance and rashness and keep to plain living and hard struggle in our style of work and that we should be on the lookout against the corrosive influence of bourgeoisie ideology and should oppose bureaucratism which would alienate us from the masses.

30. The living soul of Mao Zedong Thought is the stand, viewpoint and method embodied in its component parts mentioned above. This stand, viewpoint and method boil down to three basic points: to seek truth from facts, the mass line, and independence. Comrade Mao Zedong applied dialectical and historical materialism to the entire work of the proletarian party, giving shape to this stand, viewpoint and method so characteristic of Chinese Communists in the course of the Chinese revolution and its arduous, protracted struggles and thus enriching Marxism-Leninism. They find expression not only in such important works as

Oppose Book Worship, On Practice, On Contradiction, Preface and Postscript to "Rural Surveys," Some Questions Concerning Methods of Leadership and Where Do Correct Ideas Come From?, but also in all his scientific writings and in the revolutionary activities of the Chinese Communists.

1)   Seeking truth from facts. This means preceding from reality and combining theory and practice, that is, integrating the universal principles of Marxism-Leninism with the concrete practice of the Chinese revolution. Comrade Mao Zedong was always against studying Marxism in isolation from the realities of Chinese society and the Chinese revolution. As early as 1930, he opposed blind book worship by emphasizing that investigation and study is the first step in all work and that one has no right to speak without investigation. On the eve of the rectification movement in Yanan, he affirmed that subjectivism is a formidable enemy of the Communist Party, a manifestation of impurity in Party spirit. These brilliant theses helped people break through the shackles of dogmatism and greatly emancipate their minds. While summarizing the experience and lessons of the Chinese revolution in his philosophical works and many other works rich in philosophical content, Comrade Mao Zedong showed great profundity in expounding and enriching the Marxist theory of knowledge and dialectics. He stressed that the dialectical materialist theory of knowledge is the dynamic, revolutionary theory of reflection and that full scope should be given to man's conscious dynamic role which is based on and is in conformity with objective reality. Basing himself on social practice, he comprehensively and systematically elaborated the dialectical materialist theory on the sources, the process and the purpose of knowledge and on the criterion of truth. He said that as a rule, correct knowledge can be arrived at and developed only after many repetitions of the process leading from matter to consciousness and then back to matter, that is, leading from practice to knowledge and then back to practice. He pointed out that truth exists by contrast with falsehood and grows in struggle with it, that truth is inexhaustible and that the truth of any piece of knowledge, namely, whether it corresponds to objective reality, can ultimately be decided only through social practice. He further elaborated the law of the unity of opposites, the nucleus of Marxist dialectics. He indicated that we should not only study the universality of contradiction in objective existence, but, what is more important, we should study the particularity of contradiction, and that we should resolve contradictions which are different in nature by different methods. Therefore, dialectics should not be viewed as a formula to be learnt by rote and applied mechanically, but should be closely linked with practice and with investigation and study and should be applied flexibly. He forged philosophy into a sharp weapon in

the hands of the proletariat and the people for knowing and changing the world. His distinguished works on China's revolutionary war, in particular, provide outstandingly shining examples of applying and developing the Marxist theory of knowledge and dialectics in practice. Our Party must always adhere to the above ideological line formulated by Comrade Mao Zedong.

2) The mass line means everything for the masses, reliance on the masses in everything and "from the masses, to the masses." The Party's mass line in all its work has come into being through the systematic application in all its activities of the Marxist-Leninist principle that the people are the makers of history. It is a summation of our Party's invaluable historical experience in conducting revolutionary activities over the years under difficult circumstances in which the enemy's strength far outstripped ours. Comrade Mao Zedong stressed time and again that as long as we rely on the people, believe firmly in the inexhaustible creative power of the masses and hence trust and identify ourselves with them, no enemy can crush us while we can eventually crush every enemy and overcome every difficulty. He also pointed out that in leading the masses in all practical work, the leadership can form its correct ideas only by adopting the method of "from the masses, to the masses" and by combining the leadership with the masses and combining the general call with particular guidance. This means concentrating the ideas of the masses and turning them into systematic ideas, then going to the masses so that the ideas are persevered in and carried through, and testing the correctness of these ideas in the practice of the masses. And this process goes on, over and over again, so that the understanding of the leadership becomes more correct, keener and richer each time. This is how Comrade Mao Zedong united the Marxist theory of knowledge with the Party's mass line. As the vanguard of the proletariat, the Party exists and fights for the interests of the people. But it always constitutes only a small part of the people, so that isolation from the people will render all the Party's struggles and ideals devoid of content as well as impossible of success. To persevere in the revolution and advance the socialist cause, our Party must uphold the mass line.

3) Independence and self-reliance are the inevitable corollary of carrying out the Chinese revolution and construction by proceeding from Chinese reality and relying on the masses. The proletarian revolution is an internationalist cause which calls for the mutual support of the proletariat of different countries. But for the cause to triumph, each proletariat should primarily base itself on its own country's realities, rely on the efforts of its own masses and revolutionary forces, integrate the universal principles of

Marxism-Leninism with the concrete practice of its own revolution and thus achieve victory. Comrade Mao Zedong always stressed that our policy should rest on our own strength and that we should find our own road of advance in accordance with our own conditions. In a vast country like China, we must all the more rely mainly on our own efforts to promote the revolution and construction. We must be determined to carry the struggle through to the end and must have faith in the hundreds of millions of Chinese people and rely on their wisdom and strength; otherwise, it will be impossible for our revolution and construction to succeed or to be consolidated even if success is won. Of course China's revolution and national construction are not and cannot be carried on in isolation from the rest of the world. It is always necessary for us to try to win foreign aid and, in particular to learn all that is advanced and beneficial from other countries. The closed-door policy, blind opposition to everything foreign and any theory or practice of great-nation chauvinism are all entirely wrong. At the same time, although China is still comparatively backward economically and culturally, we must maintain our own national dignity and confidence and there must be no slavishness or submissiveness in an form in dealing with big, powerful or rich countries. Under the leadership of the Party and Comrade Mao Zedong, no matter what difficulty we encountered, we never wavered, whether before or after the founding of New China, is our determination to remain independent and self-reliant and we never submitted to any pressure from outside; we showed the dauntless and heroic spirit of the Chinese Communist Party and the Chinese people. We stand for the peaceful coexistence of the people of all countries and their mutual assistance on an equal footing. While upholding our own independence. The road of revolution and construction suited to the characteristics of a country has to be explored, decided on and blazed by its own people. No one has the right to impose his views on others. Only under these conditions can there be genuine internationalism. Otherwise, there can only be hegemonism. We will always adhere to this principled stand in our international relations.

31. Mao Zedong Thought is the valuable spiritual asset of our Party. It will be our guide to action for a long time to come. The Party leaders and the large group of cadres nurtured by Marxism-Leninism and Mao Zedong Thought were the backbone forces in winning great victories for our cause; they are and will remain our treasured mainstay in the cause of socialist modernization. While many of Comrade Mao Zedong's important works were written during the periods of new-democratic revolution and the socialist transformation, we must still constantly study them. This is not only because one cannot cut the past off from the present and failure of understand the past will hamper our understanding of

present-day problems, but also because many of the basic theories, principles and scientific approaches set forth in these works are of universal significance and provide us with invaluable guidance now and will continue to do so in the future. Therefore, we must continue to uphold Mao Zedong Thought, study it in earnest and apply its stand, viewpoint and method in studying the new situation and solving the new problems arising in the course of practice. Mao Zedong Thought has added much that is new to the treasure-house of Marxist-Leninist theory. We must combine our study of the scientific works of Comrade Mao Zedong with that of the scientific writings of Marx, Engels, Lenin and Stalin. It is entirely wrong to try to negate the scientific value of Mao Zedong Thought and to deny its guiding role in our revolution and construction just because Comrade Mao Zedong made mistakes in his later years. And it is likewise entirely wrong to adopt a dogmatic attitude towards the sayings of Comrade Mao Zedong to regard whatever he said as the immutable truth which must be mechanically applied everywhere, and to be unwilling to admit honestly that the made mistakes in his later years, and even try to stick to them in our new activities. Both these attitudes fail to make a distinction between Mao Zedong Thought -- a scientific theory formed and tested over a long period of time -- and the mistakes Comrade Mao Zedong made in his later years. And it is absolutely necessary that this distinction should be made. We must treasure all the positive experience obtained in the course of integrating the universal principles of Marxism-Leninism with the concrete practice of China's revolution and construction over fifty years or so, apply and carry forward this experience in our new work, enrich and develop Party theory with new principles and new conclusions corresponding to reality, so as to ensure the continued progress of our cause along the scientific course of Marxism-Leninism and Mao Zedong Thought.

Unite and Strive to Build a Powerful, Modern Socialist China

32. The objective of our Party's struggle in the new historical period is to turn China step by step into a powerful socialist country with modern agriculture, industry, national defence and science and technology and with a high level of democracy and culture. We must also accomplish the great cause of reunification of the country by getting Taiwan to return to the embrace of the motherland. The fundamental aim of summing up the historical experience of the thirty-two years since the founding of the People's Republic is to accomplish the great objective of building a powerful and modern socialist country by further rallying the will and strength of the whole Party, the whole army and the whole people on the basis of upholding the four fundamental principles, namely, upholding the socialist road, the people's democratic dictatorship (i.e., the dictatorship of the proletariat), the leadership of the Communist Party, and Marxism-Leninism and Mao Zedong Thought. These four principles constitute the

common political basis of the unity of the whole Party and the unity of the whole people as well as the basic guarantee for the realization of socialist modernization. Any word or deed which deviates from these four principles is wrong. Any word or deed which denies or undermines these four principles cannot be tolerated.

33. Socialism and socialism alone can save China. This is the unalterable conclusion drawn by all our people from their own experience over the past century or so; it likewise constitutes our fundamental historical experience in the thirty-two years since the founding of our People's Republic. Although our socialist system is still in its early phase of development, China has undoubtedly established a socialist system and entered the stage of socialist society. Any view denying this basic fact is wrong. Under socialism, we have achieved successes which were absolutely impossible in old China. This is a preliminary and at the same time convincing manifestation of the superiority of the socialist system. The fact that we have been and are able to overcome all kinds of difficulties through our own efforts testifies to its great vitality. Of course, our system will have to undergo a long process of development before it can be perfected. Given the premise that we uphold the basic system of socialism, therefore, we must strive to reform those specific features which are not in keeping with the expansion of the productive forces and the interests of the people, and to staunchly combat all activities detrimental to socialism. With the development of our cause, the immense superiority of socialism will become more and more apparent.

34. Without the Chinese Communist Party, there would have been no New China. Likewise, without the Chinese Communist Party, there would be no modern socialist China. The Chinese Communist Party is a proletarian party armed with Marxism-Leninism and Mao Zedong Thought and imbued with a strict sense of discipline and the spirit of self-criticism, and its ultimate historical mission is to realize communism. Without the leadership of such a party, without the flesh-and-blood ties it has formed with the masses through protracted struggles and without its painstaking and effective work among the people and the high prestige it consequently enjoys, our country -- for a variety of reasons, both internal and external -- would inexorably fall apart and the future of our nation and people would inexorably be forfeited. The Party leadership cannot be exempt from mistakes, but there is no doubt that it can correct them by relying on the close unity between the Party and the people, and in no case should one use the Party's mistakes as a pretext for weakening, breaking away from or even sabotaging its leadership. That would only lead to even greater mistakes and court grievous disasters. We must improve Party leadership in order to uphold it. We must resolutely overcome the many shortcomings that still exist in our Party's style of thinking and work, in its system of organization and leadership and in its contacts with the masses. So long as we earnestly uphold and constantly improve

Party leadership, our Party will definitely be better able to undertake the tremendous tasks entrusted to it by history.

35. Since the Third Plenary Session of its Eleventh Central Committee, our Party has gradually mapped out the correct path for socialist modernization suited to China's conditions. In the course of practice, the path will be broadened and become more clearly defined, but, in essence, the key pointers can already be determined on the basis of the summing up of the negative as well as positive experience since the founding of the People's Republic, and particularly of the lessons of the "cultural revolution."

1) After socialist transformation was fundamentally completed, the principle contradiction our country has had to resolve is that between the growing material and cultural needs of the people and the backwardness of social production. It was imperative that the focus of Party and government work be shifted to socialist modernization centering on economic construction and that the people's material and cultural life be gradually improved by means of an immense expansion of productive forces. In the final analysis, the mistake we made in the past was that we failed to persevere in making this strategic shift. What is more, the preposterous view opposing the so-called "theory of the unique importance of productive forces," a view diametrically opposed to historical materialism was put forward during the "cultural revolution." We must never deviate from this for except in the event of large-scale invasion by foreign enemy (and even then it will still be necessary to carry on such economic construction as wartime conditions require and permit). All our Party work must be subordinated to and serve this central task -- economic construction. All our Party cadres, and particularly those in economic departments, must diligently study economic theory and economic practice as well as science and technology.

2) In our socialist economic construction we must strive to reach the goal of modernization systematically and in stages, according to the conditions and resources of our country. The prolonged "Left" mistakes we made in our economic work in the past consisted chiefly of departing from Chinese realities, trying to exceed our actual capabilities and ignoring the economic returns of construction and management as well as the scientific confirmation of our economic plans, policies and measures, with the concomitants of colossal waste and losses. We must adopt a scientific attitude, gain a thorough knowledge of the realities and make a deep analysis of the situation, earnestly listen to the opinions of the cadres, masses and specialists of the various fields and try out best to act in

accordance with objective economic and natural laws and bring about a proportionate and harmonious development of the various branches of economy. We must keep in mind the fundamental fact that China's economy and culture are still relatively backward. At the same time, we must keep in mind such favorable domestic and international conditions as the achievements we have already scored and the experience we have gained in our economic construction and the expansion of economic and technological exchanges with foreign countries, and we must make full use of these favorable conditions. We must oppose both impetuosity and passivity.

3) The reform and improvement of the socialist relations of production must be in conformity with the level of the productive forces and conducive to the expansion of production. The state economy and the collective economy are the basic forms of the Chinese economy. The working people's individual economy within certain prescribed limits is a necessary complement to public economy. It is necessary to establish specific systems of management and distribution suited to the various sectors of the economy. It is necessary to have planned economy and at the same time give play to the supplementary, regulatory role of the market on the basis of public ownership. We must strive to promote commodity production and exchange on a socialist basis. There is no rigid pattern for the development of the socialist relations of production. At every stage our task is to create those specific forms of the relations of production that correspond to the needs of the growing productive forces and facilitate their continued advance.

4) Class struggle no longer constitutes the principal contradiction after the exploiters have been eliminated as classes. However, owing to certain domestic factors and influences from abroad, class struggle will continue to exist within certain limits for a long time to come and may even grow acute under certain conditions. It is necessary to oppose both the view that the scope of class struggle must be enlarged and the view that it has died out. It is imperative to maintain a high level of vigilance and conduct effective struggle against all those who are hostile to socialism and try to sabotage it in the political, economic, ideological and cultural fields and in community life. We must correctly understand that there are diverse social contradictions in Chinese society which do not fall within the scope of class struggle and that methods other than class struggle must be used for their appropriate revolution. Otherwise, social stability and unity will be jeopardized. We must unswervingly unite all forces that can be united with and consolidate and expand the patriotic united front.

5) A fundamental task of the socialist revolution is gradually to establish a highly democratic socialist political system. Inadequate attention was paid to this matter after the founding of the People's Republic, and this was one of the major factors contributing to the initiation of the "cultural revolution." Here is a grievous lesson for us to learn. It is necessary to strengthen the building of state organs at all levels in accordance with the principle of democratic centralism, make the people's political power, gradually realize direct popular participation in the democratic process at the grass roots of political power and community life and, in particular, stress democratic management by the working classes in urban and rural enterprises over the affairs of their establishments. It is essential to consolidate the people's democratic dictatorship, improve our Constitution and laws and ensure their strict observance and inviolability. We must turn the socialist legal system into a powerful instrument for protecting the rights of the people, ensuring order in production, work and other activities, punishing criminals and cracking down on the disruptive activities of class enemies. The kind of chaotic situation that obtained in the "cultural revolution" must never be allowed to happen again in any sphere.

6) Life under socialism must attain a high ethical and cultural level. We must firmly eradicate such gross fallacies as the denigration of education, science and culture and discrimination against intellectuals, fallacies which had long existed and found extreme express during the "cultural revolution"; we must strive to raise the status and expand the role of education, science and culture in our drive for modernization. We unequivocally affirm that, together with the workers and peasants, the intellectuals are a force to rely on in the cause of socialism and that it is impossible to carry out socialist construction without culture and the intellectuals. It is imperative for the whole Party to engage in a more diligent study of Marxist theories, of the past and present in China and abroad, and of the different branches of the natural and social sciences. We must strengthen and improve ideological and political work and educate the people and youth in the Marxist world outlook and communist morality; we must persistently carry out the educational policy which calls for an all-round development morally, intellectually and physically, for being both red and expert, for integration of the intellectuals with the workers and peasants and the combination of mental and physical labor; and we must counter the influence of decadent bourgeois ideology and the decadent remnants of feudal ideology, overcome the influence of petty-bourgeois ideology and foster the patriotism which puts the interest of the

motherland above everything else and the pioneer spirit of selfless devotion to modernization.

7) It is of profound significance to our multi-national country to improve and promote socialist relations among our various nationalities and strengthen national unity. In the past, particularly during the "cultural revolution," we committed, on the question of nationalities, the grave mistake of widening the scope of class struggle and wronged a large number of cadres and masses of the minority nationalities. In our work among them, we did not show due respect for their right to autonomy. We must never forget this lesson. We must have a clear understanding that relations among our nationalities today are, in the main, relations among the working people of the various nationalities. It is necessary to persist in their regional autonomy and enact laws and regulations to ensure this autonomy and their decision-making power in applying Party and government policies according to the actual conditions in their regions. We must take effective measures to assist economic and cultural development in regions inhabited by minority nationalities, actively train and promote cadres from among them and resolutely oppose all words and deeds undermining national unity and equality. It is imperative to continue to implement the policy of freedom of religious belief. To uphold the four fundamental principles does not mean that religious believers should renounce their faith but that they must not engage in propaganda against Marxism-Leninism and Mao Zedong Thought and that they must not interfere with politics and education in their religious activities.

8) In the present international situation in which the danger of war still exists, it is necessary to strengthen the modernization of our national defence. The building up of national defence must be in keeping with the building up of the economy. The People's Liberation Army should strengthen its military training, political work, logistic service and study of military science and further raise its combat effectiveness so as gradually to become a still more powerful modern revolutionary army. It is necessary to restore and carry forward the fine tradition of unity inside the army, between the army and the government and between the army and the people. The building of the people's militia must also be further strengthened.

9) In our external relations, we must continue to oppose imperialism, hegemonism, colonialism and racism, and safeguard world peace. We must actively promote relations and economic and cultural exchanges with other countries on the basis of the Five Principles of Peaceful Coexistence.

We must uphold proletarian internationalism and support the cause of the liberation of oppressed nations, the national construction of newly independent countries and the just struggles of the peoples everywhere.

10) In the light of the lessons of the "cultural revolution" and the present situation in the Party, it is imperative to build up a sound system of democratic centralism inside the Party. We must carry out the Marxist principle of the exercise of collective Party leadership by leaders who have emerged from mass struggles and who combine political integrity with professional competence, and we must prohibit the personality cult in any form. It is imperative to uphold the prestige of Party leaders and at the same time ensure that their activities come under the supervision of the Party and the people. We must have a high degree of centralism based on a high degree of democracy and insist that the minority is subordinate to the majority, the individual to the organization, the lower to the higher level and the entire membership to the Central Committee. The style of work of a political party in power is a matter that determines its very existence. Party organizations at all levels and all Party cadres must go deep among the masses, plunge themselves into practical struggle, remain modest and prudent, share weal and woe with the masses and firmly overcome bureaucratism. We must properly wield the weapon of criticism and self-criticism, overcome erroneous ideas that deviate from the Party's correct principles, uproot factionalism, oppose anarchism and ultra-individualism and eradicate such unhealthy tendencies as the practice of seeking perks and privileges. We must consolidate the Party organization, purify the Party ranks and weed out degenerate elements who oppress and bully the people. In exercising leadership over state affairs and work in the economic and cultural fields as well as community life, the Party must correctly handle its relations with other organizations, ensure by every means the effective functioning of the organs of state power and administrative, judicial and economic and cultural organizations and see to it that trade unions, the Youth League, the Women's Federation, the Science and Technology Association, the Federation of Literary and Art Circles and other mass organizations carry out their work responsibly and on their own initiative. The Party must strengthen its co-operation with public figures outside the Party, give full play to the role of the Chinese People's Political Consultations with democratic parties and personages without party affiliation on major issues of state affairs and respect their opinions and the opinions of specialists in various fields. As with other social organizations, Party organizations at all levels must conduct their activities within the limits permitted by the Constitution and the law.

36. In firmly correcting the mistake of the so-called "continued revolution under the dictatorship of the proletariat," a slogan which was advanced during the "cultural revolution" and which called for the overthrow of one class by another, we absolutely do not mean that the tasks of the revolution have been accomplished and that there is no need to carry on revolutionary struggles with determination. Socialism aims not just at eliminating all systems of exploitation and all exploiting classes but also at greatly expanding the productive forces, improving and developing the socialist relations of production and the superstructure and, on this basis, gradually eliminating all class differences and all major social distinctions and inequalities which are chiefly due to the inadequate development of the productive forces until communism is finally realized. This is a great revolution, unprecedented in human history. Our present endeavours to build a modern socialist China constitutes but one stage of this great revolution. Differing from the revolutions before the overthrow of the system of exploitation, this solution is carried out not through fierce class confrontation and conflict, but through the strength of the socialist system itself, under leadership, step by step and in an orderly way. This revolution which has entered the period of peaceful development is more profound and arduous than any previous revolution and will not only take a very long historical period to accomplish but also demand the unswerving and disciplined hard work and heroic sacrifices of many generations. In this historical period of peaceful development, revolution can never be plain sailing. There are still overt and covert enemies and other saboteurs who watch for opportunities to create trouble. We must maintain high revolutionary vigilance and be ready at all times to come out boldly to safeguard the interests of the revolution. In this new historical period, the whole membership of the Chinese Communist Party and the whole people must never cease to cherish lofty revolutionary ideals, maintain a dynamic revolutionary fighting spirit and carry China's great socialist revolution and socialist construction through to the end.

37. Repeated assessment of our successes and failures, of our correct and incorrect practices, of the thirty-two years since the founding of our People's Republic, and particularly deliberation over and review of the events of the past few years, have helped to raise immensely the political consciousness of all Party comrades and of all patriots. Obviously, our Party now has a higher level of understanding of socialist revolution and construction than at any other period since liberation. Our Party has both the courage to acknowledge and correct its mistakes and the determination and ability to prevent repetition of the serious mistakes of the past. After all, from a long-term historical point of view the mistakes and setbacks of our Party were only temporary whereas the consequent steeling of our Party and people, the greater maturity of the core force formed among our Party cadres through protracted struggle, the growing superiority of our socialist system and the increasingly keen and common aspiration of our Party,

army and people for the prosperity of the motherland will be decisive factors in the long run. A great future is in store for our socialist cause and for the Chinese people in their hundreds of millions.

38. Inner-Party unity and unity between the Party and the people are the basic guarantee for new victories in our socialist modernization. Whatever the difficulties, as long as the Party is closely united and remains closely united with the people, our Party and the cause of socialism it leads will certainly prosper day by day.

The Resolution on Certain Questions in the History of Our Party unanimously adopted in 1945 by the Enlarged Seventh Plenary Session of the Sixth Central Committee of the Party unified the thinking of the whole Party, consolidated its unity, promoted the rapid advance of the people's revolutionary cause and accelerated its eventual triumph. The Sixth Plenary Session of the Eleventh Central Committee of the Party believes that the present resolution it has unanimously adopted will play a similar historical role. This session calls upon the whole Party, the whole army and the people of all our nationalities to act under the great banner of Marxism-Leninism and Mao Zedong Thought, closely rally around the Central Committee of the Party, preserve the spirit of the legendary Foolish Old Man who removed mountains and work together as one in defiance of all difficulties so as to turn China step by step into a powerful modern socialist country which is highly democratic and highly cultured. Our goal must be attained! Our goal can unquestionably be attained!

*****

DOCUMENT NO. 5

MATERIAL FOR STUDYING THE "RESOLUTION ON CERTAIN QUESTIONS IN THE HISTORY OF OUR PARTY SINCE THE FOUNDING OF THE STATE

(**Jenmin Jihpao**, Beijing, July 21, 1981;
FBIS-CHI, July 22, 1981)

A GREAT TURNING POINT IN HISTORY

The smashing of the counterrevolutionary Jiang Qing clique has enabled our country to enter a new historical period.

The Third Plenary Session of the Eleventh CCP Central Committee is a great turning point of far-reaching significance in the history of our party since the founding of the state.

COMRADE HUA GUOFENG'S CONTRIBUTIONS AND MISTAKES

The "resolution" fully affirms the role played by Comrade Hua Guofeng in smashing the counterrevolutionary Jiang Qing clique and the useful work he did after that. However, in the two years prior to the third plenary session, he continued to make "leftist" errors in guiding ideology:

--He promoted and was tardy in correcting the "two whatevers."

--He procrastinated and obstructed the work of reinstating veteran cadres and redressing unjust, false and wrong cases.

--He accepted and fostered the personality cult.

Apart from this, he should also be held responsible for impetuously seeking quick results in economic work and for continuing certain other "leftist" policies. Obviously, under his leadership it is impossible to correct "leftist" errors within the party and all the more impossible to restore the party's fine traditions.

THE FAR-REACHING SIGNIFICANCE OF
THE THIRD PLENARY SESSION

It put an end to the situation of advancing haltingly in our work, began to correct conscientiously and comprehensively the "leftist" errors made before and during the "Great Cultural Revolution," reestablished the ideological, political and organizational lines of Marxism and instituted a series of significant changes in leadership work.

--It established the guiding policy of emancipating the mind, using our brains, seeking truth from facts and uniting as one in looking forward to the future.

--It made the strategic decision to shift the focus of work to socialist modernization.

--It put forth the task of strengthening socialist democracy and the socialist system.

--It examined and redressed a number of major unjust, false and wrong cases in the history of the party and settled the controversy on the merits and faults, rights and wrongs of some prominent leaders.

Apart from all these, the plenary session also elected additional members to the leadership organs of the Central Committee.

Since then, our party has taken the initiative in restoring order out of chaos. After carrying out the heavy tasks of construction and reform, a very good situation has appeared in both the economic and political spheres of our country. We still have mistakes and shortcomings and there are still many difficulties ahead. However, the course of our victorious advance has been cleared and the prestige of our party among the people is daily improving.

THE THIRD PLENARY SESSION OF
THE ELEVENTH PARTY CENTRAL COMMITTEE

The Third Plenary Session of the Eleventh CCP Central Committee was held in Beijing from 18 to 22 December 1978. Before the session, the CCP Central Committee convened a work meeting to make full preparations for it. The meeting was attended by 169 members and 112 alternate members of the CCP Central Committee. Responsible cadres of various localities and the departments of the central authorities concerned were also present as delegates without the right to vote.

The third plenary session was a turning point of profound historic significance in the history of our party since the founding of new China. It put an end to the situation in which the party's work had been stagnating since October 1976 and began to conscientiously and adequately correct the leftist mistakes committed before and during the "Great Cultural Revolution."

The third plenary session reestablished the Marxist ideological line of the party. It resolutely repudiated the erroneous guiding principle of "two whatevers" ("We must resolutely uphold whatever policy decision Chairman Mao made and unswervingly carry out whatever Chairman Mao instructed"), highly evaluated the discussion on the criterion for truth and emphasized Comrade Mao Zedong's great role in our protracted revolutionary struggle. The session pointed out that the lofty task of the party Central Committee in the theoretical field is to assume the leadership. It educated the entire party and people throughout the country so that they would historically and scientifically understand the great contributions of Comrade Mao Zedong, comprehensively and accurately master the scientific system of Mao Zedong Thought and combine the general principle of Marxism-Leninism-Mao Zedong Thought with the with the specific practice of the socialist modernization and construction and develop it under the new historical conditions. The session defined the guiding principle of emancipating our minds, using our brains, seeking truth from facts and uniting as one to look ahead.

The third plenary session reestablished the Marxist political line. It decisively abandoned the slogan "taking class struggle as the key link" which was unsuitable to the socialist society and reached a strategic decision of shifting our work focus to the socialist modernization. It aroused the attention of the whole nation to the problem of severe imbalance in the proportional relations in our national economy. The plenary session thoroughly discussed the problem of agriculture and maintained that at present the whole party should concentrate its main efforts on promoting the development of agriculture and approved the proposal of distributing the two documents "Decision of the CCP Central Committee on Several Questions Concerning the Acceleration of the Development of Agricultural (Draft)" and "Working Rules and Regulations of the People's Communes in Rural Areas (Draft for Trial Implementation)" and implementing them on a trial basis. The plenary session discussed and accepted in principle the arrangements for the national economic plan for 1979 and 1980. It proposed that the State Council present it to the second session of the Fifth NPC for approval after amendment.

The plenary session called on the entire party and army and people of various nationalities throughout the country to work with one heart and one mind to further develop the political situation of stability and unity and carry out the new Long March aimed at building our country into a modern and powerful country.

The third plenary session also reestablished the Marxist organizational line. It thoroughly discussed some important events which occurred during the "Great Cultural Revolution," examined and redressed a number of false charges, wrong sentences and frameup cases and solved the problems concerning the merits and faults of some important leaders. It also decided to annul the erroneous documents issued by the central authorities on "Combating the Rightist Wind of Reversing Verdicts" and the Tiananmen incident, examined and corrected the erroneous conclusions about Comrades Peng Dehuai, Tao Zhu, Bo Yibo, Yang Shangkun and others and reversed the verdicts on the "renegade clique composed of sixty-one persons."

The plenary session elected Comrade Chen Yun as a vice chairman of the CCP Central Committee and Comrades Deng Yingchao, Hu Yaobang and Wang Zhen as members of the Political Bureau of the CCP Central Committee. It formed the central Discipline Inspection Committee and elected Comrade Chen Yun as its first secretary, Comrade Deng Yingchao as the second secretary, Comrade Hu Yaobang as the third secretary, Comrade Huang Kecheng as executive secretary and Comrade Wang Heshou as deputy secretary.

Due to the practical changes of the party's life since the eleventh party congress and the urgent needs of the present party's work, the plenary session elected nine comrades such as Huang Kecheng and others as members of the CCP Central Committee, and these decisions will be endorsed retroactively by the twelfth party congress.

Since the third plenary session, the party has taken the initiative of restoring order out of chaos and solved in a planned way many problems left over from the past and other new problems arising in practical life. The party has also carried out strenuous tasks of construction and reforms. All this has brought about an excellent situation in our country's economic and political arenas.

THE "TWO WHATEVERS" AND
THE DISCUSSION ON THE CRITERION OF TRUTH

The full form of the two whatevers reads: "We must resolutely uphold whatever policy decision Chairman Mao made and unswervingly carry out whatever Chairman Mao instructed." This phrasing first appeared in the draft of a speech prepared by Comrade Hua Guofeng in January 1977. Afterwards it was officially put forward on 7 February of the same year in an editorial in *Renmin Ribao, Hongqi* and *Jiefang Junbao* entitled "Study of the Documents Well and Grasp the Key Link," and became an erroneous guiding principle pushed by Comrade Hua Guofeng. The cadres, especially the old cadres, had varying opinions on this guiding principle. Comrade Hua Guofeng persistently followed the viewpoint of the "two whatevers" and even during the central work conference in Mary 1977 he was still saying that criticizing Deng was correct and that no reversal of verdict could be made on the Tiananmen incident. In April, while people were marking the first anniversary of the "5 April movement," he again arrested people, he delayed and obstructed the course of restoring work to old cadres and rehabilitating victims of miscarriages of justice; he continued to uphold the old personality cult, and also created and accepted his own personality cult. In the eleventh party congress political work report, far from correcting the erroneous theories, policies and slogans of the "Great Cultural Revolution," he actually fully affirmed these things; he continued to carry out a number of leftist economic policies, and so on. The facts have shown that the promotion of the erroneous guiding principle of the "two whatevers" seriously hampered the work of turning chaos to order.

Comrade Deng Xiaoping held that the "two whatevers" violated Marxism. He clearly pointed out in a 10 April 1977 letter to the Central Committee: "We must forever apply accurate and complete Mao Zedong Thought to guide the whole party, the whole army and the people of the whole country, and to victoriously push forward the cause of the party and socialism and the history of international communism." He solemnly declared that we could not uphold erroneous things and the things turned upside down by the "gang of four." Comrade Deng Xiaoping's letter represented the common desire of the comrades of the whole party. It was in fact the harbinger of the discussion on the criterion of truth and the high tide of emancipation of the mind that followed it.

On 9 May 1978, the internal publication "Lilun Dongtai (Theory Trends)" of the central party school under Comrade Hu Yaobang's leadership carried for the first time an article entitled "Practice Is the Sole Criterion for Testing Truth," which appeared openly the next day in *Guangming Ribao* under the signature of a contributing commentator. This article clearly reiterated a basic principle of the Marxist theory of cognition: "Only social practice can test whether a theory correctly reflects objective reality and is true." It also sharply pointed out, "We must dare to touch and to get clear the rights and wrongs" regarding the "forbidden areas" set up by the Gang of Four to shackle people's thinking.

Obviously, this was a negation in fundamental theory of the "two whatevers." This article aroused strong response throughout the whole party, and the great discussion on the "two whatevers" and on taking practice as the sole criterion for testing truth rapidly got underway throughout the whole country. This started in June 1978 and reached a high tide in November of the same year. Although it encountered obstruction and suppression by Hua Guofeng, Wang Dongxing and other comrades, thanks to the support of Comrades Deng Xiaoping, Chen Yun and many other old comrades, by carrying out this discussion the comrades of the whole party enhanced their awareness of Marxism-Leninism and emancipated themselves from the spiritual shackles of the rampant personality cult and dogmatism of the past. Party secretaries of the great majority of provinces, municipalities and autonomous regions and military region commanders enthusiastically published articles or interviews in the press, upholding practice as the sole criterion for testing truth and opposing the erroneous guiding principle of the "two whatevers."

The Third Plenary Session of the Eleventh Central Committee in December 1978 gave high evaluation to the discussion on practice as the sole criterion for testing truth, holding that it was of far-reaching historical significance for promoting the emancipation of the mind of the comrades of the whole party and the people of the whole country and correcting the ideological line. The erroneous guiding principle of the "two whatevers" was curbed from then on.

THE ELEVENTH PARTY CONGRESS

The eleventh national party congress was held in Beijing from 12 to 18 August 1977. The congress was attended by 1,510 delegates, representing the more than 35 million party members.

Comrade Hua Guofeng presided at this congress. The congress held a preparatory meeting on 11 August, which elected the presidium and adopted the three items on the agenda of the congress which had been proposed by the third plenary session of the Tenth Central Committee: 1) The political report of the Central Committee; 2) revision of the CCP constitution, and the report on revision of the constitution; 3) election of Central Committee members.

During the congress, Comrade Hua Guofeng delivered a "political report" on behalf of the CCP Central Committee; Comrade Ye Jianying delivered a "report on revision of the party constitution," and Comrade Deng Xiaoping delivered the "closing speech." The congress adopted a "Resolution on the Political Report," a "Resolution on the (Draft) Revision of the Party Constitution," and the new "CCP constitution."

In his political report Comrade Hua Guofeng proposed eight tasks to the whole party and army and the people of the entire country for "bringing about great orders;" in his closing speech, Comrade Deng xiaoping stressed that our party must revive and carry forward its fine traditions and work style of following the mass line, seeking truth from facts, carrying out criticism and self-criticism and of being modest and prudent, refraining from arrogance and impetuosity, struggling hard amid difficulties, promoting democratic centralism and so on. He again proposed the great goal of striving to build China into a powerful socialist state before the end of the century.

This congress played a positive role in exposing and criticizing the Gang of Four and mobilizing the whole party to build China into a powerful modern socialist country. However, due to the limitations imposed by historical conditions at the time and the erroneous influence of Comrade Hua Guofeng, this congress was not able to correct the erroneous theory, policies and slogans of the "Great Cultural Revolution," such as "persistently continue the revolution under the dictatorship of the proletariat," "persistently follow the party's basic line" and so on; on the contrary, these things were affirmed. Although the new party constitution made many revisions of that adopted by the "10th party congress," it still retained some of the expressions used during the "Great Cultural Revolution" and failed to fundamentally negate the constitutions adopted by the "ninth and tenth party congresses" under the manipulations of Lin Biao and "gang of four."

In conclusion, the congress elected the Eleventh Central Committee with 201 members and 132 alternate members.

REHABILITATING THE VICTIMS OF MISCARRIAGES OF JUSTICE

Due to the previous leftist errors of the "Great Cultural Revolution," and in particular the savage persecution of old cadres carried out by the Lin Biao and Jing Qing counterrevolutionary cliques, many miscarriages of justice had existed for many years among party cadres and members and among the masses. The number of these cases was shocking. In the wake of the development of the work of turning chaos to order carried out by the Central Committee, many victims and their family members strongly demanded rehabilitation. However, from 1976 to 1977, rehabilitation work was unable to proceed smoothly due to the erroneous guiding principle of the "two whatevers" pushed by Comrade Hua Guofeng; and in fact new miscarriages of justice continued to occur. This caused unhappiness among the cadres and masses.

Document Nos. 1 - 6

In October 1977, while presiding over the work of the central party school, Comrade Hu Yaobang guided the comrades concerned to investigate and study the cadre issue. On this basis he wrote a long article entitled "Rectify the Rights and Wrongs in the Cadre Line That Were Reversed by the 'Gang of Four'" (carried in *Renmin Ribao* on 7 October 1977). This article broke through the bindings of the "two whatevers," and called for rapidly and correctly solving the cadre problem and liberating large numbers of cadres who for various reasons had not been rehabilitated or assigned work. The article said, "We must act with boldness, dare to break through obstacles, and dare to overturn the erroneous conclusions drawn during the screening of cadres carried out by the 'gang of four' and company. We must overturn and get rid of all unfair slanders heaped on the cadres." Within a short period after the publication of this article, the Central Committee received thousands of letters from all parts of the country enthusiastically hailing the article and demanding the implementation of the proletarian policies for cadres, intellectuals, patriotic figures, and so on. Following that, the Central Committee appointed Comrade Hu Yaobang director of the Organization Department to lead the work of this department and the departments concerned throughout the country in rehabilitating the victims of miscarriages of justice. As a result, this work gathered speed.

As instructed by the Central Committee, *Renmin Ribao* published numerous contributing commentator's articles, strongly appealing: "Victims of miscarriages of justice must be cleared and rehabilitated and trumpeted-up cases must be rectified." A 15 November 1978 article entitled "Seek Truth From Facts and Set Wrongs to Right" again reiterated the party's consistent guiding principles of correcting mistakes, and clearly pointed out that "if someone is found to have been erroneously criticized, no matter by whom, the organization department of the corresponding level has the full right to correct the case." It also specifically stipulated that the work of rehabilitating the cadres should be completed in the first half of 1979.

The Third Plenary Session of the Eleventh Central Committee in December 1978 resolutely criticized the erroneous guiding principle of the "two whatevers," and started all-round serious correction of the leftist errors of the "Great Cultural Revolution" and the period prior to it. A number of major miscarriages of justice in the history of the party were reviewed and solved. The whole country achieved very great success in rehabilitation work. During this period, the Central Committee and the local authorities also carried out work to completely correct the cases of those who had been erroneously labeled rightists during the 1957 antirightist struggle. They also distinguished between small traders, hawkers and handicraft workers, who were originally laborers, and bourgeois industrialists and businessmen. The whole party and the people of the whole country supported and welcomed these measures.

THE RESPONSIBILITY SYSTEM LINKING
REMUNERATION TO OUTPUT

Since the Third Plenary Session of the Eleventh Central Committee, the rural areas have promoted various types of responsibility system linking remuneration to output. The various types are as follows:

1. Specialized contracting with remuneration linked to output: Under unified management by the production team, division of labor and cooperation is practiced, with agricultural, forestry, animal husbandry, sideline production, fishery, industrial and commercial tasks being contracted out according to the skills and specialties of the laborers. The production tasks in each trade, following the principle of acting for the convenience of production and the benefit of management, are contracted out to various kinds of specialized teams, groups, households and workers, and remuneration is calculated according to output. This is known as the "four specialized, one link" responsibility system.

2. Contracting production for work groups, with remuneration linked to output: Laborers with different kinds of skills in a production team are divided into different work groups and arable land, farm tools sown areas, output targets, manure, seed and so on are then allocated to each group. The production team assigns each group fixed work, output, production costs, and rewards or fines for exceeding or failing to fulfill targets and remuneration is finally calculated according to the production achievement of each group. The production team carries out the accounting and distribution in a unified way. This method frequently changes "great tumult" into "small tumult," and is currently being gradually reduced.

3. Linking remuneration to output for each laborer, under unified leadership: This method upholds the "three unchanging things and four unified things," that is, it upholds no change in collective ownership, in the principle of distribution according to work, or in the basic accounting unit, and adopts unified sowing plans, and unified use of draft animals and farm tools, unified allocation of the labor force and unified accounting and distribution. Under these conditions, land and production quotas are assigned according to labor force or a proportion of total population to labor force, distribution is calculated according to output, and proportional or all-round rewards or fines are practiced.

4. Fixing output quotas for each household: The production team divides up the farmland for each household according to the number of its laborers or to the proportion of total population to laborers. The team signs contracts with the households and assigns them contractual responsibilities in respect to output (or output value), work points, and consumption, and hands out rewards for overfulfilling plans and fines for failure to fulfill them. The production team carries out unified accounting and distribution regarding the portion of production done under these contracts, and hands out all-round or proportional rewards or fines, as appropriate, for the portion of plan overfulfilled or not fulfilled.

5. Assigning full responsibilities to the households: Under the premise of upholding public ownership of the basic means of production, the production team contracts the farmland to the households according to the number of laborers or to the proportion of total population to laborers; draft animals and farm tools are permanently handed over to the households to look after and use. Quotas in respect of state procurement plans and collective retention of produce are worked out for each household, and the fulfillment of contract tasks is assured by the form of economic contracts. To put it simply, this means "ensuring the state's requirements, retaining sufficient produce for the collective, and keeping all the rest oneself." The masses praise this form, saying: "Handing over full responsibilities is a straightforward affair with not twists." At present the various responsibility systems are being constantly developed and changed. The general tendency is for constant promotion of the system linking remuneration to output and a gradual decline in system that do not link remuneration to output.

*****

DOCUMENT NO. 6

DIFFERENTIATE MAO FROM MAO ZEDONG THOUGHT

**Understanding the Documents of the Sixth Plenary
Session of the CCP Central Committee**

by

Wu Lu

(**Jenmin Jihpao**, Beijing, July 24, 1981;
FBIS-CHI, July 27, 1981)

The "Resolution on Certain Questions in the History of Our Party Since the Founding of the PRC" has differentiated the scientific theory of Mao Zedong Thought long-tested by history from the mistakes made by Comrade Mao Zedong in his later years. This is very necessary in correctly understanding Mao Zedong Thought and upholding and applying Marxism-Leninism-Mao Zedong Thought as a guide to Chinese revolution and construction in the new historical period. One very important point about the study of the "resolution" is to pay attention to such differentiation.

Mao Zedong Thought illuminated the course of the Chinese revolution from setbacks to victory, and led the Chinese people onto the broad socialist path, so that the most profound social reform in the history of China was completed. This is clear to everyone. Comrade Mao Zedong made serious mistakes in his later years, especially the "Great Cultural Revolution" initiated by him which brought great disaster to the party and the people. This cannot be denied. The tremendous contributions made by him are without parallel, while the mistake of the "Great Cultural Revolution" affected the whole situation and was of a long duration. Such a contradictory historical phenomenon influenced certain comrades within a period of time. They assumed two erroneous attitudes toward Mao Zedong Thought. They negated the scientific value of Mao Zedong Thought and negated the guiding role of Mao Zedong Thought in the Chinese revolution and in construction because Mao Zedong made mistakes in his later years. Or they negated the mistakes made by Comrade Mao Zedong in his later years and promoted the "two whatevers" in an attempt to uphold Comrade Mao Zedong's wrong viewpoints in the course of new practice. The "resolution" has differentiated the scientific theory of Mao Zedong Thought from the mistakes made by Comrade Mao Zedong in his later years -- providing us with an effective key in our rectifying the above two erroneous attitudes toward Mao Zedong Thought.

Here the major problem is: What is called Mao Zedong Thought? Is Comrade Mao Zedong's personal way of thinking to be called Mao Zedong Thought?

On this problem, there was an open discussion as early as at the seventh national CCP congress: Mao Zedong Thought was a product of the general principles of Marxism-Leninism and the concrete practice of the Chinese revolution. In the "resolution," it was clearly stated: "Mao Zedong Thought is the application and development of Marxism-Leninism in China; is the correct theory and principle and the summation of experiences about the Chinese revolution proved by practice; and is the crystallization of the collective wisdom of the Chinese Communist Party. Many outstanding leaders of our party have made important contributions toward its formation and development. Comrade Mao Zedong's scientific works are the concentrated embodiment of it."

As far as Comrade Mao Zedong the individual is concerned, he was not a born Marxist. Just as he stated many times, he in his early years was a religious believer, a believer in Confucius and also a believer in idealism and democratic reformism. Only later did he discover Marxism. Obviously, we cannot incorporate all the ideas of his early years into Mao Zedong Thought.

Not every viewpoint put forth by Comrade Mao Zedong even in the later period when he, then a Marxist, applied Marxism-Leninism in studying the reality of the Chinese revolution and put forth a number of new conclusions, that is, during the time when Mao Zedong Thought took shape, should be incorporated in Mao Zedong Thought. In his speech entitled "The Working Principles of the 'Seventh CCP Congress'" published recently, Comrade Mao Zedong said: "I have also committed mistakes before."

"In 1927, I wrote an article, applying the Marxist viewpoint. However, as I did not have a Marxist viewpoint toward economic problems, the passage on economic problems was wrong. Moreover, I also made many mistakes in my work, whether in the military and political sphere or in party affairs, over the past decades and more. I did not put down these mistakes in writing, but his does not mean that I did not make them. Judging by actual history and the true situation, I made mistakes." Comrade Mao Zedong made this speech when the seventh national CCP congress took Mao Zedong Thought as the ideology guiding the

Chinese revolution and put this in writing into the party constitution. This shows that even at that time, the party and Comrade Mao Zedong himself did not mix Comrade Mao Zedong's mistakes and his lack of the Marxist viewpoint with Mao Zedong Thought.

Some comrades hold that during his later years, Comrade Mao Zedong did not make mistakes just in an article and lack the Marxist viewpoint toward a specific question but went against Marxism when dealing with a number of major issues. So, they say that Mao Zedong Thought should not mentioned again. They even hold that if Mao Zedong Thought is to be upheld, his mistakes during his later years should also be mentioned. This viewpoint is incorrect. Actually, during his later years, Comrade Mao Zedong did not make mistakes in just some individual problems. The principal thesis of the "Great Cultural Revolution" initiated by him was summed up as the "Theory of continued revolution under the dictatorship of the proletariat," which was certainly not a mistake represented by an individual conclusion. And yet, we should not mix Comrade Mao Zedong's erroneous proposals during his later years with Mao Zedong Thought. Mao Zedong Thought is a product of the integration of the universal principles of Marxism-Leninism with the concrete practice of the Chinese revolution. The erroneous leftist thesis of the "Great Cultural Revolution" initiated by Comrade Mao Zedong during his later years conformed neither with the universal principles of Marxism-Leninism nor with the reality of China. Its assessment of the class relations and the political conditions of our party and state was entirely wrong. Therefore, we definitely should differentiate Comrade Mao Zedong's mistakes during his later years from Mao Zedong Thought which is a scientific theory which took shape after being tested for a long period of time.

This differentiation is of vital significance in the development of the Chinese revolution. If we uphold the erroneous leftist thesis of the "Great Cultural Revolution" initiated by Comrade Mao Zedong and take it as the scientific theory of Mao Zedong Thought, we shall sink deeper and deeper in the quagmire of the "left." If we negate Mao Zedong Thought just because Comrade Mao Zedong committed mistakes during his later years, we shall be pacing up and down in the fog. Since the Third Plenary Session of the Eleventh CCP Central Committee, the CCP Central Committee has adopted a very prudent attitude toward the appraisal of Mao Zedong Thought. On the one hand, it firmly rectified the mistakes committed by Comrade Mao Zedong during his later years and has scored remarkable results in eliminating chaos and restoring order in various spheres. On the other hand, it has firmly resisted the wave of erroneous ideas of a few people to negate Mao Zedong Thought. While eliminating chaos and restoring order in the past few years, we have made criticism and established new things without going beyond the scope of the scientific theory of Mao Zedong Thought. Now, the "Resolution" has theoretically differentiated Mao Zedong Thought from the mistakes committed by Comrade Mao Zedong during his later years. Through serious study and by unifying the thinking of all party members on the basis of the "Resolution," we surely can accomplish with faster and better results our task of eliminating chaos and restoring order on all fronts and advance firmly toward the great goal of building a powerful modern socialist China.

*****

NOTES

1. The double-track system for labour refers to a combination of the system of the eight-hour day in factories, rural areas and government offices with a system of part-time work and part-time study in factories and rural areas. The double-track system for education means a system of full-time schooling combined with a system of part-time work and part-time study.

CHAPTER TWO

THE TRIAL OF THE GANG OF FOUR

The trial of Mao Tse-tung's widow, Chiang Ch'ing and her principal supporters--the so-called Gang of Four began on November 20, 1960. The trial lasted for three months with the verdict being delivered on January 23, 1981.

The two documents contained in Chapter Ten are the Indictment of the Special Procurate (Document No. 7), and the Written Judgement of the Special Court (Document No. 8).

In fact, the indictment of the Gang of Four charged a total of seventeen people--including the late Lin Piao and several of his family and supporters who were also dead--with a variety of serious crimes including conspiracy to overthrow the government of China and murder Chairman Mao. It is clear from the lengthy "indictment" that the guilt of the accused was already well established in the minds of their accusers.

The written judgement, not surprisingly, found all ten of the living defendants guilty as charged. Chiang Ch'ing, who had refused legal counsel and chosen to defend herself, was sentenced to death with a two-year reprieve and permanent loss of her political rights. The others were sentenced to a variety of lesser penalties ranging down to sixteen years in prison.

*****

DOCUMENTS

7. "Indictment of the Special Procuratorate," **Beijing Review**, No. 48, December 1, 1980.

8. "Written Judgement of the Special Court under the Supreme People's Court of the People's Republic of China," January 23, 1981, **New China News Agency**, Beijing, January 25, 1981; **FBIS - CHI**, January 26, 1981.

*****

DOCUMENT NO. 7

INDICTMENT OF THE SPECIAL PROCURATORATE

(**Beijing Review**, No. 48, December 1, 1980)

The Special Court under the Supreme People's Court started trying the ten principal culprits of the "Lin Biao and Jiang Qing counter-revolutionary cliques" on November 20. The following is the full text of the indictment drawn up by the Special Procuratorate under the Supreme People's Procuratorate of the People's Republic of China. -- *Beijing Review* Ed.

November 2, 1980.

To the Special Court under the Supreme People's Court of the People's Republic of China:

The Ministry of Public Security of the People's Republic of China, after concluding its investigation, has referred the case of the plot by the Lin Biao and Jiang Qing counter-revolutionary cliques to overthrow the political power of the dictatorship of the proletariat to the Supreme People's Procuratorate of the People's Republic of China for examination and prosecution.

Having examined the case, the Special Procuratorate under the Supreme People's Procuratorate confirms that the principal culprits of the Lin Biao and Jiang Qing counter-revolutionary cliques, namely Lin Biao, Jiang Qing, Kang Sheng, Zhang Chunqiao, Yao Wenyuan, Wang Hongwen, Chen Boda, Xie Fuzhi, Ye Qun, Huang Yongsheng, Wu Faxian, Li Zuopeng, Qiu Huizuo, Lin Liguo, Zhou Yuchi and Jiang Tengjiao, acted in collusion during the "great cultural revolution" and, taking advantage of their positions and the power at their disposal, framed and persecuted Communist Party and state leaders in a premeditated way in an attempt to usurp Party leadership and state power and overthrow the political power of the dictatorship of the proletariat. They did this by resorting to all kinds of intrigues and using every possible means, legal or illegal, overt or covert, by pen or by gun. In September 1971, after the failure of the plot to murder Chairman Mao Zedong and stage an armed counter-revolutionary coup d'etat by Lin Biao, Ye Qun, Lin Liguo, Zhou Yuchi and Jiang Tengjiao, Lin Biao and others fled the country in defection, and the counter-revolutionary clique headed by him was exposed and crushed. The counter-revolutionary gang of four of Jiang Qing, Zhang Chunqiao, Yao Wenyuan and Wang Hongwen, with Jiang Qing at the head, carried on its counter-revolutionary conspiratorial activities until it was exposed and smashed in October 1976. The Lin Biao and Jiang Qing counter-revolutionary cliques brought untold disasters to our country and nation.

The Lin Biao and Jiang Qing counter-revolutionary cliques committed the following crimes:

I

Frame-Up and Persecution of Party and State Leaders and Plotting to Overthrow The Political Power of the Dictatorship of the Proletariat

To overthrow the political power of the dictatorship of the proletariat, the Lin Biao and Jiang Qing counter-revolutionary cliques framed and persecuted Party and state leaders and leading cadres in all walks of life in a premeditated way.

1) They instigated the persecution of Party and state leaders at all levels in an attempt to seize leadership. On January 23, 1967, Lin Biao plotted the usurpation of power, saying, "All power, be it at the top, middle or lower levels, should be seized. In some cases, this should be done soon, in others later." "This may be done at the top or lower levels, or done in co-ordination at both levels." He also instigated the persecution of leading cadres. He said, "Put some of them in custody, cap some with tall paper hats, and search and ransack the homes of others." "It is necessary to use measures such as the 'jet aircraft' (forcing a person to bow with both hands raised over the back like the swept-back wings of a jet plane--Tr.) against people like Peng Zhen, Luo Ruiqing, Lu Dingyi and Yang Shangkun."

Zhang Chunqiao said in Shanghai on January 22, 1967, "Our aim in the Great Proletarian Cultural Revolution has always been to seize power, from the grass roots to the central organizations, including powers of the Party, the government, as well as in the financial, cultural and other fields." "We must seize power everywhere." With regard to veteran cadres he said in Shanghai in April, "All of them are bad" and "None shall be spared!" From 1967 to 1975, he said on many other occasions in Shanghai and Beijing that "the great cultural revolution" meant "a change of dynasty." In plotting to usurp power and effect a "change of dynasty," the Lin Biao and Jiang Qing counter-revolutionary cliques laid bare their counter-revolutionary objective of overthrowing the political power of the proletarian dictatorship.

2) They brought false charges against and persecuted Liu Shaoqi, Chairman of the People's Republic of China and Vice-Chairman of the Central Committee of the Communist Party of China (C.P.C.). In August 1966, when Liu Shaoqi was still Chairman of the Peoples's Republic of China (P.R.C.) and was re-elected to the Standing Committee of the Political Bureau of the C.P.C. Central Committee, Lin Biao instructed Ye Qun to summon Lei Yingfu twice, on August 11 and 12, to her presence. Lei Yingfu was then deputy director of the Operations Department of the Headquarters of the General Staff of the Chinese People's Liberation Army (P.L.A.). She provided him verbally with material containing false charges fabricated by Lin Biao and herself against Liu Shaoqi and instructed him to put these charges in writing. On August 13, Lin Biao read what Lei had written. At his residence, Lin told Lei the next day that "it will look more political" if Lei would write an accompanying letter addressed to Lin Biao and Chairman Mao Zedong, so that Lin could write his comments on the letter before forwarding it to the Chairman. On the same day, Lin Biao sent Lei Yingfu's letter together with his material incriminating Liu Shaoqi to Jiang Qing for her to "consider forwarding" them to the Chairman.

On the afternoon of December 18, 1966, Zhang Chunqiao met privately with Kuai Dafu, a student of Qinghua University, in the reception room at the west gate of Zhongnanhai, Beijing. He said, "That a couple of persons in the Central Committee who put forward the reactionary bourgeois line have not yet surrendered.... You young revolutionary fighters should unite, carry forward your thoroughgoing revolutionary spirit and flog the cur that has fallen into the water. Make their very names stink. Don't stop halfway." Incited by Zhang, Kuai organized a demonstration in Beijing on December 25. The demonstrators put up slogans and big-character posters, handed out leaflets and shouted demagogically, "Down with Liu Shaoqi!" and "Down with Deng Xiaoping!"

In July 1967, Jiang Qing, Kang Sheng and Chen Boda decided without authorization that Liu Shaoqi should be repudiated and struggled against. Qi Benyu, a member of the "Cultural Revolution Group under the C.P.C. Central Committee," organized a "rally for repudiating and struggling against Liu Shaoqi."

on July 18 of the same year; the residence of Liu Shaoqi and Wang Guangmei was searched and ransacked and the two were persecuted physically. During July and August 1967, Kang Sheng, Xie Fuzhi and Qi Benyu incited people to organize a "frontline for getting Liu Shaoqi out of Zhongnanhai," surround the place and attempt to break into the State Council.

Jiang Qing assumed direct control of the "group for inquiring into the special case of Liu Shaoqi and Wang Guangmei" and directed its work in collusion with Kang Sheng and Xie Fuzhi. They resorted to extorting confessions through torture an rigging up false evidence in order to vilify Liu Shaoqi and Wang Guangmei as "renegades," "enemy agents" and "counter-revolutionaries." From May to October 1967, acting on her own, Jiang Qing made the decision to arrest and imprison Yang Yichen, Deputy Governor of Hebei Province; Yang Chengzuo, a professor of the China People's University in Beijing; Wang Guangen, a citizen of Tianjin (originally assistant manager of the former Fengtian Cotton Mill); Liu Shaoqi's former cook Hao Miao; and seven others. When Yang Chengzuo was critically ill, Jiang Qing said to the group for inquiring into the special case, "Step up the interrogation to squeeze out of him what we need before he dies." Yang Chengzuo died of afflictions. Wang Guangen was also persecuted to death. On October 23, 1967, Xie Fuzhi said to the special case group, "It is necessary to be firm and ruthless in interrogation. . . . It is necessary to carry out group interrogation for hours at a time until confessions are obtained." In order to frame Wang Guangmei as an "enemy agent," Jiang Qing and Xie Fuzhi ordered the interrogation and torture of Zhang Zhongyi, a professor of the Hebei Provincial Normal College in Beijing who was critically ill. Zhang was tortured to death. In order to frame Liu Shaoqi as a "renegade," they extorted confessions from Ding Juequn, who worked with Liu Shaoqi in the workers' movement in Wuhan in 1927, and Meng Yongqian, who was arrested with Liu Shaoqi in Shenyang in 1929. On September 25, 1967, Ding declared in prison that the confession he was compelled to write "does not strictly conform to facts." Between June 15, 1967 and March 18, 1969, Meng wrote twenty statements in prison declaring that what he had written about Liu Shaoqi under duress "was mere fabrication" and should be withdrawn. But all their requests for correction and appeals were withheld and not allowed to be submitted to higher authorities. Liu Shaoqi was persecuted to death.

3) Jiang Qing and Kang Sheng cooked up false charges to persecute Members of the Eighth C.P.C. Central Committee. On July 21, 1968, Kang Sheng wrote a strictly confidential letter. On the envelope he wrote "Important. To be forwarded immediately to and personally opened by Comrade Jiang Qing." In the letter, he wrote, "Enclosed please find the name list you have asked for." On this list drawn up by Kang Sheng in his own handwriting, 88 of the 193 Members and

Alternate Members of the Eighth C.P.C. Central Committee were falsely charged as "enemy agents," "renegades," "elements having illicit relations with foreign countries" or "anti-Party elements." Another seven were classified as having been temporarily "removed from their posts but not yet included in the special cases" and twenty-nine were classified as "having committed mistakes or needing to be subjected to investigation for their historical records." Later, the great majority of them were also framed and persecuted by Kang Sheng and others.

Among the Party and state leaders and the first secretaries of the regional bureaus of the Central Committee of the Communist Party who were thus framed were:

Members and Alternate Members of the Political Bureau of the C.P.C. Central Committee: Liu Shaoqi, Zhu De, Chen Yun, Deng Xiaoping, Peng Zhen, Chen Yi, Peng Dehuai, He Long, Li Xiannian, Tan Zhenlin, Li Jingquan, Tao Zhu, Xu Xiangqian, Nie Rongzhen, Ye Jianying, Ulanhu, Zhang Wentian, Lu Dingyi, Bo Yibo and Song Renqiong.

General Secretary of the C.P.C. Central Committee Deng Xiaoping; Members and Alternate Members of the Secretariat of the C.P.C. Central Committee: Peng Zhen, Wang Jiaxiang, Tan Zhenlin, Li Xiannian, Lu Dingyi, Luo Ruiqing, Tao Zhu, Ye Jianying, Liu Ningyi, Liu Lantao, Yang Shangkun and Hu Qiaomu.

Vice-Premiers of the State Council: Chen Yun, Deng Xiaoping, He Long, Chen Yi, Ulanhu, Li Xiannian, Tan Zhenlin, Nie Rongzhen, Bo Yibo, Lu Dingyi, Luo Ruiqing and Tao Zhu.

Vice-Chairmen of the Military Commission of the C.P.C. Central Committee: He Long, Nie Rongzhen, Chen Yi, Xu Xiangqian and Ye Jianying.

First secretaries of the regional bureaus of the C.P.C. Central Committee: Song Renqiong, Liu Lantao, Li Jingquan and Wang Renzhong.

Other Members and Alternate Members of the C.P.C. Central Committee: Xiao Jingguang, Su Yu, Xiao Ke, Chen Shaomin, Wang Zhen, Zeng Shan, Ouyang Qin, Wang Shusheng, Wang Enmao, Deng Hua, Deng Zihui, Tan Zheng, Liu Xiao, Li Weihan, Yang Xiufeng, Zhang Jichun, Cheng Zihua, Wu Xiuquan, Qian Ying, Wang Congwu, Ma Mingfang, Li Baohua, Xu Guangda, Lin Tie, Zheng Weisan, Xu Haidong, Xiao Hua, Hu Yaobang, Xi Zhongxun, An Ziwen, Lu Zhengcao, Zhang Jingwu, Liao Chengzhi, Ye Fei, Yang Xianzhen, Zhang Dingcheng, Shu Tong, Pan Zili, Yang Yong, Huang Huoqing, Chen Manyuan, Su

Zhenhua, Feng Baiju, Fan Wenlan, Li Jianzhen, Feng Baiju, Fan Wenlan, Li Jianzhen, Gao Kelin, Zhong Qiguang, Jiang Hua, Li Zhimin, Yang Chengwu, Zhang Hanfu, Shuai Mengqi, Liu Ren, Wan Yi, Zhou Yang, Xu Zirong, Liu Lanbo, Kui Bi, Ou Mengjue, Zhu Dehai, Zhang Qilong, Ma Wenrui, Wang Shitai, Liao Hansheng, Hong Xuezhi, Zhang Yun, Xu Bing, Liao Luyan, Song Shilun, Zhou Huan, Chen Pixian, Zhao Jianmin, Qian Junrui, Jiang Nanxiang, Han Guang, Li Chang, Wang Heshou, Chen Zhengren, Zhao Yimin, Kong Yuan, Zhang Su, Yang Yichen, Zhao Boping, Zhang Aiping, Yao Yilin, Wang Feng, Fang Yi, Wang Shangrong, Liu Zhen, Zhang Jingfu, Li Jiebo, Liao Zhigao, Jiang Weiqing, Tan Qilong, Zhang Zhongliang and Zhang Pinghua.

4) Chen Boda, Xie Fuzhi and Wu Faxian made use of the case of the "Extraordinary Central Committee of the Communist Party of China" leaflet, which had been unearthed in Tianjin in November 1967, to frame and persecute Party and state leaders under the pretext of tracking down the "behind-the-scene bosses." On April 28 and August 19, 1968, when they received Zhao Dengcheng, then a member of the leading group of the Ministry of Public Security, and others, Chen Boda said that the unearthing of the case was merely "the beginning." And he added, "It is not the end. The bosses are hidden behind the scenes, and they are no ordinary persons, for ordinary people aren't capable of doing such a thing. It isn't the act of one individual. Very likely, there's an organization behind all this." Xie Fuzhi cut in saying, "Yes, it's merely the beginning, not the end." "Somebody from the notorious Liu-Deng headquarters is at the root of it all." Wu Faxian said, "Who else can it be but Capitalist Roader No. 2?" In December 1968, while tracking down the "behind-the-scenes bosses," Xie Fuzhi, Zhao Dengcheng and others cooked up the false case of a "Chinese Communist Party (M-L)," with Zhu De alleged as "secretary" of its central committee, Chen Yi as "deputy secretary and concurrently minister of defence," and Li Fuchun as "premier." Its members allegedly included Dong Biwu, Ye Jianying, Li Xiannian, He Long, Liu Bocheng, Xu Xiangqian, Nie Rongzhen, Tan Zhenlin, Yu Qiuli, Wang Zhen and Liao Chengzhi, who were falsely accused of having "illicit relations with foreign countries," "making preparations for an armed insurrection" and attempting to "stage a coup." Even up to August 21, 1969, Xie Fuzhi told those who were responsible for inquiring into the case, "Be firm and keep up your inquiries, for some evidence is still lacking. Verbal confessions made by those jailed can be used as evidence, too."

5) Kang Sheng and his wife Cao Yiou instructed Guo Yufeng, who was in charge of the Organization Department of the C.P.C. Central Committee, to provide an August 23, 1968 a fabricated "Report on the Political Background of Members of the Control Commission of the C.P.C. Central Committee." In the report, 37 of the 60 Members and Alternate Members of the Control Commission

of the Eighth C.P.C. Central Committee were falsely labelled "renegades," "enemy agents" or "counter-revolutionary revisionists." They were: Liu Lantao, Wang Congwu, Qian Ying, Liu Xiwu, Shuai Mengqi, Li Yunchang, Wang Weigang, Yang Zhihua, Li Shiying, Li Chuli, Ma Mingfang, Gong Zirong, Chen Shaomin, Fang Zhongru, Liu Yaxiong, Zhang Ziyi, Wang Hefeng, Liu Shenzhi, Li Peizhi, Zhou Zhongying, Chen Peng, Chen Zenggu, Zheng Ping, Xue Zizheng, Gao Kelin, Ji Yatai, Wang Shiying, Qiu Jin, Wu Gaizhi, Ma Guorui, Zhang Dingcheng, Wu Defeng, Zhang Jiafu, Liao Suhua, Gong Fengchun, Li Jingying and Xiao Hua.

6) Kang Sheng and Cao Yiou instructed Guo Yufeng to fabricate on August 27, 1968 a "Report on the Political Background of Members of the Standing Committee of the Third National People's Congress," which was subsequently revised and finalized by Kang Sheng himself. In the report, 60 of the 115 Members were framed as "renegades," "suspected enemy agents," "counter-revolutionary revisionists, capitalist roaders or anti-Party, anti-socialist and anti-Mao Zedong Thought elements" and "highly dubious characters." They were: Chairman of the Standing Committee Zhu De; Vice-Chairman of the Standing Committee Peng Zhen, Li Jingquan, Lin Feng, Liu Ningyi and Zhang Zhizhong; and Members Chen Shaomin, Yang Zhihua, Shuai Mengqi, Zhao Yimin, Qian Ying, Liu Yaxiong, Li Da, Xu Liqing, Wang Shitai, Hu Ziang, Lui Lanbo, Xu Bing, Xu Zirong, Zhang Jingwu, Yang Shangkun, Li Yanlu, Han Guang, Mei Gongbin, Wang Kunlun, Nan Hanchen, Gong Yinbing, Cao Mengjun, Shi Liang, Tang Shengzhi, Kong Yuan, Hu Yaobang, Xie Fumin, Luo Qiong, Wu Lengxi, Zhang Su, Wu Xinyu, Ma Chungu, Yu Aifeng, Liu Changsheng, Gu Dacun, Zhou Li, Zhao Shoushan, Hu Yuzhi, Hu Qiaomu, Liang Sicheng, Tong Dizhou, Ye Zhupei, Chen Qiyou, Wang Weizhou, Ye Jianying, Lin Qiangyun, Guo Jian, Yang Yunyu, Hua Luogeng, Zhao Zhongyao, Chen Shaoxian, Zhao Jiuzhang, Mao Yisheng and Hu Juewen.

7) Kang Sheng and Cao Yiou instructed Guo Yufeng to fabricate on August 27, 1968 a "Report on the Political Background of Member of the Standing Committee of the Fourth National Committee of the Chinese People's Political Consultative Conference," which was subsequently revised and finalized by Kang Sheng himself. In the report, 74 of the 159 Members were falsely accused of being "renegades," "suspected renegades," "enemy agents," "suspected enemy agents," "Kuomintang agents," "counter-revolutionary revisionist," or "having illicit relations with foreign countries." They were Vice-Chairmen Peng Zhen, Liu Lantao, Song Renqiong, Xu Bing and Gao Chongmin; and Members Wang Congwu, Liu Xiwu, Ping Jiesan, Yang Dongchun, Li Chuli, Wang Weigang, Zhang Ziyi, Li Yunchang, Gong Zirong, Li Chulee, Cao Ying, Liu Qingyang, Kong Xiangzhen, Ma Huizhi, Zhang Youyu, Zhang Yun, Wang Zhaohua, Zhou Yang, Wu Gaizhi, He Changgong, Lin Xiude, Tang Tianji, Zhu

Yunshan, Su Ziheng, Gong Tianmin, Zou Dapeng, An Ziwen, Chu Tunan, Wang Jinxiang, Li Lisan, Zeng Xianzhi, Sa Kongliao, Zhang Xiuyan, Ji Yatai, Yu Yifu, Ha Fenga, Wang Shiying, Liu Xiao, Yan Baohang, Yang Qiqing, Sun Qimeng, Zhao Puchu, Che Ziangchen, Bainqen Erdini Qoigyi Gyaincain, Wang Jiaxiang, Wu Xiuquan, Zhang Zhizhong, Sun Xiaocun, Shi Liang, Chu Xuefan, Liu Fei, Zhang Xiaoqian, Cun Shusheng, Yu Dafu, Zheng Weisan, Chen Guodong, Gao Wenhua, Wang Zigang, Zhang Bangying, Hu Keshi, Li Chang, He Cheng, Zhong Huilan, Wu Hongbin, Fu Lianzhang, Jin Rubai, Chen Qiyou, Xiong Qinglai and Zhang Jingfu.

8) The frame-up and persecution of Zhou Enlai, Vice-Chairman of the C.P.C. Central Committee and Premier of the State Council. In October 1974, Jiang Qing falsely accused Zhou Enlai and others of conspiracy, saying, "Those people in the State Council often maintain illicit contact with each other on the pretext of discussing work. . . . The Premier is the boss behind the scenes." On October 17, 1974, the gang of four, namely Jiang Qing, Zhang Chunqiao, Yao Wenyuan and Wang Hongwen, hatched a plot in Building No. 17 at Diao Yu Tai in Beijing and the following day sent Wang Hongwen to Changsha to make a false and insinuating report to Chairman Mao Zedong there. He said, "Although the Premier is ill and hospitalized, he is busy summoning people for talks far into the night. Almost every day someone goes to his place. Deng Xiaoping, Ye Jianying and Li Xiannian are frequent visitors." And he added, "The atmosphere in Beijing now is very much like that of the Lushan Meeting." He was falsely accusing Zhou Enlai, Deng Xiaoping and others of engaging in activities to usurp power as Lin Biao had been during the 1970 Lushan Meeting. In 1974, Jiang Qing, Zhang Chunqiao and Yao Wenyuan instructed Chi Qun, then secretary of the C.P.C. Committee of Qinghua University, Xie Jingyi, then secretary of the Beijing Municipal Committee of the C.P.C., Lu Ying, editor-in-chief of *Renmin Ribao (People's Daily)*, Zhu Yongjia, then head of the Shanghai Writing Group, and others to make use of the media to stir up nationwide criticism of the "big Confucian of our time," the "chief minister" and the "Duke of Zhou," thus attacking Zhou Enlai by innuendo.

9) The frame-up and persecution of Zhu De, Vice-Chairman of the C.P.C. Central Committee and Chairman of the Standing Committee of the National People's Congress. From September 1966 to December 1968, Lin Biao, Zhang Chunqiao, Wu Faxian, Qiu Huizuo and others slandered Zhu De and falsely accused him of being a "sinister commander," an "old-line opportunist" and a "warlord" and of "harboring wild ambitions to become the leader."

At the end of January 1967, at the instigation of Qi Benyu, some people from the China People's University put up large-size slogans in Beijing, which read "Down with Zhu De." Presently the "Liaison Centre for Ferreting Out Zhu De" was set up and a plot was under way to hold meetings to repudiate him. On March 4, Qi Benyu received some people from the China People's University and incited them to continue with their persecution of Zhu De. He said, "If you do it yourselves, you will succeed. But if you tell people that I'm behind all this, you won't succeed. You think you're smart. Actually you're a bunch of fatheads. It's up to you to decide whether you go on or not."

10) The frame-up and persecution of Deng Xiaoping, Member of the Standing Committee of the Political Bureau of the C.P.C. Central Committee, General Secretary of the Central Committee and Vice-Premier of the State Council. On December 6, 1966, Lin Biao slandered Deng Xiaoping as a "member of a sinister gang" and an "anti-Party element." And on January 29, 1967, Kang Sheng vilified Deng Xiaoping, saying that he was a "Khrushchov-type person."

On October 4, 1974, Chairman Mao Zedong proposed that Deng Xiaoping be First Vice-President of the State Council. In an attempt to prevent Deng Xiaoping from taking office, Jiang Qing, Zhang Chunqiao, Yao Wenyuan, and Wang Hongwen conspired together on October 17 in Building No. 17 at Diao Yu Tai in Beijing and had Wang Hongwen go to Changsha the following day to report to Chairman Mao Zedong with the false charge that Zhou Enlai, Deng Xiaoping and others were engaged in activities to seize power.

From February to May 1976, Jiang Qing, Zhang Chunqiao, Yao Wenyuan and Mao Yuanxin, another key member of the Jiang Qing counter-revolutionary clique, went a step further in their false accusations against Deng Xiaoping. The C.P.C. Central Committee's Document No. 1 of 1975 had carried the appointment of Deng Xiaoping as Vice-Chairman of the Military Commission of the C.P.C. Central Committee and concurrently Chief of the General staff, of the P.L.A. and the C.P.C. Central Committee's Document No. 1 of 1976 had carried the appointment of Hua Guofeng as Acting Premier of the State Council. Regarding these two documents, Zhang Chunqiao wrote on February 3, 1976, "Here is yet another Document No. 1. Last year there was a Document No. 1. This is truly a case of inflated arrogance at an upturn in fortune. Moving up so fast and so hurriedly spells a downfall that will be just as rapid," and he quoted a classical poem:

A year ends amidst the crepitation of
firecrackers,
An easterly breeze has warmed the New
Year's wine.

*The doors of every household are bathed in
the sunshine,
A new peach-wood lintel charm invariably
replaces the old.*

This again revealed Zhang Chunqiao's counter-revolutionary ambition to effect a "change of dynasty." On February 22, Mao Yuanxin said to Ma Tianshui and Xu Jingxian, then vice-chairmen of the Shanghai Municipal Revolutionary Committee, and others that Deng Xiaoping "worships things foreign and sells out the sovereignty of the country" and that he "represents the interests of the comprador bourgeoisie," was trying to bring about an "all-around retrogression" and so "there would be a change in the nature of the state." On March 2, at a forum of the leading members from a number of provinces and autonomous regions, Jiang Qing maligned Deng Xiaoping, calling him a "counter-revolutionary double-dealer," the "general manager of a rumor-mongering company," a "fascist," a "big quisling" and a "representative of the comprador bourgeoisie." On April 26, Jiang Qing falsely charged that Deng Xiaoping, like Lin Biao, had "big and small fleets" (gangs formed to carry out plots and assassinations--Tr.) and that "their fleets operated in about the same way in some cases, and differently in others. Deng's small fleets are, however, more active." On April 5, Zhang Chunqiao slanderously accused Deng Xiaoping of being a "Nagy." On May 16, in an article entitled "There Is Really a Bourgeoisie Within the Party -- Analysis of the Counter-Revolutionary Political Incident at Tian An Men Square," which *Renmin Ribao (People's Daily)* sent him for finalization, Yao Wenyuan added that Deng Xiaoping "is the chief boss behind this counter-revolutionary political incident."

11) The frame-up and persecution of Chen Yi, Member of the Political Bureau of the C.P.C. Central Committee, Vice-Premier of the State Council and Vice-Chairman of the Military Commission of the C.P.C. Central Committee. On August 7, 1967, Wang Li, a member of the "Cultural Revolution Group under the C.P.C. Central Committee," said, "Picking on Chen Yi is of course correct in orientation." He added, "What's wrong with the slogan 'Down with Liu (Shaoqi), Deng (Xiaoping) and Chen (Yi)?'" He was agitating people to usurp leadership over foreign affairs. In November 1968, upon Zhang Chunqiao's instruction, Wang Hongwen, Xu Jingxian and others compiled a *Collection of Chen Yi's Reactionary Views and Utterances* while nominally preparing documents for the forthcoming C.P.C. Ninth National Congress. This fabricated *Collection* was distributed in the study class of deputies from Shanghai to the Ninth National Party Congress and in it Chen Yi was falsely accused of "capitulating to imperialism, revisionism and reaction" and "whipping up public opinion for restoring capitalism." At the same time, they collected and compiled another seventy-six copies of material, running to a total of 1,163 pages, which carried

false charges against Ye Jianying, Li Xiannian, Chen Yun, Chen Yi, Nie Rongzhen, Li Fuchun, Tan Zhenlin and others.

12) The frame-up and persecution of Peng Dehuai, Member of the Political Bureau of the C.P.C. Central Committee. In July 1967, when Kang Sheng, Chen Boda and Qi Benyu received Han Aijing and other students of the Beijing Aeronautical Engineering Institute, Qi Benyu made arrangements with them for the repudiation and persecution of Peng Dehuai. On November 3, 1970, Huang Yongsheng examined and approved a report prepared by the special case group, which contained the proposal that "Peng Dehuai be dismissed from all posts inside and outside the Party, expelled from the Party for good, sentenced to life imprisonment and deprived of civil rights for life." Peng Dehuai was persecuted to death.

13) The frame-up and persecution of He Long, Member of the Political Bureau of the C.P.C. Central Committee, Vice-Premier of the State Council and Vice-Chairman of the Military Commission of the C.P.C. Central Committee. In the summer of 1966, at a students' rally at the Beijing Normal University and at meetings of the "Cultural Revolution Group under the C.P.C. Central Committee," Kang Sheng falsely charged He Long and Peng Zhen with "secretly deploying troops to stage a February mutiny," In August 1966, Lin Biao instructed Wu Faxian to fabricate material accusing He Long of plotting to usurp leadership in the Air Force. On September 3, Wu Faxian sent Lin Biao the material he had prepared. Between late August and early September, Ye Qun spoke to Song Zhiguo, then chief of the Guards Division of the General Office of the C.P.C. Central Committee's Military Commission, giving an oral account of what she had fabricated in order to frame He Long. Then she directed him to put the material in writing, saying, "Make it sound as if you were giving me the information yourself, and not as if I had directed you to do so." From September 7 to 24 Song Zhiguo sent Lin Biao four collections of material which he had prepared for framing He Long. On May 16, 1968, Kang Sheng went a step further in maligning He Long by saying, "Judging He Long's present behavior in the light of his betrayal of the revolution and surrender to the enemy in the past, it is inconceivable that he is not now engaged in active counter-revolutionary activities. The past provides the clue to present." He Long was persecuted to death.

14) The frame-up and persecution of Xu Xiangqian, Member of the Political Bureau of the C.P.C. Central Committee and Vice-Chairman of its Military Commission. In April 1967, Kuai Dafu, at Ye Qun's instigation, sent people to collect material for framing Xu Xiangqian and Ye Jianying and published a slanderous article entitled "Bombard Xu Xiangqian--Down With Xu Xiangqian, the Military Counterpart of Liu (Shaoqi) and Deng (Xiaoping)." In

June that year, Qiu Huizuo instructed Wang Xike, then director of the "cultural revolution office" of the P.L.A. General Logistics Department, and some others to concoct material vilifying Xu Xiangqian and to edit and print leaflets slandering him as a "big time-bomb" planted in the Party and army and a "typical careerist and conspirator" and putting forward the slogan "Down with Xu Xiangqian."

15) The frame-up and persecution of Nie Rongzhen, Member of the Political Bureau of the C.P.C. Central Committee, Vice-Premier of the State Council and Vice-Chairman of the Military Commission of the C.P.C. Central Committee. In April 1968, Lin Biao ordered the Beijing Units of the P.L.A. to convene an enlarged Party committee meeting so as to engineer the repudiation of what they called "mountain-stronghold mentality of northern China." He then sent Huang Yongsheng, Wu Faxian and Xie Fuzhi to the meeting. Jiang Qing and Chen Boda falsely charged Nie Rongzhen with being the boss behind those with the "mountain-stronghold mentality of northern China" and plotted to overthrow him. In November of the same year, Huang Yongsheng slandered Nie Rongzhen, saying that "he has never done anything good all his life" and that "these people will never give up. Whenever the climate is right, they're up to something." On January 5, 1971, Jiang Qing slandered Nie Rongzhen and others, saying that they had been "bad people in the saddle" in northern China.

16) The frame-up and persecution of Ye Jianying, Member of the Political Bureau and of the Secretariat of the C.P.C. Central Committee and Vice-Chairman of its Military Commission. On June 23, 1967, Huang Yongsheng approved the "Report for Instructions on Investigation for the Purpose of Rounding Up Renegades," submitted by the head of the military control commission stationed in the Guangzhou Municipal Public Security Bureau, and its appendix, "Plan for Investigation, No. 1," which was directed against Ye Jianying, whom they were scheming to persecute. In June 1968, making use of the false charges he concocted in Guangzhou against Deputy Commander Wen Niansheng and others of the Guangzhou Units of the P.L.A., Huang Yongsheng launched an investigation concerning the so-called "sinister line." He later submitted to Ye Qun extorted confessions, charging Ye Jianying and others with having called "covert meetings" and "trying to usurp Party and state leadership by plotting a counter-revolutionary coup."

On April 3, 1968, Li Zuopeng, together with Wang Hongkun, then second political commissar of the Navy, and Zhang Xiuchuan, then director of the Navy's Political Department, wrote material in which they trumped up charges alleging that "He (Long) and Ye (Jianying) attempted to seize the command of the armed forces to oppose the Party" in co-ordination with Liu (Shaoqi), Deng (Xiaoping) and Tao (Zhu).

17) The frame-up and persecution of Lu Dingyi, Alternate Member of the Political Bureau of the C.P.C. Central Committee and Member of its Secretariat, Vice-Premier of the State Council and Director of the Propaganda Department of the C.P.C. Central Committee. In May 1966, Lin Biao trumped up charges against Lu Dingyi, labelling him a "counter-revolutionary." Jiang Qing, Kang Sheng, Chen Boda, Xie Fuzhi, Wu Faxian and others slandered him as a "renegade," "hidden traitor" and "special agent of the Bureau of Investigation and Statistics of the Kuomintang Government's Military Council." Chen Boda said that Lu Dingyi should be "handed to the Red Guards for trial." At the instigation and under the direction of the Lin Biao and Jiang Qing counter-revolutionary cliques, nine deputy directors of the Propaganda Department of the C.P.C. Central Committee were slandered as being "renegades," "enemy agents" or "Kuomintang elements."

18) The frame-up and persecution of Luo Ruiqing, Member of the Secretariat of the C.P.C. Central Committee, Vice-Premier of the State Council and Chief of the General Staff of the P.L.A. Lin Biao, Ye Qun, Kang Sheng, Xie Fuzhi, Huang Yongsheng, Wu Faxian, Li Zuopeng and others trumped up charges against him, alleging that he had "illicit relations with foreign countries," was a "hidden traitor" and a "counter-revolutionary who has committed heinous crimes" and had "hatched a major scheme" against the Navy.

19) Besides those people mentioned in Items (3), (4), (5), (6) and (7), others who were framed and persecuted by the Lin Biao and Jiang Qing counter-revolutionary cliques and the principal members of their factional setups include the following leading members of various departments under the C.P.C. Central Committee, various ministries and commissions under the State Council, and the C.P.C. committees and the people's governments in various provinces, autonomous regions and municipalities directly under the Central Government, and also high-ranking P.L.A. cadres: Kang Keqing, Jia Tuofu, Zhou Rongxin, Gu Mu, Lu Dong, Gao Yang, Duan Junyi, Liu Jie, Sun Zhiyuan, Wang Zheng, Zhang Linzhi, Liu Yumin, Sun Daguang, Yuan Baohua, He Wei, Qian Xinzhong, Xiao Wangdong, Wan Xiaotang, Zhang Huaisan, Zhao Lin, Zhao Ziyang, Wu Zhipu, Yan Hongyan, Wei Wenbo, Zeng Xisheng, Hui Yuyu, Wang Yanchun, Fang Zhichun, Wen Minsheng, Wei Heng, Huo Shilian, Yang Zhilin, Wang Zhao, Yang Jingren, Fu Qiutao, Liu Shaowen, Liang Biye, Liu Zhijian, Li Jukui, Rao Zhengxi, Li Yao, Peng Jiaqing, Tang Ping, Zhao Erlu, Xiao Xiangrong, Wang Ping, Cai Shunli, Liu Daosheng, Du Yide, Tao Yong, Fang Zhengping, Cheng Jun, Xu Shenji, Zhang Tingfa, Nie Fengzhi, Wu Fushan, Wu Kehua, Ouyang Yi, Liu He, He Jinnian, Cheng Shicai, Dun Xingyun, Tan Youlin, Cui Tianmin, Fu Chongbi, Zhuang Tian, Yan Fusheng, Chen Zaidao, Zhong, Hanhua, Yang Xiushan, Tang Jinlong, Liu Peishan, Liu Zhuanlian, Zhang Zhonghan, Huang Xinting, Guo

Linxiang, Gan Weihan, Yuan Shengping, Yang Jiarui, Qin Jiwei, Hu Ronggui, Kong Fei, Ting Mao and Wang Qimei.

20) The frame-up and persecution of leading cadres of the Organization Department of the C.P.C. Central Committee and usurpation and control of vital organizational power of the Party Central Committee. In January 1968, Kang Sheng ordered Guo Yufeng to produce charts and reports to frame up charges against Zhang Wentian, Chen Yun, Peng Zhen, Deng Xiaoping and An Ziwen, who had successively served as director of the Organization Department of the C.P.C. Central Committee since 1937. They were falsely accused of being "renegades," "enemy agents," "elements who oppose the Party, socialism and Mao Zedong Thought," or "any combination of these." Twenty-two people, who had at one time or another served as deputy directors of the Organization Department, were falsely charged with being "renegades," "enemy agents," elements maintaining illicit relations with foreign countries," or "elements who oppose the Party, socialism and Mao Zedong Thought." It was also alleged that a "counter-revolutionary clique" had entrenched itself in the Organization Department, which had become "a sinister den" and had "established a nationwide network of counter-revolution which recruited renegades to form a clique to pursue selfish interests." And it was proposed that the Organization Department "be disbanded and abolished."

21) The frame-up and persecution of leading cadres of the public security organs, the procuratorial organs and the courts at various levels, and usurpation and control of the instruments of the dictatorship of the proletariat. At the instigation and under the direction of the Lin Biao and Jiang Qing counter-revolutionary cliques, the nation's public security, procuratorial and judicial organs were completely destroyed. Xie Fuzhi incited people to "smash the public security, procuratorial and judicial organs" all over the country. Zhang Dingcheng, Chief Procurator of the Supreme People's Procuratorate, Yang Xiufeng, President of the Supreme People's Court, and large numbers of cadres and policemen working in the public security organs, the procuratorial organs and the courts at various levels were framed and persecuted. Kang Sheng, Xie Fuzhi and others concocted false charges against the Ministry of Public Security, alleging that there was a so-called "underground sinister ministry of public security headed by Luo Ruiqing." With the exception of Xie Fuzhi himself and one vice-minister who held other posts concurrently, all the vice-ministers of the then Ministry of Public Security were arrested and imprisoned. Vice-Minister Xu Zirong was persecuted to death.

22) In January 1967, Lin Biao Personally attached the comment, "I fully approve," to the slogan put forward by Guan Feng, Wang Li and other members

of the "Cultural Revolution Group under the C.P.C. Central Committee," that is, "Thoroughly expose the handful of capitalist roaders in power in the People's Liberation Army." They plotted to plunge the armed forces into chaos.

In order to control the armed forces, Lin Biao fabricated charges against large numbers of cadres and masses in the Headquarters of the P.L.A. General Staff and framed and persecuted them. In April 1968, Huang Yongsheng said at the Headquarters of the General Staff, "Quite a few bad people have surfaced here, people such as Huang Kecheng, Luo Ruiqing, Zhang Aiping and Wang Shangrong," and "the verdicts against them can never be reversed; they must never be allowed to stage a comeback."

On July 25, 1967, Lin Biao called for the "thorough smashing of that Palace of Hell -- the General Political Department of the People's Liberation Army." On many occasions Lin Biao and Ye Qun slandered Luo Ronghuan and Tan Zheng, former directors of the General Political Department. They trumped up charges, alleging that there was a "Luo (Ruiqing) -- Liang (Biye) anti-Party clique." Huang Yongsheng vilified the General Political Department, saying that it "has been recruiting renegades during the reign of several directors." Qiu Huizuo also slandered it, saying that it was "not much different from the Kuomintang secret service." He took an active part in the conspiratorial activities to "thoroughly smash the General Political Department." Large numbers of cadres and masses of the department were framed and persecuted. Four comrades who had been its director or deputy directors and another twenty who had been heads and deputy heads of its various sections were imprisoned and investigated owing to the false charge of attempting to "usurp leadership over the Army and oppose the Party" and of being "renegades," "enemy agents" or "active counter-revolutionaries." Yuan Ziqin, Wang Bing and fifteen other persons were persecuted to death.

On Mary 5, 1974, Jiang Qing and Zhang Chunqiao gave an audience to Chen Yading, former deputy head of the cultural section of the P.L.A. General Political Department, and others. Jiang Qing said, "Chen Yading, we have invited you here today in order to straighten things out in the Army." She added, "It seems that we have to seize power. Chen Yading, why don't you go and do it? In my opinion, we might as well let Chen Yading take charge of the Army's cultural work." She also said to him and others, "You should kindle a prairie fire," thus instigating them to grab power in the Army by throwing it into disorder.

23) Through Chen Boda and Yao Wenyuan, the Lin Biao and Jiang Qing counter-revolutionary cliques controlled the mass media and instigated the

overthrow of the political power of the dictatorship of the proletariat. In June 1966, Chen Boda organized people to write and cleared such editorials as "Sweep Away All the Monsters and Demons," thus trying to shape counter-revolutionary public opinion so that the Lin Biao and Jiang Qing counter-revolutionary cliques might usurp power after throwing the whole country into chaos. From 1974 to 1976, Jiang Qing, Zhang Chunqiao and Yao Wenyuan instructed the "Liang Xiao" writing group of Qinghua and Beijing Universities, the "Luo Siding" writing group in Shanghai, the "Chi Heng" writing group of the magazine *Hongqi (Red Flag)* and the "Tang Xiaowen" writing group of the Higher Party School of the C.P.C. Central Committee to spread counter-revolutionary, demagogic propaganda. In the spring of 1976, Yao Wen-yuan personally revised and cleared such articles as "From Bourgeois Democrats to Capitalist roaders" published in *Honggi (Red Flag)* and *Renmin Ribao (People's Daily)*. He and Zhang Chunqiao also cleared speeches prepared for Ma Tianshui and Xu Jingxian. In these articles and speeches, they vilified veteran cadres in leading organs of the Party, government and army at various levels as "bourgeois democrats," "capitalist roaders" or "long-time capitalist roaders" and instigated further persecution of them.

At the end of March 1976, slogans written in bold characters opposing Zhang Chunqiao appeared in Nanjing. Yao Wenyuan slandered the people who had put up the slogans, calling them "counter-revolutionaries." He said to Lu Ying, "It seems there's a command office stirring up this adverse, counter-revolutionary current." He added, "The situation in Beijing merits attention." Prompted by Yao Wenyuan, Lu Ying dispatched people to Tian An Men Square to collect and compile material which was then adulterated by Yao Wenyuan. Thus the revolutionary words and deeds of the masses opposing the gang of four, commemorating Zhou Enlai and supporting Deng Xiaoping were made out to be "counter-revolutionary speeches and slogans" and a "manifestation of last-ditch struggle and frenzied counterattack by the declining, moribund forces." The masses themselves were vilified as "a handful of bad elements" and "counter-revolutionaries." Yao Wenyuan even called for the "execution of a bunch of them."

From January to September 1976, at the instigation of Yao Wenyuan and Wang Hongwen, Lu Ying dispatched people to certain departments of the Party and the Government as well as to Fujian, Jiangxi, Zhejiang, Jiangsu, Sichuan, Yunnan, Heilongjiang and other provinces. There they collected material which they distorted to frame leading cadres in the Party, government and army, calling them "unrepentant capitalist roaders" or "capitalist roaders still travelling the capitalist road," and accusing them of "having organized landlords' restitution corps" and "trying to reverse correct verdicts and stage a comeback."

II

The Persecution and Suppression of
Large Numbers of Cadres and Masses

In order to seize Party and state leadership and establish their counter-revolutionary rule, the Lin Biao and Jiang Qing counter-revolutionary cliques incited beating, smashing and looting, whipped up violence, and trumped up false charges, thus persecuting and suppressing large numbers of cadres and people.

24) At the instigation and under the direction of Lin Biao, Jiang Qing, Kang Sheng and Xie Fuzhi, seven secretaries of the Beijing Municipal Committee of the C.P.C., including Liu Ren, Zheng Tianxiang, Wan Li and Deng Tuo, and six deputy mayors, including Wu Han and Yue Songsheng, were charged with being "enemy agents," "renegades," "counter-revolutionary revisionists," "reactionary capitalists" or "reactionary academic authorities." In January 1968, Kang Sheng falsely charged Liu Ren and deputy mayors Feng Jiping, Cui Yueli and others with "selling out vital secrets of the Party, government and army and betraying the Party and the nation." And he gave instructions, saying that "the ordinary methods of dealing with criminals cannot be used in their case," and that "we should put them in handcuffs and carry out sudden, gruelling interrogations." In May of the same year, Kang Sheng and Xie Fuzhi concocted the case of a "counter-revolutionary clique within the former Beijing Municipal Public Security Bureau, headed by Feng Jiping and Xing Xiangsheng," falsely accusing Feng Jiping and others of "carrying out espionage in collaboration with U.S. and Chiang Kai-shek's spies." Liu Ren, Deng Tuo, Wu Han and Yue Songsheng were persecuted to death.

25) In January 1968, Zhang Chunqiao and Yao Wenyuan slandered the Shanghai Municipal Committee of the C.P.C., saying that it was a "stubborn stronghold of the bourgeoisie" and consisted of an "evil bunch." They falsely accused Chen Pixian, its first secretary, of being "an extremely cunning and treacherous counter-revolutionary double-dealer" and "the most dangerous enemy of the proletariat," and framed up the charge of "renegade" against Cao Diqiu, a secretary of the municipal Party committee and mayor of Shanghai. At the instigation and under the direction of Zhang Chunqiao and Yao Wenyuan, 17 people, who were secretaries or standing committee members of the Party's shanghai municipal committee and mayor or deputy mayors of the municipality, were falsely charged with being "renegades," "enemy agents," "capitalist roaders" or "counter-revolutionaries." Cao Diqiu and deputy mayor Jin Zhonghua were persecuted to death.

26) In December 1967, Chen Boda said in Tangshan that the C.P.C. organization in eastern Hebei Province "was probably a party of Kuomintang-Communist co-operation, and in fact it might be the Kuomintang members and renegades who were playing a dominant role here." A case was trumped up at his instigation, and more than 84,000 Party cadres and masses in eastern Hebei Province were framed and persecuted. Zhang Wenhao and 2,954 others were persecuted to death.

27) On January 21, 1968, at the Jingxi Hotel in Beijing, Kang Sheng slandered Zhao Jianmin, secretary of the Yunnan Provincial Committee of the C.P.C., saying to his face, "You are a renegade . . . I can tell. Forty years' experience in revolutionary work gives me this kind of intuition . . . you have a deep-seated class hatred." He falsely accused Zhao Jianmin of carrying out the plans of a group of Kuomintang agents in Yunnan and of "trying to take advantage of the Great Cultural Revolution to create chaos in the border areas." Kang Sheng and Xie Fuzhi forbade Zhao Jianmin to argue, and Xie announced Zhao's arrest then and there. Thus at the instigation of Kang Sheng and Xie Fuzhi, the "case of enemy agent Zhao Jianmin" was fabricated, leading to the frame-up and persecution of large numbers of cadres and masses in Yunnan, over 14,000 of whom died as a result.

28) Under the pretext of digging out the so-called "Inner Mongolian People's Revolutionary Party," Kang Sheng framed and persecuted large numbers of cadres and masses in Inner Mongolia and sabotaged the unity between the various nationalities. On February 4, 1968, he said, "The Inner Mongolian People's Revolutionary Party is still active underground. When we begin to ferret out its members, we may overdo it a little, but we needn't be worried about that." Again, on February 4, 1969, he said, "There are members of the Inner Mongolian People's Revolutionary Party inside the army too. This is a very serious matter." Xie Fuzhi said, "The Inner Mongolian People's Revolutionary Party is disguised as a Communist Party but actually it is not. We must wipe it out." At the instigation of Kang Sheng and Xie Fuzhi, more than 346,000 cadres and other people in the Inner Mongolian Autonomous Region were framed and persecuted in the case of the "Inner Mongolian People's Revolutionary Party" and other false cases, and 16,222 persons died of persecution.

29) In 1967, Kang Sheng and others trumped up the case of a "Xinjiang renegade clique." One hundred and thirty-one Party cadres, who had been arrested and imprisoned in September 1942 by Sheng Shicai, a Xinjiang warlord, were falsely accused of having "surrendered to the enemy, betrayed the revolution" and "concealed themselves inside our Party" and of forming a "renegade clique."

Ninety-two cadres, including Ma Mingfang, Zhang Ziyi, Yang Zhihua and Fang Zhichun, were persecuted, and Ma Mingfang and 25 others died as a result.

30)　In February 1947, in accordance with a decision of the Northeast Bureau of the C.P.C. Central Committee which had been approved by the Central Committee in 1945, Lu Zhengcao, Wan Yi, Zhang Xuesi, Jia Tao, Liu Lanbo, Li Youwen, Yu Yifu and 35 others jointly sent a telegraph to Chiang Kai-shek through the Xinhua News Agency in Yanan, demanding the release of Zhang Xueliang. From 1967 to 1969, the Lin Biao and Jiang Qing counter-revolutionary cliques and their key members distorted the facts about this incident, accused them of engaging in a "major, long premeditated, counter-revolutionary scheme to betray the Party and capitulate to the enemy" and fabricated the case of a "counter-revolutionary 'northeast gang' that betrayed the Party and capitulated to the enemy," framing and persecuting ninety persons. Zhang Xuesi, Jia Tao, Che Xiangchen and Chen Xianzhou were persecuted to death.

31)　The counter-revolutionary cliques of Lin Biao and Jiang Qing falsely accused the underground organizations of the C.P.C. in Beiping, Shanghai, Tianjin, Guangdong, Sichuan, Yunnan and other places of having "recruited renegades" during the War of Resistance Against Japan and the Liberation War and of being a "Kuomintang," a "renegade party" and a "U.S.-Chiang special detachment." The Lin Biao and Jiang Qing counter-revolutionary cliques decided to "make the underground Party organization the first target of attack." Consequently, large numbers of leaders and members of these underground Party organizations and many ordinary people who had fought heroically against the enemy were charged with being "renegades," "hidden traitors," "Japanese agents," "Kuomintang agents," "U.S. agents," "spies" or "counter-revolutionarics."

In October 1967, Huang Yongsheng, in collusion with Liu Xingyuan, then political commissar of the P.L.A. Guangzhou Units, and others, decided to investigate the history of the underground C.P.C. organization in Guangdong and set up a special group for this purpose. They slandered the underground Party organization as having "recruited renegades," and alleged that a number of "renegades," "enemy agents" and "spies" had sneaked in. This was the false case of "the Guangdong underground Party organization," which led to the framing and persecution of more than 7,100 people. Lin Qiangyun and eight-four others were persecuted to death.

32)　The Lin Biao counter-revolutionary clique trumped up false charges against large numbers of people in the P.L.A. Over 80,000 people were framed and persecuted, of whom 1,169 died.

From May 1967 to November 1970, Huang Yongsheng, in collusion with Liu Xingyuan, concocted the case of a "counter-revolutionary clique" in the P.L.A. Guangzhou Units, falsely accusing Deputy Commander Wen Niansheng and others of attempting to "usurp power by staging a coup." More than 700 cadres were implicated. Wen Niansheng and some others were persecuted to death.

Wu Faxian, in collusion with Wang Fei, then deputy chief of staff of the Air Force Command, and Liang Pu, its chief of staff, framed and persecuted large numbers of cadres and the rank and file in the Air Force. Wu Faxian said, "If you don't strike them down, they will turn around and pounce on us and have us beheaded." He laid false charges against a number of leading cadres in the Air Forces, alleging that they were "conducting underground activities" in an attempt to "seize power" and "stage a coup." Wu Faxian directly framed and persecuted 174 persons, among whom Gu Qian and Liu Shanben were persecuted to death.

Li Zuopeng, in collusion with Wang Hongkun and Zhang Xiuchuan, framed and persecuted a large number of cadres and rank and file in the Navy. In January 1968, Li Zuopeng said that working on special cases was equivalent to "the Communist Party dealing blows at the Kuomintang." In October of the same year he again said that there should be "fierce attacks, vigorous charges and hot pursuit." Li Zuopeng directly framed and persecuted 120 persons, among whom Lei Yongtong and two others were persecuted to death.

Qiu Huizuo, in league with Chen Pang, then deputy director of the General Logistics Department of the P.L.A., set up a kangaroo court in the department to extort confessions through torture. Qiu Huizuo said that there should be "ruthless struggle," "ruthless interrogation" and "ruthless dictatorship." Large numbers of cadres and rank and file were framed and persecuted. Qui Huizuo directly framed and persecuted 462 people. Eight people, including Shen Maoxing and Wang Shuchen, died as a result.

33) In order to suppress the "Workers' Red Detachment," a mass organization in Shanghai, and seize Party and government leadership there, Zhang Chunqiao made a phone call from Beijing to his wife, Li Wenjing, in Shanghai on December 28, 1966. He said to her, "The fruits of victory mustn't be snatched by the Red Detachment. Tell the revolutionary rebels that they mustn't just stand idly by." Li Wenjing told Xu Jingxian about the phone call, who then passed on the message. At the instigation of Zhang Chunqiao and others, Wang Hongwen worked in collusion with Geng Jinzhang, a criminal guilty of beating, smashing and looting, and organized and directed a number of people who were ignorant of the real situation to attack the "Workers' Red Detachment." This armed clash, known as the Kangping Road Incident resulted in 91 injured or maimed.

On August 4, 1967, Wang Hongwen engineered and directed an armed attack on the mass organization known as the "Rebel Headquarters of the Revolutionary Alliance of the Shanghai Diesel Engine Plant." Six hundred and fifty people were imprisoned or injured. Afterwards, Zhang Chunqiao acclaimed Wang Hongwen as "our commanding officer" and "leader of the working class in Shanghai."

34) In May 1967, while in Jinan, Zhang Chunqiao and Yao Wenyuan supported the suppression of the local masses by Wang Xiaoyu, then chairman of the Shandong Provincial Revolutionary Committee. Zhang said to him, "You'll have my support if you're strong." Thereupon, on May 7, Wang Xiaoyu engineered a violent incident in the compound of the provincial revolutionary committee, resulting in 388 persons arrested and imprisoned. Afterwards, Zhang Chunqiao and Yao Wenyuan again expressed their support of Wang Xiaoyu and congratulated him on his "victory in battle."

35) In October 1966, Jiang Qing collaborated with Ye Qun in ordering Jiang Tengjiao to search and ransack the homes of a number of writers and artists in Shanghai. Ye Qun asked Wu Faxian to summon Jiang Tengjiao to Beijing, where she said to him, "One of Comrade Jiang Qing's letters has fallen into the hands of Zheng Junli, Gu Eryi and company. It's not clear who has the letter now, but you can organize some people to search the homes of five persons including Zheng Junli, Gu Eryi, Zhao Dan and Tong Zhiling. Bring here all the letters, diaries, notebooks and suchlike you can lay your hands on." And she added, "Keep this absolutely secret." After returning to Shanghai, Jiang Tengjiao got together more than forty people. They disguised themselves as Red Guards and, in the small hours of October 9, searched the homes of Zhao Dan, Zheng Junli, Tong Zhiling, Chen Liting and Gu Eryi. Jiang Tengjiao sent what they had got hold of in two batches to Ye Qun's residence in Beijing. In January 1967, under Jiang Qing's personal supervision, Xie Fuzhi and Ye Qun burnt all the letters, photos and other material relating to Jiang Qing, which had been obtained in the search.

36) While in Shanghai in 1967, Zhang Chunqiao order a counter-revolutionary secret service organization there -- the "You Xuetao Group" (code name "244") -- to undertake the special tasks of fascist espionage such as tailing, shadowing, kidnapping, ransacking people's homes, taking people into custody, secretly interrogating and torturing them, and gathering intelligence. From November 1967 to March 1968, this organization collected or fabricated for Zhang Chunqiao's use slanderous information on ninety-seven leading cadres of the East China Bureau of the C.P.C. Central Committee. It drew up a "Diagram Showing the Relationships Between Persons Working for the Sinister Line in the East China

Bureau" and compiled 300 issues of the publications *Minesweeping Bulletin* and *Trends*. All told, it provided over one million words in intelligence material, trumping up cases to persecute 183 cadres and other people. In the winter of 1967 and the spring of 1968, this organization sent people to Jiangsu, Zhejiang and other places to carry out espionage. It falsely charged the leading Party government and army cadres in eastern China with "organizing an underground armed detachment south of the Changjiang River" and "plotting a mutiny." On October 26, 1967, Wang Shaoyang, then vice-chairman of the Shanghai Municipal Revolutionary Committee, relayed Zhang Chunqiao's words to You Xuetao, "Be careful. You can spy on others, but they can spy on you too." In its "Summary of the Year's Work" submitted to Zhang Chunqiao on November 30, 1968, this organization said that it had been "fighting on a special front" and that "over the past year our work has been mainly covert struggle against the enemy. . . . From the central down to the local levels, we have directly or indirectly kicked the backsides of many bigshots." Zhang Chunqiao expressed his approval by writing "Thanks, Comrades" on the summary.

37) From 1974 to 1976, Jiang Qing, Zhang Chunqiao and Yao Wenyuan instructed Chi Qun and Xie Jingyi to use their base of activity at Qinghua University to make secret contacts and exchange information with key members of the Jiang Qing counter-revolutionary clique in certain departments of the C.P.C. Central Committee and the State Council and in Shanghai and Liaoning. They collected records of speeches made by some leading cadres of various provincial Party committees and documents of these committees and wrote up such material as *The Capitalist Roaders Are Still Travelling the Capitalist Road* and *Information for Reference* to frame leading Party, government and army cadres.

38) As a result of instigation and instructions from the Lin Biao and Jiang Qing counter-revolutionary cliques and their backbone elements, frame-ups were ubiquitous in the country. Falsely charged and persecuted to disability or death were numerous cadres and other people in the various democratic parties, in people's organizations such as trade unions, the Communist Youth League and women's federations, and in the cultural, educational, scientific, technological, journalistic, publishing, public health and physical culture circles as well as large numbers of returned overseas Chinese.

The falsely charged and persecuted leading members of the various democratic parties were: Deng Baoshan, Vice-Chairman of the Central Committee of the Revolutionary Committee of the Kuomintang; Gao Chongmin and Wu Han, Vice-Chairmen of the Central Committee of the China Democratic League; Sun Qimeng, Vice-Chairman of the Central Committee of the China Democratic National Construction Association; Che Xiangchen, Vice-Chairman of the Central

Committee of the China Association for Promoting Democracy; Zhou Gucheng, member of the Presidium of the Central Committee of the Chinese Peasants' and Workers' Democratic Party; and Pan Shu, Vice-Chairman of the Central Committee of the Jiu San (September the Third) Society. Large numbers of standing committee members and members and alternate members of the central committees of the various democratic parties as well as the All-China Federation of Industry and Commerce were falsely charged and persecuted, among whom Huang Shaohong, Mei Gongbin, Chu Xichun, Gao Chongmin, Liu Qingyang, Pan Guangdan, Liu-Wang Liming, Liu Nianyi, Wang Xingyao, Tang Xunze, Xu Chongqing, Li Pingxin, Chen Linrui, Zheng Tianbao, Wang Jiaji, Liu Xiying, Zhang Xi, Wang Tianqiang and others died in consequence.

In the literary and art circles, more than 2,600 people were falsely charged and persecuted in the Ministry of Culture and units directly under it alone. Noted writers and well-known art workers including Lao She, Zhao Shuli, Zhou Xinfang, Gai Jiaotian, Pan Tianshou, Ying Yunwei, Zheng Junli and Sun Weishi died in consequence.

In the educational circles, more than 142,000 cadres and teachers in units under the Ministry of Education and in seventeen provinces and municipalities were falsely charged and persecuted. Noted professors including Xiong Qinglai, Jain Bozan, He Sijing, Wang Shourong, Gu Yuzhen, Li Guangtian, Rao Yutai, Li Pansui and Ma Te died in consequence of such persecution.

In the scientific and technological circles, more than 53,000 scientists and technicians in units directly affiliated to the Chinese Academy of Sciences, two research institutes under the Seventh Ministry of Machine-Building and seventeen provinces and municipalities were falsely charged and persecuted. Noted scientists such as geophysicists Zhao Jiuzhang, metallurgist Ye Zhupei, theoretical physicist Zhang Zongsui, entomologist Liu Chongle, taxonomist Chen Huanyong, and metal ceramist Zhou Ren died in consequence of such persecution.

In the health circles, more than 500 of the 674 professors and associate professors in the 14 medical colleges and institutes directly led by the Ministry of Public Health were falsely charged and persecuted. Such famous medical scientists as pathologist Hu Zhengxiang, pharmacologist Zhang Changshao, specialist in thoracic surgery Ji Suhua, specialist in acupuncture Lu Shouyan, and physicians of traditional Chinese medicine Ye Xichun and Li Zhongren were persecuted to death.

In the physical culture circles, large numbers of cadres, coaches and sportsmen were falsely charged and persecuted. Outstanding coaches such as Fu Zifang, Rong Guotuan and Jiang Yongning were victimized to death.

Also falsely charged and persecuted were large numbers of model workers of national renown, among whom Meng Tai and Shi Chuanxiang died in consequence.

In nineteen provinces and municipalities, over 13,000 returned overseas Chinese and overseas Chinese family members were falsely charged and persecuted, of whom 281 died in consequence. Such well-known figures in the field of overseas Chinese affairs as Fang Fang, Xu Li, Huang Jie, Chen Xujing, Huang Qinshu and Chen Manyun were persecuted to death.

Also persecuted on the false charges of being "renegades," "enemy agents," "counter-revolutionaries" or "lackeys of capitalist roaders" were innumerable cadres and other people working in various Party, government and army organs, in enterprises and establishments, rural people's communes and production brigades and teams as well as in urban neighborhood committees throughout the country.

III

Plotting to Assassinate Chairman Mao Zedong and Engineer an Armed Counter-Revolutionary Coup d'Etat

After the failure of their conspiracy to usurp Party and state leadership through "peaceful transition," the Lin Biao counter-revolutionary clique plotted to stage an armed counter-revolutionary coup d'etat and assassinate Chairman Mao Zedong.

39) In October 1969, Lin Biao instructed Wu Faxian to make his son Lin Liguo deputy director of the General Office and concurrently deputy chief of the Operations Department of the Air Force Command. On October 18, Wu Faxian called together Lin Liguo, Wang Fei and Zhou Yuchi, another deputy director of the General Office of the Air Force Command, and said, "You are to report everything concerning the Air Force to Comrade Liguo. Everything is at his disposal and under his command." In this way Wu illicitly put command of the Air Force in the hands of Lin Liguo. Zhou Yuchi and Wang Fei successively passed on this message to the standing committee of the Air Force Party committee at one of its working sessions, and to the offices under the Air Force Command. Lin Liguo formed an "investigation group" in collaboration with Zhou

Yuchi, Wang Fei and others. On the evening of May 2, 1970, when Lin Biao received Lin Liguo, Zhou Yuchi, Wang Fei and Liu Peifeng, then a section head under the Air Force Command's General Office, he asked them who their leader was. On May 3, Zhou Yuchi, Wang Fei and others held a meeting to pledge allegiance to Lin Biao and made Lin Liguo their "leader." In October 1970, the "investigation group" headed by Lin Liguo was reorganized into a "joint fleet." Ye Qun gave code names to Zhou Yuchi, Wang Fei and others. The "joint fleet" constituted the backbone force in Lin Biao's plot to assassinate Chairman Mao Zedong and stage and armed counter-revolutionary coup d'etat.

From 1970 to September 13, 1971, under the direction of Lin Liguo and Zhou Yuchi, Hu Ping, deputy chief-of-staff of the Air Force Command, Wang Weiguo, political commissar of the P.L.A. Unit 7341, Mi Jianong, political commissar of the Guangzhou Branch of the Civil Aviation Administration of China (CAAC) and Gu Tongzhou, chief-of-staff of the Air Force Headquarters of the Guangzhou Units, and others set up secret centres of activity in Beijing, Shanghai and Guangzhou. These centres were used by Lin Liguo and others for liaison purposes and for storing arms and ammunition, wireless sets, bugging devices and confidential Party and government, documents.

40) From September 1970 onwards, Lin Biao stepped up his preparations for an armed counter-revolutionary coup d'etat. In February 1971, after plotting with Ye Qun and Lin Liguo in Shzhou, Lin Biao sent Lin Liguo to Shanghai, where from March 21 to 24, he called together such chief members of the "joining fleet" as Zhou Yuchi, Yu Xinye, a deputy section head under the General Office of the Air Force Command, and Li Weixin, then a deputy section head under the Political Department of the P.L.A. Unit 7341, and mapped out a plan for the armed counter-revolutionary coup -- *Outline "Project 571."* They assessed the situation, worked out the outline of implementation and decided on the slogans and tactics. They called for "gaining the upper hand by striking first militarily" and plotted to launch an armed counter-revolutionary coup d'etat to "seize nationwide political power" or bring about "a situation of rival regimes" by taking advantage of "some high-level meeting to catch all in one net" or "using special means such as bombs, the 543 (code name for a kind of guided missile--Tr.), traffic accidents, assassination, kidnapping and urban guerrilla squads. They also plotted to "seek Soviet help to tie down domestic and foreign forces."

On March 31, 1971, while in Shanghai, Lin Liguo, implementing the plan for establishing a "command team" as described in the *Outline of "Project 571,"* summoned Jiang Tengjiao, Wang Weiguo, Chen Liyun, political commissar of the P.L.A. Unit 7350, and Zhou Jianping, deputy commander of the Air Force of the Nanjing Units of the P.L.A., to a secret meeting at which Zhou Jianping was made "head" in Nanjing, Wang Weiguo "head" in Shanghai and Chen Liyun "head" in Hangzhou. Jiang Tengjiao was to be "responsible for liaison between the three places with a view to co-ordination and concerted operation."

In March 1971, instructed by Lin Liguo, Mi Jianong organized a "combat detachment" in Guangzhou. He made its members take an oath of allegiance to Lin Biao and Lin Liguo, and worked out argots and code words for communication.

In April 1971, Lin Liguo directed Wang Weiguo to set up a "training corps" in Shanghai in preparation for the armed counter-revolutionary coup. Trainees were taught special skills in arresting people, hand-to-hand fighting, the use of various kinds of light weapons and driving motor vehicles.

41) On the evening of September 5, 1971, Zhou Yuchi and Yu Xinye telephoned Gu Tongzhou to find out what Chairman Mao Zedong had said in Changsha to some leading personnel. The information thus obtained was secretly reported to Lin Liguo and Ye Qun at once, and Gu Tongzhou sent a written report to Ye Qun. On September 6, Li Zuopeng, then in Wuhan, received a confidential report from Liu Feng, political commissar of the P.L.A. Wuhan Units, containing Chairman Mao Zedong's conversations with some leading personnel assembled in the city. Li Zuopeng returned to Beijing the same day and separately tipped off Huang Yongsheng and Qiu Huizuo. That very night Huang Yongsheng phoned Ye Qun about this, who was then in Beidaihe. After receiving the secret information from Gu Tongzhou and Huang Yongsheng, Lin Biao and Ye Qun made up their minds to assassinate Chairman Mao Zedong. On September 7, Lin Liguo issued the order for first-degree combat readiness to the "joint fleet." On September 8, Lin Biao issued the following handwritten order for the armed coup: "Expect you to act according to the order transmitted by Comrades Liguo and Yuchi." On the same day, Lin Liguo brought from Ye Qun in Beidaihe a sealed document addressed to Huang Yongsheng personally. It was to be delivered by Wang Fei. On the morning of September 10, Wang Fei delivered the sealed document to Huang Yongsheng. On that same day Huang Yongsheng repeatedly contacted Ye Qun, making five phone calls to her. The two longest calls lasted 90 and 135 minutes respectively. Also on that day, Liu Peifeng brought a letter to Huang Yongsheng from Lin Biao in Beidaihe, in which Lin wrote: "Comrade Yongsheng, I miss you very much and hope that you will be optimistic at all times. Take care of your health. If you have any problems, consult Comrade Wang Fei directly." The letter was given to Wang Fei by Lin Liguo and Zhou Yuchi, and Wang was instructed to deliver it to Huang Yongsheng when necessary. From September 8 to 11, at their secret centres at the Air Force Academy and the Xijiao Airport of Beijing, Lin Liguo and Zhou Yuchi separately

relayed Lin Biao's handwritten order for an armed coup to Liu Peifeng, Jiang Tengjiao, Wang Fei, Li Weixin, Lu Min, chief of the Operations Department of the Air Force Command, Liu Shiying, deputy director of its General Office, Cheng Hongzhen, secretary of the office, Guan Guangile, political commissar of the P.L.A. Unit 0190, and others. They worked out the details for assassinating Chairman Mao Zedong. Jiang Tengjiao was appointed frontline commander for action in the Shanghai area. They plotted to attack Chairman Mao Zedong's train with flame throwers and 40-mm. bazookas, dynamite the Shuofang Railway Bridge near Suzhou, bomb the train from the air, or blow up the oil depot in Shanghai, near which the special train would pull up, and then assassinate the Chairman in the ensuing commotion, or let Wang Weiguo carry out the murder when he was being received by Chairman Mao Zedong.

Meanwhile, Lin Biao and Ye Qun were making preparations for fleeing south to Guangzhou where they would set up a separate Party central committee, and also for defection to another county. On September 10, 1971, they ordered Zhou Yuchi and others to obtain from the Air Force Command maps showing where radar units were deployed in northern, northeastern and northwestern China, frequency tables of the radio stations in neighboring countries which could be used for navigation purposes, maps showing air lines leading from Beijing to Ulan Bator and Irkutsk and the location of their airports and the latter's call signs and radio frequency tables, as well as information concerning the airports in the Guangzhou and Fuzhou areas.

42)   On the evening of September 11, 1971, Wang Weiguo secretly telephoned Lin Liguo and Zhou Yuchi, informing them that Chairman Mao Zedong had already left Shanghai for Beijing. When Lin Biao and Ye Qun learnt that their plot to murder Chairman Mao Zedong had fallen through, they planned to flee south to Guangzhou, taking along Huang Yongsheng, Wu Faxian, Li Zuopeng and Qiu Huizuo, and set up a separate Party central committee there to split the nation. They also planned to "launch a pincer attack from north to south in alliance with the Soviet Union should fighting be necessary." On September 12, Lin Liguo and Zhou Yuchi separately told Jiang Tengjiao, Wang Fei, Yu Xinye, Hu Ping and Wang Yongkui, a deputy section chief in the Intelligence Department of the Air Force Command, to make preparations for the flight south. Hu Ping and company had eight planes ready to leave for Guangzhou and helped Lin Liguo to fly to Shanhaiguan on special plane 256, which was then assigned for the use of Lin Biao, Ye Qun and Lin Liguo in Beidaihe. Wang Fei, Yu Xinye and He Dequan, chief of the Intelligence Department of the Air Force Command, prepared the name list of those who were to flee south, assigned duties and made specific plans for action. Around 10 o'clock that evening, Premier Zhou Enlai inquired about the details concerning the flight of special plane 256 to

Shanhaiguan and ordered it to return to Beijing at once. Hu Ping lied, saying that the plane was on a training flight to Shanhaiguan and had developed engine trouble. Thus, he refused to carry out Premier Zhou's order. Meanwhile, he telephoned Zhou Yuchi and tipped him off on what had happened.

Late at night on September 12, 1971, Lin Biao, Ye Qun and Lin Liguo received a secret report that Premier Zhou Enlai had been making inquiries about the special plane. Thereupon, they hurried to the Shanhaiguan Airport with Liu Peifeng and others, scrambled on to the plane and ordered it to start taxiing without waiting for the co-pilot, navigator and radio operator to board and the lights to be turned on. The aircraft took off at 00:32 hours on September 13 and crashed near Undur Khan in Mongolia, killing all those abroad.

At 03:15 hours on September 13, 1971, Zhou Yuchi, Yu Xinye and Li Weixing hijacked helicopter 3685 at Beijing's Shahe Airport in an attempt to flee the country, taking with them piles of confidential state documents and large amounts of U.S. dollars which they had got hold of illicitly. After seeing through their intention, pilot Chen Xiuwen took steps to fly the helicopter back to Huairou County, a suburb of Beijing, but was killed by Zhou Yuchi when the helicopter landed.

43) Before Lin Biao's defection, Premier Zhou Enlai had made the decision that special plane 256 "cannot take off without a joint order from four persons," namely Zhou Enlai, Huang Yongsheng, Wu Faxian and Li Zuopeng. However, when relaying this directive to those in charge of the Navy's Shanhaiguan Airport, Li Zuopeng distorted it, saying, "The plane must not be allowed to take off unless one of the four leading officials gives the order." He added, "If anyone gives you such an order, you must report it to me. You will be held responsible for this." At 00:20 hours on September 13, when special plane 256 was getting ready to take off but its engines were not yet started, the airport leadership phoned Li Zuopeng asking what they should do if the plane were to take off forcibly. Instead of taking any measures to prevent the plane from taking off, Li Zuopeng said evasively, "You may report directly to the Premier and ask for his instructions." He was procrastinating so that Lin Biao could have enough time to escape. Afterwards, Li Zuopeng tried to cover up his crime by altering the logbook entry of the relevant phone calls.

44) After Lin Biao's defection on September 13, 1971, Huang Yongsheng, Wu Faxian, Qiu Huizuo and others separately destroyed such incriminating evidence as their correspondence with Lin Biao and Ye Qun, notebooks, photographs and other material, in an attempt to cover up the crimes of the counter-revolutionary clique.

IV

Plotting Armed Rebellion in Shanghai

Zhang Chunqiao, Yao Wenyuan and Wang Hongwen, as well as Ma Tianshui, Xu Jingxian, Wang Xiuzhen and company, made Shanghai their base, built up their own armed force and plotted an armed rebellion in the face of their impending doom.

45) In July 1967, Zhang Chunqiao wrote in a report he finalized: "We must use the gun to protect revolution made with the pen," and instructed Wang Hongwen and others to organize in Shanghai an armed force under their control. In September 1973, Wang Hongwen said to Wang Xiuzhen, "A national general headquarters must be set up for the people's militia. I will take charge of it myself." In March 1974, Wang again said to her, "The army must not be allowed to lead the militia whose command should be in the hands of the [Shanghai] municipal Party committee." On many occasions in January and August 1975, Wang Hongwen said to Ma Tianshui, Xu Jingxian and Wang Xiuzhen in Beijing and Shanghai, "What worries me most is that the army is not in our hands." He added, "We must be on the alert against the danger of the revisionists taking power" and "We must be prepared for guerrilla warfare." In February 1976, he said, "It's Chunqiao and me who organized the People's Militia in Shanghai." And he added, "I'm certainly going to keep firm control over it. You must run it well for me. . . . They army isn't so reliable."

46) On May 7, 1976, when talking in Beijing with Chen Jide, a member of the Shanghai writing group, Yao Wenyuan said, "The Great Cultural Revolution is an example of violence, so is the Tian An Men Square Incident. And the outcome of future struggles will have to be decided through violence too." On returning to Shanghai, Chen Jide communicated Yao's views to Ma Tianshui, Xu Jingxian and others. In August of the same year, Yao Wenyuan personally revised and approved an article by the Shanghai writing group, entitled "Strengthen the Building of the Workers' Militia," which was later published in *Hongqi (Red Flag)*. To prepare public opinion for violent suppression and armed rebellion, the article called for the struggle of the workers' militia against "the bourgeoisie inside the Party."

47) In August 1976, Ding Sheng, head of the Nanjing Units of the P.L.A., arrived in Shanghai and had a secret talk with Ma Tianshui, Xu Jingxian and Wang Xiuzhen at Yanan Hotel till midnight. Ding Sheng said, "My biggest worry is Unit 6453. . . . I haven't the slightest control over it. . . . Several of its

divisions are deployed along the Wuxi-Suzhou-Shanghai line. This ia a big headache. . . . You must be prepared for any eventuality." Immediately afterwards, Ma Tianshui looked into the arming of the militia. Altogether, 74,220 rifles, 300 artillery pieces and more than 10 million rounds of ammunition were handed out in no time, as a concrete measure in preparation for an armed rebellion. On September 21 of the same year, Zhang Chunqiao received Xu Jingxian along in Beijing. After hearing about Ding Sheng's secret talk with Ma Tianshui, Xu Jingxian and Wang Xiuzhen in Shanghai and about the hurried handout of weapons, Zhang Chunqiao said, "Be careful, keep your eyes open for new trends in the class struggle." On September 23, Wang Hongwen made a telephone call to Wang Xiuzhen, saying, "Be on your guard, for the struggle isn't over yet. The bourgeoisie inside the Party will not be reconciled to defeat. Someone or other is sure to try to reinstate Deng Xiaoping."

48) On October 6, 1976, the gang of Jiang Qing, Zhang Chunqiao, Yao Wenyuan and Wang Hongwen was smashed. On October 8, Xu Jingxian and Wang Xiuzhen sent to Beijing Miao Wenjin, secretary of Jin Zumin, who was in charge of the preparatory group for the reorganization of the All-China Federation of Trade Unions, to find out what had happened. They laid down a secret code for contact purposes. That evening, Miao Wenjin and Zhu Jiayao, a member of the leading Party group in the Ministry of Public Security, made a phone call to Kang Ningyi, political commissar of the Security Section of the C.P.C. Shanghai Municipal Committee, asking him to tell Wang Xiuzhen that the worst had befallen Jiang Qing, Zhang Chunqiao, Yao Wenyuan and Wang Hongwen, using the code "My mother has contracted myocardial infarction." Soon afterwards, Zhu Jiayao phoned Kang Ningyi again, asking him to tell Wang Xiuzhen, "People have been assembled and locked up. They can no longer move about." So Xu Jingxian and Wang Xiuzhen immediately called an emergency mobilization meeting. They decided to "fight it out." They said, "Send the militia into action. If we cannot keep up the fight for a week, five or three days will suffice to let the whole world know what's happening." Then and there, Xu Jingxian wrote an order to assemble and deploy 33,500 militiamen. A command team and two secret command posts were set up for the armed rebellion, and the newspapers and broadcasting stations in Shanghai were instructed to act in co-ordination. Li Binshan, deputy political commissar of the Shanghai Garrison, Shi Shangying and Zhong Dingdong, who were in charge of the Shanghai militia headquarters, and others drew up an initial plan for the armed rebellion, which was then approved by Wang Xiuzhen. Xue Ganqing and Xu Chenghu, deputy secretaries of the Party committee of the Shanghai Municipal Public Security Bureau, worked out the bureau's programme for action. On October 9, Shi Shangying called a meeting of the militia leaders of ten districts and of the five militia divisions directly under the command of the Shanghai Municipal Revolutionary Committee and ordered them to muster their

forces and see to it that there were enough motor vehicles and drivers and that their arms and ammunition matched. Over 27,000 rifles and artillery pieces and 225 motor vehicles were assigned for use. A large quantity of food and other material was made available. Fifteen transmitter-receivers were installed at the command posts in the Jiangnan Shipyards and the China Textile Machinery Plant and at the militia headquarters of the various districts so as to link them up through telecommunications. Zhong Dingdong drew up more specific operation plans, code named "Han No. 1" and "Fang No. 2," for the armed rebellion. The decided to throw up three cordons between the heart of Shanghai and its outskirts in order to bring under control the city's administrative centre, railway stations, wharves, airports, harbors, the Pujiang River Tunnel, bridges and other main transport routes. Pass words and argots were also worked out. On October 12, they planned to publish a "Message to the People of Shanghai and the Whole Country" and drafted twenty-one counter-revolutionary slogans. On the evening of the same day, Wang Shaoyong and Zhu Yongjia, together with Huang Tao and Chen Ada, who were leading members of the group in charge of industries and communications under the Shanghai Municipal Revolutionary Committee, and others, met to plan production stoppages through strikes, parades and demonstrations, and the acquiring of control over the press and radio stations and blockade of the news released by the central media. They planned to cut off the supply of electricity at the grid, barricade airport runways with steel ingots and scuttle ships to block the river mouth at Wusongkou. They put forward the counter-revolutionary slogans: "Return Jiang Qing to us," "Return Chunqiao to us," "Return Wenyuan to us" and "Return Hongwen to us," readying themselves for "a life-and-death struggle." The above-mentioned facts established that the two counter-revolutionary cliques of Lin Biao and Jiang Qing framed and persecuted the Chairman of the People's Republic of China, the Chairman of the Standing Committee of the National People's Congress, the Premier of the State Council, the General Secretary of the Central Committee of the Chinese Communist Party and other leaders of the Party and state, persecuted and suppressed large numbers of cadres and people, plotted to assassinate Chairman Mao Zedong and planned to engineer an armed rebellion, and that they are counter-revolutionary cliques whose aim is to overthrow the political power of the dictatorship of the proletariate. Their felonies have been proved by a host of conclusive evidence. The people of all nationalities of the country, and in particular, the large numbers of cadres and other people who were framed, persecuted or implicated, are witnesses to their criminal activities. And so are those who, for a time, were hoodwinked or misled by them.

In accordance with the provisions of Article 9 of the Criminal Law of the People's Republic of China with regard to the application of law, this procuratorate affirms that the following ten principal culprits have violated the

Criminal Law of the People's Republic of China and have committed the offence of attempting to overthrow the government and split the state, the offence of attempting to engineer an armed rebellion, the offence of having people injured or murdered for counter-revolutionary ends, the offence of framing and persecuting people for counter-revolutionary ends, the offence of organizing and leading counter-revolutionary cliques, the offence of conducting demagogical propaganda for counter-revolutionary ends, the offence of extorting confessions by torture, and the offence of illegally detaining people, and that they should be duly prosecuted according to their criminal liability. This Procuratorate hereby institutes, according to law, a public prosecution against these ten principal accused:

Defendant Jiang Qing, female, 67, of Zhucheng County, Shandong Province. Member of the Tenth Central Committee of the Communist Party of China (C.P.C.) and its Political Bureau prior to her arrest. Now in custody;

Defendant Zhang Chunqiao, male, 63, of Juye County, Shandong Province. Member of the Tenth C.P.C. Central Committee, its Political Bureau and the Bureau's Standing Committee, vice-premier of the State Council, director of the General Political Department of the Chinese People's Liberation Army (P.L.A.), first secretary of the Shanghai Municipal Committee of the C.P.C., and chairman of the Shanghai Municipal Revolutionary Committee prior to his arrest. Now in custody;

Defendant Yao Wenyuan, male, 49, of Zhuji County, Zhejiang Province. Member of the Tenth C.P.C. Central Committee and its Political Bureau, second secretary of the Shanghai Municipal Committee of the C.P.C., and vice-chairman of the Shanghai Municipal Revolutionary Committee prior to his arrest. Now in custody;

Defendant Wang Hongwen, male, 45, of Changchun, Jilin Province. Member of the Tenth C.P.C. Central Committee, its Political Bureau and the Bureau's Standing Committee, vice-chairman of the C.P.C. Central Committee, secretary of the Shanghai Municipal Committee of the C.P.C., and vice-chairman of the Shanghai Municipal Revolutionary Committee prior to his arrest. Now in custody;

Defendant Chen Boda, male, 76, of Huian County, Fujian Province. Member of the Ninth C.P.C. Central Committee, its Political Bureau and the Bureau's Standing Committee prior to his arrest. Now in custody;

Defendant Huang Yongsheng, male, 70, of Xianning County, Hubei Province. Member of the Ninth C.P.C. Central Committee and its Political Bureau, and chief of the General Staff of the P.L.A. prior to his arrest. Now in custody;

Defendant Wu Faxian, male 65, of Yongfeng County, Jiangxi Province. Member of the Ninth C.P.C. Central Committee and its Political Bureau, and deputy chief of the P.L.A. General Staff and concurrently commander of the P.L.A. Air Force prior to his arrest. Now in custody;

Defendant Li Zuopeng, male, 66, of Jian County, Jiangxi Province. Member of the Ninth C.P.C. Central Committee and its Political Bureau, and deputy chief of the P.L.A. General Staff and concurrently first political commissar of the P.L.A. Navy prior to his arrest. Now in custody;

Defendant Qiu Huizuo, male, 66, of Xingguo County, Jiangxi Province. Member of the Ninth C.P.C. Central Committee and its Political Bureau, and deputy chief of the P.L.A. General Staff and concurrently director of the P.L.A. General Logistics Department prior to his arrest. Now in custody; and

Defendant Jiang Tengjiao, male, 61, of Hongan County, Hubei Province. Air Force political commissar of the P.L.A. Nanjing Units prior to his arrest. Now in custody.

In accordance with Item 5, Article 11, of the Law of Criminal Procedure of the People's Republic of China, no criminal liability shall be pursued against those defendants who are dead. In this case, they are Lin Biao, Kang Sheng, Xie Fuzhi, Ye Qun, Lin Liguo and Zhou Yuchi, who were also principal culprits of the Lin Biao and Jiang Qing counter-revolutionary cliques. The other defendants involved in this will be dealt with separately.

Huang Huoqing

Chief Procurator of the Supreme People's Procuratorate of the People's Republic of China and concurrently Chief of the Special Procuratorate under the Supreme People's Procuratorate.

*****

DOCUMENT NO. 8

WRITTEN JUDGEMENT OF THE SPECIAL COURT
OF THE SPECIAL COURT UNDER THE SUPREME
PEOPLE'S COURT OF THE PEOPLE'S REPUBLIC OF CHINA
January 23, 1981

(**New China News Agency**, Beijing, January 25, 1981;
FBIS-CHI January 26, 1981)

The prosecutors: Huang Huoqing, chief procurator of the Supreme People's Procuratorate and concurrently chief of the Special Procuratorate; Yu Ping and Shi Jinqian, deputy chiefs of the Special Procuratorate; and procurators Ma Chunyi, Wang Wenlin, Wang Fang, Wang Zhenzhong, Wang Pusheng, Wang Yaoqing, Feng Changyi, Qu Wenda, Zhu Zongzheng, Jiang Wen, Sun Shufeng, Li Tianxiang, Shen Jianliang, Zhang Zhongru, Zhang Yingjie, Zhang Zhaoqi, Meng Qing'en, Tu Men, Zhong Shuqin, Yuan Tongjiang and Jing Yusong.

The defendant, Jiang Qing, female, 67, of Zhucheng County, Shandong Province. Formerly deputy head of the "Cultural Revolution group under the Central Committee: of the Communist Party of China and a member of the Political Bureau of the ninth and tenth CCP Central Committees. Now in custody.

The defendant, Zhang Chunqiao, male, 63, of Juye County, Shandong Province. Formerly deputy head of the "Cultural Revolution group under the CCP Central Committee," a member of the Political Bureau of the ninth CCP Central Committee, a Standing Committee member of the Political Bureau of the tenth CCP Central Committee and chairman of the Shanghai Municipal Revolutionary Committee. Now in custody.

The defendant, Yao Wenyuan, male, 49, of Zhuji County, Zhejiang Province. Formerly a member of the "Cultural Revolution group under the CCP Central Committee," a member of the Political Bureau of the ninth and tenth CCP Central Committees and vice-chairman of the Shanghai Municipal Revolutionary Committee. Now in custody.

The defendant, Wang Hongwen, male, 46, of Changchun City, Jilin Province. Formerly vice-chairman of the tenth CCP Central Committee and vice-chairman of the Shanghai Municipal Revolutionary Committee. Now in custody.

The defendant, Chen Boda, male, 76, of Huian County, Fujian Province. Formerly head of the "Cultural Revolution group under the CCP Central Committee" and a Standing Committee member of the Political Bureau of the eighth and ninth CCP Central Committees. Now in custody.

The defendant, Huang Yongsheng, male, 70, of Xianning County, Hubei Province. Formerly chief of the General Staff of the Chinese People's Liberation Army. Now in custody.

The defendant, Wu Faxian, male, 65, of Yongfeng County, Jiangxi Province. Formerly deputy chief of the PLA General Staff and concurrently commander of the air force. Now in custody.

The defendant, Li Zuopeng, male, 66, of Jian County, Jiangxi Province. Formerly deputy chief of the PLA General Staff and concurrently first political commissar of the Navy. Now in custody.

The defendant, Qui Huizuo, male, 66, of Xingguo County, Jiangxi Province. Formerly deputy chief of the PLA General Staff and concurrently director of the General Logistics Department. Now in custody.

The defendant, Jiang Tengjiao, male, 61, of Hongan County, Hubei Province. Formerly air force political commissar of the PLA Nanjing units. Now in custody.

The advocates: defence lawyers Han Xuezhang and Zhang Zhong for the defendant Yao Wenyuan; defence lawyers Gan Yupei and Fu Zhiren for the defendant Chen Boda; defence lawyers Ma Kechang and Zhou Hengyuan for the defendant Wu Faxian; defence layers Ehang Sizhi and Su Huiyu for the defendant Li Zuopeng; defence lawyers Wang Shunhua and Zhou Kuizheng for the defendant Jiang Tengjiao.

The other defendants, Jiang Qing, Zhang Chunqiao, Wang Hongwen, Huang Yongsheng and Qiu Huizuo, did not entrust their defence to any lawyers, nor did they request the Special Court to assign advocates for them.

The Special Court under the Supreme People's Court of the People's Republic of China was set up in line with the "decision on the establishment of a Special Procuratorate under the Supreme People's Procuratorate and a Special Court under the Supreme People's Court to prosecute and try the principal defendants in the case of the Lin Biao and Jiang Qing counter-revolutionary cliques," which was adopted at the sixteenth meeting of the Standing Committee of the Fifth National People's Congress held on September 29, 1980. The task of this court, as defined by the decision, is trying the principal defendants in the case of the Lin Biao and Jiang Qing counter-revolutionary cliques.

On November 5, 1980, the Special Procuratorate brought before this court the case of the Lin Biao and Jiang Qing counter-revolutionary cliques plotting to overthrow the political power of the dictatorship of the proletariat, and lodged a public prosecution against the defendants, Jiang Qing, Zhang Chunqiao, Yao Wenyuan, Wang Hongwen, Chen Boda, Huang Yongsheng, Wu Faxian, Li Zuopeng, Qiu Huizuo and Jiang Tengjiao.

Article 9 of the criminal law of the People's Republic of China states: "If an act performed after the founding of the People's Republic of China and prior to the enforcement of the present law was not deemed an offence under the laws, decrees and policies then in force, these laws, decrees and policies shall be the standard. If the act was deemed an offence under the said laws, decrees and policies and is also subject to prosecution under section 8, chapter 4, of the general provisions of the present law, the standard of criminal liability shall also be the said laws, decrees and policies. But if the act is not deemed an offence or the penalty for the offence is lighter under the present law, the present law shall apply." In line with the criminal law of the People's Republic of China and the law of the criminal procedure of the People's Republic of China, this court tried the principal defendants in the case of the Lin Biao and Jiang Qing counter-revolutionary cliques in Beijing from November 20, 1980, to January 25, 1981. This court listened to the speeches of public prosecutors in support of the public prosecution, interrogated the defendants and listened to their depositions, defences and final statements, heard the speeches of the advocates, the testimonies of the witnesses and the accounts of some of the victims, and verified various pieces of evidence directly relating to the case.

This court confirms that the counter-revolutionary clique headed by Lin Biao and the counter-revolutionary clique headed by Jiang Qing were both counter-revolutionary cliques that carried our conspiratorial activities for the purpose of seizing the supreme power of the party and the state. These two counter-revolutionary cliques had the common criminal motives and purpose of overthrowing the people's democratic dictatorship, namely the dictatorship of the proletariat (including the state organs and military institutions and, in the present case, also including the Chinese Communist Party, the force that exercises leadership over the above-mentioned organs and institutions) in China, conspired together in committing criminal offenses, and thus formed a counter-revolutionary alliance. The principal culprits in the case of the Lin Biao and Jiang Qing counter-revolutionary cliques are the defendants, Jiang Qing, Zhang Chunqiao, Yao Wenyuan, Wang Hongwen, Chen Boda, Huang Yongsheng, Wu Faxian, Li Zuopeng, Qiu Huizuo and Jiang Tengjiao, as well as the following who are dead: Lin Biao (formerly vice-chairman of the eighth and ninth CCP Central Committee and minister of national defence), Kang Sheng (formerly adviser to the "Cultural Revolution group under the CCP Central Committee and vice-chairman of the tenth CCP Central Committee), Xie Fuzhi (formerly a member of the Political Bureau of the ninth CCP Central Committee and minister of public security), Ye Qun (formerly a member of the Political Bureau of the ninth CCP Central Committee and the wife of Lin Biao), Lin Liguo (formerly deputy chief of the Operations Department of the PLA air force headquarters and the son of Lin Biao) and Zhou Yuchi (formerly deputy director of the General Office of the PLA air force headquarters).

It was in the decade of turmoil known as the "Great Cultural Revolution" that the Lin Biao and Jiang Qing counter-revolutionary cliques carried out their counter-revolutionary criminal activities. During the "Great Cultural Revolution." The political life of the state became extremely abnormal, and the socialist legal system was seriously undermined. Taking advantage of their positions and power at that time and resorting to every possible means, overt and covert, by pen and by gun, the Lin Biao and Jiang Qing counter-revolutionary cliques framed and persecuted state leaders and leaders of the Chinese Communist Party and the democratic parties in a premeditated way, conspired to overthrow the government and sabotage the army, suppressed and persecuted large numbers of cadres, intellectuals and ordinary people from various social strata, poisoned the minds of large numbers of young people, and endangered the life and property and right of autonomy of the people of various national minorities. The Lin Biao counter-revolutionary clique plotted to stage an armed coup d'etat and conspired to assassinate Chairman Mao Zedong. The Jiang Qing counter-revolutionary clique plotted to stage an armed rebellion in Shanghai. The criminal activities of the Lin Biao and Jiang Qing counter-revolutionary cliques lasted for a whole decade, bringing calamities to all fields of work and all regions across the country, subjecting the system of the people's democratic dictatorship and socialist public order in our country to extraordinarily grave danger, inflicting very great damage upon the national economy and all other undertakings, and causing enormous disasters to the people of all nationalities in the country.

The acts of the principal culprits in the case of the Lin Biao and Jiang Qing counter-revolutionary cliques, which endangered the state and society, constitute criminal offenses both under the law of the People's Republic of China which came into force on January 1, 1980. The duty of this court is to hear the criminal offenses committed by the principal culprits in the case of the Lin Biao and Jiang Qing counter-revolutionary cliques and pursue their criminal liability, in strict accordance with the criminal law of the People's Republic of China. This court does not handle other problems of the defendants that do not fall into the category of criminal offenses.

The offenses committed by the principal culprits in the case of the Lin Biao and Jiang Qing counter-revolutionary cliques are as follows:

The Lin Biao and Jiang Qing counter-revolutionary cliques plotted to subvert the government and overthrow the people's democratic dictatorship in China. While formulating the policy for seizing party and state leadership, Lin Biao said on January 23, 1967: "All power, be it at the top, middle or lower levels, should be seized. In some cases, this should be done soon, in others later. . . . This may be done at the top or lower levels, or done in co-ordination at both levels." Zhang Chunqiao said on January 22: "We must seize power everywhere." From 1967 to 1975, Zhang Chunqiao declared on many occasions that "the Great Cultural Revolution" meant "a change of dynasty." Although the above-mentioned counter-revolutionary aim of the Lin Biao and Jiang Qing counter-revolutionary cliques could not entirely succeed owing to resistance from the party, the government and the people, they did succeed over a fairly long period of time in seriously disrupting government and the people, they did succeed over a fairly long period of time in seriously disrupting government institutions and affecting their work, seriously undermining the people's public security organs, the people's procuratorates and people's courts.

They controlled leadership in the Departments of Organization and Propaganda under the Central Committee of the Communist Party of China, and the departments of culture, education, health, and seized leadership in most of the provinces, autonomous regions and municipalities directly under the central government, for a time "smashed" the General Political Department of the Chinese People's Liberation Army and seized part of the leadership in some military institutions.

The Lin Biao and Jiang Qing counter-revolutionary cliques worked hand in glove in scheming to frame and persecute Liu Shaoqi, chairman of the People's Republic of China. In August of 1966, Lin Biao asked Ye Qun to dictate to Lei Yingfu, deputy director of the Operations Department of the headquarters of the PLA General Staff, material containing false charges they had fabricated against Liu Shaoqi, and they instructed Lei Yingfu to put these charges in writing. In

December of the same year, Zhang Chunqiao privately summoned Kuai Dafu, a student at Qinghua University, and instigated him to organize a demonstration and agitate first of all in society at large of "overthrowing Liu Shaoqi," In July of 1967, Jiang Qing, in collusion with Kang Sheng and Chen Boda, decided to have Liu Shaoqi persecuted physically, depriving him of his freedom of action ever since. Beginning from May of 1967, Jiang Qing assumed direct control of the "group for inquiring into the special case of Liu Shaoqi and Wang Guangmei" and, in collusion with Kang Sheng and Xie Fuzhi, directed the group to extort confessions from people arrested and imprisoned and rig up false evidence vilifying Liu Shaoqi as "renegade," "enemy agent" and "counter-revolutionary." In 1967, in order to fabricate false evidence against Liu Shaoqi, Jiang Qing made the decision to arrest and imprison Yang Yichen, deputy governor of Hebei Province (formerly a worker in the Organization Department of the CPC Manchuria provincial committee); Yang Chengzuo, a professor at the China People's University (formerly a professor at the Catholic University in Beijing and Wang Guangmei's teacher); Wang Guang'en, a citizen of Tianjin (formerly assistant manager of the Fengtian cotton mill); Hao Miao, Liu Shaoqi's cook, and seven others. When Yang Chengzuo was critically ill, Jiang Qing said to members of the special case group: "Step up the interrogation to squeeze out of him what we need before he dies." As a result of this decision made by Jiang Qing, Yang Chengzuo was hounded to death. The special case group under her control also persecuted Wang Guangen to death. In collusion with Xie Fuzhi, Jiang Qing ordered people to extort confessions repeatedly from Zhang Zhongyi, a professor at the Hebei Beijing Normal College (formerly a professor at the Catholic University in Beijing and Wang Guangmei's teacher), who was critically ill, so that he died barely two hours after an interrogation to extort confessions from him. In order to rig up false evidence and frame Liu Shaoqi as a "renegade," Jiang Qing, along with Kang Sheng, Xie Fuzhi and others, ordered the special case group to extort confessions from Ding Juequn, who worked with Liu Shaoqi in the workers' movement in Wuhan in 1927, and Meng Yongqian, who was arrested at the same time as Liu Shaoqi in Shenyang in 1929. As a result of the framing by Jiang Qing and others, Liu Shaoqi was imprisoned and persecuted to death.

The Lin Biao and Jiang Qing counter-revolutionary cliques framed and persecuted other party and state leaders. In July of 1967, Qi Benyu, a member of the "Cultural Revolution group under the CCP Central Committee," with the approval of Kang Sheng, instigated Han Aijing, a student at the Beijing Aeronautical Engineering Institute, to subject Peng Dehuai, a member of the Political Bureau of the CCP Central Committee, to physical persecution. As a result, Peng Dehuai was severely wounded with several ribs fractured. On November 3, 1970, Huang Yongsheng agreed to the proposal raised by the group in charge of the special case of Peng Dehuai, that Peng Dehuai be "sentenced to life imprisonment and deprived of civil rights for life," in order to continue persecuting him. Peng Dehuai was later tormented to death because of the framing and persecution by the Lin Biao and Jiang Qing counter-revolutionary cliques. In July of 1966, Kang Sheng falsely charged He Long, vice-premier and vice-chairman of the Military Commission of the CCP Central Committee, with "deploying troops to stage a February mutiny" in Beijing. In August of the same year, Lin Biao instructed Wu Faxian to fabricate charges against He Long. In April of 1968, Li Zuopeng and others falsely charged He Long and others with "usurping army leadership and opposing the party." Framed by Lin Biao, Kang Sheng and others, He Long was imprisoned and tormented to death. On June 23, 1967, Huang Yongsheng approved the "report for instruction on investigation for the purpose of rounding up renegades," which was submitted by the head of the Military Control Commission stationed in the Guangzhou Municipal Public Security Bureau, and its appendix, "Plan for Investigation, No 1," in a scheme to frame Ye Jianying, vice-chairman of the military Commission of the CCP Central Committee as a "renegade." In June of 1968, Huang Yongsheng turned over to Ye Qun the materials charging Ye Jianying with "plotting a counter-revolutionary coup." In August of 1968, Huang Yongsheng and Wu Faxian fabricated facts and framed Luo Ruiqing, vice-premier of the State Council, as a "counter-revolutionary who has committed heinous crimes." From late 1966 to 1968, Chen Boda on quite a few occasions framed Lu Dingyi, vice-premier of the State Council, as an "active counter-revolutionary," "renegade" and "hidden traitor," and decided to have his health ruined.

On July 21, 1968, Jiang Qing and Kang Sheng drew up a list of names, aiming at framing members of the eighth CCP Central Committee. In August of the same year, Kang Sheng again drew up lists of names aimed at framing members of the Standing Committee of the third National People's Congress and Standing Committee members of the fourth national committee of the Chinese People's Political Consultative Conference. In December of the same year, Xie Fuzhi rigged up the case of a "Chinese Communist Party (Marxist-Leninist)," with still another list of names. On these four lists, 103 members and alternate members of the eighth CCP Central Committee, 52 members of the third NPC Standing Committee and 76 Standing Committee members of the fourth CPPCC National Committee were labelled "enemy agents," "renegades," "elements having illicit relations with foreign countries," "counter-revolutionaries," "suspected renegades" or "suspected enemy agents." The people framed were subsequently persecuted.

They included the chairman and seven vice-chairmen of the NPC Standing Committee, 12 vice-premiers of the State Council, 22 members and alternate members of the Political Bureau of the CCP Central Committee, the general secretary and 13 members and alternate members of the Secretariat of the CCP Central Committee, six vice-chairmen of the Military Commission of the CCP Central Committee, and 11 leading members of various democratic parties. From 1966 to 1970, Jiang Qing at various meetings named 24 members and alternate members of the eighth CCP Central Committee and hurled false charges at them, so that they were persecuted one after another. After Jiang Qing named and made false accusations against Zhang Linzhi, minister of coal industry, he was illegally incarcerated and subsequently died of serious injuries from beating.

The Lin Biao and Jiang Qing counter-revolutionary cliques framed and persecuted large numbers of officers of the Chinese People's Liberation Army in an attempt to put it under their complete control. On July 25, 1967, Lin Biao called for the "thorough smashing of the PLA General Political Department." Huang Yongsheng, Wu Faxian, Li Zuopeng and Qui Huizuo respectively framed and persecuted large numbers of officers in the headquarters of the General Staff, the General Political Department, the General Logistics Department, the air force and they navy of the Chinese People's Liberation Army. The Lin Biao and Jiang Qing counter-revolutionary cliques cooked up so many false cases in the Chinese People's Liberation Army that over 80,000 people were framed and persecuted, of whom 1,169 died under persecution.

The Lin Biao and Jiang Qing counter-revolutionary cliques framed and persecuted party and government leaders at various levels in an attempt to seize departmental and regional leadership that they had not yet got hold of. In January of 1968, Kang Sheng and others framed cadres in the Organization Department of the CPC Central Committee and directly controlled leadership in that department. The Lin Biao and Jiang Qing counter-revolutionary cliques framed and persecuted large numbers of cadres and people's policemen in people's public security organs, people's procuratorates and people's courts at various levels, of whom 1,565 were hounded to death. The Lin Biao and Jiang Qing counter-revolutionary cliques framed and persecuted large numbers of cadres in various provinces, autonomous regions and municipalities directly under the central government. Under the instruction and instigation of Kang Sheng, Xie Fuzhi and others, leadership of Beijing Municipality was seized and thirteen of its leading cadres were framed and persecuted. Liu Ren and Deng Tuo, secretaries of the municipal party committee, and Vice-Mayors Wu Han and Yue Songsheng, were persecuted to death. Leadership of Shanghai Municipality was seized and twelve of its leading cadres were framed and persecuted as a result of the instruction and instigation of Zhang Chunqiao and Yao Wenyuan. Mayor Cao Diqiu and Vice-Mayor Jin Zhonghua died from persecution. In 1967 and 1968, Zhang Chunqiao directly manipulated and ordered the "You Xuetao group" in Shanghai to undertake such special tasks of espionage as tailing, shadowing, kidnapping, ransacking people's homes, taking people into custody, extorting confessions by torture, and fabricating intelligence. The group trumped up false cases, framed and persecuted cadres and ordinary people, and falsely charged leading cadres in east China with "organizing an underground armed detachment south of the Changjiang (Yangtze) River" and "plotting a mutiny."

The Lin Biao and Jiang Qing counter-revolutionary cliques created large numbers of false cases, inciting beating, smashing and looting throughout the country, and persecuted large numbers of cadres and ordinary people. In 1967, Kang Sheng and others trumped up the case of a "Xinjiang renegade clique." In 1967 and 1968, Huang Yongsheng and company concocted, one after another, the case of a "Guangdong underground party organization" and that of a "counter-revolutionary clique" in the PLA Guangzhou units. Under Chen Boda's instigation, a false case in eastern Hebei Province brought serious consequences with a large number of cadres and ordinary people persecuted in 1967. Kang Sheng and Xie Fuzhi rigged up the case of "enemy agent Zhao Jianmin" in Yunnan in 1968. In the same year, because of the agitation of Kang Sheng and Xie Fuzhi, the false case of an "Inner Mongolian People's Revolutionary Party" entailed disastrous consequences, with large numbers of cadres and ordinary people persecuted or hounded to death or disability. Between 1967 and 1969, the case of a "counter-revolutionary 'northeast gang' that betrayed the party and capitulated to the enemy" was trumped up under the agitation of the Lin Biao and Jiang Qing counter-revolutionary cliques. In October of 1966, Jiang Qing collaborated with Ye Qun in ordering Jiang Tengjiao to carry out an unlawful search in Shanghai of the homes of Zheng Junli, Zhao Dan, Gu Eryi, Tong Zhiling and Chen Liting, who were later persecuted physically. False cases concocted under the instruction and instigation of the Lin Biao and Jiang Qing counter-revolutionary cliques led to the framing and persecution of large numbers of cadres and ordinary members of Communist Party, government and army organs at various levels and various democratic parties and people's organizations, cadres and other people in various circles and returned Overseas Chinese. Among those well-known figures in various circles who were persecuted to death were: noted writers and artists including Lao She, Zhao Shuli, Zhou Xinfang, Gai Jiaotian, Pan Tianshou, Ying Yunwei, Zheng Junli and Sun Weishi; noted professors including Xiong Qinglai, Jian Bozan, He Sijing, Wang Shourong, Gu Yuzhen, Li Guangtian, Rao Yutai, Liu Pansui and Ma Te; noted scientists including Zhao Jiuzhang, Ye Zhupei, Zhang Zongsui, Liu Chongle, Chen Huanyong and Zhou Ren; famous medical specialists including Hu Zhengxiang, Zhang Changshao, Ji Suhua, Lu Shouyan, Ye Xichun and Li Zhongren; outstanding sports coaches including Fu Qifang, Rong Guotuan and Jiang Yongning; well-known model workers including Meng Tai and Shi Chuanxiang; and well-known figures in Overseas Chinese affairs including Fang Fang, Xu Li, Huang Jie, Chen Xujing, Huang Qinshu and

Chen Manyun. The Lin Biao and Jiang Qing counter-revolutionary cliques seriously disrupted national unity and had large numbers of cadres and ordinary people of various minority nationalities cruelly persecuted. As a result, Ji Yatai and others were persecuted to death.

The Lin Biao and Jiang Qing counter-revolutionary cliques instigated large-scale incidents of violence among mass organizations throughout the country, attempting thus to seize power and cruelly suppress the people. At the instigation of Zhang Chunqiao, and armed clash, known as the Kangping Road incident, was triggered off in Shanghai on December 28, 1966, resulting in 91 injured and setting a vile precedent for seizing power by instigating violent incidents throughout the country.

With the support of Zhang Chunqiao and Yao Wenyuan, Wang Xiayu, then chairman of the Shandong Provincial Revolutionary Committee, engineered in May of 1967 a violent incident in the compound of the provincial Revolutionary Committee in Jinan, resulting in 388 persons arrested and imprisoned. On August 4 of the same year, Wang Hongwen organized and directed people to surround and attack the Shanghai diesel engine plant, resulting in 650 people imprisoned, injured or maimed.

The Lin Biao and Jiang Qing counter-revolutionary cliques each plotted to seize supreme party and state power for itself. While they formed an alliance, their sharp contradictions remained. In 1969, Lin Biao was designated successor to Chairman Mao Zedong. In 1970, Lin Biao realized that the forces of Jiang Qing, Zhang Chunqiao and company were growing in such a manner as to surpass his own, so he plotted to "take over" the leadership ahead of schedule. While well aware that Jiang Qing could never succeed in her ambitions, Lin Biao knew that it was impossible for Chairman Mao Zedong to support his "take-over" in advance. Therefore, in September of 1971, the Lin Biao counter-revolutionary clique decided to cast off its mask and stage an armed coup and assassinate Chairman Mao Zedong. As early as October of 1969, Wu Faxian, commander of the air force, turned over to Lin Liguo all power to place the air force under his command and at his disposal. In October of 1970, Lin Liguo organized a secret backbone force for the armed coup, which he named the "joining fleet." In March of 1971, Lin Liguo, Zhou Yuchi and others mapped out in Shanghai a plan for the armed coup, which they named "outline of 'project 571'." In line with the plan for establishing a "command team" as described in the "outline," Lin Liguo summoned Jiang Tengjiao and Wang Weiguo, political commissar of the fourth army of the air force, Chen Liyun, political commissar of the fifth army of the air force, and Zhou Jianping, deputy commander of the air force of the PLA Nanjing units, to a secret meeting in Shanghai on March 31, at which Jiang Tengjiao was put in charge of liaison between the three places of Nanjing, Shanghai and Hangzhou with a view to coordination and concerted operation. On September 5 and 6 of the same year, after receiving secret reports first from Zhou Yuchi and then from Huang Yongsheng about Chairman Mao Zedong's talks which showed that he was aware of Lin Biao's scheme to seize power, Lin Biao and Ye Qun decided to take action to assassinate Chairman Mao Zedong on his inspection tour and stage an armed coup. On September 8, Lin Biao issued the following hand-written order for the armed coup: "Expect you to act according to the order transmitted by Comrades Liguo and Yuchi." Lin Liguo and Zhou Yuchi then gave detailed assignments to Jiang Tengjiao and Wang Fei, deputy chief-of-staff of the air force head quarters, and other key members of the "joint fleet." While the Lin Biao counter-revolutionary clique was plotting intensively for the armed coup, Chairman Mao Zedong, having been alerted by their plot, suddenly changed his itinerary and safely returned to Beijing on September 12.

After the failure of their plan for the assassination, Lin Biao then made preparations for fleeing south with Huang Yongsheng, Wu Faxian, Li Zuopeng and Qui Huizuo to Guangzhou, the base where he was prepared to stage the armed coup, in an attempt to set up a separate central government there and split the state. At Lin Biao's order, Hu Ping, deputy chief-of-staff of the air force headquarters, had eight planes ready for the flight south to Guangzhou.

On September 12, he secretly despatched the special plane, No. 256, to Shanhaiguan for the use of Lin Biao, Ye Qun and Lin Liguo, who were then in Beidaihe. At a few minutes past 10 o'clock that evening, Premier Zhou Enlai inquired about the unexpected despatch of the special plane, No. 256, to Shanhaiguan and ordered that it be brought back to Beijing at once. Hu Ping lied, saying that the special plane, No. 256, had gone to Shanhaiguan on a training flight and had developed engine trouble, refusing to carry out the order for bringing it back to Beijing. Meanwhile, he reported to Zhou Yuchi that the premier had inquired about the movement of the plane. Zhou Yuchi in turn reported this to Lin Liguo. While issuing directives to those in charge of the navy aviation corps' Shanhaiguan airport, first at 23:35 hours on September 12 and then at 00:06 hours on September 13, Li Zuopeng distorted Premier Zhou Enlai's directive that the special plane, No. 256, "cannot take off without a joint order from four persons," namely, Zhou Enlai, Huang Yongsheng, Wu Faxian and Li Zuopeng, saying, "the plane must not be allowed to take off unless one of the four leading officials gives the order." At 00:20 hours on September 13, when Pen Hao, director of the navy aviation corps' Shanhaiguan airport, who had discovered the abnormal situation at the time, phoned Li Zuopeng, asking what they should do if the plane were to take off forcibly, Li Zuopeng still did not take any measure to prevent the plane from taking off, thus enabling Lin Biao, Ye Qun and

Lin Liguo to defect by the special plane, No. 256. Learning that Premier Zhou Enlai had inquired about the special plane's flight to Shanhaiguan, Lin Biao decided it was impossible to carry out the plan of fleeing south to Guangzhou and setting up a separate government there. So they boarded the plane and took off forcibly at 00:32 hours on September 13 to flee abroad in defection. The plane crashed on the way, killing all those aboard.

After learning about Lin Biao's defection, Zhou Yuchi and others seized the helicopter, No. 3685, in Beijing and took off at 03:15 hours on September 13 to flee the country, but the helicopter was forced to land. Large amounts of confidential state documents stolen by Lin Biao counter-revolutionary clique and its plans for an armed coup were captured from the helicopter.

After Lin Biao and others died on their flight abroad, the Jiang Qing counter-revolutionary clique, in an attempt to seize party and state leadership, carried on criminal activities to frame and persecute leading members at various levels. From 1974 to 1976, the Jiang Qing counter-revolutionary clique instructed writing groups such as "Liang Xiao," "Chi Heng" and "Luo Siding" to carrying out counter-revolutionary agitation for vilifying leading cadres at various levels who had just returned to their posts as "having turned from bourgeois democrats to capitalists roaders," thus becoming targets of their so-called continued revolution. In 1976, Jiang Qing, Zhang Chunqiao, Yao Wenyuan and Wang Hongwen created new disturbances throughout the country and framed and persecuted large numbers of leading cadres with the ultimate objective of subverting the government. In March Jiang Qing, in a talk with leading members from twelve provinces and autonomous regions, named a number of leading cadres at central and local levels and hurled false changes at them. In the same year, Zhang Chunqiao instigated Ma Tianshui and Xu Jingxian, vice-chairmen of the Shanghai Municipal Revolutionary Committee, to speak at a meeting attended by more than 10,000 people in Shanghai and vilify leading cadres who had resumed work as "turning from bourgeois democrats to capitalist roaders."

In the same year, Wang Hongwen and Yao Wenyuan ordered Lu ying, editor-in chief of the *People's Daily*, to despatch people to some departments of the State Council and some provinces to cook up materials according to their intentions for framing veteran cadres who had resumed work as "having organized landlords' restitution corps" and "trying to reverse correct verdicts and stage a comeback." They used the materials to justify their seizure of power from those departments and regions which were not yet under their control. From March to May of 1976, the Jiang Qing counter-revolutionary clique made up stories, slandering ordinary people in Nanjing, Beijing and other places who honoured the memory of Premier Zhou Enlai as "counter-revolutionaries." The clique also vilified Vice-Premier Deng Xiaoping as "the chief boss behind the counter-revolutionary political incident" at Tiananmen Square and agitated for large scale suppression and persecution of cadres and ordinary people.

Zhang Chunqiao and Wang Hongwen, principal culprits in the case of the Jiang Qing counter-revolutionary clique, made Shanghai their base for building and expanding a "militia force" under their direct control. As early as August of 1967, a report cleared by Zhang Chunqiao, entitled "Plans of the Shanghai Municipal Revolutionary Committee for Setting Up the 'Verbal Attack and Armed Defence' Headquarters," called for "using the gun to protect revolution made with the pen" and for vigorously building up armed forces under their control. From 1973 to 1976, Wang Hongwen said on many occasions to Ma Tianshui, Xu Jingxian and Wang Xiuzhen, key members of the Jiang Qing counter-revolutionary clique in Shanghai, that "the army must not be allowed to lead the militia," that "It's Chunqiao and me who organized the people's militia in Shanghai," that "You must run it well for me," that "What worries me most is that the army is not in our hands," and that "we must be prepared for guerrilla warfare," urging them to step up the expansion of the "militia force." The Jiang Qing counter-revolutionary clique planned to use this armed force which they regarded as their own to engineer an armed rebellion in Shanghai. In August of 1976, Ding Sheng, a remaining confederate of the Lin Biao clique who had thrown his lot with the Jiang Qing counter-revolutionary clique and commander of the PLA Nanjing units at the time, arrived in Shanghai. He told Ma Tianshui, Xu Jingxian and Wang Xiuzhen, "my biggest worry is unit 6453" stationed near Shanghai, that "I have no control over it" and that "you must be prepared for any eventuality." Ma Tianshui then made a decision and 74,220 rifles, 300 artillery pieces and more than 10 million rounds of ammunition were issued from a munitions depot under their control to the "militia." On September 21, after being briefed in Beijing by Xu Jingxian about Ding Sheng's talk and about the hand-out of weapons to the "militia," Zhang Chunqiao said to Xu Jingxian: "Keep your eyes open for new trends in the class struggle." On September 23, Wang Hongwen made a telephone call to Wang Xiuzhen, saying: "be on your guard, for the struggle isn't over yet. The bourgeoisie inside the party will not be reconciled to defeat." On October 8, after learning that Jiang Qing, Zhang Chunqiao, Yao Wenyuan and Wang Hongwen had been taken into custody, Xu Jingxian, Wang Xiuzhen and others decided to stage an armed rebellion. The command teams they had organized for the armed rebellion then moved into their command posts, and fifteen transmitter-receivers were installed to link them up by telecommunications.

They also assemble and deployed 33,500 "militiamen." On October 9, Shi Shangying, who was in charge of the Shanghai militia headquarters, ordered that the "militia" be concentrated with over 27,000 guns and artillery pieces of various types. On October 12, Zhong Dingdong, another member, in charge of the Shanghai militia headquarters, drew up two specific operation plans, code-named "Han No. 1" and "Fang No. 2." On the evening of the same day, Wang Shaoyong, vice-chairman of the Shanghai Municipal Revolutionary Committee, Zhu Yongjia, leading member of the shanghai writing group, Chen Ada, leading member of the industrial and communication group of the Shanghai Municipal Revolutionary Committee, and others met to plan production stoppages, strikes, parades and demonstrations. They put forward the counter-revolutionary slogans "Return Jiang Qing to Us," "Return Chunqiao to us," "Return Wenyuan to Us" and "Return Hongwen to Us," readying themselves for "a life-and-death struggle." Thanks to the powerful measures adopted by the party Central Committee and the struggle waged by the people of Shanghai, their scheme for an armed coup failed to materialize.

This court has held a total of forty-two sessions for investigation and debate, during which forty-nine witnesses and victims appeared in court to testify, and 873 pieces of evidence were examined. The above-mentioned offenses committed by the Lin Biao and Jiang Qing counter-revolutionary cliques have been verified by great amounts of material and documentary evidence, conclusions of expert corroboration, testimonies of witnesses and statements of victims. The facts are clear and the evidence conclusive.

Since Lin Biao, Kang Sheng, Xie Fuzhi, Ye Qun, Lin Liguo and Zhou Yuchi, who were among the 16 principal culprits in the case of the Lin Biao and Jiang Qing counter-revolutionary cliques, are dead, the Special Procuratorate under the Supreme People's Procuratorate decides not to pursue their criminal liability, in accordance with article 11 of the law of criminal procedure of the People's Republic of China. The Special Procuratorate also decides that except Jiang Qing and the other nine principal culprits, the other defendants in the case will be dealt with separately according to law. Following are the offenses committed by Jiang Qing, Zhang Chunqiao, Yao Wenyuan, Wang Hongwen, Chen Boda, Huang Yongsheng, Wu Faxian, Li Zuopeng, Qiu Huizuo and Jiang Tengjiao, for which they should be held criminally liable as confirmed by this court:

(1) The defendant, Jiang Qing, who acted as a ringleader in organizing and leading a counter-revolutionary clique for the purpose of overthrowing the people's democratic dictatorship, was a principal culprit in the case of the counter-revolutionary clique. Jiang Qing framed and persecuted Liu Shaoqi, chairman of the People's Republic of China. Working in collaboration with Kang Sheng and Chen Boda, she decided in July of 1967 to have Liu Shaoqi persecuted physically and hence deprived of the freedom on action. From May of 1967, Jiang Qing assumed direct control of the "group for inquiring into the special case of Liu

Shaoqi and Wang Guangmei" and, in collusion with Kang Sheng and Xie Fuzhi, ordered the group to extort confessions from those arrested and put in custody, concoct false evidence and frame Liu Shaoqi as a "renegade," "enemy agent" and "counter-revolutionary." In order to rig up false evidence and persecute Liu Shaoqi, Jiang Qing made the decision in 1967 to arrest and imprison Yang Yichen, Yang Changzuo, Wang Guangen, Hao Miao and seven others. When Yang Chengzuo was critically ill, Jiang Qing decided to "step up the interrogation" on him. As a result, Yang Chengzuo was persecuted to death.

The special case group under Jiang Qing's direction also had Wang Guangen persecuted to death. In collusion with Xie Fuzhi, Jiang Qing ordered that repeated actions be taken to extort confessions from Zhang Zhongyi who was critically ill. As a result, he died just two hours after an interrogation. In collaboration with Kang Sheng, Xie Fuzhi and others, Jiang Qing instructed the special case group to extract confessions from Ding Juequn and Meng Yongqian and rig up false evidence for framing Liu Shaoqi as a "renegade." As a result of the false charges made by Jiang Qing and others, Liu Shaoqi was imprisoned and persecuted to death.

On July 21, 1968, Jiang Qing worked hand in glove with Kang Sheng in cooking up such false charges as "renegade," "enemy agent" or "element having illicit relations with foreign countries" against 88 members and alternate members of the eight Central Committee of the Communist Party of China.

From 1966 to 1970, Jiang Qing named twenty-four members and alternate members of the eighth CCP Central Committee and hurled false charges at them at various meetings. As a result, they were persecuted one after another.

On December 14, 1966, Jiang Qing attacked Zhang Linzhi (minister of coal industry) by name on false charges. As a result, Zhang Linzhi was illegally incarcerated and beaten up, and he later died from serious wounds. On December 27 of the same year, Jiang Qing smeared Shi Chuanxiang, a national model worker and a street cleaner in Beijing, as a "scab." Shi Chuanxiang thus suffered serious maltreatment and later died from torment.

In October of 1966, Jiang Qing collaborated with Ye Qun in ordering Jiang Tengjiao to search and ransack the homes of Zheng Junli and four other persons in Shanghai, which was against the law. As a result, they were persecuted physically.

In 1976, Jiang Qing worked hand in glove with Zhang Chunqiao, Yao Wenyuan and Wang Hongwen to create new disturbances across the country. In a talk to leading members of 12 provinces and autonomous regions in March of the same year, Jiang Qing attacked a number of central and local leading cadres by name on false charges.

Jiang Qing was a ringleader of the Lin Biao and Jiang Qing counter-revolutionary cliques. She bore direct or indirect responsibilities for all the offenses, committed during the decade of turmoil by the counter-revolutionary clique she organized and led, of endangering the People's Republic of China, working to overthrow the government and tyrannizing the people.

The defendant, Jiang Qing, has been found guilty of organizing and leading a counter-revolutionary clique as provided in article 98 of the criminal law of the People's Republic of China, of plotting to overthrow the government as provided in article 92, of conducting propaganda and agitation for counter-revolutionary purposes as provided in article 102, and of framing and persecuting people as provided in article 138. She caused particularly grave harm to the state and the people in a particularly flagrant way.

(2) The defendant, Zhang Chunqiao, who collaborated with Jiang Qing in organizing the leading a counter-revolutionary clique for the purpose of overthrowing the people's democratic dictatorship, was a principal culprit in the case of the counter-revolutionary clique.

As the initiator and an all-time instigator and plotter in seizing power from the people's democratic political power during the decade of turmoil, [he] caused extremely grave harm to the state and the people.

In January of 1967, Zhang Chunqiao said: "We must seize power everywhere." From 1967 to 1975, he said on many occasions that "the Great Cultural Revolution" meant "a change of dynasty." He worked hand in glove with Jiang Qing in leading their counter-revolutionary clique in a great deal of activities aimed at usurping party and state leadership.

In order to seize leadership of Shanghai Municipality, Zhang Chunqiao triggered off an armed clash in Shanghai on December 28, 1966, known as the Kangping Road incident, which resulted in 91 injured. In May of 1967, he supported Wang Xiaoyu to engineer a violent incident in Jinan, which resulted in 388 persons arrested and imprisoned.

In December of 1966, Zhang Chunqiao summoned Kuai Dafu alone and instructed him to organize a demonstration and agitate for "overthrowing Liu Shaoqi" for the first time in society at large.

Leadership of Shanghai Municipality was seized under Zhang Chunqiao's instruction and instigation. Twelve leading cadres of the municipality were labelled "renegades," "enemy agents" or "counter-revolutionaries." Cao Diqiu and Jin Zhonghua were persecuted to death.

Controlled and directed by Zhang Chunqiao, the "You Xuetao group" carried out special tasks of espionage, trumped up cases to persecute cadres and other people, and falsely charged leading cadres in east China with "organizing an underground armed detachment south of the Changjiang (Yangtze) River" and "plotting a mutiny."

In 1976, Zhang Chunqiao collaborated with Jiang Qing, Yao Wenyuan and Wang Hongwen in creating new disturbances across the country. In March of the same year, Zhang Chunqiao instructed Ma Tianshui and Xu Jingxian to smear, at a mass meeting of 10,000 people in Shanghai, those leading cadres who had resumed work as having turned "from bourgeois democrats into capitalist roaders" and become targets of what they called continued revolution.

Zhang Chunqiao in collusion with Wang Hongwen and others, made Shanghai their base for building up a "militia force" under their direct control, and plotted an armed rebellion there.

The defendant, Zhang Chunqiao, has been found guilty of organizing and leading a counter-revolutionary clique as provided in article 98 of the criminal law of the People's Republic of China, of scheming to overthrow the government as provided in article 92, of plotting an armed rebellion as provided in article 93, of conducting propaganda and agitation for counter-revolutionary purposes as provided in article 102, and of framing and persecuting people as provided in article 138. He caused particularly grave harm to the state and the people in a particularly flagrant way.

(3) The defendant, Yao Wenyuan, who organized and led a counter-revolutionary clique for the purpose of overthrowing the people's democratic dictatorship, was a principal culprit in the case of the counter-revolutionary clique. He took an active part in Jiang Qing's activities to seize supreme power.

Yao Wenyuan directly controlled the mass media and conducted propaganda and agitation for counter-revolutionary ends over a long period. From 1974 to 1976, he instructed writing groups including "Liang Xiao," "Chi Heng" and "Luo Siding" to vilify leading cadres at various levels who had resumed work, accusing them of having turned "from bourgeois democrats into capitalist roaders" and become targets of the so-called continued revolution, thus agitating for framing and persecuting them.

In 1967, Yao Wenyuan took an active part in seizing leadership of Shanghai Municipality. IIe joined in framing leading cadres of the municipality including Cao Diqiu.

Yao Wenyuan was one of those who supported Wang Xiaoyu's plan to engineer a violent incident in Jinan in May of 1967.

In 1976, Yao Wenyuan collaborated with Jiang Qing, Zhang Chunqiao and Wang Hongwen in creating new disturbances across the country. From January to September of the same year, he instructed Lu Ying to despatch people to some departments of the State Council and some provinces to fabricate materials according to their intentions so as to frame those leading cadres who had resumed work. From March to May of the same year, Yao Wenyuan, by trumping up charges, smeared people in Nanjing, Beijing and other places who mourned the death of Premier Zhou Enlai as "counter-revolutionaries," falsely charged Deng Xiaoping with being the "chief boss behind the counter-revolutionary political incident" at Tiananmen Square, and agitated for suppressing and persecuting large numbers of cadres and ordinary people.

The defendant, Yao Wenyuan, has been found guilty of organizing and leading a counter-revolutionary clique as provided in article 98 of the criminal law of the People's Republic of China, of plotting to overthrow the government as provided in article 92, of conducting propaganda and agitation for counter-revolutionary ends as provided in article 102, and of framing and persecuting people as provided in article 138.

(4) The defendant, Wang Hongwen, who organized and led a counter-revolutionary clique for the purpose of overthrowing the people's democratic dictatorship, was a principal culprit in the case of the counter-revolutionary clique. He took an active part in Jiang Qing's activities to seize supreme power.

On December 28, 1966, Wang Hongwen participated in triggering off the Kangping Road incident of violence, which resulted in ninety-one injured. On August 4, 1967, he organized and directed people to surround and attack the Shanghai diesel engine plant, and 650 people were imprisoned, wounded or maimed.

In 1976, Wang Hongwen collaborated with Jiang Qing, Zhang Chunqiao and Yao Wenyuan in creating new disturbances across the country. He instructed

Lu Ying to despatch people to a number of provinces to fabricate materials according to their intentions for framing leading cadres who had resumed work.

Working in collusion with Zhang Chunqiao, Wang Hongwen made Shanghai their base for building up a "militia force" under their direct control. He instructed Ma Tianshui, Xu Jingxian and Wang Xiuzhen time and again to step up the expansion of the "militia force," and plotted an armed rebellion in Shanghai.

The defendant, Wang Hongwen, has been found guilty of organizing and leading a counter-revolutionary clique as provided in article 98 of the criminal law of the People's Republic of China, of conspiring to overthrow the government as provided in article 92, of instigating an armed rebellion as provided in article 93, of causing injury to people for counter-revolutionary purposes as provided in article 101, and of framing and persecuting people as provided in article 138.

(5) The defendant, Chen Boda, who played an active part in a counter-revolutionary clique for the purpose of overthrowing the people's democratic dictatorship, was a principal culprit in the case of the counter-revolutionary clique. He took an active part in the activities of Lin Biao and Jiang Qing to seize supreme power.

Chen Boda controlled the mass media and conducted propaganda and agitation for counter-revolutionary purposes. In 1966, he raised such slogans as "sweep away all monsters and demons" and whipped up extensive framing and persecution of cadres and ordinary people.

In July of 1967, Chen Boda collaborated with Jiang Qing and Kang Sheng in deciding to have Liu Shaoqi persecuted physically and deprived of his freedom of action ever since. From late 1966 to 1968, Chen Boda on quite a few occasions smeared Lu Dingyi, vice-premier of the State Council, as an "active counter-revolutionary," "renegade" and "hidden traitor," and decided to have his health ruined.

In December of 1967, Chen Boda said in Tangshan that the CCP organization in eastern Hebei Province "was probably a party of Kuomintang-communist cooperation, and in fact it might be the Kuomintang members, or renegades, who were playing a dominant role here." A case was thus trumped up at his instigation, which brought serious consequences, with many cadres and ordinary people in eastern Hebei persecuted.

The defendant, Chen Boda, has been found guilty of actively joining a counter-revolutionary clique as provided in article 98 of the criminal law of the

People's Republic of China, of conspiring to overthrow the government as provided in article 92, of conducting propaganda and agitation for counter-revolutionary purposes as provided in article 102, and of framing and persecuting people as provided in article 138.

(6) The defendant, Huang Yongsheng, who organized and led a counter-revolutionary clique for the purpose of overthrowing the people's democratic dictatorship, was a principal culprit in the case of the counter-revolutionary clique. He actively participated in Lin Biao's activities to seize supreme power.

On November 3, 1970, Huang Yongsheng agreed to the proposal raised by the group in charge of the special case of Peng Dehuai that "Peng Dehuai be dismissed from all posts inside and outside the party, expelled from the party for good, sentenced to life imprisonment and deprived of civil rights for life." As a result, Peng Dehuai was subsequently persecuted.

In June of 1967, Huang Yongsheng approved the "Report for Instruction on Investigation for the Purpose of Rounding Up Renegades," which was submitted by the head of the Military Control Commission stationed in the Guangzhou Municipal Public Security Bureau, and its appendix, "Plan for Investigation, No. 1," scheming to frame Ye Jianying as a "renegade." In June of 1968, he turned over to Ye Qun materials falsely charging Ye Jianying with "plotting a counter-revolutionary coup."

In 1968, Huang Yongsheng, in collaboration with Wu Faxian, fabricated charges against Luo Ruiqing, smearing him as a "counter-revolutionary who has committed heinous crimes." Huang Yongsheng also framed leading cadres in the headquarters of the PLA General Staff. In December of the same year, he slandered the PLA General Political Department as "recruiting renegades" and took an active part in Lin Biao's criminal activities for the "thorough smashing of the PLA General Political Department."

From October of 1967 to March of 1968, Huang Yongsheng proposed to investigate the history of the underground CCP organization in Guangdong Province before liberation and decided to examine the records of Wen Niansheng, deputy commander of the PLA Guangzhou units, and others. This gave rise to the false cases of the "Guangdong underground party organization" and a "counter-revolutionary clique" in the PLA Guangzhou units. As a result, large numbers of cadres and ordinary people were framed and persecuted, and the vice-governor of Guangdong, Lin Qiangyun, and Wen Niansheng were persecuted to death.

On September 6, 1971, Huang Yongsheng secretly informed Lin Biao of Chairman Mao Zedong's talks which showed he was aware that Lin Biao was conspiring to seize power. This prompted Lin Biao decision to take action to assassinate Chairman Mao Zedong and engineer an armed coup d'etat.

The defendant, Huang Yongsheng, has been found guilty of organizing and leading a counter-revolutionary clique as provided in article 98 of the criminal law of the People's Republic of China, of conspiring to overthrow the government as provided in article 92, and of framing and persecuting people as provided in article 138.

(7) The defendant, Wu Faxian, who organized and led a counter-revolutionary clique for the purpose of overthrowing the people's democratic dictatorship, was a principal culprit in the case of the counter-revolutionary clique. He actively participated in Lin Biao's activities to seize supreme power.

Receiving Lin Biao's instructions in August of 1966, Wu Faxian had materials prepared on September 3, accusing He Long of plotting to seize leadership in the air force, and sent them to Lin Biao. In August of 1968, Wu Faxian, in collaboration with Huang Yongsheng, fabricated charges against Luo Ruiqing, smearing him as a "counter-revolutionary who has committed heinous crimes."

Wu Faxian laid false charges against a number of leading cadres in the air force, alleging that they attempted to "seize power." He approved the detention and persecution of 174 cadres and rank-and-filers in the air force, among whom Gu Qian, chief of staff of the air force command of the PLA Nanjing units, and Liu Shanben, deputy superintendent of the Air Force Academy, were persecuted to death.

In October of 1969, Wu Faxian turned over to Lin Liguo all power to place the air force under his command and at his disposal, thus enabling him to form a "joint fleet," which constituted the backbone force in the plot of the Lin Biao counter-revolutionary clique to assassinate Chairman Mao Zedong and stage an armed coup d'etat.

The defendant, Wu Faxian, has been found guilty of organizing and leading a counter-revolutionary clique as provided in article 98 of the criminal law of the People's Republic of China, of conspiring to overthrow the government as provided in article 92, and of persecuting people on false charges as provided in article 138.

(8)   The defendant, Li Zuopeng, who organized and led a counter-revolutionary clique for the purpose of overthrowing the people's democratic dictatorship, was a principal culprit in the case of the counter-revolutionary clique. Li Zuopeng took an active part in Lin Biao's activities to seize supreme power.

In April of 1968, he falsely accused He Long and others of trying to "usurp army leadership and oppose the party." He attacked 120 cadres in the navy by name on false charges.

At 11:35 p.m. on September 12 and at 00:06 a.m. on September 13, 1971, Li Zuopeng twice distorted Premier Zhou Enlai's directive just before the defection of Lin Biao and Ye Qun. When Pan Hao, director of the navy aviation corps' Shanhaiguan airport, in an emergency phone call at 00:20 a.m. on September 13, asked for instruction on what he should do if the plane were to take off forcibly, Li Zuopeng did not take any measure to prevent the take-off, thus allowing Lin Biao to escape abroad by air. Afterwards, Li Zuopeng tried to cover up his crime by altering the log-book entry of the relevant phone calls.

The defendant, Li Zuopeng, has been found guilty of organizing and leading a counter-revolutionary clique as provided in article 98 of the criminal law of the People's Republic of China, of conspiring to overthrow the government as provided in article 92, and of framing and persecuting people as provided in article 138.

(9)   The defendant, Qiu Huizuo, who organized and led a counter-revolutionary clique for the purpose of overthrowing the people's democratic dictatorship, was a principal culprit in the case of the counter-revolutionary clique. Qiu Huizuo took an active party in Lin Biao's activities to seize supreme power.

In 1967, Qiu Huizuo instructed some persons to steal the archives of the PLA General Political Department and framed cadres in the department. He played an important role in Lin Biao's criminal activities of "smashing the General Political Department."

Between 1967 and 1971, Qiu Huizuo set up a kangaroo court in the PlA General Logistics Department to extort confessions through torture, and directly framed and persecuted 462 cadres and ordinary people, among who Tang Ping, Zhou Changgeng, Gu Zizhuang, Zhang Shusen, Shen Maoxing, Wang Shuchen, Zhang Lingdou and Hua Diping were persecuted to death.

The defendant, Qiu Huizuo, has been found guilty of organizing and leading a counter-revolutionary clique as provided in article 98 of the criminal law of the People's Republic of China, of conspiring to overthrow the government as provided in article 92, and of framing and persecuting people as provided in article 138.

(10) The defendant, Jiang Tengjiao, who played an active role in the counter-revolutionary clique for the purpose of overthrowing the people's democratic dictatorship, was a principal culprit in the case of the counter-revolutionary clique.

On March 31, 1971, Jiang Tengjiao attended a secret meeting called by Lin Liguo in Shanghai to establish a "command team" for an armed coup, at which he was made the person responsible for liaison between the three places of Nanjing, Shanghai and Hangzhou "with a view to coordination and concerted operation." Having received, via Lin Liguo, a hand-written order from Lin Biao on September 8 for an armed coup, Jiang Tengjiao took part in working out the details for assassinating Chairman Mao Zedong, and assumed the position of first-line commander for action in the Shanghai area. Following the failure of the plot to murder Chairman Mao Zedong, Jiang Tengjiao took an active part in the counter-revolutionary action of Lin Biao and Ye Qun in preparing for fleeing south to Guangzhou.

The defendant, Jiang Tengjiao, has been found guilty of playing an active role in a counter-revolutionary clique as provided in article 98 of the criminal law of the People's Republic of China, of instigating an armed rebellion as provided in article 93, and of attempting to kill people for counter-revolutionary purposes as provided in article 101.

Among the above-mentioned defendants, Wang Hongwen, Chen Boda, Wu Faxian, Li Zuopeng, Qiu Huizuo and Jiang Tengjiao each gave an account of the offenses he had committed. Jiang Tengjiao confessed his offenses the day after Lin Biao's defection. Wu Faxian, Qiu Huizuo and Jiang Tengjiao exposed crimes committed by Lin Biao, Jiang Qing and other co-defendants in the case. Huang Yongsheng confessed some of his offenses. Yao Wenyuan described his offenses as mistakes and denied that they were crimes. Zhang Chunqiao refused to answer the questions put to him by the bench. Jiang Qing disrupted order in court.

In view of the facts, nature and degree of the offenses Jiang Qing and the other nine defendants committed and the damage they did to society, and in accordance with articles 90, 92, 93, 98, 101, 102, 103 and 138, as well as articles 20, 43, 53 and 64, of the criminal law of the People's Republic of China, this court now passes the following judgement:

Jiang Qing is sentenced to death with a two-year reprieve and permanent deprivation of political rights; Zhang Chunqiao is sentenced to death with a two-year reprieve and permanent deprivation of political rights; Yao Wenyuan is sentenced to 20 years' imprisonment and deprivation of political rights for five years; Wang Hongwen is sentenced to life imprisonment and permanent deprivation of political rights; Chen Boda is sentenced to 18 years' imprisonment and deprivation of political rights for five years; Huang Yongsheng is sentenced to 18 years' imprisonment and deprivation of political rights for five years; Wu Faxian is sentenced to 17 years' imprisonment and deprivation of political rights for five years; Li Zuopeng is sentenced to 17 years' imprisonment and deprivation of political rights for five years; Qiu Huizuo is sentenced to 16 years imprisonment and deprivation of political rights for five years; Jiang Tengjiao is sentenced to 18 years' imprisonment and deprivation of political rights for five years.

To fixed terms of imprisonment for those above who are sentenced to such a penalty shall run from the first day of enforcement of the sentences where an offender has been held in prior custody, the duration of such custody shall be deducted from the term of imprisonment at the rate of one day for each day spent in prior custody.

This judgement is final.

*****

CHAPTER THREE

NEW RURAL SOCIETAL POLICIES

Chapter Three contains documents which provide a glimpse of the major changes which took place in Chinese rural and agricultural policies between 1978 and 1982.

Document No. 9, is a long article by Hu Ch'iao-mu, President of the Chinese Academy of Social Sciences offering a theoretical justification for reforming the economy and pushing ahead with the Four Modernizations. Quoting Marx and Engels as well as Lenin, Stalin and Mao Tse-tung, Hu argued that the desired reforms were fully consistent with the ultimate progress toward socialism.

Document No. 10 is an internal Party document reporting a decision by the Central Committee of the Chinese Communist Party regarding the agricultural reforms. While maintaining the people's communes as the basic unit of organization in the countryside, the decision stressed the need for more attention to greater pay for more work and for the ability of the peasants to work private plots and to develop sideline occupations. The article by Yu Guoyao (Document No. 11) published in the *Kuangming Daily* defended the new agricultural policies and the efforts to promote the acceleration of agricultural production.

By 1982, more than 90 percent of the production teams in China had adopted some form of the "responsibility system" (Document No. 12). While maintaining that Chinese agriculture must adhere to the "road of socialist collectivization," the article acknowledges many production teams had begun to operate with "each household as a basic unit."

A short time after the publication of Document No. 12, the *Beijing Review* published another article explaining the decision of the leadership to abolish the people's communes as a governmental administrative unit and to re-establish the township level of government (Document No. 13). While maintaining that the communes had been a great success, the article stated that the old arrangement was no longer satisfactory under the new conditions of agricultural reform.

*****

DOCUMENTS

9.   Hu Ch'iao-mu, "Act in Accordance with Economic Laws, Step Up the Four Modernizations," **Jenmin Jihpao**, Beijing, October 6, 1978; **FBIS-CHI**, 11 October 1978.

10.   "Decision of the Central Committee of the Communist Party of China on Some Questions Concerning the Acceleration of Agricultural Development -- A Document of the Central Committee of the Chinese Communist Party, *Chung-fa* (1979) No. 4," Part I, **Issues & Studies**, Vol. XV, No 7, July 1979; Part II, **Issues & Studies**, Vol. XV, No. 8, August 1979.

11.   Yu Guoyao, "Applying Economic Means to Readjusting the Irrational Structure of Agriculture -- Discussion on Agricultural Modernization," **Kuangming Jihpao**, Beijing, January 17, 1980; **FBIS-CHI**, 5 February 1980.

12.   "A Programme for Current Agricultural Work," **Beijing Review**, No. 24, June 14, 1982.

13.   Song Dahan and Zhang Chunsheng, "Important Change in the System of People's Communes," **Beijing Review**, No. 29, July 19, 1982.

*****

DOCUMENT NO. 9

ACT IN ACCORDANCE WITH ECONOMIC LAWS,

STEP UP THE FOUR MODERNIZATIONS

by

Hu Ch'iao-mu
President, Chinese Academy of Social Sciences

(**Jenmin Jihpao**, Beijing, October 6, 1978;
FBIS - CHI, October 11, 1978)

In his speech to the National Finance and Trade Conference on Learning From Taching and Tachai, Comrade Hua Kuo-feng pointed out: "Some comrades still do not adequately recognize the importance of studying, mastering and applying the economic laws of socialism. They have gone so far as to imagine that it is possible to put politics in command while neglecting objective economic laws and that acknowledgment of economic laws means negating putting politics in command; this view is entirely wrong. We must put proletarian politics in command of our economic work and must do things according to objective economic laws, these two aspects being a unity. Leading cadres at all levels in the party should strive to bring politics and economics together and raise the quality of their economic management. This is of key significance for the rapid development of the national economy and demands particularly close attention.

The above instruction given by Comrade Hua Kuo-feng is indeed of "key significance for the rapid development of the national economy and demands particularly close attention." This article will relate some experiences and put forward a number of proposals on the need of doing our economic work according to objective economic laws.

I. The Objectiveness of Economic Laws

On many occasions, Marx, Engels, Lenin, Stalin and Comrade Mao Tse-tung discussed the objectiveness of economic laws. Touching on the necessity of proportional distribution of social labor, Marx regarded it as a natural law, saying that "natural laws can by no means be repealed. The thing that can change under different historical conditions is the **form** through which these laws can materialize."[1]

Lenin pointed out that the social economic formation could not possibly "be changed at will by the superior officers (or by the will of society of the government,)" that its development "goes through a natural historical process," and that the law of its development "is not only independent of but determines man's will, mentality and aspirations."[2] Comrade Mao Tse-tung said: "For us the socialist economy is in many respects a still unknown realm of necessity"[3] and "we should continue investigating in our future practice so that we can find the inherent laws and use them to serve socialism."[4]

As a result of our inadequate understanding and efforts in publicizing these instructions, especially because of the pernicious influence of Lin Piao and the Gang of Four, many cadres leading our industrial, agricultural and other economic work still do not recognize or do not want to recognize economic laws and their objectiveness. They take the wills of society, the government and the superior officers as economic laws. They consider that economic laws can change according to political needs and that acknowledgment of this means putting politics in command of economic affairs.

These comrades forget that "politics is the most concentrated expression of economics."[5] Politics itself cannot create a law beyond the objective economic laws and impose it on economics. In light of economic development laws, the task of the party's correct political leadership is precisely to do its utmost to guide our socialist economic work according to objective laws. (Practice shows that it is a very complicated and arduous task.) Only by doing so can it be possible to guarantee the political purpose of this work and guarantee the identity of the political leadership and the people's interests. It is our view that Comrade Hua Kuo-feng exactly meant this when he said putting proletarian politics in command and doing things according to objective economic laws are a unity.

Affirming the objectiveness of economic laws, it is necessary to solve these two questions 1) Can the social system of socialism guarantee that our economy develops automatically, rapidly and in a planned way? 2) Why do the capitalist countries' economic management methods have merits worthy of our learning?

On the first question, Marx and Engels many times pointed out that in capitalist society "from its very beginning there never existed any conscious social regulation of production,"[6] and that all production in bourgeois society "is regulated not by commonly formulated plans, but by blind laws, and these blind laws, with spontaneous force, play their role in the storms of periodical crises in commerce."[7]   In socialist society, conscious social regulation of production is effected by state plans.   From this we can conclude that in socialist society the economy assuredly will develop faster than in capitalist society and assuredly will create much higher labor productivity than under capitalism. Generally speaking, socialist economy has proved that it develops faster than capitalist economy and can develop at an even faster speed, and that it is entirely possible for socialist economy to bring about much higher labor productivity.   In fact, however, sometimes and in some aspects, socialist economy has developed at a slower pace than capitalist economy and has failed to create higher labor productivity. Why? The reasons are: First, in countries that have undergone socialist revolution, economic and cultural development lagged behind the developed capitalist countries to begin with.   In these countries, the forces of small producers and feudal influence were more powerful, and despite socialist revolution, the forces of various backward habits of small producers and feudalism continued to exist for a long time in many fields and to seriously hinder the normal, rapid development of socialist economy.   Second, as a newborn system, socialist society is not yet consolidated and still has to use a considerably large portion of its strength to deal with the hostile forces at home and abroad.   Third, a socialist country's national economic plan is a kind of conscious social regulation of production.   This is unprecedented in history.   It is a very difficult task for the people to skillfully apply the objective economic laws in order to correctly formulate and implement plans; this involves a rather long process of learning and practicing.

Comrade Mao Tse-tung said: The socialist relations of production "are in correspondence with the growth of the productive forces, but these relations are still far from perfect, and this imperfection stands in contradiction to the growth of the productive forces."[8]   Moreover, there is correspondence as well as contradiction between the superstructure and the economic base.

As we know, Engels long ago repeatedly pointed out that while state power can help the economy develop faster, it can also work the other way, and thus political power may cause great damage to economic development and may cause much waste in manpower and material resources. Although what Engels referred to was past history, practice has shown that even a socialist country cannot guarantee that its political power will never cause great harm to its economic development.

Stalin said: "We must not confuse our yearly plan and five-year plan with the objective economic laws governing the planned and proportionate development of the national economy."[9]   He pointed out: Socialist relations of production often fall behind the growth of the productive forces and, if handled improperly, they still can become an extremely serious obstacle to, even conflict with, the continued growth of the productive forces. In fact, conflict is not only caused by the contradiction between the relations of production and the continued development of the productive forces, but also caused by mistakes made by state organs in organizing economic work.

In his report at the Fourteenth Congress of the CPSU in 1925, Stalin pointed out: "In capitalist countries, any mistake of a more serious nature and any more serious phenomenon of overproduction or serious discrepancy between production and total demand unavoidably will have to be corrected by some crises. . . . In capitalist countries, economic, commercial and financial crises only touch certain capitalist groups (Stalin at this time could not foresee the great 1929 crisis--editor)."[10] But in our country it is different. Each time there is a serious stagnation in commerce and production or a miscalculation in our economy, it will not be ended by a crisis in a single field, and it certainly will deal a blow to the entire national economy. Every crisis, be it commercial, financial or industrial, can become a national crisis in our country. The situation referred to by Stalin occurred in the Soviet Union both before and after he made that report, and it also occurred in China. Thus it can be seen that the socialist system itself cannot automatically guarantee that we will act according to objective economic laws, nor can it automatically guarantee that our economy will always develop rapidly in a planned way.

The system of socialist society gives us the possibility to act in accordance with objective laws. This is a superiority of the socialist system that has been found lacking throughout the history of the national economic development under the capitalist system. Turning a possibility into a reality, however, requires strenuous efforts and inevitably goes through twists and turns. In Comrade Mao Tse-tung's words, this is the price we have to pay. In order to reduce the twists and turns in the course of development, the socialist economic system has to integrate itself closely with the socialist political system or, in other words, the people's democratic system, and with economic, managerial and natural sciences. In short, the socialist economy means highly socialized mass production based on the public ownership system. When the superiority of the socialist system is correctly put to use and objective laws are adhered to in handling our affairs, we will have a tremendous strength, unprecedented in human history, for rapidly developing our economy. If we do not study and observe objective laws but act blindly in accordance with the will of our superior officers and take things for granted, some departments, and even the entire national economy, will stagnate or go backward and the people, in their tens of millions or even in their hundreds of millions, will suffer.

In addition to giving us a great possibility to act in accordance with objective economic laws, the socialist system also gives us the absolute necessity and grave historic duty of acting in accordance with these laws. It has been nearly thirty years since our country was founded and we can no longer attribute our mistakes to lack of experience. In order to rapidly achieve the four modernizations, we now need all the more to conscientiously sum up both positive and negative experiences, consciously act in accordance with objective economic laws and enthusiastically give full play to the superiority of the socialist system.

As for the second question, Comrade Mao Tse-tung said: "In the industrially developed countries they run their enterprises with fewer people and greater efficiency and they know how to run business. All this should be learned well in accordance with our own principles in order to improve our work."[11] Since production in a capitalist society is not adjusted in accordance with a jointly formulated plan but in accordance with blind laws, why do its economic management methods have merits for us to learn from? Speaking as a whole, the capitalist economy is not planned. The individual enterprises generally have their own plans. Marx said: "The internal division of labor of a factory plays a pre-planned role; the internal division of labor of a society plays an inherent, silent role of natural necessity."[12] So, the entire non-planned social production of capitalism does not mean that the capitalist enterprises do not have their own internal plans. Marx long ago emphatically pointed out the dual nature of the capitalist enterprise management; that is, "the special function engendered by the nature of the course of social labor that belongs to this course" and the "the function of exploitation in the course of social labor." The former is indispensable to all kinds of social labor under various systems.

"Direct social labor or common labor of all large sizes does need, more or less, to be commanded so as to coordinate with the activities of the individuals and carry out the various general functions engendered by the entire production campaign -- a campaign which is different from that of the independent organs of the entire operation."[13] Of course, these functions include the function of planning. The planned management and other management systems within capitalist factories in the early years have now been developed into a modern, highly efficient planned management and other management systems of the big companies, and planned management and other management systems also exist in one way or another within a certain economic department of a country (take U.S. agricultural production and management, for example). Within these areas, the bourgeoisie has been doing things consciously according to objective laws of economy (naturally, this does not change the capitalist nature of their economy nor can it help them avoid any crisis). And due to a long period of practice, the bourgeoisie has accumulated a relatively rich experience in using these laws skillfully. This is precisely what Marx meant that it is the first function of the capitalist enterprise management that the proletariat can and must learn from the bourgeoisie.

Lenin said: "Only those who understand that **without learning** from the trust organizers **it is impossible** to create or implement socialism are worthy of being called communists. This is because socialism is not a utopian idea, but calls on the vanguard of the proletariat, after it has seized political power, to master and use the things created by the trusts. Unless our proletarian political party learns from the first-rate capitalist experts the ability to organize large-scale trust production, then **nowhere else** can this ability be learned."[14] "Some people . . . say that it is possible to build socialism without learning from the bourgeoisie. I think this is the psychology of the people in central Africa. We cannot imagine what other socialism there is except the socialism based on the sum total of the experiences gained by the huge capitalist culture."[15] The proletarian political power "cannot be maintained by relying merely on dictatorship, violence and coercion. Only be grasping all the civilized, technically advanced, progressive experiences of capitalism and by using all the people who possess such experiences can it be maintained."[16]

Lenin said these things more than half a century ago, but they are still applicable in principle. We learn from the bourgeoisie in an analytical and selective manner and from the proletarian and socialist stand, not from the bourgeois and capitalist stand. This is why Comrade Mao Tsetung viewed learning in a principled manner. Of course, in the learning process we must prevent and correct the tendency of thinking that all foreign things are good and that China can rely on foreign countries instead of on her own efforts to accomplish the four modernizations. But this is not the main danger at present. The main dangers at present are the attitudes of smugness, inertia, and parochial arrogance, as pointed out repeatedly by Comrade Hua Kuo-feng, and the poisonous influence of the fallacy spread by the Gang of Four to regard self-reliance and learning advanced things from foreign countries as opposed to each other. While adhering to the principle of self-reliance, we not only should not reject learning advanced things from foreign countries, but, as previously mentioned, must make learning advanced foreign things a requirement. Otherwise, we will sink with the doctrine of trailing behind at a snail's pace, and we cannot possibly succeed in building socialism, or we will be defeated by our enemies before we can successfully build socialism. We must combine the superiority of the socialist system with the advanced science and technology and advanced managerial experiences of the developed capitalist countries and combine all the useful things from the experience of foreign countries with our own concrete conditions and successful experiences. Only in this way can we quickly increase our ability to do things according to objective economic laws and to accelerate the pace of the four modernizations.

With the downfall of the Gang of Four, the economic situation has fundamentally changed, the speed of production has increased and production order has greatly improved. But, as Comrade Hua Kuo-feng pointed out, our managerial level is still very low. In other words, our level in doing things according to economic laws is still very low. At present, our industry and agriculture still cannot organize production totally based on the requirements of the state, the masses and export. The varieties, specifications, quality and quantities of our products still cannot fully meet plans. As a result, some items, which we need and can produce, are not produced in sufficient quantities, while some items being produced are not needed, causing oversupply and waste. Our capacity of power and raw-material supplies is still not fully in proportion with the requirements of production and capital construction. As a result, work stoppages and idleness frequently occur. We still have not seriously promoted specialization and coordination. Many enterprises are established as "make-everything-you-need" enterprises, big or small. Therefore, technical progress is very slow, labor productivity is very low and costs are very high. In general, our enterprises pay little attention to economic results, and the phenomenon that there is no fixed number of workers and staff members, no fixed production quotas, no examination of quality and no accounting of costs is widespread, causing much waste in manpower and material and financial resources.

Because we have not been good at unifying the interests of the state, the enterprises and the staff and workers, our efforts in urging leaders of enterprises and the vast numbers of staff and workers to take the initiative and pay attention to enterprise management and improvement have not fully achieved their intended role as an economic motive force. All this shows that our level in acting according to the economic laws is still quite low. This problem deserves our serious attention in order to quickly solve it.

II. Act According to Economic Laws

To accelerate the four modernizations, we must act according to economic laws to raise our economic management level. There are many economic laws. Here we will only offer some views on three problems, namely, the law of proportionate development in a planned way, the law of value, and unification of interests of the state, enterprises and the individual.

First of all it is necessary to obey the law of proportionate development in a planned way.

Marx said: "Economic use of time and planned distribution of working time among the different departments of production are still the primary economic laws in a collective-based society. We can even say that they are laws of a very high degree."[17] Because making economic use of time comes under the laws of value, we will discuss it later. Here let use first discuss the question of planned distribution of working time. To meet objective needs, class societies in the past also proportionately distributed social labor. But this was not done consciously in a planned way. Our socialist economy can and must develop proportionately in a planned way. This is a basic character of our socialist economy. If we can truly develop our economy proportionately in a planned way, we can then achieve sustained, steady and rapid economic growth and can avoid anarchist or semi-anarchist states and their ensuing consequences of wide fluctuations in development speed, and continuously expand our socialist reproduction and create reliable material resource to raise the people's material and cultural living standards. Because of the long sabotage of Lin Piao and the Gang of Four, at present our national economic base is still in a "semi-planned" status. To improve our economic management work, it is necessary first of all to transform the semi-planned status to a fully planned status. Our planning must obey, reflect and employ the law of proportionate development in a planned way and take into consideration the interests of the state (including interests of the central organs and local interests), the collective interests of the industrial and agricultural enterprises and the individual interests of workers.

State plans should be formulated by taking into consideration the needs of various sides and all possibilities and, after repeated calculations and comprehensive balancing, they should not leave any loopholes. Additions should not be made to local plans by each level. Production or capital construction projects outside state plans should be included in local plans at the various levels. There should be direct and indirect plans. State plans are a combination of these two types of plans. Production targets issued by the state must be integrated into the enterprises' production contracts to solve current contradictions between supply and demand and between production and needs.

Strengthening enterprise management may produce contradictions between central and local organs, among departments and between the state and the enterprises. This situation is more likely now than before due to the long interference and sabotage of Lin Piao and the Gang of Four. But these contradictions can and must be resolved with the principle of overall planning and all-round consideration. In our planning work, we must give full play to local initiative. Otherwise, our plans cannot reflect the desires of all the people, nor can they be effective. But local initiative must yield to the state's overall interests. It is correct and justified for the various provinces to demand industrialization.

Adapting to local conditions, the various provinces must develop their local industry to a high level and must be able to produce the most needed daily industrial products as well as products for supporting agricultural production. But this does not mean that each province must build an independent and complete industrial system. This is certainly not necessary at present. Even in the long-range future it also may be unnecessary. Because the various provinces are vastly different from one another in resources, if, by disregarding local conditions, each province strives to be self-contained and self-sufficient, it is bound to cause a tremendous waste of both manpower and material resources and delay the nation's four modernizations. In the United States, a developed capitalist nation, each state has its own emphasis on industrial and agricultural development. Western European countries also help supply one another's needs. This method, instead of hindering, has accelerated modernization in these countries.

We must follow Comrade Mao Tse-tung's teaching by effecting overall planning and all-round consideration and taking the 800 million Chinese people into consideration in everything we do. If we cannot resolve contradictions between the central and local organs and each level makes its own additions to state plans and causes discrepancies in state plans by attaching many production and capital construction projects not included in the original state plans, then we will not be able to accelerate the four modernizations, raise our economic management and technological production levels or even carry on normal production; our capital construction projects cannot be completed for long periods of time and put into production; and our procurement personnel will be rushing here, there and everywhere. These chaotic conditions will certainly create an adventurist's paradise for the newborn bourgeois class elements.

Proportionate development of a planned national economy calls for effective specialization and coordination. It is an inevitable law governing modern mass production. It is also the most important method for raising production technology and labor efficiency, improving product quality and cutting the consumption of energy, raw and other materials and production costs. Marx said: "A nation's level of productivity is most clearly reflected by the degree of division of labor of that nation."[18] Lenin said: "Technical progress is bound to promote specialization in the various production departments," and "to raise the productivity of workers who are engaged in producing a certain part of the whole product, it is necessary to specialize production of this part."[19] Over the past twenty to thirty years, each day has brought new changes to the world's scientific technology. Specialized division of labor has become more meticulous and precise, and the scope of coordination has become larger and larger.

To fully develop our national economy, we must, under unified state planning, do a real good job in specialized division of labor and in promoting inter-department, inter-area and inter-enterprise coordination. Only by repeated balancing work and calculations under the condition of proportionately developing the economy in a planned way can we arrive at a correct answer to the question of which products are suitable for specialized productions and which are suitable for consolidated production, whether certain specialized productions are within the scope of the province and municipality, or that of the zone of the state, and which are the relatively economical organizations for supplying raw and other material, fuel, power, parts and accessories to the various enterprises. For example, a problem currently prevailing among enterprises is big and complete and small but complete. In a certain sense, this situation is inevitable at present. But if we cannot do a good job in specialized division of labor and wide coordination within all of society, this problem will be difficult to solve and will even continue to develop. Only by organizing specialized production of parts and accessories by professions and areas so as to insure supplies, by organizing specialized maintenance plants to give customers satisfactory service, and by assigning society's various specialized service trades the tasks of marketing, transportation, service of staff and workers and other such services can we really solve this problem.

Next, it is necessary to obey the law of value.

The law of value is a universal law in commodity economics. The fundamental point of this law is that the value of a commodity is determined by the working time needed by society to product it. The price of a commodity is based on its value. Exchange of commodities is done according to the principle of equal value. Under socialist conditions, the production and flow of commodities will continue to exist for a long time to come. They still require vigorous development in China. The law of value still plays an inalienable role in our economic life. While formulating and implementing plans, we must employ the law of value to reflect its requirements; we must demand that all enterprises (including national defense industries) strictly economize on the use of time, continuously achieve the optimum ratio between the costs of labor and materials (or the co-called "materialized labor" costs) and the economic effect, strictly apply economic accounting and strive to reduce per-unit cost and raise labor productivity and capital interest return. Otherwise, we are liable to cause tremendous losses and create confusion for our socialist cause. Each enterprise and its workers must never waste even one minute of time, or the enterprise or individual will be held responsible and charged for the loss. Without obeying the objective law of value, it is impossible to strictly obey the law of proportionate development in a planned way. Marx said: "The law of commodity value is decided by how much time society can use of the entire time under its control to produce each kind of a particular commodity."[20] Thus, the law of proportionate planned development and the law of value are inseparable and violators of these laws cannot avoid punishment.

Stalin said: A socialist society which produces commodities cannot do without the law of value. This is not a bad thing, "because this situation teaches our economic personnel to continuously improve production methods, reduce production costs, carry out economic accounting and make the enterprises earn profits. This is a very fine school of practice which enables our cadres in economic work to rapidly mature and become true leaders of socialist production in its present developing stage."[21] Only by settling accounts can we implement that objective law of value.

Comrade Mao Tse-tung said: "This law is a great school. Only by applying it can we educate our tens of millions of cadres and hundreds of millions of people and build our socialism and communism. Otherwise it would all be impossible."[22]

In nearly 30 years since the founding of our country, our cadres and masses have persistently studied in this great school. They have really mastered measurable skills, made measurable contributions and therefore guaranteed development of our national economy. However, due to the interference and sabotage by Lin Piao and the Gang of Four, our revolutionary teacher's directive could not be carried out and our planned economy suffered serious losses. To eliminate some confusions in our economy created by Lin Piao and the Gang of Four, we must apply the law of value to implement economic accounting. We must continuously improve our socialist economic management by keeping accounts to calculate the created value (production departments) or the realized value (circulation departments) and the consumption of materialized labor and living labor in production and circulation and review the results of our management. In order to apply the law of value to economic accounting, we must see to it that the prices we set can correctly reflect value. We should apply the law of value to institute our policy on price so that our planned price can help reasonably adjust the relationship between the interests of the state, the collective and the individual and the relationship between workers and peasants. In this way we can bring into full play the positive adjusting role of planned price for social production.

By having the plan come first and price second, we mean that we first of all draw up our plan in accordance with our social demands, and then we set reasonable prices for all kinds of products so that these prices serve the plan. We do not separate price form plan. Price is based on, but not absolutely equal to, value. If a price is set higher, the unit which produces the product will earn more profit. The converse is also true. Therefore, price is a major instrument of our planned economy. We must be good at handling this instrument. The Gang of Four did not allow anyone to pay attention to profits and bludgeoned anyone who did. Therefore, it was out of the question to apply the law of value, to use price as an instrument for carrying out the plan. As a result, the following occurred: Units concerned were not very willing to produce products urgently needed in society, such as ceramics, frying pans and other similar daily commodities, because they were procured at prices lower than those of industrial ceramic products and iron tubes. These units were blamed for "putting profit in command." Now that the Gang of Four has fallen, nobody is indiscriminately labeling others as "putting profit in command." We should appropriately raise the prices of commonly used ceramics and frying pans so that the law of value can play its role in helping fulfill the plan.

When Stalin said the law of value had only some influence at most on production under the socialist system instead of playing an adjusting role for production, he went too far. Marx said: "After elimination of the capitalist way of production and in the situation in which social production still exists, the determination of price still plays a dominant role in the following sense: Adjustment of labor time, distribution of social labor in all different production and bookkeeping (refers to accounting and other work--**JMJP** editor) will become more important than ever."[23] This was the viewpoint which Marx repeatedly explained. It helps us understand that the law of value does not fail to play an adjusting role for production under the socialist system. Our practice in economic construction also proves this point. While drawing up the state plan, we may and should implement the policy on price to bring into full play the adjusting role of the law of value for production.

The economic accounting system was seriously undermined when the Gang of Four were rampant. No distinction was made between those who worked and those how did not, between those who did more work and those who did less, between those who did heavy and those who did light work and between those who did a good job and those who did a poor one. Thus, the consumption of living labor was not calculated or supervised at all. Workers of some units did no work all year round, but received wages as usual; in some units, only casual workers worked, while regular workers did not; they took care of personal matters or fooled around. Now this state of affairs has been considerably changed, but not thoroughly enough.

For example, if thousands of workers at a certain construction project actually work only 5 to 5.5 hours a day on a long-term basis, more than 10,000 hours of labor a day will be lost. The state of affairs where labor is not calculated is not only an economic question, but also a serious political question damaging the attitude toward labor and the revolutionary qualities of the working class of our country. How can we still turn a blind eye to it and not make every effort to solve the question? Over a long period of time, many enterprises have not calculated or supervised their materialized labor and have willfully wasted raw and other materials and failed to calculate fixed funds and working capital, let alone how much value and profits they have earned.

This situation where there is no calculation or supervision is a fundamental reason why our enterprise management is disrupted. To eliminate chaos and restore order now, we must apply the law of value, strengthen economic accounting and, by using a target in kind and target in value, following the principle of to each according to his work, and linking enterprise management with the material interests of each staff and worker, must improve management and create a prerequisite for realization of the modernization of management. Without the above-mentioned calculation and supervision, all other measures for improving management are out of the question. In practicing economic accounting, we must make every possible effort to accurately indicate how much value has been actually earned and how much living labor and materialized labor have been consumed. By "making every possible effort," we mean it is actually impossible to accurately do so. In this regard there are many difficulties not easy to surmount; however, we still should make every effort possible to do so.

Third, it is necessary to guarantee the unity of interests between the state, the enterprise and the individual.

Comrade Mao Tse-tung, said: "Consideration must be given to both sides, not to just one, whether they are the state and the factory, the state and the worker, the factory and the worker, the state and the cooperative, the state and the peasant, or the cooperative and the peasant."[24] The unity of interests between the state, the production unit and the individual producer is determined by the socialist system. The inevitable reflection of the unity of interests is one of the fundamental laws of the socialist economic management system. In the past, when considering the question of the management system, we used to be more concerned about the relationship between higher levels and lower levels inside the state or about the relationship between the central authorities and the local authorities. In other words, we were more concerned about the question of centralization and decentralization. Such consideration was of course necessary. This was to implement Comrade Mao Tse-tung's directive on correctly handling well the relationship between the central authorities and the local authorities. But we gave less concern to the question of guaranteeing the unity of interests between the state, the enterprise and the individual in terms of the economic relationship. This showed that we failed to fully implement Comrade Mao Tse-tung's entire directive on this question. In fact, no matter how we divide the work between higher levels and lower levels and no matter who manages enterprises, we have to fist take into consideration the economic relationship between the state, the enterprise and the individual. This is because first of all the fundamental aim of socialist economy is to raise the people's (certainly including staff and workers) level of material and cultural well-being. If we do not consider the interests of staff and workers, we are violating the fundamental aim of the socialist economy. The second reason is that since staff and workers and the enterprises to which they belong are direct producers and organizers of production, the rapid development of production cannot possibly be guaranteed if we do not first take their interests into consideration. The third reason is that neither the central state organ nor the local state organ has a relatively clear understanding of the urgent needs in an enterprise's economic activities, because neither is the administrative organization directly responsible for the economic task. Therefore, inappropriate centralization or decentralization often results in damaging the development of economic construction. This is the so-called "centralization causes death; decentralization causes disorder." The question will be further discussed later.

Comrade Hua Kuo-feng repeatedly instructed: If there is not objective reason, we should make a distinction between those enterprises run well and those run poorly and between those making profits and those suffering deficits. This involved the question of the relationship between the state and the enterprise. Handling the relationship between the state and the enterprise well is of important significance to accelerating realization of the four modernizations. Whether or not we handle the relationship between the state and the enterprise, but also directly concerns the interests of each individual staff and worker. Because the enterprise under the system of socialist ownership by the whole people is the basic unit of socialist economy, the relationship between the worker and the state is closely linked with the relationship between the enterprise and the state.

In handling the relationship between the state and the enterprise, we should regard implementation of the state's unified plan as the basic prerequisite. Under this prerequisite we must also consider the requirements of the law of value. We must, under the unified plan of the state, clearly understand the economic responsibility of both the state and the enterprise.

At present it is necessary to consider the possibility of suitably expanding the enterprises' authorities so that the leaderships of various enterprise and the masses will take the initiative and concern themselves with the enterprises' economic activities. Previously it was stipulated in the 70-point decision on industry that the state practices the "five fixes" among the enterprises, while the enterprises provide the state with the "five guarantees." The thirty-point decision on industry again puts forward the "five fixes" and the eight economic and technical norms for the evaluation of enterprise. This is an important issue. We must further conduct investigation and study, and improve all the rules concerned. The current eight norms do not include a norm on the use of fixed assets. This is not conducive to making enterprises make good use of investments and create even greater wealth for the state. It looks like we have to solve this issue when we study how to improve management.[25]

The "fixes" and "guarantees" manifest the responsibilities of both the state and enterprises. On the one hand, it is necessary to provide and guarantee the conditions needed by enterprises to carry out normal production. The state and coordinating units should be held responsible economically if they fail to provide this guarantee and thus hamper the normal operations of enterprises in production. On the other hand, it is also essential to strictly assign the tasks that enterprises should fulfill. Enterprises that fulfill all their tasks should be given certain rewards. For example, some funds should be left to enterprises for rewarding advanced collectives and individuals, improving the workers' well-being and expanding production. If enterprises and individuals fail to fulfill their tasks, they should be held economically responsible.

Lenin said: "Various trusts and enterprises are built on the foundation of the economic accounting system, precisely because they are responsible for themselves and they are fully responsible in making sure that their own enterprises do not lose money. If they fail to do so, I think they should stand trail and all the managers should be punished by having all their properties confiscated and their freedom stripped off over a long period (perhaps they may be released on parole after a certain period)."[26]

We must adhere to the principle illustrated in Lenin's instruction to give awards to enterprises that have run themselves well and made money, and punish those that do not run themselves well and lose money. Legal action must be taken against the responsible leaders of enterprises where management is alarmingly chaotic, laws and discipline are defied and there are heavy financial losses. They should be punished or fined. New leading groups must be organized to replace the old ones. Those derelict in their duties must not be left unpunished by the law.

In short, running enterprises well not only benefits the state but also all workers and leaders of enterprises, whereas failing to do so harms the workers of enterprises, particularly the leaders. We must directly link the interest of the state, the collective and the individual together and help everyone in an enterprise to be concerned about the fulfillment of state plans and about the results of enterprise management from the point of material interests.

The Gang of Four opposed efforts to integrate the interests of individuals with those of the collective, and basically denied the interests of individuals. This is an entirely reactionary pseudo-leftist and genuinely rightist ideological trend that runs counter to Marxism-Leninism. The basic purpose of all communists is to work for the interest of the majority of people. If communists fail to work for the interests of the majority of people, then why do the masses need the Communist Party and why should they support it? The interests of the majority of people naturally mean the interests of the collective as well as the interests of the individual. Lenin said: "We say that we must build all the major departments of the national economy on the concern for the interests of the individuals, carry out joint discussions and assign some people to assume sole responsibility for doing this work well. However, we have suffered every step we make, because we fail to adhere to this principle.[27] In essence, are we not all suffering every step we make? Therefore, Comrade Mao Tsetung said it well: "All empty talk is useless. We must give material benefits to the people that they can see for themselves."[28]

To properly handle the question of one's material benefit, we must resolutely implement the principles "from each according to his ability: and "to each according to his work." Comrade Hua Kuo-feng pointed out recently: Now that we have determined the general policy and we also have the principle and auxiliary principles, what we should do now is to implement them quickly; what should be calculated on a piecework basis should be done so and whoever should receive bonuses should receive them. We should not be besieged by all kinds of worries.

The practice of tens of millions of people over a long period of time has proven that, during the historical period of socialist society, the national economy will be strengthened and the socialist system further consolidated and developed by implementing the principle "to each according to his work," and that the national economy will not be able to develop and the socialist system will be impaired when the principle "to each according to his work" is not implemented. This is an economic law independent of man's will. If people do their work according to this law, they will be rewarded; otherwise they will be punished.

According to the State Bureau of Labor, during the first 5-year plan period, gross industrial production increased at an average of 18 percent annually, labor productivity increased at an average annual rate of 8.7 percent, and workers' wages increased at an average of 7.4 percent annually. During that period, the industrial growth of 59 percent depended on raising labor productivity. But after 1958, wages did not increase in due time and growth of labor productivity was not normal. As a result industrial growth depended entirely or for the most part on increasing the number of workers. If the growth of labor productivity could be maintained at 8.7 percent annually, the 1977 labor productivity by the workers of the industrial, capital construction, and communications and transportation sectors should be three times the current rate. In other words, the total number of workers could be two-thirds less. Is this lesson thorough enough? Now that we are reinstating this law, it is certain that we can achieve good results. As a matter of fact, we already have achieved good results in certain areas.

Comrade Li Hsien-nien once pointed out that in the past, whenever a pay raise was mentioned, the financial comrades always worried that it would tip the balance between revenue and expenditures; but the results of year-end accounting showed that the profit revenue by the state-run enterprises was still increasing, and it was still the Ministry of Finance which "made the fortune." This is a very good conclusion of our practical experience over the last 20 years and more.

At any rate, when we do our work according to economic law we must persist in putting politics in command in the first place and never put politics in a secondary position. On the contrary, we must uphold the party's leadership and the mass line before we can correctly solve all sorts of problems and surmount all sorts of obstacles in the course of our work. The Gang of Four's pernicious influence must be eradicated, the offensive launched by the newborn bourgeoisie must be crushed, and certain forces of habit and all kinds of erroneous tendencies which exist among our comrades must be combated. For example, some people might indulge in economism and slacken political work on the pretext of following the economic law; or they might ignore the plight of the masses, use coercion and force on the pretext of putting politics in command; or they might do all sorts of evils on other pretexts. All this must be dealt with by strengthening the party leadership, by genuinely putting the proletarian politics in command and by unifying everybody's understanding of the long-range and fundamental interests.

In short, putting proletarian politics in command and working according to objective law should go hand in hand. Without putting proletarian politics in command we cannot uphold the socialist orientation, resolutely implement the party's line, principles and policies and cannot firmly realize the general task for the new period; on the other hand, the Marxist method of putting politics in command must be in accord with economic law, and acting rashly and subjectively by denying and violating economic law will certainly cause economic and political losses and will completely violate the fundamental principles of putting proletarian politics in command.

III. Expand the Economic Organizations and the Role of the Economic Means

The socialist system requires the entire country's production to proceed according to plan, and this has created more planning organizations and industrial management organizations in socialist countries than in capitalist countries. These organizations are necessary, but are they too many considering the total number throughout the country? And would it be more effective if these organizations handed over their economic administration to the economic organizations, which will handle such work by economic means? This is a question we must consider seriously.

In his work "State and Revolution," Lenin thought that the state apparatus of the dictatorship of the proletariat should be very simple because its work in economic administration "has been simplified to the extreme by capitalism." But now we realize that the work has not been simplified as Lenin had thought. The scope of our administrative work is still too large, and many pompous but inefficient organizations have been unnecessarily established. And they have prevented us from utilizing the already simplified system left by capitalism and prevented us from managing the economy according to economic laws.

Administrative measures are always necessary and scientific management of an economic organization can be shown by its scientific administration. The socialist states' economic administrative departments can fully master the methods of scientific management, work according to economic laws, and attain the goal of simplification, unity, efficiency, economy and being unbureaucratic. But economic administration cannot primarily depend on purely administrative methods. This is because:

First, purely administrative methods often mean applying the work methods of ordinary administrative organizations (which do not have economic responsibilities and economic accounting systems) on the economic aspects. Instead of striving to study, adapt and use economic laws to administer economic work, they tend to consider administrative conveniences and require their economic activities be mechanically adapted to administrative systems, channels and division. This has abetted the large and comprehensive or small and comprehensive enterprise structure.

It has also abetted gratis transfers, gratis supply and gratis reimbursement; abetted the supply system, which disregards economic responsibilities and economic accounting; and abetted bureaucratization of economic activities and the officially supervised industry and commerce, as well as the belief that the will of the society, the government and higher authorities are almighty. All this would give rise to the mistakes of commanding subjectively and unscrupulously.

Second, because of these methods, the levels of economic management and economic activities would develop according to the levels and activities of the administrative organizations. This would cause duplication, red tape, much time spent in processing paperwork and unresolved problems, thus immensely hindering the efficiency of economic work and wasting opportunities for economic activities.

Third, the administrative structure, be it hierarchial or departmental, often cannot adapt to the structure of product supply and marketing and to the objective needs of other economic activities. Thus the replacement of economic classification by administrative classification will not only confuse the flow of commodities and materials and cause overstocking, but sometimes will even ridiculously disrupt rational economic ties, causing man-made economic disruptions and blockades, destroying commodity flow and allocation of products and obstructing normal economic development.

Fourth, purely administrative methods often cannot correctly and reflect in a timely way the relationship of material benefits between the central and local departments, and the relationship among the local departments, and it usually takes a long time before such a situation is reflected in the leading departments and corrected. Since the administrative leadership bears no direct economic responsibilities for the enterprises' profits or losses, it is not sensitive to, and lacks concern for, good or bad enterprises management, its judgment and decision will hardly be quick, correct, efficient, and it is apt to cause losses to the state, the enterprises, the workers and the consumers.

Fifth, relying on pure administrative measures is not good for bringing into play the initiative and creativeness of lower-level localities, enterprises and the broad masses of staffers and workers. It will also deprive the enterprises of their inherent power and often make those enterprise leaders, staffers and workers who desire progress and possess revolutionary enthusiasm feel that they find no scope for their energies or at least cannot make sufficient and effective use of their energies. All they can do is wait for arrangements and instructions of their superiors. What a big loss, both tangible and intangible! For this reason, the scope of management's relying on pure administrative measures should be reduced to the minimum, and maximum volume of economic work should be switched from the government administrative scope to that of enterprise operation. The entrprises themselves should also reduce the scope of management's relying on pure administration measures to the minimum, and expand the scope of management by relying on economic measures.

To enlarge the role of economic organization and measures, it is necessary to effect a series of economic reorganizations and reforms and tackle a series of concrete problems. We offer suggestions on only four aspects:

1. Popularize the Contract System

The contract system is being implemented in many fields of our country's economic work. Practice shows that this is a more effective form which must be vigorously popularized. Normally the contract system is one under which a contract is signed directly by and between two enterprises.

In signing the contract, they always make more careful consideration of their respective economic interests and advance more careful and practical proposals to each other. Moreover, the contract is signed out of their own will and for mutual binding without any factors of coercion and commandism. Any shortcomings can be easily remedied, without the necessity of seeking approval through channels.

The contract system can be implemented between grassroots enterprises, among producers, suppliers and sellers, between big and specialized companies, between local companies themselves and between various types of companies and grassroots enterprises so as to improve the efficiency of economic work, insure the conduct of economic activities in a planned manner and lighten the burdens of administrative organs at all levels. Furthermore, we think that the contract system may also be introduced between the state and enterprises (including industrial and agricultural enterprises, enterprises owned by all people and those of collective ownership) and even between the central authorities and the localities, between the localities themselves, between localities of different levels and between enterprises and their staff and workers. The contract system, if implemented between the state and enterprises, will especially play an important role in clearly defining the responsibilities of both the state and the enterprises, enhancing the enterprises' initiative and improving the chaotic conditions presently existing in economic management.

In order to have the contract system effectively and correctly play its role, it is still necessary, first of all, to put proletarian politics in command. Meanwhile, necessary support and guarantees by many other economic factors are also essential. It is not true that all problems will automatically be solve and everything will be in order with implementation of the contract system. But it is certain and without doubt that the adoption of this system is good for developing the national economy in a planned manner and accelerating the growth of the national economy, conducive to the development of specialization and cooperation in production; helpful in fulfilling in an all-round way the economic and technical targets, primarily the targets of quality and variety and power conservation, fuel, raw materials and supplies; good for bringing the role of the law of value into play, strengthening economic accounting and enhancing labor productivity and capital profitability; conducive to vigorously overcoming bureaucracy and extravagance, extensively promoting and the mass line and greatly enhancing the level of economic management; and helpful in training economic management personnel.

2. Develop Specialized Companies

In the draft "Decision on Some Problems in Accelerating Industrial Development" worked out by the central authorities, it is stated: "Organizing specialized production is an inevitable tendency of the development of modernized industries, the all-embracing complexes, large or small, will not only cause serious extravagance but also adversely hinder the progress of productive techniques and impede the enhancement of labor productivity." Lenin said: "When the scattered enterprises have organized themselves into a syndicate, there will be noticeable frugality. This is told in economics and also clearly illustrated by all syndicates, cartels and trusts."[29]

The experience of developed capitalist countries tells us that to organize specialization and cooperation according to different trades and localities and organize scattered enterprises into specialized companies (including national companies, regional companies, incorporation of enterprises of the same trade and incorporation of enterprises of related trades) is not only an inevitable trend in modern industrial development but also an objective demand in developing industry at high speed and with high standards. In the early 1960's we made some attempts in this respect.

We set up on a trial basis thirteen specialized companies under the industrial and communications departments of the central government and also ran some others in certain provinces and municipalities, such as the various specialized companies in Shanghai and the silk companies in Chekiang. Except those set up in Shanghai, all the other specialized companies operated for a short time.

Despite interference by Liu Shao-chi and Chen Po-ta, coupled with inexperience as well as shortcomings and mistakes in work, these companies still played a certain role in promoting the development of production. Take for example the aluminum company established by the Ministry of Metallurgical Industry with the approval of the State Council in October 1964. The production of raw materials, semifinished products and auxiliary materials was incorporated in one specialized company, thereby bringing about close cooperation and coordination in the order of work at both higher and lower levels. Moreover, the company's management was placed under centralized leadership, kept in touch with production units, eliminated unnecessary channels and had flexibility in operation. As a result, production developed rapidly. After the suspension of operation of the aluminum company, little increase in output was registered in the 10-year period from 1966 to 1976. However, the amount of state investment during these 10 years was five times that of 1965 and 1966.

Similar conditions existed in other specialized companies before and after their establishment. The shortcomings in their operation in the past were that they failed to consider the interests of the localities. For example, the tobacco company absorbed all the revenues collectible by the localities on tobacco sales and gave little consideration to the interests of the peasants in non-traditional tobacco-producing areas. There will be no difficulty in solving problems like this in the future. Hereafter, all specialized companies run by the various ministries of the central government should consider the interests of the localities while those operated by the localities should also be subject to the supervision of the departments concerned of the central government.

Changing the backward production form of all-embracing complexes, large or small, into socialist specialized companies organized for the sake of specialization and cooperation is a deep going transformation from the economic base to the sphere of superstructure. It is a heavy and complicated task requiring a sound policy and involving many factors, which must be carried out in a planned way and step by step on the basis of investigations and study, through unified planning and serious experimentation at selected places and by adopting an active but careful policy.

3. Strengthen the Bank's Role

Lenin said: **Socialism cannot be realized without a big bank**. A big bank **is** the state organ **needed** by us in realizing socialism, and we can . . . turn it into a **bigger** more democratic and more all-embracing organ. At that time, quantity will be transferred into quality. A unified and huge state bank, together with its offices in various villages and factories . . . is a state **book-keeping organ**, and a state **calculating organ** for production and distribution of products, and may also be called **a backbone** in a socialist society.[30]

Since liberation, the bank has done work in many fields and has accumulated an abundance of experiences. Comrade Hua Kuo-feng said: "We must fully utilize finance, banking and credit in promoting and supervise economic undertakings."[31] The bank is the nation's accounting, credit and payments center. It has branches throughout the country. Many economic management functions of the state can be performed by the bank. The bank can perform these functions more flexibly and efficiently than administrative organs. The bank can also promote and supervise all undertakings of the enterprises.

Before the Cultural Revolution, our state bank effectively promoted and supervised the enterprises' various activities through credit loans and funds appropriations. At that time, the bank made loans to the enterprises on three conditions: A) The enterprise had a material guarantee for the loan; B) the enterprise had legitimate plans approved by higher level authorities; and C) the enterprise guaranteed repayments on time. These conditions served well at that time. But over the past dozen years or so, because of interference and sabotage by Lin Piao and the Gang of Four, these fine measures were negated. Now the bank is only concerned with wage funds and a part of the capital construction investments and plays only a insignificant role in enterprise operations. This is also an evil result of relying only on administrative measures (such as notes endorsed by the head of an administrative organ) instead of relying on economic measures. To rapidly raise the level of economic management and end confusion in many industrial and commercial enterprises and capital construction units, we must revive and vigorously strengthen the bank's role.

4. Develop Economic Legislation and the Economic Judicial System

While implementing the contract system, developing specialized companies, strengthening the bank's role and promoting other measures as mentioned above, we expect various complicated disputes to arise. To rapidly, fairly and correctly solve these disputes, we must strengthen economic legislation and economic judicial work; reflect the interests of the state, the enterprises and the individual staff members and workers as well as the relationship between these interests when issuing laws; and charge the judicial organs with the job of handling problems according to the law. Otherwise, we cannot carry out the above mentioned measures and may even retrogress to the old way of solely relying on administrative actions. Although at present we have a nominal contract system, many contracts cannot be fulfilled or cannot be thoroughly fulfilled. Even if an enterprise is fined for failure to fulfill a contract, the fine is either listed as a production cost or made up from the enterprise's profit without directly affecting the immediate interests of enterprise's leaders, staff members and workers. We have issued many fine rules and regulations, but frequently they are not strictly legal and lack clear binding power. To insure that these rules and regulations are lawful and to give them clearly defined power, not only must we issue strict legislation regarding economic matters and carry out extensive propaganda work among the people of the whole nation, but we must also set up strict economic judicial organs to sternly handle, in accord with legal procedures, all enterprises or individual violating economic laws.

IV. Seriously Implement the Policy of Taking Agriculture as the Foundation

In developing the national economy, we must take agriculture as the foundation. This is a fundamental experience in economic history. Following the physiocrats, Marx further expounded and proved this experience. Comrade Mao Tse-tung prescribed it as a basic principle for our nation's socialist construction. This principle is entirely correct. Whether or not our national economy can have sustained, steady and rapid growth largely depends on whether or not we can rapidly develop our agriculture. The 10-year program sets a production target for the nation of 800 billion catties of grain by 1985. It is a target that has a vital bearing on the whole situation. Now that the central organs have decided to accelerate the four modernizations, it has become even more important for us to accelerate agricultural development.

After the Gang of Four was smashed, the party Central Committee headed by Chairman Hua and many provincial leading organs proposed and adopted many important measures to gradually improve the agricultural situation. These measures have been warmly supported by peasants throughout the nation.

Because of the interference and sabotage of Liu Shao-chi, Lin Piao and, particularly, the Gang of Four, plus the defects in our own work, the agriculture situation is still serious. The average per-capita grain distribution in 1977 only matched that of 1955. This shows that grain increases were only sufficient to compensate for increases in consumption caused by population growth and by industrial use. To change the situation of protracted slow agricultural development, we must also make a series of important decisions including vigorously developing the livestock and forestry industries as well as commune and brigade-run industries and joint agricultural-industrial enterprises. Here we will only discuss two principle issues based on a number of directives issued by Comrades Mao Tsetung and Hua Kuo-feng and the party Central Committee.

First, minimize the scissors diffferentialin the exchange prices of industrial and agricultural products.

Application of the law of value in the socialist economy definitely requires exchanges of industrial and agricultural products at equal value in order to eliminate the scissors differential between them. Comrade Mao Tsetung gave a specific instruction more than twenty years ago: **"In the exchange of industrial and agricultural products we follow a policy of narrowing the price scissors, a policy of exchanging equal or roughly equal values."**[32] Comrade Hua Kuo-feng said in his report to the Fifth NPC, "the law of value must be consciously applied under the guidance of the unified state plan. We must earnestly study the price parities between industrial and agricultural products.... To promote production, we must appropriately raise the purchase price of agricultural products and, as costs are cut down, properly reduce the prices of manufactured goods, especially those produced to support agriculture." Comrade Li Hsien-nien at the National Capital Construction Conference reaffirmed this policy, which had long since been decided upon by the party Central Committee, pointing out that the present task is to formulate a plan to implement the policy after thorough investigation. Therefore, narrowing the scissors differential is the party's established policy and a proper plan has to be formulated to insure that the policy is implemented.

It should be pointed out here that in the twenty-nine years since the founding of the PRC, the purchase price for agricultural products has doubled while the retail price of industrial products increased 28 percent. Although the difference between the two has been gradually narrowed it is still too large. The big scissors differential and the slow rate at which the differential has been narrowed dampens the peasants' enthusiasm to develop production. Except from those areas that have fared a little better, peasants in many areas after a year's toil may increase production but have little or no increase in income. In a few places they even had a reduction in income despite increase production. There are many reasons for this. The existence of the scissors differential, however, is the most important reason.   If this situation remains unchanged it will hinder rapid agricultural development, the movement to learn from Tachai in agriculture, agricultural modernization and full implementation of the various rural policies. The situation is unfavorable for the consolidation of the worker-peasant alliance, narrowing the gap between workers and peasants and between town and country, and implementation of the principle of taking agriculture as the foundation. Adjustment of the parity rate of industrial and agricultural products is a complicated matter and requires the solution of many concrete problems and problems related to policy. However, the difficulties can be overcome. If the overwhelming majority of the peasants have lessened burdens and increased incomes it will be possible to fully implement the principle of taking agriculture as the foundation and will greatly enhance the acceleration of agricultural development, rural development and agricultural modernization. Many seemingly insurmountable difficulties will be overcome.

If the burdens are not lessened it will be very difficult to change the situation prevailing during the past twenty years in which the development of agricultural was slow. Thus, the four modernizations will be hampered. Obviously, a modern, rich and powerful socialist China can never be built on top of a poverty-stricken and backward countryside.

Second, truly affirm the peasants' collective ownership and the production teams' own rights.

Comrade Mao Tse-tung at the March 1959 second Chengchow conference poignantly criticized the wrongdoing of taking away, without compensation, fruits of labor of the peasants and production teams. The revised draft regulation on people's commune work (the sixty-article document), formulated under the personal guidance of Comrade Mao Tse-tung in 1961, emphasized protection of the production teams' right to run their own affairs. In this draft regulation, the production brigade was designated as the basic accounting unit. Later, the production team was designated as the basic accounting unit. As a result, the production teams' right to run their own affairs should have been increased. However, due to the interference and sabotage by Lin Piao and the Gang of Four, this problem remained unsolved during the past ten years. In a considerable number of localities, the peasants' collective ownership has not been protected and recognized. The number of places in which this ownership has not been completely protected and recognized is still greater.

Wherever a commune and farming are not run democratically, the peasants' collective ownership and in turn the socialist economic and political systems that affect 700 million peasants are actually not recognized. Why was there such a phenomenon throughout the country as found in Hsianghsiang, where the production team's burden was unnecessarily purposely increased? Why were there such incidences as found in Hsuni and many other counties, where peasants' personal rights were violated? Why could certain leading organizations arbitrarily order the peasants to pull and uproot all they planted and replace it with other crops without bearing legal and economic responsibilities for the losses incurred? Why could certain leading organizations, without the peasants' consent after discussion, order the transition, from the production team to the production brigade, of the function of the basic accounting unit of the people's communes in one or more than one country and the liquidation of various rights of the commune members? This shows that many comrades do not bear in mind such things as the peasants' collective ownership, the right to run their own affairs in the production teams, production brigades and people's communes and the various basic systems of the people's communes. Therefore, the collective economic rights and interests of the commune and its subordinate units, and even the property and personal rights of individual commune members, were freely disposed of by the higher level and by one or several leaders, including cadres of the commune and its subordinate levels, while the organizations at the various levels of the commune, the meetings of the representatives of the commune members and of the commune members themselves were totally ignored.

The party Central Committee headed by Comrade Hua Kuo-feng has resolutely corrected such wrongdoings, fully embodying the desire of the masses of peasants. Yet, not only the party's policy but the state's clear-cut, mistake-free and rock-firm systems are needed to thoroughly solve this problem. The constitution stipulates that the state insures the consolidation and development of the socialist economy of collective ownership by the working people, that the state prohibits encroachment upon the socialist public property and that commune members may farm shall plots of land for personal needs and engage in limited household sideline production. These are all very good but not quite enough. That is why there are still people who feel no qualms in violating these stipulations. This shows that to thoroughly solve this problem, special laws and courts are needed to firmly punish whosoever dares to violate this law.

To safeguard the people's commune's collective ownership, all enterprises, organizations and PLA units (except otherwise stipulated by law) of the state should adopt the contract system in their economic relations with the commune or its subordinate units. This should also be adopted in the economic relations between communes, between production brigades, between production teams between communes and production brigades on the one hand and the production teams on the other, and between communes and its subordinate units on the one hand and the commune members on the other. The contract should be entered into according to set procedures and in a democratic way. Communes and their subordinate units as well as the commune members may refuse to honor any demand beyond the contract terms and have the right to demand compensation for losses resulting from the other party's violation of these terms.

Only thus can there be genuine collective ownership. Only on this basis can peasants realize that they are the masters of their own fate, the production team, the production brigade, the commune and the state. Only thus will they really, enthusiastically and boldly develop agricultural production and build a modern socialist countryside. This will by no means weaken but certainly strengthen the leadership of the party and the state over the peasants and will by no means hamper but certainly guarantee the transition under really ripe conditions.

To accelerate the development of agricultural production and modernization, it is also necessary to popularize the various specialized agricultural techniques and specialized production, develop farm crop processing and other industries in the countryside according to state plans, develop forestry, animal breeding and fishery industries, develop education and culture in the countryside and greatly raise the scientific and technical level of all the peasants, particularly the youths. All this will not be difficult to implement step by step provided the peasants' income is increased, the right of the communes and their subordinate units to run their own affairs is protected and the commune is run in a democratic way.

To bring forth the peasants' enthusiasm for production, it is naturally necessary to implement the socialist principle of to each according to his work and more pay for more work, to run the commune in a democratic way, to make accounts open to the public and to fully carry out the central authorities' various rural work policies and directives. Here we will not go into details on all of them.

V. Strengthen the Study of Economics and Raise its Level

Engels said: The proletarian political party's "entire theoretical content was produced by the study of political economy."[33] Economics is a science for studying economic laws. To be able to act according to economic laws, we must step up the popularization of the study of economics and raise its level. We are developing our country's socialist construction and realizing the four socialist modernizations on an unprecedented large scale and with an unprecedented speed in Chinese history. This calls for vastly expanding our country's economics-study contingent, because we must study many economic problems, many of which require meticulous and quantitative study. In addition to the great deal of work now being carried out by the various units, we still need many specialized economic research organs (including research activities in the universities) to assist the state organs. At present our economic research contingent is really too weak.

In our economic research work, we must study many important theoretical problems as well as many important practical ones. We must study and sum up

China's construction experiences as well as those of foreign countries. In the field of economic science, like any other major science, many new subjects are being developed at present.

We are faced with a host of important and complicated problems, such as the formulation of plans and management systems for these plans, adjustments to wages and prices, expansion of foreign trade, introduction of foreign technologies and the resulting financial problems.

NOTES

1. *Selected Works of Marx and Engels*, "Marx to Ludwig Kugelmann" (July 11, 1868), Vol. IV, p. 368.

2. *Selected Works of Lenin*, "Who Are the 'Friends of the People' and How Did They Attack the Social Democrats?" (1894), Vol. I, pp. 10 and 33.

3. "Talk at an Enlarged Working Conference Convened by the CCP Central Committee" (January 30, 1962).

4. "Sum Up the Ten Years," (June 18, 1966).

5. *Selected Works of Lenin*, "On Trade Unions, the Current Situation and Trotsky's Mistakes" (December 30, 1920), Vol. XXXII, p. 15.

6. *Selected Works of Marx and Engels*, "Marx to Ludwig Kugelmann" (July 11, 1868), Vol. IV, p. 369.

7. *Selected Works of Marx and Engels*, "Families and the Origins of Private Ownership and States" (1884), Vol. IV, p. 171.

8. *Selected Works of Mao Tsetung*, "On the Correct Handling of Contradictions Among the People" (February 22, 1957), Vol. V, p. 374.

9. *The Problems of Socialist Economy in the Soviet Union* (1961), p. 5, 1962 edition, People's Publishing House.

10. *Complete Works of Stalin*, Vol. VII, p. 248.

11. *Selected Works of Mao Tsetung*, "On the Ten Major Relations" (April 25, 1956), Vol. V, p. 287.

12. *Complete Works of Marx and Engels*, "On Capital: Vol. I," (1867), Vol. XXIII, p. 394.

13. *Ibid.*, pp. 367-368.

14. *Selected Works of Lenin*, "On Infantilism of 'Leftists' and the Petty Bourgeoisie" (1918), Vol. III, p. 555.

15. *Complete Works of Lenin*, "Conference of the All-Russia Central Executive Council" (1920), Vol. XXVII, p. 285.

16. *Complete Works of Lenin*, "Speech at the Third All-Russia Congress of Water Transport Workers" (1920), Vol. XXX, p. 395.

17. *An Outline of a Critique of Political Economy* (1857-1858), Book I, p. 112, 1975 edition, People's Publishing House.

18. *Complete Works of Marx and Engels*, "German Ideology" (1845-1846), Vol. III, p. 24.

19. *Complete Works of Lenin*, "On So-Called Market Problems" (1893), Vol. I, pp. 84-85.

20. *Complete Works of Marx and Engels*, "On Capital," Vol. I, (1867), Vol. XXIII, p. 394.

21. *Problems of Socialist Economy in the Soviet Union* (1952), p. 15, 1961 edition, People's Publishing House.

22. "A Comment on 'A Report on the Proceedings of the Five-Level Cadres Conference'" (March 30, 1959), quoted from Comrade Hua Kuo-feng's speech at the National Finance and Trade Conference held on 7 July to learn from Teaching and Tachai.

23. *Complete Works of Marx and Engels*, Vol. XXV, "On Capital," Vol. III, (1894), p. 963.

24. *Selected Works of Mao Tsetung*, 24. "On the 10 Major Relationships" (April 25, 1956), Vol. V, p. 275.

25. "70-Point Regulations for Industry," that is, "Draft Work Regulations for State-Run Industrial Enterprise" issued by the CCP Central Committee on September 16, 1961.

"Five fixes" and "five guarantees" are stipulations of the "70-Point Regulations for Industry." "Five fixes" are production conditions provided to enterprise by the state and production requirements for enterprise fixed by the state. The "five fixes" are: A) The fixing of production plans and scale; B) the fixing of the number of personnel and organizations; C) the fixing of supply sources and consumption quotas for principal raw and other materials, fuel, power and tools; D) the fixing of set assets and circulating funds; and E) the fixing of coordination and cooperation. The "five guarantees" are enterprise' obligations to the state. They are: A) Guarantee of quantity, quality and variety of products; B) guarantee not to exceed the total wage quota; C) guarantee to fulfill the cost plan and do everything possible to reduce production costs; D) guarantee to fulfill the profit plan; and E) guarantee the life of major equipment in a fixed period of time.

The "30-Point Regulations for Industry" refers to the "Resolution (Draft) on Some Problems of Accelerating Industrial Development" issued by the CCP Central Committee in April 1978.

The eight economic and technological targets are those for an all-round check up of enterprises' production and management set by the "30-Point Regulations for Industry." The targets are: A) Output; B) product variety; C) quality; D) consumption; E) labor productivity; F) costs; G) profits; and H) appropriation of circulating funds.

26. *Complete Works of Lenin*, "To the Financial Commissariat" (February 1, 1922), Vol. XXXV, p. 549.

27. *Complete Works of Lenin*, "New Economic Policy and Tasks for the Political Education Bureau" (1921), Vol. XXXIII, p 51

28. *Selected Works of Mao Tsetung*, "Economic and Financial Problems (1942), p. 876, the Northeast Bookstore Edition.

29. *Selected Works of Lenin*, "Where Is the Road Out in the Face of Great Calamities?" (1917), Vol III, p. 150.

30. *Selected Works of Lenin*, "Can the Bolsheviks Maintain Political Power?" (from late September to October 1, 1917), Vol III, p.311

31. "Report on the Government's Work at First Session of the Fifth NPC," (6 February 1978).

32. *Selected Works of Mao Tsetung*, "On The Ten Major Relationships" (April 25, 1956), Vol. V, p. 274.

33. *Selected Works of Marx and Engels*, "Karl Marx' Critique of Political Economy" (August 1859), Vol. II, p. 116.

DOCUMENT NO. 10

DECISION OF THE CENTRAL COMMITTEE OF THE COMMUNIST PARTY OF CHINA ON SOME QUESTIONS CONCERNING THE ACCELERATION OF AGRICULTURAL DEVELOPMENT (Draft)

A Document of the Central Committee of the Chinese Communist Party, *Chung-fa* (1979) No. 4

Part I

(**Issues & Studies**, Vol. XV, No. 7, July 1979)

Part II

(**Issues & Studies**, Vol. XV, No. 8, August 1979)

Part I

Circular of the Central Committee of the Communist Party of China

Party Committees in Various Provinces, Municipalities, and Autonomous Regions; Party Committees in Various Military Regions, Military Districts, and Field Armies; Party Committees and Groups in Departments, Ministries, and Commissions of the Central and State Organs; Party Committees at the Military Commission, Various Headquarters, and Branches of the Armed Forces, and Party Groups of People's Organizations:

Issued to you now are "Decisions of the Central Committee of the Communist Party of China on Some Questions Concerning the Acceleration of Agricultural Development" (Draft), and "Regulations on the Work in the Rural People's Communes" (Draft for Trial Use). The third plenary session of the Eleventh Central Committee has ratified these two documents in principle and agreed to distribute them to the provinces, municipalities, and autonomous regions for discussion, trial use, and suggestions for further revision. The Party committees and groups should distribute copies of these two documents to the people's communes quickly, before the busy period of spring planting, transmit the contents of the documents to the cadres and commune members in the mass rural areas, organize them for study and discussion, and then implement the documents on a trial basis. This should be done in time to involve the socialist initiative of the masses of cadres and commune members in promoting the great growth of agricultural production.

The Party committees in the various provinces, municipalities, and autonomous regions, the Party committees and groups of the departments, ministries, and commissions of the central and state organs, as well as the Party groups in the people's organizations should submit the suggestions for revising the "Decisions" and the "New 60 Articles" collected in their own regions or units to the Central Committee in the first half of 1979 and again by the end of November 1979. The suggestions for revision from the army will be gathered by the General Political Department which will be responsible for submitting them to the Central Committee. After revision, the Central Committee will formally issue these two documents. This winter or next spring you should again organize the rural cadres and commune members for study and discussion. These documents should be used to train rural cadres, to integrate conscientiously their experience, and to raise the level of ideological policy. It is expected that any difficulties with or suggestions about this directive will be presented to the Central Committee.

Central Committee of the Communist
Party of China January 11, 1989

(Issued by the Administrative Office of the
Central Committee of the Communist Party
of China on January 14, 1979)

**Decisions of the Central Committee of the Communist
Party of China on Some Questions Concerning the
Acceleration of Agricultural Development (Draft)**

(Approved in principle by the Third Plenary Session of the Eleventh Central Committee of the Communist Party of China on December 22, 1978).

The great task of building socialism which our people have undertaken has entered into a new historical phase in which we will rapidly realize the four modernizations. As of 1979, the emphasis in the work of our Party and state should shift to socialist modernization. Our primary task now is to concentrate our main energy and efforts on developing our currently backward agriculture as fast as possible because agriculture is the foundation of the national economy and the rapid development of agriculture is the foundation for realizing the four modernizations. Only by rapidly increasing agricultural production and realizing step-by-step agriculture modernization can the peasants, who account for 80 percent of our population, become prosperous, the whole national economy flourishing, the worker-peasant alliance strengthened, and our socialists system and the proletarian dictatorship consolidated. For this reason, the Central Committee has made the following decisions:

I.   Unifying the Views within the Party on Our Agricultural Problems

To accelerate agricultural development, comrades throughout the Party should have a unified and correct view of our agricultural status quo and historical experiences.

Since the founding of the People's Republic, under the guidance of Chairman Mao's revolutionary line, our country has triumphantly carried out the socialist reform of agriculture through the hard struggle of our several hundred million peasants and mass cadres. Grain yields have increased 1.5 times and the yields of industrial crops, forestry, animal husbandry, side-occupations, and fishing have each grown at its own speed. In some areas agricultural development is relatively conspicuous. A large number of water conservancy projects of all sizes have been completed. About one third of the arable land has been converted into stable high yield fields. In addition, there have been marked increases in the production of chemical fertilizers, farm machinery, and drainage and irrigation machinery, and in the consumption of rural electricity. On the whole, however, the pace of agricultural development in our nation for the past twenty years has not been fast and strikingly sharp contradictions still remain between our agricultural development and the needs of our people and the four modernizations. Between 1957 and 1977 our population grew by 300 million, of this non-farming population accounted for 40 million. At the same time the amount of cultivated land decreased by more than 100 million *mou* due to capital construction. Therefore, although per-unit yield and grain production had grown by 1977, the average grain ration for each person was still a little less than in 1957, and more than 100 million people in the rural areas suffered from a lack of grain. In 1977 the average annual income per capita among agricultural population was only sixty-odd *yuan*. In Nearly one-fourth of the production teams average income per capita was under forty *yuan*. The average annual accumulation of production brigades did not reach ten thousand *yuan*. For some areas it was difficult even to have a surplus for replanting. Unless agricultural development can be accelerated, industrial and other construction projects cannot be well developed, and, as a result, the four modernizations will remain far from realization. Therefore, the attention of the comrades of whole Party must be called fully to the importance and urgency of problems concerning our agriculture.

In the past twenty-nine year have been ups and downs in our agricultural development the speed of development was faster in the early period and slower, even retrograde, in the latter part. During the three years of restoration after liberation and the subsequent period of the first five-year plan, we accomplished a nation-wide land reform and scored a great victory in the agricultural socialist reform. A large-scale socialist economic construction was thus developed in order, and a large growth in agricultural production was achieved. The average annual growth rate of the national grain production for these eight years was 7 percent. The masses' revolutionary fervor of bold thinking and action in 1958 when the "Great Leap Forward" movement was launched was indeed very precious. Nevertheless, as we lacked experience and were unable to keep a cool head at that time in leading the nationwide socialist collective agriculture, and were eager to effect the transition to communism prematurely, this plus the influence of an exaggerated working style, lack of direction, excessive requisition, as well as severe natural calamities, caused serious damage to our agriculture in the late 1950s and the early 1960s. Under the leadership of the Party Central Committee, Comrade Mao Tse-tung, and Comrade Chou En-lai, and through the efforts of the whole Party and the people, we redressed the shortcomings and mistakes of our work and overcame difficulties, making it possible to restore agriculture and attain new development. During the ten years of the Cultural Revolution, Lin Piao together with the Gang of Four put forth their ultra-left counter-revolutionary revisionist line; they used the club of the "Theory of Productivity" to attack cadres and masses who insisted on grasping revolution and promoting production. They seriously undermined Party organizations at various levels, its policies, and excellent traditional style in the rural areas, and damaged the collective economy as well as the worker-peasant alliance and greatly frustrated the initiative of the mass peasants cadres. It is only due to the persistence of the mass cadres and masses in resisting the perverted actions of Lin Piao and the Gang of Four that our agricultural could maintain slow-footed development through the 1970s.

The agricultural development in our country over the past twenty years shows us that we must have a correct estimate of and policy toward class struggle after we complete the socialist reform, and maintain with extreme care the necessary social and political stability; otherwise, the productive forces and the relations of production will be sabotaged, which will surely result in a slow-down of agricultural development. At the same time, we must act in line with the objective laws of economic development in our work. In the past, in some policies, we did not recognize that agriculture was the foundation of the national economy. Some policies and measures we adopted hindered the peasants' socialist initiative for production. The state did not support agriculture adequately and agricultural policies were also not fully effective. The improvement of agricultural technology was not really regarded as an important task. For a long time research and education in the agricultural sciences did not receive the attention they deserved and there was little attention paid to the principle of all-round development of farming, forestry, animal husbandry, and fishing. All these failures are also obstacles to the rapid development of agriculture. Therefore, to accelerate the restoration and development of agriculture, we have to bear firmly in mind the following experiences and lessons:

1) We must maintain long-term political stability and unity. Without this, it will be impossible to modernize agricultural within this century. In the past two years, with the eradication of the Gang of Four, the whole country has been politically stable and united, which was achieved by strenuous effort. We must cherish and guard this political stability and unity and do our utmost to further develop this great asset.

2) To maintain stability and unity, we must correctly understand and manage class struggle in the rural areas, and in all areas, and correctly educate the peasants in socialism to prevent the revival of left deviationism. Since the movement for agricultural co-operation was initiated, there have been class struggles in the rural areas. However, class enemies who are hostile to socialism and insist on capitalism are only a minimal part of our population. Therefore, either to ignore or to exaggerate class struggle is erroneous. There is only a handful of class enemies seeking to sabotage us and these we must attack adamantly. It is utterly unacceptable to confuse these two qualitatively different contradictions and arbitrarily inflate the scope of contradictions to hurt good men. The long-term practice of struggle demonstrates that the mass peasants of our country firmly support the Party's leadership and follow the socialist road. During the struggle to modernize agriculture, we should better rely on and bring into full play their initiative. As for the small group of peasants with the spontaneous tendency toward capitalism, we must apply patient persuasion and education in order to help them overcome this weakness self-consciously. Here, we should first of all, draw a distinction between socialism and capitalism. The diversified undertakings of the communes, brigades, and teams are part of the socialist economy; small plots of land for private use by commune members, their domestic side-occupations, and village fairs are legitimate adjuncts of the socialist economy.

It is not permitted to criticize them and ban them as capitalist. "To each according to his work" and "more pay for more work" are the socialist principles of distribution; it is absolutely not permitted to reject them as capitalist principles. The system of three levels of ownership with the production team as the basic accounting unit, which suits our current level of agriculture productivity, may not be changed wilfully to enable so-called "wanton transition."

3) We must concentrate our energy and efforts on improving agricultural techniques to promote agricultural productivity. The Party's principle line on agricultural problems is to improve agricultural techniques based on agricultural collectivization. This principle line should be kept in mind at all times; otherwise, neither can we consolidate the worker-peasant alliance nor can we conquer capitalism with socialism. Thus we would violate the basic interests of the Party and the people. Much emphasis should be placed upon agricultural capital construction as well as on the development of industries run by communes, brigades, and teams in the rural areas. This is because they have played a conspicuous role in transforming natural conditions for agricultural production and in raising the material ability of the peasants to expand reproduction.

4) We must pursue, in a sustained and stable way, the Party's current rural policies. Those policies proved effective by practice should not be changed lightly lest we should break faith with the people and frustrate the peasants' initiative. At the same time, erroneous policies which hinder the peasants' initiative to produce and to develop agricultural productivity should also be resolutely modified and remedied.

5) We must firmly carry out the guiding principle of taking agricultural as the foundation. The Central Committee, the State Council, together with the ministries and commissions in charge of economic work, should take particular care and strive to implement and fulfill this guiding principle. When working out the national economic plan, we should sequence the priorities as agriculture, light industry, and then heavy industry, and balance agriculture and industry. The state, cities, and the units in charge of industry, science, and education must strengthen their support of techniques and materials for agriculture.

6) We must resolutely and fully develop simultaneously farming, forestry, animal husbandry, side-occupations, and fishing; take grain as the key link and ensure well-rounded development; and adapt to local conditions and select the crops appropriate to certain areas. Since grain production enables us to feed the population of 900 million as well as prepare for war and natural disasters, we must attend most closely to it. Meanwhile, we must make full use of our superior natural conditions and tap the full variety of resources to ensure the complete

development of farming, forestry, animal husbandry, side-occupations, and fishing. Grain and industrial crops should be developed appropriately and selectively in accordance with the features of various areas. We should transform step by step our current mix of agricultural products in which undue emphasis is placed on grain rather than industrial crops and little importance is attached to forestry, animal husbandry, and fishing. We must also plan to transform the food structure of our people which has relied excessively on grain in preference to other edibles.

7) We must strengthen the leadership over agriculture in accordance with objective reality, effectively act in line with the economic regulations and laws of nature, and work in accordance with the mass interests and democratic methods. We must never abuse administrative directives, give orders blindly, and act abruptly without regard to the complexity of the situation. Having smashed the Gang of Four, the biggest obstacle to our progress has been removed. It is now possible to make the best use of various favorable conditions, which give us the confidence that we can speed up agricultural development successfully. We possess the excellent socialist system, abundant natural resources, 800 million industrious and brave peasants, and a large group of steeled cadres. Our industry has been quite developed, and, with further development, can certainly assume the responsibility of equipping agriculture with modern technology. In addition to 1.5 million *mou* of land already cultivated, there are still vast wastelands, prairies, forests, and mountain areas fit for forestry and pasturage, as well as fresh and sea waters fit for fishing. On the whole, there are many favorable conditions for developing agriculture. Only if we conscientiously sum up the positive and negative experiences of the past, hold the ideological line that "practice is the sole criterion for testing truth," constantly study new problems, and sum up new experiences, can we eventually bring into play all positive factors to achieve the great goal of agricultural modernization within this century.

II.   Twenty-Five Policies and Measures Currently Set for Developing Agricultural Productivity

In terms of our agricultural modernization, the level of productivity in the rural areas is quite low; the peasants are poverty-stricken; the peasants' ability to expand reproduction is very weak; and the superiority of the socialist agricultural economy is far from fully utilized. Therefore, we must make every effort to adopt a series of policies and measures in the next two or three years that will accelerate agricultural development, lighten the burdens on the peasants, and increase the peasants' income. On this basis, we can then carry out agricultural modernization step by step.

The primary origin of policies toward agriculture and the rural economy is engaging the socialist initiative of our 800 million peasants. As we ideologically strengthen the socialist education of the peasants, we must, economically, simultaneously attend to their material well-being and, politically, effectively protect their democratic rights. If we ignore material well-being and democratic rights, it will be impossible to arouse spontaneous initiative in any classes. All of our policies for developing productivity must be judged by whether or not these policies can engage the initiative of the laborers to produce. Next, we must effectively strengthen the state's material and technical support for agriculture, thus providing agriculture with advanced technology and equipment. Without support of this kind, it will be impossible to develop agriculture swiftly, based simply on the peasants' material strength and initiative. Realizing mechanization and modernization will be out of the question. Only when the peasants' initiative is fully engaged can the state's support be fully exploited; only when the state strengthens its support for agriculture, can the peasants' initiative upsurge and crest. Both sides complement each other.

Proceeding from this, the Central Committee holds that the following twenty-five policies toward agriculture and the rural economy, and measures to increase production must be adopted in light of the current situation:

1) The people's communes are socialist economic organizations collectively owned by the laboring masses. The right of ownership and autonomy vested in the people's communes, production brigades, and production teams must be protected effectively by the laws of the state. No unit or individual may wilfully seize or encroach upon their interests. According to the premise of persisting along the socialist orientation, adhering to the laws of the state, and accepting the plans and directions of the state, all the basic accounting units of the people's communes have the right: to grow plants in a manner and timing suitable to local conditions; to decide what measures to take to increase production; to select methods of management and administration, to distribute their own products and cash; and finally to resist blind directions by any leadership.

2) No unit or individual is permitted under any conditions to commander the labor, land, livestock, machinery, funds, products, or materials of any production team. The various departments of the state are absolutely forbidden to burden commune members with additional work when sponsoring various enterprises and undertakings in the rural areas (excluding those sponsored by the peasants themselves), unless it is required by the laws and regulations of the state. The departments of the state must persist in the principle of voluntariness and mutual benefit when they sponsor the agricultural capital construction and develop enterprises to be run by the communes, brigades, and teams. No unit is allowed

to requisition labor from the communes, brigades, and teams, unless for state projects. In that case, the units should also sign contracts with and provide reasonable payment for the workers contracted as well as for casual workers requisitioned for state projects.

3) The economic organizations at various levels of the people's communes must conscientiously implement the principle of "to each according to his work, more pay for more work, less pay for less work, equal pay for equal work by men and women." They must strengthen the control over fixed production quotas, work out payment in accordance with the amount and quality of the work done, set up the necessary systems of reward and penalty, and resolutely rectify equalitarianism. The organizations may calculate work points on the basis of fixed production quotas, or on the basis of working hours together with the assessment; also they may distribute the responsibilities to work groups with the unified accounting and allocation by the production brigades, and may calculate the payment for labors on the basis of output with a reward for over-production. Fixing output quotas based on the individual household and distributing land to the individual peasant household are both prohibited. As for the distribution of rations, the organizations can use the general practice of distribution according to working points and basic rations in a ratio of 3:7 or 4:6, or based on other proper ways agreed to by a majority of commune members. The basic ration for each should be given by grade with fixed quotas. With the development of the collective economy, we must administer collective welfare undertakings carefully, step by step, so that the life of the old, weak, orphaned, widowed, ill, or disabled in the communes can be guaranteed.

4) Small plots of land for private use by commune members, their domestic side-occupations, and village fairs are necessary adjuncts to a socialist economy, and should not be criticized as the so-called "tail of capitalism." On the contrary, while we consolidate and develop the collective economy, we must simultaneously encourage and assist the peasants to manage domestic side-occupations, thus increasing their personal income and invigorating the rural economy.

5) The people's communes should continue to steadily implement the system of three levels of ownership with the production team as the basic accounting unit. They must then concentrate energy and efforts on developing productivity in the rural areas. It is forbidden to transfer the basic accounting unit to upper levels hastily without filling all requirements. The transfer of units which meet the requirements must be submitted to the provincial leading organs of the first level for approval.

6) The investment of the state in agriculture in the next three to five years will be raised gradually to 18 percent of total investment in capital construction. The expenditure on agriculture projects and aids to the communes, brigades, and teams, will also be raised to 8 percent out of the state's total expenditure. Local revenue should be mainly spent on agriculture and agricultural industries.

7) The annual loans to agriculture given by the state from now until 1985 will be more than double the amount up till now. The long-term low-interest or minimal-interest loans should be floated in a planned way. The period of the loans may be ten or fifteen years; some may even be extended to the end of the century. It has been decided to reestablish the China Agricultural Bank to meet the demand for developing credit facilities in the rural areas.

8) The requisition price of grain should be raised by 20 percent, starting when the summer grain is marketed in 1979; the price for amounts requisitioned above the quota should be raised by an additional 50 per cent. The requisition price for cotton, oil-bearing and sugar crops, livestock by-products, and forestry products should also be raised step by step, depending on the concrete conditions. The factory price and market price of farm machinery, chemical fertilizers, insecticides, plastics, and other manufactured goods for farm use will be cut by 10 to 15 percent in 1979 and 1980 due to reduced production costs, and these benefits will, in general, be passed on to the peasants. After the requisition price of farm products is raised, the market price of all grain should remain unchanged, and the selling price of other farm products needed for daily life must be kept stable. If some prices have to be raised, appropriate subsidies should be given to the consumers. From now on, we must also continue to make the necessary adjustments in the disparity of prices between industrial and agricultural products on the basis of the situation of the national economy and the principle of exchange at equal value.

9) For a fairly long period to come, the national figures for the state requisitions of grain will continue to be based on the five-year quotas of 1971-1975. From 1979, these grain requisitions will be reduced by 5 billion catties so as to lighten the burden on the peasants and to develop production. The rice areas where the average annual grain ration for each is under 400 catties and the side crops areas where the average annual ration for each is under 300 catties should be free from grain requisition. The grain requisition must never be excessive.

10) It is necessary to continue firmly to devote considerable time and energy, in a manner appropriate to local conditions, to doing the farmland capital construction well, building irrigation works, improving conditions for production, promoting the ability to counter natural disasters, and establishing farming fields

which give stable and high yields irrespective of drought or excessive rain. By 1985, the irrigated areas in our country should be increased from current 700 million to more than 900 million *mou*; the acreage of the stable and high yields should be increased from the current 500 million to 700 million *mou*. The states should go on establishing a number of large scale primary conservation projects; local organizations should be conscientiously engaged in the middle and small-scale construction projects and manufacture complete sets of equipment. To carry on farmland construction in a way that combines the large, middle, and small-scale projects, it is necessary to follow the mass line, plan conscientiously, practice the combination of specialized teams and the mass work, stress substantial results, assure high quality, and reject formalism.

11) While making full use of the already cultivated land, the state-run farms and the people's communes should simultaneously open up wasteland and also reclaim land from the sea, enlarging the cultivated acreage by more than 120 million *mous* by 1985. The land newly reclaimed for cultivation by the communes, brigades, and teams will be exempted from the levy and requisitions of grain for five years from the first year of harvesting. While opening up wasteland or reclaiming a tract from the sea, keeping the natural ecological balance must be considered. It is prohibited to ruin forests, pasture lands, and fishery resources, or to block the storing and venting of flood waters. All organs, groups, army units, enterprises, and schools are prohibited from wantonly commandeering the cultivated land, pasture, and forest land of the people's communes and farms. Necessary capital construction must also effectively save land for use and commandeer as little as possible of the cultivated land. The land law should be stipulated and promulgated as soon as possible.

12) The state-run farms should be run well and vigorously so that they can supply the state with more commodities, grain, industrial crops, and other farm and side-line products. The amount of marketable grain the state-run farms submit to the state should be raised from some 3 billion catties in the present year to around 10 billion catties by 1985. The farms running a deficit should turn the deficit into a profit within a stated time. The staff and workers of the farms which are run well and make big profits may enjoy a rise in personal income. The profits of the state-run farms gaining before 1985 should, instead of being submitted to the state, be used to expand reproduction, to engage in diverse economic undertakings, to build industries for the processing of agricultural and animal products, and to develop commercial links to sell the farms' products. On the other hand, integrated complexes of agriculture, industry, and commerce should be established as soon as possible so that they can play an exemplary role in the course of agricultural modernization.

13) It is necessary to increase rapidly the output of chemical fertilizers, insecticides, plastics, and various herbicides, to stock up fully on farm manure, to increase the amounts of green manure, and to expand energetically stalk fields. The total output of chemical fertilizers should amount to more than 80 million tons by 1985. Also, with care, the proportion among nitrogen, phosphate, and potassium fertilizers should be able to remain reasonable. The output of various insecticides, herbicides, and plastic products for agricultural use should increase significantly. On the other hand, we must broadly promote scientific use of chemical fertilizers and the scientific application of chemical insecticides so as to enlarge the effects of chemical fertilizers and insecticides.

14) It is necessary to select, breed superior seeds, and then introduce them and encourage their use. While the seed plots of brigades and teams as well as the nurseries for propagating superior seed which are owned by the counties and people's communes are all set in order, the seed production centers should immediately be established by each province, prefecture, and county in order to realize step-by-step the specialization of seed production, the mechanization of processing, the standardization of quality, and the regionalization of the cropping technique and seed types. Codes and conventions should also be formulated to improve the management system of the seed companies, to perfect the selection of seed types and the propagation of superior seed, and to popularize the operation and administration of the seed inspection and testing to prevent seed deterioration and admixture. Also, the seed law should be stipulated and promulgated as early as possible. With respect to the supply of superior seed, the quality must be high, the price favorable, and the increase in output be guaranteed.

15) The pace of agricultural mechanization should be quickened. By 1985 about 80 percent of the main agricultural work should be mechanized. It is necessary to really straighten out agriculture, raise quality, and reduce costs so that standardization, structuring, and generalization can be achieved step by step. The problems concerning manufacturing complete sets of farm mechanical implements as well supplying parts and accessories should be conscientiously resolved. The current problems in supplying complete sets of equipment for hitching to tractors should be resolved within the next two or three years so that the farming efficiency of tractors can be doubled. From now on, tractors and complete sets of farm machinery for hitching to tractors should be produced in proportion. In order to give impetus to the great and hard undertaking of agricultural mechanization, to unify the management of the design, manufacture, supply, and maintenance of farm machinery, and to develop scientific research in this field, it is decided to reestablish the Ministry of Farm Machinery (however no bureaus of farm machinery will be set up by provinces, municipalities, or autonomous regions). There are two ways to establish tractor stations: one is by having the

communes, brigades, and teams buy the tractors themselves, and those who are short of capital will ask the state for loans; the second is that the state will set up tractor stations for communes, brigades, and teams, and charge reasonable fees. The former way is preferred.

16) At the time the production of grain is being developed, close attention must be given simultaneously to the various industrial crops including cotton, oil-bearing and sugar crops, as well as forestry, animal husbandry, side-occupations, and fishing so that the policy of simultaneously developing grain and industrial crop production can be implemented. To implement the policy of simultaneous developing of farming, forestry, animal husbandry, side-occupations, and fishing, all positive factors should be brought into full play. All applicable resources should be exploited and put into use step by step, thus making for a prosperous agricultural and forest economy. By 1985 grain output must reach 800 billion catties, cotton output 72 million *tan* (unit equivalent to 100 catties), oil-bearing crops 160 million *tan*, and targets for forestry, animal husbandry, side-occupations, and fishing must also be achieved.

17) By 1985 thriving afforestation should be guaranteed to have reached 400 million *mou*. Energy and efforts should be concentrated on the five key construction projects: (1) building the forest shelter belt which will stretch for several ten thousand *li* along Northwest China, North China, and Northeast China; (2) building in North China, the Central Plain, and Northeast China patchworks of cultivated fields and forest which are afforested on all sides (3) developing the production of fast growing timbers in the provinces located south of the Yangtze River; (4) establishing economic forestry centers in South and North China; (5) reclaiming the ruined land in the forest belt in Northeast China. In all the desolate mountains and wastelands afforestation is possible, the various localities should map out a practical and feasible program to afforest them within a stated time. Efforts should be made to adopt advanced technology and to strengthen the multi-purpose use of forest resources. It is necessary to fell trees in a reasonable way, to breed energetically, to introduce, and extend superior tree breeds, and to attend to the production of oil and foodstuffs from wood plants. It is also necessary to promulgate the forestry law as soon as possible, to preserve forests effectively, to prohibit strictly the wanton felling of trees, to modify resolutely the erroneous decisions which emphasized felling trees rather than reforesting and ignored the importance of management, and to strictly prevent forest fire.

18) It is necessary to vigorously develop and stress the importance of animal husbandry. By 1985 the total number of heads of livestock must grow by 30 percent and the output of meat grow from current 15 billion catties to more than 35 billion catties. It is also important to continue to encourage the families

of commune members to raise pigs and sheep, to develop energetically the collective raising of pigs and sheep, to improve actively the animal breeding stock, to strengthen the development of prairies, and grassy hills and slopes in cultivation zones, to build irrigation works, to improve grass seed, to utilize the pasture land for rotational grazing, and to raise the number of livestock it can bear. A number of modern livestock stalls, poultry yards, slaughter houses, refrigeration houses, and processing factories for livestock products should also be established in a planned way in pasturage zones and suburbs.

19) Aquatic resources should be utilized reasonably and fishery production be accelerated so that the output of aquatic products can be raised from the current 4 million tons to 7 million tons by 1985. In addition to promulgating the fishery law and the regulations on the protection and propagation of aquatic resources as soon as possible, it is also necessary to strengthen strenuously the administration of fisheries. We must develop fresh-water as well as sea-water cultivation of fish or other aquatics, expand the areas which can gain high yields from intensive cultivation, develop fish cultivation in suburbs and factories, explore energetically the offshore fishing grounds, and adopt advanced technology and equipment to speed up modernization in fishing, cultivation, processing, storing, and shipping.

20) The enterprises run by the communes, brigades, and teams must be broadly developed. By 1985 the total value of the output of these enterprises in the revenue of the people's communes (at all three levels) should grow from current 28 percent to more than 50 percent. Those agricultural and side-line products which can be processed economically and reasonably in rural areas should be transferred step by step to the enterprises run by the communes, brigades, and teams for processing. The factories in cities should distribute in a planned way these processing undertakings to those enterprises, offering them equipment and technical instruction. The state must continue the policy of exempting these enterprises from taxation or taxing them minimally, according to the situation.

21) The principle of exchange at equal value should be conscientiously and thoroughly implemented in commercial work and, the exchange of goods between the city and the countryside should be handled carefully. When purchasing side-line products from the countryside, it is necessary to negotiate prices on the basis of the quality of the products. It is forbidden to degrade the level of products for cutting prices. The capital goods and daily necessities needed by the countryside should be supplied in time and they must be of good quality and at reasonable prices. Except for the materials requisitioned by the state such as grain, cotton, and oil, all other agricultural and side-line products should be purchased through signed contracts in which the amounts of products assigned by

the upper level or agreed upon by both sides are clearly stated; it is forbidden to complete the purchase by force or order. The various provinces can conduct experiments in selected places in a selected county on whether or not supply and marketing co-operatives at the primary level in the countryside should be operated by the people's communes. Then, based on the results of these experiments, they will determine whether or not the supply and marketing co-operatives can be made commercial organizations of the people's communes when conditions prove satisfactory.

22) Efforts should be made to develop agricultural exports and imports. The state has decided to allot a special amount of foreign exchange to aid various provinces, municipalities, and autonomous regions to develop the industrial crops, local and special products, livestock, side-occupations, fishing, and processing undertakings concerned. The products which sell well in the international market, earn substantial foreign exchange, and regain quickly the capital invested should be produced under the state's unified program; concrete methods of production should be mapped out by the State Planning Commission and the departments concerned.

23) Some areas in Northwest China and Southwest China, some old revolutionary bases, remote mountain areas, areas inhabited by minority nationalities, and border areas have long suffered from low yields and grain deficits. As a result, the masses living there are poverty-stricken. The speed with which the production of these areas is developed concerns not only the national economy but also politics. The state Council should set up a special committee composed of the responsible cadres from the departments concerned, empowered to plan and organize all possible manpower and material resources for these areas, supporting these areas financially, materially, and technically in key aspects, and helping them to develop production so that they are able to lift themselves from poverty.

24) It is necessary to continue resolutely and strenuously to carry on the family planning and conscientiously do a good job in propaganda education in this aspect. Methods which are backward and inappropriate should be rectified. The medical services and supplies should be ensured; and every effort should be made to keep the population growth rate under 1 per cent by 1980.

25) Protecting and bringing into full play the initiative of the grassroot cadres in the mass areas is one of the key factors for speeding agricultural development. Most cadres at the primary level in the countryside are good or relatively good. They have lived with the mass peasants for months or years. They have been exposed to hardship without any complaints, combated with

natural disasters, transformed undesirable local conditions, and made great contribution to our agriculture. Except a few bad elements cadres who make mistakes should be assisted with education to remedy their mistakes and to proceed. A number of mistakes made by the primary level cadres in their work were caused by the inappropriateness or vagueness of the tasks or policies laid down by the Central Committee and the upper levels, which ought to be held responsible for these mistakes. The erroneous, false, and wrong cases involving the cadres at the primary level which have occurred in past political movement should be completely redressed by discriminating the nature of the cases. The income of cadres in the production brigades should be higher than that of the local laborers at the same grade. Cadres who perform well in their work should be given citations and material rewards. It is necessary to work out special plans to strengthen the training and education of the cadres in political, cultural, administrative, and specialized technical aspects. It must be insisted that the cadres be elected on schedule from the various levels in the people's communes, production brigades, and production teams by representative conferences of commune members or general meetings of commune members. Cadres who do not please the broad masses may be dismissed as the occasion demands by representative conferences or the general meetings. Various financial accounts should be made public on schedule on the basis of democratic management on which the communes, brigades, and teams insist. The democratic style of cadres should be strenuously brought into full play and the stability of the ranks of cadres be maintained. The Party committees at various levels should continue to pay special attention to the mass movement which urges "In agriculture, learn from Tachai and popularize the experience of Tachai," and combine this movement closely with the thorough implementation of the policies and measures mentioned above, and with the great goal of agricultural modernization. Also, the various Party committees should guide the mass cadres and peasants in continuously holding firm the learning from Tachai's basic experience; they must perpetually maintain and bring into full play the revolutionary spirit of self-reliance and hard struggle. At the same time, the various Party committees should resolutely carry on the Party's policies toward agriculture and the rural economy, study the best domestic and foreign experiences, try their best to obtain a firm grasp of advanced science and technology, and learn to manage the modern great agriculture. Our tasks change rapidly and new types will emerge constantly. Tachai and other advanced units in the country should divide themselves into two and strenuously create new achievements as well as new experiences so as to make a new contribution to the acceleration of our agricultural development.

(Translated by Liu Fang-ying)

Part II

III. The Blueprint for the Modernization of Agriculture

To modernize agriculture completely and to change the rural landscape thoroughly is a great revolution unprecedented in our history. The thorough implementation of the twenty-five policies listed above is just the first step we will take in the new long march on the agricultural front. As we strenuously take this step, we must continue simultaneously to investigate and study, learn from experiences of advanced units at home and advanced countries abroad, concentrate on mapping out a complete program, prepare new measures attentively, resolutely arrange for the problems which we can anticipate, organize all possible resources, and solidly do our best to guarantee a success in this first step.

1) To realize the modernization of agriculture, we urgently need to equip our rural cadres and farming technicians with the knowledge of agricultural science and technology. We need a number of experts in modern agricultural science and technology, and an enormous battalion of technicians in agricultural science and technology. We also need a number of qualified agricultural colleges or institutions to train talented people in agricultural science and technology as well as in administration and management. We must greatly raise the level of science, technology, and culture among the peasants, particularly young peasants. Since it will take up to ten or even more years to complete these tasks, we must embark on them now, and not relax for a moment. Also, we must rectify thoroughly some erroneous points of view. These hold, for example, that agriculture can be modernized without highly modern science research and education, that both research and educational institutes in agricultural science are dispensable, that the modernization of agriculture has nothing to do with the governing agricultural organs at various levels or with modern scientific and technological centers, and that experts need not be actively involved in agricultural development. We must quickly recover and strengthen the necessary conditions for research and teaching. The central government should run some key institutes of advanced agricultural research and higher education; the various provinces, municipalities, autonomous regions and prefectures should run agricultural research institutes, agricultural colleges, and secondary agricultural technical schools; counties should run certain institutes of agricultural science, agricultural service stations, and training schools in agricultural technology. Various localities should work out a program for and then as soon as possible begin training cadres in rotation from communes, brigades, and teams, developing the farm machinery technicians and agricultural technicians whom the rural areas need desperately. It is therefore important to train all cadres in rotation within the next several years.

Each commune, brigade, or team should be equipped with enough qualified machinery technicians and agricultural technicians. Since intellectual youth sent down to the countryside have reached a certain level of culture and have had some practical experience, we must encourage them mentally and materially to commit themselves to farming and enroll them according to their skills in institutions of agriculture or secondary schools of agricultural technology for advanced study, conscientiously educating them to be the backbone of modern agricultural development. The Ministry of Education, the Ministry of Agriculture, and other departments concerned should work out concrete programs for these ideas by the first half of 1979 and put them into practice beginning in the latter half of 1979.

2) In order to modernize agriculture, it is essential to complete first all farm mechanization, rural electrification, water conservancy projects, and to promote the use of chemical fertilizers and insecticides. We must energetically introduce, manufacture the advanced farm machinery which best suits for us, and then expand our use of it in a planned way. In order to take full advantage of the benefits of agricultural mechanization and to raise productivity as much as possible we must manufacture farm machinery in complete sets and maintain it well. We should strive to build small-scale hydroelectric and thermal power generating stations in the countryside according to local resources and conditions. Meanwhile, marsh gas, wind power, and solar energy should be fully utilized in terms of developing energy for agricultural use. It is also necessary to develop farm land irrigation and prairie irrigation facilities in a manner appropriate to local conditions. According to the variable features of the North and South, mountains and plains, paddy fields and dry fields, we may employ all possible means of irrigation, stage by stage, so that we are able to carry out over-all irrigation in the rural areas and make it possible to facilitate drainage and irrigation and to achieve stable and high yields. Apart from this, we must accelerate the development of chemical products for farm use to enable the high-speed development of agriculture, gradually equipping our agriculture with plenty of chemical products for farm use such as chemical fertilizers, insecticides, plastic sheeting, herbicides which are of excellent quality and good price. In compliance with the demands of agricultural modernization, the Ministry of Agriculture and Forestry, the Ministry of agriculture, the ministry of Water conservancy and Power, the Ministry of Chemical Industries should cooperate closely. Between 1979 and 1980 they must work out the long-term all-around programs for farm mechanization, rural electrification, water conservancy construction, and the expanded use of chemical products, as well as feasible plans for each year, and then they must execute these programs thoroughly and conscientiously.

3) To modernize agriculture, we must arrange the sectors of agriculture rationally, carry out regionalization and specialization in production, and expand

steadily the degree of socialization of agricultural production. Otherwise, neither over-all farm mechanization nor the comprehensive adoption of a system of advanced science and technology is possible on a large scale. As to the arrangement of regionalization and specialization in our agriculture, we should not only conscientiously study experiences of the advanced countries but also investigate and study our agricultural situation according to factual local situations. Departments concerned in the State Council and various localities should map out programs and organize all possible resources by the end of 1979 so that we may accomplish the nationwide surveys of our natural conditions such as soil and climate as well as of our social conditions such as population, communications, transportation, industry and commerce, science, and education within the next three years. On this basis, the departments and localities together with experienced peasants and rural cadres should work out step by step programs together for specialized regional production the spheres and to the degrees appropriate; programs should also be prepared for coordinating agriculture, forestry, animal husbandry, fishing, industry, side-occupations, import and export trade, communications, transportation, science, education, finance, and banking with each other. While developing well-designed programs, we should make down-to-earth experiments in these programs, approaching them in an orderly way and systematically practicing and integrating experiences.

4) The main part of the state's investment in agriculture must be spent to establish a number of production centers for marketable grains, industrial crops, animal husbandry, fishing, and forestry. These centers can be the enlarged state-run farms, or newly reclaimed state-run farms; they may also be set up through the cooperation of several people's communes. These centers will be charged with building great modern agricultural enterprises of high labor productivity and marketability by employing advanced equipment and adopting scientific methods of production and management. In addition to managing agriculture and animal husbandry, they will also be engaged in processing agricultural and sideline products as well as in commercial work, thus these enterprises will gradually develop into integrated complexes of agriculture, industry, and commerce. After these centers are established, the supply of materials to the state including commodities, grain, cotton, oil-bearing and sugar crops, fruit, livestock products, aquatic products, and forest products will be better provided for. Developing centers of commodities and agricultural products is one of the important strategic measures to build great socialist agriculture. We must concentrate all the investment of the state necessary on this measure and administer these centers vigorously in the same way we administer the important industrial construction projects. Departments concerned in the State Council should work with various localities in preparing by the end of 1979 a feasible program for this.

5) Modern industry, communications and transportation are indispensable to modernizing agriculture. Within the next two or three years, in accordance with the features of our agriculture, the requirements for agricultural modernization, and variable local conditions and demands of production, we must make an over-all plan and arrange all agricultural industries rationally, in line with the principle of specialization and coordination. In doing this, we should, economically and rationally, produce the various farm machines and chemical industrial products for farm use in quantity, while we raise the quality, and reduce the cost of production at the same time. Departments concerned including the Ministry of Farm Machinery and the Ministry of Chemical Industry should establish according to actual demands a certain number of specialized companies to effectively improve agricultural industries by strengthening the operation and management of these companies and paying close attention to economy and efficiency. The Ministry of Farm Machinery should set up gradually in accordance with economic zones the service centers for farm machinery at the local level. These companies will be expected to provide, in a centralized way, supply, maintenance, rental, retrieval, and technical instruction for farm machinery and chemical products; this will expedite the use of these farm materials and reduce the expenditures by the communes, brigades, and teams. As for communication and transportation, we must strive to build highways which will link the cities to the countryside. Also, it is essential to open traffic between counties and between communes and strengthen the construction of communications within pasturage, forestry, and fishing areas by 1985.

6) It is necessary to modernize economically and rationally the processing industries for agricultural and animal husbandry products so that they are able to adapt to and even accelerate the modernization of agriculture. From an economic point of view, these processing industries for agricultural and animal husbandry products should be located in the producing centers to make use of local resources and products and this will also enable them to coordinate with the local communications and transportation so as to expedite the sale and supply between cities and the countryside. The Ministry of Agriculture and Forestry, the Ministry of Light Industry, the Ministry of Textile Industry, the Ministry of Commerce, and the All-China Federation of Supply and Marketing Co-operatives, together with other departments concerned in the State Council, should confer with provinces, municipalities, and autonomous regions, and then seriously put their heads together to work out a construction program in this aspect within 1979.

7) Developing the small cities and towns and strengthening the aid of cities to the countryside are requisite for accelerating modernization, realizing the four modernizations, and narrowing the gap between cities and the countryside and between workers and peasants. We now have 800 million population and 300

million laborers in our rural areas. As agricultural modernization progresses, a good portion of the labor force can be saved. We must not and need not let these spare laborers be involved in industries and other construction projects in cities and then remain there. We must strengthen with extreme care the development of small cities and towns and equip them with modern industry, communications, commerce, services, education, science, culture, and public health; this will convert them stage by stage into advanced bases for changing the look of the countryside of our country. Our country now has some 2,000 counties; in these counties there are relatively developed towns, and there are people's communes whose enterprises have been developed to a certain extent. It is necessary to first intensively work out programs which comply with the needs and possibilities of economic development and then develop these relatively developed places step by step. Also, big cities may exert their force by putting up satellite towns around in the countryside on their perimeters, thus further strengthening their aid to agriculture. Peking, Shanghai, Tientsin, Shenyang, Wuhan and other municipalities which have the capability to do so should be charged with promoting the modernization of agriculture in several counties under the unified leadership of the municipal Party committees. This program should be mapped out by the end of 1979 and put into practice as soon as possible. In doing this, the principle of exchange at equal value should be adhered to between the economy of ownership by the whole people and the economy of collective ownership. Both production and exchange should be included in the scope of the State's plans. It is important not to confuse these two categories of economy. Further, it is forbidden to engage in illegal barter and dishonest activities such as making a deal under the table, giving a party, or offering a bribe.

8) To modernize agriculture, we must thoroughly implement the principle of concentrating our force to fight a war of annihilation. We should make progress in various sectors of agriculture one by one and stage by stage; that is to say, we advance in waves rather than disperse the movement in breadth like spreading sand. Complete sets of farm machinery should be manufactured in a centralized way so that their power can be fully exerted. Areas with favorable conditions may be given priority and more support to develop agricultural modernization; while areas with unsatisfactory conditions will thus take the back seat and receive less support. It is not bad to see the output of the areas which receive the priority and support grow conspicuously and the per capital income of peasants living there rise. In that case, these areas will then play an exemplary role in promoting a nationwide modernization of agriculture. It is important to complete the modernization of agriculture within the first several years in the selected areas (whose population should account for five per cent of our whole population). In doing this, there will be some 40 million people enjoying first a rise of personal income, a figure which could be that of the population of a rather

big country in the world. Apart from this, the domestic market will be accordingly expanded to a large extent. This will surely be an outstanding achievement. We must make every effort to expand the population of these advanced areas to 10 per cent out of the national population by 1985. The State Planning Commission, the Ministry of Agriculture and Forestry, and other departments concerned should confer with various provinces, municipalities, and autonomous regions about this strategic outline. They should work out programs by the end of 1979 and submit them to the Central Committee and the State Council.

IV. Strengthening the Leadership of the Party and Government over Agriculture

To promote speedily the production of agriculture and develop energetically a great modern agriculture is the grand task of the whole Party and people. It is important to mobilize the whole Party and the whole country for the modernization of agriculture. The leading Party and government organs from the central to local levels should give agriculture the first priority, regard agricultural modernization as a significant goal for long-term struggle, and effectively strengthen their leadership in commanding the great forces to fight this unprecedented great battle.

For a long time, some Party committees, government organs, and operation departments have formulated general measures about instruction and management in agriculture simply according to the methods laid down in the administrative decrees, and they would ask their subordinate levels as well as rural communes, brigades, and teams to carry them out mechanically. Since this kind of leadership which just executes the will of the upper levels estranges itself from the reality and the masses, the measures they institute always lead to undesirable effects and frustrate the peasants' initiative. This not only damages agricultural production but also impedes the vigor and development of the rural economy. This erroneous way of doing things should be rectified conscientiously.

Party committees at various levels should execute the Party's line, principle, and policy effectively, accelerate the development of agriculture, and carry out stage by stage the great policy of modernizing agriculture. Meanwhile, they must strive to do a good job in ideological and political work with the mass cadres and peasants, combine political work and economic work skillfully, and guarantee success in production and construction. In the concrete work of agricultural production and construction, it is necessary to encourage the operation units at various levels to function properly, and to organize them to do their duties independently. Party committees do not necessarily take interest in everything and meddle with everything because the involvement of Party committees in concrete operations work will make them neglect Party work and interfere with administrative work. This will not only prevent the government departments and agricultural enterprises and units from completing the work which they are empowered, authorized, responsible, and scheduled to do, but will also weaken the Party's leadership, thus impairing the leadership function of the Party.

The state's administrative units should take charge of agriculture independently and can perform satisfactorily a great deal of the administrative work such as the mapping out of programs for nationwide or regional production and construction, the control of river systems, water conservancy construction projects of all sizes, the establishment of production centers for marketable grain, industrial crops, animal husbandry, and fishing, and the construction of key forestry areas and pastures. The primary work on the modernization of agriculture includes the research and planning for mechanization, the investigation of soil conditions and the creation of soil restoration programs, the research into and improvement of agricultural science and technology, the planning for a execution of agricultural education, appropriate investment in agriculture, the distribution of materials, and the creation and management of seed companies, fertilizer companies, feed companies, and farm machinery service companies. All these are the duties of the agricultural units at various levels and of the operation units concerned. They are responsible for doing them well. However, in the past, some of this work was left out of consideration; some was done unsatisfactory. To change this situation and effectively strengthen this work, the Central Committee has decided to set up the State Agricultural Commission which will be charged with making studies and then putting forth the guidelines and policies for agricultural production and construction; this body will assume the unified leadership over the departments concerned in the State Council to map out far-reaching programs and annual plans, to provide over-all planning and arrangement for the distribution and use of agricultural capital and materials, to review, set, and guide the operation of the important agricultural construction projects either nationwide or conducted by several provinces or several departments, to coordinate skillfully the work among the ministries concerning agriculture, between agricultural departments and other departments, between the central and local departments, and to solve the important problems concerning agricultural work.

The central and local departments should establish a clear division of labor in managing agriculture and understand the distinction between positions and responsibilities. The projects involving the whole country or several provinces should be put under the charge of the central departments; the projects involving a single province or several counties should be put under the charge of the provincial departments. The same applies to prefectures and counties. That is to say, the upper level must not monopolize things which should be done by lower level and let the lower level bring their initiative into full play.

Administrative organs at various levels should and must make essential plans for and give guidance to the production and construction of the rural collective economic units. While formulating plans, it is necessary to follow the mass line; to conduct comprehensive investigation, study, deliberation, and discussion from top to bottom; and to achieve a comprehensive balance. It is forbidden to force communes, brigades, and teams to perform these plans in the name of administrative decrees, unless it is required by the law. They should be permitted to safeguard, their autonomy in this aspect as much as is suitable to the timing and local conditions under the state's unified planning and instruction. Also, when operation departments and scientific and technology institutes give instructions in scientific farming to communes, brigades, and terms, they should try their utmost to make the instructions scientific and suitable for local conditions, to follow the principle of mass voluntariness, and to adopt extensively the methods of setting up an example for all, which we have promoted for years and has been successful, in order to avert arbitrary orders and blind directions.

To meet the needs of a revolution like the modernization of agriculture, we must improve completely our leadership style and methods; restore and persist in our fine traditions of seeking truth from facts, maintaining contact with the masses, and promoting democracy; raise the level of leadership and the level of art which leads; enhance through practice abilities in and talents for leading modern agriculture; resolutely act in line with objective economic laws and the laws of nature; firmly overcome the undesirable styles which do not care to proceed from reality, to stress economy and efficiency, or to follow the mass line; adamantly combat bureaucraticism and formalism; reject all things which do not solve problems but squander in vain a great deal of manpower and materials such as meetings, summonses, briefings, inspections, visits of this kind and various circular routings of official documents. Also we must resolutely carry out the system of personal responsibility by committing fixed responsibilities to specified personnel so as to eliminate the situation in which no one is responsible for a certain part of the work.

Learning is of key importance. Our cadres at various levels, leading cadres in particular, should not only continue conscientiously to study the Marxist-Leninist theory, and make every effort to grasp completely and exactly the system of Mao Tse-tung Thought and the Party's line and policy, but also should posses the necessary knowledge of agricultural science and technology as well as of economics, and study the advanced management methods in agriculture, educating themselves strenuously as specialists for special fields. It is important to conduct regularly strict evaluation for cadres, especially leading cadres, to institute distinctions between right and wrong, between merits and faults, and to dispense rewards and penalties impartially. Cadres who study energetically, perform their work satisfactorily, display good working style, and are bold to emancipate their minds, who raise problems and then study and solve them, deserve rewards and promotion. Cadres who are always averse to study, working long as outsiders, parrot what others say, and thus delay the work should be transferred or given due punishment. Since our task is quite arduous and burdensome, we must seek out talented people with extreme care, train and employ them. In doing this, we will create a grand rank of cadres who possess ability and political integrity and are able to lead and manage modern agriculture to accomplish this great revolution on our agricultural front.

Regulations on the Work in the Rural People's Communes (Draft for Trial Use) (Approved in Principle by the Third Plenary Session of the Eleventh Central Committee of the Communist Party of China on December 22, 1978)

Preamble

The "Regulations on the Work in the Rural People's Communes (Revised Draft)," also known as the "60 Articles," was instituted under Comrade Mao Tse-tung's personal direction and approved after discussion by the Tenth Plenary Session of the Eighth Party Central Committee. Since it was implemented on a trial basis in the rural areas in 1962, it has played an important and historical role in promoting the consolidation of the people's commune system and the development of agricultural production. During the Great Cultural Revolution, Lin Piao and the Gang of Four sabotaged the Party's rural policies and the thorough implementation of the "60 Articles," causing grave damage to our agricultural development.

The Party Central Committee headed by Comrade Hua Kuo-feng has directed the whole Party, the whole army, and the people of all our nationalities to smash the Anti-Party Clique of Wang Hung-wen, Chang Ch'un-chiao, Chiang Ch'ing, and Yao Wen-yuan. Our socialist revolution and construction has now entered into a new period of development. Now, the focus of the work of the whole Party and whole country has turned to socialist modernization. Under new historical conditions, according to the general line and task for the new period and to the new situation emerging in our rural development, the Party Central

Committee now reiterates directly the rural policies put forth in the original "60 Articles," makes necessary revision, and supplements them.

The trial use of the new "60 Articles" will certainly mobilize our rural areas and encourage hundreds of millions of members of the people's communes to make greater contributions to the modernization of agriculture, the four modernizations, and the general tasks for the new period.

Chapter I

The Character and Basic Task of a People's Commune in the Current Phase

Article 1: A rural people's communes is a socialist economic organization which is collectively owned by the laboring masses to develop simultaneously farming, forestry, animal husbandry, side-occupations, and fishing, and to integrate agriculture, industry, and commerce. Collective ownership by the people's commune and ownership by the whole people are the two forms of socialist economy. They should support each other and jointly enhance the prosperity of our national economy.

Article 2: The people's congress and the revolutionary committee of a people's commune are the basic organizations of state power as well as the leading bodies of the collective economy. The people's congress of a people's commune is the representative conference of the members of a people's commune. The leadership of the revolutionary committee of a people's commune over the commune's economic organizations and enterprises should be in line with objective laws and ensure that their accounting practices be strictly independent.

Article 3: The basic tasks of a people's commune are to raise high the banner of Mao Tse-tung Thought and to grasp class struggle, struggle for production, and scientific experiment simultaneously and persistently. They must take production and construction as their central focus in order to develop constantly the socialist collective economy and to modernize agriculture by the end of the century. A people's commune should improve the material and cultural life of the masses of commune members step by step by developing production. It should supply more grain, meat, other foodstuff, industrial materials, and other products to the state. The state in turn should support the collective economy of the people's communes strenuously and on many fronts.

Article 4: When fulfilling its task of modernizing agriculture, a people's commune should continuously foster. Tachai's revolutionary spirit, adhere to the principle that Marxist-Leninism, and Mao Tse-tung Thought take the precedence over all else; it should persist in self-reliance and hard struggle, uphold the communist style of patriotism and the love of collectivism, go all out, aim high, and achieve greater, faster, better, and more economical results in developing production

Article 5: The organizations at various levels of a people's commune must implement conscientiously the socialist principle of distribution and the current phase of the Party's basic rural economic policies. They must pursue the principle of "From each according to his ability, and to each according to his work," ensure more pay for more work done, object to false equalitarianism, hold fast to the principles of voluntariness, mutual benefit and exchange at equal value, and forbid strictly "equalitarianism and indiscriminate transfer of manpower, land, daft animals, farm tools, funds, and so on." Also they should perform their task of requisitioning grain for the state conscientiously and adhere to the policy which sets the quotas for the state requisitions of grain on a five-year basis, and never requisition excessive amounts of grain. Further, they should execute the state's policies on prices and rewards correctly, encourage the peasants to sell their agricultural and side-line products to the state, take care simultaneously of the interests of the state, the collectives, and the individual, increase commune members' income based on the increase in production, and allow commune members to manage small private plots and domestic side-occupations, and to participate in legal village fairs.

Chapter II

The System of Administration

Article 6: The people's communes must now implement steadily and continuously the system of three levels of ownership with the production teams as the basic accounting unit, and they must make concerted efforts to develop rural production. It is forbidden to transfer the basic accounting unit without meeting the requirements. Those transfers which meet the requirements must be submitted to the provincial organs of the fist level for approval. The communes and brigades should be geared to the needs of the production brigades, mobilize the masses for the efficient administration of the production teams being careful to especially help poor teams change their circumstances, and develop the economy of brigades and teams energetically. Usually, the sizes of the communes, brigades, and teams should remained unchanged; any necessary adjustments in size should be discussed and approved by a general meeting of commune members or a representative conference of commune members, and then be submitted separately to the provincial, prefecture and county organs for ratification.

Article 7: It is necessary to protect the ownership of the organizations at various levels of a people's commune. No units and individuals may commandeer its land, woods, pastures, beaches, water, labor force, livestock, farm tools or machinery, industrial equipment, capital, materials, or products. Any requisitions of land by the state or for collective construction should be strictly according to the law; the less cultivated is land they commandeer, the better. No rural land including houses and centers may be rented to sold.

Article 8: It is necessary to respect the autonomy vested in the basic accounting units of a people's commune. According to the premise of persisting in the socialist orientation and accepting the planning and instruction of the state, all the basic accounting units of a people's commune have certain rights: to plant in a manner and timing suitable to local conditions, to decide how to increase production, to select methods of management and administration, to distribute their own products and cash, and to resist blind direction by any leaders or government organs.

Article 9: The organizations at various levels of a people's commune should implement the principle of democratic centralism. The representative conferences of members of a people's commune and of a production brigade, and a general meeting of commune members are the organs with authority at various levels of a people's commune. The representatives should be elected by commune or brigade members by secret vote. Elections should be held every two years and the members have the rights of supervision and recall. A representative conference of the members of a people's commune should be held at least twice annually; a representative conference of members of a production brigade should be held at least once every season; and a general meeting of a production team should be held at least once a month. The administrative organs at various levels of a people's commune are the revolutionary committee of a people's commune, the management committee of a production brigade and the management committee of a production team. The chairman, vice-chairman, and members of the revolutionary committee of a people's commune, the director, deputy director, and members of the management committee of a production brigade, and the leader, deputy leader, and members of the management committee of a production team should be elected by representative conferences or a general meeting; the term of office is two years. Officials who are just, work conscientiously, and gain the support of the masses may be reelected for a second term; incompetent officials may be dismissed as the occasion demands. On important issues including production and capital construction, operation and management, distribution, supply and marketing, credit, and the collective welfare, the administrative organs at various levels of a people's commune should extensively seek suggestions from the masses, and then let the authorized organs at various levels make their decisions in a democratic way. Decisions must not be made by only a few cadres. The administrative organs should be responsible to the organs in authority at the same level and report their work on schedule.

Article 10: In addition to having specified personnel manage administrative work, the revolutionary committee of people's commune should concentrate its main energy and efforts on strengthening its leadership over production and construction. It may, if necessary, set up a management committee for production to handle the management of agricultural production, capital construction, farm machinery, enterprises run by the communes and brigades, and financial administration.

Article 11: To modernize agriculture constantly, the state should train talented people to serve in the organizations at various levels of the people's communes, gradually equipping these organizations with technicians in farming, forestry, animal husbandry, and fishing, and with able accountants.

Chapter III

All-Around Development of Farming, Forestry, Animal Husbandry, Side-Occupations, and Fishing

Article 12: The People's communes should simultaneously develop farming, forestry, animal husbandry, side-occupations, and fishing, taking grain as the key link; they must ensure well-rounded development, adapt to local conditions, and select the crops appropriate to their areas. It is particularly important to give equal emphasis to farming, forestry; and animal husbandry. Areas producing grain should put the main emphasis on grain production, arranging grain and industrial crops rationally. Forestry, pasturage, and fishing areas should concentrate solely or in part on forestry, animal husbandry, or fishing. The centralized production areas for industrial crops should give first priority to the planting of industrial crops. The suburbs should primarily grow vegetables and fruit, raise poultry, and cultivate fish.

Article 13: Serious efforts should be made to develop grain production and ensure a steady and rapid increase in grain production. In increasing grain production, emphasis should be put on raising the output of the land already cultivated. In order not to erode agricultural land, wood lands, and prairies, the communes, brigades, or teams which own wasteland fit for cultivation may open up this wasteland only in a planned way with the approval of the county revolutionary committee. The land newly reclaimed for cultivation will be exempted from grain requisitions for five years from the first year of harvesting.

Article 14: It is necessary to mobilize the masses to reforest the motherland. All the mountains, wastelands, and sandy areas fit for reforestation should be reforested and allowed to grow grass cover. It is important to seal off the mountains for reforestation and to expand the acreage having grass cover. Special efforts should be made to reforest those areas which suffer from sever soil erosion and damage from wind and sand, and those in the suburbs. The communes and brigades may claim ownership of the woods and meadows they create. It is also necessary to mechanize forestry, to breed superior seeds and healthy seedlings, to raise the survival rate in reforestation, to make possible fast growth, high quality, and luxuriant production, to establish a strict system for felling trees and reforestation. Strong emphasis should be placed on reforestation so that both felling and reforestation can be combined. A convention for preserving forest lands must be formulated to prohibit strictly the wanton felling of trees or the opening up of wastelands by destroying forest. Also, forest fires must be absolutely prevented. Those who perform meritorious service in preserving forests should be given citations and rewards; those who violate the law by destroying forests should be punished according to the law.

Article 15: It is necessary to develop animal husbandry vigorously and to enhance its relative importance in the agricultural economy. Serious efforts should be made to develop the raising of livestock such as pigs, cattle, sheep, rabbits, chickens, ducks and geese in a manner appropriate to local conditions. It is important to continue to encourage the families of commune members to raise pigs, and to develop the pig-breeding energetically. Land should be set aside for growing feed crops for collective pig-breeding. The breeding of pigs and sheep by commune members should be subsidized collectively by the state by providing a certain quantity of feed. When purchasing pigs from the producers, the state should sell them feed as encouragement to continue raising. Feed production centers and feed processing plants should be set up in a planned way; and farms for breeding pigs, chickens, dairy cows, beef cattle, and sheep should be mechanized and managed in the same way we manage factories. In pasturage areas, semi-pasturage areas, and mountains fit for grazing, it is necessary to strictly prohibit destruction of prairies, to strengthen construction of pasture land, to build irrigation facilities, and to raise the degree of mechanization. Localities where animal-power is still used for cultivation should feed and breed draft animals with extreme care, employ them rationally, select animal keepers strictly, and establish a system of responsibility for feeding and management as well as a system of rewards. As mechanization develops, it is necessary to change in a planned way from raising draft animals to raising beef cattle and dairy cows; it is also necessary to administer the veterinary stations of communes conscientiously, to breed and extend superior varieties of livestock energetically, and to do a good job of preventing and curing animal diseases.

Article 16: It is necessary to develop collective side-occupations energetically. Assuming that grain requisitions for the state and the rations for commune members will not be affects, the communes may fund flour mills and bean curd workshops. Also, they may undertake, according to local conditions, side-occupations such as short-distance transportation, knitting, gathering, sericulture, and apiculture. Materials for the side-occupations can be supplied in a collective and centralized way, then be processed by commune members. Products of the side-occupations should be centrally marketed.

Article 17: It is necessary to develop fishing and other aquatic undertakings energetically, to strengthen fresh- and seawater cultivation of fish, to expand areas which are able to gain high yields from intensive cultivation, to manage fish cultivation in the same way we manage factories, to explore the offshore fishing grounds strenuously, to improve fishing techniques, and to accelerate mechanization in catching, cultivation, processing, storing, and shipping fish. Efforts should be made to protect water surface and aquatic resources, to forbid all harmful tools and means for catching fish, to execute strictly the regulations on preserving areas and periods in which fishing is forbidden to prevent water pollution scrupulously, to do a good job in preventing and curing fish disease, and to organize those fishermen living on boats and solve properly the problems concerning their production centers and their settlement on the land.

Chapter IV

Farmland Capital Construction

Article 18: Farmland capital construction is a great socialist task which must accord with local conditions and the principle of comprehensive management of mountains, waters, fields, forest, and roads and which must consider the improvement of the soil conditions and the control of rivers as the core. It is necessary to completely follow the mass line, to prepare programs conscientiously, to manage in an orderly, unified and progressive manner, and to build stable and high yield fields. In developing farmland capital construction, it is important to adapt to local conditions, stress efficiency, ensure high quality, throw formalism aside, determine our exact orientation, make concentrated efforts to develop techniques, manufacture complete sets of equipment to secure full efficiency, and not destroy the topsoil when levelling the ground. Immediate increases in production should be ensured; and the use of mechanized or semi-mechanized implements be promoted to raise the efficiency of operation.

Article 19: Farmland capital construction may be coordinated with certain organizations if the projects demand. It is necessary to adhere to the principle of voluntariness and mutual benefits as well as exchange at equal value in the course of coordination. The state should invest in large and middle-size backbone projects as sponsors, providing them subsidiary grain. The investment and subsidiary grain needed by other coordination projects should be provided by the beneficiary units; the projects with financial difficulties should properly be subsidized by the state or the communes. The communes or brigades which are non-beneficiary but contribute laboring force may be exempted from investing money and subsidizing grain. To ensure higher annual production, sudden mass efforts should be combined with ongoing specialized work. To requisition labor force for their specialized teams, the counties, communes, and brigades must coordinate with the basic accounting units and make an over-all plan. As a rule, the requisitioned labor force may account for 5 percent of general laboring force; 10 percent at most. The mechanized specialized teams should be employed first.

Article 20: For irrigation facilities and hydropower stations which have already been completed we should set up corresponding managing bodies or appoint specified personnel to provide them scientific and centralized management, to strengthen maintenance, to ensure economic accounting, to strictly save water and electricity, and to charge all fees for water and electricity consumed. Water resources should be utilized comprehensively to raise fish and ducks, grow aquatic crops, and develop diverse economic undertakings.

Chapter V

Farm Mechanization

Article 21: Mechanization is the basic hope for the peasants. The state should help the people's communes work out concrete programs, according to local conditions, to speed up farm mechanization and electrification as well as raise labor productivity unceasingly. The communes or brigades may buy farm machinery and establish farm machinery stations by themselves; those who are short of capital may ask the state for loans. The state also may set up farm machinery stations for the communes or brigades. It is essential to strengthen the management in farm machinery stations and farm machinery teams and to practice independent economic accounting. Farm machinery stations or teams should sign contracts with the basic accounting units, specifying their responsibilities and fees. Stations or teams which perform their tasks satisfactorily and thus increase production should be given rewards; stations or teams which perform unsatisfactorily and thus reduce production should pay compensation. In accordance with the principle of volunatriness and mutual benefits, it is acceptable to coordinate the use of farm machinery.

Article 22: It is necessary to train farm machinery technicians in a planned way, to build a battalion of farm machinery technicians both red and expert, and to set up a perfect system for managing farm machinery. Farm machinery technicians should be trained strictly by specialized schools or training classes and earn their certificates through tests which prove their qualifications. It is also necessary to establish a system for evaluating, appraising, and giving rewards or penalties to farm machinery technicians, and a system for using, maintaining, and repairing farm machinery and electric equipment; we must follow strictly the regulations on safe operations, prohibit stringently operating against the regulations and driving without licenses. There should be quality standards, fixed quotas on work, and fixed quotas for oil consumption in operating farm machinery. Cost accounting for each unit of machinery must be practiced.

Article 23: The ministers should support farm mechanization vigorously. The units concerning agricultural production and supply should provide farm machinery of the types and quality required at good prices and in complete sets, and they must ensure enough parts and accessories. Also they must ensure prompt supply. Substandard products will not be allowed to leave the factories. Substandard products which have left the factories should be repaired free of charge, replaced, or refunded; and the compensation should be paid to the members of the communes or brigades. In addition, the state should pursue a policy of favorable prices on oil and electricity for farm use.

Chapter VI

Scientific Farming

Article 24: The people's communes should promote scientific experimentation energetically, make every effort to extend advanced technology, implement fully the Eight-Point Charter for Agriculture, and practice scientific farming in a manner appropriate to local conditions so as to achieve stable and high yields with low cost: 1) They should devote every effort to improving the soil conditions, make general surveys of the soil on schedule, file information on the soil, adopt measures to improve the soil in accordance with its situation, and set up schemes for fertilization; 2) they should explore the sources of fertilizers extensively, apply fertilizers rationally, stock up on farm manure, increase the amounts of green manure, apply additional chemical fertilizers scientifically, energetically utilize marsh gas, wind power, and solar energy, expand energy sources for agricultural use, and expand stalk fields; 3) they should improve the conditions for irrigation constantly, do a good job in soil conservation, build a scientific drainage and irrigation system, and practice reasonable drainage and irrigation; 4) they should breed and popularize superior seed energetically and step by step standardize seeds for ordinary fields; 5) they should innovate upon the farming system and agricultural techniques to fully utilized local sunlight, heat, and water and to cultivate the productivity to the soil, making the innovations in the farming system and agricultural techniques and the modernization of agricultural complement each other; 6) they should protect crops carefully, study the periodicity of the occurrence of local diseases and insect damage conscientiously, make prompt and correct observations and reports, carry out comprehensive prevention and treatment, promote biological control energetically, and extend the use of agricultural insecticides and herbicides of deep effect and low toxicity; 7) they should do a good job in forecasting the weather which is likely to cause disasters, and adopt efficient measures to resist natural disasters; 8) they should strengthen the comprehensive investigation, development, and utilization of agricultural resources, develop energetically technical innovation in forestry, animal husbandry, and fishing, extend the use of advanced technology, set up measures to increase production through experimentation, follow the mass line, and never execute decrees by force.

Article 25:   Communes should set up agricultural scientific and technological stations, as brigades should sections; production teams should set up groups for agricultural science and technology or appoint technicians. Under the instruction of upper level research departments in agricultural science, these units should demonstrate and extend the use of advanced science and technology. It is necessary to bring into full play the functions of agricultural technical personnel, to confer the official title of technicians upon them, to set up a system of technical responsibilities, to implement evaluation, promotion, reward and punishment, to effect conscientiously the three-in-one combination consisting of cadres, technicians, and the mass commune members, and to cultivate experimental plots with care.   Technical personnel should vigorously put forward measures to increase production and supervise the practice of these measures. Leadership cadres should listen with care to the suggestions from technicians and experienced peasants, and take the lead in learning science and technology.

Article 26: It is necessary to mobilize the masses for learning science and technology, and strive to raise the level of science and culture among the commune members.   The state should build additional agricultural technical schools, rural primary and high schools, and night schools, provide courses concerning agricultural science and technology and short-term technical training classes, make extensive use of newspapers and periodicals on science and technology, radio broadcasts, television, movies, and slides to spread the knowledge of science and technology; it is also necessary to have experienced peasants impart their technical knowledge to others, and give citations and rewards to those who have inventions or creations in science and technology and who make contributions in the spread of technology.

Chapter VII

Enterprises Run by the Communes and Brigades

Article 27: Assuming that agricultural production is well-developed and meets local resources, conditions and social demands, the rural people's communes must build enterprises vigorously and systematically. In developing enterprises run by the communes and brigades, the communes must adhere to a socialist orientation to serve agricultural production, the mass livelihood, large-scale industries, and export, and stick to self-reliance. Also, they must make full use of local resources to sponsor industries appropriate to local conditions such as the planting, cultivation, and processing of agricultural and side-line products mining, building, farm machinery, transportation, and so on. Under the state's unified supervision, agricultural and side-line products which can be processed economically and rationally in the rural areas should be transferred step by step to the enterprises run by the communes and brigades for processing. The communes and brigades in pasturage areas and forest areas which measure up to the requirements should also develop the processing of livestock and forest products energetically. Factories, mines and other enterprises in cities should distribute products or parts suitable for production by the commune - or brigade-run enterprises to them in a planned way, providing them equipment and technical instruction. The state should include the enterprises run by the communes or brigades into its economic plans step by step by signing contracts on supply, production, and marketing with them. The enterprises not included in the state's economic plans are allowed to produce and market their products by themselves. Both the enterprises and the units concerned must observe the signed contracts earnestly, stress credit, and shoulder economic responsibility. Integrated complexes, planned industries, capital construction of communications, and commercial supply and marketing may be sponsored jointly by several communes, brigades, or communes and brigades together. Departments in charge of materials, finance, banking, and science and technology should support energetically these enterprises in the financial, material, and technical aspects. The state should make a policy of exempting these enterprises from taxation or taxing them minimally.

Article 28: The communes and brigades should consult the basic accounting units for the labor force they need for their enterprises, and then make over-all arrangements. Payment for the requisitioned labor should generally be equal to that for farm workers at the same grade. It is acceptable to use the general practice of "appraising work done by factories, calculating work-points earned by brigades, settling accounts jointly between factories and brigades, and distributing payment by brigades." Some enterprises may practice the wages system, giving their technicians technical subsidies. The staff and workers belonging to the enterprises under the system of ownership by the whole people and to the handicraft co-operatives which are placed under or incorporated into the enterprises run by the communes or brigades should be given their original wages, labor insurance, and other forms of welfare treatment. The craftsmen scattered around the countryside should be admitted to the enterprises run by the communes or brigades or be organized to work around the countryside: it is also necessary to lay down reasonable ways of calculating payment for these craftsmen.

Article 29: The major part of the capital needed by enterprises run by communes and brigades should be accumulated by the enterprises themselves. With the approval of the mass of commune members, a small sum of public reserve funds of the commune or brigade can be drawn on for building the enterprises. A good portion of the state's investment in the people's communes as financial aid should be used to support poor communes or brigades in developing their enterprises. The loans provided by the state-run banks to the enterprises run by the communes or brigades should be scrupulously controlled and properly used. The representative conferences have the right to decide how to use the profits in the enterprises. In addition to investment to enlarge the enterprises' production, the profits will mainly be used to purchase additional farm machinery, to develop capital farmland construction, and to aid the poorer brigades to develop production; furthermore, a portion of the profits may also be distributed to commune members. It is necessary to straighten out the administration and operation of these enterprises, to establish a system of responsibilities, to exercise control over fixed quotas, to do economic accounting carefully and to strive to raise the quality of goods produced. No unit or individual has the right to use the capital of these enterprises, or is allowed to take advantage of the enterprises to take more than is due, to give parties or presents, to waste or be extravagant, to hand out jobs to associates, or to speculate for profit.

Chapter VIII

Supply, Marketing, and Credit

Article 30: Placing the supply and marketing co-operatives at the primary level in the rural areas under the control of the people's communes has been successful in a series of experiments at selected spots. Now they will become the commercial organizations of the collective economy of the people's communes, and be the supply and marketing departments for the people's communes. The operation of these co-operatives is under the guidance of the supply and marketing co-operatives at the upper level. The rural supply and marketing centers are guided by both supply and marketing co-operatives and the brigades, but they are mainly guided in business operations work by supply and marketing co-operatives. The functions of these primary supply and marketing co-operatives are: to implement thoroughly the principles which will develop the economy and ensure supply; to organize and support energetically the ability of communes and brigades to develop diverse undertakings; to supply the productive materials and daily necessities needed by the collectives and commune members; and to purchase and market successfully the agricultural and side-line products and certain amounts of the products of enterprises run the communes or brigades. In purchasing these products, it is necessary to negotiate prices based on the quality of products. It is forbidden to downgrade the goods and cut prices. Timing, quality, and quantity should be guaranteed when supplying the materials. When the collectives exchange products with or sell products to commune members, they must not cheat them with inferior goods. The supply and marketing co-operatives of the communes should practice independent accounting, strengthen their operation and administration, expand their capital accumulation, increase the strength of the collective energy of the people's communes, and sell more industrial products to encourage those communes and brigades which supply the state relatively more grain, cotton, oil, pigs, and other agricultural and side-line products.

Article 31: The rural credit co-operatives are the banking sector of the collective economy of the people's communes and their business operations are under the guidance of the agricultural banks at the upper level. The credit co-operatives should energetically encourage commune members to save and deposit their money in the co-operatives, organize the capital efficiently, support the development of production, and issue loans to commune members to solve their financial difficulties.

Article 32: Rural trade fairs are necessary adjuncts to a socialist commerce. Commune members have the right to market in the trade fairs, making up what one lacks by what another has in surplus. No unit or individual is allowed to meddle with these fairs. Commune members are also permitted to sell and buy small amounts of grain or oil-bearing crops through the trade fairs after they have provided what the state requisitions. Also, they may negotiate prices with the grain departments in buying or selling grain. The livestock market should be opened under guidance. The management of the rural trade fairs should be strengthened to deal a firm blow to the opportunists.

(Translated by Liu Fang-ying)

Part III

Chapter IX

Management

Article 33:   The organizations at all levels of the people's communes should strive to raise the standards of economic managements, and to uphold the democratic administration.   They must be diligent and thrifty in running the communes, and conscientiously plan the management of labor, finance, and materials.   To raise labor productivity constantly and reduce production costs, the communes organizations should carry out economic accounting, conduct economic analysis, and stress efficiency.

Article 34: It is important to strengthen planned management.   Under the state's planning and instruction, the commune organizations should, in accordance with the factual situation, map out annual plans for production, capital construction, the employment of the labor force, the allocation of revenues and expenditures, and the distribution of income and profits.   Also they must prepare far-reaching construction programs for commune members as high goals for their struggle.   The target set up for production should be properly high and realistic, but leave an appropriate margin for unforeseen circumstances.   The various statistical figures on which working plans are based should be verified scrupulously.   When preparing plans, it is necessary to follow the mass line.   After full deliberation and discussion by the masses, the plans should be approved through discussion by representative conferences or general meetings.   The upper level may readjust these plans by means of consultation but not force. Furthermore, it is essential to let each commune member understand clearly and early in the year the distribution of the whole year's output, the labor he ought to contribute, the amount of fertilizers he should employ, and the grain and cash he will share.

Article 35: The organization of labor should be strengthened and a strict system of accountability for production should be established.   Efforts should be made to organize all able-bodied persons to participate in productive activities, and to evaluate and assign in a democratic way the basic attendance dates which fully and partially able-bodied males and females are required to contribute.   Regardless of whether or not they are independent accounting units, all groups and individuals must--according to the demands of production in farming, forestry, animal husbandry, fishing, industry, and side-occupations--accept responsibility for their post.   In this way they can implement a system for specifying staff, tasks, quality, payments, rewards, and penalties. It is forbidden to fix output quotas or to distribute the land according to the individual households.

Article 36: It is important to control fixed output quotas, and to practice the evaluation of work done and the calculation of work points. The commune organizations should fix labor quotas for field work, if this is suitable, and assign work on this basis; the field work done should be verified and evaluated. In fixing labor quotas and evaluating labor achievements, the quality of the work should be considered first. It is important to evaluate the work done by each commune member and calculate his work points based on the quality as well as the amount of his labor. Payment for work which is laborious or needs high technical skill should be raised appropriately. The commune organizations may calculate work points on the basis of fixed output quotas, or on the basis of hours worked plus assessment; also they may distribute the responsibilities to work groups, keeping unified accounting and allocation in the hands of the production brigades; they may also calculate the payment for laborers on the basis of output with a reward for over-production. The concrete methods of calculating work points should be decided by commune members through discussion. No matter what methods the commune organizations adopt, they must perform ideological and political work conscientiously and educate commune members to love collective labor. Regardless of sex or age, cadres or commune members, there is equal pay for equal work. In addition, they must distribute labor handbooks to commune members and make public monthly the work points earned by commune members and the account.

Article 37: Socialist labor competitions should be held and labor discipline should be strictly executed. Model workers and advanced collectives should be selected through annual appraisal. Collectives and individuals who perform well and make great contributions should be given citations and rewards; collectives and individuals who violate labor discipline and thus cause losses should be re-educated by criticism or be made to pay compensation, according to their different situations. These rewards and penalties should be given in a democratic way rather than arbitrarily by a few cadres.

Article 38: Non-productive personnel, workers for non-productive purposes, and the labor force not belonging to the production brigades should be strictly limited in order to ensure enough labor for the agriculture front. No unit is allowed to requisition labor from the communes or brigades, unless it is for state projects. In that case, the units should sign contracts with and provide reasonable payment for the workers contracted as well as for temporary workers requisitioned for state projects. When communes or brigades need to requisition labor for their own production and construction, they must consult the production teams and reach an agreement with them. Production teams have the right to reject any requisition violating the above principles. The communes should not set up art troupes and sports teams which do not contribute to production; production brigades should not employ broadcasters, operators, or messengers, who divorce themselves from productive activities. As for barefoot doctors, it is necessary to fix their production quotas and give them fixed subsides. Cultural and athletic activities should be conducted in free time. Militia training should place equal emphasis on labor and military training, and not affect production.

Article 39: Financial affairs should be handled in a democratic way. Efforts should be made to establish a sound system for financial accounting, to maintain strict financial and economic discipline, and to set up sound systems for budgets and final financial statements, audits, and management. The budgets, supplementary budgets, and final financial statements to be submitted should be decided by representatives conferences and general meetings. Accountants and treasurers have the right to reject any expenditures inconsistent with the systems and procedures established. Credit financial accounting should be practiced stringently. Those brigades, production teams, and enterprises run by the communes and brigades, and other units which also adopt independent accounting should convene democratic conferences on schedule about financial administration, making public their revenues and expenditures. Communes members have the right to raise questions, criticize and make suggestions on these financial affairs; also democratic conferences of this kind have the right to veto unreasonable expenditures. Expenses for non-productive purposes should be kept under strict control. It is forbidden to be extravagant and wasteful. Furthermore, it is prohibited to construct buildings, halls, hostels, or centers without authorization, to eat and drink extravagantly, or given personal parties and gifts. From now on, those who appropriate public funds for personal parties and gifts should pay compensation. Moreover, a sound system of assistance and guidance for accounting should be set up and educational activities should be developed for financial accounting. Accountants of the production brigades, production teams, and the enterprises run by the communes and brigades should train in rotation annually so as to provide a battalion of financial accountants both red and expert.

Article 40: Management in materials should be particularly strengthened, especially in fixed assets. Materials such as grain, agricultural products, chemical fertilizers, and insecticides should be classified and listed before they are stored, and then should be properly kept. The store-room keepers have the right to reject the delivery of any materials inconsistent with the systems and procedures. Fixed assets including farm machinery, industrial equipment, electricity generation equipment, irrigation facilities, and draft animals should also be listed. Furthermore, it is important to check the state of machinery, equipment, and facilities, and the physical situation of draft animals on schedule, to carry on strictly the maintenance of equipment and feeding of animals, and to carry out a system of responsibility for employing these fixed assets. Serious actions should be taken to find those responsible for unusual losses in fixed assets.

Article 41: All accounting units should regard the review of accounts, materials, cash, and work points as a permanent system. They should, with the masses' assistance, conscientiously check these matters once or twice annually. In the course of review, it is important to continue socialist education and be serious about policies and discipline. Properties embezzled or stolen should be returned or repaid. Serious cases should be handled according to the law. Public funds appropriated should be returned within a stated time. Accountants who have integrity and public spirit and firmly uphold socialist principles should be given citations and rewards.

Chapter X

The Distribution of Income

Article 42: When people's communes distribute their income, they should pay equal attention to the interests of the state, collective, and individuals, setting up reasonable proportion for reserve and distribution. In case of a normal year, the people's communes should strive to increase the income of 90 percent of their commune members and maintain the income of other 10 percent without decrease; failures to maintain the income of commune members should be remedied as soon as possible. In addition, communes should try their best to lay aside enough funds for production and keep the fees for management under strict control, which generally should not exceed .05 percent of the gross distributable revenue. As usual, public reserve funds may account for around 5 percent of this revenue, with the exception of high-income brigades which may properly set aside more income for public reserve funds. Public welfare funds should generally be limited to less than 2 to 4 percent of the distributable revenue. It is also important to set aside depreciation funds for fixed assets such as farm machinery and industrial equipment, as well as funds for grain reserves, if they are necessary. The plan for the distribution of income should be approved through discussion by representative conferences and general meetings.

Article 43: Concerning the distribution of grain, the people's communes should first arrange, in compliance with the policies, food grain for commune members, then they should reserve enough grain for seed and necessary fodder crops, and provide the grain requisitions for the state. Surplus grain may be used to develop animal husbandry or be processed. It is also acceptable to set aside a certain amount of grain as reserves and labor subsidy. Concrete arrangements should be decided through discussion by representative conferences or general meetings. The communes should perform conscientiously the task of providing grain for the state and should implement the policy concerning the five-year plan for requisitioning grain. Excess grain produced may be partially set aside and partially sold to the state, which should raise the price for this grain to encourage the producers. Grain output should be calculated based on the figures on the final statements submitted by the accounting units, with the output from the private plots excluded. Communes or brigades whose per capital ration of food grain is lower than the minimum for state grain requisitions should be exempted. It is essential not to requisition grain excessively. Unless necessary for readjusting grain varieties, a basic accounting unit is forbidden to purchase and market grain in the same year. In the communes or brigades which provide the state more commodity grain and oil-bearing crops on a per capita basis, the ration of food grain and oil for each person should be higher. Assuming that they have met the state's requisitions, communes and brigades engaged in the production of industrial crops, vegetables, lumber, and fish should be ensured food grain ration equal to that for adjacent grain producing areas. Proper food grain rations should also be provided for pasturage areas.

Article 44: In the distribution of rations, it is acceptable to use the general practice of integrating basic rations with distribution according to work points, or to use the practice of distribution according to work points plus the consideration for special cases, or to implement other methods chosen by a majority of commune members. Areas where commune members received higher food grain rations may carry out distribution through self-assessment and public discussion. In the first mode of distribution, the food grain given for work points and the basic food grain ration should be in a ratio of 3:7 or 4:6. The basic food grain ration for each should be given by grade with fixed quotas. Whatever the case, the grain should be so distributed that it can facilitate mobilizing labor aggressiveness of commune members and contribute to promoting birth control. At the same time, proper care should be given to the dependents of martyrs and servicemen as well as to needy households.

Article 45: The normal distribution for commune members should be ensured. Households with too many members but little man-power should be assigned appropriate field work and helped to develop domestic side-occupations so that they are able to increase their income, rather than overdraw. Neither cadres nor commune members may borrow grain or ask for a loan from the accounting units. Efforts should be made to clear the debts owed for years and formulate measures for repayment according to situations. The dependents of cadres, the staff and workers under the government organizations and state's enterprises and undertakings who live in the countryside should energetically participate in collective productive activities. If their labor income is not sufficient to pay for their food grain, they should submit money without delay. Goods should be distributed rationally so as to avoid the overdrawing caused by the over-distribution of goods on a per capita basis. The enterprises and undertakings sponsored by state departments should not transfer their unreasonable burdens which are inconsistent with policy to the collectives and commune members.

Chapter XI

Cultural and Welfare Undertakings

Article 46: Organizations at various levels of the people's communes should establish rural elementary and secondary schools so that all school-age children may go to school, gradually popularizing secondary education. The public should gradually assume control of all rural secondary schools and most elementary schools. Also, elementary schools in poverty-stricken and border areas should gradually be taken over by the public. No unit or individual is allowed to deduct or appropriate the state's subsidy for educational expenditures. To wipe out illiteracy, it is necessary to administer the rural night schools and libraries well, and organize the peasants to study politics, culture, science, and technology. Commune organizations should also develop spare time literary and athletic activities to create a vigorous cultural life for their members. Meanwhile, they must strengthen their work in rural public health, and make prevention their basic policy. They must constantly promote patriotic public health campaigns aiming at eliminating pests, calamities, and diseases, build public health centers for the communes and co-operative medical stations for the brigades, and raise the medical skills of the barefoot doctors. Furthermore, they must strive to do a good gob in planned parenthood, keeping the population growth rate under effective control.

Article 47: A system for protecting laborers should be established and undertakings for the collective welfare should be developed energetically. Proper medical treatment and subsidies should be given to the commune members who are injured or disabled due to official assignments. Dependents of commune members who died while discharging official assignments should be given commiseration and assistance. In assigning jobs, special consideration should be provided for female commune members undergoing physiological changes and growing teenagers. To strike a proper balance between work and leisure, it is necessary to implement a vacation system. Commune members who have lost their independence as they have become old, weak, orphaned, widowed, or disabled should be given support. The commune members who meet with unfortunate incidents or difficulties in earning their livelihood should be subsidized after discussion and endorsement by the masses of commune members. Preferential treatment should also be given to the dependents of martyrs and servicemen and to the disabled servicemen who have difficulties in earning their livelihood. The model workers and old cadres who had made contributions to the revolution but have lost the ability to work should be properly subsidized with additional work points. The basic accounting units may implement a system for old-age pensions, if they are able to do so. It is also acceptable to build child-care centers, kindergartens, and sewing groups to lessen the household burdens of commune members.

Article 48: The living circumstances of commune members should be improved as production is developed. In accordance with the principles of benefiting production, of facilitating life, of giving due consideration to public health, and of commandeering land already cultivated as little as possible, the communes should work out unified programs for the construction of residential quarters: houses may be constructed by the collectives, to be rented and occupied by commune members; in addition, commune members may construct houses by themselves.

Chapter XII

Domestic Side-Occupations of Commune Members

Article 49: The domestic side-occupations of the members of the people's communes are necessary adjuncts of a socialist economy. Assuming that they will not affect the development of the collective economy, commune members have the right to manage domestic side-occupations, with which no unit or individual is allowed to interfere: 1) Commune members may cultivate their private plots distributed by the collectives; commune members in the pasturage or mountain areas may have a few private animals; private land will usually account for 5 to 7 percent of the cultivated land owned by the production teams and this percentage may not be expanded or transferred. If there is a disparity in the sizes of private plots caused by changes in population, a readjustment may be made after approval by the counties on the basis of the current population, but the total area of private plots may not be changed; 2) Commune members may raise pigs sheep, chickens, ducks, rabbits, and geese; households which measure up to the requirements may raise dairy cows or beef cattle; 3) Commune members may engage in knitting, embroidery, gathering, fishing, sericulture, apiculture, and so on; 4) Commune members may plant fruit trees and bamboo in land around their houses, which should belong to commune members themselves.

Chapter XIII

Commune Members

Article 50: Commune members are the masters of the people's communes. They are vested with the following rights: 1) Commune members who have reached the age of eighteen have the right to vote and to be elected; 2) They may participate in discussion, raise suggestions, put questions to a vote, and supervise administrative work and economic work in production, distribution, finance, supply and market, credit, and collective welfare; 3) They may criticize violations of the law and discipline by cadres or report their accusations to the cadres' superiors; none are allowed to obstruct, forestall, or attack them, or to retaliate for their criticism and accusations; 4) Living and productive materials such as houses, farming tools, and implements legally owned by commune members and their deposits in banks or credit co-operatives should belong to commune members forever; none are permitted to encroach upon their ownership; commune members of other nationalities should enjoy equal rights; the status of the commune members with a family background of landlords and rich peasants should be regarded as same as that of other commune members and enjoy the equal rights; they should not be discriminated against, and at the same time their children must not be regarded as descendants of landlords or of rich peasants.

Article 51: Members of the people's communes should assume the following duties: 1) They must adhere to the state's constitution, policies, decrees, and carry out the resolutions adopted by representative conferences or general meetings; 2) They must abide by labor discipline and the management system conscientiously, and fulfil the fixed basic labor attendance dates and responsibilities in applying fertilizers; 3) They must take good care of property of the state and collectives; 4) They must sharpen their vigilance and struggle with all counterrevolutionary sabotage activities.

Article 52: Landlords, rich peasants, counterrevolutionaries, base elements, and new-born bourgeois elements who are still not fully reformed should be reformed under mass supervision; the masses should help them turn over a new leaf and give them a way out. Landlords, rich peasants, counterrevolutionaries, and bad elements, who have abided by government decrees, been engaged in honest labor, and not committed crimes for years, should be freed from their designations and treated the same as other commune members after being evaluated by the masses and approved by the county revolutionary committees.

Chapter XIV

Cadres

Article 53: Cadres at all levels of the people's communes should take the lead in upholding the socialist orientation and the modernization of agriculture. The governing organs at the upper levels should care for the work, study, and life of cadres in the communes and brigades, strengthen their education and training, and support their work. Cadres of the communes and brigades should strive to study politics, culture, science, technology, as well as management, to raise their political consciousness, and to master the business operations, thus educating themselves to be red and expert.

Article 54: Cadres at all levels of the people's communes are the servants of the people. They must serve the people whole-heatedly, and implement conscientiously the three main rules of discipline and the eight points for attention, which are laid down for Party and state cadres. The three main rules of discipline are: 1) conscientiously execute the policies set forth by the Party Central Committee and state decrees, and participate energetically in socialist construction; 2) implement democratic centralism; and 3) reflect the true situation. The eight points for attention are: 1) care for the life of the masses; 2) take part in collective labor; 3) deal with people on an equal footing; 4) consult the masses about their work and be fair and square in running affairs; 5) identify themselves with the masses and not hold themselves aloof from the masses; 6) investigate before making pronouncements; 7) act in accordance with factual situations; 8) raise the proletarian class-consciousness and meanwhile raise the political level.

Article 55: Cadres at all levels of the people's communes must take the lead in restoring and promoting the Party's excellent tradition and work style, persist in integrating theory with practice, keep in close contact with the masses, and uphold the style of hard struggle, truth-seeking, criticism, and self-criticism. They should tell truth, act with sincerity and candor, and be honest. It is absolutely forbidden to resort to deception, to oppress the people, to hide the truth from higher authority, or to execute decrees by force and give blind directions. It is also prohibited to ride roughshod over the people, to beat or scold the people, to stifle democracy or take revenge. Furthermore, cadres will never be allowed to attain private or personal ends in the name of official duties, to make under-the-table deals, to eat or take more than is their due, or to commit corruption and share in bribes.

Article 56: The insistence on cadre participation in collective productive activities is essential to the socialist system. With the exception of the old, weak, ill, and disabled, the cadres of the communes should engage in at least sixty days of physical labor and the cadres of the production brigades at least 120 days. Cadres who engage in labor for more than the days stipulated should be given citations. In case counties or units above counties summon the cadres of the communes or brigades to conferences, they should bear these cadres' travel and food expenses and subsidize them for their lost working time. The cadres should submit these subsidies to the brigades in exchange for working points. The brigades should not employ the cadres or personnel who divorce themselves from productive activities. Senior cadres in the brigades should be given fixed subsidies. The number of cadres receiving fixed subsidies in a brigade will usually be three to five, depending on its size; each may be subsidized with work points of 150 labor days annually. The addition or deduction of the subsidized work points for cadres at the end of a year should be decided by commune members themselves. The cadres who successfully manage a project which contributes a conspicuous increase in production should be awarded an additional 10 to 30 percent of their subsidized work points; The cadres who poorly manage a project which thus causes a decrease in production should be punished by a dedication of 10 to 20 percent of their subsidized work points. Other cadres of the brigades and production teams should also be subsidized for the loss of working time and be appraised by commune members at the end of a year, receiving rewards or penalties for their performance. The gross number of work points given to the cadres of a brigade and its production teams as fixed subsidies and subsidies for the loss of working time in a whole year should not exceed 2 percent of the gross work points of a brigade. Relatively large brigades should keep these subsidiary work points under 1.5 percent.

Chapter XV

Political Work

Article 57: The organizations at various levels of the people's communes must strengthen the ideological and political work, carry out propaganda among the masses, mobilize and organize the masses to struggle to fulfill the general task of the new period: 1) They should organize cadres and commune members to study the works of Marx, Lenin, and Mao Tse-tung, publicize at all times the domestic and international situation and Party's policies, engage in education in class and the revolutionary tradition, inculcate the masses of peasants consistently with a socialist ideology, criticize the tendency toward capitalism, and advocate the principle of integrating collective interests with individual ones; 2) They should unite more than 95 percent of the masses and cadres to attack sabotage activities by the small handful of class enemies as well as the offensives of capitalist forces and to safeguard the socialist public ownership; 3) To do a good job in political work, they should promote socialist democracy as extensively as possible, ensure the right of commune members to take part in managing the collective economy, reject the poor feudal and bureaucratic style in working, and mobilize commune members' socialist enthusiasm to the fullest extent possible; 4) In doing political work, they should uphold the integration of theory and practice, proceed from the personal experiences of the peasants, and combine the economic work so as to ensure a smooth fulfillment of tasks in production and construction; in doing this, they should not adopt measures as simple and crude as formalism; 5) They should promote the socialist new morality and fashion, innovate upon the old customs and habits, do away with feudalism and superstitions, fight against mercenary or arranged marriage, and overcome the concept of clan.

Article 58: According to the situation of production, the communes and brigades should check up on Party and commune organizations, rectify the working style on schedule, and straighten out the leadership groups in key units. Emphasis should be placed on rectifying the ideological style and on the necessary reorganization of units. For the cadres committing mistakes, the communes or brigades should adhere to the principle of learning from the past mistakes to avoid future ones and curing the sickness to save the patients, educating them to rectify their mistakes conscientiously and advance continuously. For those alien class elements, political degenerates, and new-born bourgeois elements who have wormed their way into the Party and the ranks of cadres, the communes or brigades should resolutely comb them out in accordance with the organic regulations and with the approval of the upper levels so as to purify the Party organizations and ranks of cadres.

Article 59: The Party organizations in the people's communes should keep in close contact with the masses, and play a leading and nuclear role in the organizations at various levels of the people's commune. They should bring the revolutionary committees and management committees into full play rather than trying to monopolize their duties. The secretaries of the commune Party committees and the secretaries of Party branches in the brigades should not concurrently assume the chairmanship of the commune revolutionary committees or directorship of the brigades. The Chinese Communist Youth League and the Women's Federation should play an exemplary and leading role in rural production and construction. The Party organizations should also strengthen militia work, putting militia work on a solid basis organizationally, politically, and militarily. Furthermore, they should ensure that the armed militia are effectively in the hands of the activist elements of poor, lower-middle peasants' origin, who are politically reliable.

Supplemental Provisions

Article 60: The revolutionary committees of various provinces, municipalities, and autonomous regions may formulate supplemental rules pinpointing special local problems on the basis of the principles laid down in these regulations.

> The Administrative Office of the Central
> Committee of the Communist Party of China
> (Issued on January 14, 1979)
> [Translated by Liu Fang-ying]

DOCUMENT NO. 11

APPLYING ECONOMIC MEANS TO READJUSTING
THE IRRATIONAL STRUCTURE OF AGRICULTURE

Discussion on Agricultural Modernization

by

Yu Guoyao

(**Kuangming Jihpao**, Beijing, January 17, 1980;
FBIS-CHI, February 5, 1980)

In implementing the eight-character principle for economic development, it is important to readjust the irrational economic structure in agriculture and gradually help our agriculture become reasonably distributed, developed in an all-round manner and advanced enough to satisfy the needs of the people and the growth of our industries. This important question also involves gradually changing our countryside into a land of plenty where diverse economic undertakings in agriculture, industry and commerce form integrated complexes. To realize this goal, it is very important to study how to apply economic means in readjusting the economic structure of our economy.

On the Solution of the Grain Problem by Economic Means

Our agriculture's present economic structure is irrational. There are still tendencies to pay exclusive attention to producing grain while overlooking forestry, animal husbandry and other cash crops. It is not simply a question of understanding. It is also a practical question because grain, in a sense, is in short supply. Due to the slow progress on the agricultural front over the past twenty-five years or so, we still have to import grain, cotton (to be used for reexport after processing), oil and sugar. The question of doing a good job in planning the importation of grain, cotton, oil and sugar and in applying economic means to accelerate the readjustment of the economic structure or our agriculture is well worth studying. Now let me explain this question by making two calculations. First, let us see if importing grain according to the needs entailed by our plans to accelerate the readjustment of the economic structure of agriculture is better than importing less grain, which will result in a certain deceleration in the readjustment process. Take the Mantong and Yancheng cotton growing areas for instance. If the state is able to provide them a billion *jin* of grain to permit them to concentrate on the production of cotton, they will overfill their production plans by a margin of 4 million *dan* by 1985. That means we can substantially reduce cotton imports in the future. If we base our calculations on current international market rates, 4 million *dan* of cotton can be swapped for 6 billion *jin* of grain. On the whole, this is sufficient for the grain needs in all cotton-growing areas in our country. Once the grain problem is ironed out in the cotton growing areas throughout the country, we will not have to import any more cotton. It is the same with areas growing oil-bearing or sugar crops. If these areas can be helped to care less about the grain problem, they can plan their production in line with local natural conditions, which are most favorable for producing oils or sugar, and increase their outputs. We now come to the second item for calculation. If the state increases the importation of chemical fertilizer to be supplied to grain growing areas and accelerates the development of marketable grain production, there will be more marketable grain available to facilitate the readjustment of the economic structure of our agriculture. At present, if the state increases the importation of urea by 2 million tons per year especially for areas producing marketable grains, we can reap an additional 6-7 billion *jin* of marketable grain at the estimated rate of 1 *jin* of urea for an additional production of 3 *jin* of grain. If we import 1 million tons more of phosphate fertilizer, we can gather in 8-9 billion more in of marketable grain (calculated on the basis of the state and the grain growing locality sharing the additional output by a ratio of 6 to 4 or even on a 50-50 basis). The state can then utilize this marketable grain to readjust our agricultural structure. In about 3 to 5 years, the very irrational distribution of various crops in the country will be rectified. Practice has proven that if the grain problem is allowed to remain unsolved and if commune members must pay the state grain tax in full when their grain rations are barely sufficient, it will be very difficult to imagine that the peasants will actively develop forestry, animal husbandry or the production of cash crops. If appropriate changes are not made in this respect, it will be difficult to change the situation where various localities stick to the practice of only growing grain. It will also be impossible to change the mentality that equates agriculture with the production of grain.

On the Question of Contract Systems for Farm Produce Purchases

It is worth studying whether it is feasible to arrange the procurement of farm produce, in addition to grain and cotton, on the basis of a contract system. Practicing the contract system means the state only sets production quotas, purchase quotas and planting plans for the reference of the communes and production brigades and no longer monopolizes the purchases and marketing of farm produce. To promote agricultural zoning and specialization, it is naturally necessary to strengthen greatly the mutual cooperation among provinces, prefectures and counties from now on. If such cooperation is conducted on the basis of the contract system, we can remedy the situation where there is only a kind of vertical relationship in dealings in farm and animal products (namely, the localities only come in touch with the central administration), while there is no horizontal relationships (namely, there has been no contact among different localities). With such a change, the Commodities exchange market, in which both vertical and horizontal relationships can exist simultaneously, will be greatly expanded. For example, Guangdong, Fujian and Guangxi are ideal places for growing sugarcane, but the Changjiang Delta is not. However, the Changjiang Delta is good for cultivating grain. For a long time, arable land for producing high-yield sugarcane crops was allocated for growing grain, while other fields unsuitable for growing sugarcane, but suitable for grain, were used to grow sugarcane. This is a waste of arable land, manpower and material resources. Take sugarcane production for instance. On a national average, to obtain 1 ton of sugar we currently need to use more than 4 *mu* of land. However, in the Zhujiang Delta in Guangdong, it takes only 1.7 *mu* to yield the same amount of sugar. If the cooperation among provinces and regions is brought into effect, Guangdong, Fujian and Guangxi can then concentrate on sugarcane production while the provinces in the Changjiang Delta can specialize in cultivating grain. These areas can obtain the sugar or grain they need by signing contracts for the exchanges of such products. This method will give full scope to the special natural advantages each individual locality may have over others, and it will benefit the state and the localities as well as the peasants.

**On the Question of What Percentage of the
Foreign Exchange Earned from the Export of Farm
and Animal Products Is to Be Turned Over**

Since the founding of the PRC, a third of our country's foreign exchange earnings has come from the export of agricultural and sideline products. Another third has come from processed agricultural and sideline products. This represents two-thirds of our total foreign exchange revenue. However, the foreign exchange does not go to the departments or localities that actually produce these exports or materials for processing. This is detrimental to mobilizing the initiative of these departments or localities. If the past practice which allowed the Foreign Trade Ministry "to be the sole holder of the purse" is changed, if a new method is introduced in which a certain percentage of foreign exchange obtained from exporting farm and sideline products is turned over to the state coffers and if individual provinces and regions are encouraged to establish direct contact with the international market, the enthusiasm of various regions will be greatly aroused in developing production, exploiting the natural advantages of their localities by all means and producing more and better agricultural and sideline products. Take soybean production in the northeast for instance. The amount of soybeans currently available for export is less than the amount solicited by orders received from abroad. One of the reasons for this has been the inappropriate price fixing of grain and soybeans in our agricultural front. Conditions have made it less profitable to grow soybean than to grow corn. As a result, Yushu County in Jilin Province, long famous for being the "hometown" of soybeans," has now become a "corn belt." If the method is adopted by which the state and the locality can each receive a certain percentage of the foreign exchange earned while letting the localities sell their agricultural and sideline products directly on the international market, we can expect the restoration and further development of soybean production in Yushu Country. They will naturally only be too willing to grow more soybeans since they could then acquire more foreign exchange with which to buy badly needed advanced equipment and technology from abroad. In this way, the solution to the disproportionate development of the production of soybeans and corn could be made much easier.

*****

DOCUMENT NO. 12

A PROGRAMME FOR CURRENT AGRICULTURAL WORK

(Beijing Review, No. 24, June 14, 1982)

The "Summary of the National Conference on Rural Work" released by the CPC Central Committee on April 6 is another programmatic document on the Party's work in rural areas, following the adoption of the Decisions on Some Questions Concerning the Acceleration of Agricultural Development (Draft) (see "Beijing Review," No. 11, 1979) at the Third Plenary Session of the Party's Eleventh Central Committee held in 1978.

The conference was held by the Party Central Committee towards the end of 1981. The programme systematically sums up the experiences gained in the recent years' readjustment and restructuring of the rural economy. It defines and solves some new problems encountered in practical work and charts further measures for rural development. Following is a slightly abridged translation of the document.-- ***Beijing Review** Ed.*

At the heels of the adoption of the decision on accelerating agricultural development, the Party Central Committee decided upon a series of measures to raise the purchasing prices of farm produce, to maximize the effectiveness of the responsibility system for agricultural production and to develop a diversified economy. Meanwhile, it carried out economic readjustment and restructuring in rural areas. All of these were enthusiastically accepted by the peasants and boosted the growth of rural economy.

The peasants have raised a number of questions encountered in practice. These must be solved in good time so as to ensure sustained, all-round development.

The Responsibility System

(1) More than 90 percent of the production teams across the nation have adopted some form of the responsibility system. The large-scale changes have come to an end, and the focus of our work is to sum up experience, perfect the system and stabilize the situation.

The progress in cstablishing the system mirrors the strong desire of the peasants to boost socialist agriculture in line with concrete conditions. The system has proved adaptable to numerous widely divergent areas. Egalitarianism with "everyone sharing the meal in the same big pot," which long pervaded the collective economy, has been overcome. By improving the organizations of the labor force and the methods of remuneration, the system changed the long-standing overconcentration of power in the hands of managers and the mechanical application of operational policies.

The collective economy, with a range of organizational scales and methods of operation, is still the major rural economic form. Coexistent with it are state farms, and the household-based economy which is playing a supplementary role. This structurally varied socialist agricultural economy is conducive to the development of the social productive forces and the full display of the superiority of the socialist system. It will undoubtedly have a positive influence on our rural economic construction and on social development as a whole.

Various localities' successful implementation of the Party's policies on agriculture, formulated after the Third Plenary Session of the Eleventh Party Central Committee, indicates the overall correctness of policies.

Since the transformation is so extensive and complicated, involving hundreds of millions of people, the emergence of problems is predictably unavoidable. We should strive to maximize the effectiveness of the responsibility system for agricultural production. From now on, except in a few districts and communes and production brigades, the responsibility system should be stabilized in the rural areas as a whole. Leaders at various levels should conduct thorough investigations of the grass-roots organizations to help sum up their experiences and solve problems in order to further improve the system.

(2)   Chinese agriculture must adhere to the road of socialist collectivization. The public ownership of land and other basic means of production will remain unchanged for a long time to come. So will the responsibility system for agricultural production for the collective economy.

The various forms of responsibility system in force at present include paying remuneration according to the short-term contract, paying seasonal remuneration for specialized farm work done, also according to a contract, fixing output quotas based on production group s[1] and allotting work to individual households.[2] Whatever form is currently being implemented should remain in force unless the peasants demand changes.

Some people believe that the production responsibility system is just a form of "allotting work to individual households," which means individual farming achieved by dividing up the collective land and properties.   This is a misunderstanding.

Since the implementation of "allotting work to individual households," many production teams have begun to operate with each household as a basic unit, responsible for their own gains and losses. But this is based on the public ownership of the land, with the peasants and the production teams maintaining a contracting relationship.

The collective still administers the utilization of the land, large-size farm tools and water conservancy facilities. The production team subjects itself to the guidance of the state plan and retains a portion of the earnings to provide subsidies for members of revolutionary martyr's families, soldiers' defendants and people who have financial difficulties.

Some production teams also engage in agricultural capital construction under unified planning. These activities differ from the private individual economy that existed before the co-operative transformation of agricultural economy. With the development of the productive forces, this form of responsibility system will gradually develop and improve.

(3) In introducing the responsibility system for production, more than 80 per cent of the production teams have adopted the methods of paying remuneration according to output. Generally speaking, this form calls for contracting. It can co-ordinate appropriately the relationship between the collective and individual interests, simultaneously displaying the role of collectively unified management and the individual peasant's power of decision-making. Hence its welcome among the peasants.

The various forms of responsibility system are the result of flexible implementation of contracting in light of local conditions. In some places with poor economic development, there are no distinct technical divisions, farming is the main economic activity, and collective sideline occupations are undeveloped. There the land is contracted out according to the proportion of labor power to the number of persons, or according to the average ability of the labor force. In the relatively economically developed communes and production teams which have highly specialized technical and occupational divisions, contracts are written for each economic specialty, such as farming, forestry, animal husbandry, sideline occupation, fishery or industry. In some places, the two methods are introduced in a mixed way to suit local conditions.

Some odd jobs may be contracted to the individual laborer or household. Those that need co-operation may be contracted out to groups. Whatever the form, it only reflects the scale of the labor organization required, and is not itself an indication of progress or regression.

Allotting work to individual laborers, households or production groups is a very simple methods of production welcomed by the peasant masses. With this method, peasants hand over to the collective only a defined portion of their yield and there is no need for book-keepers to determine work-points for them. But it is suitable only in places where scattered operations or management are most needed. In other places where sideline occupations account for a significant portion of the earnings, and there are complexities in the economic relationships and the utilization of labor, the equal exchange of labor needs a unified calculating standard for unified distribution in order to balance reasonably the earnings in various occupational categories.

In summary, each form of contracting has its own adaptability and limitation at a given place and under a given condition. Therefore, different methods are appropriate to different jobs.

(4) While establishing and perfecting the production responsibility system in agriculture, it is necessary to maintain the collective ownership of the land and pay earnest attention to the protection and rational utilization of cultivated land.

The utilization of land, vegetable gardens, forest land, grassland, water surface and beaches as well as barren mountain slopes and land owned by the collective must accord with the unified planning and arrangements of the collective. No unit or individual is allowed to occupy them randomly. The collective retains ownership of the small plots of land and mountain slopes distributed to commune members for their long-term private use as well as of the land allotted to them for building houses.

The peasants are strictly forbidden to build houses, dig graves or remove soil on land contracted out to them. If contracted land is bought, sold, rented, given away or wasted, the collective has the right to reclaim it. Peasants who do not have enough strength to till their plots, or who decide to do other jobs, should return the land to the collective.

China has a large population but little cultivated land. Therefore, it is an important state policy to control the growth of the population and protect cultivated land. Strict controls should be exercised over the occupation of cultivated land, especially of vegetable-growing land on the outskirts of cities, by government offices, enterprises, organizations, army units, schools, communes, production brigades or teams. Cases of illegal or irrational occupation of land should be corrected and dealt with.

Public buildings, production facilities, trees and other public property on the collectively owned land are a part of the socialist public accumulation. They are also the foundation upon which the collective economy can be further developed, so they must be properly protected. Suitable management techniques conducive to production may be adopted. Wanton destruction of them is not allowed.

(5) It is necessary to closely integrate perfection of the responsibility system with the goal of achieving an overall development of agricultural production. The current drive to diversify the economy and develop commodity production is a response to urgent demands from the broad masses of peasants. Development must keep pace with such demands. Production teams must draw up lands for the overall development of agriculture, forestry, animal husbandry, sideline occupations, fishery, industry and commerce in line with their specific conditions. They must also make a good arrangement of the labor force and adopt suitable forms of the responsibility system.

(6) Production teams which use contracts to implement the responsibility system must clearly define the rights and obligations of the parties to the contract. Because contracting is the main medium in the managerial work of the collective economy, it must be done with all might. Furthermore, the contracts must stipulate the parties' contributions towards the construction of public utilities, their family planning quotas and their quotas of grain for the state.

Improving Rural Commodity Circulation

(7) The current financial resources of the state require a basic stabilization of the purchasing prices for agricultural and sideline products during the foreseeable future. We cannot pin our hope of increasing the peasants' income on raising purchasing prices or lowering purchasing quotas. We can only depend on the development of commodity production and production of more marketable goods.

(8) Agricultural economy is an important part of the national economy and its major component must be the planned economy, with regulation by the market playing a supplementary role. The policy of state monopoly of purchasing and marketing of grain, cotton, edible oil and other products must be upheld.

Reasonable and basic quotas for second-priority agricultural and sideline products (such as meat, poultry and eggs), which are decided by the sate, should remain unchanged for a few years. On products for which it is difficult to determine purchasing quotas, a reasonable ratio should be ascertained between the proportion purchased by the state and that kept by the individual producers.

As for that portion above the basic quotas, the state may purchase all of some products, it may purchase a portion of other products, while still others should be left entirely to the communes and production teams or the individual peasants.

The prices of products that exceed the basic quotas should be allowed to fluctuate within a certain range in line with the supply and demand of the market. Peasants on the outskirts of cities should be encouraged to grow more vegetables. Long-standing vegetable-growing plots should not be used for other purposes so that the vegetable supply to the cities can be guaranteed and improved. The contract system must be publicized and gradually adopted in order to improve the co-ordination between the tasks set by the state plan and the peasants' own priorities for production.

(9) Supply and marketing co-operatives in the countryside are a major channel for economic exchanges between the cities and the countryside. They are also a bond to promote economic integration in the rural areas. These co-operatives should be gradually reformed. Each province can choose one or two counties to carry out the following experiment: Run the supply and marketing co-operatives at the grass-roots level as a form of co-operative commerce; take in more shares from the production teams and individual peasants on a voluntary basis; distribute the profit in the form of dividends according to the amount of shares and amount of agricultural and sideline products sold to the state; introduce democratic management and combine the management of the co-operative with the economic interests of the peasants.

(10) It is necessary to open up and strengthen the channels of commodity circulation by every available means. The state commercial departments and rural supply and marketing co-operatives must make full use of existing institutions, overcome the limitations in communication between the localities, organize commodity circulation according to economic laws and do a good job in marketing.

(11) It is necessary to carry out on-the-spot processing, select the choice products and to comprehensively utilize agricultural and sideline products under the precondition that the established quotas are handed over to the state. In addition to the development of processing industries run by the communes and production brigades or teams in the rural areas, the commercial departments can also process agricultural and sideline products they purchase, or process them

together with the communes and production teams, or they can entrust the job to peasant households.

Agricultural Science and Technology

(12)   Agriculture can absorb the fruits of scientific and technological research in many fields and thus become a knowledge-intensive productive sector. While giving full play to our country's traditional agricultural techniques, wider use of the results of modern science and technology of reap greater economic results and maintain the ecological environment with less investment and lower consumption of energy will change the outlook of our countryside.

(13)   In carrying out agricultural scientific research, it is necessary to mobilize all forces to work out a plan for key projects, such as breeding higher quality varieties of crops, improving the cropping system and cultivation techniques, scientific application of fertilizer and rational use of water, developing new effective and low-toxic insecticides and publicizing agricultural mechanization in a selective manner.

(14)   It is necessary to restore and strengthen the institutions for popularizing agricultural technology at various levels and to reinforce the contingents of technical personnel. Stress should be placed on improving those at the county level. Organizations responsible for popularizing technological findings, plant protection measures and soil and fertilizer information should gradually be combined. They should be centrally managed, with a reasonable division of labor and should co-ordinate with each other so as to fully utilize the results of scientific and technical research in production.

(15)   Agricultural work such as resource surveys and agricultural zoning must be done well so as to provide a scientific basis for the exploitation, utilization and protection of natural resources and for readjustment of the structure of agricultural production. At present, stress should be placed on surveys of soil, water and biological resources and surveys of key areas. Particular attention should be paid to strengthening the protection of agricultural resources and halting the deterioration of the ecological environment in some places. We should make efforts in defining agricultural zones at the county level and, on this basis, draw up a general plan for utilizing land and building up the countryside.

(16)   Departments concerned should make efforts to consolidate and strengthen the leading bodies of colleges and universities of agricultural sciences and improve their working conditions. Middle schools at or below the country level should include agricultural courses in their curriculums. Some middle

schools in the rural areas may be converted into agricultural technical schools. Both agricultural colleges and secondary agricultural technical schools should shoulder the task of training cadres who are now working in the countryside.

(17)   The vast countryside is presently experiencing an upsurge in the number of peasants seeking to learn and use science.   Agroscientists and agrotechnicians should devote their energy to agricultural production and unselfishly give the peasants whatever assistance they can provide.   In the future, graduates of colleges and universities as well as secondary vocational schools will be assigned jobs as technicians at the commune level every year. They will enjoy the same status as cadres.   All localities may hold examinations for self-taught peasant technicians at regular intervals, issue diplomas and grant technical subsidies to them.   They should find employment for the most accomplished.

Enhancing Economic Results and Improving Production Conditions

(18)   Like other sectors, in agricultural production, great importance should be attached to economic results and tapping potentials.

During the readjustment period, investments in agriculture are limited and efforts should be made to maximize results with these minimal investments. Agricultural work must stress improving the per-unit yield and increasing labor productivity in farming, cultivation and industrial and sideline occupations. The increase of grain and cash crops mainly depends on intensive farming and improvement of medium- and low-yielding plots.   Other sectors should also make efforts to improve economic results.

(19)   A rational production structure should be established in accordance with the requirements of the all-round development of farming, forestry, animal husbandry, sideline production and fishery.   The past error of developing a single-product economy should be avoided.   Attention must be paid to co-ordinating the rational distribution of agricultural production in the country on the one hand and local development plans suited to specific conditions on the other.   All localities must implement the policy of "never slackening the grain production and vigorously carrying out the diversified economy."   In the utilization of the land, major efforts should be made to gradually convert the cultivated plots which are not suitable to grain production but are suitable to other crops.   Cotton and sugar-bearing crops which are urgently needed by the state, should be developed in suitable areas.   Diversified economy should be vigorously developed.   Emphasis is to be on the development of mountainous areas, water surface, beaches and grasslands and on household animal raising.

The development of the diversified economy should be a combined effort of the collective and the individuals. The existing enterprises run by communes and production brigades should be straightened out. Administration and democratic management should be improved. At the present stage, in some areas many items will mainly be managed by the peasant families. The policy of supporting household sideline occupations and skilful individual peasants should be implemented. Assistance and guidance in the fields of funds, techniques and supply and marketing must be provided. At the same time, attention must be paid to the requirements of the development of production. Co-operation and association must be promoted between individuals, and between individuals and the collective. Co-operation and association between communes and production brigades in the localities and those in other areas are also allowed.

(20) The weak links of our national economy are forestry and animal husbandry. Effective measures should be taken to restore and develop them as quickly as possible.

The 1981 state resolutions on the protection of the forest and other questions on the development of forestry and the decision to develop afforestation through participation from the whole people should be earnestly implemented.

In the rural areas, effective measures and policies encouraging the development of animal husbandry should be carried out down to the households, making full use of the favorable conditions of the abundant labor force, equipment and fodder there. On the basis of investigations, the ownership of the pastoral areas should be specified so as to better protect and build up the pastoral areas. On the vast frontiers as well as on barren hills and uncultivated areas, aeroplane sowing, tree and grass planting should be continuously carried out in a planned way.

(21) Since the founding of the People's Republic in 1949, great achievements have been chalked up in irrigation, but great waste and losses still exist. In the future, large-scale water conservancy construction should be carried out in accordance with the overall plan. Those water conservancy works which require much investment but yield little benefit should be suspended. Attention must be paid to scientific management of those works which have gone into operation. Small-scale construction of water conservancy works must be carried on and substantial results must be stressed. Advanced irrigation techniques and cultivation measures should be popularized.

The mechanization of agriculture must be carried out step by step. For a fairly long time to come, mechanization, semi-mechanization and hand tools are to be developed simultaneously; and manpower, animals and power energy should all be used. Farmland capital construction and technical biological measures should be combined.

Energetic efforts should be made to increase the production of phosphorus and potash fertilizer and fertilizer containing microelements, thus improving the composition of the chemical fertilizer and raising the effects of their application. Attention must be paid to the utilization of farmyard and green manure and leguminous plants. Compost made of stalks should be returned to the farmland so as to regulate the chemical and physical functions of the soil and increase the soil's organic matter. Chemical fertilizer supplies to the medium- and low-yielding areas should be increased and efforts must be made to produce pesticide with high efficiency and low toxicity.

(22) The accounting units of the collective economy must establish an economic accounting system and carefully analyze economic activities in order to reduce the cost of production.

Strengthening Ideological Work and Organization at the Grass-Roots Level

(23) In recent years, the Party has done a great deal of work in rural areas and has achieved remarkable results. However, laxness and weak ideological and political work still exists in some rural areas. Effective measures must be taken to improve this situation.

The broad masses of peasants are willing to take the socialist road under the leadership of the Party. But at the present stage, some peasants still retain the ideologies and habits left over from the old society. They need the constant education and correct guidance given by the political party of the working class.

In the winter of 1981 and the spring of 1982, the central task for leaders in various localities should be to educate the peasants in the light of their problems in work and in ideology centering around the consolidation of the responsibility system so as to make them understand: China must adhere to the road of socialist collectivization of agriculture; the public ownership will not change for a long period of time; nor will the responsibility system in production; and none of the interests of the state, the collective or the individuals should be neglected. The production portion designated for the collective and the state quotas must be fulfilled. The peasants must be clear that in the past three years, the state has done its utmost to give consideration to the interests of the peasants, and the peasants should give their consideration to the difficulties of the state. They should make efforts to develop production, increase commodities and make further contributions.

(24) The implementation of the Party's policies and the fulfillment of various tasks in the rural areas depend on the organizations at the grass-roots level, including the Party organization, the administration organization, the economic organization and the mass organizations.

At present, weakness in the leadership in some localities has caused paralysis or semi-paralysis in the leading bodies of some production teams. The result is that no one is responsible for certain kinds of work. Leading groups in the communes and production brigades should be well organized in order to improve the production responsibility system.

As collective economic organizations, production brigades and production teams should retain authority over essential economic functions. They should rationally distribute the plots to individuals, take good care of the cultivated land and use them well, draw up production plans, arrange work in capital construction, popularize new techniques, sign contracts with the peasants and carry them out, fulfill the state purchasing quotas, designate the portion of products for the collective, and take care of the families of the martyrs and armymen and those with financial difficulties.

(25) Party organizations at the grass-roots level in the countryside are the force at the core leading the broad masses forward. The Party and its members united and led the peasants to wage great revolutionary wars and carry out land reform and the co-operative movement in the past. Now China is living in a era of great changes and developments. Members of the Party in power should carry forward the traditions of wholeheartedly serving the people, and should unite and lead the peasants in readjusting and restructuring the rural economy, thus contributing to the modernization of agriculture. At present, they should stand in the forefront of the peasants and lead them to improve the responsibility system in production.

Starting in 1982, with the county or the communes as a unit, Party members in the rural areas, particularly the commune and production brigades cadres, should be trained by rotation in a planned way during the slack seasons. They should be organized to study the "resolution on Certain Questions in the History of Our Party Since the Founding of the People's Republic of China" and the various policies of the Party in the rural areas, to sum up experiences in the spirit of rectification, to unfold criticism and self-criticism and to enhance their awareness. The Party branches in the rural areas should become staunch fighting nuclei, thus securing the Party's leadership over the administrative organizations, economic organizations and mass organizations and ensuring the fulfillment of various tasks.

*****

NOTES

1. Under both these forms, peasants contract with the production teams to produce a particular quantity of a crop or product. This amount must be delivered to the collective, with the remainder going partly or wholly to the peasants themselves as reward. As members of the collective they also receive an allotment which is apportioned from the collective produce. The specialization contracts divide labor according to specialized jobs while the production-group contracts do no specify a division of labor.

2. The contractors deliver to the production teams the part retained by the collective, with the remaining part belonging to the peasants themselves. They do not receive an allotment from collective distribution.

DOCUMENT NO. 13

IMPORTANT CHANGE IN THE SYSTEM
OF PEOPLE'S COMMUNES

by

Song Dahan and Zhang Chunsheng

(**Beijing Review**, No. 29, July 19, 1982)

In the "Notes From the Editors" column in issue No. 13, 1982, we examined the possibility of changing the present system of rural people's communes, which combine government administration with commune management. Here two members of the Commission for Legal Affairs of the NPC Standing Committee further explain the reasons for the change and the steps involved. --Beijing Review Ed.

The Draft of the Revised Constitution of the People's Republic of China stipulates the re-establishment of township governments and retains the people's communes as collective economic organizations which no longer function as a level of political power. The suggestion for the changes was made after summing up long years of experience with the commune system. It answers the needs of boosting the rural collective economy and strengthening political power at the grass-roots level in the new period of socialist construction.

The people's commune system was founded in 1958. Later, adjustments were made as to its scale and management powers. This led to the institution of the system of "three-level ownership by the commune, production brigade and production team, with the production team as the basic accounting unit." At the same time the communes function as a level of political power. This has remained intact until today.

At present, a medium-sized people's commune is roughly the size of a township of earlier years. It governs the work and lives of more than 10,000 persons in some 2,000 peasant families. A commune is divided into production brigades and a production brigade is sub-divided into production teams. Usually a production team embraces 20-30 peasant households having more than 100 people.

Since the second half of last year, the Commission for Legal Affairs of the NPC Standing Committee has sent investigators to several provinces to study the rural economy.

Based on the opinions of commune members, local cadres and economists, the investigators unanimously agreed that the communes have played a positive role in organizing large-scale farmland capital construction and the construction of water conservancy projects and in running rural sideline occupations by pooling labor power and capital. These improved agricultural production conditions and boosted the development of the rural economy in some areas.

However, some insurmountable contradictions exist because the economic organizations and the organs of political power are identical. Therefore changes should be made step by step.

Advantages of Separation

The advantages of separating government administration from commune management, that is, the establishment of a township level of political power while retaining the people's communes as collective economic organizations, are:

(1) It is conducive to maintaining the independent management of the rural collective economic organizations.

One of the important aspects of China's current economic restructuring in both urban and rural areas is the expansion of the decision-making rights of economic organizations under the guidance of a unified state plan. Rural collective economic organizations have independent material interests and should have more decision-making rights in management than state-owned enterprises. Only thus can the enthusiasm of laborers be mobilized to improve business management and economic effects.

Under the present system of combining government administration with commune management, too much administrative interference makes independent business accounting difficult. For instance, before the system has changed, government-imposed unpaid labor required from the Xiangyand People's Commune in Sichuan Province averaged 10 percent of its total amount of labor every year. Furthermore, the commune itself also used the labor power and funds of the production teams without remuneration, thus interfering with team production and distribution.

Since the Party's policies for accelerating the growth of agriculture were formulated in 1978 at the Third Plenary Session of the Eleventh Party Central Committee, the localities have made great efforts to expand the decision-making rights of the production teams. Successes have already been achieved in this field. But encroachments upon the rights and interests of the teams continue to occur. Thus, without changing the present system, independent management in collective economic organizations cannot be guaranteed legally or institutionally.

(2) It is conducive to the development of a socialized and specialized rural economy.

In recent years, the rural areas have expanded from single grain crop economies to all-round development of numerous undertakings. Division of work according to specialties has gradually become the norm in agricultural production. The ratio of commodities in farm output has been raised. Rural economic activities that cross administration divisions, such as business transactions with city factories, have been increasing. Trans-team, trans-commune and trans-regional economic joint enterprises, such as agricultural-industrial-commercial complexes and other companies dealing with seeds, plant protection, agrotechnology and farm machinery have emerged.

The divergence between the original administrative regions and the scope of present economic activities has become clear. An agricultural-industrial-commercial complex may embrace several communes, or even factories and other enterprises in the urban area. Therefore, maintaining a common government administration and commune management is obviously not beneficial to the growth of production.

(3) It is conducive to scientific management.

Under the present system of combining government administration with commune management, the administrative centre of a commune is quite large. Commune cadres often hold too many posts and cannot concentrate their efforts on economic affairs. Because most of these cadres are paid by the government regardless of the success or failure of the collective economy, it is hard to evoke in them a sense of economic responsibility and enthusiasm. In addition, because they are simultaneously government administrators and economic managers, the cadres must attend to every aspect of the work and lives of the peasants. It is hard to establish a strict responsibility system in their work. The separation of the two will enable the local government to supervise and give guidance to the grass-roots level through planning, finances, taxation, bank loans and commodity pricing. It will free grass-roots rural economic organizations to manage their own production and business affairs.

(4) It is conducive to strengthening political power at the grass roots.

Since 1979, the production responsibility system has been popularized throughout the country. The material interests of individual peasants are now recognized and protected. This mobilizes the peasants' initiative for production. As a result, the tasks of mediating disputes, maintaining public security, tax collection, village construction and providing welfare facilities have become heavier. They require stronger local political organizations.

However, under the present system, when the busy farming seasons come, commune leaders have to devote all their energy to production. Their work as political leaders cannot but be weakened. The separation of the two will lead to the establishment of township governments and villagers committees that can devote all their time to political power building and administration. This will contribute to peace and stability in the rural areas.

Step-by-Step Change

The separation of government administration from commune management is a big issue which involves the political and economic life of the 800 million Chinese peasants. It will have a great impact on the development of China's countryside. The state will institute the reforms cautiously in order to ensure the smooth progress of production and other work.

If the people of the whole country agree to separate government administration from commune management after their discussion of the draft of the revised Constitution, then once the Constitution has been formally adopted by the National People's Congress, the government will conduct experiments on a larger scale than the current trials done in several counties. Experiences will be summed up and on this basis, concrete laws and policies will be formulated. It will take several years to complete this reform step by step in the light of local situations.

The draft of the revised Constitution states clearly that the people's communes will continue to be form of collective economic organizations in the rural areas after their function as a level of government administration has been removed.   The separation of government administration from commune management will not change the ownership of the communes, production brigades and teams with regard to their enterprises and other collective property. The name of the commune may still be used, or the communes may be reorganized into other suitable economic organizations.   During the experiment in Sichuan Province, some communes have changed into agricultural-industrial-commercial complexes and some production teams into agricultural producers' co-operatives.

The successful experiment in three counties in Sichuan, which divided the work and responsibility of the rural Party organizations, political power organs and economic organizations, resulted in much more clearly defined responsibilities after the separation.   The over-concentration of power in the hands of a few people in the political, economic and cultural fields was eliminated.   This was conducive to giving play to democracy and to effecting democratic management within economic organizations.   As a result, the rural economy grew and the peasants' income increased by a big margin. Work improved in every field.

*****

CHAPTER FOUR

PARTY WORK STYLE
AND "SOCIALIST SPIRITUAL CIVILIZATION"

The documents in Chapter Four are concerned principally with the problems associated with Communist Party leadership. The documents especially express a concern with inner-Party discipline and with the spirit of Party members and their commitment to Communist principles.

In Document No. 14, a speech to a Party Central Committee Work Conference, veteran Party leader Ch'en Yun gave a blunt assessment of the problems of inner-Party discipline and spirit. He lamented, "To be sure, people of my age will be able to rekindle the Yenan spirit probably only in our next life." Document No. 15 is a *People's Daily* editorial on the subject of Party work style which made favorable reference to another strong speech by Ch'en Yun.

Document No. 16 is a long speech by Teng Hsiao-p'ing at a 1980 Party Central Committee Working Conference. Teng stressed his support for the important "adjustments" in Party policy adopted at the Third Plenum of the Eleventh Central Committee which were discussed in Chapter Eleven. Teng also stressed the importance of Party leadership, which he called the "nucleus of the Four Basic Principles," and of improving Party working style.

Both Documents Nos. 17 and 18 carry on the theme of improving Party working style and correcting mistakes in order to push forward the reform policies. Documents Nos. 19 and 21 call on the Chinese people to emulate Lei Feng a model young PLA soldier who died in 1962 and was the subject of a huge nationwide emulation campaign during the 1960s. Document No. 20 focuses on the fight against "rampant" corruption among Party members and cadres. Document No. 22 is an attack on "bourgeois liberalization," which once again stresses the importance of maintaining Party leadership.

*****

DOCUMENTS

14. "Ch'en Yun's, Speech at the CPC Central Committee Work Conference, April 1979," **Issues & Studies**, Vol. 16, No. 4, April 1980.

15. "Fully Understand the Extreme Importance of Correcting the Party Work Style," **Jenmin Jihpao** editorial, December 11, 1980; **FBIS-CHI**, December 12, 1980.

16. Teng Hsiao-p'ing, "Carrying Through the Principles of Adjustment, Improving the Work of the Party and Guaranteeing Stability and Solidarity--A Speech by Teng Hsiao-p'ing at the CPC Central Working Conference," Beijing, by Teng Hsiao-p'ing December 25, 1980, **Issues & Studies**, Vol. XVII, No. 7, July 1981.

17. "Eliminate 'Leftist' Influence to Push the Work of the Whole Province in a Better Way," Excerpts of the February 20 editorial in **Hunan Ribao**, **Jenmin Jihpao**, Beijing, February 24, 1981; **FBIS-CHI**, February 25, 1981.

18. "Building Socialist Spiritual Civilization," **Beijing Review**, No. 10, March 9, 1981.

19. "Carry Forward the Spirit of Lei Feng," **Beijing Review**, No. 10, March 9, 1981.

20. "Be a Sober-Minded Marxist," **Beijing Review**, No. 12, March 22, 1981.

21. "Young People Learn from Lei Feng," **Beijing Review**, No. 14, April 4, 1982.

22. Hu Qiao-mu, "On Bourgeois Liberalization and Other Problems," **Beijing Review**, No. 23, June 7, 1982.

*****

DOCUMENT NO. 14

CH'EN YUN'S SPEECH AT THE CPC CENTRAL COMMITTEE WORK CONFERENCE
April 1979
(**Issues & Studies**, Vol. 16, No. 4, April 1980)

"Nobody Speaks the Truth at Meetings"

Usually whenever there is a meeting, not a few people come forward to air their views. But things that can really be solved at meetings are too few in number. What is said are often things that should not have been said. But nobody talks about things that should have been talked about. Why can't we say fewer unnecessary words? What's wrong with saving some human energy?

There have been quite a few meetings since the Third Plenum, but what good is it if they cannot solve problems? For the last two days I have listened with patience at this meeting and feel something is not quite right; some comrades have wanted to speak but decided not to upon second thought. This is a matter for us to think about. Did they have some unspeakable grievances which they had wanted to express in order to give vent to their pent-up feelings? Class contradictions in society are already much too complicated and it is surprising that contradictions within the Party are even more complicated. In the interest of the whole Party, I cannot but state my views although this may offend some people.

Some comrades may have reasons to regret for having advanced me to this post, but it is not too late [for them to change their mind.] If they are not pleased with me, they may just keep me on as a figurehead. For example, they may assign me as a member of the Politburo without letting me do anything. Anyway, there have been many such precedents, and the [Party] Central for quite some time used to ask some people to stand aside without giving any explanation to Party members or even the Party representatives. Isn't it true that Liu Shao-ch'i, Ho lung, P'eng Te-huai and T'ao Chu all died with reasons unknown? Had it not been for criticisms from the higher level and pressures from the lower level, those branded earlier as traitors would continue to be regarded as such, and those branded as counter-revolutionaries would continue to be so condemned. Things would go on like this indefinitely. If people's life which is so very important can be handled so callously, how can anybody be so surprised that people's aspirations should remain unfulfilled? To be sure, people of my age will be able to rekindle the Yenan spirit probably only in our next life.

"Tolling the Bell as Long as One Is a Monk"

Last month, I called Comrade Wu Te to my place to discuss something. At first, I was afraid that it might not be easy for me to talk with him on that matter and, at least, I had to make an effort to be circumspect as he might be involved in it. But my judgment proved to be wrong. Comrade Wu Te said in the end: "People like me can be promoted or demoted from my present position only once more. Even if there should be a second time, what can be made known to me will be limited." Isn't it the same with me? The four modernizations will be realized in A.D. 2000. Can we live long enough to see it? Thinking of this, I feel much more peaceful inside myself. How many people there must be in the country who like us have already waited thirty years and will have to continue to wait for another twenty or thirty years? This is really [according to an old Chinese saying], "Do not waste time when young and feel mournful when old." The Pa Pao Shan [cemetery] has no room for many more people. Since we shan't be able to see the "four modernizations" realized in our lifetime and cannot all go to Pa Pao Shan, we have to do what is expected of us. In such a circumstances, what is the use of talking about Marxism-Leninism? That being so, to wait passively is what the clever people will do.

"Cadres' Thinking Is Degenerated and Their Life Corrupted"

At this moment, what needs to be solved first is not only questions concerning economic readjustment but also those concerning the people's mind. To put it more explicitly, the morale of the Party, the army and the people should be restored. No decision can be made if there is no confidence [in the future]. This meeting has already lasted for several days. Could it be possible that nobody has perceived this point? Actually, every one has noticed it, but no one wants to say anything. Otherwise, it would lead to many more questions including class status, historical background and ideological consciousness, and few people will have the necessary courage to turn around to take a look at the footprints we have left behind us. In the final analysis, this is the root problem. It is an impasse that could not be solved in the past two years. Why is it we feared nothing and not even feared being annihilated during the period of revolution, but fear everything now? Could it be because of the comfortable life we are leading now? For transportation, we travel by cars and do not have to walk; for housing, we have luxurious Western-style buildings. In the past, we did not dare to keep too many things in our house, and even if we must, we put them in places not easily noticeable to others. When the Red Guards confiscated the properties of some people during the Cultural Revolution, the things ferreted out from under the beds of some leading comrades were more valuable than those found in conspicuous places. We do not have this kind of fear now. Who among you comrades present here does not have an air conditioner, a washing machine and a refrigerator in your house? Take the TV set for example, please raise your hand if the one in your house is not imported from some foreign country! The one in my house is a "Siemens" product. Our mode of transportation and housing conditions being what they are, we need not say any more about food and clothing. For inspection trips, we take airplanes. Wherever we go, there are people to wait on us. This, of course, is good. Is there anybody who prefers to lead a bitter life instead of a good life? If I had known that I would have to suffer hardship for more than ten years, I, Ch'en Yun, not to mention others, would have been the first one to follow Chang Kuo-t'ao when he left Yenan for Chungking to see Chiang Kai-shek. One becomes more scared when he leads a more comfortable life. What is there to be afraid of? One is afraid of losing his power. Mao Tse-tung also had this kind of fear because he was a human being but not a god. That is why he said: "Don't get yourself beheaded before you know the reason." In order not to lose one's head, one has to hold on to power. Take Pao Cheng, [an upright official in Sung Dynasty known for his strictness in upholding the sanctity of law] for instance, he righted wrongs for people and feared not even the emperor's relatives. But he could not sleep one night when he found that his official seal had been stolen. However, no one alone will be able to secure power. Only by forming factions can people secure their power and positions. As a result, there naturally are parties outside the Party, and factions within the Party. No faction dares to be careless in dealing with other factions, and they would rather suspect others than believe in them. This is the way they treat other factions, and don't they do the same to comrades of their own faction? Everyone feels insecure and is on guard all the time. What would happen if we should let it go on like this? Think it over for yourselves!

"Liu Shao-ch'i Made One Mistake, Teng Hsiao-p'ing Adds One Half"

You said that Liu Shao-ch'i made many mistakes and it appears that since he took part in the revolution he had been sometimes on the left and other times on the right, sometimes had participated in the revolution and other times refused to participate in it and even betrayed it and finally became a counter-revolutionary element himself. In my opinion, Liu Shao-ch'i did not make many mistakes, but he made a fatal one. Which one? What he really should not have done was to serve as the state chairman in 1959, thereby placing himself at the forefront while there were the first and the second fronts. Speaking of this matter, both Teng Hsiao-p'ing and I were also wrong in pushing him into that unlucky position. What about Comrade Teng Hsiao-p'ing? He made one and a half mistakes, one half more than Liu Shao-ch'i's. Teng made that one half mistake at the time of the Cultural Revolution. What is that one mistake? He really should not have delivered that speech at the Eighth Congress voicing his opposition to personality cult shortly after Stalin's death and in doing so, he violated the taboo. As a result, he had a record of three ups and three downs in his career. Wasn't this true?

"We Are Afraid of People Who Take a Passive Attitude and Not Participate in Production, and People Who Actively Pick Other's Faults"

We used to say: "The class struggle in society will surely be reflected in the Party." There is nothing wrong with this observation. However, isn't the factional struggle, or, we shall say, the power struggle in the Party, also reflected in society? Since Marxism-Leninism puts emphasis on dialectics, how can it overlook this point? What is reflected in society? It is not mass movement but mass struggle. Why can't we understand in the past more than ten years that the content of mass struggle is the same as that of class struggle? Fortunately at least, some people have understood this. We have noticed it, and we cannot cover it up. The ordinary people want to lift the lid. Once the lid is lifted, we probably will lose our power. Who wants to lose his power? Because no one is willing to lose his power, he is sure to be afraid. Afraid of whom? Those who seek to disclose our shortcomings. It is those small people that one is afraid of.

At present, we are afraid of two kinds of people more so than we are fearful of the Soviet revisionists. These two kinds of people have been mentioned before: One kind of people take a passive attitude and we can do nothing about it. They cope with dynamics with inaction and place themselves in undefeatable positions. If there are too many of this kind of people, our production will lag behind and our society will not make any progress. If our society does not move forward, the life of our Party will come to a stop. How serious is it? This has already resulted in the lackluster situation as it exists today although outwardly we seem to have made some magnificent achievements. The second kind of people are those who take an active attitude. What are they being active about? Not active in production but active in picking others' faults. It is not that we do not know how to deal with them, but is that it will take considerable effort. If we do not put them under control, they will dig here and there until finally there is a big hole at the foot of the wall. We can stand some pain and even shed some blood if necessary, but once we talk about someone digging at the foot of the wall, we have to do our best to stop it because it will be too much to endure and make us lose our power. There is no better solution.

"People Will Not Be Deceived by Lies and It Is Not a Good Idea to Wait"

How did these two kinds of people come into being? In my opinion, there are four reasons, I don't know if you agree with me:

(1) Because they now understand the things that previously had no idea of. For example, [they now know that] workers in foreign countries lead a better life than workers in our country. This single point will suffice to explain the whole thing.

(2) They do not want to listen to empty words they have heard before. For example, [they have been told that] the situation in our country is excellent, but they still need coupons to buy food and have to line up for shopping. They are still hungry after shouting slogans.

(3) They do not want to die as martyrs to their ideals but want instead to have some real benefits. For example, what they want only is a better life here and now, and even if Communism is a paradise, the next generation can have it.

(4) They have become tired of waiting. For example, they have already waited thirty years and yet they will have to wait another thirty years. Just as we ourselves have found waiting hard to endure, they, of course, are not happy waiting any longer. Moreover, they want justice. What justice? The cadres have improved their lot while the common people are still tossing on the boundless sea of hard life.

"Political Calls, Criticisms and Struggles Are All Useless"

It won't do to deal with this kind of people with administrative decrees or ordinary political sermons, not to say criticism and struggle. We are now in a dilemma, not knowing whether to arrest them or to let them go on. Sometimes it is more troublesome for us to arrest them than to leave them alone. Let's put it this way: "It is easy to arrest a man but difficult to release him." Take Wei Ching-sheng, for instance. We can neither arrest him nor release him. Comrade Lin Hu-chia asked me what to do. I told him: "As you arrested the man, it is you who should decide whether the man should be sentenced or released. After all, it is up to the person who has tied the bell in the first place to untie it." What's the use asking the Commission for Inspection of Discipline of the Party Central

Committee? We are not gods and cannot think of better tactics either. In my opinion, we could have done no better at the time than talking with him, having him take a look around the country and visit some factories to see how conscientiously our workers are doing and then try to dissuade him. Some people were afraid that President Carter may change his China policy because of his espousal of human rights if the foreign press should attack us on the Wei case. I do not worry about it. Carter has ten or a hundred reasons for normalizing relations with us, but human rights are not among them. Don't look for troubles. It is domestic issues we need to worry about.

"There Are the Best, the Second Best and the Worst Policies, It Is Better to Follow the Second Best Policy"

Some comrades may want to ask: "Where should we begin at the present time when there are a host of problems?" With regard to this question, why don't we see, first of all, what solutions we have to the current problems and then study where to begin. It is more practical that way.

Several days ago, I intentionally went to Chiuhsienchiao and a few other places where I had talks with some commune members and cadres. Later, I talked with some factory workers and middle school and college students at Fengt'ai. I came away with a stronger belief in the correctness of my viewpoint that there are three options, namely, the best, the second best, and the worst policies to tackle our problems:

(1) The first one is a thorough elimination of all existing impediments, including the sacred label, even at the risk of causing its advocate to lose his power. Do we still need the Party leadership? We couldn't care less. But as far as I can see, no one would accept such a thorough way of doing things. Let's say no more about it!

(2) Although the second one is not aimed at solving things so thoroughly, it can at least improve the current situation to a certain extent. Make a large-scale readjustment of the economic relationships and perform a minor operation without demolishing the existing political institutions. Currently, this policy will most likely be acceptable to a majority of people and can get quick results.

(3) The third one is to maintain the status quo. Although we must not prescribe medicines recklessly in hope to cure our illness, we would be able to do nothing but apply local treatments to ease the pain and use only such remedial resources as are available. I dare not say there will be no disturbances within eight or ten years, but we can safely see three to five years down the road! As

to what will happen after that, I am afraid it is beyond our ability to do anything about it, because by that time, many of us shall have been buried underneath the ground for a long time.

Let's study how to perform the kind of operation under the second option! I'll show you a simple and easily understood example. Just think, why people in factories show no interest when they hear someone mention that "the four modernizations will be realized by the end of the twentieth century and that the major production targets will reach certain level by 1990," but get excited when they hear that an extra amount of pork will be made available in the afternoon; why they will hurry up in their work when they are told that whoever finishes his work earlier can go home earlier. Dancing is not easy and as a matter of fact, people sweat more in dancing than working, and yet people enjoy dancing and never get tired? Why so many people admire things foreign and want to go abroad? I think it is better to find answers to these questions before we decide where to begin the operation.

"Have Enough Food and Loosen the Control over People's Thought Are the Most Important Things"

"To the people, food is heaven (of primary importance)." "What's the most important questions? The answer is food." All leaders know to say the same thing. It is one thing if conditions do not permit and quite another if conditions do permit. During the war against Japan, there were chaos and social upheavals, and battles were incessant. Therefore, it was not surprising that some people died of starvation at the time of natural calamities and man-made disasters. But is it acceptable to one's sense of justice if people are still dying of starvation at a time of peace, years after the storm of revolution had passed? From the Great Leap Forward up till now, there have been reports about people dying of starvation. How can anyone say that the situation is good and [when reporting the situation, the news media always say that] it is not just good, but excellent and that the situation is getting better day after day? Not long ago, some people who appealed to the higher authority for justice in individual cases were found to be dying of illness or hunger on streets in Peking. Is the Public Security Bureau of the Peking Municipality a corpse-gathering team? Why doesn't it feed those corpses to the wolves? Once we settle questions concerning food, housing, clothing and daily necessities, people can lead a better life. People will not get nervous and we'll have no trouble if we supply the people with sufficient food and loosen up a bit the control over their thinking instead of holding it in a tight grip, conduct more literary and athletic activities, and pay more attention to their work load and give them enough time to rest. Unity, tensions, solemnity and liveliness. In the present circumstances we lack for unity and liveliness but have too much solemnity and tensions. If we grasp well these questions, we'll have no trouble at all. Of course, if we want to improve our livelihood, build up our country, increase production and truly make some outstanding achievements, it will not do if we just shout some empty slogans, work out some grand but impractical projects, or set up some targets. Rather, we should view a thing from near to the afar and deduct it from the distant to the present and then carry it out step by step. At this meeting, I also want to express some of my opinions on the planned readjustment of our national economy.

"For the Settlement of Economic Problems, It is Necessary First to Carry out Political Renovation"

Today we are confronted with many difficulties. Some of them have resulted from the objective situation while others are caused by man-made factors. In the matter of objective situation, we are limited by many unfavorable conditions in the implementation of our economic development plans. As a result, we achieved little despite our herculean efforts. Many comrades have commented on this point. What about the man-made factors? Few people have talked about this question at the meeting in the past two days. Is it possible that this question does not exist? Yes, and definitely it does exist! And there are many such questions. Shouldn't the man-made factors also be given due attention? The causes for our current economic problems did not begin today or yesterday. "A sheet of ice three feet in thickness takes more than one cold day to form." The same theory is applicable here.

Economic problems have long existed in our society. Since the liberation of our country, economic questions have never been thoroughly resolved. The situation has changed back and forth many times. Sometimes the situation was better because we had a better sense of proportion, followed a right policy and took a comparatively correct approach. Otherwise, there would have been many more problems and our country would have found itself in even greater financial straits. I do not mean to discourage you. In the thirty years since liberation, there were very few leaders who correctly understood the laws of economic development and who could provide good guidance in economic matters. Not a few economists have ridiculed us by saying that "The Communists seized the country on horseback but did not know how to rule it after they dismounted." Although this observation is not completely correct, it is not far from the truth. The question lies not in the Party itself but in the fact that many comrades in our Party have no idea even today of the "close relationship between the economic foundation and the superstructure." They always tend to overlook special features of economics and apply political theories to economic issues. If by luck or by chance, they should succeed once or twice, they become more unmindful of the long-range objectives. Consequently, they run into difficulties for the eight and tenth time. Confronted with this kind of problem, they do not make a conscientious effort to learn from the past failures or to discover the economic laws. How can they retrieve a hopeless situation? On the contrary, they become even more opinionated, make changes here and there and quote writings on Marxism-Leninism out of context, and, moreover, cover up their own mistaken policies with economic theories that were applicable only to Britain at the time of the Industrial Revolution. As a result, what they have done not only is of no help to economic development but makes the situation worse. Lin Piao and the Gang of Four have been accused of doing things this way. But was everything alright and were there no problems before the Gang of Four appeared on the scene? As far as I can see, it wasn't so. Not to mention other things, weren't the problems that emerged at the end of the 1950's and at the beginning of the 1960's a reflection of this kind of questions? In 1961, I called the attention of Comrades Mao Tse-tung, Liu Shao-ch'i and Teng Hsiao-p'ing to the "interdependent relationship between economy and politics." Probably I said that too early, but this was the fact.

India's Madame Indira Gandhi went down in defeat; Pakistan was finally separated into the east and west parts; Soviet Union's Malenkov was thrown out of power; and Cambodia's Pol Pot, faced with various kinds of domestic problems, had to return to the mountains to engage in guerrilla warfare against the Vietnamese intruders. All these are closely related with economic difficulties. If we look at things from the opposite side, and let us suppose that people like Lin Piao and the Gang of Four had successfully settled the people's food problem, thereby allowing them to live in relative affluence, I am afraid that even if they had failed politically it would not have been so easy for us to smash in one stroke their conspiracy of usurping the political power in October 1976. If the people do not have enough food and enough clothing, they would not listen to whatever you may have to say, even if you have countless good reasons!

"Socialist Nations Also Need to Have Accumulations"

The fundamental difference between socialism and capitalism lies in who owns the means of production: One practices capitalism by the state, the other practices capitalism by individuals. Although they follow different ways of production and distribution, the two have something in common: both need to have accumulations. We cannot say that the socialist nations need not have accumulations because they practice state capitalism. Without accumulations, production cannot be developed. Without accumulations, there will be no distribution and no redistribution which is based on the development of productivity. Here, distribution refers to social distribution. The urge to lessen the burden on the participating peasants as was put forth in the "Hsianghsiang experiment" was aimed at achieving a reasonable distribution. We cannot over-emphasize distribution at the expense of production, nor can we over-emphasize production at the expense of distribution. The relationship between production and accumulations is the same. When there is production, there are accumulations. With accumulations, it will be possible for us to have reproduction. If we do not accumulate capital but make high-sounding statements about increasing production, it sounds like a high-brow music which can be appreciated by only a few people. I do not know whether this simile is appropriate.

All right, after spending so much time making explanations, let's go back to the main topic. In the days before the Cultural Revolution, although our country sometimes suffered hardships, our production did show a significant development, and we made a greater progress in economic development as compared with the pre-liberation days and we naturally accumulated some capital and experience needed for modernization. All this came from our efforts in the first ten or more years after liberation. However, during the more than ten years of the Cultural Revolution, production was disrupted, economic growth was retarded and then stopped. Not only were there no accumulations to speak of, even the past accumulations were gradually squandered. A country is like a human body. If a man suffers from a long illness, his vitality will be exhausted for lack of replenishment. As a result, his constitution will be greatly impaired. Even if he recovers from his illness by having injections and taking medicines, he cannot be considered as a strong man. If we ask this man just out of the sick bed to take not only a hundred-meter dash but also a three thousand-meter race, he will be out of breath before he runs ten steps. If we do not ask him to stop right away but make him to run continuously, I am afraid that another ten more steps will kill him before the terminus is in sight. Isn't it true?

"Long-Time Coordination of All Sectors Is Necessary for the Increasing of Accumulations"

By accumulations is meant not only the accumulation of capital but also of technology, resources and experience. It would make a most beautiful picture if the targets of the four modernizations can be fulfilled. I also hope to be able to live another twenty years. I shall die contented if I can hear about it -- I don't have to see it -- one moment before my eyes are closed. Probably few people would not like to see such a beautiful picture. However, on the other hand, I want to ask, whether we have accumulated the labor force, the materials, the capital, the experience and the technology needed for the realization of the four modernizations? Have we or have we not? Speak aloud! No, I don't mean sometime in the future, I mean now, today! Have we? Why? You dare not say?

I would say this: "It's just as good as nothing if we have accumulated some but not much." That is to say, we do not have them. This is not a case of pessimism. This is seeking truth from facts. From nothing to something, there should be a process, and such a process is indispensable.

With regard to experience, we can accumulate it through practice and meanwhile, we can learn from the rich experience of the advanced countries. It is of great important to us to bring in advanced scientific and technology know-how and knowledge from foreign countries and to continue to learn from the advanced countries by inviting their scholars to our country or sending our students to study in their countries. We have made some efforts in this respect, but we will not be able to learn all the things right away. There must be a process.

With respect to resources, our country has many. However, not all of them can be used right away. Some still lie deep underneath the ground waiting for us to explore and exploit them. The same thing is true with agriculture. The potential is great. Much of our land has not yet been cultivated and the mountains and forests are waiting for us to open them up. They cannot be made productive at once. Besides time, we shall need to have capital.

With respect to labor force, our country has the largest population in the world, totalling 950,000,000, larger than the total population of some continents. "There will be more people at work if the population is increased." However, with more people, there will be more mouths, divergent opinions and the need of more food to feed them, and inevitably not a few disputes will also arise. We must look at both the bad and the good aspects of everything not just the good aspects. However, the greatest problem today lies elsewhere and not among those I have described. The real problem is that we have too few people with modern knowledge. Not a few people can write big-character posters, or are well versed in speech, or can fully display their talents during a debate, but there are really too few people who can operate automatic machines, design factories and big buildings, manufacture airplanes and steamships, or know how to use computers. What can we do? We have to train them. Doesn't it take time and money to train people?

I am not going to touch on any other things. What I have said is already enough to pinpoint the problem. It is a matter of vital importance that we lack for capital and technology and this is holding us back as we try to move toward the four modernizations. Contradictions should be solved whenever they are discovered and the major ones must be solved first. This is one of the basic reasons why we have proposed to readjust our national economy.

"Agriculture Takes the Lead, Attention Be Given to Ten Questions"

One is to solve the problem of how to feed the population by bringing into full play the people's enthusiasm for socialist construction; the other is to solve the problem of accumulations, thereby laying a solid foundation for the realization of the four modernizations. If agricultural production cannot reach the desired target, and if the production of food stuff and light industrial goods needed to meet the people's daily necessities remain at the previous levels, we will never be able to solve questions concerning food, housing, clothing and consumer goods for more than 900,000,000 people. Our light industries have never been given due attention and our agriculture has always been in a backward state because, in the past long years, we have failed to free ourselves from the Soviet model of economic development: heavy industries come first and then light industries, industry first and then agriculture, large-scale ones first and then small-scale ones, the central government comes first and then the local areas. With regard to agriculture, not only mechanization is not realized, even the per *mu* yield has remained at the previous level. Neither can agriculture provide more raw materials for industry, nor can the rural areas provide industry with any sizeable quantity of technology and any large number of laborers. In order to alter this situation, we should rearrange the position of the four modernizations, and rearrange the proportionate relationships between the various construction projects.

(1) Production and distribution: We do not mean to overlook production, but what is of concern to peasants throughout the country is distribution and not production. The more important thing for us to do is to work out a reasonable system of distribution. The "Tachai-type system of registering work points" should be discarded because it is against the socialist principle of "more pay for more work." We should allow the "five kinds of disparities" to exist in the rural areas; there is a disparity between the rich and the poor production teams, between the strong labor force and the weak labor force, between technical work and non-technical work, between the household with a greater labor force and the one with a small labor force, and between men and women, between adults and children and between lazy peasants and diligent peasants. Only with reasonable distribution can the peasants' income be raised and their enthusiasm for production be mobilized. The state, the collective and the individual should all be taken care of. At first, the state should lighten the peasants' burden, raise the purchase price of agricultural by-products by 20% to 100%, offer more agricultural loans, and reduce public accumulations to ensure that the collectives and the individuals can both enjoy increased distribution.

(2) Long-range planning and short-range program: Long-range planning is not unnecessary. However, in formulating long-range plans, we should not just

issue instructions without taking concrete measures. Most of the villages in our country do not have the necessary conditions for adopting a ten-year or twenty-year development plan. Let's begin with short-range ones. By so doing, the people will be able to see them and have a feeling for them and will then have confidence in them. In places lacking the necessary conditions, it will probably be better for them to work out plans to run for one or two years. When the conditions are ready, they can formulate plans to run for two years, three years or five years. Any plan for more than five years can be adopted only when short-range plans have already been implemented for sometime. All plans should be formulated on an objective and scientific basis, so that they can be carried out within the capability of locality concerned, that they are adaptable to local conditions and that they leave sufficient margin for unforeseen circumstances. In evaluating a unit, our judgement should not be made according to the plan it has formulated but on the things it has done.

(3) Questions concerning the organizational structure of communes: Views differ on whether the people's communes have been run well or badly. We cannot make a final verdict yet. If the commune system is abolished, it will cause many big and complicated problems which cannot be solved within a short period of time. What we can do is to gradually reform or abolish those organizations and institutions which are not adaptable or are impeding the development of productivity. It is better to do things in accordance with the natural tendency. However, the production, distribution and labor force in the rural areas should be arranged with the production team as the basis. The communes should not assume arbitrary power and wilfully interfere with everything; they are the units which exercise leadership and give guidance but must not monopolize everything. They can make decisions on any arrangement which directly affects the production team's agricultural production only after they have asked instructions from their superior-level units. The "tendency of equalitarianism and indiscriminate transfer of manpower, land, draught animals, farm tools, funds, etc." should end right now.

(4) The principle for the development of agriculture, forestry, pasturage, side-occupations, and fishery: Food production, of course, is the major task of agricultural development. This is said with the whole country in view and not with regard to certain production units only. In some places where it is not suitable to grow grain, why should we plant it even though we know that it will not yield a single grain of food? To change grasslands into grain-producing areas, leaving pasturage completely unattended and causing cattle and sheep to become scarce may be China's great invention in the world today. It's really a farce! Our principle is that agricultural units should make their development plans in accordance with local conditions. They should make different plans in accordance with the climate, and the conditions of water conservancy and soil in their

respective places. They can either engage in one kind of production or comprehensively develop many kinds of production. Try our best to make sure that we have sufficient food and have even some to spare.

(5) Agricultural mechanization: Agricultural mechanization is the decisive factor in changing the style of agricultural production. The state should enhance the level of agricultural mechanization, raise the purchase price of agricultural products and by-products and extend more credit loans by making direct and indirect investments, in order to enable the rural populace to have more capital to buy agricultural machines. One more item is to be added now, that is, the increase of 10% to 20% foreign exchange for the purchase of agro-scientific instruments, equipment and machinery. Also, we should train a large number of experts in this field by making the best use of the intellectual youths in the rural and mountainous areas and regarding them as one of the essential links [of the realization of agricultural mechanization]. Meanwhile, we should develop technical skills along scientific lines.

(6) Class relationship: We should mobilize the enthusiasm of not just a certain section of the people but all kinds of people. The five categories of elements will also have an important role to play if their enthusiasm is mobilized. In the rural areas, therefore, the class relationship should not become more strained, the contradiction should not become more sharp and the struggle should not get more bitter; because in the family of a landlord who has four sons, four daughters-in-law and more than ten grandchildren, if one man opposes us and ten others assume a passive attitude, the number of people thus involved will be considerable. Among the five categories of elements, there are eight kinds of objects, twenty-two kinds of people and numerous other suspects and problem persons. Among the 950,000,000 population in our country, if we ask 200,000,000 good people to watch over 200,000,000 bad people, then how many people will be left to take part in production? We should take into consideration not only one's class or family background but his performance. That is why Chairman Mao himself once said: "I also have rightist friends, Chang Chih-chung being one of them." In our socialist society why are we not allowed to have friends who belong to the five categories of elements? As many of them should be exempted from their stigmatizations as possible. We would rather see their stigmatizations removed than preserved. If the stress and strain of class relationship is relaxed, benefits can be guaranteed. If the policy is well formulated and well implemented, there will be fewer divergent opinions in the country. Once their mind is emancipated, they can immediately be mobilized. By so doing, the problem of an adequate labor force can be solved.

(7) Economic policies for the rural areas: The vital point in formulating economic policies for the rural areas is admission of the fact that our villages are backward, this including the application of science and education; admission of the three great differences [differences between urban and rural areas, between workers and peasants and between those engaged in mental labor and others in manual labor]; and admission that the idea of private ownership and the social force of the old habits have existed to a serious extent for a long time in the past and that they cannot be easily overcome. Conditions determining the formulation of economic policies in the rural areas are many. Among them, the most controversial and changeable ones include questions concerning the production and distribution systems and the *San tzu i pao* [the extension of plots for private use, the extension of free markets, the increase of small enterprises with sole responsibility for their own profits or losses, and the fixing of output quotas based on individuals households], and mainly, the questions concerning private plots and village trade fairs, that is, the free markets. Actually, these are two sides of one question, that is, the questions concerning the preservation of private properties and the right to freely distribute one's properties. The private plots and free markets should be allowed to exist and should be protected. Free markets should be prosperous, supplies to the urban areas should be sufficient. Lighten the pressure on the state's capacity to supply the daily necessities and raise the peasants' income. This is where enthusiasm for production comes from. Many comrades miscalculated and failed to understand that if the peasants' income is raised, the state stands to benefit the most. The State Council recently issued a price index for consumers in the rural areas. You may take a look at it. So long as the vast number of peasants have a higher consuming power, the state need not worry about not having enough money to use. Why don't we follow this policy which brings us benefits and no harm? But why have so many comrades not noticed this point?

(8) Reasonable allocation: In our effort to promote regional agricultural planning, we should not only readjust the allocation of the varieties of plants but should readjust many other things, such as the allocation of population, construction projects, and water resources. Of course, there should be a reasonable arrangement as to the allocation of such supportive industries as basic construction on the farms, agricultural meteorology, the building of power stations in the rural areas, radio and communications systems, transportation and communication system, and the popularization of scientific and technical knowledge in the rural areas. Some of these are of a long-term nature while others are of a short-term nature. They are to be carried out step by step and group by group. For example, the current allocation of agricultural population is very unreasonable. More than 90% of our population are living in less than 40% of the total land areas, while the remaining 10% live in 60% of the total land areas. On one side, there is a

lack of labor force, and on the other, a surplus of labor force. In many places where the land is not arid, natural disasters have appeared frequently. Since the soil structure has been destroyed, the water resources are insufficient, the weather condition is not good, and the acreage of arable land is reduced while more land is used for industrial purposes. One is lucky to have one *mu* of [arable] land. In coastal areas likes Chaochou and Swatow in the Kwangtung province, each person has an average of three-tenths a *mu* of [arable] land. Therefore, in the densely populated areas where there is a surplus of labor force, the most important thing in readjustment is not to replace labor force with machinery, but to increase the unit yield of crops, and if possible, increase the acreage of arable land, and pay attention to the planting of catching crops in order to increase the utility of the arable land. On the other hand, in places where the population is small and the area is enormous, we should ease the burden of labor force shortage by engaging in mechanization, in order to increase the acreage of arable land and productivity. In order to realize such a reasonable allocation, we need not only arrangement by the Party Central Committee but also coordination in the local areas.

(9) Strengthen the agro-science studies and agro-meteorological work, prevent natural disasters, make comprehensive planning, take good measures to protect agriculture, natural resources and environment, increase the production of chemical fertilizers and the supply of pesticides to prevent plant diseases and insect pests.

(10) Questions concerning support: Support to industry by agriculture and support to cities by villages can be effected on the condition that the two sides can exchange things or services of equal values. On the contrary, it is not necessary for the support to agriculture by industry and support to rural areas by cities to have conditions. For example, in the three autumn works [autumn harvesting, sowing and ploughing], the urban labor force should provide mechanical products for the use of rural production teams, the state should grant long-term and low-interest and even interest-free loans to villages, but the cities must not be allowed to buy agricultural products sold from villages on long-term and low-term credit. This is how things should be done and no more explanation is necessary. But today, in supporting the production teams and establishing direct contacts with production teams, many factories do not act this way but seize upon the opportunity to squeeze the production teams. The barter system exists between production teams but not between rural production teams and factories. For industry to support agriculture, we should put an end to the phenomenon of asking high prices and engaging in secret dealings. We should lower the prices of the farm machinery and farming tools needed for agricultural production, and lower the costs for the maintenance of various farming tools -- the purchase of spare parts and accessories, as well as wages in payment for services. But for those

consumer goods transported to the rural areas but not for agricultural production purposes, especially those which are in short supply and need the distributed and helped, their prices should be raised depending on different kinds of goods and in accordance with the laws of supply and demand. In this way, a large amount of money can be withdrawn from circulation while the consuming power is being increased in order to accumulate more capital for industrial and urban development purposes. We can practice the policy of having low prices in one sector and high prices in another sector. To sell at low prices is to patronize production and to sell at high prices is to get back more money for the sake of accumulations.

[Translated by Yun-hua Kao]

*****

DOCUMENT NO. 15

FULLY UNDERSTAND THE EXTREME IMPORTANCE
OF CORRECTING THE PARTY WORK STYLE

Jenmin Jihpao editorial, December 11, 1980;

FBIS-CHI, December 12, 1980

At the third symposium on implementing the "guiding principle" sponsored recently by the Discipline Inspection Commission of the CCP Central Committee, Comrade Chen Yun pointed out that the issue of the ruling party's work style is one that concerns the party's survival. Therefore, the issue of the party work style must be firmly grasped on a permanent basis. To study and implement the guidelines of this meeting and the opinions of Comrade Chen Yun has extreme, important significance in correcting the party work style, ensuring the implementation of the party's lines, principles and policies, consolidating and developing the political situation of stability and unity and uniting the whole party and the entire people to work wholeheartedly for the four modernizations.

The issue of party work style, whether we view it from historical experience or from the present actual situation, is an important issue that our whole party, particularly the high-ranking cadres, must seriously consider.

Our party is a proletarian political party. Not only did we lead the entire nation to overthrow the reactionary rule of the Kuomintang, but we have, after assuming the political power of the whole country, thoroughly transformed the old China, built the socialist new China and will eventually realize the noblest and most perfect idea of man -- communism. Historical experience has borne out that it is a fundamental change in quality for a proletarian political party to become the ruling party of the whole country from a state of being oppressed, encircled and suppressed. This change confronted us with a series of new problems; how to guard against inroads on the party organism is of particular importance.

Historically, when our party was not yet the ruling party of the whole country, our party work style was relatively good even after we assumed political power in the revolutionary base. This is "the Yanan work style." That was highly praised by people until now. No doubt the formation of this fine party work style was because of the correct leadership, education and care of the party Central Committee, but it was also closely related to the position and circumstances of our party at that time. In those days, struggles were ruthless and the circumstances difficult. If we had not had a good party work style, the people would not have supported us and we could not have won the victory in the revolutionary war. Even the existence of our party and ourselves would have been in doubt. Therefore, in those days our whole party from top to bottom worked conscientiously, engaged in hard struggles, paid attention to the well-being of the masses and maintained close ties with them. This was an extremely important reason for the victory of the Chinese revolution.

In the preliminary post-liberation period, our party work style was still relatively good and generally praised by the people of the whole country. However, as the party scored one victory after another, some comrades became arrogant, forgetting the party's ultimate aim and the masses who had shared trials and tribulations with us, mistakenly regarded the leading role of our party as the role of the ruler and set themselves up as rulers high above the people. They claimed credit for themselves and became arrogant, setting themselves high above others, abusing the power given by the party and the people to seek personal gains and pursue special privileges. Certain people even became morally degenerate and violated law and discipline. The party's work style was gravely damaged during the 10-year period of unprecedented calamity.

This posed an important issue in our new Long March which we could not but seriously and conscientiously try to resolve. That is why the party, soon after the smashing of the "gang of four," regarded correcting the party work style as an important matter for bringing order out of chaos, and the party Central Committee drew up and made public the "guiding principles for inner-party political life." Its purpose was to use these laws formulated within the party to arouse the whole party to pay attention to the unhealthy tendencies and mobilize the masses to struggle against them. We must admit that since the "guiding principles" were made public, we have made considerable progress in improving the party work style. However, just as this meeting has pointed out, the party work style, compared to the preliminary post-liberation period, has not been fundamentally improved and great efforts are still required from us.

Why is it that the party work style has not been fundamentally improved four years or so after the smashing of the "gang of four?" The reasons are many, but the most important is that quite a number of comrades have not truly realized the extreme important of the ruling party's work style. Some comrades do not pay attention at all to the issue of correcting the party's bad work style, deeming it as a small, unimportant matter. Some even consider grasping party work style would hinder stability and unity. Some stress that they are too busy building the four modernizations and cannot spare time for grasping party work style, and so on and so forth.

All such views which regard grasping party work style as antagonistic to stability and unity and the four modernizations are completely wrong and very harmful. What must stability, unity and the four modernizations rely on? They must all rely on the enthusiasm and initiative of the broad masses of people in building socialism. To mobilize the masses' enthusiasm and initiativeness of course relies on the correctness of the party's lines, principles and policies, but a good party work style is also a must. On the contrary, if the party's style of work is not good, if we feign compliance with the party's lines, principles and policies, if we do not solve issues which should be and can be solved, if we do badly what should be and can be done well, if we take the attitude of subjectivism and bureaucratism when encountering difficulties, if we ignore the interests of the state and the people and show no concern for the well-being of the people and the masses, if we haggle over every bit of our own personal interests and the interests of our family by all means and even violate law and discipline to engage in all

kinds of scandal and bad things to the detriment of the interests of the masses --
how then can we mobilize the enthusiasm and initiative of the masses?

Without the enthusiasm and initiative of the people and the masses that
engenders the political situation of stability and unity, how can we do a good job
for the four modernizations? What is worth special attention is that if we allow
the unhealthy phenomenon of bad party work styles to continue to develop, not
only stability and unity cannot be promoted but the four modernizations cannot be
carried out, and it would seriously divorce our party from the people and the
masses. Thus a great danger could exist. Even the enlightened feudal rulers knew
the truth that "water can float a boat and can capsize it." Cannot we Communist
Party members understand this truth? Thus is can be seen that what Comrade
Chen Yun pointed out -- "The issue of the ruling party's work style is one that
concerns the party's survival" -- is not merely an exaggeration to scare people but
a timely alarm for the whole party. Comrades of the whole party must try to
understand the deep meaning of Comrade Chen Yun's statement, be determined
to improve the party work style, further strengthen the close ties between the party
and the masses, increase the fighting capability of the party in order to enable it
to shoulder the heavy responsibility in leading the construction of the four
modernizations.

Rectifying the unhealthy work style within the party is a sharp and
complex struggle which will encounter obstructions from all quarters. Therefore
it is imperative for us to foster the spirit of putting daring above all else.
Comrades of the discipline inspection departments, in particular, must not be afraid
of offending people and must uphold justice on issues that require them to
distinguish right and wrong and adhere to principle. In the face of major issues
of principle, they must assume a clear-cut stand, adhere to principle, be impartial
and incorruptible and do their work justly. We must realize that unhealthy party
style has a complex historical and social background, and since the problem is a
long-standing one, it has created many other problems which must be tackled
constantly and persistently and not just one or two times. Therefore, it is
necessary to carry out education on party regulations and rules throughout the
party according to plan so as to help the broad masses of party members
understand the party's fine traditions and fine work style. At the same time we
must improve the system of party life and carry out criticism and self-criticism
with actual problems in mind so as to raise the consciousness of party members
and cadres of resisting unhealthy tendencies. Typical cases should be used to
serve the purpose of appropriately carrying out criticism and self-criticism in
newspapers and in journals.

*****

DOCUMENT NO. 16

CARRYING THROUGH THE PRINCIPLES OF ADJUSTMENT,
IMPROVING THE WORK OF THE PARTY AND
GUARANTEEING STABILITY AND SOLIDARITY

A Speech by Teng Hsiao-p'ing at the
CCP Central Working Conference

Beijing, December 25, 1980

(Issues & Studies, Vol. XVII, No. 7, July 1981)

I fully agree with Comrade Ch'en Yun's speech. For a whole series of questions this speech accurately summed up the experiences and lessons of our thirty-one years of economic work, and provided long-term guiding principles for the future.

I also fully agree with Comrade Chao Tzu-yang's speech, and the arrangements passed by the Central Finance and Economics Team of the 1981 plan.

Following the Third Plenary Session of the Eleventh Central Committee in December 1978, Comrade Ch'en Yun was responsible for finance and economic work; he brought up the principle of adjustment that was decided upon by the Central Working Conference in April last year. But knowledge of this throughout the Party was much less than unanimous and very shallow, and so the execution left much to be desired. Only now has there been a change in this situation, and the adjustment this time is a further carrying through of that principle.

As Comrade Ch'en Yun said, this is a healthy and sober adjustment. It requires retreat in some aspects -- and retreat to a sufficient degree. In other areas, primarily agriculture, light industry and production related to daily necessities, energy and communications construction, and scientific, educational, health, and cultural endeavors, we must continue developing as rapidly as possible. The enterprise, industry, and construction units involved in this continued development must conscientiously carry out rectification, enhance management standards, improve the operation and technical capabilities of staff and workers, heighten the production and working efficiency of labor, give full play to the activeness and creativity of staff and workers, and reduce all kinds of waste to a minimum.

Why should the question of adjustment or partial retreat arise in the process of the Four Modernizations? This is because without adjustment, or without retreat or with insufficient retreat where retreat is called for, our economy cannot advance steadily. Because of the historical situation prior to Liberation, and because of the long-term haste to produce results following the first five-year plan, a severe imbalance always existed in our economy. This, plus the decade of destruction brought about by the Great Cultural Revolution and the two years of confusion immediately following the smashing of the Gang of Four developed into even greater imbalances in finance, credit, commodities and foreign exchange revenues and expenditures in the period just before and after the Third Plenary Session. To alter this situation is completely consistent with the rectification of leftist errors by the Third Plenary Session and with the general principle of basing everything on particular considerations, and is an essential condition for the realization of modernization. The ineffective implementation of adjustment over the past two years has brought about a large amount of financial red ink, excessive currency issuance, and continued price rises. Without a conscientious adjustment, we will not be able to smoothly carry out our modernization construction. Only through adequate retreat in certain areas will we be able to achieve an overall ability and initiative, and put our economy as a whole on the road to healthy development.

This "adequate retreat in certain areas" means primarily that there must be adequate retreat in capital construction; that enterprises with inadequate conditions for production will be shut down, closed up, merged, switched to other operations, or have their production reduced; and that administrative expenditures (including outlays for defense and the administrative and management expenditures for all enterprise and industrial units) will be curtailed so that revenues and expenditures in financial administration and loan operations can be balanced. Productive enterprise construction, administrative measures, and improvement in the people's livelihood must be carried out in full consideration of the available resources. This is the principle of "seeking truth from facts." A resolute determination to do this shows that our thought is truly liberated, and that we have thrown off the shackles of the leftist errors in guiding principles of years past.

It has been difficult to unify thinking within the Party regarding this problem over the past two years, and it will obviously take a lot of work to unify the thinking of all the country's people. We must explain clearly to the people why we cannot but go ahead with adjustment, what problems may appear during adjustment, and what results completion of the adjustment will bring. Only in this way will the people understand the necessity of further adjustment, will they believe that the Party and the government are really thinking of the basic benefit of all the people and the steady carrying out of modernization, and will they support us. The accomplishment of this part of the work is extremely important, and we must not hope that it can be taken care of by giving cursory orders.

Economic adjustment is a big matter, changing the 1981 plan and budget passed by the National People's Congress this year and affecting the work and life of all the nation's people. The State Council, therefore, is asked to make a report on it to the Standing Committee of the National People's Congress in the near future. When the report is made public, it may be used as the basic material for spreading propaganda among and giving explanation to the people of the whole country.

This further adjustment of the economy is for the purpose of setting our feet firmly on the ground and advancing steadily, and carrying out the Four Modernizations with more confidence and attaining their goals more advantageously. As to what kind of route to travel and what kind of steps to take in the attainment of modernization, this will require us to continue casting off all the old and new frames and structures, to gain a clear and accurate knowledge of the interrelationships among the various factors in our national situation and economic activity, and then based on this to accurately determine the principles of our long-range plan and finally set our hands to working out a realistic and practicable sixth five-year plan. If only everyone in the country advances in an orderly and step-by-step manner with solidarity and unanimity, then we will be able to pass the next twenty years with confidence and bring our country to the standard of a well-to-do society, and afterwards continue progress toward an even higher level of modernization.

Over the thirty-one years since the establishment of the country we have truly committed a considerable number of errors, including serious ones and have undergone numerous tribulations; this has brought no small amount of harm to the people, and has slowed down the progress of socialist construction. But after thirty-one years of effort our industrial, communications, and enterprise units have increased to almost 400,000; the fixed capital of state enterprises has grown nearly 20-fold from the period immediately following Liberation; we have cultivated a great number of workers and close to ten million specialists; and we have built up relatively complete industrial and national economic systems. Life for people over the country is much better than before Liberation. In comparison with a number of relatively large developing countries, our accomplishments have been greater and our construction faster. Over these past few years, and especially at this conference, we have concentrated on investigating the shortcomings and errors of the past and on making accurate conclusions from the positive and negative lessons of experiences and this has allowed us to arrange our overall construction deployment on a realistic and dependable foundation. If we depend on the material conditions and economic working principles mentioned above and continue strengthening and improving Party guidance, manifesting the superiority of the socialist system and the activeness and creativity of all the nation's races, using our abundant resources more rationally, ceaselessly cause our work to become more closely tied to actual conditions; and if we regularly draw conclusions from new experiences, and strive to avoid and make timely investigation of new shortcomings and errors, then our work of socialist modernization will surely be able to steadily attain its goal and our future will be infinitely bright. In view of this, our present adjustment is not a retreat but an advance.

The Party's Third Plenary Session asked the entire Party to liberate thinking, activate minds, seek truth from facts, look forward in solidarity and unanimity, and study new situations and solve new problems. Over the two years since then we have set a series of policies and carried out a series of reforms in accordance with this guiding thought, and have achieved obvious accomplishments. In April last year we proposed adjustment, and at the same time reform, rectification, and enhancement. The broad masses of the people and the cadres have faithfully supported the correct decisions by the Party on the one hand, and on the other hand have worried about when this policy might change. This fear of reversal and tribulation is completely understandable.

Is this adjustment, then, to alter the directions and policies of the post-Third Plenary Session period? Absolutely not. As I said above, this adjustment is a continuation and development of the correct directions and policies that followed the Third Plenary Session about seeking truth from facts and rectifying leftist errors. If it can be said that there is any change, then the change involves elimination of the defects, still existing in our work, that are inconsistent with the spirit of the Third Plenary Session -- that is, elimination of ideas out of accord with reality and of the high index of subjectivism. This is precisely what the Third Plenary Session line demands that we do.

To assure the smooth execution of this adjustment, we must unwaveringly continue to carry out all of the effective directions, policies, and measures that have been undertaken since the Third Plenary Session.

We must hold resolutely to the Four Basic Principles -- the socialist road; the people's democratic dictatorship, or the dictatorship of the proletariat; the leadership of the Party; and Marxism-Leninism and Mao Tse-tung's thought. No one can be allowed to shake them, and suitable legal forms must be used to establish them firmly.

The nucleus of the Four Basic Principles is holding to the leadership of the Party. We have said repeatedly that a large country such as China would be ripped asunder and all would come to naught without the leadership of the Communist Party. Any attempt from within the Party or outside it to weaken, depart from, cancel, or oppose Party leadership must be met with criticism, education, and -- if necessary -- struggle. This is the key to the success of the Four Modernizations, and to the success or failure of the current adjustment.

If the leadership of the Party is to be maintained, it must be improved and the Party's working style advanced. Our Party's work among the masses today is somewhat weaker than it was before the Great Cultural Revolution, and our working methods are also rough in some places; all of this hinders contact between the Party and the people. Many of the problems of economic adjustment can be easily overcome only by greatly strengthening contact between the Party and the people, and by going deep among the masses and doing thought and political work there. The improper ways of a small minority of Party members and cadres are most unfavorable to the recovery of Party prestige among the people. I agree with what Comrade Ch'en Yun said about the question of Party style being a question of the life or death of the ruling Party. To strictly carry out the "Guiding Principles for Inner-Party Political Life" and resolutely and tirelessly rectify the various improper styles, we must be particularly resolute in opposing the erroneous attitudes of pretended and fence-straddling observance of Party Central's lines, directions, and policies.

The directions for reforming the Party and state leadership system must be steadfastly maintained, but the methods must be cautious and the steps steady. In short, we cannot cause those who can still truly work for the Party not to work. Reform of the leadership system in basic-level units must first be experimentally carried out in a small number of units. Before complete regulations are set and promulgated, all basic-level units that are not test cases will keep to the original system. This is the principle originally proposed by Party Central. The thought, political, economic, and organizational work of all the basic-level enterprises and other units during the economic adjustment is very heavy and very difficult. To bring the various kinds of relationships within the national economy gradually into harmony and to make the benefit of the part follow the benefit of the whole, certain items of construction will be halted and certain enterprises will be shut down, closed up, merged switched to other operations, or otherwise have their production reduced. For all the personnel of these three types of units, planned training must be carried out and arrangements must be made for their livelihood. It will be far from easy to accomplish this work. We hope that comrades at all organizational levels -- especially those working at the basic level -- will manifest our glorious tradition, take the nation's and the masses' troubles upon themselves with patience and with a single mind, and permit themselves no laxity of mood at all. When we are in the face of adversity is precisely the time for our Party members and cadres at all organizational levels -- particularly the old Party members and cadres -- to hold faithfully to their posts body and soul and face up to another trial. Party Central is confident that they will not fail to carry out this charge by the Party and the people.

We will continue the development of socialist democracy and the perfection of the rule of law. This has been Party Central's unshakable principle following the Third Plenary Session, and no wavering about it will be permitted in the future. Our democratic system is still incomplete in places, and a set of laws, rules, and regulations must be formulated to systematize and legalize our democracy. Socialist democracy and the socialist rule of law are inseparable. Democracy without the socialist rule of law, without the leadership of the Party, and without discipline and order is no socialist democracy at all. Such a situation would only make our nation fall into an anarchic state again, and would make it even more difficult for the country to be democratized, for the nation's economy to develop, and for the people's livelihood to be improved.

In life within the Party and within national politics, we must truly carry out democratic centralism and collective leadership. We must resolutely rectify such defects as a minority of people refusing to carry out decisions taken collectively. Under present circumstances it is especially necessary to reiterate and stress the principle of the individual obeying the organization, the minority obeying the majority, the lower ranks obeying the higher ranks, and the entire Party obeying Party Central. Within the Party, the military, and the governmental system, we must resolutely resist everything that does not respect Party, military, and government discipline.

We must strengthen disciplinary and rule of law eduction in all party and administration organs, the military enterprises, schools, and the entire populace. Discipline that is not covered by regulations or for which the regulations are incomplete or unreasonable must be speedily regulated or have the regulations improved. Beginning from the time students enter colleges, middle schools, or primary schools, workers enter the factories, soldiers enter the military, and staff personnel take up their positions, they must study and follow the necessary discipline. All undisciplined, anarchic, lawbreaking phenomena must be resolutely opposed and rectified; otherwise we will never be able to build up socialism and bring about modernization. Reasonable discipline and socialist democracy are not only not mutually opposed, but they mutually guarantee each other.

We must continue overcoming the excess concentration of authority. Steadily, and step-by-step, we must carry out a system of cadre retirement, and we must abolish the system of lifetime leadership cadre positions that actually exists. The various aspects of political and livelihood treatment of these retirees will be properly arranged one by one.

Over the past year, Party Central has stressed many times that the old cadres must take the selection and cultivation of young and middle-aged cadres as their first and most solemn duty. Other work done improperly is cause for self-criticism, but this work done improperly is the commission of a historical error. If this work is done properly, our endeavor can continue in full confidence and our old cadres will once again have made a great contribution to the Party and the people. We hope that all of the old comrades have a high level of awareness concerning this matter.

Under the precondition of holding to the socialist road, we will make younger, intellectualize, and specialize our cadres, and will work out a gradual completion of a cadre system as a guaranty. Of course, revolutionization must come before this so-called making younger, intellectualization, and specialization, and that is why we say there is a precondition of holding to the socialist road. This does not mean that comrades of talent and virtue, who are eager to learn and are in good health, will be removed if they fail to meet these three conditions, or one or two of them; age requirements, especially, cannot be called immutable. If we depart from our present cadre corps, we will not be able to complete any of our tasks and it will be impossible for us to make the cadres younger, and all the rest. We must see, however, that this is a strategic question. Our cadre crops must become younger, more intellectual, more understanding of its business. Some comrades have a inadequate understanding of the importance in this matter even today; there are historical and practical reasons for this and a general patient and painstaking propaganda effort must be made to explain it. Suitable stages must be set for the execution of this effort. The "first enter and then exit" idea proposed by a Shanghai comrade means this: first absorb young comrades of virtue and ability (including industrial, agricultural, and intellectual comrades) into the leadership ranks, so that they can work there and the old cadres can pass on their skills to the younger generation so that they can truly fulfill their jobs and only then will the old cadres who cannot uphold their work be retired. This is a good idea. Of course, this cannot be accomplished by one fell swoop; concrete steps must be decided in accordance with the concrete situation.

Many units are currently overstaffed. During this economic adjustment, all or part of the work forces of some enterprises may stop work. In addition to arranging for the cadres and other personnel of these units to work in rotation at such productive jobs as reforestation, road repair, city administration construction, and health facilities, the concerned areas and departments should carry out regulation training of these people, heighten the awareness and ability of all cadres and workers in this training, and then put them through a selection process so that those of superior ability can be discovered and chosen. Adjustment is an active measure that must be taken for the accomplishment of modernization, and training is an important aspect of this measure. Everybody often talks about increasing investment in intellectual education, and the use of this opportunity to carry out a planned education of a large group of cadres and workers to heighten their level of politics, culture, technology, and management would be a very effective way to invest in intellectual education. We must make the whole body of cadres and workers understand the great significance of this kind of training, and gradually change the training into a regular system that is used with the whole body of cadres and workers.

Very good accomplishments have been made in reforming the economic structure and the economic system. We must consolidate the accomplishments already made, sum up the experiences we have had, and analyze and resolve the new problems that have appeared in the reform process. I fully concur with the opinions of Comrades Ch'en Yun and Chao Tzu-yang that for a period of time in the future our emphasis must be on adjustment, with reform serving adjustment and being beneficial to it instead of obstructing it. The pace of reform needs to be slowed down a bit, but this is no change of any sort in direction.

The decisions of the Third Plenary Session concerning agriculture, and this year's document No. 75, have been abundantly proven effective; they will continue to be carried through, and we must be careful to solve the problems that come up during the execution whenever they occur. We cannot copy the methods of places like Western countries and Russia in our agricultural modernization; we must work out a way that is consistent with conditions in China under the socialist system.

The number of test units under this year's expanded enterprise autonomy has topped 6,000. The collective production value of these units constitutes about sixty per cent of the total value of the nation's industrial production. We have started working to find ways to bring the benefit of the nation, the enterprises, and the workers together more effectively, and to mobilize the active nature of all sectors. The scope of test points will not be expanded next year; the emphasis will instead be on summing up experience, consolidation, and enhancement.

The carrying out of a high level of collective unity in the midst of adjustment is absolutely essential. But reform measures that have proven effective in various areas cannot be reversed; we must continue putting life into our economy and manifesting the active nature of local areas, enterprises, and workers. Of course, we must prevent blindness, and especially the self-aggrandizing tendency to work for the benefit of oneself and one's position at the expense of the benefit of the nation and the people. In this respect we must stipulate more detailed laws to avoid distortions and abuse of autonomy.

We must continue to find ways of managing things primarily through the various forms of collective economy and individual labor, and by making as many arrangements as possible for the unemployed. We must truly guarantee reasonable benefits for group and individual laborers, and at the same time prevent illegal activities by strengthening industrial and commercial management.

The decision to establish a number of special zones in the provinces of Kwangtung [Guangdong] and Fukien [Fujian] will continue to be carried out; but the steps and methods must serve the purpose of adjustment, and the pace can be slowed down a bit.

Under the preconditions of independent sovereignty and self-reliance, we will continue to carry out the set of policies that have already been determined concerning opening the economy to the outside, and we will draw conclusions from our experiences and make improvements accordingly. Because of our many years of self-imposed isolation we have no experience at this, and for this we have paid dearly. The responsibility for this lies mainly with Party Central, and I must take the responsibility for myself.

We will continue to carry out an external policy of opposition, hegemonism and preservation of world peace. If this policy is carried out well, we might be able to win a peaceful construction environment for a relatively long period of time.

It is precisely because we determined and carried out the set of correct directions and policies described above following the Third Plenary Session that we have created fairly good conditions for the present economic adjustment. If only we continue holding to these practicable directions and policies, we can surely achieve our expected goals in this adjustment.

Comrade Ch'en Yun said that whether or not our economic and political situation can develop steadily is closely related to whether or not our economic and propaganda work is done well. The reason why he brought up propaganda at the same time as economics is that on the one hand he warns us to make a clear-headed assessment of the accomplishments and shortcomings of propaganda work, and on the other hand he wants our propaganda work in the future to be able to accommodate the economic and political situation and to help, rather than hinder, the smooth progress of the work of adjustment.

The propaganda work we speak of here in fact includes all of the Party's thought and political work. The economic adjustment is a very difficult and complicated task; we already see quite a number of problems involved in it, and we will run into more problems that we do not now expect. To complete this task and guarantee unanimity of thought and action throughout the Party, we must effectively strengthen and improve the Party's broad, penetrating, and painstaking thought and political work.

Discussion of the question of the criterion of truth has had a great motivating utility in the accomplishments we have made during the past few years in political, economic, and organizational reforms and on our various battle lines. Theoretical, propaganda, journalistic, education and cultural and art workers, along with the Party cadres at various levels, have together made important contributions in the richly effective work of the past few years, and they should be given adequate acknowledgement. Overall, accomplishments in the various aspects of work of the thought battle lines are of primary importance.

To liberate thought is to unite thought with actuality and subjectiveness with objectiveness, and that is seeking truth from facts. From now on, to truly hold to the seeking of truth from facts in all our work we must liberate thought. To feel that the liberation of thought has gone far enough or even too far is obviously incorrect.

I must point out, however, that there are still serious shortcomings in our propaganda work -- primarily a failure to propagandize the Four Basic Principles aggressively, confidently, and persuasively, and to vigorously carry out a struggle against seriously erroneous thinking that is opposed to the Four Basic Principles. There is really still confusion in the thought of some comrades; some people feel, for example, that holding to the Four Basic Principles will obstruct the liberation of thought, that strengthening the socialist rule of law will hinder socialist democracy, that carrying out correct criticism of erroneous ideas is a violation of the "double hundred" directions, and the like.

This confused thinking has definite social and historical reasons, of course, and we certainly cannot deal with it through violent and simple methods. This is not to say, however, that we can let this kind of confused thinking run its natural course, that we need take no effective measures to deal with it. This situation in fact supplies a favorable condition, in one respect, for the activities of those who fear only the absence of chaos in the world. An especially serious aspect of this is that very few people come out in print or within the Party to wage solemn thought combat against these inaccurate ideas and errors in thought trends, or even against those who openly and boldly oppose Party leadership and socialist concepts. A number of people with ties to illegal organizations have been especially active of late, wantonly making anti-Party and anti-socialist statements on all sorts of pretexts. These danger signals should be sufficient to arouse the entire Party, populace, and youth to vigilance!

The strengthening of thought and political work, and the improvement of propaganda work, have already been taken as an extremely important mission, now facing the comrades of the entire Party, for guaranteeing the smooth execution of this adjustment and for consolidating the stable and unified political situation.

The most important aspect of the improvement in the leadership of the Party that we speak of is the strengthening of thought and political work. Party Central feels that in principle, all levels of the Party organization should turn over as much as possible of their daily administrative and operational work to the government and operational departments; besides firmly grasping policies of direction and deciding on the utilization of important cadres, the Party's leadership agencies should reserve most of their time and energy for thought and political work -- the work of the people and the masses. If this cannot be accomplished at once, thought and political work must at least be given a high priority; otherwise it will be impossible to improve or strengthen the leadership of the Party.

In strengthening thought and political work, emphasis must be given to solving the following problems:

Concerning an assessment of the Party's work following the establishment of the country, the great accomplishments of the thirty-one-year period must definitely be affirmed and the errors and shortcomings must be solemnly criticized, but the picture must not be painted all black. Even such a grave error as the Great

Cultural Revolution cannot be called "counter-revolutionary." We must unshakably hold fast to this kind of "seeking truth from facts" standpoint.

By the same token, Comrade Mao Tse-tung's contributions are primary and his errors secondary; this assessment is consistent with reality and there can be no suspicion or denial of it. Comrade Mao's errors can in no wise be considered a question of his individual quality. If the question is not viewed in this way, then the attitude used is not one of Marxism-Leninism or of historical materialism. It is very plain that to emotionally build up his errors too much would only damage the image of our Party and our country, harm the prestige of the Party and the socialist system, and dissipate the unity of the entire Party, the entire military, and all the races of the whole country.

Our guiding thinking is still Mao Tse-tung Thought, which the test of experience has proven accurate, and it must be held to and expanded in concert with actual conditions; we must also carry out propaganda about it in the certainly of our correctness, and no lagging will be permitted. Much confusion can be avoided by separating Mao Tse-tung Thought from the thought of his later years. But this is not to say, of course, that Comrade Mao never expressed any correct ideas in his later years.

It is a fact that there is a heterodox wind blowing in the Party, and that a very small minority of leadership cadres are engaged in working for special privilege; Party Central is resolved about this, and is successively solving problems in this respect. The utility of accurate newspaper criticism must be affirmed; but care must be taken not to take individual phenomena as general phenomena, and partial things must not be expanded to cover the whole. It is certainly not true that all Party members or even a majority of them, are blowing with the heterodox wind, and that all or a majority of leadership cadres are maneuvering for special privilege. There is not, nor can there be, any so-called "bureaucratic class." In our propaganda, we must prevent the formation among the masses of all kinds of impressions that are out of step with reality.

We must, through thought and political work, strengthen organization and discipline throughout the Party. Organizations at all levels, and each Party member, must act in accordance with Party regulations, and all actions must be in accordance with the decisions of higher-level organizations; it is especially essential to maintain a political unanimity with Party Central. This point is extremely important right now, and whoever violates it will be subject to the punishment of Party discipline. In its disciplinary investigation work, the Party must take this as its current focus. We must educate the comrades of the entire Party to promote a spirit of selflessness, of service to the overall situation, incorruptibility, and holding to communist thought and communist virtue. The socialist country that we want to build must have a high level of spiritual as well as material civilization. This so-called spiritual civilization refers not only to education, science, and culture (though this is absolutely necessary) but also to the revolutionary stances and principles of Communist thought, ideals, beliefs, virtues, and discipline, as well as comradely relations between people and the like. This does not require particularly good material conditions nor particularly high educational levels. Have we not participated in the revolution up to now on the basis of the scientific theories of Marxism? Besides depending on correct political directions from Yenan times up to the New China, have we not depended on this precious revolutionary spirit to attract the people of the entire country as well as friendly people abroad? How can socialism be built up without this kind of spiritual civilization, without Communist thought, without Communist virtue? The more the Party and the government carry out policies of economic reform and opening up to the outside, the more must Party members, and especially high-ranking Party authorities, put a high grade of emphasis on, and personally work vigorously for, Communist thought and virtue. Otherwise we will be spiritually disarmed, and then how will we be able to educate the young people and lead the nation and the populace in building socialism? In the time of the new democratic revolution, we are determined to use the thought system of Communism as guidance for all our work, to use Communist virtue to restrain the speech and actions of Communist Party members and progressive elements, to advocate and honor wholehearted service to the people, "the individual serving the organization," "selflessness," "working not for oneself but only for others," and "fearing neither hardship nor death." Now that we have entered a socialist period, there are people who actually mount criticisms against these solemn revolutionary slogans; not only has this wild criticism not been effectively countered, but it has even received the sympathy and support of some people within our own ranks. Can any Communist Party member with a Party and revolutionary nature allow this kind of situation to continue?

Comrade Mao Tse-tung said that a person must have a bit of spirit. Under the guidance of correct political directions and based on the analysis of actual conditions during the long-term revolutionary war, we developed a spirit of revolution and hard work, of strict adherence to discipline and self-sacrifice, of selflessness and others first, of suppressing all enemies and all hardships, and of holding to revolutionary optimism and of eradicating all difficulties in the pursuit of victory; and we did achieve a great victory. We must also manifest this kind of spirit in carrying out socialist construction and the Four Modernizations under the correct leadership of the Party. A Communist Party member without this spirit can absolutely not be considered a qualified Party member. Further, we must call loudly for using the force of example to extend this kind of spirit among all the people and the youth so that it will become the main support of the People's Republic of China, a source of inspiration for all those in the world who seek revolution and progress, and a source of admiration for people throughout the world with a spiritual emptiness and distressed thinking.

We must vigorously strengthen the Party's organization and contact between Party members and the masses, and we must frequently and truthfully report to the masses on the country's conditions and difficulties and on the Party's work and policies. We must resolutely criticize and rectify all kinds of errors that depart from the people and care nothing for the people's hardships. The masses are the source of all our strength and mass lines and viewpoints are our precious heirlooms. The Party organization, Party members, and Party cadres must become one with the people; they must absolutely not stand opposed to the people. Any Party organization that seriously departs from the people and cannot correct itself loses the source of its strength and will surely be defeated and abandoned by the people. Comrades of all the Party and cadres of all levels, especially leadership cadres, must keep this point always in mind and use it as a standard for inspecting all their speech and actions. We must strive to help the masses solve all problems that can be solved. For problems temporarily incapable of solution, patient and sincere explanations must be made to the masses.

We must continue criticizing and opposing the lingering influence of feudalism in thought and politics both inside and outside the Party, and we must continue eradicating this influence by instituting and perfecting all kinds of systems and laws consistent with socialist principles. At the same time we must criticize and oppose tendencies toward the worship of capitalism and the liberation of the bourgeois class; the corrupt bourgeois thinking of doing harm to others to benefit oneself, seeking nothing but profit, and looking at everything in terms of money; and anarchism and extreme individualism. We will continue having contacts with Western countries friendly to us and learning what the capitalist countries have that is useful to us, but we must carry the above-mentioned struggle to the end in the areas of thought and politics. We must foster a spirit of patriotism and heighten national self-confidence. Otherwise, it will be impossible for us to build socialism and we will be corroded away by all kinds of capitalist forces.

We will strengthen political, situational, thought, life philosophy, and ethical education in schools at all levels.

We will vigorously strengthen work with trade union and women's federations, as well as with Communist Youth League, Young Vanguards, and students' associations. We must strive to make our young people into youths with ideals, ethics, knowledge, and health, and with a will to make contributions to the people, to the fatherland, and to humanity. From childhood, good habits of adherence to discipline, courtesy, and preservation of the public benefit should be cultivated in them.

We must heighten the confidence of comrades throughout the Party in building a modernized socialist power; through the influence and attraction of the model actions of Party members in all posts, we will have aroused spirits, solidarity, and concentrated attention, and will achieve our great objective. We must propagandize, recover, and develop the Yenan spirit, the spirit that immediately followed revolution, and the early 1960s spirit of overcoming difficulties. Before we can teach and consolidate the masses and heighten their confidence, we must first solidly establish our own confidence.

Whether our stable and united political situation continues being consolidated or meets with destruction is the key to the success or failure of the present adjustment. If our stable and united political situation is destroyed, then it will be impossible to carry out the work of adjustment.

It has been discovered in a number of locals that a small handful of people who fear only the absence of chaos are just now using the methods of the Great Cultural Revolution to incite and cause trouble, and some people are even calling for something like carrying out a second Great Cultural Revolution. Word is frequently heard of a minority of fringe youths in individual places stirring up trouble, of active collusion between illegal organizations controlled by a small minority of bad leaders and illegal publications, of the public issuance of anti-Party and anti-socialist statements, of the distribution of counter-revolutionary pamphlets, of the spreading of political rumors, of the activities of remnant forces of the Gang of Four, of murder and arson, of manufacturing explosions, of robbery and thievery, of rape and gang-rape, of dealing in white slavery, and of organized prostitution; of the spread of such criminal activities as smuggling and tax evasion, opportunism, fraud and bribe-taking, twisting of the law to solicit bribes, and the selling and taking of narcotics; and of the ceaseless occurrence of such serious illegal and anti-disciplinary behavior as the revelation and sale of national secrets, the wanton granting of bonuses in intentional violation of regulations, the raising of commodity prices, and the disturbing of the market. We must not take these phenomena lightly. Some of these things are the activities of counter-revolutionary elements, some are counter-strikes by remnants of Lin Piao and the Gang of Four, some are destructive acts by those who fear only the absence of chaos, some are a return of the old ideas of the exploiting class remnants, and some are the result of severe corrosion by the thought and ways of feudalism and the bourgeois class. In terms of nature, one type of this consists of contradictions between ourselves and the enemy, and one type is a reflection of differing levels of internal class struggle among the people. This shows that while class struggle is no longer the principal contradiction in our society, it does in fact still exist and must not be underestimated. If this is not taken care of in a timely and discriminating fashion, but the different-natured problems described above are allowed to spread and converge together, then it will pose a very serious threat to our stable and united situation. Some of our comrades do not yet have an adequate understanding of the importance of these kinds of activity, so they fail to strike at them forcefully or even let them run free.

For this reason we must strengthen the state organizations of the people's democratic dictatorship; resolutely attack, divide, and destroy the forces described above that are destructive of stability and unity; resolutely attack, divide, and destroy the remnant forces of the Lin Piao - Chiang Ch'ing cliques; and resolutely attack, prevent, and put a stop to all kinds of criminal activity.

Consolidation and development of the stable and united political situation is the common desire of people of the entire country. We must carry out well our thought and political work toward the broad masses, and mobilize and organize them to take positive action and carry out an effective struggle against all kinds of forces destructive of stability and unity. In carrying out this kind of struggle we cannot adopt the past method of using political movements; we must follow the principles of the socialist rule of law. So in addition to the issuing of related instructions in the Party, it is suggested that the Standing Committee of the National People's Congress and the State Council also promulgate related regulations and laws. The necessary legal measures, plus thought and political work by the entire Party, propaganda by newspapers and magazines, and education by the schools, can bring about common standards of action for the entire Party, the whole military, and all the people. In this way, some of the present confused conditions can be gradually resolved.

To assure stability and unity, it is suggested that state agencies pass appropriate laws stipulating that mediation must be tired before there are work or study stoppages, approval must be sought and a time and place designated before there are parades or demonstrations; the collusion between different units and different areas be prohibited, and that the activities of illegal organizations and the printing of illegal publications be banned.

This is political struggle, but it must be carried out within the confines of the law. Power must be used, but preparations must be adequate, steps taken must be steady, and there must be appropriate restraint. Serious sabotage activities must not only be struck at, but struck at many times. Comrades of the whole Party and all the cadres must work in accordance with the Constitution and the law, and learn how to use legal weapons (including such economic weapons as fines and heavy taxes) to carry out struggles against anti-Party and anti-socialist forces and all sorts of criminal elements. This is a new subject that we are being asked to master as quickly as possible for the present and future development of socialist democracy and the strengthening of the socialist rule of law.

We must vigorously strengthen the construction and working of legal and public security agencies, and enhance the political and operational quality of the personnel of these agencies.

We must select a group of good workers, cadres, and soldiers from among the basic construction ranks and discharged military personnel and train them to expand and strengthen the administrative, legal, public security, and the civil police.

In places where there are serious disturbances, the local governments may, if it is deemed truly necessary and after careful consideration and thorough preparation, institute martial law and utilize trained troops to restore and maintain normal order in society, production, and working. Necessary training in the rule of law must be given to commanders throughout the military.

Party committees at all levels must strengthen their leadership and organize the concerned departments to work out a unified deployment, take effective measures, carry out a general mobilization on all battle lines, and resolutely and steadily perform the work of guaranteeing a stable and united political situation.

Some people will say that in doing this we are retrenching and not liberalizing any more, and that the directions of the Third Plenary Session have been changed. This is completely wrong. Party Central has said that there as never any question of "liberation" toward the activities of counter-revolutionary elements, anti-Party and anti-socialist elements, and criminal elements; it has always advocated that these people cannot be let free and allowed to carry on their mischief. There will also be people who will say that we speak only of dictatorship now and not democracy. This too is completely wrong. From the establishment of the People's Republic of China up until most recent times -- except for the ten years of chaos that do not count -- we have always resolutely practiced dictatorship against all opposing forces, counter-revolutionary elements, and criminal elements who seriously threaten social order; these people are definitely not to be treated with kid gloves.

This involved the question of how to perceive and carry out the people's democratic dictatorship. Comrade Mao said that the alliance of democracy among the people and dictatorship against counter-revolutionary cliques is the people's democratic dictatorship. In substance this is also the dictatorship of the proletariat, but the name "people's democratic dictatorship" is more appropriate to our national circumstances. The democratic rights of the people were trampled upon during the period of depredation by Lin Piao and the Gang of Four; following the smashing of the Gang of Four, and especially after the Third Plenary Session, we have been striving to develop democracy. So far this work has been carried out very insufficiently, and we must continue striving. As I said before we must resolutely and steadily continue carrying out various reforms of the political and economic system. The overall direction of these reforms is toward developing and guaranteeing democracy within the Party and developing and guaranteeing the people's democracy.

Now, as we resolutely and unshakably continue the work of developing socialist democracy, we ask comrades of the entire party and the people of the whole country to maintain a high level of vigilance and resolutely attack all kinds of anti-Party, anti-socialist, and criminal activities. This is because if such activity is not attached, it not only will be very difficult to carry out economic adjustment but there will also be a grave threat to the people's democratic rights and even to their right to exist. If these people are allowed to run rampant and create confusion every where, then in some places, some departments, and some units, the democratic rights of a majority of the people will once again be trampled upon, just as they were during the Great Cultural Revolution; it will be impossible to maintain the stable, united, and lively situation throughout the whole country, much less consolidate and expand that situation; our present fine political and economic situation, seldom seen since the establishment of the country, will again receive setbacks; and the improvements already gained in the people's livelihood will be lost. The vast majority of cadres, Party members, and members of the masses throughout the country have fresh memories of the hardships of the Great Cultural Revolution period. How can we permit those "rebel cliques" who closely followed Lin Piao and the Gang of Four, and the small number of bad chiefs who are carrying on their policies, to mount a second Great Cultural Revolution? They must not be allowed to succeed in even a single place, a single department, or a single unit, much less in the whole country. But in individual units and places they are already causing unrestrained disturbances, and the masses in those places are already furious at this situation. Under these conditions can we do other but resolutely rise up and protect the people's benefit?

Marxist theory and real life teach up repeatedly that an effective dictatorship can be exercised against a small minority of enemies only when the vast majority enjoy a high level of democracy, and that the only way to fully guarantee the rights of the vast majority is to exercise dictatorship over the small enemy minority. Thus to use the nation's suppressive strength to attack and dissolve all kinds of counter-revolutionary subversive elements, anti-Party and anti-socialist elements, and serious criminal elements under the present conditions, and to preserve social stability, is completely consistent with what the people and socialist modernization demand.

In sum, the carrying out of further adjustment in the economy and the carrying out of further stability in politics are all for the purpose of carrying through with the integrated directions that have been in effect since the Third Plenary Session. If we thoroughly carry through with those directions, our endeavor will surely be victorious.

DOCUMENT NO. 17

ELIMINATE "LEFTIST" INFLUENCE TO PUSH THE WORK OF THE WHOLE PROVINCE IN A BETTER WAY

Excerpts of the February 20 Editorial in Hunan Ribao

Jenmin Jihpao, Beijing, February 24, 1981;

FBIS-CHI, February 25, 1981

Since the Third Plenary Session, party organizations at all levels in our province (Hunan) have done a lot of work in implementing the line, principles and policies stipulated by the session. Generally speaking, the political and economic situation in Hunan is quite good. However, the process of implementing the spirit of the third plenary session shows that the central issue most deserving consideration is that some of our cadres lack morale and unity. A number of contrary opinions have accumulated between upper and lower levels and between left and right among the cadres. We must have a clear understanding about this and make a clear-headed appraisal. We would rather overestimate than underestimate the situation -- judging things to be a bit too serious and a bit too complicated.

Why do some people lack morale and unity? There is a profound historical reason for this. We need to analyze correctly and sum up our province's historical experiences and lessons in the past thirty years. Comrades familiar with conditions in Hunan all know that the province went in for many leftist things in the various political movements starting with the end of the 1950s. Many good comrades were harmed as a result. After the Gang of Four was smashed, our province conducted excessive publicity for the individual due to the ideological bindings of the "two whatevers," belatedly understood the importance of the discussion on practice as the sole criterion for testing truth, and failed to get a sufficient grasp of it. As a result, the influence of leftist thinking was never seriously and completely cleared away. Some people were even blindly complacent and arrogant. Although they had been influenced by leftism and done erroneous leftists things, they did not feel that these things were either leftist or erroneous. They were therefore never very straightforward and decisive in solving problems left over from history. This is why some cadres lack morale and unity. Hence, to solve the problem of lack of morale and unity among the cadres, we must start with education and adopt the method of keeping in touch with reality, recalling history, summing up work, and spontaneously taking stock of one's own thinking, in order to eliminate completely leftist influence and truly enhance the ideological and theoretical level of the cadres and their grasp of policies. Through education, we should ensure that after cool reflection, everyone will truly feel that the current line, principles and policies of the Central Committee are correct and will thus firmly maintain political unanimity with the Central Committee. We must soberly understand that generally speaking, there are only distinctions between more and less, between deep and shallow, and between late and early awareness, as far as leftist things among the cadres are concerned; there is no distinction between possession and non-possession of such things. Unless this issue is clearly stated, certain comrades may only criticize leftist things in the upper levels and in other people without eradicating them from themselves, and they may also continue to apply leftist viewpoints and methods to regard the upper levels and other people. Meanwhile, we must clearly understand that in recalling history, our aim is to sum up experience, learn lessons and raise the cadres' ideological consciousness. It is not our aim to get entangled with settling old accounts and hold individuals responsible.

We must energetically consolidate and carry forward the political situation of stability and unity. Regarding certain shortcomings and mistakes inevitable in past and future work, we must continue to maintain the self-criticism spirit of seeking truth from facts and being open and aboveboard. We must have the courage to lead the way in solving existing problems. We must also dare to criticize and correct what is wrong and dare to cope with those who act against the law. We must have a clear-cut and not a vague attitude toward problems about what is right or wrong ideologically, rural policies, economic readjustment, and so forth. All cadres must take the whole situation into consideration, cherish the great ambitious of the proletariat and consciously promote stability and unity. Our province's investigation work, generally speaking, is satisfactory. In our approach toward those subjected to investigation, we must seek truth from facts. We must treat a mistake as it is without adding to it. We must continue to thoroughly reverse verdicts on those framed or wrongly accused. In solving problems left over from history, we must adopt a decisive, and not indecisive, approach. If some comrades who fought the Gang of Four were wrongly treated in the past, they must be thoroughly rehabilitated and cleared. If some people use the correct line that they followed in the past as capital, if they insist that they have always been right despite the wrong line followed by them, and if they make trouble and launch improper activities against the party, they must be unhesitatingly subject to criticism and education and even struggle.

*****

DOCUMENT NO. 18

BUILDING SOCIALIST SPIRITUAL CIVILIZATION

(**Beijing Review**, No. 10, March 9, 1981)

Li Chang, Vice-President of the Chinese Academy of Sciences, in a letter to a leading member of the Party Central Committee last December, proposed that the goal of "building socialist spiritual civilization" should be put forward. It received due attention. The text of the letter follows. -- **B.R.** Ed.

The Third Plenary Session of the Eleventh Party Central Committee signified that our country has entered a new era of socialist construction. The central task for the whole Party and the people of all nationalities throughout the country is to bring about the four modernizations. Over the past two years, the ideal of working hard for the realization of the four modernizations has struck root in the hearts of the people.

In the revised draft of the Constitution of the Communist Party of China, the Party's general task at the present stage was formulated as: "Unite the people of all nationalities, work with one heart and one mind, achieve greater, faster, better and more economical results in developing socialist economy in a planned and proportionate way and build a modern and powerful socialist country with highly developed democracy and civilization." This is a more comprehensive formulation; following its adoption at the forthcoming Twelfth National Congress of the Party, it will surely play a still more significant role as the basis for uniting the actions of the whole Party and the people of all nationalities at the present stage.

Since the Fifth Plenary Session of the Eleventh Party Central Committee, inspired by the idea of "improving and strengthening the party leadership," I have felt all along that, after the ten disastrous years of the "cultural revolution," there still exists within the Party the pernicious influence of the ultra-Left line of the gang of four, remnants of the factional ideology of feudalism, selfish individualism of the bourgeoisie, anarchism of the petty-bourgeoisie and colonial ideas which worship things foreign. Under these influences, ideological demands inside and outside the Party have grown somewhat slack. Therefore it is necessary for the Party Central Committee to put forward a clear-cut and effective general slogan to guide the actions of the whole Party and the people all over the country, comparable to "Down with Japanese imperialism!" in the War of Resistance Against Japan and "Down with Chiang Kai-shek, liberate the whole country!" in the War of Liberation. It would serve to strengthen ideological and political work, and mobilize all the people of the country to accomplish the arduous task which history has entrusted to us.

In fact, we now have a general goal, that is, to "bring about the four modernizations." Among our people, there is no one who does not support it. But I feel that, along with the general goal of realizing the four modernizations, we should also consider putting forward a goal of "building socialist spiritual civilization." The phrase itself first appeared in Vice-Chairman Ye's 1979 speech at the meeting in celebration of the thirtieth anniversary of the founding of the People's Republic of China.

I consider that the socialist spiritual civilization includes a concrete aspect (such as well-developed education and thriving sciences, literature and art) as well as an ideological aspect (such as social ethics, traditions and customs). For example, by ideals we mean dedication to the people's cause and building the socialist motherland, whereas moral concepts imply identification of individual interests with the interests of the people and, when the two fall into contradiction, subordination of personal interests to the overall interests of the people. Moral concepts also refer to democracy and unity, hard work and plain living, eagerness to acquire an education, attaching importance to the development of science, paying attention to personal and public hygiene and being polite and courteous.

The first aspect (concrete) may be carried forward by people working in those fields while the latter (ideological aspect) would involve the efforts of all the Chinese people. While we are working to achieve the four modernizations, we must also strive to build socialist spiritual civilization, that is, mobilizing all workers, peasants, commercial and trade people, students, soldiers, men, women, old and young, for this task, so that the broad masses may concentrate on a clear-cut, revolutionary, patriotic objective. This in turn will propel the advance of the country's modernization programme.

To put forward the goal of building socialist spiritual civilization will give the slogan. "Be both red and expert" a new content. Now people know clearly what "expert" means. If we say someone is "expert," we mean that he has worked hard in his field of study and reached a certain professional level. If we say someone is "red," could we understand it as this way now: he has worked hard for the building of socialist spiritual civilization and he himself has met the requirements of the civilization?

At the same time, to put forward the goal of building socialist spiritual civilization will raise clear-cut and strict demands on members of the Communist Party and Communist Youth League. In addition to doing a good job at their own posts and doing their bit for the four modernizations, Party members must play an exemplary role, and League members a vanguard role, in uniting comrades they are working with to strive for the building of the socialist spiritual civilization.

I believe that, if the Party Central Committee can emphatically put forward the goal of "bringing about the four modernizations and building socialist spiritual civilization," it will enable people to form a clear view of the future, to advance with one heart and one mind, to be hard-working and live plainly, to increase production and practice economy at the present stage when the country is carrying out a big readjustment of the economy. It was wrong for Lin Biao and the gang of four to emphasize the primacy of the spiritual role. However, we should not overlook the fact that spirit can play a definite role.

During the War of Resistance Against Japan, we were poor and faced many difficulties, yet when people, Chinese or foreign, came to Yanan and other anti-Japanese democratic base areas, they felt that they had come to a new world which was full of revolutionary spirit. They believed that the hope of the whole Chinese nation could be seen there, and that these places were a stronghold for the world's anti-fascist war at the time. In the early post-liberation days, we were poorer than we are now and there were also difficulties. But as soon as foreigners arrived in Shenzhen and Guangzhou, they felt they had arrived in a plain-living, clean country with a revolutionary spirit and excellent social ethics. Some people even said that there was no need to lock their doors at night and that no one pocketed lost articles picked up in the street.

Now, our Party can and should rid itself of the damage by Lin Biao and the gang of four and the pernicious influence of the "Left" deviationist line, purify its thinking, enhance its revolutionary vigour, find the road to the four modernizations suited to China's conditions and stride ahead.

*****

DOCUMENT NO. 19

CARRY FORWARD THE SPIRIT OF LEI FENG

(**Beijing Review**, No. 10, March 9, 1981)

On February 19, the General Political Department of the People's Liberation Army issued a circular calling on the whole army to further unfold the movement to learn from Lei Feng, a young PLA soldier who died while on duty in 1962.

Lei Feng was a man of noble moral character and was imbued with communist ideals. He was dedicated to serving the public without any thought of himself. During his off hours, he often spent his time helping others. On March 5, 1963, Chairman Mao wrote an inscription calling on the people throughout the country to learn from Lei Feng, which later became a nationwide movement, particularly among the young people.

Renmin Ribao recently published a report on how the PLA unit in which Lei Feng served has carried forward the spirit of this selfless PLA fighter. In fact the officers and men of this unit started emulating Lei Feng as early as 1960. Over the past twenty years, they have worked selflessly for the public interest and done many good things for the people. For instance, they have built houses, highways and school buildings for the minority peoples in the remote border areas and sunk wells for the fishermen living by the seaside. And they have rescued children who fell into the rivers, intercepted startled horses, donated blood for patients who were seriously ill, and done many other good turns for the people.

On March 1, hundreds of thousands of youngsters and tens of thousands of officers and men of the People's Liberation Army in Beijing carried out activities emulating Lie Feng and doing good things for the public. They swept the streets, cleaned up public recreation centers, helped the people's police in maintaining traffic order, publicized politeness and took part in farm work or in building parks in the city.

It was the first day of "Learning From Lei Feng Week" sponsored by the office in charge of education of children and youth under the Beijing municipal party committee and the Beijing municipal committee of the Communist Youth League. Responsible members of the Beijing municipal Party committee, the municipal people's government and the PLA units stationed in Beijing also took part in these activities.

The movement to learn from Lei Feng is not only carried out in the army units and among the youngsters. In fact, people all over the country are learning from him.

Peng Yixiang, 61, is a barber in the port city of Tianjin in north China. Before liberation he served as an apprentice and lived in misery. Liberation brought him happiness but he has never forgotten his sufferings in the old society. Since the restoration of the bonus system in 1978, he has deposited his monthly bonus in the bank and used the money to help people in difficulty or to buy hair-clippers, hair scissors and other instruments for his barbershop. In addition he spent 300 yuan to buy two electric fans and a few umbrellas for the convenience of the customers.

Hu Asu, a retired woman worker in Shanghai, lived frugally. When she died, she gave her entire savings totalling more than 10,000 yuan to the state. She said in her will: "I endured untold sufferings in the old society. The new society and Chairman Mao have given me happiness. What I have now has all been given my by the state. I wish to donate all my savings to the state after I die." She is praised by the people as a fine example of the working class.

*****

DOCUMENT NO. 20

BE A SOBER-MINDED MARXIST

(**Beijing Review**, No. 12, March 22, 1982)

*The following is a slightly abridged translation of an article carried in "Renmin Ribao" by its commentator on May 15. Subheads are ours.--**B.R.** Ed.*

Smuggling, selling smuggled articles, embezzlement, bribery, speculation, swindling, and other illegal and criminal activities that shift huge amounts of state and collective property into private possession have become rampant in the economic field in the last two or three years. What deserves particular attention is the fact that some Party members, cadres and even some leading cadres have taken part in such illegal and criminal activities. Although they make up only a very small part of the vast contingents of Party members and cadres, they have greatly harmed the Party's prestige. If their activities remain unchecked, this would surely mean the destruction of the socialist cause and the revolutionary fruits achieved by the Party and the people through decades of arduous struggle. We should have a thorough understanding of this great danger and be highly vigilant against it.

Danger of "Peaceful Evolution"

There is no denying that through the untiring efforts of all Party members since the downfall of the gang of four more than five years ago, and especially since the Third Plenary Session of the Eleventh Party Central Committee, the Party and the nation have averted a grave crisis resulting from the ten years of domestic turmoil and have returned to the road towards prosperity. This is an undeniable fundamental historic fact which our descendants will never forget. But does this mean that there will not be any significant dangers other than war for our Party, our nation and our socialist cause? Certainly not. Even in times of peace, there is still the danger that could weaken our Party and lead it towards "peaceful evolution." In the economic field, criminal offenses are fare more serious than during the "san fan" [three-anti] and "wu fan" [five-anti] movements[1] thirty years ago. In the ideological and cultural arenas and in social morality, the influence of decadent bourgeois ideas and feudal remnants and the phenomena of worshipping foreign things have grown on a scale rarely seen since the birth of New China.

What is the major source of the danger? We are right in our frequent assertions that we should guard against any attempt to invade and subvert China from abroad and against any actions taken by the remnants of the overthrown Lin Biao and Jiang Qing counter-revolutionary cliques. But at the same time we should clearly bear in mind that our Party, the vanguard of the working class, is the force that is leading this big country of China. So long as our Party remains sound and healthy, effectively wards off erosion by unhealthy tendencies, does not become rotten itself and always stays in close touch with the people, then no enemy force in the world can have its way in destroying us. In this sense, the main danger is from no source other than the degeneration of certain weak-willed members inside our Party.

The Focus of the Problem

For the Party itself, the focus of the problem lies with the middle- and high-ranking leaders within the Party. If our leading cadres at the middle and high levels are staunch, sober-minded and active Marxists, they can set a good example for the whole Party and the Party will be strong enough to overcome all things that are mistaken. In 1938, Comrade Mao Zedong said in his article "The Role of the Chinese Communist Party in the National War": "So far as shouldering the main responsibility of leadership is concerned, our Party's fighting capacity will be much greater and our task of defeating Japanese imperialism will be more quickly accomplished if there are one or two hundred comrades with a grasp of Marxism-Leninism which is systematic and not fragmentary, genuine and not hollow."

This point of view of Comrade Mao Zedong's is very profound and important. He put the figure at 100 or 200 at that time. Now, the historical conditions have changed and we need 10,000 or 20,000 today. Our Party's fighting capacity will greatly increase if 10,000 to 20,000 of our cadres can really become staunch, sober-minded and active Marxists. So long as our Party is strong and healthy, we are sure to accomplish our socialist modernization programme, no matter how arduous it is. On the contrary, it would be very dangerous if some of our middle- and high-ranking cadres become corrupt and degenerate in peace time and if this tendency is not checked soon enough but is allowed to spread instead.

From the analysis above, we can see that it is completely correct and necessary for the Party Central Committee to decide to deal resolute blows at illegal and criminal activities in the economic field and to stress meting out severe punishments for Party members and cadres, especially leading cadres, who commit illegal and criminal offenses. This struggle is indeed connected with the life and death of our party as well as the prosperity of our state. It is a severe test for all Party members and cadres as to what attitude they should adopt towards the struggle. It is necessary for us to strengthen communist ideological education within the Party, and among the Party cadres, especially among those middle- and high-ranking cadres.

Cadres of the Party, especially leading cadres at the middle and high levels, must review and really grasp Comrade Mao Zedong's theory and tactics of both unity and struggle in the united front work. They should follow his teachings of fighting against both Left-deviationist closed-doorism and Right-deviationist capitulationism; of both taking into consideration the interests of our allies and maintaining the ideological, political and organization independence of the proletarian Party; of both adopting different social policies under different conditions and seriously and resolutely maintaining the communist purity of Party members under whatever conditions. They must also creatively apply these theories and tactics under the new historical conditions when China has adopted an open policy towards the outside world and flexible domestic policies to enliven the economy.

The cadres of the Party, especially the middle- and high-ranking cadres, must strengthen their Party spirit, abide by Party discipline and keep their heads clear in the new situation and in face of new tasks. Our Party will be able to weather all storms so long as these cadres play their role as the mainstay of the nation.

*****

NOTES

1. This refers to the movement against three evils (corruption, waste and bureaucracy) launched among state functionaries at the end of 1951, and the movement against five evils (bribery of government workers, tax evasion, theft of state property, cheating on government contracts, and stealing economic information for private speculation) launched among capitalist industrialists and businessmen at the beginning of 1952.

*****

DOCUMENT NO. 21

YOUNG PEOPLE LEARN FROM LEI FENG

(**Beijing Review**, No. 14, April 4, 1982)

Every childless, elderly disabled person in Beijing is looked after by young volunteers.

Caring for the elderly and the handicapped is one aspect of the campaign to "learn from Lei Feng" and to serve the people. Lei Feng, a squad leader in the People's Liberation Army, did numerous good deeds for the people before he died at his post in 1962 at the age of twenty-two. He has since been cited throughout the country as a model of serving the people.

In Beijing more than 100,000 young people have formed 10,000 "learn from Lei Feng groups." Each group is assigned to one or two old people in its neighborhood and helps them with household chores and shopping or other work.

Young people in other municipalities and provinces have also organized "service groups," "care-offering teams" and "learn from Lei Feng groups" to provide services for childless elderly and handicapped people, revolutionary martyrs' families, and the families of men and women in the armed services.

The Beijing municipal committee of the Communist Youth League and the Beijing Youth Research Society recently cosponsored a forum on learning from Lei Feng attended by eighty people including theoreticians, cadres in charge of youth work, and advanced individuals and representatives of advanced collectives in learning from Lei Feng.

Addressing the forum participants, Gan Baolu, a philosophy lecturer at the Beijing Teachers' University, said that moral models and principles reflect the economic and social relations in a society. Every ruling class, sets up its own models to maintain its rule and interests. In feudal society, filial piety and loyalty to one's superiors were stressed, whereas in socialist society, the emphasis is on people like Lei Feng who serve the people wholeheartedly. "Like a road sign showing the way, revolutionary models encourage, educate and inspire people to go forward," she said.

Another speaker, Li Yanjie of the Beijing Normal College, whose lectures on socialist ethics and aesthetics have been warmly received by young people and students from all over the country, said that he had come across many people like Lei Feng all over China. He quoted the words of many young people he had spoken with the show that the Lei Feng spirit has blossomed and borne fruits among the present-day younger generation.

Advanced individuals and representatives of advanced collectives present at the forum talked of their experiences in learning from Lei Feng and in educating young people in the Lei Feng spirit.

*****

DOCUMENT NO. 22

HU QIAO-MU ON BOURGEOIS LIBERALIZATION AND OTHER PROBLEMS

(**Beijing Review**, No. 23, June 7, 1982)

*What is the essence of the bourgeois liberalization tendency now being criticized in China? Why should intellectual products be treated as anything but commodities? What are the criteria for literature and art? All these issues were dealt with by Hu Qiaomu in a speech made at the forum on ideological questions sponsored by the propaganda department of the Chinese Communist Party Central Committee in August last year (excerpts appeared in **Beijing Review**, issue No. 4 this year). In April the author, a Member of the Secretariat of the Party Central Committee, made the following important revisions and additions while preparing the speech for publication in booklet form. (**B.R.** Ed.)*

Bourgeois Liberalization

Why is it that we call violations of our society's four fundamental principles[1] the bourgeois liberalization tendency? Freedom in a capitalist country is first and foremost the freedom of the capitalists to exploit hired laborers and to maintain bourgeois private ownership. That is the essence of bourgeois freedom. All the other freedoms, such as the freedom of speech, press, assembly and association, the freedom to run for office and the freedom to adopt the two- and multi-party system, are derived from it and serve it.

The bourgeois liberalization tendency in China today is characterized by publicizing and advocating bourgeois freedoms calling for the adoption of the bourgeois parliamentarism, including the two-party system, campaigning for office, bourgeois freedoms of speech, press, assembly and association, bourgeois individualism and even anarchism to a certain extent.

Its advocates also promote bourgeois profit-seeking mentality and behavior, the bourgeois way of life, vulgar tastes and its standards of morality and the arts. They try to transplant the capitalist system and their worship for the capitalist world into China's political, economic, social as well as cultural life. They negate, oppose and undermine in principle the socialist cause in China and the Chinese Communist Party's leadership over it.

The essence of this bourgeois ideological tendency lies in consciously or unconsciously demanding China forsake the socialist road and install the so-called capitalist liberal system in the political, economic, social and cultural arenas. Thus we call it the bourgeois liberalization tendency.

Clarifying the implication and characteristics of this tendency will help us prevent abuse of the term and make demarcation lines between issues. For instance, to criticize the decision of a certain Party organization, its work or one of its leaders is the proper democratic right of a Communist Party member or a citizen, which should be labelled neither as negating or opposing the Party's leadership, nor as bourgeois liberalization.

It is necessary for the development of science and the arts in China that the Constitution and laws guarantee academic freedom and the freedom of artistic creation. This also has nothing to do with bourgeois liberalization. Unquestionably, within institutions of scientific research and the arts, the relationship between collective plans and the freedom of individual activities must be dealt with properly. But generally speaking, this does not involved bourgeois liberalization.

On the other hand, we do not hesitate to wage resolute struggle against anyone who negates, opposes or undermines China's socialist cause and the leadership of the Chinese Communist Party over it and demands that socialist democracy and the socialist system be replaced by the bourgeois liberal system, no matter how much he denies that he is doing so.

Erroneous Tendency of Commercializing Intellectual Products

In a socialist society, a large number of intellectual products are circulated like material products. The fundamental purpose of producing both material and intellectual products is to satisfy the material and intellectual needs of the people.

To this end, those who turn out intellectual products should not only strive to increase them quantitatively but also improve them qualitatively. That is to say, efforts should be made to ensure that the content of each intellectual product is patriotic, revolutionary and ideologically sound, so that they can give people worthwhile intellectual entertainment and inspiration.

No intellectual products can be allowed to stray from their intellectual purposes and be circulated blindly like commodities. In sum, we must not "turn our eyes towards money."

If intellectual products deviate from the fundamental purpose of satisfying the needs of the people and instead chase after money, they will also deviate from the fundamental principle of socialism and there will be no basic difference between the intellectual products of our socialist society and those of a capitalist society.

In a capitalist society, both material and intellectual products are produced as commodities, with the sole purpose of making profits. Anything can be sold out there in order to make money, even the conscience, personality and physical body. To make money, many capitalist producers of intellectual products can, unscrupulously and almost without restriction, produce vulgar, decadent and reactionary products that poison and corrode the mental outlook of the people.

The laissez-faire production of intellectual products is one of the reasons behind the insoluble intellectual crisis in the capitalist world.

At present, some units in China that turn out intellectual products such as the editorial boards of newspapers, magazines and publishing houses and also some art and literary departments, to a lesser or greater extent, are too concerned with the marketability of their products. This stems from the error in their guiding thinking and defects in management. They do not set high standards for their publications and performances in the light of the needs of the people who are engaged in the modernization drive and in accordance with the principle of socialism, but "turn their eyes towards money."

As a result, some things with conspicuously negative and corrosive influences have become the vogue of the day. Some people even openly advocate that publications and other cultural undertakings should not be operated only by the state and the people's organizations, that individuals should be allowed to run them.

This tendency towards bourgeois liberalization in cultural fields has an undeniable influence on the emergence of various wrong views and has added to the flooding of bourgeois ideological and therefore warrants serious attention and effective correction.

The Criteria for Art and Literature

A piece of work should be assessed by its ideological content and its artistic form. As a whole, the ideological content includes political views, social views, philosophy, historical views, ethical views and artistic views. These views are not abstract but connected with the images, subject-matters and plots of the work as well as the life the work reflects.

Therefore, when assessing the ideological content of a work, we must not only analyze its political views and its political inclination but also its other ideological content and its concept of value towards life. Only thus can a comprehensive appraisal of the work be made. Without such an appraisal, the work will inevitably be treated as merely an illustration of a political view.

Even a piece of work with an obvious political inclination includes other ideological content than its state politics, unless it is not a literary one. Therefore, it is inadequate to consider the political view or the political inclination as the only ideological content of a work (although, of course, it is absolutely important and necessary for a revolutionary writer to have a revolutionary political view or a revolutionary political inclination) and to use political criteria as the primary criteria to judge a piece. To act otherwise would inevitably lead to crude interferences in the creation of literary and art works and hinder the healthy development of creativity as well as literary and art criticism.

*****

NOTES

1. The four fundamental principles are adherence to the socialist road, the people's democratic dictatorship, i.e., the dictatorship of the proletariat, the leadership of the Communist Party, and Marxism-Leninism and Mao Zedong Thought.

CHAPTER FIVE

REFORMERS IN COMMAND

The documents in this final chapter reflect the triumph and consolidation of the victory of the reform faction in Chinese politics led by Teng Hsiao-p'ing.

Document No. 23, an editorial in the Party theoretical journal **Red Flag**, attacked the "Two Whatevers," that is, the leftist ideas of the followers of Mao and of Hua Guo-feng. The editorial asserted that the "specter" of these policies still "haunted" China and must be guarded against.

Document No. 24, repeats the theme which we saw in Chapter One that the "Thought" of Mao Tse-tung is not Mao's alone, but represents the collective historical wisdom of the entire Chinese Communist Party. As the essay puts it, Mao's Thought "is also the product of the wisdom of his comrades-in-arms."

Repeating again a theme which was stressed in Chapter Four, Hu Yao-pang's speech on ideological issues (Document No. 25) focuses on party leadership and spirit. Citing a speech by Teng, Hu criticized "lax and weak leadership" especially in ideological work.

Documents Nos. 26 and 27 are two speeches by Chao Tzu-yang. The first, a very long report on government work delivered to the Fifth National People's Congress, stressed that the main item on the agenda was "economic work." Chao reported on the successes of the reforms and the guidelines for future development. The second address by Chao was delivered to the National Industrial and Communications Work Conference. Chao stressed the importance of real economic results rather than "inflated speech" and "exaggerations" of growth rates by officials. Chao also criticized the "blind increase of output" for its own sake. He also stressed the importance of leadership in enterprise reorganization and readjustment.

Part of Teng's modernization drive involved an attempt to replace older -- especially more leftist -- cadres with younger leaders more committed to reform.

Document Nos. 23 - 30

Document No. 28 deals with the policies intended to encourage the retirement of elderly cadres who are described as the "precious riches" of the Party.

Questions about whether the reform policies were consistent with the goal of building socialism are the subject of Document No. 29. The essay argues that these policies are indeed consistent with the goals of the revolution and that, in fact, "only socialism can save China."

Document No. 30 announces plans to convene the Twelfth CPC Congress on September 1, 1982.

*****

DOCUMENTS

23.   "Spectre of 'Two Whatevers' Still Haunts China," **Hongqi [Red Flag]**, No. 22, Beijing, November 16, 1980; **FBIS-CHI,** December 9, 1980.

24.   "How to Define Mao Zedong Thought: Changes over Forty Years," **Beijing Review**, No. 9, March 2, 1981.

25.   "Hu Yao-pang's Speech Delivered at the 'Meeting on Issues Concerning the Ideological Front,'" August 3, 1981, **Issues & Studies**, Vol. XX, No. 1, January 1984.

26.   Zhao Ziyang, "The Present Economic Situation and the Principles for Future Economic Construction -- Report on the Work of the Government Delivered by Premier Zhao Ziyang at the Fourth Session of the Fifth National People's Congress on November 30 and December 1, 1981." **Beijing Review**, No. 51, December 21, 1981.

27.   Zhao Ziyang, "Several Questions on the Current Economic Work -- Report Delivered by Premier Zhao Ziyang at the National Industrial and Communications Work Conference," Tianjin, March 30, 1982; **Hongqi,** No. 7, 1982; **Jenmin Jihpao**, Beijing, March 30, 1982; **FBIS-CHI**, April 1, 1982.

28.   "The CCP Central Committee's Decisions Concerning the Establishment of a Retirement System for Elderly Cadres," February 20, 1982, **Issues & Studies**, Vol. XX, No. 8, August 1984.

29.   Feng Wenbin, "Nature of Chinese Society Today," **Beijing Review**, Nos. 23, 25 and 26, June 8, 22, and 29, 1981.

30.   "Central Committee Session Announces: Party Congress to Open Sept. 1," **Beijing Review**, No. 33, August 16, 1982.

*****

DOCUMENT NO. 23

SPECTER OF 'TWO WHATEVERS' STILL HAUNTS CHINA

(Hongqi [Red Flag], No. 22, Beijing, November 16, 1980;
FBIS-CHI, December 9, 1980)

We still remember that a few years ago, the specter of the theory of the "Two Whatevers" was haunting every corner of our country. Was there anyone who did not strictly observe the tenet of the "two Whatevers?" After the discussion on the criterion to test truth and the implementation of the spirit of the Third Plenary Session of the Eleventh Party Central Committee, we came to realize that "our present policies are correct and the previous ones were wrong." With the restoration of the party's dialectical ideological line, it seemed as if "whatever" has vanished from sight.

Has the problem of the emancipation of the mind been completely solved? Has the spirit of the Third Plenary Session been accepted by all? The answer is no. Some people have "stubbornly resisted" or "hindered" the implementation of the spirit. Since they are not people in our camp, we do not want to talk about them too much in this article. As for our own comrades, some of them have still cast doubt upon, hesitated about, taken a wait-and-see attitude or even borne resentment against the party's decisions and policies adopted since the Third

Plenary Session. This has actually shown that the soul of "whatever" refuses to leave. Whither this soul, haunting about? After making considerable efforts to detect and trace it, we have finally located it. "Whatever" has been changed into "but." Let us listen to what they are saying:

"It is right to take practice as a criterion to test truth, but it is not an erroneous act to use revolutionary theory to judge what is right and what is wrong."

"It is right to emancipate the mind, but we should not go so far in this 'emancipation' campaign as to discard the teachings of the revolutionary teacher!"

"It is absolutely necessary to oppose the ultra-leftist ideas, but we should not oppose them from the rightist standpoint!"

"It is right that we should not talk about class struggle every day, but we should follow a key link to carry out our production!"

"It is right to allot private plots to peasants and encourage them to develop their household sideline production, but we should not lose our bearings!"

They say so and so, ranging from the criterion of truth to the system of job responsibility in production. These instances of "but" defy enumeration.

After studying the text, we find out that the trick of this sentence pattern lies in the subordinate clause beginning with "but." If we only looked at the main clause, we would have wrong thought that the speakers had completely accepted the principles of taking practice as the criterion for testing truth, encouraging the emancipation of the mind and attaching importance to production, and that they had favored the party's economic policy. In a word, that they had fully supported the spirit of the Third Plenary Session. However, the main clause is only an empty shot and the substance is embodied in the subordinate clause to insignificance amid sweet smiles and gentle manner. In other words, "but" of today is still a shadow of "whatever" of yesterday!

A few years ago, it was not a sin to believe in the theory of the "Two Whatevers," and the act of changing "whatever" into "but" cannot but be considered small progress now. However, if a person is still indifferent to the excellent situation brought about by the Third Plenary Session and worries about the fact that many newborn things do not conform with a single "quotation" or "instruction," we can only say that his mind is incorrigibly ossified. Ours is a country ruled by feudal autocracy for several thousand years, and Lin Biao, Jiang

Qing and company frenziedly created modern superstitions for a decade or so. The pernicious influence of the past several thousand years and ten years of catastrophe led some people to live in fear of the "divine emperor." It has only been not more than two years since the convening of the Third Plenary Session. How can the ideas of the "Two Whatevers" be "destroyed overnight?"

Today, we are marching toward the four modernizations and continuing to emancipate our minds. If we still deem it necessary to criticize the theory of the "Two Whatevers" which enormously harmed us in the past, we should effectively deal with the variety of "whatever " -- the problem of "but." We should "apply proper antidotes to heart disease." A few years ago, he wrote out a prescription of taking practice as the criterion for testing truth for the patients who suffered from the disease of "whatever." Today, there is no harm applying the same antidote to the disease of "but" so that the patients will have sharper eyes and stronger minds. To implement the party's line, guiding principles and policies more effectively, it is absolutely necessary to strengthen our ideological and political work.

*****

DOCUMENT NO. 24

HOW TO DEFINE MAO ZEDONG THOUGHT: CHANGES OVER FORTY YEARS

(Beijing Review, No. 9, March 2, 1981)

Mao Zedong Thought is Marxism as applied in the Chinese revolution. The fruit of a prolonged struggle, it has been accepted as an invaluable asset of our Party and our country. The formulation of the term Mao Zedong Thought and the whole Party's understanding of it have only evolved through a long, complicated process.

Formulating "Mao Zedong Thought"

During the 1942 rectification campaign in Yanan, Mao Zedong was acknowledged by Zhou Enlai, Liu Shaoqi and Zhu De as a great revolutionary who had integrated the universal truth of Marxism with the concrete practice of the Chinese revolution.

Liu Shaoqi said in his report of July 4, 1943 to mark the twenty-second anniversary of the founding of the Chinese Communist Party: "All cadres and all Party members must study conscientiously the historical experience of the Chinese Party over the past twenty-two years; they must study conscientiously Comrade Mao Zedong's theories on the Chinese revolution and other aspects; they must arm themselves with the thought of Comrade Mao Zedong and adopt his ideological system to combat Menshevik thinking inside the Party."

The Resolution on Certain Questions in the History of Our Party adopted in April 1945 by the Enlarged Seventh Plenary Session of the Sixth Central Committee of the Chinese Communist Party observed: "Ever since its birth in 1921, the Communist Party of China has made the integration of the universal truth of Marxism-Leninism with the concrete practice of the Chinese revolution of guiding principle in all its work, and Comrade Mao Zedong's theory and practice of the Chinese revolution represent this integration."

The concept of "Mao Zedong Thought" was first articulated in May 1945 when Liu Shaoqi said at the Party's Seventh National Congress: "Mao Zedong Thought means the continuation and development of Marxism in the national, democratic revolution in a colonial, semi-colonial and semi-feudal country of our time; it is a fine prototype of Marxism with a given national character." The Party Constitution adopted at that time also said: "The Communist Party of China takes Mao Zedong Thought -- the thought of unity of Marxist-Leninist theory with the practice of the Chinese revolution -- as the guiding principle in all its work and opposes any dogmatist or empiricist deviations."

When the American correspondent Anna Louise Strong interviewed Liu Shaoqi in Yanan between January and February 1947, he said: "Mao Zedong's great achievement lies in his transformation of Marxism from its European form into an Asiatic form," that is, "he has created a Chinese type or a so-called Asiatic type of Marxism."

In his report to the First All-China Youth Congress on May 7, 1949, Zhou Enlai said: "Chairman Mao has applied the truth of the world revolution -- the universal truth of Marxism-Leninism -- to China and integrated it with the revolutionary practice in China to become Mao Zedong Thought." "Mao Zedong Thought has the distinct feature of giving concrete expression to universal truth and applying it on Chinese soil."

Personally, Mao Zedong never regarded Mao Zedong Thought as the thought of an individual but an expression of the collective wisdom of the Chinese Communist Party and the Chinese people. During the 1942 rectification campaign in Yanan when students of the Party School under the Party Central Committee were discussing what was meant by Mao Zedong Thought, Mao Zedong made it clear that Mao Zedong Thought was not just his own thinking, but something that had been written in blood by millions upon millions of martyrs and represented the collective wisdom of the Chinese Communist Party and the Chinese people. "My personal thoughts," he added, "are developing, and I, too, am liable to make mistakes."

In August 1948, Wu Yuzhang contemplated proposing in a speech he was to deliver at the opening of the North China University that Mao Zedong Thought be changed into Mao Zedong-ism. When he sent a telegram to Mao Zedong, the Chairman replied: "This expression is most inappropriate. There is no such thing as Mao Zedong-ism. The issue is not one of 'mainly studying Mao Zedong-ism,' but of it being necessary to call on students to study the theories of Marx, Engels, Lenin and Stalin and the experience of the Chinese revolution."

In the 1950s

In the early years of New China, our Party adhered to the formulation "Mao Zedong Thought" that had been accepted at the Seventh National Party Congress and stressed the need to be careful and modest in giving publicity to Mao Zedong Thought.

But then in 1954, Mao Zedong proposed that the formulation "Mao Zedong Thought" not be used any more to avoid possible misinterpretations. Accordingly, the Department of propaganda under the Party Central Committee issued a special circular on this matter. "'Mao Zedong Thought' is the 'very thought of the unity of Marxist-Leninist theory with one concrete practice of the Chinese revolution.'" "Our advice is that comrades inside the Party, when writing an article or addressing a meeting, should act in accordance with this directive of Comrade Mao Zedong's. When expounding the Party Constitution or important Party documents or resolutions of the past, however, there is no need to make any change but keep to the original. We should, however, explain to the public that 'Mao Zedong Thought' itself is Marxism-Leninism to avoid giving people the false impression that they are two different things. When Comrade Mao Zedong is involved in an article or a speech, the wording 'the works by Mao Zedong' may be used."

When preparations were being made for the Eight National Party Congress in 1956, Mao Zedong once again proposed not to use the formulation "Mao Zedong Thought" in Party documents. Consequently, the Party Constitution adopted by the congress dropped the term "Mao Zedong Thought" and replaced it with the following: "The Communist Party of China takes Marxism-Leninism as its guide to action"; "the Party in its activities upholds the principle of integrating the universal truth of Marxism- Leninism with the actual practice of China's revolutionary struggle, and combats all doctrinaire or empiricist deviations."

Late 50s and Early 60s

Towards the end of the 1950s, Khrushchov wantonly attacked Mao Zedong Thought and stirred up an anti-China adverse current around the world. At home, while a large-scale struggle was being waged against so-called "Right opportunism," something abnormal appeared in the political life of our Party and state. Following the Lushan Meeting in 1959, some responsible members of the Party Central Committee went back to the formulation "Mao Zedong Thought." Meanwhile, Lin Biao, who was then the defense minister, and Kang Sheng took this opportunity to create confusion and freely distort things.

At the meeting of senior army cadres held in September and October 1959, Lin Biao said: "What is Marxism-Leninism of today? The thought of our Chairman Mao of course." He also claimed that studying Mao Zedong's works was "the short cut to Marxism-Leninist studies," "an investment that returns real good profit." In early 1966, Lin Biao had Mao Zedong Thought further absolutized. "Mao Zedong Thought," he declared, "is the acme of contemporary Marxism-Leninism, the highest and liveliest Marxism-Leninism." Kang Sheng said many things more or less to the same effect.

During the said period, some leading comrades in our Party and the Department of Propaganda under the Party Central Committee opposed the fallacies brought forward their own views on the proper way to publicize Mao Zedong Thought. They maintained that "we must not draw a parallel between Mao Zedong Thought and Marxism-Leninism" -- a view shared by Mao Zedong himself in 1961, "nor look at Mao Zedong's works and sayings as a dogma," and they must not be "simplified and vulgarized."

In November 15, 1963, Zhou Enlai pointed out explicitly at the Nineteenth Session of the Supreme State Conference: "Mao Zedong Thought was brought about and established in the midst of adhering to what is right and revising what is wrong."

On September 30, 1964, in a letter of reply to an old comrade, Liu Shaoqi said: "Our principle is to learn from all who know the truth, not just from those in high places." "We must not accept Mao Zedong's works and sayings as a dogma just as we must not accept the theories of Marx and Lenin as a dogma. You should analyze the actual state of affairs in your locality, in the spirit and essence of Mao Zedong Thought and correctly sum up the practical experiences there, and draw up the correct policies, plans and steps in your forthcoming work." When Mao Zedong saw the letter, he sent a note to Liu Shaoqi with a comment: Have read your letter and feel it's really great.

Between 1966 and 1976

In the "cultural revolution" (1966-76), to seize Party and state leadership, Lin Biao, the gang of four and Kang Sheng launched a mammoth campaign to deify the leader and distort Mao Zedong Thought in a vain attempt to transform it into a religious faith.

Lin Biao said at an enlarged meeting of the Political Bureau of the Party Central Committee in May 1966: "Chairman Mao has inherited, defended and developed Marxism-Leninism with genius, creatively and comprehensively and has brought it to a higher and completely new stage. Mao Zedong's Though is Marxism-Leninism of the era in which imperialism is heading for total collapse and socialism is advancing to worldwide victory." Later Zhang Chunqiao inserted this statement into Lin Biao's foreword to the second edition of *Quotations From Chairman Mao*.

In August 1966, Lin Biao said: "Do everything in accordance with Chairman Mao's thinking." "We must resolutely carry out the Chairman's instructions, carry out both what we understand and what we don't."

Kang Sheng, in the same period, declared that "Mao Zedong Thought has become the banner of the international communist movement in our era." "For or against China's great cultural revolution, for or against Mao Zedong Thought--this has become the line of demarcation, the watershed, between Marxism and revisionism."

During this period Mao Zedong criticized Lin Biao, the gang of four and Kang Sheng and rejected their wrong formulations. He wrote comments on a document, saying: "Please note, from now on do not use expressions like 'the highest and the liveliest . . .' 'acme,' and the 'supreme directives.'" In regard to those formulations in the widely circulated foreword to the second edition of *Quotations From Chairman Mao*, Mao Zedong said: "We are still in the era of imperialism and the proletarian revolution." He asked to delete some portions and actually struck out himself the phrase "with genius, creatively and comprehensively." Mao Zedong time and again emphatically warned against judging the merit of a Party in a foreign country by whether it has accepted or rejected Mao Zedong Thought. He also said that in contacts with Parties of other countries, the Chinese Communist Party could only, and just, stick to this kind of formulation: integrating the universal truth of Marxism-Leninism with the concrete practice in the revolution in that particular country.

After the Downfall of the Gang

Following the collapse of the gang of four in October 1976, our Party gradually rectified the distortions and alterations of Mao Zedong Thought by Lin Biao, the gang of four and Kang Sheng, and repudiated their pernicious influence. But struggle has continued over the issue of what should be the correct approach to Mao Zedong Thought.

On February 7, 1977 the joint editorial of *Renmin Ribao, Hongqi* and *Jiefangjun Bao* wrote: "We'll resolutely adhere to whatever policy decision made by Chairman Mao, we'll always follow unswervingly whatever directive of Chairman Mao."

On April 10, 1977, Deng Xiaoping in a letter to the Party Central Committee, countering the two "whatevers," put forward the formulation of using the correct, comprehensive Mao Zedong Thought to guide our whole Party, whole army and the whole population.

On December 22, 1978, the Third Plenary Session of the Eleventh Central Committee of the Chinese Communist Party pointed out: "The lofty task of the Party Central Committee on the theoretical front is to lead and educate the whole Party and the people of the whole country to recognize Comrade Mao Zedong's great feats in a historical and scientific perspective, comprehensively and correctly grasp the scientific system of Mao Zedong Thought and integrate the universal principles of Marxism-Leninism-Mao Zedong Thought with the concrete practice of socialist modernization and develop it under the new historical conditions."

In September 1979, Ye Jianying in his speech at the meeting in celebration of the thirtieth anniversary of the founding of the People's Republic of China said: "Marxism-Leninism develops through the revolutionary struggles of the people in different countries. It cannot be monopolized or ossified by anyone in whatever form. Mao Zedong Thought is Marxism-Leninism as applied and developed in the Chinese revolution. It is the result of integrating the universal truth of Marxism-Leninism with the concrete practice of the Chinese revolution." "We Chinese Communists and Chinese people call this development of Marxism-Leninism in the Chinese revolution Mao Zedong Thought. We hold that all our victories were achieved under the guidance of Mao Zedong Thought, without which there would be no New China Today." "Of course, Mao Zedong Thought is not the product of Mao Zedong's personal wisdom alone, it is also the product of the wisdom of his comrades-in-arms, the Party and the revolutionary people, and, as he once pointed out, it emerged from the 'collective struggles of the Party and the people.'"

When interviewed by the Italian journalist Oriana Falaci on August 21 and 23, 1980, Deng Xiaoping said: "Chairman Mao's greatest feat was integrating Marxism-Leninism with the reality of the Chinese revolution and showing a way for China to achieve a victorious revolution. It must be said that prior to the 60s or prior to the end of the 50s, many of his thoughts brought us victories and some basic principles he put forward are very correct. .... Unfortunately, in the later years of his life, especially in the 'cultural revolution,' he made mistakes, and no small mistakes at that, bring many misfortunes to our Party, country and people. You known our Party in the Yanan days epitomized Chairman Mao's thinking in various fields as Mao Zedong Thought and made it the guiding thought of our Party. It was exactly because we followed this road that we were able to seize great victory for the revolution. Of course, Mao Zedong Thought is not a personal creation by Comrade Mao Zedong alone; revolutionaries of the older generation all had a part in founding and developing Mao Zedong Thought, which consists mainly of Comrade Mao Zedong's thought. But, because of victory, he became not so prudent and in his later years, bit by bit, some unhealthy factors and unhealthy ideas, mostly 'Leftist' ideas began to come to the fore. A considerable part of them ran counter to his original thought, to his former excellent, correct stand, his style of work included." "We will continue to adhere to Mao Zedong Thought. Mao Zedong Thought is the correct part of Chairman Mao's thinking in his lifetime. Mao Zedong Thought not only led our revolution to victory but should also remain an invaluable asset of the Chinese party and country, now and in the future."

(An abridged translation of an article in "Hongqi" magazine, No. 2, 1981.)

*****

DOCUMENT NO. 25

HU YAO-PANG'S SPEECH DELIVERED AT THE "MEETING ON
ISSUES CONCERNING THE IDEOLOGICAL FRONT"

August 3, 1981

(**Issues & Studies**, Vol XX, No. 1, January 1984)

I'll speak first and give six opinions.

My first opinion is on the objective of this meeting.

The Propaganda Department of the Party Central Committee called this meeting in accordance with a decision of the Secretariat of the CCP Central Committee. Over 320 people are attending the meeting, including comrades of the Party Central Committee and the relevant State Council departments, comrades of provincial, municipal and autonomous regional CCP committees, comrades from theoretical, literary and artistic, journalist and publishing circles, and comrades of the armed services. What is this meeting called? It is called the "Meeting on Issues Concerning the Ideological Front." What will be the topic under discussion? We will discuss Comrade Teng Hsiao-p'ing's July 17 talk on this question.

Since the convention of the Sixth Plenum [of the Eleventh CCP Central Committee in June 1981], Comrade Hsiao-p'ing has given two important talks: one, given to Comrades Wan Li, Yu Ch'iu-li, Ku Mu and Yao I-lin, concerned problems on the economic front. The transcript of that talk has not been put in order. What I meant to say is that it should be put in order. The keynote of that speech was that economic development should be advanced by all possible means and the speed of economic development should be kept as high as possible. We who are in power will be to blame if the economy cannot be pushed forward. The other talk was given on July 17 to five comrades, Wang Jen-chung, Chu Mu-chih, Chou Yang, Tseng T'ao and Hu Chi-wei, and concerned issues on the ideological front. Our Secretariat considered these two talks by Comrade Hsiao-p'ing to be very important. Since both of these questions, one concerning economic work, and the other concerning ideological work, will have great bearing on the overall situation in the latter half of this year, we have to discuss them further. Some preparatory work is to be done concerning economic work during August and September. Comrades of our Secretariat are to be sent down to make investigations, and the Party committees in the ministries and commissions under the State Council, and those in the provinces, municipalities and autonomous regions have to submit reports to the Party Central Committee before the end of August. We are prepared to hold a one-week-long meeting at the end of September and the beginning of October, in which about one thousand comrades from the Central organizations will participate. To convene the ideological conference before the economic conference may be seen as an indication that ideology is taking the lead or that it is in first place. It is only natural that progress on the ideological front should run ahead.

My second opinion concerns the gist of Comrade Hsiao-p'ing's July 17 talk.

What was the basic and central point of Comrade Hsiao-p'ing's talk of over 2,700 characters. I'll put it in one sentence: Our Party's leadership over ideological work is weak and lax and we should overcome this tendency. We should comprehend this subject, for only then will we be able to solve the problem through deep research.

What I have to say here is that the draft of this talk was revised twice before being finalized by Comrade Hsiao-p'ing, and it is to be issued as a Party Central Committee document.

Comrade Hsiao-p'ing said: "We have to discuss issues concerning the ideological front with the propaganda departments, especially those issues concerning literary and art work. Remarkable achievements have been made by the Party in guiding ideological work and literary and art work, and this fact should be affirmed. But there is also a tendency to do things in an oversimplified and crude way, and this should not be denied or ignored. The question that merits more attention today is that of lax and weak leadership." From this, it is clear that the focal point of our work is to be the overcoming of weak and lax leadership over ideological work. In his talk, Comrade Hsiao-p'ing emphasized questions concerning literary and art work. This is because he has recently been particularly concerned with the problems confronting literary and artistic circles. But it should be made clear here that the major point of his talk was that we should overcome the problem of weak and lax leadership over ideological work. The implications of this are not limited to the literary and art front or the ideological front itself. Therefore, we should understand that the aim of this meeting is to face up to the fact that our Party's leadership over ideological work is weak and lax. That is to say:

First, as Comrade Hsiao-p'ing has said, weak and lax leadership over ideological work is not limited to any individual department, place or unit. Rather, it is a problem prevalent throughout the Party. To consider the strengthening of leadership over ideological work as something relating only to certain areas is to play down the significance of Comrade Hsiao- p'ing's talk. Leadership over ideological work is to be strengthened not only on the ideological front, but also on the economic front and in the armed forces.

Secondly, while discussing this problem, the first thing for us to do is not to find out who is to blame but to find out the reason why leadership over ideological front is weak and lax. We should examine whether there are historical reasons, leadership reasons or subjective reasons and then work out measures to overcome the weakness and laxity and to unify and strengthen our leadership on the ideological front. The emphasis should not be on finding out who should bear the greater blame. Otherwise, we will only be striving for personal fame. How can we then handle the work well? Of course, from the point of view of summing up experiences, it is all right to ascertain where the responsibility lies. However, our major purpose is not to affix responsibility on any individuals but to find out the reason and then work out measures for its solution. It is important for us to adopt this kind of attitude. If we adopt an incorrect attitude, we may very possibly deviate from the right road and even take to evil ways. If we have to investigate and affix responsibility, who should bear the responsibility for the weak and lax leadership over ideological work? Probably it is the Secretariat of the Party Central Committee that should be held responsible because we in the Secretariat are in charge of ideological work. And among us, it is the general secretary who should be held responsible because it is he who supervises this work. Of course, the Secretariat of the Party Central Committee should not bear all the responsibility. Otherwise, it would be tantamount to saying that only the Secretariat of the Party Central Committee is weak and lax while all other units are strong. Probably it is not justifiable for us to say this. Every unit and leading cadre should think this over: Am I strong or weak? Have I acted in unison or have I been lax in this respect? One can only learn something through self-examination.

Thirdly, it is even more important that we should work out measures and ways to overcome our weakness and laxity and make ourselves staunch and vigorous. We should not engage in massive criticism and struggle or raise a hue and cry just because we have been weak in the past and now want to be strong. No, that will not do. If we fail to work out the correct way to overcome our weakness and strengthen our leadership, we will very likely commit again our past mistakes and, probably before this meeting is concluded, there will be people at the lower levels passing on the message that we should "fight against the Rightists" again. It is not correct for them to say so. Anyway, we should never again forget the following words of Comrade Mao Tse-tung in his "On the Correct Handling of Contradictions Among the People": "Ideological struggle is not like other forms of struggle. The only method to be used in this struggle is that of painstaking reasoning and not crude coercion." For ideological issues, "it is only by employing the method of discussion, criticism and reasoning that we can really foster correct ideas and overcome wrong ones, and that we can really settle issues." To be staunch is not to act rashly, nor to raise a hue and cry, nor to wantonly criticize and struggle. One cannot be considered staunch if he acts rashly, raises a hue and cry and wantonly criticizes and struggles.

My third opinion concerns how we should correctly deal with historical experiences in ideological criticism and struggle.

To overcome the weak and lax leadership on the ideological front, and to make the leadership united and strong, we should correctly deal with historical experiences.

What historical experience should we begin with? In my opinion, we should begin with Comrade Mao Tse-tung's "On the Correct Handling of Contradictions Among the People" which was published in February 1957. In that article, he advanced for the first time the theory that socialist society is replete with contradictions and that socialist society should advance by revealing and resolving contradictions. Comrade Mao Tse-tung said in this article that there are two types of contradictions in socialist society and that different principles and methods should be used to resolve these contradictions. He added that the contradictions between ourselves and the enemy, if properly handled, can be transformed into non-antagonistic ones, and the antagonistic elements can, if the policy is well handled, be transformed into a new type of people who can support themselves by their own labor; and that the contradictions among the people, if not properly handled, can be intensified into those between ourselves and the enemy. This work of Comrade Mao's is a great contribution and it was a new acquisition with which he enriched the treasure-house of Marxism during the socialist period. This question has also been included in the resolution of the Sixth Plenum, both in the chapter concerning Mao Tse-tung Thought and in the last chapter. In this work, Comrade Mao Tse-tung reiterated the formula for resolving contradictions among the people ideologically and politically: one should start with desire for unity, resolve contradictions through criticism or struggle and arrive at a new unity on a new basis. This method was epitomized during the Yenan period in the formula "unity , criticism, unity." This method was elaborated more thoroughly in 1957. In the early years after the founding of our state, Comrade Mao Tse-tung placed strong emphasis on the words -- "on a new basis." All Party members agree that this work of Comrade Mao Tse-tung's is brilliant. Although several paragraphs were added after the struggle against the Rightists and some of the wording was not in tune with the basic point of the work and the basic principle laid down at the "Eight [CCP National] Congress," these parts can be easily identified and they do not impair the value of the work. It was, is, and always will be a Marxist work to guide us.

However, right after Comrade Mao Tse-tung advanced these theories, problems appeared. What were those problems? The problem was that in our practical work, we did not implement his correct viewpoints. Nor did he himself do so. He spoke these words in February 1957 and his article was published in June [the same year]. Comrade Mao Tse-tung left us a great ideological treasure. However, in practical work, we, even including Comrade Mao himself, have violated his correct principle. In the twenty years from the anti-Rightist struggle to his death, the two different types of contradiction were confused first in problems of a local nature and then in overall problems. As a result, many of the contradictions among the people were exaggerated into contradictions between ourselves and the enemy. The long-standing and effective work style of the Party which entails integrating theory with practice, forging close links with the masses and practicing self-criticism was destroyed. During the "Great Cultural Revolution," the good habits of criticism and self-criticism were used as an excuse to engage in factional activities and as an amulet. The method of criticism (it was then called giving judgment, and that judgment was by default in reality) turned out to be ruthless struggle and merciless blows which were even more serious than those in the days of the Wang Ming line. Comrade Mao Tse-tung himself committed these mistakes, and many of our comrades in the Party, or it can be said a majority of comrades (including myself), have committed these mistakes to varying degrees. The mistakes committee by some comrades are serious, while the mistakes committed by others may not be so serious; some became aware of them earlier, others later, and some may not be aware of them even now. As a result, once they find out that there are going to be ideological struggles and criticism and self-criticism, many comrades both within and outside the Party get very worried, they have lingering fears and feel skeptical and threatened. This is understandable. Actually, these were the major mistakes committed over the last twenty years. Nevertheless, there are some other people who hold a different attitude. Once they find out that there is to be an ideological struggle and that there will be criticism and self-criticism, they take a strong aversion to it and boycott and oppose it. They criticize and attack others but do not accept criticism from others, let alone self-criticism. This kind of mentality is dangerous and harmful and is in violation of Marxism and the Four Basic Principles. This question should be raised incisively at this meeting. From the time of our ancestors, from Marx, Engels, Chairman Mao, right down to the present Party Central Committee and our proletarian Party, has it been possible to go without criticism and self-criticism? Comrade Mao Tse-tung said in his work "On Coalition Government":

> Conscientious practice of self-criticism is still another hallmark distinguishing our Party from all other political parties. As we say, dust will accumulate if a room is not cleaned regularly, our faces will get dirty if they are not washed regularly. Our comrades' minds and our Party's work may also collect dust, and also need sweeping and washing. The proverb "Running water is never stale and a door-hinge is never worm-eaten" means that constant motion prevents the inroads of germs and other organisms. To check up regularly on our work and in the process develop a democratic style of work, to fear neither criticism nor self-criticism. . . this is the only effective way to prevent all kinds of political dust and germs from contaminating the minds of our comrades and the body of our Party.

Is there any other effective way? All our Party members should consider this question. Can you solve problems by arresting those people who have committed mistakes? Or will it do if you forget them or even kowtow to them? Of course not. The most effective way is to develop criticism and self-criticism. Therefore, those people who feel aversion to, boycott and oppose criticisms and self-criticism actually run counter to Marxism and are in violation of the Four Basic Principles. This is something that each of our revolutionists should understand.

We have had two kinds of historical experiences, not just one. First, we have had correct historical experiences. That is to say, when we have established and persisted in the three good styles of work which entail integrating theory with practice, forging close links with the masses and practicing criticism and self-criticisms. It is just because we have persisted in the three styles of work that our Party has achieved marked development. Think back over the history of our Party. We practiced criticism and self-criticism at the Tsunyi Conference. The "Seventh Party Congress" proved to be a success just because we conducted a rectification campaign in advance. That is to say, we developed criticism and self-criticism. We have conducted such campaigns three times since the smashing of the Gang of Four: The first time was at the Third Plenum [of the Eleventh

CCP Central Committee on December 1978]. It is generally agreed that the Third Plenum was a success. The reason for its success was that we set things to right by conducting criticism and self-criticism and struggle. Without criticism and self-criticism and the necessary struggle, some of our comrades present here, Comrade Yang Shang-k'un, for example, could not have been rehabilitated. Therefore, it was just because of the struggle that the Third Plenum was a success. The second time was at the enlarged meeting of the Politburo held in November and December last year, and the third time was at the Sixth Plenum. All these meetings were held after criticism and self-criticism and the necessary struggles. The resolution on the history of our Party was finalized after many revisions had been made. In the repeated discussion of that resolution, didn't we frequently make criticisms and self-criticisms? Moreover, the resolution is in itself a most penetrating self-criticism. Therefore, the first kind of experience we have had is a correct historical experience. Our Party prospers whenever we adhere to these three fine styles of work. Without them it is impossible for our Party to prosper. This is a kind of historical experience.

The other kind of experience we have had is an erroneous historical experience, and, since the founding of our state, the "Great Cultural Revolution" was a typical example of this. [This kind of experience] involves unlimited criticism and indiscriminate struggle. We have made it clear that we will never again and should never again conduct this kind of unlimited criticism and indiscriminate struggle.

However, some comrades often think only of the erroneous historical experiences, totally neglecting the fact that we also have had correct historical experiences. When talking about the restoration of the fine traditions of our Party, some comrades think only of one thing, that is, seeking truth from facts. They do not remember other things, including the forming of close ties with the masses and criticism and self-criticism. If we fail to form close ties with the masses, take the mass line and conduct the necessary criticism and even struggle, our efforts to seek truth from facts will become empty talk. The three fine styles of work are inseparable. In my "July 1" talk (it was not all my own work, but a collective work which was discussed by the Secretariat and the Politburo and revised by dozens of people), I said the following: We have learned many things from frustrations and mistakes; and we will continue to learn many more things. I meant that we have learned many things from both correct and erroneous historical experiences and that we want to and will learn many more things. There are things we have not learned yet. I didn't mean to say that there is anyone, such as the comrades of the Party Central Committee or least of all myself, Hu Yao-pang, who has learned everything. We should by no means say that. We still have many things to learn. In my opinion, many of our comrades have not learned how to correctly develop criticism and self-criticism. Our meeting this time is aimed at solving this problem.

My fourth opinion is that all our Party members should learn to use the weapon of criticism and self-criticism to strengthen our unity and improve our work.

Our socialist system which has not long been established and has been seriously sabotaged by Lin Piao and the Gang of Four is confronted with many problems. We will meet great difficulties and have to cope with heavy tasks. The people have high expectation of us. We should take note of the general situation in our country. Facing us are the two types of contradiction which Comrade Mao Tse-tung mentioned before. One is the contradiction between the enemy and ourselves, or contradictions of that nature. We should not treat these lightly. In our resolution on the history of our Party, we have done away with the theories of "taking class struggle as the key link" and of "continuing the revolution under the dictatorship of the proletariat" in accordance with the lessons of history and the actual situation. Meanwhile, we have affirmed the theory that "class struggle will continue to exist." In accordance with Comrade Hsiao-p'ing's opinion, I said the following in my "July 1" talk: "We are dedicated to the strengthening of socialist democracy and legal system. We are also dedicated to the improvement and perfection of the socialist political system." These words are a call to strengthen the people's democratic dictatorship, to correctly carry out class struggle and correctly handle contradictions between the enemy and ourselves. We will not deal with these questions at length here.

We are now also facing the other type of contradiction which exists in still larger numbers. As Comrade Hsiao-p'ing said in his talks, this type of contradiction may be intensified and lead to disorder if it is not well handled. If this type of contradiction is handled in the following two ways, it will lead to disorder: if we fail to carry out eduction and criticism and ignore this type of contradiction; if education and criticism are not properly conducted. Generally speaking, the contradictions which exist in still greater numbers are the contradictions among the people themselves. I am going to talk about two questions concerning this type of contradiction: The first concerns important matters of principle, firstly the question whether to uphold or to suspect and oppose the Four Basic Principles; and in political matters, the open distribution of some seriously erroneous opinions, including some very harmful literary and art works. The other question concerns engagement in factional activities, bureaucratism, serious irresponsibility in work and other erroneous styles of work. These two kinds of question are always mutually related and interlocked. On the 29th of the last month, I gave a short speech to the graduates of the Sixth Class of the Central Party School. I said that in my opinion we had failed to effect a fundamental change for the better in three respects in the nearly five years since the smashing of the Gang of Four: the first is in the work style of the Party, the second is in the atmosphere of society, and the third is in social order. In some places, three kinds of comrades have been isolated. The first kind of comrades are those who supported the line adopted since the Third Plenum. The second kind are those who actively do their work and have made remarkable achievements. The third kind are those who dare to uphold principles, speak justly and struggle against erroneous opinions and styles of work. These three types of people are good comrades. What is implied by the isolation of these good comrades? We should be quick to realize that there are still problems and a large number of contradictions and negative phenomena and factors in our country, our Party and our society. The main problem is that our Party members do not have a correct political-ideological consciousness. In the face of this phenomenon, what should we do? There are two ways from which we can choose: to neglect it or to bestir ourselves to make criticism or we might say fearless criticism. As justice is on our side and on the side of the people, what should we be afraid of? Justice is on our side. Erroneous work styles and opinions cannot draw much support from the people because they do not stand for the interests of the people. Only if we are bold and assured, that is if we dauntlessly make criticisms and exposures, will we be able to restore and enhance our good traditions.

Some comrades say that there are people who refuse or are opposed to making criticisms because they do not understand the situation and do not understand the true facts. This seems to be reasonable. However, it is not really acceptable. In my view, an honest, sober and good person would not obstinately oppose our decision to make criticism before he has a clear understanding of the truth and can clearly distinguish right from wrong. At the most, he would remain silent or hesitant. His attitude would be: Ah, dare I criticize this? Is it all right to criticize it? Let me think about it. For example, at the Sixth Plenum we criticized not only Comrade Mao Tse-tung but also someone who is now a leading comrade. People who are honest, sober and good may say: "Well, I don't know why we should criticize yet another comrade. Let me think it over." He would not obstinately oppose our decision. Those who obstinately oppose the decision to make criticisms may be divided into the following three categories: The first category of people consists of those who are opinionated. Instead of making investigations, they are conceited and maintain that they have a clear understanding of everything. The second category consists of those who have certain erroneous feelings. It is not that they do not understand the truth. They do have some understanding of the truth. However, when they look at a problem, they are opinionated and have the wrong feelings. The third category consists of people who have ulterior motives. Instead of criticizing correctly, they criticize those who want to criticize correctly. They not only intend to criticize them but also intend to knock them down. Therefore, we should investigate and analyze those who are obstinately opposed to making criticisms. I think that our comrades in the Party Central Committee organizations, on the Party committees of the ministries and in the provincial and municipal organizations should investigate and analyze new situations and questions so that they have some idea of how things develop.

In his talks, Comrade Hsiao-p'ing also mentioned another situation. He said: "Today, there are people who think of themselves as heroes. Everything seems to be all right when they are not criticized. But once they are criticized, they are more popular than ever." How come? Comrades, let's recall two things that happened in recent years: One was that quite a few people sympathized with a counter-revolutionary who was held in custody after selling state secrets to foreigners. Instead of criticizing and redeeming that counter-revolutionary who vilified our Party, our country, our socialist system and our people, those people wantonly vilified us when they saw that he was pronounced guilty for having sold state secrets and broken the criminal law. There were not many of those people. The second thing was that many people have supported Comrade Pai Hua and written to him since our recent criticism of him. We should make an analysis to see who these people are that have written to him. We should learn from Lu Hsun. In 1936, a Trotskyist wrote a letter to Lu Hsun saying how good and brilliant he was. Knowing the background of the man, Lu Hsun looked at it and said, that's the kind of man who is flattering me, I'll write back and give him a scolding. If I become complacent just because he wrote to flatter me, wouldn't I be equating myself with the enemy? What would I think of myself if I were to preen myself just because the enemy has applauded me? Only those people who are muddleheaded, have the wrong kind of feelings or are counter-revolutionary would show sympathy for those who are criticized justly. Of course, not all the people who wrote to Pai Hua are evil-doers. Among them, many just lack a clear understanding. But here I want to call Comrade Pai Hua's attention to the fact that he should have a clear understanding of the serious mistakes he has committed and correct them with a feeling of deep remorse. He should not argue about whether the articles criticizing him were perfect or not and feel he is wronged. Still less should he feel comforted and take it as [an expression of] "deep love in the spring" that he has received many letters of support. He should be no means think like that! The real "deep love in the spring" is the severe criticism which gives us pain for a while rather than the "sympathy" showed to us after we have been criticized. All of us should take heed of this question, otherwise we'll really come to grief. Leading cadres should have a clear understanding of this phenomenon. Why are there some people who support comrades who have been criticized for committing mistakes? What are their intentions? We should keep a sober mind.

As for how we should develop criticism, there are many good experiences in the history of our Party. There are also regulations in the draft of our new Party constitution. Detailed regulations on this are also included in the twelve guiding principles for inner Party political life passed by the Party Central Committee. In these principles, a demarcation has been emphatically drawn between correct criticism and the so-called "coming down with a big stick." In my opinion, it is not that we do not have rules and regulations. When we say that we have to carry out proper and normal ideological struggle and develop necessary criticism and self-criticism, it does not mean that we do not have rules and regulations. We have many of them. It is not appropriate for us to ask the Party Central Committee to draw up any more rules and regulations. Since the smashing of the Gang of Four, we have summed up historical experiences and drawn up many rules and regulations. The problem today is that we have not carried them out, and what is most important, the political and organizational life of our Party is not healthy. Ours is a great Party. Our Party organizations have been established in every place and every department in our country. Is there any place where our Party organizations are not established? Party branches and Party members are everywhere. The major problem is that we do not have a healthy Party life, and our Party committees do not exercise effective leadership, do not discuss the questions that should be handled by them, do not take the lead in many things and do not take the mass line. They ask what they should do if deviations appear in the course of criticism and self-criticism. As long as you persist in the principle and take the mass line, there will not be any deviations. At least, there will not be any serious deviations. Not long ago, the Party Central Committee held a work conference in Hopei, in which more than 200 Hopei comrades took part. This is also an example of taking the mass line. We conducted a poll one day, gathering opinions as to which cadres above the district and municipal levels in Hopei should be transferred to other places. It was a secret poll. Those who took part in the poll were not allowed to collaborate with one another. They were allowed either to cast secret ballots or to write their names on them. Their voting on the question as to which comrades should be transferred was to be submitted to the Party Central Committee and the provincial Party committee for reference. Members of the standing committee of the provincial Party committee were not invited to join the voting. Of the 201 Hopei comrades, 181 cast their ballots. The ballots suggested that many comrades should be transferred (not dismissed from their posts, expelled from the Party, or have disciplinary action taken against them). From this, we know that we will be able to avoid mistakes by taking the mass line. Therefore, I think the most important thing is not that we do not have rules and regulations but that we have not conscientiously implemented them.

Comrade Mao Tse-tung said that it is not difficult to handle criticism and self-criticism correctly. In his words, "The reason why the rectification campaign which aimed at 'learning from past mistakes to avoid future ones, and curing the sickness to save the patient' produced such a great effect was because we developed a correct but not distorted, and earnest but not perfunctory criticism and self-criticism." We should make correct but not distorted criticism, for otherwise, you cannot reason things out. We should make earnest but not perfunctory self-criticism. Our comrades who were in Yenan in 1945 may still remember the fact that Wang Ming's self-criticism was perfunctory while Comrade Po Ku's was in earnest. Whether one is sincere in making self-criticism does not depend on whether one's written confession is long, but it depends on whether one is sincere of hypocritical. Therefore, only if our Party committees take the lead and grasp this issue, and stick to principles and conscientiously put into practice the policy lines, will we be able to handle criticism and self-criticism well. As our criticism and self-criticism is aimed at reaching a new unity on a new basis, we should stick to principles. Now, the first thing for you to do is to keep your actions in step with the Party Central Committee and the Sixth Plenum, and, more important, you should uphold the Four Basic Principles which have been reiterated by the Party Central Committee time and again and were emphasized again at the Sixth Plenum. This is the basis on which the whole Party, the whole army and all nationalities can unite. While analyzing history and the present situation, we should take as our criterion the resolutions laid down at the Sixth Plenum. Otherwise, what else can be used as our criterion for developing criticism and self-criticism and on what basis will we be able to unite?

My fifth opinion concerns leadership over the ideological issues in theoretical, literary and artistic, journalistic and publishing circles.

Why should we concentrate on this question? It is because our discussion this time is focused on issues on the ideological front. In our theoretical, literary and artistic, journalistic and publishing circles, our leadership over ideological issues is lax and weak. To put it briefly, the way to solve questions in these circles is to affirm three things and to do work well in three respects.

What are the three things to be affirmed? First, we should affirm that remarkable achievements have been made. In recent years, remarkable achievements have been made in journalistic, theoretical, publishing, literary and artistic and educational circles and in the study of social sciences. Second, we should affirm that a majority of our comrades are good. Third, the Party Central Committee will continue to persist in its policy toward intellectuals, and its policy concerning ideological work and literary and art work. These are the three things to be affirmed and we don't have to elaborate on them any further here.

What are the three things to be done well?

The first thing is to handle the criticism of the film scenario "Unrequited Love" properly. Why do we hold out on this question? It is because although the *Liberation Army Daily* and some other newspapers and periodicals began to criticize "Unrequited Love" in April, and Comrade Hsiao-p'ing has made a correct appraisal of the *Liberation Army Daily* criticism, those organizations concerned, such as the China Federation of Literary and Art Circles, the Chinese Writers' Association and the Chinese Film Artists' Association, have not started yet. This is a strong indication that leadership over the ideological front is weak and lax, and this is a typical problem in ideological circle. As this question is of great significance, those who are hostile to us are eager to know what we are going to do about it. Therefore, we should promptly and conscientiously solve it. At the end of his speech, Comrade Hsiao-p'ing also said: "The *Liberation Army Daily* does not have to publish any more criticism of 'Unrequited Love,' but the *Literature Gazette* should have some high quality article written to develop criticism of it. When you have finished those articles, you should publish them in the *Literature Gazette* and have them reprinted in the *People's Daily*." It is a task of pressing importance to the literary and art front and the whole ideological front. The most important thing is that we should make it clear ideologically why we should make up for a missed lesson. Why do we have to make up a lesson in the criticism of "Unrequited Love"? This is because, first, "Unrequited Love" is not an isolated problem. There are quite a few erroneous opinions and writings which deviate from the socialist road and from the Party's leadership and engage in liberalization like "Unrequited Love." We should soberly criticize this erroneous tendency and should not let it develop unchecked. Secondly, many people both within and outside our country wantonly distorted our criticism of "Unrequited Love" and disseminated a lot of provocative and instigating opinions. Let's stop this way of doing things and get off to a new start, otherwise we'll meet with all kinds of obstructions in making criticisms. As I have just said, many provocative opinions were expressed both within and outside out country after we tried a counter-revolutionary element who sold our state secrets to foreigners. Immediately after the publication of our articles in the recent criticism of "Unrequited Love," some newspapers in Hong Kong which harbored malicious intentions published articles under the following line from [the Sung poet] Hsin Ch'i-chi: "How can we stand the repeated storms, the spring passed in a hurry." Our criticism started in April, the spring time. What they meant was how many more struggles can our country endure. We had just begun the movement to let "a hundred flowers blossom," spring had just arrived, but that spring soon passed. They distributed a lot of material, up until June or July. Since they have distributed so much provocative material, how can we handle our ideological work if we do not clarify all these things? If this problem is not thrashed out, how can we carry on our criticism and self-criticism? If we are weak and helpless to start with, how can we toughen ourselves up? Therefore, it is necessary for us to make up this lesson. This problem could have been settled more easily when it first appeared, but I did not pay attention to it at that time. Hence, I am partly responsible. The situation would have been better if we had asked the China Federation of Literary and Art Circles to hold a forum at which some writers and artists could have made impartial appraisals of "Unrequited Love." Only now have we come to realize that we did not take the mass line at that time, and that we should have taken the mass line. Anyway, we should do it now, and then have the *Literature Gazette* publish articles, as Comrade Hsiao-p'ing has said. Those articles should be well written, and should not be composed carelessly. May our critics of literature and arts display their talents to the utmost. On the eve of the liberation of our country, Comrade Mao Tse-tung wrote articles criticizing D.G. Acheson's "White Paper." He wrote five articles in a month or so. Today, we have not even penned one critical article in half a year. Is it really so difficult? If the critical article were well written, it would serve to educate people and Comrade Pai Hua himself. After he received a lot of letters, Comrade Pai Hua felt that he was supported by the masses. On this question, we should review the argument I have just made: Why not analyze the question? Today, apart from the *Literature Gazette's* articles, many other old, middle-aged and young writers can also take up cudgels on behalf of this just cause. However, to avoid a joint attack, we should know when and where to stop. As there are many things which deserve our criticism, we should not direct the attack all at one person or one work. Instead of bludgeoning Comrade Pai Hua, we should help him out of a desire for unity, as he has also written some good works. However, since "Unrequited Love" is disadvantageous to the people and socialism, it needs to be criticized! Do you not dare to say so? In February last year, the situation was not so good as it is this year. At that time, Comrade Chou Yang and I went all out to criticize the drama "If Only I Were Real" and we dared to say that it was no good. When something is good, we say it is good, and when something is not good, we say it is not good. We should distinguish right from wrong. Comrade Hsiao-p'ing demands great things from our senior writers, asking them to pass on experience, help and set an example to some middle-aged and young writers. This is a good way of doing things. We should criticize Comrade Pai Hua and some other comrades in order to help them cleanse themselves. I feel that it would be good for them. On some material I read recently, I wrote some comments about two or three middle-aged and young writers. My intentions in doing so were entirely good. Comrades, unnecessary criticism does people harm. Some people are killed by flattery and others are killed by rebukes. There is a film called "The Bitter Fruit" which tells the story of a sister's negligence in giving proper education to her younger brother which resulted in the latter committing serious mistakes. Historical experiences show that if one only kowtows but does not criticize, this is called metaphysics, and it invites disaster. This is true for children, young people, our Party members and our cadres, including senior ones. We old fellows are always grateful to Comrade Mao Tse-tung for his correct criticism. The only thing we do not agree with was that he labelled us counter-revolutionary capitalist-roaders. We do not agree with that. Since I am not a capitalist-roader, how could you charge me with being a capitalist-roader? At spring festival 1957, Comrade Mao Tse-tung criticized me, saying that although the Central Committee of the Communist Youth League had held a meeting of activists, we only pretended to be active. That's putting it too strongly. After thinking his words over, I decided to do my work meticulously. Why were we criticized for pretending to be active? His reason was that the CYL Congress was not a success despite the successful activists' meeting. He also said that we should investigate this problem. Without criticism and self-criticism, our Party would decline and fall. In my "July 1" talk which has been ratified by the Party Central Committee, there is one place where I specifically talked about this question. That was in my fourth point, where I said that we should correctly develop criticism and self-criticism if our Party is to keep young forever. Think this over, comrades, this is the first thing that should be taken care of.

The second thing that should be taken care of is that the Party Central Committee and the Party committees at provincial, municipal and autonomous regional levels (not including those at or below district level, except in cases which the provincial and municipal committees consider necessary) should examine the opinions and writings recently published by theoretical, literary and artistic, journalistic and publishing circles. Those creations published since the Sixth Plenum should be examined in accordance with the spirit laid down at the Sixth Plenum, and some of the major mistakes discovered should be criticized. This chiefly concerns the Central and the provincial, municipal and autonomous regional levels. This work started with the convocation of the work conference of the CCP Central Committee at the end of last year. The scope of attack should not be wide because that would be disadvantageous to us. Why do we say that the work started with the convocation of the Central Committee work conference held at the end of last year? It is because at that meeting, Comrade Hsiao-p'ing, on behalf of the Party Central Committee, mentioned that question again, and the text of his talk was issued in the name of the CCP Central Committee. Will you please examine the erroneous opinions and writings published by theoretical, literary and artistic, journalistic and publishing circles since the convocation of the Central Committee work conference in December last year, and develop criticism against the main ones. Mistaken opinions and writings have appeared in some provinces. In some other provinces where no mistakes have been made, we should not lack subtlety. Criticism should be to the point and be fair and reasonable and should not be made in an exaggerated or distorted manner, and we certainly should not make joint attacks. Criticism and self-criticism are everyday tasks which should not be done in a hurry but should be carried out case by case in a down-to-earth manner. The key to the handling of this question is in Comrade Hsiao-p'ing's talk on the ideological issues in our Party. This is an important task which requires us to uphold the Four Basic Principles and the "double hundred" principle, and to oppose the tendency toward liberalization. It is not something that can be finished perfunctorily within two or three days. You must think this over. For some problems of secondary importance, you may just hold a meeting and criticize them orally. The method of criticism is something we should pay attention to. Criticism may be handled in four ways: The first way is to write articles and criticize by name; the second way is to write articles but not to criticize by name; the third way is to make oral criticism only, so as to render help and education; and the fourth way is to publish self-criticisms. Not many people should be criticized by name. Before criticizing by name, Party committees in those places should submit the case to the Propaganda Department of the Party Central Committee for approval, so that a mass movement or a joint attack from all sides does not result. Don't you think it is appropriate to do it like this? We should criticize a case at a time, not all at once. Comrades, there is nothing wrong with that. Only few cadres in charge of ideological work have been criticized by name. Among Party workers, however, several dozens have been criticized by name. These include secretaries of county Party committees and district Party committees, ministers, and even vice premiers. Whenever cadres of their profession are criticized by name, why do people in ideological circle always complain and charge that an anti-Rightist tendency is on the rise? But why, whenever the Party or government cadres are criticized by name, do they always say that they deserve criticism and maintain that they should be treated more severely? This is not a good mentality and it is illogical to have this kind of thinking. I find that for many years now, there have been some quite unhealthy tendencies prevalent in intellectual circles (not involving everybody, just a minority) and they have not been overcome in all that long period of time. For example, some people argued that their writings should not be revised, not even a single work, otherwise they would lose their own style. Before passing down a decision, the Party Central Committee is used to having it discussed by many people, and no one takes offense. I admit that there are differences between political documents and literary works because literary works should have their own style. However, if they have significant political implications, others are entitled to judge them. While emphasizing their style, writers should also listen to others people's opinions. Otherwise, what is the use of literary criticism?

The third thing that should be done well is that the ideological work departments at the two levels of the Party Central Committee and the provincial, municipal and autonomous regional Party committees should make a marked turn for the better, or a marked progress in their leadership over ideological work. Which departments are these? They include the Party schools, social science research departments, propaganda departments, journals and periodicals, radio, publishing and literature and the arts. They should all make greater progress in their leadership over ideological work. Writers, artists and ideological theorists who are Party members should bear in mind first their Party membership and then their professions. Since they are Party members, what they should do first is observe Party discipline as Comrade Hsiao-p'ing said in his talks. To adhere to the Four Basic Principles is the basic discipline to be observed. If Party members do not observe discipline, how can the Party lead the masses? Our whole Party, Party committees at all levels, and leadership organizations on all fronts should make greater progress and make a turn for the better in their leadership over ideological work. What kind of turn for the better should they make? I can give you only one principle, that is, to seek truth from facts and adopt and the right remedies to correct shortcomings. We should solve problems which have appeared in all places and on all fronts. Wherever there are problems, we should concentrate our efforts to solve them. In short, we should adopt the right remedies to correct shortcomings and to seek truth from facts.

My last opinion involves questions concerning our faith.

Questions concerning our future have been dealt with at our Sixth Plenum, in the resolution on historical issues, in the communique of the Plenum and the "July 1" talks. Articles 37 and 38 of the resolution on historical issues dealt precisely with questions concerning our future. And they reflect the common conviction of the whole Party, the whole army and people of all nationalities. It is imperative for us to have faith in our undertakings. We want to point out again that we should have two objectives in our undertakings: One is the building of a high level of socialist material civilization and the other is the building of a high level of socialist spiritual civilization. Is it possible for us to realize these two high levels of civilization? In our documents, we have enumerated a lot of favorable conditions. As for the actual situation, that is not bad, either. Take for example agricultural production which has been stepped up ahead of other fields or production. It is Comrade Wan Li who is in charge of agricultural work, and I am glad to say that agricultural production has increased at a faster rate than production in other fields. Instead of a drop in production, wheat output this year will increase by 50, 60 or even 70 billion catties. If it increases by 60 billion catties, that means it will have increased by three million tons. There is sure to be a bumper harvest this year. It is not that we can see into the future. It is that we have made investigations before we came to that judgment. We send hundreds of thousands of people each day to make investigations in the lower level units. Our Secretariat can say the following words definitely: We are still making progress in tapping the potential of agricultural production. We do not know whether cotton output this year will be over three billion kilograms. How much can we turn out next year? We have also made progress in industry, especially light industry and the textile industry. Nevertheless, I want to point out here that although there is a great potential for output, our production results are not satisfactory. Therefore, we should go all out to step up our industrial production as much as possible next year. Don't be bothered by those people who say odd things or put up reactionary slogans, as only two or three thousand slogans have been put up. If there were one thousand slogans, it would mean that out of a population of 1,000,000,000, there would be only one slogan for every 1,000,000 people. That does not count for anything. It is impossible that all the people will support the Party. However, it is possible to have 95 percent or 98 percent of them stand by Marxism- Leninism, Mao Tse-tung's thought and the Party Central Committee rather than by erroneous opinions or contemptible scoundrels. Some of our comrades are always care-ridden. In my opinion, the major reason for them to be care-ridden is that they have not gone deeply into the masses to try to understand the practical situation. Without going deeply into the masses and the cadres, our thinking will be superficial. It is imperative for us to go deeply into the masses, into the cadres and into matters so as to grasp the essential issues. Therefore, it can be said that we have favorable conditions and that we have a bright future. Nevertheless, the basic issue is, in the final analysis, our own efforts. Our leading cadres in particular should take the lead in work. In my recent speech at the Central Party School, I mentioned one thing, that is, when we made resolutions on historical events before July 1, 1981, we dealt with part history, especially the history of our predecessors. Since July 1, 1981, however, we who are in the leadership posts should be writing our own history. If we do not pay attention to the writing of our own history, other people will write our history in three or five years time. Will our history be glorious or inglorious? Therefore, we, especially those of us who are in the prime of life, should value ourselves and go all out. Of course, old comrades are not comparable with young ones because they are old and need more rest. Except for eight hours of sleep (eight hours of sleep are necessary), those comrades who are in the prime of their life and those comrades who can still work for the Party should exert all their efforts. In short, on the fronts of building material and spiritual civilization, our comrades who are in leadership posts should be full of confidence, go all out, go deep into reality, unite with the masses, exert all their efforts and improve their work with the weapon of criticism and self-criticism. The bright and great future is sure to come.

(Translated by Y. H. Kao)

*****

DOCUMENT NO. 26

THE PRESENT ECONOMIC SITUATION AND THE PRINCIPLES FOR FUTURE ECONOMIC CONSTRUCTION

Report on the Work of the Government Delivered at the
Fourth Session of the Fifth National People's Congress
on November 30 and December 1, 1981

ZHAO ZIYANG

Premier of the State Council

(**Beijing Review**, No. 51, December 21, 1981)

Fellow Deputies,

Fourteen months have passed since the Third Session of the Fifth National People's Congress in September last year. During this period the government has submitted six reports on its work in both domestic and foreign affairs to the Standing Committee of the National People's Congress. In accordance with the decision of the Standing Committee, the main item on the agenda of the present session is economic work. It is the central task of the State Council and governments at all levels and the question of greatest concern to the people of all our nationalities and to all our fellow deputies.

On behalf of the State Council. I now submit to the present session for discussion and approval a report on the present economic situation, the principles for future economic construction and the prospects for China's economic development.

I. The Present Economic Situation

In 1981 we have made headway in economic work in the course of consolidating achievements, overcoming difficulties and progressively summing up experience and improving our understanding.

After the Third Session of the Fifth National People's Congress, the State Council made a further comprehensive analysis of the economic situation and trend and identified some major problems calling for immediate solution. From 1979 on, we substantially increased state expenditures for improving the people's living standards. On the whole, this was the right thing to do, even though the steps we took were a bit too hasty. At the same time, capital construction expenditures were not reduced as much as called for, and administrative expenses kept going up. Hence, total expenditures exceeded revenues. For two consecutive years, 1979 and 1980, there were very large financial deficits, too much currency was put into circulation, and prices rose. Without vigorous counter-measures, there would again have been a financial deficit of more than 10 billion yuan in 1981. With such a deficit, the improvement in the people's living conditions in the past few years would have been forfeited and the disproportions in our national economy aggravated, there would have been serious confusion in the country's economic life, and it would have been hard to strengthen our political stability and unity.

In view of all this, the State Council convened a plenary session in October 1980, followed in November by a conference to discuss economic work attended by provincial governors, the mayors of the three municipalities directly under the central authority and the chairmen of the autonomous regions. In December 1980 the Central Committee of the Communist Party of China held a working conference which, on the basis of a realistic nationwide appraisal, took a major policy decision for further economic readjustment and for the achievement of greater political stability.

In February 1981, on the proposal of the Central Committee of the Party, the State Council submitted a report on the further readjustment of the national economy of the 17th meeting of the Standing Committee of the National People's Congress. It proposed necessary revisions of the 1981 national economic plan and financial estimates with the aim of achieving a basic balance within 1981 between state revenues and expenditures and between credit receipts and payments and, in the main, stabilizing commodity prices. The Standing Committee of the National People's Congress examined and approved these revisions.

Since the beginning of 1981, governments at all levels have resolutely carried out with marked success a series of emergency measures for further readjustment the national economy. On the basis of our achievements in the past 11 months, I can now confidently report to this session that the 1981 national economic plan will be fulfilled and our objective of stabilizing the national economy will essentially be realized. Despite extensive economic readjustment and despite this year's serious natural calamities, the total output value of agriculture and industry in 1981 will not go down, but, on the contrary, will increase by more than 3 percent over that of 1980. The overall economic situation is better than anticipated. Our national economy has embarked on the path of steady growth.

Economic stability is manifested, first of all, in the basic balance between state revenues and expenditures and between credit receipts and payments. Since the winter of 1980-81, through their united and concerted efforts, the State Council and governments at all levels have strengthened centralized leadership, tightened financial and price controls, rigorously curtailed capital construction and administrative expenditures, economized on other spending and explored new sources of revenue so as to ensure the implementation of the 1981 budget. The financial deficit for the year is expected to drop to 2.7 billion yuan, from 17 billion yuan in 1979 and 12.7 billion yuan in 1980. It is no easy matter for any country to eliminate large financial deficits and basically balance its budget in a short time. We have done it relatively smoothly, thanks to the hard work of all our people and the full trust they have shown in the government. This proves the complete correctness of the policy decisions of the Central Committee of the Party and the State Council and the great superiority of our socialist system. On behalf of the Central Committee of the Party and the State Council I express thanks to the people of all nationalities for their trust and support.

With the achievement of the basic balance between revenues and expenditures, commodity prices are stable in the main. The rise in the general price index in 1981 has been smaller than last year's. Prices of daily necessities have been kept stable. However, the prices of some items have risen, especially those of vegetables which went up by quite a bit in some localities. We must try to solve this problem resolutely and conscientiously by increasing production, supplying more and better commodities, tightening price and market control and strictly enforcing price regulations.

The steady development of the Chinese economy depends on an overall increase in agricultural production. Although many regions have suffered serious floods and droughts in 1981, agricultural prospects in the country as a whole are bright. It is estimated that total grain output may approach the 1979 level, which would make 1981 the second peak year since the founding of the People's Republic. A new breakthrough has occurred in cotton production following the previous all-time record of 1980. Output of oil-bearing crops has risen by about 17 percent following big successive increases in the three previous years. Output of sugar-yielding crops should register an increase of more than 10 percent over 1980. New successes have been scored in forestry, animal husbandry and fisheries. Enterprises run by communes and production brigades and teams have continued to make progress; household sideline occupations have grown even faster. A dynamic atmosphere prevails throughout the countryside, with commune members rejoicing over their successes, and agricultural production is on the threshold of vigorous growth. Everyone who has the well-being of the 800 million peasants at heart rejoices over this. Our achievements would be inconceivable without the conscientious fulfillment of the principles and policies on rural work put forward by the Party and government since the Third Plenary Session of the 11th Central Committee of the Party in December 1978.

This year, many regions in China suffered from floods or droughts, which were of a gravity rarely known in our history. With unstinted help from the other regions the ensuing difficulties were overcome through the concerted effort of the Party and government cadres, the commanders and fighters of the People's Liberation Army and the broad masses in the affected areas. Production was rapidly resumed, great care was taken of the people's livelihood, and society is in good order. The exceptionally dangerous floods on the upper reaches of the Changjiang (Yangtze River) and Huanghe (Yellow River) were finally brought under control through the heroic efforts of the armymen and people fighting along their banks. The Gezhou Dam water-control project on the Changjiang and the Longyangxia and Liujiaxia hydroelectric power stations along the Huanghe withstood extraordinary flood crests. The Chengdu-Kunming and Baoji-Chengdu Railways and the Baoji-Tianshui section of the Longhai Railway, which had been severely damaged by floods and mud-rock flow, were very quickly re-opened to traffic. All these accomplishments won the admiration of people at home and abroad who were deeply concerned about conditions in the afflicted areas. On behalf of the State Council, I wish to warmly greet and express our deep respect to the people and cadres in these areas, and to PLA commanders and fighters, railway workers and staff who took part in the struggle against natural calamities and in the later relief work.

In light industry, production rose markedly thanks to the principle of stressing the manufacture of goods for everyday consumption and to the adoption of a series of detailed measures. It is estimated that the total output value of textile and other light industries for 1981 will show an increase of 12 percent over 1980. The output of durable consumer goods such as wrist watches, bicycles, sewing machines, TV sets, washing machines and electric fans has increased by double-digit percentages or in some cases several-fold. Output of such major items as cotton yarn and cloth, chemical fibers, sugar, paper and cigarettes will reach or exceed the planned targets. Light industry and textile products are now available in better designs and quality an in richer variety. The output of medium- and high-grade products has markedly increased, and articles of daily use are available in more varieties. Great changes in our markets as compared with previous years are apparent to all. Substantial increases in the output of goods for everyday consumption, continuing over several years, have played a major role in meeting the needs of people in town and country, created a thriving market, reinvigorated the economy, enabled all industry to maintain a certain rate of growth and increased financial revenues.

In heavy industry, which is now being readjusted, the year 1981 will witness a decrease of about 5 percent in output value as compared with 1980. This has resulted from the following circumstances: A number of heavy industrial enterprises have suspended production of grossly overstocked items whose manufacture entails high energy consumption. These cutbacks are necessary and rational, for they enable us to transfer the energy thus saved to light industry. A considerable number of heavy industrial enterprises, which have long engaged mainly in serving capital construction, have found their production dropping in 1981 as a result of the much curtailed investment in capital construction and the corresponding decreasing orders for equipment and other production goods. This is inevitable in the course of readjusting the service orientation and product mix of heavy industry. Also, some heavy industrial enterprises were switched to the manufacture of other products later than they should have been, thus causing a drop in the production of some items, which could have been avoided. This happened because some comrades were slow to act, failing fully to understand the necessity of readjusting the service orientation and product mix of heavy industry. Efforts are being made to overcome this tendency. In the latter half of 1981, much has been done in heavy industry to change the orientation of its service, to cut back on products in excess supply and to increase the output of items most needed by the people and of export items. Here, initial successes have been achieved so that heavy industrial production began to pick up in the fourth quarter. Besides, geological prospecting has yielded fairly good results in the past year. The departments of railway, water, highway and air transport and of posts and ttelecommunicationsare fulfilling their plans satisfactorily, so that the transport of various important materials and the passengers is basically ensured.

The appropriate curtailment of capital construction is an important aspect of this year's work in economic readjustment. The problem of overextension of capital construction is being resolved step by step, and utilization of investment in this field is more rational than before. Total expenditure on capital construction were cut down to 30 billion yuan in February this year when the national plan was being revised. Later, 8 billion yuan were added, of which 3.5 billion have been used in building more housing projects and the remainder in increasing capacity in the production of goods for everyday consumption, in developing the oil industry and the transport services, and in resuming a number of badly needed projects whose equipment and technology are introduced from abroad. The emphasis in capital construction this year has first of all been on textile and other light industries which have an important bearing on the people's standard of living, and then on energy, building materials and transport and communications. The proportions going to education, science, culture, public health and urban utilities have been raised in varying degrees. The first stage of the Gezhou Dam water-control project which had started several years ago was speeded up, so that the river was open to navigation in June 1981 and the first 170,000-kilowatt generator set went into trial operation and began to generate electricity. The three big chemical fibre plants in Liaoyang, Tianjin and Sichuan have basically been completed and put into commission. Over 90 percent of the projects scheduled to go into full operation in 1981 can be completed according to plan. This is a rate unknown for many years.

Scientific research is playing an important role, guided as it is by the correct principle of the close integration of research with economic construction. The pace has been quickened and there has been substantial progress in applying the latest results of scientific research, in popularizing new technology in agriculture, industry, national defence and other fields. In 1980, altogether more than 2,600 major research projects were successful, and there will be still more successes in 1981. About 50 percent of the results have been applied to production. The popularization of such improved strains as hybrid paddy rice and "Lumian" Cotton Seed No. 1 over large areas has greatly contributed to the increased output of grain and cotton. During 1981 industrial departments have trail-produced or experimented with about 10,000 new products and technologies, half of which have been applied in regular production. Extensive use of new technologies, techniques and materials has steadily raised the technical level of industry. The successful launching of three satellites with one carrier rocket points to a new achievement in our science and technology following the launching of a carrier rocket to a prescribed area in the Pacific last year.

Domestic and foreign trade has expanded. More commodities are now supplied to the home market and consumer demand is being met fairly well. The volume of retail sales for 1981, according to estimates, should register a 9 percent increase over 1980. To achieve a balance between the supply of commodities and social purchasing power, it was originally planned to release several billion yuan's worth of commodity inventories. But as both purchases and sales have grown considerably, instead of going down commodity inventories are expected to increase by nearly 10 billion yuan. There has been a fairly big increase both in trade handled by urban and rural collectively owned establishments and in trade run by individuals as a supplement to state-operated and collective commerce. These forms have complemented state-owned stores, restaurants and service trades with respect to the increase in the number of stores, variety of goods, scope of services and business hours, thus providing more conveniences for the people. Further progress has been made in economic and technical exchanges with foreign countries, and the total volume of imports and exports in 1981 will have increased considerably over the previous year. More solid and perceptibly successful work has been done with regard to joint ventures involving Chinese and foreign investment, compensatory trade, the processing of materials for foreign businessmen, and the import of advanced technology and key equipment.

The living standards of the people have continued to improve. With the overall increase in agricultural production, rural income has gone up noticeably following the fairly big rise in the two previous years. There are more and more peasant families, production teams, production brigades, communes and counties whose income has gone up by a big margin. In 1979, there were 1,622 production brigades whose members each received an average of over 300 yuan from the distribution of collective income. The number rose to 5,569 in 1980 and it will be even higher in 1981. Especially gratifying is the fact that production and the people's living standards have gone up considerably, and profound changes have taken place in areas such as western Shandong, eastern Henan, northern Jiangsu and the area north of the Huaihe River where production used to be low because of poor natural conditions. An important indicator of the improvement in peasant living conditions is the large-scale construction of housing in rural areas where, according to incomplete statistics, new houses with about 900 million square meters of floor space have been added in the past three years. In the cities and towns, 4.77 million people were assigned jobs from January to September 1981. It has been decided to raise the pay of primary and middle school teachers, of some medical personnel and of physical culture workers as of October this year. Despite the big reduction in capital construction expenditures, the financing of housing projects for workers and staff has remained at last year's level, and close to 80 million square meters of new residential space in cities and towns will be completed by the end of 1981. With better planning of auxiliary projects providing water, electricity and public transport, more floor space will be commissioned than last year, resulting in improved urban housing conditions. Bank savings in the urban and rural areas increased by 9.5 billion yuan between January and October 1982, reaching 49.4 billion yuan. This is a striking indication of the improvement in the living standards of the masses of the people as well as of their confidence in the development of the economy.

The above facts amply show that the principles guiding the further readjustment of our economy are correct, our course of development is sound and our achievements are considerable. The task of readjustment is a very challenging one. We had anticipated that troubles of one sort or another might crop up. But progress has been fairly smooth, with no really big troubles at all, and the few troubles that did occur were quickly resolved. Through the current readjustment, we have essentially achieved the aim of stabilizing the overall economic situation and of further consolidating and developing a political situation characterized by stability, unity and liveliness.

The setting forth of the principle of readjusting, restructuring, consolidating and improving the national economy marked a fundamental turn in our economic work under the guidance of the correct line formulated at the Third Plenary Session of the Eleventh Central Committee of the Party.

Beginning from 1979, we set about readjusting our rural policy to ensure the production teams power of decision. Many different forms of the system of responsibility for production have been practiced in our vast rural areas in the last three years. This system represents a new form of management and distribution for our socialist agriculture in the specific conditions of China's countryside. We have firmly grasped two important links: the establishment and perfecting of the responsibility system and the development of diversified undertakings. Meanwhile, we have made significant increases in the purchasing prices of farm and sideline products and decided to import a certain quantity of food grains every year. All this has been of great help in readjusting crop patterns, developing a diversified rural economy in accordance with actual conditions and rehabilitating the rural areas.

Readjustment in industry is somewhat different from that in agriculture. In industry, the main stress is on readjusting the proportions between its different branches, coupled with the necessary restructuring. As regards the readjustment of the ratio between light and heavy industry, measures have been taken -- since the policy decision in late 1980 to further readjust the national economy -- to give top priority to the development of light industry in the following spheres: the supply of raw and semi-finished materials and energy; bank loans; tapping potential, and carrying out technical innovations and transformation; capital construction; the use of foreign exchange and imported technology; and transport and communications. In 1981, beginning with key industrial cities, co-operation for specialized functions and through different forms of economic association has been organized for the mass production of certain items, with factories producing brand-name and quality products as the foundation. At the same time, arrangements have been made for such enterprises in the heavy and national defence industries as have the necessary conditions to produce durable consumer goods which meet the needs of the people. All these factors account for the sustained increase in the proportion of the total industrial output value produced by light industry. A bigger section of heavy industry is able to give direct service to light industry and agriculture, thus making the internal structure of our industry as a whole more rational. In the last three years, we have also gradually enhanced the power of decision of enterprises, introduced the system of economic responsibility, carried out the principle of distribution according to work, and striven to bring into play the supplementary role of regulation through the market under the guidance of the state plan. All these initial reforms have helped to invigorate our industrial enterprises, to overcome the widespread phenomenon of egalitarianism with "everybody sharing food from the same big pot," and to develop the initiative of enterprises and of their workers and staff.

Conspicuous changes have also taken place in the distribution of national income. With increased purchasing prices for farm and sideline products and the reduction of tax burdens in some rural areas, state revenue fell by 52 billion yuan from 1979 to 1981 while peasant income increased accordingly. In the same period, the state provided jobs for more than 20 million people in towns and cities, raised the wages and salaries of workers and staff and applied the bonus system. The consequent increase in state expenditures and reduction in state revenues, taken together, provided a total of 40.5 billion yuan for an increase in the income of workers and staff. The reduction of state revenues in the countryside and the cities thus totalled 92.5 billion yuan, or 54 percent more than the estimated figure of 60 billion yuan. Moreover, price subsidies from the state for diesel oil and electricity used in agricultural production, farm machines, chemical fertilizer, coal for civilian use, and imported food grains, cotton and sugar amounted to 23.4 billion yuan. Thanks to this series of effective measures for solving some of the problems piled up over the years and improving urban and rural living standards, the share of consumption in the national income went up from 63.5 percent in 1978 to about 70 percent in 1981 while the share of accumulation fell from 36.5 to about 30 percent. It can be said that a marked change for the better has taken place in the serious disproportion between consumption and accumulation left over from the past.

Although we have scored striking successes in economic readjustment in the past year, it should be noted that the latent dangers in our national economy have not been completely eliminated. The basic balance between revenues and expenditures this year is not yet a stable one, because it has been achieved mainly by curtailing financial outlays. Therefore, more arduous work is needed for a pretty long period to enable us to maintain the basic financial and credit balance, increase the production of consumer goods to match rising purchasing power and keep prices essentially stable, so that the economy can develop harmoniously and the financial and economic situation can take a fundamental turn for the better. Implementing the principle of readjustment, restructuring, consolidation and improvement is a matter of overall importance, bearing directly on the country's long-term interests. Without awareness and conscientiousness on this score, repetition of the mistakes made many times in the past is still possible.

It was at the Second Session of the Fifth National People's Congress held in June 1979, that the State Council proposed the tasks of readjusting, restructuring, consolidating and improving the economy within three years. Through practice, we have since gained a deeper understanding of this principle. As far as readjustment is concerned, we should not only readjust the proportions between industry and agriculture, between light and heavy industries and between accumulation and consumption: we should also readjust the product mix, the technological makeup, the line-up of enterprises and the organizational structure so as to rationalize the overall structure of our national economy. Therefore, economic readjustment covers a much wider range than we first envisaged. The overall restructuring of the economic management system will take an even longer period. For this reason, the State Council holds that it is necessary to carry on with the principle of readjustment, restructuring, consolidation and improvement for another five years or a little longer, beginning from 1981. This is the way to gain a firm foothold and to lay a solid foundation for sounder development in the future.

Fellow deputies,

The present economic situation in our country is good. Things have been getting better and better quarter by quarter in 1981. Compared with the corresponding periods of 1980, the gross value of industrial output dropped by 0.2 percent in the first quarter but increased by 1.7 percent in the second and by 3 percent in the third, while in October it went up by 10.6 percent. Our economic prospects for 1982 and, of course, for subsequent years are unquestionably better.

The successes we have achieved in economic construction in the past year are due to the common efforts of all our people under the leadership of the Chinese Communist Party. The workers, peasants, intellectuals and cadres on the economic front have been very diligent and hard-working. The cadres and masses in the fields of education, science, culture, the mass media, publishing, public health, politics and law, foreign affairs, etc., have brought their initiative and creativeness into full play in their work and scored significant achievements in the drive for socialist modernization centered on economic construction. In sports, good news has kept pouring in this year. Recently the Chinese Women's Volleyball Team won a world championship for the first time. Their victory inspires the people of all our nationalities who are working hard for the modernization programme. On behalf of the State Council, I take this opportunity to extend our sincere greetings to comrades on the above fronts. The Chinese People's Liberation Army has firmly carried out the line, principles and policies laid down by the Central Committee of the Party, strengthened ideological and political work, intensified military training, enhanced its sense of organization and its discipline, safeguarded and taken an active part in socialist construction and continued to play its role of pillar of the people's democratic dictatorship. PLA units and militiamen in the frontier regions and the heroes defending the Koulin and Faka Mountains on the border between China and Vietnam are on guard every minute against provocations and incursions by the imperialists and hegemonists, thus defending the sacred frontiers of the motherland. Public security and judicial workers throughout the country have made outstanding contributions to the maintenance of public order, the struggle against criminals and the education and remolding of delinquents. On behalf of the State Council, I would like to take this opportunity to pay high tribute to the PLA commanders and fighters, the militiamen and public security workers.

II. Principles for Future Economic Construction

In continuing to readjust the national economy, we must strive not only to solve the problem of large financial deficits and to control prices so as to eliminate potential dangers and speedily achieve overall stability in the economic situation; we should, on this basis, also strive to achieve the steady advance and sound growth of the economy. For this purpose, we must thoroughly change the conventional methods evolved over the years under the influence of the "Left" ideology and, proceeding from the actual conditions in China, blaze a new trail characterized by a fairly steady tempo and better economic results, yielding more substantial benefits to the people.

The crux of the problem is to do all we can to get better economic results in areas of production, construction and circulation. We have undergone major twists and turns in our economic construction since the founding of the People's Republic. But on the whole we have obtained notable success. In 1980, as compared with 1952, the year economic recovery was completed, the total output value of industry and agriculture had increased 9.1 times, national income 5.2 times, and industrial fixed assets 27 times, and the average consumption level of the people had increased by 100 percent. All this fully shows that progress in our economic construction has been fairly rapid under socialism. At the same time, we can see that the increase in our national income in the 32 years has been much less than that in the total value of industrial and agricultural output, and, further, that the people's standard of living has lagged far behind the national income. The results of our economic construction have not been what they should be, and the improvement in the people's living standards has not been commensurate with the labor they have contributed.

There are subjective as well as objective reasons for the unsatisfactory results of China's economic construction. Our country was very backward economically and culturally before liberation and for long years after liberation, there have been threats or even aggression by alien hostile forces, so we have had to concentrate our financial and material resources on the speedy development of heavy industry in order to lay the foundations for industrialization and strengthen national defence. Owing to prolonged blockade by imperialism and social-imperialism, China has been seriously obstructed from utilizing the advanced technology and managerial experience of foreign countries. Our country has a big and rapidly growing population so that a fair measure of the social wealth created by expanding production has to be consumed by the additional population, which adversely affects the raising of the living standards of the people as a whole. In addition to these objective reasons, long-standing "Left" mistakes in our guidelines for economic construction prevented us in many of our efforts from acting in conformity with objective economic laws. Coupled with the disruption during the decade-long "cultural revolution," this could not but seriously hamper us in giving effect to the superiority of our socialist system, it could not but impede our economic construction and detract from its results. The influence and consequences of the "Left" ideology which formerly guided economic work cannot possibly be eliminated in a short time. To this day, many major targets in our plans, in terms of anticipated economic results, are not only below the level of the economically advanced countries but also below that reached in China in the past. The setup of production, the product mix, the technological makeup, the line-up of enterprises, the organizational structure, the geographical distribution of industries and other economic undertakings, all these features of our country's economy as a whole are far from rational, and there are many defects in our system of economic management. These are the biggest obstacles to the attainment of better economic results. From now on we must tackle all economic problems with better economic problems with better economic results as the fundamental objective, ensuring a more satisfactory sustained development of our economy.

To blaze a new trail in our economic construction for the attainment of better economic results, we must conscientiously implement the ten principles set out below, which embody the general principle of readjusting, restructuring, consolidating and improving the national economy, and sum up our experience in the past thirty-two years, and particularly in the past three years.

1. Accelerate the development of agriculture by relying on correct policies and on science. Agricultural is the foundation of the national economy, and all-round development of the rural economy is the key to all-round growth of our whole economy. The state will gradually increase its investment in agriculture but will not be able to increase it by much. The growth of agricultural production and other rural development will therefore continue to rely mainly on correct policies and on science.

Socialist agriculture was established in China long ago, and it has since been consolidated. The broad masses of peasants have an immense reservoir of enthusiasm for socialism. On the one hand, they want to stick to the path of socialist collectivization of agriculture, to public ownership of land and other basic means of production. On the other hand, they demand an end to the over-concentration of power in the managerial system and arbitrary directions in the sphere of production, and to egalitarianism and a number of irrational burdens in the sphere of distribution. In the last three years, we have broken the shackles of "Left" ideology and carried out some necessary readjustment in the relations of production in rural areas by respecting the decision-making power of the production teams and introducing various forms of the system of responsibility for production. This has enhanced the enthusiasm of the peasants in their work and led to better use of the material and technical conditions built up over the years, once again liberating the productive forces in agriculture. We must earnestly study and review the new conditions and problems that have emerged in the course of practice, adhere unwaveringly to the path of socialist collectivization and public ownership of land and other basic means of production responsibility in agriculture, and strive to improve the different types of the responsibility system and our other rural economic policies.

To develop the rural economy, we must first of all, put existing arable land to more rational use. At the same time, we must take measures, step by step, to utilize properly and fully China's vast expanses of hilly land and mountainous areas, broad grasslands, big and small rivers, numerous lakes and ponds, beaches and territorial waters. In the past, our vision in agricultural production was often limited to existing cultivated land and to grain production, which increasingly cramped our efforts. Henceforth we should stress the concept of all-round development, mobilizing the more than 300 million peasants capable of full-time labor to explore new possibilities in production and promote diversified undertakings and household sideline occupations so as to advance production both intensively and extensively. Our policy is to spare no effort in promoting grain production and diversified undertakings. While ensuring the steady development of grain cultivation, we must also ensure an increase in the production of such cash crops as cotton, oil-bearing crops, hemp, silk, tea, sugar-yielding crops, vegetables, tobacco, fruit and medicinal materials and sundry products, as well as other farm and subsidiary products. We must consolidate and expand the bases for producing marketable grain, continue to make a success of the state farms and land reclamation, and strive to increase yields per unit area. While actively expanding the production of cash crops, we must make their geographical distribution more rational. Peasants in suburban districts should engage mainly in vegetable growing, and it is essential to ensure the area sown to vegetables. We should strive to protect the existing grasslands, use them rationally, step up their development, rear as much livestock as possible and at the same time encourage the raising of domestic animals and poultry in the vast countryside, and so significantly develop animal husbandry. In a word, our great motherland has all kinds of inexhaustible resources and it is full of vitality. We can certainly achieve the all-round development of farming, forestry, animal husbandry, sideline occupations and fisheries, provided we emancipate our minds, work realistically, rely on the masses, devise appropriate methods and turn human talents and land and other material resources to good account.

Our country has a vast population but not enough arable land; this contradiction will become more and more acute as the population increases. Our state policy should therefore be to treasure and use every inch of land rationally. We must survey China's agricultural resources and draw up plans for agricultural regionalization and the comprehensive use of land on nationwide, provincial and county levels, as well as for the planned use of land by the communes, production brigades and teams. We must encourage scientific farming. As regards existing farmland, we should gradually accomplish the general improvement and utilization of the alkaline soil in the Huanghe, Huaihe and Haihe river basins and of the red soil in southern China and, relying mainly on the local people and their experience, apply the achievements of the relevant scientific research of the past two decades. Use of farmland for capital construction, even where it is unavoidable, should be strictly limited. There must be planning in the building of houses in rural areas and unlawful seizure or misuse of farmland is absolutely impermissible.

Water is a major material resource; the way it is exploited and used has a direct bearing on the development not only of agriculture but also of the whole economy. We failed to pay enough attention to this in the past. Now we should do adequate research and conduct sufficient publicity among the masses and cadres so that they understand the importance of preserving, rationally using, saving and developing water resources. Our water resources are distributed very unevenly and are utilized inadequately and irrationally. That is why a serious water shortage is felt in some places where it already severely affects the people's living conditions and industrial and agricultural production. In conjunction with the nationwide improvement of farmland, we must conduct comprehensive surveys of water resources and prospecting for them, and draw up plans for their rational use. We should gradually bring them under unified management, work earnestly for thrift in their use and prevent their pollution. Existing water conservancy works should be well maintained and properly used so as to yield the maximum benefit.

China's afforested area and the percentage of its forest cover are small, there is grievous soil erosion, and the ecological balance is increasingly being impaired. If we fail to find an effective solution to this problem, we shall be committing a historical error whose consequences may afflict future generations. To change the situation, we must take immediate and effective measures to forbid indiscriminate felling, prevent fires, diseases and insect pests in the forests, and launch a national afforestation drive. Present emphasis should be on planting fuel trees. In villages, suburban districts and coastal and frontier regions where conditions permit the planting of groves of timber or fruit trees, it is necessary to organize specialized afforestation groups with production teams and brigades or communes as the unit and to put the work on a permanent basis. Forestry departments should stress the preservation and expansion of existing forest bases, the active reforestation of denuded lands, and the promotion of the multi-purpose use of forest resources. Meanwhile, efforts should be made to plant trees and grass and conserve water and soil along the upper reaches of the Huanghe, Changjiang and other rivers. The State Council has prepared a Resolution on a Nationwide Campaign for Obligatory Tree Planting, which will be submitted to this session for examination and then promulgated and implemented.

While developing the entire rural economy which embraces crop-framing, forestry, animal husbandry, sideline occupations and fisheries, we must also consider and make arrangements for overall rural development. Transport and communication services, small hydropower stations, methane gas installations, the manufacture of building materials, the building industry, the processing of farm and sideline products, the construction of public amenities in towns and villages, commerce and service trades, bank credit, culture, education, physical culture, public health work -- all these can and should be developed in a planned way according to the needs and possibilities. We have immense labor, power in the countryside and there is no need to worry about being short of people to do the work. The problem is, firstly, how to get them to do these things willingly and actively, which means that correct policies are needed; and, secondly, how to work efficiently and achieve good results, which calls for the proper application of science and technology. In everything they undertake people in all trades and professions should work out specific policies in the light of their own conditions and apply the relevant science and technology and appropriate methods of management. It is necessary to link the readjustment of the relations of production with the development of the productive forces in the countryside, make rational use of the labor of the hundreds of millions of peasants, carry out farmland capital construction and water conservancy projects, and improve production conditions so as to secure the all-round development of the rural economy and bring greater prosperity to our new socialist countryside.

To blaze a new trail for agriculture so that it will develop with relatively little investment and high economic returns, stress must be laid on research in, and popularization of, agricultural science and technology and on combining the achievements of modern research in these spheres with China's fine traditions of intensive farming in order to wrest more farm products from nature to meet our needs. Since the founding of the People's Republic, much has been done in research in agricultural science and technology and in their popularization, and with substantial results. The cultivation and popularization of some improved seed strains has often yielded economic returns scores or even hundreds of times the cost of research on them. This has fully demonstrated the power of intellectual investment in scientific research. We hope that the departments concerned will concentrate greater efforts and, within a relatively short time, achieve further notable successes in breeding and popularizing fine seed strains, improving farming methods and crop patterns, changing the composition of chemical fertilizers, applying fertilizer rationally, producing highly efficient farm chemicals low in poisonous residue, and popularizing selected and suitable farm machinery.

For progress in agriculture we rely on correct policies and science. But it is the cadres and scientific and technical personnel in the rural areas who implement the policies and apply the science. With the introduction of various forms of system of responsibility for production, a profound change has taken place in the relations between cadres and scientific and technical personnel on the one hand and the peasant masses on the other, promoting generally closer relations between them. People everywhere respect and are grateful to our rural cadres and scientific and technical personnel working gloriously and arduously in the forefront of agricultural production. We should show particular concern for them politically, vocationally and in their daily life, and take concrete measures to encourage them to continue to do their best.

2. Give prominence to the development of consumer goods industries and further adjust the service orientation of heavy industry. With the situation in the countryside constantly improving, agriculture is providing more and more raw materials for light industry, and the cash income of people in both country and town is rising year by year. This gives tremendous impetus to the development of consumer goods industries, whose accelerated development will, through exchange, promote the growth of agriculture, heavy industry and domestic and foreign trade, and better satisfy the demand of the people for a higher standard of living. Concurrently, it will increase state revenues, stabilize prices and provide more jobs, thus helping consolidate political stability and unity. Vigorous promotion of the production of consumer goods will also help rationalize the whole structure of the economy and properly resolve the contradiction between accumulation and consumption. We must give prominence to the development of consumer goods industries for a long time yet. Therefore we should ensure that their requirements are met with regard to the supply of energy and materials, the allotment of loans and investments, the allocation of scientific and technical personnel, the selection of topics for scientific research and the introduction of foreign technology and equipment.

The prospects are bright and the potential immense for the growth of the consumer goods industries. At present, urban and rural people badly need durable consumer goods, textiles, foodstuffs including beverages, building materials for civilian use, chemical products for daily use, stationery and medical supplies. Goods for tourism an other services are also needed. The departments concerned are now mapping out plans for developing these trades. Taking full advantage of our rich natural resources and abundant labor power, we should build more labor-intensive enterprises turning out consumer goods; such enterprises need less investment but yield quicker returns. Giving due consideration to both town and country, to both domestic and foreign markets, and to the special needs of the minority nationalities, a balance must be struck between supply, production and marketing, planning and market surveys and forecasts improved, and blindness in production eliminated. While increasing the output of medium- and high-grade goods, the production of less profitable run-of-the-mill goods and small items liked and needed by the broad masses should on no account be neglected. Stress must be laid on better quality, so as to turn out more readily marketable goods new in design, rich in variety, fine in quality and low in price. There must be no stress on quantity at the expense of quality, and rough and slipshod methods of manufacture should be checked. Shanghai, Tianjin and other old industrial bases should make full use of their advantages and potential in expanding consumer goods industries and try to co-operate with other cites and areas, helping them with their skills and experience in operation and management to boost their production of consumer goods. Localities must ensure the fulfillment of their quotas in purchasing raw materials for the consumer goods industries and sending them to other areas. In the distribution of raw materials, we must give priority to the needs of the old industrial bases.

Under present conditions, faster growth in the production of consumer goods will promote the expansion of heavy industry and definitely not hinder it. The growth of the former will set more and higher demands on the latter. According to the Marxist theory of reproduction, the more harmonious the relations between the two departments of social production, i.e., the production of the means of production and the production of the means of subsistence, and the faster the exchange and turnover, the more rapid will be the growth of the whole economy. The maintenance of a harmonious development of these two departments is our long-term policy. We should now radically change the long-standing tendency of one-sided emphasis on the development of heavy industry and on making some of its sectors serve new construction projects. Apart from producing certain durable consumer goods, in its future development our heavy industry must attend to the more important take of readjusting its orientation, enlarging its scope, raising the quality of its services and improving its adaptability, so that it can give better service to agriculture and the consumer goods industries, the technical transformation of the economy, exports and the modernization of our national defense. Such is the way forward for our heavy industry. The better and more energetically its orientation and internal structure are readjusted, the greater the scope for its initiative.

Much basic work needs to be done in developing heavy industry. As its production cycle is, in general, relatively long, we must start right now to design and manufacture the equipment that will be required years later by projects in the infrastructure like those in energy and transport. We must pay great attention to preparatory work of all kinds, such as prospecting for energy and mineral resources and designing projects to exploit them; to scientific research, the technical testing and technological designing of major new products; and to the training of competent personal, technical transformation and renewal of equipment -- all these tasks must be accomplished in good time. All workers and staff members in heavy industry departments should exert themselves in such work which is indispensable to our modernization programme.

3. Raise the energy utilization ratio and promote the building of the energy industry and transport. The energy industry and transport are now the weak links in the chain of our economic development. Whether our economy can keep on growing at a comparatively high speed and whether a new expansion will come about depends largely on the proper solution of the problems of energy and transport.

Our policy for solving the energy problem is to lay equal stress on exploiting energy resources and on practicing economy in its consumption, while giving priority to saving energy now and in the near future. Our output of energy at present is exceeded only by that of the United States, the Soviet Union and Saudi Arabia, but our national income per unit of energy consumed is much lower than that of many countries and even lower than our own former highest level. China's waste of energy is shocking, but it also indicates a remarkable potential for energy savings. In the last few years, energy conservation and reduced consumption have been effected mainly through readjusting the structure of light and heavy industry, and little has been achieved through improved management and technical transformation. It is imperative to set strict demands in these respects, take most rigorous measures, set stringent energy consumption quotas for different products, shut down those factories which waste too much energy and whose products fail to meet social needs, and also gradually and systematically carry out the technical transformation of backward energy-guzzling production facilities and technologies in order to ensure success in our task of economizing on oil, coal and power. We must first strive to surpass our own record in national income per unit of energy consumed. Then we must try, gradually, to approach the levels of the world's industrially developed countries.

There are fewer than ten countries whose annual output of petroleum exceeds 100 million tons, and China is one of them. This output constitutes an immense item of wealth for our country. The rational use of this wealth is essential for securing better economic results for the whole of society. At present, 40 million tons of petroleum are burnt as fuel each years, a large proportion of which should not have been so used. The waste is enormous. The State Council has decided to take the necessary measures in the next ten years to replace oil consumption by coal consumption, saving petroleum for processing at home or for export, and to use the revenues thus derived for building our energy industry and transport. Our crude oil processing is still at a low level, so that many components which can be used as industrial chemicals have yet to be cracked or separated for optimal utilization. The value China derives from 100 million tons of petroleum is far less than in industrially developed countries, which constitute another enormous waste. We must go all out to reorganize and transform existing oil refineries and petrochemical enterprises, raise the level of crude oil processing and promote the comprehensive utilization of petrochemicals. This will not only add to China's exports but also help increase the production of such products as chemical fibers, plastics and synthetic rubber, thus providing more consumer goods for the market. In a word, effective utilization of our 100 million tons of petroleum is important for attaining better economic results, increasing revenues and improving the economic situation; all departments and units must pay special attention to this task and make concerted and strenuous efforts to accomplish it.

In the production and exploitation of energy, long-term development as well as immediate needs must be taken into account. China is very rich in coal reserves. In exploiting them we should lay stress on transforming and expanding existing coal mines now and in the near future. New mines to be opened should mainly be small and medium-sized ones, involving small investments and a shorter construction cycle and yielding faster results. As for large mines, their construction and commissioning should be staggered, so that they can turn out more coal sooner. Efforts should be concentrated on extracting coal in Shanxi Province; at the same time appropriate arrangements should be made for mining in the provinces of Henan, Shandong, Anhui, Heilongjiang and Guizhou, and in Inner Mongolia. In production and construction in the power industry, we should strive to build thermal power plants and hydroelectric stations suiting local conditions, with the focus gradually shifting to the construction of hydroelectric stations. Villages with water power resources should try to build small hydroelectric stations so as to relieve the shortage of energy, reduce pollution and cut down the cost of generation. In production and construction in the oil industry, it is necessary to effect the technical transformation of the Daqing and other oil-fields, tap their potential and renovate them, try to keep total output at 100 million tons in the next few years and at the same time muster funds for opening up new oil-fields. Efforts must be redoubled to make a general survey of petroleum and natural gas resources and to prospect for them and also to increase our reserves so as to create the necessary conditions for future development.

The deputies and people of all our nationalities have shown great concern about the exploration of offshore oil. I am delighted to report that gratifying progress has been made. We have completed a general seismological survey of part of the South China Sea and the southern waters of the Yellow Sea. A number of exploratory wells in the Bohai Sea and the Beibu Gulf have started to produce oil. Our oil industry's prospects are bright. In accordance with the principle of mutual benefit, the government has decided to invite tenders from foreign firms in the near future and, with their co-operation, to step up exploration and open and build up new oil-fields as soon as possible. Not long ago, some people asserted that China's oil output would gradually fall so that before long she would become not an exporter but an importer of oil. I can assure you that this definitely will not happen.

The building of the energy industry and transport should go hand in hand, with the latter starting up a bit earlier. Only thus can excavated coal, for instance, be moved out in time. For a number of years the central authorities should give top priority to the needs of transport including the building of harbors, when allocating investments for construction. Railway sections with low transport capacity and harbors with low handling capacity should be the first to undergo technical transformation. The departments in charge of transport and water conservancy should jointly strive to adjust inland water transport and dredge the channels so as to greatly increase inland water transport potentialities. At the same time, we should make full use of our offshore transport potentialities, mobilize all possible forces to step up highway construction and organize vehicles of every kind of reinforce short-distance transportation. Efforts should be made to hasten the growth of postal and telecommunications services. Every means should be used to adapt transport to the needs of expanded production and construction throughout the economy.

4. Carry out technical transformation step by step in key units and make the maximum use of existing enterprises. Not only will technical transformation and the updating of equipment in existing enterprises in industry and transport bring about a change in the present situation of dearth of assignments to heavy industry, ensuring a definite growth rate for our economy and an increase in productive capacity; they will also help raise our industrial techniques to a new level and pave the way and build up reserves for the modernization of our entire economy in the years to come. This is the key to smoother economic development. In the past, we carried on expanded reproduction chiefly by building new factories, which had to be done in the period of laying the foundation for industrialization. Now that China already has several hundred thousand enterprises in industry and transport, we will have to rely chiefly on the technical transformation of existing enterprises and on their initiative for expanded reproduction in the future. The good results obtained by many enterprises in this regard indicate that this course will yield faster results and bigger economic returns and call for smaller investments than the building of new enterprises.

China should follow her own road in the light of her own conditions in the technical transformation of existing enterprises. Our country is rich in manpower but short of funds, and for a considerably long period it must therefore not expect to equip all enterprises with the most advanced technology, nor should it one-sidedly pursue automation. Closely centering around the effort to secure better economic results, our technical transformation should include the following features: (1) economizing on energy and raw and semi-finished materials, reducing their consumption and lower production costs; (2) changing the product mix, upgrading and updating products, and improving their properties and quality, so as to meet the needs of markets at home and abroad; and (3) making rational use of resources and raising the level of comprehensive utilization.

The work of technical transformation calls for both overall plans and detailed requirements for different trades. It should first be done well in the industrially developed key cities and a number of key enterprises, and undertaken group after group and at different times. It must not be undertaken without prior study or without consideration for economic results. Nor should there be a general rush into action, with each unit going its own way. Proceeding from their specific conditions, all trades should formulate correct policies with respect to technical equipment and map out overall plans for technical transformation and for the updating of their equipment so as to carry out such transformation and renovation after adequate preparations. The machine-building industry must be transformed and reorganized early; it should endeavour to design and manufacture sophisticated machines and equipment to meet the needs of technical transformation plans should be included in the state programme. Transformation projects must be arranged and carried out one by one.

The equipment in a number of our key enterprises is outdated, low in efficiency and high in energy consumption; it should be systematically replaced with more efficient machinery. However, this should be done within our capabilities. Under existing conditions, what most enterprises can accomplish is mainly to add or update a few key installations, improve technology, perfect operating procedures and promote the designing and trial manufacture of new products. It is necessary to arouse the masses of workers and staff members to make rationalization proposals for the renovation of production techniques.

To promote effective technical transformation, in allocating investments for fixed assets we should make unified arrangements for the use of funds for both capital construction and technical transformation. Fairly soon, new policies should be framed for the updating of equipment, which should be in keeping with our conditions and conducive to the growth of our economy. The depreciation rate for fixed assets should be increased gradually in the light of the differing conditions in each trade or enterprise, so as to appropriately shorten the cycle for updating their equipment. From now on, depreciation funds, funds for expanding production drawn from profits retained by enterprises and relevant funds allocated by departments at a higher level should all be used for technical transformation and the updating of equipment. Both the distribution and use of these funds should be included in the financial and credit plans; they must not be used for the construction of new projects or other purposes. Where conditions permit, some enterprises can make use of a certain amount of foreign investment, combining their technical transformation with the import of technology.

5. Carry out the all-round consolidation and necessary restructuring of enterprises by groups. To tap the potential of existing enterprises, secure better economic results and increase state revenues, it is imperative that the all-round consolidation of enterprises be carried out in groups and in a planned way.

In the course of consolidation, special attention must now be given to the following four tasks: (1) strengthening and perfecting the system of economic responsibility, improving the operation and management of enterprises and doing a good job in overall planning, quality control and business accounting; (2) reorganizing work units, arranging production according to a fixed number of workers and fixed quotas, systematically training all workers and staff and firmly overcoming overstaffing and laxity; (3) strengthening work discipline and strictly enforcing regulations concerning rewards and disciplinary sanctions -- persons doing good work should be commended and given rewards, but as for serious violators of work discipline who refuse to mend their ways despite repeated admonitions, the enterprise has the right to mete out economic or administrative penalties, or, in the worst cases, to ask them to leave or simply discharge them in accordance with the relevant regulations; and (4) strengthening financial discipline, improving financial and accounting rules and regulations and tightening financial control; in cases of breaches of financial discipline such as fraud, embezzlement, retention of profits which ought to be turned over to the state and evasion of taxes, the persons and the leading cadres concerned should be made to bear the economic and legal responsibility. To carry out the above tasks, special efforts must be made to reorganize leading bodies by putting an end to laxity, flabbiness, overstaffing and keeping on people who are too old, phenomena which exist in some leading organizations, and by promoting young and middle-aged cadres and technical personnel to leading posts. It is also necessary to strengthen the system under which the factory director assumes full responsibility under the leadership of the Party committee and the system of congresses of workers and staff, and to improve the organization of leadership and control of production technology and management headed by the factory director.

With regard to the consolidation of enterprises, to implement and perfect the system of economic responsibility in a planned and orderly way it is first necessary to define the economic responsibility of the enterprise to the state and of the workers and staff to the enterprise; at the same time the enterprise should be granted a measure of economic authority, and the enterprise and workers and staff should be given due economic benefits, so as to combine responsibility, authority and benefit, bring into play the initiative of the enterprise and of the workers and staff, improve enterprise management, perfect business accounting within the factory and raise production. The enforcement of the system of economic responsibility can effectively solve the grave production of egalitarianism with "everybody sharing food from the same big pot," which now exists among enterprises and among the workers and staff in individual enterprises; thus both the enterprise and its workers and staff will be motivated to run the enterprise well and tap its potential. This is a key to the successful running of socialist enterprises. We must fully understanding the profound, far-reaching significance of this system and, in the course of steadily implementing it, strive to work out different forms of the system to suit the different trades and enterprises. Two things are to be avoided -- rushing headlong into mass action and imposing uniformity on all enterprises. When implementing the responsibility system, it is necessary to set advanced average quotas, improve the quality of products, lower costs, accelerate the turnover of circulating funds and turn out readily marketable goods, and arbitrary raising of prices in violation of state discipline should not be allowed. Effective measures must be taken to exercise closer supervision over the enterprise and to formulate regulations and methods for applying them to accounting, wages and salaries, bonuses and welfare. In distributing surplus revenue, we must uphold the principle that the state should receive the largest share first and that the enterprise should retain a major part of the rest. In no case should the rate of growth of the portion of profits retained by the enterprise exceed the rate of growth either of production or of the overall profit. It is imperative to be firm in stopping dishonest practices that impair the interests of the state and the people. All this, if accompanied by effective ideological and political work, will help the enterprise and its workers and staff to realize clearly where their fundamental interest lie, guiding them in the right direction and heightening their enthusiasm for better operation and management and achieving better economic results.

We should carry out the consolidation of enterprises step by step, taking into account the experiences gained in selected enterprises and their popularization in other enterprises, and try to complete it by groups in two or three years. For the first group, about 300 enterprises of special importance to the national economy are to be selected; it will take six months or a little longer to accomplish their consolidation. After this experience has been summed up, other enterprises will be consolidated, group by group. In principle, the task of consolidation should be carried out under the leadership of the Party organization within the enterprise. To assist in this task, leading comrades in all industrial ministries and departments under the State Council and those in charge of industry in the provinces, municipalities and autonomous regions as well as those in the departments concerned at all levels should head groups of cadres going down to the grassroots units for study and investigation and the summing up of experience. Departments at all level should draw up plans, organize their implementation and provide better guidance so as to ensure practical results in the process of consolidation. We must guard against just going through the motions and reducing consolidation to a formality. While carrying on the consolidation of enterprises, we must also consolidate and strengthen the work of departments in charge of them.

The consolidation of an enterprise should go hand in hand with its readjustment and restructuring. First of all, with regard to enterprises whose products are in excess supply and of very poor quality and whose consumption of energy and raw and semi-finished materials is too high, or which have incurred losses over the years and cause serious pollution, we should unhesitatingly apply the policy of shutting them down, or suspending their operation, or amalgamating them with other enterprises, or switching them to the manufacture of other products, on the merits of each case. The state will then be able to allocate its limited amount of energy and raw and semi-finished materials to enterprises which can turn out fine quality products with low consumption rates and better economic results. The number of small iron plants run by prefectures and counties throughout the country has been cut from 466 to 276, and the latter have improved their management. As a result, the coke ratio in iron smelting has fallen from 950 kg to 705 kg per ton, the cost of pig iron from 303 yuan to 243 yuan and the total loss incurred by these plants from 630 million yuan to 100 million yuan. This shows that the proper application of the policy of "shutting down, suspension, amalgamation or switching" is of substantial economic significance. The State Council has already instructed the departments concerned to set appropriate requirements for the operation of factories belonging to different industries and turning out different products, and the minimum requirements for batch production, quality and material consumption. Factories and enterprises that fail to meet these requirements within a certain time limit must either suspend production pending consolidation, or close down. In energy-deficient areas in eastern and northeastern China, strict restrictions must be placed on products whose manufacture consumes a lot of energy, and their production should as far as possible be transferred to areas where energy supply is relatively sufficient so as to help ensure a regional balance between energy supply and demand. All localities and departments concerned should adopt an overall point of view, taking the interests of the whole into consideration and subordinating the interests of the part to those of the whole; they should ensure that state property is protected during the implementation of the policy of "shutting down, suspension, amalgamation or switching," and they should make suitable arrangements for political study, vocational training and labor for the workers and staff in enterprises that suspend production. To conduct the political and vocational training of the workers and staff during the time left open when production is suspended wholly or partly is a way of developing our intellectual resources at very low cost but to very good effect. Now that the workers and staff in enterprises operating at full capacity are devoting whatever time is available to study, it is all the more incumbent upon those in the enterprises operating very much under capacity, and especially in enterprises that shut down or suspend operations, to make use of the valuable time gained for study. Such study will, in fact, expand our production potential and pave the way for future development.

6. Raise more construction funds and use them thriftily through improved methods of acquisition, accumulation and spending. Financial difficulties and lack of funds are a serious problem in our present task of economic construction. The fundamental solution is to adopt correct policies which will arouse the initiative of all the workers and staff, all enterprises and all local authorities so that they will work hard to increase production, practice economy, oppose waste and achieve better economic results. This is the correct way to "make a fortune," so to speak. Great possibilities for increasing revenue and cutting expenditures remain to be tapped in the various spheres of the economy. On the current scale of production, if all industrial enterprises cut down the cost production by 1 percent, they can add 2 billion yuan to the state's annual revenues. Our circulating funds have far surpassed what is needed. Faster turnover -- reducing it by say 2-3 percent -- will mean the saving of 7 to 10 billion yuan. The building cycles for many large and medium-sized projects are rather long; efforts to shorten them will considerably reduce expenditures on builders' wages, and earlier completion and commissioning will enable these projects to provide the state with more profits and taxes. If only we try hard, we can surely translate the objective possibilities for increasing revenues and reducing expenditures into realities. It will thus become possible not only to maintain a basic balance between revenues and expenditures but also to raise more funds for production and construction.

The first task of all economic departments is to try by every means to increase production and revenue and add to the wealth of society. This is the basis for the solution of our financial problems. With growing production and more social wealth, the state will have abundant financial resources. The financial departments should do their best to help the economic departments to increase production and income, and at the same time efficiently perform their supervisory functions by ensuring the rational use of funds and preventing waste. The economic departments for their part should closely cooperate with the financial departments in the effective accumulation and use of funds. In addition to collecting taxes and profits from various production units that should be collected, governments at all levels should find more ways and try harder to aid and develop production so as to increase revenue. We must not, on account of financial difficulties, abandon reforms that not only help release the initiative of local authorities, enterprises and workers and staff members but also contribute to the overall interest. Otherwise we will block the channels for increasing production and revenue and thus aggravate problems of finance.

With the widespread increase in income, appropriate measures should be taken in financial, taxation and other respects to ensure a basic balance between revenues and expenditures. Taxation and customs must be strengthened, taxes should be restored on certain items and imposed on others, the state monopoly on sales of tobacco and alcoholic drinks should be maintained and every form of tax evasion checked, so that the state can collect all funds that should be collected and concentrate all funds that should be concentrated. Besides, it is necessary to use a determinate part of the deposits of local authorities, enterprises and individuals as funds for construction and to do this through bank credit in a planned way. We can thus not only turn a considerable proportion of idle funds and consumption funds into construction funds but also partly mitigate the contradiction between growing purchasing power and the supply of commodities, thus reducing pressure on the market. This will benefit both the depositors and the state. The method of replacing financial allocations for many capital construction projects by bank loans has proved fruitful, and its application should be actively extended. Other measures such as issuing bonds and conducting insurance and trust operations may be adopted to raise funds. At the same time, we should keep fund raising under control and guard against credit inflation. The role of banks in the accumulation, transfer and unified control of credit funds should be strengthened.

With the growing briskness of the economy and the greater financial powers of the local authorities and enterprises, more and more extra-budgetary funds have become available. At present, they are equal to half our budgetary revenues and so can play a very important role when combined with budgetary funds and used rationally according to plan and under overall arrangements. Many projects can be financed by extra-budgetary funds, which means reducing the state's burdens. From now on, the central authorities should gradually diminish the scope of their financial investments and concentrate them on energy, transport and new industries. Projects involving short investment cycles and yielding fairly large profits as well as urban construction projects should be financed as far a possible by local authorities or by enterprises. At the same time, measures to strengthen financial supervision should be taken and strict discipline enforced. Effective protection should be given to the legitimate interests of enterprises, departments and local authorities, while strictly preventing them from making unlawful gains.

In short, it is possible to overcome our financial difficulties and there are enormous potentialities for increasing production and economizing on expenditures. Everything depends on our own efforts. Take the city of Fushun, which is mainly engaged in heavy industry. Owning to economic readjustment, many of its enterprises are very short of orders this year and their output has dropped. From the conventional point of view, this should have led to a fall in their profits and income, and nothing would have been more "natural." But the comrades in Fushun's financial and economic departments took a different view. Mobilizing the masses in every possible way to tap potential, they worked out and successfully implemented thirty measures to prevent a reduction in income despite lowered production. A fair number of enterprises elsewhere have also succeeded in increasing both production and income, or in cutting down expenditures and increasing income. All comrades in our financial and economic departments should follow the example of Fushun, study the new conditions and problems confronting them and explore new ways to solve financial problems. People in all trades, from top to bottom, must perfect ways to acquire, accumulate and use funds. If they stick to conventional ways of doing things, they will see their path "barred by hills and streams," but if they use new methods in the light of the new circumstances, they will find themselves on a path "shaded by willows and radiant with flowers," as the saying goes.

7. Persist in an open-door policy and enhance our capacity for self-reliant action. No longer subjected to blockades, China has established economic and trade contacts with 174 countries and regions. This is a very favorable condition for our modernization programme. Expansion of exchange is a basic feature of large-scale socialized production, and it has extended from internal trade in China to trade with the world at large. By linking our country with the world market, expanding foreign trade, importing advanced technology, utilizing foreign capital and entering into different forms of international economic and technological co-operation, we can use our strong points to make up for our weak points through international exchange on the basis of equality and mutual benefit. Far from impairing our capacity for self-reliant action, this will only serve to enhance it. In economic work, we must abandon once for all the idea of self-sufficiency, which is a characteristic of the natural economy. All ideas and actions based on keeping our door closed to the outside world and sticking to conventions are wrong, and so are ideas and actions based on relying solely on other countries and having blind faith in them.

As we still lack experience in pursuing an open-door policy and carrying out economic and technological exchanges with other countries, we must really strive to learn. We should use our domestic resources in the first place and international resources in the second; we should develop our domestic market in the first place and our role in the world market in the second; and we should master two skills, that of domestic economic management and that of foreign trade and economic exchange.

Greater exports are the key to the expansion of foreign trade. We should boldly enter the world market and strive to maintain a rate of increase of exports higher than the rate of growth of the Chinese economy. Basing ourselves on our own conditions and on demand in the world market, we should make full use of our rich natural resources and increase the export of minerals, farm and sideline products and local specialists. We should make full use of our fine traditional skills and techniques and increase the export of arts and crafts articles, traditional textiles and other light industrial products. We should make full use of our abundant labor power to process materials for foreign businessmen. And we should make full use of our existing industrial bases and increase our exports of mechanical and electrical products and processed nonferrous or rare metals. In the case of some products, imports may be utilized to serve the expansion of exports. Putting China's products to the test of competition in the world market will spur us to improve management, increase variety, raise quality, lower production costs and achieve better economic results.

Over the last few years there have been successes as well as failures in our imports of technology and equipment, and a summing-up is called for. We should oppose indecision and excessive causation on the one hand, and credulity and making hasty promises on the other. From now on, China should mainly import technology and single machines or key equipment which cannot be produced domestically. We should not import complete sets of equipment every time and must avoid duplicating imports. We should not import equipment without knowhow or fail to assimilate the imported technology and to popularize what we have learnt from it.

To speed up our economic construction, it is definitely necessary to utilize as much foreign capital as possible, and first of all to utilize low interest loans and loans offered on relatively favoururable terms. Here we must guard against rashness, make meticulous feasibility studies and bear economic results in mind. In the final analysis, the amount of foreign capital we can utilize is not determined by our subjective desires but by what we can do at home, that is, mainly by our ability to repay, to provide the necessary accessories and to assimilate advanced technology. The long-term loans at low interest that may be available in the near future should be used chiefly on such infrastructural projects as the development of energy and transport. Small and medium-sized enterprises turning out products much in demand on the domestic and world markets should have more access to foreign capital and to imported technology. They are very numerous, and most of them will be able speedily to raise the quantity and quality of their products if only they can import some appropriate key techniques and equipment without spending too much. Moreover, they can repay the money fairly quickly. Such use of foreign capital is favorable to the growth of production in China.

Ours is a sovereign socialist state. In accordance with the principle of equality and mutual benefit, foreigners are welcome to invest in China and launch joint ventures in opening up mines and running factories or other undertakings, but they must respect China's sovereignty and abide by her laws, policies and decrees. We have set up experimental special economic zones in Shenzhen, Zhuhai and Shantou in Guangdong Province and Xiamen in Fujian Province; our experience in this sphere should be summed up in good time. These zones should boldly introduce advanced technology and methods of management from abroad and make use of foreign capital. Our aim is to promote China's socialist modernization; we should adhere to the characteristics of the socialist system in our work in the special zones, and the workers, staff and other inhabitants should be imbued with socialist morality.

To expand economic and technology exchanges with foreign counties, we must make full use of the coastal areas, and especially the coastal cities. Shanghai, Tianjin, Guangzhou, Dalian, Qingdao, Fuzhou and Xiamen among other cities, should make a bigger contribution in this regard. We should lose no time in using different ways to train large numbers of specialists, technical personnel and sales agents for our foreign trade and other external economic affairs. They should become familiar with the world market and with economic and technological developments abroad, and so constitute an effective network of information on world business and a marketing network which provides, among other things, servicing for the articles sold. We should continue to gradually reform the existing system of managing our foreign trade and other foreign economic relations, persisting in overall arrangements by the state and unified action in dealing with other countries and at the same time arousing the initiative of the local authorities, departments and enterprises.

In short, it is our firm principle to follow an open-door policy and further economic and technological exchanges with other countries. We need international co-operation in our drive for modernization. Far-sighted personages in political and economic circles abroad understand the enormous potentialities of the Chinese market and its far-reaching significance for the steady development of the world economy. We should take stock of the current situation and work hard to expand and strengthen our contacts and co-operation with all those willing to have economic and technological exchanges with us on the basis of mutual benefit.

8. Actively and steadily reform our economic system and realize the initiative of all concerned to the full. The chief weaknesses of our previous economic structure were over- concentration of power and failure to separate the functions of the government from those of the enterprises in matters of management: another weakness was egalitarianism in distribution, with "everybody sharing food from the same big pot." In recent years, we have introduced certain reforms in agriculture, industry, finance and trade affecting the forms of ownership, planning, management and distribution. These reforms, carried out in accordance with the requirement that they serve, promote and conform with economic readjustment, have been markedly successful in mobilizing the enthusiasm of all concerned, reinvigorating the economy and advancing production. Nevertheless, they are still partial and exploratory in nature, and our work here has suffered from certain incongruities and from lack of co-ordination. The task before us is to sum up our experience in these reforms and, after careful investigation and study and repeated scientific confirmations, to draw up as soon as possible an overall plan for restructuring the economy and carry it out step by step.

The state economy and the collective economy are the basic forms of the Chinese economy. The individual economy of working people, operating within certain prescribed limits, is a necessary complement to the public economy. The vigorous development of socialist commodity production and commodity exchange in China is a necessity. The basic orientation of the structural reform of our economy should be as follows: while upholding the planned socialist economy, give scope to the supplementary role of regulation through the market and fully take into account and utilize the law of value when working out state plans; strengthen unified leadership by the state over economic activities of overall importance to the economy and the people's living standards, give different enterprises different degrees of decision-making power in their economic activities and at the same time extend the democratic rights of the workers and staff in the management of their enterprise; and change over from economic management relying solely on administrative measures to management combining economic with administrative measures and utilizing laws and regulations as well as economic levers in running the economy. In keeping with this basic orientation, we advance the following tentative ideas regarding the reform of our economic system: Gradually separate the functions of government from those of the enterprises, which should be given greater power of decision so as to make them relatively independent socialist economic units; break down the strong barriers between different localities and departments and, in accordance with the needs of co-ordination among specialized departments and of production, develop economic integration in various forms to organize the enterprises more rationally and, concurrently, establish trade associations to serve them: change over from the closed commodity circulation system with few channels but too many levels of management to an open and many-channelled system with as few levels as possible; and establish different kinds of economic centres and rationally managed economic networks by relying on big and medium-sized cities. In co-ordination with these measures, a series of reforms should be initiated in planning, statistics, finance, taxation, pricing, banking, commerce, distribution of material resources, foreign trade, labor use and the wage system.

A key problem in the reforms is the correct understanding and handling of the relations between planned economy on the one hand and regulation through the market on the other. As far back as 1956, after the basic completion of the socialist transformation of the private ownership of the means of production, Comrade Chen Yun said: "Planned production constitutes the bulk of our industrial and agricultural production, and it is complemented by free production conducted according to varied market conditions and within the limits allowed by the state plan." Comrade Chen Yun's comment is still of immediate significance in guiding our current reforms. We are of the opinion that different methods of management can be adopted for different enterprises in accordance with their importance to the national economy and the people's living standards, their different forms of ownership and the different roles, varieties and specifications of their products. Generally speaking, there are four types of enterprises and products: first type -- production is organized under state plans which are mandatory in nature. This concerns enterprises in the key branches of the economy or products vital to the economy and the people's living standards; their output value constitutes the greater part of the total output value of industry and agriculture, but the variety of their products is not large. Second type -- production is organized according to changing market conditions and within the limits permitted by the state plan; this covers miscellaneous small commodities turned out separately by numerous small enterprises or individual producers, for which it is inconvenient or impossible to enforce unified planning and management. The output value of this category accounts for only a fraction of the total output value of industry and agriculture. There are two other types between these two. In one, the major part of production comes under state planning with the rest organized by the enterprises' own decisions; on the whole, this type is generally similar to the first, but with certain differences. In the other, a principal part of production is organized by the enterprises according to changing market conditions, with the remainder coming under state planning; this type is very much like the second, though there are also certain differences between them. This entire system of management differs from our previous system of rigid control and differs still more from the capitalist market economy. Combining unified and centralized leadership of the state with the enterprises' initiative, it ensures flexible control and orderly and lively activity with better economic results and enables us to organize and develop production according to the needs of society.

Through the structural reform of the economy it is necessary to make better use of pricing, taxation and credit as economic levers, to curtail the production of goods in excessive supply and increase the production of those in short supply, to advance the reorganization of industry, readjust the levels of profit for the enterprises, impel them to improve operations and management and increase state revenue. Moreover, it is imperative to intensify work on economic legislation and give play to the guiding and supervisory roles of industrial and commercial administrations, statistics, finance, banking, etc., so that the economic activities of the enterprises will contribute to the development of the economy as a whole.

As a significant change in the system and methods of economic management, the structural reform of the economy involves a major readjustment of the economic rights and interests of the relevant parties. Both in theory and in practice, it involves many problems calling for study and solution. As we lack experience here, we should take an active attitude but steady steps. Every reform needs to be preceded by sober investigation and study, feasibility analysis and well-conceived planning, and should be popularized step by step through experiment. We should continue our probing and sum up our experience from time to time so as to advance steadily in the accomplishment of this important historical mission.

9. Raise the scientific and cultural level of all working people, and organize strong forces to tackle key scientific research projects. We must train large numbers of specialists of all grades in all lines and large numbers of competent workers for our modernization programme. This is of paramount importance. China is still rather backward in education and science, whose development thus lags behind that of the various sectors of the economy. Unless we solve this problem, we shall fail in our drive for modernization.

Our basic policy in education is clear-cut: it aims to enable those who receive an education to develop morally, intellectually and physically and become workers with both socialist consciousness and culture and become both red and expert, and to persist in the integration of mental with manual labor and of the intellectuals with the workers and peasants. The immediate task is to go a step further in implementing this policy in the light of the specific conditions of our modernization programme. Higher education must be vigorously and steadily expanded, while paying special attention to raising its quality. On the basis of painstaking investigation and study, necessary readjustments and reforms should be made with regard to the specialties offered, the system of leadership, teaching methods and the content of instruction. In addition to regular universities and colleges, spare-time, television and correspondence universities should be actively developed so as to encourage people to become educated by teaching themselves. In secondary education, the situation in which vocational schools are markedly outnumbered by general schools must be gradually changed, specialized secondary schools be increased, and large numbers of skilled workers and intermediate specialized personnel be trained to facilitate employment and raise the cultural, technical, political and ideological levels of workers and staff. At the same time, we must pay attention to the physical and mental health of the students as well as to their scholastic progress and move away from the one-sided drive to get bigger percentages of students into higher education. Recently our fellow deputy Ye Shengtao wrote an article entitled, "I Appeal," criticizing the secondary schools and some of the primary schools too for their current error of unduly stressing increased rates of admission into higher schools. Sincere and to the point the article speaks the mind of the students, their parents and teachers and other sections of the people. We hope that all those concerned will pay due attention to this problem and solve it. In primary education, too, measures should be taken to lighten the burden of the pupils so as to ensure their sound development -- physical, intellectual and moral. Schools, families and society should co-ordinate their efforts in the ideological and political education of the students. Schools at all levels must stress the teaching of Chinese history and geography, which forms a significant part of the students' education in legal matters and arrange relevant courses. Moreover, we must train large numbers of competent teachers for pre-school education, so that more pre-school children will be able to enter kindergartens and receive education suited to their physical and mental characteristics.

We must conscientiously carry out the Decision on Strengthening Education Among Workers and Staff adopted by the Central Committee of the Party and the State Council, and do it more effectively. Here I would like to speak about the education of peasants in particular. This is an important and difficult task which should be put on the agenda right away. Governments at all levels should accomplish it successfully. Evening schools, winter classes and other forms of schooling traditionally welcomed by the peasants should be popularized, but they cannot take the place of regular primary and middle schools. Having recognized the importance of acquiring scientific and general knowledge, the peasants are now keen on such studies, but at the same time some are reluctant to send their children to school because they need them in auxiliary labor. Governments at all levels should try to persuade the peasants to handle the relations between their immediate and long-term interests properly, subordinating the former to the latter.

Our basic policy for scientific and technological development is equally clear-cut. Science and technology, with their numerous branches, should serve all aspects of human life. There must be no weakening of basic research, but the stress in the development of science and technology as a whole should be on serving economic construction and, in particular, on the solution of key problems in the economy involving major economic benefits. Our present task is to employ science and technology more efficiently so that they will be a powerful productive force, a great stimulus to economic development.

To place science and technology fully at the service of the economy, it is now most necessary to apply and spread the results we have obtained in scientific and technological research. In recent years, we have accomplished much in such research and also imported a good deal of advanced technology. Drawing on these assets and making wider use of them can yield enormous results if we do it in time. We should strive to apply the results of scientific and technological research in laboratories to production, apply those gained in the national defence industry to production for both defence and civilian purposes, and apply those gained in the coastal areas to production in the hinterland, as well as assimilate foreign experience for use in China. In the past year or so, several research and designing institutions have organized various forms of association with production units and worked out new methods and systems, such as the contracting system, compensated transfers of technology, technical services, output-related responsibility in agro-technical service, and advisory agro-technical contracts. All this has helped research and designing institutions to be directly oriented towards production and to cater to the needs of increasing production; at the same time, it has provided a motive for the popularization of science and technology. It is thus highly beneficial to the development of the economy and of science and technology themselves.

Generally speaking, our science and technology are still rather backward, but they are by no means backward in every respect. For in certain fields we have already attained a fairly high level and a considerable scale in terms of size of research staff, experimental facilities, and results of research. We should in no case underestimate ourselves. To meet the fairly long-term needs of our developing economy, it is now necessary to set before all leading scientific and technological departments, all research institutions and all scientific and technological personnel the task of tackling key problems in science and technology by pooling their efforts and strengthening their co-operation. After repeated studies and confirmation by the departments and specialists concerned, we will select a number of research projects of major national economic significance and organize the efforts of all concerned to effect a breakthrough. These projects include techniques for increasing farm yields such as seed and soil improvement, water and soil conservation, plant protection and manufacture of new varieties of farm chemicals; techniques of processing and storing foodstuff, and of keeping it fresh for a long time; finishing techniques for textiles; techniques for the conservation and better utilization of energy; techniques for the multi-purpose use of coal and petroleum, techniques for the comprehensive exploitation and utilization of nonferrous metals; and research on new materials, new technologies, new equipment and new products which are of key importance to China's economic growth. Work on the above projects is important and necessary for the accelerated development of our national economy. We hope that all concerned will give it adequate attention. Our achievements in science and technology are already at the point where we can conquer a number of difficult problems. We are convinced that our scientific and technological personnel have both the will and the ability to make a breakthrough in these major projects.

10. Proceed from the concept of everything for the people and make overall arrangements for production, construction and the people's livelihood. The fundamental purpose of socialist revolution and construction is continuously to raise the productive forces in order to meet the growing material and cultural needs of the people step by step. In the final analysis, our economic construction is aimed at resolving the contradiction between the growing material and cultural needs of the people and our still backward productive forces.

For a rather long period in the past we one-sidedly stressed capital construction to the neglect of improvements in the people's standard of living. And in capital construction, we one-sidedly stressed expanding heavy industry to the neglect of the consumer goods industry, housing and urban public utilities. This led to poor economic results, and the people's standard of living could not be improved to the extent that it should have been. Beginning from the Third Plenary Session of the Eleventh Central Committee of the Party held in December 1978, we have further summed up our experiences, resolutely corrected this deviation and have done our best to improve the people's standard of living, significantly raising the real income and the level of consumption of the overwhelming majority of the people in town and country. The state will continue to make appropriate readjustments in the relationship between the economic interests of the state, the collective and the individual, eliminate irrationalities in the wage and bonus system, and build more houses for workers and staff and more urban public utilities, schools and hospitals. To give top priority to the people's interests and, first and foremost, to satisfy their basic everyday needs in handling the relationship between production and construction and the living conditions of the people-- henceforth this is the principle to which we must firmly adhere.

However, improvement in the people's standard of living must be based on the growth of production. As production can only grow gradually, the standard of living can likewise only be improved gradually, and we cannot go too fast. Both theory and practice have proved that improvements in the people's standard of living cannot run ahead of the growth of production and the increase in labor productivity, that the increase in the people's purchasing power must be commensurate with that in the supply of consumer goods and that the portion of the national income going for accumulation must increase at a certain rate and proportion. All these are objective economic laws. If they are violated, if attention is paid only to improving the people's livelihood today and not to production and construction and if we are too demanding or hasty in our expectations of a higher standard of living, the long-term fundamental interests of the country and people are bound to suffer. The present practice of handing out bonuses indiscriminately must be sternly checked. Investigations must be made to establish the responsibility of those engaged in such unlawful practices as seeking self-interest at the public expense and damaging the interests of the state to benefit one's own unit. Leading cadres in some enterprises and other units damage the interests of the state in various ways in order to accommodate to the demands of certain individuals who give no heed to the overall public interest. This is absolutely impermissible.

To ensure the gradual raising of the people's standard of living, we must unswervingly persist in our effort to control population growth. There are two possibilities here: either to control population growth strictly and effectively so that the living standards of the entire people can improve step by step and national construction can expand year by year, or to fail to enforce strict and effective control, allowing the population to grow substantially, in which case the people's standard of living cannot be raised and economic, cultural and defence construction cannot be carried out successfully. Either one or the other. Rigorous enforcement of family planning and strict control of population growth is a long-term strategic task. The stress in family planning should be on the rural area which have more than 80 percent of the population. Since the introduction of various forms of the responsibility system for agricultural production, the existing measures for control over population growth have not been able to cope with the new situation, and an upturn in the birth rate has been reported in some places. We must not allow this situation to develop unchecked. Governments at all levels must strengthen their leadership over family planning work, steadily raise the consciousness of the masses with regard to it through painstaking and meticulous publicity and education, and constantly promote scientific research to improve family planning techniques. The measures taken in many areas to reward couples who limit themselves to a single child and to restrict the practice of having two or more children, should be continued. Meanwhile, all acts violating law and discipline in the enforcement of such measures must be firmly opposed and prevented. It is our policy to control population growth while raising the quality of the population. For the interests of the people and the future of the nation, we call on people throughout the country to strive unremittingly to achieve the goal of keeping China's population within 1,200 million by the end of this century.

Fellow deputies,

Ours is a unified multinational country. Our 10 principles for economic construction are, in general, all applicable to the minority nationality areas. But they should be implemented with due consideration to specific local characteristics and conditions. Since the liberation of the entire country, much progress has been made in agriculture, animal husbandry, industry, transport, education, science, culture and public health service in the minority nationality areas, where the material and cultural life of the people has sharply improved. In particular, we reaffirmed last year that the right of the minority nationalities to regional autonomy must be respected and that the national autonomous areas should be allowed to adopt specific policies suited to their economic conditions and national characteristics. This policy has led to favorable results in the economic development of the minority nationality areas and should be persevered in. The state should render the necessary financial, material and technical aid to these areas in order to help the minority nationalities increase production, achieve prosperity, raise their cultural level and enjoy a higher standard of living. It has been the consistent policy of our Party and government to carry out among the people and cadres of all nationality policy, develop and improve socialist relations between the various nationalities, promote their unity and mutual assistance, treat them all as equals, and help develop the economy and culture in the minority areas. This policy must be unwaveringly implemented at all times and under all circumstances.

The ten principles for economic construction proposed by the State Council touch on a wide range of questions. What I would like to stress is that only today and not before has it become at all possible to put them forward fairly concretely and systematically, because before we lacked the necessary practice and because the various problems arising from the development of our economy and their interrelations had not yet revealed themselves as clearly as now, and as a consequence people could not then gain the necessary understanding and arrive at the necessary judgments and conclusions. Not long ago, the Central Committee of the Party accomplished the historic task of making an overall assessment of the Party's history since the founding of the People's Republic. This has enabled us to make a better review of our successes and failures in economic construction, re-evaluate our gains and losses and put forward the principles and policies which I have discussed above. The Resolution on Certain Questions in the History of Our Party Since the Founding of the People's Republic of China made a scientific analysis of Mao Zedong Thought and clearly separated it from Comrade Mao Zedong's mistakes in his later years, thus re-establishing the true nature of Mao Zedong Thought. The theories of Mao Zedong Thought concerning socialist construction and the stand, viewpoint and method running through the whole of Mao Zedong Thought have consequently become more powerful instruments than ever for studying our country's economic problems. Our fellow deputies can see that the principles for economic construction proposed by the State Council are guided by Mao Zedong Thought, which integrates the universal truth of Marxism-Leninism with the concrete practice of China's revolution and construction. It is from Mao Zedong Thought that they derive their basic spirit and ideas. After these 10 principles have been discussed, amended and adopted at this session, they will be repeatedly tested in practice in all fields so that they can be continually supplemented and revised and become better suited to the realities of our country.

III. Prospects for China's Economic Development

While endeavouring to accomplish the economic tasks before it, the State Council is still drafting the Sixth Five-Year Plan for the development of the national economy. This plan will have significant change in both its guiding ideas and its concrete arrangements, so that it will fully embody the prerequisites for the further carrying out of the policy of readjustment, restructuring, consolidation and improvement of the economy, provide a new approach to national economic development and also embody the ten principles expounded above, and especially their central idea of achieving better economic results. We began studying the plan's basic outlines and principal targets last year. But as we were pre-occupied with further economic readjustments and wished to work out the plan more carefully, we have not yet completed the draft. The State Council will submit the draft plan when it is ready to the National People's Congress for examination and approval. In this report, I can only deal with some of the salient points of the plan now being drawn up.

The primary goal of the Sixth Five-Year Plan is to strive for a fundamental improvement in China's economic and financial situation. In the course of the plan, the rate of growth of the national income should equal or approach the rate of growth of the total output value of industry and agriculture. And with regard to the distribution of the national income, the ratio of the accumulation fund should be reasonably reduced while that of the consumption fund should be appropriately increased in order to raise the people's standard of living. During the plan period, our main efforts should be concentrated on readjusting the economic structure, consolidating existing enterprises and carrying out the technical transformation of key enterprises. We will thus accumulate the strength and lay a more solid foundation for the further technical transformation of existing industry and transport during the Seventh Five-Year Plan.

We need five years or more to make further readjustments not only in the relationships between the different sectors of the national economy and within the individual sectors, but also in the setup of production, the product mix, the technological makeup, the line-up of enterprises, and the organizational structure, so as to gradually rationalize them along with the gradual, overall reform of the various forms of the system of economic management. The tasks of readjustment, restructuring, consolidation and improvement of the economy will be extremely strenuous in the plan period, and such parts of the infrastructure as energy and transport will still be in the process of renovation and construction. Therefore it will be impossible for our economy to grow very rapidly during the Sixth Five-Year Plan. Of course this does not mean that we will not strive for a suitable rate of growth. But it must be a steady and realistic rate, which we can attain if we try. In other words, it must guarantee better economic results and enable the economy to accumulate strength, so laying a solid foundation for future development.

If in the plan period we can lay this solid foundation, eliminate existing defects in the economy and establish proper ratios between its sectors and harmonious relations between all its parts, we shall be able to accelerate the development of the economy on the new foundation, a development which will gather more and more momentum. We can then expect more rapid development during the Seventh Five-Year Plan, and still more rapid development in the following decade. That is to say, we shall most probably enter a new period of economic renewal in the last decade of the century. After this period of renewal begins, our economy should not only develop at a good rate, but also yield impressive practical results. The standard of living of our people should rise considerably and our education, science, technology, culture and national defence should reach a new level. Under the correct leadership of the Chinese Communist Party, we must mobilize and organize all our people to try to double and redouble China's total industrial and agricultural output value in twenty years through enhanced enthusiasm, concerted effort, arduous struggle and thrift in order to raise the level of consumption and enable the people to achieve a relatively comfortable standard of living. By that time, our economy should be in a position to take off from a new starting point, from which it will be able to advance more swiftly and catch up with the economically more developed countries.

There are good grounds for the optimistic view we have expressed on the prospects for our country's economic development.

We have already shifted the focus of all our work to socialist modernization and will unshakably persist in this orientation. The guideline for our economic work has been rectified. We have accumulated a valuable store of experience in construction, which will be further enriched and expanded in practice. We have build up a fairly extensive material and technical base which will play a bigger and bigger role. Moreover, present international conditions are favorable for our economic construction. Of course, there are also a number of adverse conditions which will inevitably affect and hinder our economic development. But, after all, they are only temporary and can be overcome, while the favorable factors are basic and enduring.

Ours is a developing country. Our rich resources are far from being well exploited and utilized. Our economic level is still rather low, and managerial, scientific and technological levels are still backward. These are undoubtedly weaknesses we should face up to. Nevertheless, these very weaknesses reveal our country's vast potential. Not only do we have our own positive and negative experience to draw on, we can also refer to and employ the advanced technological and managerial experience of other countries. There is no need to start from scratch in everything and risk following others' detours. Therefore, provided we have the correct approach, from a long-term point of view our economy will develop at a fairly quick pace.

Ours is not only a developing country, it is also a socialist country. We have achieved the public ownership of the means of production and abolished the system of exploitation of man by man. That portion of the social wealth formerly appropriated by the exploiters has reverted wholly to the people, and the growth and distribution of the entire social wealth can therefore be effected rationally and in a planned way. In this lies the fundamental superiority of the socialist system. Because of long-standing "Left" errors in the guideline for our economic work in the past and of certain defects in economic management, neither the intrinsic superiority of the socialist system nor the initiative and creativeness of the workers, peasants and intellectuals have been given full scope. The overall restructuring of the economy, the application of the system of responsibility in agricultural production, the system of economic responsibility in industry and other measures will play an important role in fully realizing the intrinsic superiority of our socialist system and in further liberating the productive forces.

With regard to the prospects for our economic development, we have to guard against two erroneous tendencies. One is pessimism about the modernization programme, stemming from failure to see the favorable conditions and consequent lack of confidence in the future. The other is the unrealistic expectation of quick results stemming from failure to see existing difficulties and the extreme arduousness and complexity of our tasks. Strategically, we must think in terms of a long period of time for construction. We must seek truth from facts, emphasize practical results, act according to our capacity and work with all our energy in order gradually and systematically to attain the magnificent goal of modernizing our agriculture, industry, national defence and science and technology.

Fellow deputies,

Next year, 1982, will be the second year of the Sixth Five-Year Plan and also the second year in the further readjustment of the economy. In order to realize our bright prospects in economic development, we must go all out and work conscientiously to achieve successes in our present work. Next year's main economic tasks are to consolidate our achievements in stabilizing the economy, continue to maintain the basic balance between revenues and expenditures in finance and credit and the basic stability of prices, and strive for better economic results, which will allow the national economy to develop a little faster than this year. The plan set for 1982 requires us to increase total agricultural and industrial output value by 4 percent instead of by 3 percent as expected while implementing the plan. Also planned is an increase in the national income of about 4 percent as compared with this year. This requires another substantial expansion in agriculture and the textile and other light industries in 1982, and in addition an increase in heavy industrial production as opposed to the decrease in 1981. With regard to the distribution of the national income, our target is to increase consumption by 5.7 percent and the total volume of retail sales by 8 percent, while accumulation is to increase by 3.2 percent and direct investments under the state budget by 5.7 percent. Expenditures for education, science, culture, public health and physical culture should increase by 5.9 percent. The collectively owned sector and the necessary individual economy of working people should be actively promoted, and various means should be adopted to provide proper employment for persons in urban areas who are waiting for jobs. The standard of living of both the urban and rural people should continue to improve. Strenuous efforts must be made to carry out the all-round consolidation of enterprises next year. Those which turn out low-quality products with high energy consumption or have long been operating at a loss must be shut down, or suspend operation, or be amalgamated with other enterprises or switch to the manufacture of other products. In order to fulfil the 1982 plan, we should do our utmost to gain better economic results and strive for noteworthy achievements in all fields, such as agricultural and industrial production, transport, capital construction, commodity circulation, finance and banking. The Draft Outline of the 1982 Plan for Economic and Social Development has been submitted to the session for discussion. I would like to suggest that the session approve it in principle. After revising it in accordance with the opinions of the deputies, the State Council will submit it to the Standing Committee of the National People's Congress for examination and approval.

Fellow deputies,

In the work of socialist modernization, we must strive for a high level of both material and cultural development. The two are inseparable. Only by so doing can we ensure the sustained growth of the national economy and the socialist orientation of material development.

Cultural development covers a wide area, but it must have as its main content the following two aspects: one is the scope and level of development of education, science, culture, art, public health and physical culture. This is an indicator of a society's level and degree of civilization. Every society develops this aspect of cultural life to suit its needs, but the socialist system demands its wider and faster development. We must tap our intellectual resources and increase intellectual investment so that a correspondence is achieved between such investment and investment in production and construction, and the requirements of economic development are consequently met. The other aspect is the orientation and level of the political, ideological and moral development of society. This is determined by the nature of the social system and, in turn, strongly reacts on the latter. Owing to complex historical and practical reasons, this problem is becoming more and more pronounced and requires immediate solution. Through effective publicity and education, political and ideological work, and work in other fields, and through promoting socialist democracy and perfecting the socialist legal system, we must enable more and more members of society to cherish the socialist and communist ideology, morality and attitude towards labor, to cultivate noble thoughts and feelings, a fine life style and aesthetic standard, a conscious law-abiding spirit and a high sense of organization and discipline, to persist in the principle of subordinating personal and partial interests to those of the whole and subordinating immediate to long-term interests, of doing everything for socialist modernization and the socialist motherland, and to develop the lofty spirit of patriotism and internationalism. In handling relations among the people, including relations between the people of different nationalities, between workers, peasants and intellectuals, between cadres and the masses, between soldiers and civilians, between the advanced and less advanced, between the well-off and those in more difficult circumstances as well as between the different participants in economic life -- the buyer and the seller, those who serve and those who receive services, the producer and the consumer -- all the members of our society should be able to respect, show concern for, unite with and help each other. They must be able to take into account the interests of the whole, observe principles, act fairly and honestly, do a good job at their posts, and serve the people and be responsible to them. In their relations with foreigners, they must be neither overbearing nor servile. In handling the relations between the ideal and the reality, they must have firm confidence in the gradual improvement of the socialist system and the certain realization of communist society in all its splendor following the development and maturity of socialist society. And to realize this ideal, they must be able at the same time to make persistent, down-to-earth efforts and adopt a correct attitude towards difficulties and the negative features of real life, neither cherishing naive illusions, nor feeling pessimistic or disillusioned in any circumstances. The development of this ideological side of cultural life is a hallmark of our socialist society as distinguished from capitalist society and other exploitative societies of the past, it is an important social, political and ideological condition for ensuring the future of our socialist economy and socialist society and represents the common aspiration and strong desire of all upright and politically conscious citizens. We have scored remarkable achievements in raising the level of our cultural life in the past year. The emergence of large numbers of advanced workers, pace-setters in the new Long March, March 8 red banner winners and other heroes and model workers on all fronts bears living testimony to this.

As you all know, Comrade Deng Xiaoping pointed out in a talk last July that trend towards bourgeois liberalization, a departure from the principles of leadership by the Communist Party and the taking the socialist road, has developed on the ideological front, and that it must be resolutely brought to an end. In his speech at the rally in commemoration of the centenary of Lu Xun's birthday last September, Comrade Hu Yaobang emphasized that, in addition to the erroneous ideas of liberalization among some people on the ideological front there are also negative factors of different kinds in our work and among our cadres. Party members and government functionaries on other fronts. In our economic life, we must continue to advocate a high ethical and cultural standard under socialism and unfold the movement of "five stresses and four points of beauty,"[1] resist and overcome the corrosive influence of exploiting class ideologies and other ideologies running counter to the socialist system, such as capitalist ideology, the survivals of feudal ideology, anarchism, ultra-individualism and bureaucratism, and oppose and crack down on unlawful or criminal activities undermining our socialist economy and socialist cause.

China was a semi-feudal and semi-colonial society for more than a century. Capitalist and slavish colonial ideology have not yet been eradicated from the minds of a part of the people. In recent years, our international contacts have sharply increased. As a result of corrosion by the corrupt ideology and life style of the foreign bourgeoisie, instances of abandonment of our national dignity have recurred in some places. This state of affairs merits our earnest attention. On the eve of nationwide victory in our revolution, Comrade Mao Zedong gave a timely warning against the bourgeoisie's "sugar-coated bullets." Now we are facing a similar situation. It is necessary to remind our government functionaries at all levels, and particularly those engaged in economic work, of the necessity of maintaining a firm stand and keeping a level head so as not to be corrupted by the decadent capitalist ideology and way of life. It is of particular importance to strengthen the work of educating the young people so that they will be better able to resist various types of erroneous ideas.

Owing to the severe damage to our fine traditions inflicted by the ten years of internal disorder and to the resurgence of certain old habits and ideas left over from the old society, there has been a recent increase in such obnoxious practices as giving lavish dinner parties and presents, trying to establish underhand connections for the sake of personal gain, demanding commissions, securing advantages through pull or influence and going in for extravagance and waste. A few economic units, economic administrative organs and their leading cadres not only turn a blind eye to such practices but even go along with them. The corrosive influence of these practices on our cadres and functionaries has been grave, causing great dissatisfaction among the masses. This problem merits the serious attention of leading organs at all levels and of all our cadres. Effective measures must be adopted to plug all loopholes and check unhealthy tendencies in our economic work.

Owing to the inadequacies in our laws and regulations covering the administrative and economic fields as well as in our management system, many weak links still exist. Furthermore, the leadership in some areas, departments or units is lax and flabby. Objectively this provides the few law-breakers and violators of discipline with openings and opportunities to carry out activities undermining the socialist economy. At present, such criminal activities as graft, embezzlement, speculation, profiteering, smuggling and tax evasion are rife in some areas. There have even been instances of open plunder of state-owned goods and materials and appropriation of other state property. What is particularly serious is that some economic units and some government functionaries connive at, shield or even directly participate in these activities, thus gravely corrupting our state organs and cadres ranks.

These phenomena must be dealt with sternly and correctly according to the merits of each case. Mistakes in the ideological sphere must be overcome through criticism and self-criticism and through political and ideological education. Those who have made serious mistakes in violation of administrative regulations and refuse to mend their ways must be disciplined. Those who have violated criminal law must be dealt with according to law, and cases of a grave nature must be dealt with severely. Heavy punishment must be meted out to all government functionaries who take part in criminal activities, and no criminality is to be tolerated. In recent years, our country has been quite active in the sphere of economic legislation and jurisdiction. A good many laws and regulations pertaining to the economy are being drafted. Economic courts have been established at most levels. Our efforts in this area still need to be greatly reinforce. Some units are unwilling to submit criminal cases in the economic field to the judicial organs, because they think that it is against their interests to do so. This is not only harmful to normal economic activities and hinders an effective crackdown on criminals but also goes directly against socialist legality. This state of affairs must therefore be changed quickly and resolutely. While learning to make use of other measures, the leading members in all government offices and economic organizations must acquire a better mastery of legal measures to maintain economic order. Besides the economic departments, all public security units, procuratorial organs, law courts, industrial and commercial administrations, customs offices and tax bureaus must co-ordinate their efforts to deal timely and heavy blows at criminals in the economic field in accordance with the laws and regulations of the state.

It must be pointed out that such criminals constitute only a tiny minority in our society. Over the past year, our governments at all levels and the broad masses have waged determined struggles against them. Naturally, after they have been punished, new ones are likely to emerge. No matter when, where and in what form they may appear, we should neither relax our vigilance against them nor let them go free. With the close co-operation of our governments at all levels, our judicial organs and our entire people, we will certainly be strong and resourceful enough to struggle against the various kinds of criminals and against the unhealthy tendencies in the economic field, so as to ensure that our socialist material development will not be impaired, and to promote the daily progress of our cultural level under socialism. We must be confident that with the development of our socialist economy, the improvement of our socialist legal system and the enhancement of our cultural level, there will be far less scope for criminal activities, and criminals will find themselves tightly encircled by the people. Socialist China will never become a paradise for a handful of saboteurs and adventurers. Such days are gone forever. Our socialist cause, our material and particularly our cultural level will advance steadily in our struggle against them.

The existing bureaucratic tendencies in our political life and economic administration are an important obstacle to our new approach to economic development and the realization of our modernization programme. At the Third Session of the Fifth National People's Congress in September 1980, the problem of eliminating bureaucratism was discussed, its causes and its various manifestations in our present administrative system were analyzed and solutions were proposed. Over the past year or so, many successes have been achieved in combating the malady of bureaucratism, especially in improving the relationship between the cadres and the masses, and there have been quite a few refreshing instances of a new style of work among the cadres. But, on the whole, the results are still not particularly satisfactory. More recently, acting on the suggestion of the Central Committee of the Party, the State Council has repeatedly studied and discussed the problem of eliminating bureaucratism. To ensure effective leadership for the modernization programme, the State Council is determined to adopt firm measures to alter the intolerably low efficiency resulting from overlapping and overstaffed administrations with their multi-tiered departments crammed full of superfluous personnel and deputy and nominal chiefs who engage in endless haggling and shifts of responsibility. The State Council has therefore adopted a decision to restructure the administration, beginning with the departments under the State Council itself, and to ensure accomplishment within a specific time limit. The restructuring of the government departments will give a powerful impetus to the enthusiasm of our cadres, to the further improvement of our work style and methods of leadership and to the readjustment and restructuring of the whole economy. Leading cadres and all functionaries of departments under the State Council should set an example of local governments at all levels in performing the task of simplifying administration and raising working efficiency. During the restructuring, there will be relatively important reductions in or merging of State Council departments, accompanied by all possible cuts in staff and fairly big changes in leadership. I would like to suggest here that the National People's Congress authorize its Standing Committee to examine and approve the restructuring plan upon its submission.

While simplifying our government structure, we should also clearly define by administrative statutes the responsibilities and the limits on the powers of the departments of the State Council and the local governments at all levels and also the powers and duties developing on them and their functionaries. Strict rules for assessing, rewarding and penalizing functionaries should be established. The habit of shirking responsibility and taking a dilatory and irresponsible attitude towards work must be resolutely rectified, and so must the bureaucratic style of work which piles up red tape without solving actual problems. In the process of simplifying our administration, we should systematically promote to leading posts at different levels outstanding young and middle-aged cadres with practical experience and a talent for leadership who are qualified ideologically, politically and professionally, so that the ranks of our leading functionaries will become revolutionized, better educated, professionally more competent and younger.

From time to time, leading cadres of the departments under the State Council and of governments at all levels should go deep among the masses, get a deeper understanding of the realities of life, make investigations and studies, and help solve actual problems at lower levels and in grass-roots units. Beginning in January next year leading comrades from the economic departments under the State Council and those in charge of economic work in the provinces, municipalities and autonomous regions will head large numbers of cadres from both central and local authorities and go down to the enterprises and help them with their all-round consolidation. Cadres at all levels, and particularly the higher leaders, must set an example in restoring and carrying forward the fine traditions of sharing weal and woe with the masses and of plain living and hard struggle which were characteristic of the period of the revolutionary wars and they early years of the People's Republic, and they must make new contributions to socialist modernization.

Fellow deputies,

Our economic construction needs close co-operation, encouragement and support from the different fronts. We must adhere to the four fundamental principles, continue to develop the political situation of stability, unity and liveliness and strive to reinforce the great unity of the whole Chinese people. The united front has always been a "magic weapon" in our revolution and it will guarantee the success of our socialist modernization. The democratic parties, the democratic personages without party affiliation and patriots in all circles have a tradition of long- term co-operation with the Communist Party in the course of our revolution and construction. Our compatriots in Taiwan, Xiang-gang (Hongkong) and Aomen (Macao) and Chinese citizens overseas have always been concerned with the construction, growing strength and unification of the motherland, thus manifesting their deep patriotism. We must conscientiously strengthen the re-education of the Party and government cadres at all levels in the policy of the united front, so that they will fully respect and pay serious attention to the suggestions advanced by personages from all circles, enable the latter to play an ample role at their respective posts and thus further consolidate and expand the patriotic united front. Acting in accordance with the policies and principles proclaimed by Ye Jianying, Chairman of the Standing Committee of the National People's Congress, and the spirit of Comrade Hu Yaobang's speech at the meeting in commemoration of the seventieth anniversary of the 1911 Revolution, we should exert ourselves in every field of work so as to promote the unification of our country at an early date, an aspiration cherished by the entire people, including the people in Taiwan. The commanders and fighters of the People's Liberation Army must heighten their state of preparedness against war, step up military and political training and make new contributions in consolidating our national defence and safeguarding socialist construction. We must continue to carry out the diplomatic lines and policies laid down for us by Comrades Mao Zedong and Zhou Enlai, lines and policies which oppose hegemonism, safeguard world peace, support the just struggles of the people of various countries and promote the cause of human progress. Under the leadership of the Communist Party of China, let us hold aloft the banner of Marxism-Leninism and Mao Zedong Thought and march forward valiantly along the road to a modern and powerful, highly democratic and culturally advanced socialist China!

*****

NOTES

1. The five stresses are: stress on decorum, manners, hygiene, discipline and morals. The four points of beauty are: beauty of the mind, language, behaviour and the environment.

*****

DOCUMENT NO. 27

SEVERAL QUESTIONS ON THE CURRENT ECONOMIC WORK

**Report Delivered By Premier Zhao Ziyang at the National
Industrial and Communications Work Conference
Tianjin, March 4, 1982**

(**Hongqi** No. 7, 1982; **Jenmin Jihpao**, Beijing,
March 30, 1982; **FBIS-CHI**, April 1, 1982)

The current national conference of industry and communications has discussed and studied measures for such issues as improving the economic results and doing a good job in this year's industrial production, communications and transport. Experiences in this regard have also been exchanged. According to everybody's view, the meeting is a successful one as it is held at an early date and it has a clear and definite guiding thought and a prominent central theme. Everybody maintains that this meeting will give a great impetus to this year's industrial and communications work. Now I would like to talk about the following questions:

I. On the Question of Raising Economic Results

On the basis of last year's remarkable achievements, our country has made further progress in industrial production since the beginning of this year. Judging from the results of January and February, the trend in production is good, and it is completely possible to fulfill this year's target of ensuring a four percent increase and striving for a five percent increase in total industrial output over last year. What we are afraid of this year is not about the problem of growth rate but about the failure to pay attention to economic results. It has been reported that there are still many cases of raising the quotas of output value at each level. While presenting the target of ensuring a four percent increase and striving for a five percent increase, the central authorities have already taken into consideration the speed of growth planned by various provinces and have incorporated this factor in the state's unified plan. However, certain localities and departments, while handing down the quotas, have raised the quotas at each level regardless of possibilities. Everybody wants to achieve a greater output value and speed up the growth. This is beyond reproach. During the period of readjustment, our country's national economic development must maintain a steady speed and we must not think that the slower the speed, the better. The issue is: We must unify speed with results. We must strive to attain the goal of having good results as well as a rapid increase in output value. It is certainly a good thing if such speed can be further accelerated; but if we only pursue output value and pay no attention to results, such a "speed" will do us more harm than good. Rather we should work in a down-to-earth manner so that our work will not be hindered by our seeking false reputation.

The main problem now is not negligence of output value, but negligence of results. Certain localities and units have made much greater efforts to increase output value than to raise economic results, or they have only verbally claimed to raise economic results but have taken no practical and effective measures to attain the goal. The State Council maintains that it is necessary to emphasize correcting the guiding thought in industrial production. This is to say that we must stress economic results and a solid, not inflated, speech. This issue of having a correct guiding thought applies not only in industrial production, but also in capital construction, circulation and other fields of the national economy.

For a long period, we ignored benefits in blind pursuit of increased output in industrial production and did a great many foolish things. In the years after 1958 and during the "Great Cultural Revolution," the output figures were considerably inflated and waste was quite serious. The lessons in this respect are very profound. This problem continued after the smashing of the gang of four. Although last year the figures were less inflated than in the past, many localities reported sharp increases in output values during the fourth quarter. This also caused some problems. Various provinces should figure out the extent of exaggerations in their growth rates in order to be sober-mined. Blind pursuit of increased output will necessarily result in the stockpiling of large qualities of goods. According to the data of the State Statistical Bureau, fifty-eight major products were excessively stocked by commercial departments at the end of 1981.

Output increase of certain products may be advantageous from the view of the part, but the result may be completely opposite if seen from the whole. For example, in East and Northeast China where energy was already in short supply, some localities greatly over-produced for export ferro-alloy and other products that consume large amounts of energy. This forced the East and Northeast China power systems to generate more electricity than the power and energy requirements. Such practices, if continued, will not only aggravate the dislocation but will also result in the recurrence of the past phenomena when "industry reported good news, commerce reported bad news, warehouses became overstocked and the financial revenue was zero." In the end, the banks were asked to issue notes to cover the deficits and the state and people suffered from it.

If it was inevitable for us to do some foolish things in the past because of our lack of experience, we should have learned from them and become wiser. We must not repeat those foolish things of the past. Comrade Xiaoping has pointed out that to pay attention to economic benefits is an extremely important policy in all work. We should tap our potential and quicken our pace in raising the economic benefits. Last year at the Fourth Session of the Fifth NPC, the State Council put forth ten principles for economic construction. The key point of these principles is to raise the economic benefits. Now that the NPC has approved these principles, we must fulfill them by our actions; they must not remain just words. This year we must have a major change and open up a new phase in raising economic benefits.

When we talk about economic results, it is first of all necessary to make clear one main point, that is, that we should spend as little living labor and as few materials as possible to produce still more products that meet society's needs. The first part of this sentence means that it is necessary to be as economical as possible and to reduce as much as possible the expenditure of living labor and materials. The second part of this sentence means that it is necessary to create more property for society, the key here being that the products must "meet the needs of society." It is not sufficient just to talk about producing more products, since that would not affect economic results. If the products are not what society needs, then the more we produce of them, the greater waste there will be. Therefore, the products we produce, including their quality, color, design and quantity, must meet the needs of society and be readily marketable. These needs are realistic and coincide with the actual level of investment and purchasing power. Society's needs are many-sided; they include the production needs and consumption needs and consist of demands in both of these two major categories. These needs change continuously with the development of production and construction and the improvement of the people's livelihood; there are different needs for different stages and each individual locality has its special needs. Whether we produce medium and high-grade products or popular goods of defendable quality, we should always meet the needs of society. Only when the products meet the needs of society can the labor expended for these products win society's approval and can we have valuable and useful products instead of having wasted labor and useless articles. Our plans should proceed from the overall situation and take into account the future and the past; they should reflect as accurately as possible society's demands and meet the needs in the development of society. Only thus can we enable the national economy to develop in coordination with plans and in a proportional manner. If the products do not meet society's needs and are not readily marketable, there can be no proportionate and coordinated development. In our economic work in the past, what we neglected was exactly this fundamental point; consequently many problems arose. Producing more products that meet the needs of society with the expenditure of as little living labor and as few materials as possible is precisely what basic socialist economic law demands, and what the law of developing the national economy according to plans and in a proportional manner calls for. A socialist country should study the needs of society well and continually satisfy the needs of society; this is the aim we communists strive for. This guiding ideology must be firmly established. In handling economic work, the whole party should concentrate its efforts on saving as much living labor and as many materials as possible and on meeting the needs of society. It should make efforts to find new ways of raising economic results.

The question of raising economic results involves various aspects and is a considerably difficult question. As to why it is not easy to succeed in meeting the needs of society, there are two main reasons: One is limited understanding. Society's needs cannot be seen clearly at once, and it is especially difficult to see them clearly beforehand. It is usually when commodities go out of stock in the markets that their shortages are noticed, and it is usually when the warehouses are filled with stockpiled commodities that their excessive qualities are discovered. This demands timely understanding of the needs of society, understanding of market changes and trends, and improvement and enhancement of the level of planning work. The other reason concerns the question of interests relations. We should ascribe definite interests to enterprises and recognize and take care of the definite interests of localities. Failing to recognize such interests will result in eating "in the same canteen as everyone else," in which situation anyone can become irresponsible. When definite interests are ascribed to them, it will be easy for departments, localities and enterprises to determine their economic activities according to their interests. Some of the policy decisions of departments, localities and enterprises meet the needs of society, but others run count to these needs. Although some products may not meet the needs of society, their production is carried on as usual; the plants share profits as usual; the localities receive a greater percentage of the profits and the commercial and supplies departments do not have to worry about overstocking of these products in the warehouses after their purchases because in the end they are completely taken care of by state finance. Consequently, falsehoods about output value continue protractedly without ever being resolved. Therefore, fundamentally, besides the demand that enterprises improve their business management and raise their scientific and technological level, raising economic results involves the questions of economic systems and economic structures and depends on the readjustment of economic structures and the reform of economic systems; there is no other way out. However, we cannot just wait and hold off our actions until the economic systems have been reformed and the economic structures have been readjusted. To solve this problem under the present situation, in which system structures and prices are all irrational, it is necessary to bring into full play the role of the leadership, namely, by strengthening guidance in planning and administrative intervention and strengthening supervision and inspection.

An important task of the planning and economic commissions at various levels is to find out the extent of stockpiling, make a concrete analysis and seriously deal with it. If the products are needed by society but are stockpiled due to problems in the circulation of commodities, efforts should be made to actively strengthen marketing work and especially to open up rural markets or, in some cases, international markets. If the products are clearly not needed by society and are in the category of impractical goods from the view of the whole, administrative and economic measures should be applied. In such cases, administrative intervention should be firmly made without any fear of giving offense. If certain products are indeed overproduced, their production should be restricted. If certain products are temporarily in short supply, there is no need for us to run headlong into producing them all at the same time. In stressing economic benefits, we should not only keep sight of the immediate benefits and the benefits to the part, but more important, we should not lose sight of the long-term benefits and the benefits to the whole. To make products meet society's needs -- in addition to readjusting plans in a timely manner in light of market changes and intervening administratively and applying economic measures -- it is necessary to strengthen market forecasting and improve planning work. At the same time, it is necessary to formulate and publish the economic and technical criteria for products and the criteria for factory construction as quickly as possible and strictly enforce these criteria in order to stop blind factory construction and blind production.

Bringing economic work to the path of raising economic benefits is the key to achieving a fundamental improvement of the financial and economic situation. We should spare no efforts to produce results in this regard. This is a new task for the vast number of cadres and workers on the economic front. It is also a new test for us all.

In the current industrial and communications work, the people's concern, as reflected in their reports, is concentrated mainly on energy and transportation issues. I will make three points: First, the Coal, Railway and Communications Ministries should make further efforts in carrying out the production, allocation and shipment of coal. Coal production was not bad in the first two months of this year and coal transportation was also good. But the implementation of the allocation plan was rather poor. Earnest measures should be taken to change this situation. Second, all localities should arrange their production in light of the energy supply situation. They should balance their industrial growth rates with the local energy supply, otherwise their goals will fall through. There are at present some localities that set very high targets for themselves and then ask the state to allocate more coal. This cannot be done. Third, energy supply cannot be expected to increase at present. The primary way out is to economize. It is necessary to save energy by every possible means. The energy shortage will not be resolved if we do not work to economize.

II. On the Question of Adhering to the Principle of Giving Highest Priority to the Planned Economy and Taking the Whole Country and the Overall Situation into Account

Comrade Chen Yun recently made a series of important instructions on economic work. He once again stressed: Our country must adhere to the principle of giving highest priority to the planned economy with market force playing a subsidiary role. In national construction, the whole country and the overall situation must be taken into account. The fundamental policy that "first we must eat, second we must construct" must be implemented. He also pointed out that the first priority task of the special economic zones is to seriously sum up experiences. These instructions all concern the major questions of principles and policies in economic construction and were put forward in light of the questions existing in our present economic life. They are of great immediate importance. They are in keeping with our economic policy of the recent years that calls for opening up our country externally and enlivening our economy internally.

Since the Third Plenary Session of the Eleventh CCP Central Committee, under the unified leadership of the state and the guidance of state planning, we have enforced the policy of opening up our country externally and enlivening our economy internally. Our orientation is correct and our achievements are the main aspect. Without these reforms, we would not have the good situation we do today. This we must first affirm. However, in implementing the policy of opening up our country externally and enlivening the economy internally, we must be sober-minded and adhere to the aforementioned several principles put forward by Comrade Chen Yun, which are also the fundamental principles and policies our party has upheld for years. They must not be forsaken or be weakened.

At present, while keeping sight of our achievements in opening up our country and enlivening our economy we must also be soberly aware that our opening up and enlivening will inevitably bring a number of problems. In this regard, we should have the courage to use the current favorable international and domestic conditions and continue to uphold the policy of opening up our country externally and enlivening our economy internally in order to promote our economic development. We must not waver over the established correct policy. At the same time, we must adequately recognize the problems brought about by this policy. We must not turn a blind eye to them or leave them alone. Today in stressing the need of giving highest priority to the planned economy and taking the whole country and the overall situation into account, our purpose is precisely to keep us sober-minded so that we can adopt measures to prevent the emergence of problems or resolve them if they have already emerged; to correctly and soundly implement the policy of opening up our country externally and enlivening our economy internally; to strengthen the position of planned economy; and to create conditions for further reforming our economic structure.

The purpose of our open-door policy is to introduce into our country foreign advanced technology and administrative knowledge as well as capital, which is useful to us in spurring our country's socialist construction. Because of the open-door policy, certain bad influences from capitalist countries will inevitably find their way into our country. Smuggling, peddling smuggled goods, speculation, swindling, corruption and accepting bribes have become rampant in certain localities and units; the capitalist living style and decadent ideology will corrode our party; certain weak-willed cadres will succumb to "sugar-coated bullets"; and our party members work style and the people's habits may be contaminated.

Our party, on several occasions in the past, when it carried out important new policies and faced new historical turning points, raised the issue that it was necessary to guard against capitalist inroads. One example was during KMT-CCP cooperation at the initial period of the era to resist Japanese aggression. The main problem needing to be resolved in those days was to combat factionalism and closed-doorism and open a new situation for the united front. At the same time, the party Central Committee explicitly pointed out that the CCP must maintain its ideological, political and organizational independence, adhere to the stand of acting independently and, keeping the initiative in our own hands, guard against problems generating from within our party. We did a very good job at that time. We took advantage of the favorable situation and, greatly expanding our strength, created a new situation. Instead of being corroded, our party became stronger.

The second example was after victory in the liberation war. After acquiring national political power, our party members entered the cities from the rural areas and faced a dazzling world of humanity with its myriad temptations. In those days, the party Central Committee and Comrade Mao Zedong quickly reminded the whole party that it was necessary to guard against the attack of "sugar-coated bullets." Later, movements against the three and five evils were carried out. In those days, our party's political, ideological and organizational situation was very sound and we withstood the test.

Now we are taking advantage of the favorable international and domestic situation and are carrying out the policy of opening our doors to foreign countries and enlivening the economy at home, and we are facing another rigorous test. This time our party is confronting a much greater and more serious influence from decadent capitalist ideology at home and abroad, particularly the influence of international capitalism, than on the previous two occasions. Moreover, after a decade of turmoil, our party's fine traditions and work style have been impaired. Therefore, during this new historical period, it is all the more necessary to quickly alert all party members to the questions of capitalist inroads. By sounding this alarm we hope we can help our party members come to their senses, heighten their spirit and strengthen their will to withstand the test.

Today, smuggling, peddling smuggled goods, speculation, swindling, corruption, accepting bribes and other crimes in the economic sphere are much more serious than during the movements to oppose the three and five evils in 1952. The inroads of such crimes on our party organizations and cadres' contingents and their pernicious influence on the entire society are quite serious. This situation, if not struggled against immediately with determination, will develop from bad to worse in certain localities and will be unstoppable in two or three years. This is a prominent expression of the inroads of capitalist ideology under the new historical conditions -- conditions of externally carrying out an open-door policy and internally enlivening the economy -- and our struggle against all sorts of crimes in the economic sphere, is an important part in our all-out struggle against capitalist inroads. This struggle is inevitable and is a protracted one. Just as Comrade Hu Yaobang pointed out: This is an extremely vital issue, which has an important bearing on our party's survival and on our country's prosperity or decline.

We must be fully aware of the seriousness, harmful effects and danger of the various crimes in the economic sphere and raise our consciousness of waging this struggle properly. If we fail to resolutely and powerfully strike at such crimes as smuggling, peddling smuggled goods, speculation, swindling, corruption and accepting bribes, not only will our building of a material civilization be seriously undermined, the building of a spiritual civilization will simply fail.

Now the activities of rebuffing economic crimes are going on simultaneously with the "courtesy month" activities and the masses have acclaimed these activities and said our country is hopeful. All units on the economic front must resolutely carry out this struggle through to the end. By no means should they act perfunctorily or superficially.

Of course, when we carry out this struggle we will not resort to the method of handling legal cases and exert special efforts to deal with major cases. This struggle will be carried out along with the overall reorganization of our enterprises and the general examination of financial affairs. We must, through reorganization and examination, find the clues, strengthen investigation and track down and seriously handle the problems so as to strike at the criminals and educate our cadres. At the same time, we must establish and improve various rules and regulations and plug loopholes so that the criminals will not be able to avail themselves of them. Doing this will spur our efforts to improve management, economic accounting and economic results.

Another conspicuous problem is the recent growth of the trend toward departmentalism, decentralism and liberalism in the economic sphere. This is another major problem which has cropped up under the new historical conditions. We have domestically implemented the policy of activating our economy, delegated some powers to the local authorities and enlarged the enterprises' decision-making powers for the purposes of whipping up the enthusiasm of the local authorities, the various departments and enterprises and the masses, turning human talents and land and other material resources to good account and vigorously developing China's national economy. Efforts to expand decision-making powers and activate the economy are also apt to foster the trend toward departmentalism, decentralism and liberalism, to weaken of socialism and to affect our efforts to take the whole country and the overall situation into consideration. Instead of surveying and dealing with problems on the basis of the overall interests of the state, some localities and units take into account the local as well as their own interests. In dealing with the higher level, they disobey the unified plans of the state and seek private gain at public expense. In dealing with the units and other localities concerned, they shift their troubles onto others and harm others to benefit themselves. In conducting foreign trade, they refuse to implement the policy of unifying as one and joining efforts to deal with foreign countries, and jostle against each other. As a result, the foreign countries reap the benefits. There are presently still many signs of people carrying out construction and production blindly in disregard of the needs in society as well as the overall and long-term interests of the state. In some localities, the tasks for state monopoly and compulsory purchase have been shirked. Economic blockade between one district and another is fairly serious. There are many examples in this respect.

Ours is a unified socialist nation. We must have a unified plan and unified domestic market. We must not allow one market for one province. If this practice is permitted, its political and economic consequences to our nation will be unimaginable. Also, for example, in the field of foreign trade, there is evidence of various districts, departments and enterprises vying with each other in cutting prices and counteracting each other's efforts. This has caused considerable damage already. The result is that by counteracting each other's efforts, the local authorities and enterprises reap some small benefits while the state suffers a great deal.

In order to strengthen centralization and unification in economic work, we must adhere to the overall plan on major issues while allowing freedom on minor issues. We must advocate centralism on major issues while allowing decentralism on minor issues. We must also correctly handle the relations between the practice of taking the whole country and the overall situation into account and the practice of whipping up local enthusiasm. The state must interfere with these erroneous practices and issue orders to eliminate them. It must not allow each one to pursue his own course.

1. In foreign trade, we must adhere to the policy of unifying as one and joining our efforts in dealing with foreign countries.

After expanding the powers of the local authorities and various departments in conducting foreign trade, we must resolutely adopt effective measures to eliminate the erroneous practice of vying with each other in dealing with foreign countries and in cutting prices. In foreign trade, it is necessary to appropriately expand the powers of the local authorities. However, at the same time, we must thoroughly solve the problem of selling products of the same category abroad in an unified manner. With a main port as a center, we must form a joint administration in exporting products of the same category in order to strengthen our coordination and management.

2. The products to be transferred according to state plans, including farm and sidelines products, must be transferred strictly according to such plans. No one is allowed to retain them for his own use or to utilize them as a means of cooperation with others or to sell them at a negotiated price.

3. We must resolutely correct the practice of enforcing economic blockade between one district and another. Except for those to be allotted or delivered according to state plans, all products which have met the standards set by the state and those products produced in accordance with state plans are permitted to be marketed throughout the country. The enterprises are authorized to select and purchase the products themselves. The party and government organs in various localities must not interfere with the enterprises. If they do, the enterprises have the right to resist such interference.

It is necessary to care for old base areas, the regions inhabited by minority people and remote areas. It is necessary to provide technology and equipment to help these areas turn out products suited for local production and achieve even greater economic development.

4. The commodity price and revenue system must be centralized and unified. Without the approval of the State Council, no locality, department or unit is allowed to change a tariff rate or reduce or increase taxes. Without the approval of the State Council, the price of any product within the limits of state commodity price control must not be increased or decreased.

Comrade Chen Yun said: The task of top priority in the special economic zones at present is to summarize experience. I think the question of earnestly summarizing experience not only prevails in the special economic zones or in the two provinces of Guangdong and Fujian, but also in the whole country. All these reforms aimed at activating the economy at home and those reforms within the foreign trade system must be reviewed and summarized to help us remain sober-minded and thoroughly solve the problems which have cropped up so that the reforms within the economic system will be healthily and extensively developed. For example, we must advocate the expansion of the enterprises' decision-making powers and the implementation of the economic responsibility system.

However, we are indeed faced with the question of how to divide profits. We must carefully study how to take into account the interests of the state, the collective and the individuals simultaneously and to determine the share belonging to the state, to the enterprises and to the individuals as well as the most appropriate form of distribution. After the expansion of the enterprises' decision-making powers, we must also strengthen the management and supervision over such enterprises accordingly. To let the local authorities adequately share some powers is necessary. However, we must study how to avoid setting up economic blockades between one locality and another, and keep from following the trends of departmentalism and decentralism that may possibly prevail and how to prevent such trends from affecting the necessary practice of centralism and unification in China's economic work and to keep them from influencing the country as a whole.

On the one hand, the foreign trade departments must pay attention to bringing into full play the enthusiasm of the units at all levels. On the other hand, they must also prevent themselves from competing against and undermining each other in front of foreign businessmen. In this respect, we must also earnestly sum up our experience. In short, the open-door policy in foreign trade and the policy of enlivening the economy domestically will not change, and the orientation for carrying out reforms remains firm. However, we must pay full attention to existing problems and sum up our experience and lessons. We are doing this precisely because we seek to do a still better job in enforcing reforms from now on.

The tentative plan for reform is:

1. The economic policies that have been put into practice generally will not be changed this year in order to maintain their stability and continuity. As far as the policy on economic benefits is concerned, the practice and level prescribed by the government last year should be generally maintained in terms of economic relationships between the state and the enterprises, and between the state and the enterprises on the one hand, and the individual on the other. However, extreme irrationalities in some individual units should be appropriately readjusted.

2. This year we should also consider what is to be done next year. By summarizing our experiences, we should put forward our views on how to complement, perfect or readjust the implemented policies and measures for next year. There appear to be three situations in this regard, one being that in which policies and measures which are effective and correct in orientation should be upheld. Another situation is that in which some policies and measures are correct in orientation but have side effects. These policies and measures should be continuously carried out if such effects can be eliminated by strengthening management. In this case, it is necessary to strengthen management in order to consolidate and improve the policies and measures. Some policies and measures

are basically correct in orientation, but their side effects cannot be eliminated for a fairly long time because management cannot keep up with the situation. In this case, an appropriate readjustment should be made. The third situation is one in which improper policies and measures should be corrected next year. No matter what reform is to be carried out, the general guideline is to combine the strengthening of centralization and unification with the activation of the economy and to bring into full play the initiative of localities, departments, enterprises and people under the guidance of state planning and the principle of taking the whole country into account.

3. It is necessary to work out as soon as possible an overall plan for reforming the economic system so that we shall have a long-term plan for reform.

III. On the Question of All-Round Consolidation and Readjustment of Enterprises

Efforts must be made to consolidate enterprises in order to achieve better economic results. Otherwise, there would be no foundation for all other work. The party Central Committee and the State Council have clearly defined the purpose and requirements of enterprise consolidation and have laid down explicit principles and policies in this regard. Now I will particularly discuss the following several points:

1. The first group of enterprises selected for consolidation this year should be big- and medium-sized key enterprises with more problems and a great potential and which urgently need to be consolidated. Many in this group should not be good enterprises; enterprises with more problems should be consolidated first. When these enterprises are consolidated well, their economic results will be raised quickly. Some enterprises that have a strong leading body and have done basic work well may carry out their consolidation by themselves or may be consolidated later. In this spirit, the lists of enterprises selected for consolidation in various localities should be adjusted.

2. Special attention should be paid to staffing enterprises leading bodies and reforming the leadership system. Judging from the streamlining of the State Council, the readjustment and strengthening of enterprise leading bodies can be carried out at a faster pace and they can become compact and efficient leading bodies.

When the central administrative structure is streamlined, it will give a tremendous stimulus to enterprises in this regard. Enterprises have many qualified cadres and technicians in their thirties or forties who are well versed in their fields of work and who have both ability and political integrity. A number of them should be selected and promoted to positions in leading bodies so that great progress can be made in having leading bodies consist of revolutionary, well-educated, professionally competent and young cadres. In this way, it will be possible to bring about a noticeable change in this regard. To achieve this purpose, there should be an age limit in selecting and appointing managers and assistant managers of enterprises and directors and deputy directors of factories during the consolidation. Except for such exceptionally big enterprises as the Anshan Iron and Steel Company and such national corporations as the China Shipping Corporation, it is necessary to select as far as possible personnel below age fifty and no older than fifty-five for managers, assistant managers, factory directors and deputy directors. Party committee secretaries and responsible persons of workers congresses may be a little older but not too old. Some comrades in enterprises who have not reached the retirement age and are still physically fit may go to the second line to serve as staff officers or advisers to do counseling work.

Some comrades have suggested that personnel with an educational level equivalent to that of a college graduate and with practical experiences be selected for directors of big key enterprises. This is a good suggestion. If it is difficult for some enterprises to select personnel with the educational level equal to that of a college graduate for their directors, they should at least select persons who have the educational level of polytechnical school graduation or those who have become qualified through self-study to be their directors. Only by properly staffing enterprises' leading bodies during the consolidation will it be possible to bring about a big change in the outlook of the enterprises.

3. It is imperative to staff various units according to their fixed number of personnel and to train workers and staff members in rotation. After streamlining the administrative structure, a large number of cadres of central organs should be organized for study and training in rotation. This is a matter of strategic significance. During the enterprises' consolidation, coupled with the institution of the economic responsibility system, it is necessary to be determined to get the surplus workers and staff members out for study and to persevere in doing so. Then, there will be a change in the educational level of all workers and staff members after a few years. If the surplus personnel should be allowed to remain in workshops and sections and on shifts, many malpractices will occur. This situation must be corrected. People in all localities should work hard in order to gain experiences in this regard.

We must strengthen leadership in a conscientious way. Party committees and governments at all levels must place the overall reorganization of enterprises on their agenda and leading comrades themselves should take charge of this task. Economic commissions at all levels as well as industrial and communications ministries, departments and bureaus must carry out this task in a practical way, and those teams assigned to work at selected units must carry out their assignments in earnest. The central authorities have decided that the organizational reform will not be initiated in provinces, municipalities and autonomous regions this year so that energies can be concentrated on enterprise reorganization and other tasks. All ministries under the State Council must assign someone to be especially in charge of this task and changes in the organs should not interfere with this task. All ministries concerned are requested to immediately hold meetings to study this task, work out plans and send out teams to work at selected units. The State Economic Commission is to be responsible for inspecting and supervising this task. We must carry out the task of reorganization in a down-to-earth manner for two or three years, promote all fundamental work at enterprises to meet the demands set by the central authorities, and greatly enhance their economic results so that there will emerge an entirely new look at the enterprises.

In connection with the enterprise reorganization, there is another problem, namely, readjustment of enterprises. Those industrial enterprises that turn out products not meeting social demands, that consume too much energy or that have long operated at a loss should be shut down, and have their operations suspended; they should be amalgamated or switched to the manufacture of other products and the practice of blindly setting up new industrial enterprises should be stopped. This is a positive measures taken to enhance the overall economic results of the society and to make the lineup of enterprises as well as the geographical distribution of industries become rational. Taking into consideration that enterprise reorganization has to be carried out as a major task, that cases of violations in economic fields have to be handled and that the reform of organs has to be promoted this year, we should be aware that a lot of work has to be done this year. In this connection, enterprise readjustment can be carried out only within a certain limit in 1982. Among those enterprises that have to be closed down or have their operations suspended first are metallurgical plants and chemical plants consuming much energy, machine-building plants and electronics plants turning out products of very poor quality, oil refineries achieving very poor economic results and some industrial enterprises run by communes or production brigades that contend with advanced enterprises for the supply of raw materials, fuel and power. Efforts should also be made to arrange their problems in order of importance and urgency, and to work out plans for enterprise readjustment as well as practical measures to deal with those enterprises that have to be closed down or have their operations suspended so as to be well prepared for promoting this task in a planned way next year.

At the same time, we must also pay attention to the promotion of major technology reforms at enterprises in a planned way. During the current period of economic readjustment, many machine-building plants are seriously in need of tasks to achieve while over 20 million *dun* of rolled steel is stocked in warehouses and the contingent of capital construction teams does not have much work to do while wages have to be paid and management expenditures have to be spent. On the other hand, plant facilities have become out of date and some of them have to be replaced with new ones. Can't we think of some way to "make a start" somewhere and activate work in various fields? We must consider the possibility of banks issuing loans to machine-building plants in the form of credit loans to sellers, of allotting rolled steel to these plants for the manufacture of new highly efficient equipment and of selling the equipment to those enterprises that need it to replace old equipment that is low in efficiency but high in energy consumption. It will not cost too much to carry out this task, for in promoting technological reforms, funds spent on equipment account for about 85 percent of the total investment under general circumstances. Some civil engineering projects have also to be completed. Since these projects will not need much funding, preparations for such projects can be made by either local units or enterprises themselves.

Once this measure is taken, overstocked rolled steel will have an outlet, machine-building industry will be reactivated, the amount of waste iron and steel that can be supplied for remelting in furnaces will be increased, metallurgical industry will be given an impetus, tax revenues for the state will be increased and a new outlook will be brought about to the technology and equipment at various plants. This was tried out at the No. 2 motor works with good results last year. We must make a start in technology reform and renewal of facilities this year. In promoting the technological reform centering on energy conservation, we must, first of all, reform technology in turning out several major products, including boilers, motor vehicles, transformers, water pumps and fanning machines as well as a number of basic parts for machines. We must do a good job in promoting technological reforms at such large enterprises as the Anshan Iron and Steel Company and the Nanjing Chemical Industrial Company, acquire some experience in this concern and then popularize their experiences.

IV. On the Question of Finance

The readjustment work was carried out conscientiously in 1981 by implementing the guidelines of the central work conference held in December, 1980. As a result, the financial situation in 1981 was better than expected. Revenues totaled 102.8 percent of the annual plans. There was a deficit of less than 2.7 billion *yuan*, the figure mentioned in the report to the Fourth Session of the Fifth National People's Congress. However, we are still confronted with considerably great difficulties in finance. As stated in the 1982 state budgets, we anticipate the expenditures to exceed revenues by 3 billion *yuan* this year. Therefore, while noting the excellent situation we must also anticipate latent dangers in financial work this year. If we fail to achieve a balance between financial revenues and expenditures in the main, the deficit will increase and it will lead to issuance of more currency. This will affect not only the basic stability of commodity prices at markets but also the situation of stability and unity.

The general guideline for this year is to consolidate and stabilize the economic achievements and march forward steadily on this basis. Whatever happens, we cannot lower our guard after having initially stabilized the economy and thus aggravate the latent danger again. To this end, the Central Committee and the State Council have asked for efforts to further implement the policy of readjustment, restructuring, reorganization and upgrading and to continuously maintain a basic balance of revenues and expenditures and of credit receipts and payments together with a basic stability of commodity prices. This is not only an economic question but also a political one.

Fundamentally speaking, to resolve a financial question, it is necessary to develop production in earnest, improve economic results and do a good job in increasing revenues and cutting expenditures. Besides continuously and energetically developing the production of consumer goods as planned, changing the service orientation of heavy industry and conscientiously reorganizing enterprises, efforts should be made to grasp the following well:

1. The purchase prices of agricultural and sideline products should be stabilized. The financial burden has become very heavy as more money is put into circulation and many different kinds of subsidies are offered. In 1981 the state gave subsidies of 32 billion *yuan* for more than 30 kinds of commodities, of which over 80 percent had something to do with the prices of agricultural and sideline products. Although agricultural and sideline product prices have increased very little in the past two years, the proportion of increased and negotiated prices is growing bigger and bigger and the actual purchase price for agricultural and sideline products is still rising steadily. Generally speaking, to solve this question we must have a stable policy and readjust measures that exceed the limit of policy and those that are drastically irrational. We must refer to the method used by Zhejiang and other places of fixing the basic figures for planned purchase and apportioned purchase of agricultural and sideline products by the state; places that had abandoned this method should restore it. By now, three years have passed for some new producing areas; next year they should think about fixing a rational purchasing task or the purchase proportion. The increased and negotiated prices for purchase exceeding the planned quota should also be readjusted and controlled.

2. The granting of bonuses should be controlled. In general they should be stabilized at last year's level within the scope of provinces, municipalities and autonomous regions this year with emphasis on doing away with egalitarianism in bonus-granting and on distribution according to work so as to make the bonuses work effectively. Indiscriminate granting of bonuses should be firmly corrected.

3. Efforts should be made to tighten financial discipline, intensify supervision and inspection and plug loopholes. At present, many enterprises have indiscriminately assigned production cost, evaded tax and rationed profits which ought to be delivered to the state. All this has reached a fairly serious degree. We must pay attention to this and solve it. The financial inspection carried out early this year which achieved good results should be continued. Problems once discovered should be dealt with expeditiously; we should not turn big problems into small ones and small problems into no problem at all.

4. Investment in capital construction must be controlled. While there is no possible major breakthrough in capital construction, an expenditure item under plan, the amount of funds raised on one's own, the funds the enterprises themselves have and the fixed capital investments made with bank loans have grown into a considerably large sum. There are many problems in this area. Various provinces, municipalities and autonomous regions should check on them. Those projects that should study how to put the funds to good use. Another problem is that some places have set up their own investment trust companies taking away bank deposits to do construction. To summarize, the amount of money available is limited and establishing an investment trust company here would mean reducing bank deposits there. This in fact amounts to diverting a part of the credit originally being used as current capital to capital construction, thus extending the capital construction line and hampering the improvement of economic results. I now reiterate that with the exception of those investment trust companies approved by the State Council or designated departments concerned, all other investment trust companies should be turned over to the banks. The job of raising and using funds should be handled exclusively by the banks and should not be done independently without them.

In short, our entire economic situation has come out of the "bottom of the pot," but the latent danger has not yet been basically eliminated. We rather assess the problem more seriously; we should never lower our guard or become unrealistically optimistic.

V.   On the Question of Intensifying Ideo-political Work

Under the new situation, ideo-political work should not be weakened but intensified.   Over the years, our political organs have been busy launching mass movements but they still lack an integrating set of experiences in doing ideo-political work well in the economic sphere.   We should make an effort to study and summarize experience in this area.   Ideo-political work should be based on the demands of the four modernizations and integrated with economic work and with the state of the mind of workers and staff in order to have a definite object in view to truly solve problems.   In discussing how to intensify ideo-political work, this conference has introduced the Daqing Oilfield's experience of strengthening the building of contingents of workers and staff and the experience of the Tianjin Caustic Soda Plant in carrying out education on the love of the party, the motherland and socialism through studying history and Chinese modern history. All this is more vivid, more realistic and convincing.   We must, through meticulous and careful ideo-political work, make the fundamental guiding principles of taking equal consideration of the interests of the state, the collectives and individuals and of "first, the people must have sufficient food; second, socialist construction must be carried out," take root in the minds of workers and staff and in work implementation as well.

Since the Third Plenary Session of the Eleventh CCP Central Committee, the party and government have made maximum efforts in improving the people's livelihood in the rural areas and cities and the great majority of the masses are satisfied.   The state of mind of the people in the cities at present is stable and upward looking on the whole.   It should also be noted that a small number of people in the cities are still not too satisfied and are grumbling.   Among them there are also elements with ulterior motives who desire to stir up trouble.   It seems that there is a necessity for choosing a suitable time this year to universally carry out a vivid education on the economic situation.   We should, through this education, reckon an overall account with the urban people and let the broad masses understand under what conditions the state solved the question of the people's livelihood since the downfall of the "gang of four," especially in the past several years since the third plenary session.   The account would cover the increase in commodity prices, people's income, state subsidies to the urban people, employment, in the total amount of wages and bonuses, in housing for workers and staff, in the sale of durable consumer goods, and in urban savings deposits. All accounts should be brought into the open.

The country has an account book.   In the three years from 1979 to 1981, jobs were found for 26 million jobless young people who returned to the cities and towns; housing covering 220 million square meters in floor space was newly completed for workers, staff and the people in the cities. The state increased subsidies of the selling price of agricultural and sideline products annually to more than 20 billion *yuan*. The total amount of wages for workers and staff in 1981 was 25.1 billion *yuan* greater than in 1978 or an increase of 44 percent; the average annual wages of workers and staff increased from 614 *yuan* in 1978 to 772 *yuan* in 1981 or an increase of 25.7 percent and so forth. Every city, every enterprise and every unit has such an account book and we should speak up with facts and figures. We must also make clear the existing problems in the spirit of seeking truth from facts. For example, for some party and government cadres, personnel engaged in scientific research, teachers and workers and staff of collective enterprises, their actual income has not been raised much and has even dropped. We should let the masses voice their opinion openly so as to help us carry out education about this situation and improve our work. Judging from results of education conducted in Shanghai, Liaoning and Xuzhou, in so doing, most of the people have come to know the truth and eliminate misunderstanding; they have realized that the party and the state have indeed made utmost efforts in the interests of the people. By reckoning accounts, workers and staff of the Shanghai No. 2 Weaving Plant who used to grumble about their livelihood problems have become even-tempered and good-humored and vigorous in work. A party branch secretary of the Ningbo Municipal Clothing Embroidery Factory made some most profound and objective remarks. She said: According to the workers, over the past several years, they have found: 1) they have more money in their pockets; 2) commodity prices have also risen; 3) they still have more money in their pocket after carefully figuring out income and expenditures; 4) the young people have higher demands. The masses of workers are very reasonable. So long as we earnestly carry out education on the economic situation, a healthy atmosphere will prevail more promisingly and there will be no room for rumors and slanders.

We should, through education on the economic situation, further lead the people to fully understand our national conditions and to foster the idea of building our country through thrift and hard work and of arduous struggle. Ours is a developing socialist country with a huge population, a weak foundation and a very burdensome construction task in all fields. Livelihood improvement can only be materialized gradually with the development of production. It is therefore wrong and unachieveable to put forth impractical and excessive demands. As to livelihood problems, we should not simply compare with the developed capitalist countries, nor should we compare with those oil-rich countries or certain countries and regions which have become prosperous by relying on processing. We have to go through a protracted hard struggle in order to build our great motherland into a more prosperous and strong country and to make all our people "comparatively well-off" for a more prosperous life later. This requires us to earnestly implement the principle of "first, the people must have sufficient food; second, socialist construction must be carried out." The people's livelihood needs to be improved gradually, but there is also a problem of doing according to one's own capability. We still have to allocate some funds, goods and materials for construction and for continuously enlarging production in order to advance toward the four modernizations. This is where the fundamental interests of the people of the whole country lie. A prosperous life will never become a reality if we only strive for enjoyment of life and divide up and eat up everything instead of carrying out construction. We must, through education, make the people correctly understand and handle well the relations between construction and livelihood and between accumulation and consumption and integrate the immediate with long-term interests.

We are deeply convinced that by striking at lawbreaking and criminal activities in the economic sphere and promoting the building of spiritual civilization together with education on the economic situation this year, the people's spirit will be greatly enhanced and the social mood will take a turn for the better.

*****

DOCUMENT NO. 28

THE CCP CENTRAL COMMITTEE'S DECISIONS CONCERNING THE ESTABLISHMENT OF A RETIREMENT SYSTEM FOR ELDERLY CADRES

(February 20, 1982)

(Issues & Studies, Vol. XX, No. 8, August 1984)

1. Ours is a great Party with a long history of struggle. In the course of over sixty years of glorious combat the Party has amassed in its ranks a large number of well-steeled old cadres, generation after generation. Of the old cadres who participated in the revolution before the founding of our state, during the four periods of the New Democratic Revolution -- the Great Revolution Period, the War of Agrarian Revolution, the Anti-Japanese War and the War of Liberation -- 2.5 million are still alive. Only a small proportion of them have retired or left

their positions, most of them are still at their posts. The problem now is that among these elderly cadres, quite a few comrades have already reached a considerable age and quite a few are on the brink of old age. Their continuing to shoulder heavy work in leadership posts has meant that our leading groups have aged to quite a serious extent. How to appropriately arrange for new cadres to take over from the old in an orderly and gradual fashion has become a major problem facing the whole Party. It has become an important part of the radical reform of our system of Party and state cadres.

Back in the late 1950s and early 1960s, the Party Central Committee and Comrade Mao Tse-tung brought up the problem of the proper replacement of old cadres by new. But because of deviations in leading ideology and mistakes in practical work, it was impossible to solve this problem. During the ten years of the Cultural Revolution, those who made up the backbone of the Party and state leadership at various levels were labelled "capitalist-roaders" and overthrown, and a whole batch of opportunists and ambitious elements were promoted to take their place. This did great damage to the Party's organizational line and organizational work which had been Marxist-Leninist and followed Mao Tse-tung Thought. It also caused the cadre system and the ranks of the cadres to fall into an unprecedented state of chaos, greatly delaying the correct solution of this problem. Now, in the new historical period, through the highly effective work done between the Third and Sixth Plenums of the Eleventh Central Committee, the historic task of correcting the chaotic state of the Party's leading ideology has been victoriously completed, and the Party's ideological, political and organizational situation has greatly improved and political conditions of stability and unity have largely been consolidated. In this situation, the Central Committee believes that the time and conditions are ripe for the question of how to use the appropriate way for new cadres to take over from the old to be put on the agenda of important items for discussion and for it to be properly solved in an orderly and steady manner.

2. Our Party's old cadres are the precious riches of the Party. Through the long and cruel revolutionary wars and the years of white terror, our Party's old cadres braved untold dangers, fearless of sacrifice and brave in struggle, to make an enormous contribution to the overthrow of reactionary rule, the liberation of our nation and our people, and the establishment of a new China. Since the foundation of our state they, together with people of all nationalities all over the country have changed a China which had long been poor and backward into a great developing socialist state with an independent and fairly complete socialist industrial and national economic system, the economy, culture and science and technology of which is reasonably well-established. During the ten years of internal chaos, the overwhelming majority of comrades among them stuck to the principles of Marxism-Leninism and Mao Tse-tung Thought and struggled with

the counter-revolutionary clique of Lin Piao and Chiang Ch'ing in various ways. In the last few years they have done a lot of work to bring order out of chaos and advance the work of building socialist modernization. The history of China's revolution and construction has repeatedly proved our Party's cadres to be a hard core force worthy of the great tasks of the Chinese people. If we had not had so many old cadres, if it had not been for the sacrifices of martyrs at every turn of the revolution and some of those elderly comrades still alive, if it had not been for the extreme hardships they had endured, the great difficulties they had encountered and the long struggle they had put up, the victory and development of the Chinese people's revolution and construction would have been difficult to imagine. Neither the Party, the army, the people of all nationalities all over the country nor future generations will forget the inexpungible historic service of the Party's old cadres, nor should they forget it.

However, after all is said and done, a considerable proportion of the old cadres who are still alive are old, weak and lacking in energy, and find it more and more difficult to bear the heavy burden of leadership work. This is a law of nature which cannot be refuted. In view of this, and to ensure that there will be people to carry on our work, to guarantee the continuity of the Party's line and policy, and guarantee the stability of our leadership, we must put a great deal of effort into selecting and cultivating tens of thousands of virtuous and talented young and middle-aged cadres who are in the prime of their life. We should get them to join in leadership work at all levels so that they can become even more effectively tried and tested and can gradually take over from our old cadres. Our old cadres should consider the work of the Party and the long-term interests of the people, recognize their overall responsibilities and happily and enthusiastically welcome and support those relatively inexperienced and youthful cadres of outstanding ability who are there to take over important leading positions. Meanwhile, they should retreat from leadership posts and keep themselves more aloof. This is an important and glorious historical responsibility for old cadres in the new historical period. In order to guarantee the proper progress of the changeover from the old cadres to new ones and to see that those cadres who are going to step down are cared for appropriately, the Party Central Committee believes that it is necessary to establish a system for elderly cadres leaving their posts, retiring, and retreating to the second line.

3. This system for elderly cadres leaving their posts, retiring, and retreating to the second line is extremely important for the normal progress and sound development of the political life of the Party and the state. We must immediately take steps to establish it systematically and perfect it, and operate it strictly and as a matter of course.

Different countries have different retirement systems, and inevitably these systems each have their peculiarities. Our system for elderly cadres leaving their posts, retiring and retreating to the second line must, of course, be based on the actual situation of our Party and our country. Only in this way can we be fair and reasonable and make sure that retiring elderly cadres get what they deserve; only then will the new and the old be able to cooperate, and the political situation of stability and unity will be consolidated and developed, only then will we be able to vigorously promote our work of building socialist modernization.

Taking into consideration the current cadre situation and the conditions for changeover, the retirement age for elderly cadres should be fixed as follows: heads and deputy heads of departments of the Central Committee and state organs, first secretaries and secretaries of provincial, municipal and autonomous regional Party committees, provincial governors and deputy governors, and the cadres in charge of provincial, municipal and autonomous regional discipline inspection commission, courts and procuratorates, should not usually be over sixty-five years old and deputies should not usually be over sixty. Heads of departments under ministries and heads of bureaus should not usually be more than sixty years old. Of course, those who have not yet reached the retiring age but find it difficult to keep up their normal work because of poor health, may take early retirement with the approval of the organization. On the other hand, those cadres who, having reached the retiring age, are still needed for work and are still able to keep up their normal work, may for a limited period of time postpone their retirement and continue to carry out leadership work.

Retreating to the second line, which includes advisory and honorary posts, is not the same as retirement. Those old cadres who are still in good health and have a fairly rich store of leadership experience and specialized knowledge but who cannot be included in the leadership for reasons of age or quota limitations, may be given certain responsibilities as consultants or may undertake investigation and research or advisory work in a certain area. Those old cadres who have made an important contribution to the work of the Party, whose prestige is rather high but who find it difficult to keep up normal leadership work (including advisory work), may be given appropriate honorary positions. But in principle, each individual should not hold more than one advisory or honorary position.

As for those famous experts, scholars and artists who originally held posts in the leadership, if they are approaching old age, they should be strongly encouraged to concentrate their precious time and energy on research and writing, they should be provided with the necessary assistance and fairly good working conditions. They may also be allowed to hold certain honorary posts, but except under special circumstances, they should not have to undertake leading executive work.

Apart from the above stipulations in principle, the Central Committee believes that it should be emphasized that it is necessary to keep a few old revolutionaries who have passed the retiring age in the Party and state leadership. Particularly in the present historical situation and in the near future, a great country like ours needs a certain number of old comrades who are rich in experience, respected, prestigious and far-seeing, who can see the situation as a whole and who still have the energy to work, to remain in their central leadership posts in the Party and the state. This is an overall necessity for the preservation of internal stability and unity and for the proper handling of international relations. It is absolutely in line with the basic interests of the Party and the people.

4. After old cadres have retired or left their posts, they must be well looked after, their basic political treatment should not change, their living conditions should not deteriorate, and care should be taken that they are given a role to play. This should be an un-shifting principle of Party and state policy.

Ours is a proletarian political party and a socialist state. Our cadres are revolutionaries by profession and have no private property. At the same time, when our old cadres retire, they may leave their original posts and cease to hold leading executive positions, but ideologically, politically and organizationally they do not retire. Communist Party members cannot "retire" or "resign" from their revolutionary will or organizational discipline. They are still Communist revolutionaries; they still have a political duty to serve and be responsible to the people. Therefore, the political treatment of retired cadres, including the reading of documents, listening to important reports, participating in important conferences and important political activities, etc., should not be changed. Living conditions, including health care and means of transportation, should not be change either.

Quite a few elderly cadres who joined the revolution before 1949 still have plenty of will power in spite of their age, and have resolved to keep up the hard struggle after retirement. This lofty revolutionary spirit deserves to be held up as a model before the whole Party, to be vigorously advocated and studied. However, the Central Committee has decided to give appropriate assistance to the many elderly cadres who, having made an important contribution during a long period of revolution, have fallen ill from overwork, whose physical condition is getting weaker and weaker and who, to various extents, are experiencing difficulties in daily life and in getting medical care.

The responsibility for fixing the actual level of assistance and the way in which it should be given lies with the Organization Department of the Central Committee. In this way we can express the solicitude of the Party and the people for the health and livelihood of old comrades. The Central Committee believes that this stipulation will be wholeheartedly approved by all comrades of the Party and people and people of all nationalities all over the country.

Services for retired cadres should be the responsibility of the department from which they retire. In principle, they should settle in the area in which they retire. If they should wish to return to their native place or settle in another suitable area, arrangements should be made for them to do so, and to make it easier for them.

In order to make plans for the solution of problems concerning the retirement of elderly cadres, the organization departments of Party committee at all levels should set up solid organizations exclusively to deal with elderly cadres. The principal comrades in charge of the Party, government and army at all levels should supervise this frequently, and include this aspect of work on the agenda of Party committees for discussion.

5. The Party Central Committee has high hopes for all elderly cadres who have retired or who are about to retire. Over the decades in which they were at work, these old comrades employed enormous energy and enthusiasm in making their individual contributions to the revolutionary endeavor of the Chinese people, and in doing this have written their own glorious history. After retirement, the most important task entrusted to them by the Party is to live a long healthy life, so that they may finish writing their glorious history. The Central Committee hopes that they will continue to show concern for the work of the Party and the fate of the country and the people, and as far as they are able, to make new contributions to the Party and the people.

After retirement, many old comrades are still enthusiastic for the work of building the material and spiritual civilization of our socialist motherland. In all ways appropriate to their circumstances they take part in various social activities, preserve their contacts with the masses, carry out social investigations, conscientiously write books which are beneficial to the people, young and old, or enthusiastically take part in socially beneficial light manual labor, thereby conscientiously doing some good for the people. They are not only very strict with themselves, but cherishing a high level of political responsibility, they also strictly educate and make strict demands on their own children and relatives. We should fully recognize that although taken individually, these things are on no spectacular scale, taken altogether they are of inestimably great and far-reaching significance to the transformation of our society, and particularly for the education of our young. Party publications should regularly and truthfully publicize and report on the deeds of these old comrades.

The Central Committee also hopes that all retired cadres and those who have retreated to the second line will learn from the older generation of proletarian revolutionaries at present working at the central level. Although these old revolutionaries have submitted to the decision of the Party Central Committee and remained in their posts in the Party and state leadership because they are needed by the Party and the people, they are public spirited, earnest and sincere enough to help comrades with less seniority and prestige, less ability and less experience then themselves to take charge. They themselves take a back seat, and what is more they see this as a glorious responsibility and a pleasant thing to do for the Party and the people. They freely allow those comrades in the front line to handle most problems of a daily nature, and they conscientiously use their rich experience and political wisdom to help comrades in the first line to think up ideas, and by combining their collective political experience and collective wisdom they respect the collective leadership of the Party Central Committee. This Marxist revolutionary spirit and scientific method is an extremely good example of the role old comrades should play in the new historical period.

The children and relatives of all retired cadres should warmly assist and support the old comrades to make their retirement a happy one. At the same time they should inherit and develop the revolutionary spirit of hard struggle of the older generation of revolutionaries, and advance along their glorious path of struggle.

6. The promotion of young and middle-aged cadres to leading positions at all levels and the retirement of old cadres are two aspects of the same problem. We should realize that in the thirty-odd years of work and struggle since the foundation of our state, the Party has actually cultivated and created a large number of outstanding young and middle-aged cadres, both virtuous and able and in the prime of their life. They are politically staunch, have a rather rich store of specialized knowledge and have leadership ability. They have been tried and tested, they are full of energy and are well-qualified to take on all kinds of leadership work. The hopes of our Party rest with them, and they are a sign that the Party has great vitality. If we fail to notice this, or fail to fully realize it, and always select leading cadres for provincial, municipal, autonomous regional, central and state bodies from among those comrades of sixty years old and above, then we will be lacking in resolution and unable to make new breakthroughs. We may bungle our task and commit unforgivable historical mistakes.

The correct criteria for selecting young and middle-aged cadres must be that they have both ability and integrity and are in the prime of their life. Firstly, we should consider their political performance, we should investigate their behavior during the Central Revolution and particularly their behavior since the Third Plenum of the Eleventh Central Committee. None of those who, having ability in a certain field, lack integrity and are unable to serve the people sincerely, may be selected for a leadership post unless they have taken active steps to reform themselves and won the forgiveness and trust of the masses. Those 'rebels' who followed Lin Piao and Chiang Ch'ing, those with serious sectarian ideas, smashers and grabbers and those who in recent years have seriously damaged the standard of Party life and committed serious economic crimes and acts of indiscipline who still occupy leadership posts, should be resolutely removed. We should not expect younger cadres to have too much leadership experience. It is only when they are given practical work to do that they will change from being inexperienced to being more experienced and more mature. On this issue, we must guard against and overcome any perfectionist ideas and promotion according to seniority. We should particularly value female cadres who have both ability and integrity and are in the prime of their life, we should not discriminate against them. The Central Committee believes that under the direction of the correct political, ideological and organizational lines since the Third Plenum of the Eleventh Central Committee, it is only necessary for us to really rely on Party organizations at all levels, on the broad masses both within and outside the Party and on old cadres rich in experience who are able to choose the right men for the right jobs, to rely on those who are good at concentrating the wisdom of the masses, and to rely on the discernment of the masses of discover and select cadres, rather than leaving the decision up to a small group of people. If only we do this we will certainly be able to select successors correctly and complete this great task. Even if some individuals are not selected correctly, or it they later fail to stand the test and turn out badly, it will not be difficult to make a timely adjustment and it will not be detrimental to the overall situation.

The Central Committee believes that it is imperative to call on all comrades of the Party to pay close attention to the historical experience of our Party. At the time when our Party first appeared on the historical scene and began to lead the countless masses in their great struggle, and even at the time of the establishment of our state, Party leaders at all levels, including those old comrades who are still with us today, were nearly all very young or quite young. In the new historical era, we should be even more confident that if we only inherit and develop the excellent tradition of our Party, thoroughly implement democratic centralism, strengthen the collective leadership, give play to the collective wisdom and rely on the help and support of our old comrades, our young and comparatively young cadres-successors will surely be able to lead the people in opening up an even more glorious future.

7. The establishment of a system for the retirement of elderly cadres and their retreat to the second line, and the appropriate solution of the problem of the transition between old and new cadres is a thoroughgoing reform of the cadre system; it is an important policy full of strategic significance which affects the further growth and development of our Party, the stability of our country and the smooth realization of the great endeavor of socialist modernization. It is a rigorous test of Party committees at all levels and it is up to all Party members to prove whether or not they can handle this great task correctly.

Our comrades should understand that to work hard when in office is an expression of responsibility toward the Party and the people; to retreat to the second line or to retire when one is getting on in years, when one's strength is no longer sufficient or when one is not up to the demands of the job, is also an expression of responsibility toward the Party and the people.

Our comrades should be imbued with the open-mindedness with which the proletariat faces the future. They should dare to break the habit of underestimating outstanding young and middle-aged cadres and welcome the development of new forces. Materialists should not despise new forces.

All cadres in office must respect those elderly cadres who have retired, should humbly ask for their assistance and devotedly care for them. They should make strict demands on themselves and look after the retired cadres. What is more, they should make efforts to create the excellent habit of respecting age and wisdom throughout society. The disgusting practice of doing the utmost for cadres when they are in office but ignoring them once they have retired must be criticized and stopped.

The Central Committee believes that if only the whole Party will pull together, take a firm stand, and refuse to give up in the face of interference or obstruction of any kind, the problem of the appropriate transition between old and new cadres will definitely be solved successfully, and a complete leadership system and cadre system appropriate to the requirements of the construction of socialist modernization will be established and these will be consolidated by means of the Party Constitution and state laws, thus creating a completely new and flourishing situation in which we have successors to carry on the revolutionary cause, so as to lay a firm foundation for the victorious completion of our magnificent historical task in the new era.

(Translated by Judith A. Fletcher)

*****

DOCUMENT NO. 29

NATURE OF CHINESE SOCIETY TODAY

by

Feng Wenbin

(**Beijing Review**, Nos. 23, 25 and 26,
June 8, 22 and 29, 1981)

During the first few years after the founding of the People's Republic in 1949, our Party had a correct line and did a fairly good job. The socialist transformation of the private ownership of the means of the production into public ownership was smooth, the economy was restored and developed quickly, the people's livelihood improved greatly, social order was excellent, and the people were full of confidence in socialism. After the basic completion of the socialist transformation of agriculture, handicrafts and capitalist industry and commerce, our Party put forward some good ideas on how socialism should be built. But we did commit many mistakes, including some serious ones, as we lacked experience and there was little successful experience for us to draw upon. We were predisposed to rash advances in our guiding ideology and made an erroneous estimate of the situation of classes and class struggle.

From 1957 to the start of the "cultural revolution" in 1966, we made some "Left" mistakes resulting in some setbacks, but they were gradually corrected. Generally speaking, socialist construction advanced along a healthy course and we made great achievements. The people remained firm in their faith in socialism.

During the "cultural revolution," Lin Biao, Kang Sheng and the gang of four made use of the "Left" mistakes in our guiding ideology to carry out counter-revolutionary sabotage and brought an unprecedented calamity to the country. It was during the ten years of great chaos in China that some capitalist countries made considerable progress in science and technology and in their national economies. This cast doubt on the superiority of socialism among some comrades, especially young comrades. These comrades are not good at analyzing the reasons why certain problems have arisen and they easily put the blame on the socialist system itself. In order to solve these problems, we must make a scientific analysis of what socialist society is, why there have been some twists and turns in China's socialist construction and how we should carry out socialist construction in China in line with our actual conditions.

Basic Features of Socialist Society

According to Marx and Lenin, socialist society is the first or preliminary stage of communist society. It differs in essence from capitalist society and in degree of maturity from advanced communist society.

Lenin said socialism means public ownership of the means of production plus the principle of distribution according to work.

Public ownership of the means of production is the most fundamental feature of socialist society. To organize production on the basis of public ownership of the means of production is a distinction of decisive significance between the socialist and the capitalist systems. The practical experience of the socialist countries shows that the form of the public ownership of the means of production is bound to vary from one country to another and from one stage of socialist development to another. For instance, China today has state economy and collective economy; within the collective economy, there are big collectives and small collectives. (Within the rural people's communes, there is ownership by the commune, by the brigade and by the production team.) In addition, there is the small sector of private economy which is regulated by the state and attached to the publicly owned economy as a necessary supplement to the socialist economy. However, the most important criteria for judging whether a society is socialist or not are whether it has established socialist public ownership of the means of production and wiped out the system of exploitation, not what form the public ownership has taken, and whether socialist public ownership has occupied a dominant position in industry, agriculture and commerce, not whether public ownership has been established for all the means of production.

Socialist economy is a combination of planned economy and commodity economy. Socialist public ownership determines that it is possible for a socialist country to conscientiously make use of the objective law of planned and proportionate development of socialist economy, to carry out planned management of the national economy, correctly handle the relationships among the various branches of the economy, distribute rationally the productive forces, make full use of manpower and material and financial resources and develop science, technology, culture and education so as to ensure a sustained and smooth development of the national economy.

At the same time, socialist economy is a commodity economy. It is a new type of commodity economy which differs from both a capitalist commodity economy and a small commodity economy. In the socialist commodity economy, labor power is no longer a commodity. It is not a kind of economic relationship in which capitalists exploit hired laborers, nor the relations among small private owners. It represents the economic relations among the laboring people (including those between the state, the collective and individual laborers) based on identity of fundamental interests. It develops in a planned way, and not in a blind, anarchic way.

The other important feature of socialist society is that it carries out the principle "from each according to his ability, to each according to his work." The productive forces, at their level of development in the stage of socialism, cannot provide society with more abundant products than this principle calls for. Consumer goods can be distributed to a laborer only according to the quantity and quality of work he has done. The more he works, the more he gets; the less he works, the less he gets. If he does not work, he gets nothing. In socialist society, labor is both the sacred right and bounden duty of all laborers. It is an honor. On the one hand, society should do everything possible to see that each laborer finds the job he likes, taking part in labor which is suited to his strong points and special knowledge. On the other hand, every laborer should take part in labor of his own accord, do his part at his post and receive his reward accordingly. "He who does not work, neither shall he eat." This is the principle everyone should follow in socialist society. Though the principle of distribution according to work differs from that of distribution according to need and it has not brought about real equality among the members of the society, it nevertheless represents a fundamental negation of the exploiting system which has lasted for several thousand years.

The third important feature of socialist society is that the people have become masters of the country. With the establishment of socialist public ownership, the laboring people have become masters of the means of production and masters of the country and society, and a new type of relationship of equality and mutual help has been established between man and man. In socialist society, a socialist democratic system is practiced in full. It guarantees that the people can exercise their rights as masters, both politically and economically. Socialist society also establishes a comprehensive legal system which embodies socialist democracy and guarantees the realization of the people's democratic rights. In socialist society, the personnel of organs of state are servants of the people whom they must serve wholeheartedly. This feature shows that socialism is not only an economic system of public ownership, but also a political system with a high degree of democracy. China's people's democratic dictatorship, or the dictatorship of the proletariat, is a political system in which the people are the masters of the country.

In a multi-national socialist country, the role of the people as masters of the country is also reflected in the new relationship of equality, unity and mutual aid between all the nationalities and their common efforts for socialist construction.

A socialist country must, in its relations with foreign countries, adopt the principle of combining patriotism and internationalism and carry out the Five Principles of Peaceful Coexistence. It should neither yield to hegemonism nor seek hegemony. If it exercised national oppression internally and sought hegemonism abroad, it would cease to be a real socialist country.

A socialist society is also distinguished by its intellectual life, which includes highly developed science and culture; communist thought, ideals, beliefs, high moral standards and discipline; revolutionary stand and principles as well as comradely relationships between man and man. It is an important task in the sphere of intellectual life of socialist society to help the masses foster ideas of serving the people wholeheartedly, being warm-hearted towards comrades, being responsible in their work, constantly perfecting their skills and thinking of others before themselves. The material civilization and intellectual civilization of socialism promote each other. The superiority of the socialist system and the development of socialist productive forces constantly enhance the mental outlook and intellectual level of the people in a socialist country. In turn, changes in the mental outlook of the people promote the development of the productive forces and the consolidation of the socialist economic and political systems. Without a highly developed socialist intellectual civilization, it would be impossible to promote the consolidation of the economic base of socialism and the development of socialist economic construction and, therefore, impossible to bring about highly developed political democracy and realize the goal of communism.

These features of socialist society make it to combine the interests of the state, the locality, the collective and the individual, rationally adjust their relations, bring the initiative from all sides into full play, rely on its own strength to solve continuously the various contradictions as they crop up in social progress and push the society forward along a healthy course.

The basic features of socialist society show that socialist society is the best social system in human history, far superior to capitalist society.

The Establishment of Socialist System

According to these fundamental features of socialist society, it should be said that with the basic completion of the socialist transformation of agriculture, handicrafts and capitalist industry and commerce, China built up in the main a socialist system and entered socialist society.

Our country's socialist system displayed its great superiority during its emergence as well as throughout the transition period when the old relations of production were transformed into new socialist relations of production. This refutes the fallacy that socialism does not suit China's conditions. During the first eight years after the founding of the People's Republic (1949-57), our country's total industrial and agricultural output value went up by an average of 14.6 percent each year, our national income by 12.6 percent and the real wages of workers and staff members by 5.5 percent. At the same time, we won the great victory of the War to Resist U.S. Aggression and Aid Korea, strengthened our national defence and consolidated our people's democratic dictatorship. During those years, our country had just started its socialist construction and there existed many difficulties in the national economy and the people's livelihood. But production rose, the national economy flourished, culture and education developed continually, the people's standard of living improved step by step, social morality was healthy, the people were full of confidence. Everybody said socialism was good.

"Without the Communist Party there would be no socialist New China" and "Only socialism can save China" -- this truth has been proved by the past several decades of history and will continue to be proved by the future practice of our socialist construction.

Some people hold the viewpoint that socialist society can only be built in a country where capitalism is highly developed. They argue that since China is backward economically and culturally, it cannot practice socialism and that it should not have plunged into socialist revolution and socialist construction after winning the nationwide victory of the new-democratic revolution. It should not start building socialism until capitalism has reached its full development.

This idea, already refuted long ago by our socialist practice, has arisen again lately in some people's minds. They claim that they are holding to the Marxist principle that China should not have gone in for socialism and that it should now go back and develop capitalism, a historical stage China missed. This view is a misinterpretation of Marxism.

It is true that Marx and Engels once predicted that socialist revolution might first succeed in Britain, France and other highly developed capitalist countries at that time. However, they did not exclude the possibility that the socialist revolution could be waged in countries where capitalism was not fully developed, much less did they define what proportion large social production should occupy in an economy before socialist revolution could be attempted. During the late 1840s Germany was still in the early stage of the industrial revolution, its level of industrialization was not high, small production was widespread and feudal rule had not been overthrown. But they pointed out at the time in *Manifesto of the Communist Party* that Germany's bourgeois revolution would be carried out with a much more developed proletariat than that of England or France at the time of their bourgeois revolutions, and that the bourgeois revolution would only be the prelude to an immediately following proletarian revolution. Later, Engels said in *The Questions of the Peasants in France and Germany* in 1894 that there was no need to wait until the results of the development of capitalist production had been revealed in an extreme form and the last small handicraft producer and the last small peasant had become the victims of large-scale capitalist production to carry out this transformation. In line with the practical experience of the Russian revolution, Lenin further developed this theory put forward by Marx and Engels. He pointed out in *Our Revolution* (1923) that it was entirely possible for the proletariat to make use of the worker-peasant alliance it established to seize political power and then, by relying on the political power of the proletariat, develop the economy and culture and realize socialism. Countering the statement of Second International opportunists that "the development of the productive forces of Russia has not attained the level that makes socialism possible," Lenin revealed a profound truth, saying: "If a definite level of culture is required for the building of socialism (although nobody can say just what that definite 'level of culture' is, for it differs in every West European country), why cannot we begin by first achieving the prerequisites for that definite level of culture in a revolutionary way, and then, with the aid of the workers' and peasants' government, proceed to overtake the other nations?"

Why China Can Bypass the Stage of Capitalist Development

Can China, after setting up the state power of the people's democratic dictatorship, enter the stage of the socialist revolution and make the transition of socialism? This question was answered in the affirmative by our Party and Comrade Mao Zedong and has also been solved in practice during the Chinese revolution. The founding of the People's Republic of China marked the end of the new-democratic revolution and the beginning of the socialist revolution. Why is it that China could bypass the stage of an independently developed capitalism and directly enter the stage of socialist revolution? Fundamentally speaking, this was decided in the process of China's historical development, which provided China with the basic conditions for taking the socialist road. In terms of the international situation, since the world had entered the epoch of imperialism and proletarian revolution, the Chinese revolution had already become a part of the world proletarian revolution and therefore it could get support from the international proletariat. As for China's domestic conditions, firstly, there were the proletariat and its political party and a solid worker-peasant alliance. What is particularly important, the proletariat occupied a dominant political position and held the revolutionary leading power firmly in its hands as a result of the establishment of the people's democratic dictatorship after the nationwide victory of the new-democratic revolution. Secondly, though China's modern factories were small in number, they were highly concentrated, with the country's biggest and most important capital concentrated in the hands of the bureaucrat-capitalists. Confiscating bureaucrat capital and turning it over to the state led by the proletariat enabled the People's Republic to control the nation's economic lifeline and make the state economy the leading sector of the whole national economy. Relying on the correct and strong leadership of the Communist Party and the leadership exercised by the state economy over the whole national economy, China carried out the socialist transformation of agriculture, handicrafts and capitalist industry and commerce, and replaced private ownership of the means of production with socialist public ownership. This fundamentally guaranteed that China, on the basis of the victory of the democratic revolution, could strike out on a non-capitalist road.

It should be pointed out that the process of historical development follows an objective law of its own, and whether or not a country must pass through the stage of an independently developed capitalism is beyond the will of man. In old China, capitalism had not developed much, and the economy was backward. This gave rise to some difficulties in building socialism. Nevertheless, after the founding of the People's Republic, we were able to make the transition to socialism by means of socialist transformation. Why then shouldn't we make full use of the advantages of the socialist system to develop our social productive forces and build a highly developed, powerful socialist material foundation? Why should we go through a stage of capitalist development which would only bring capitalist exploitation and suffering to the people?

History witnessed the phenomenon of polarization in the rural areas during the development of the peasants' individual economy after the completion of the land reform. And in the cities, with the restoration and development of capitalist economy, the bourgeoisie launched sharp attacks against socialism. This took various forms, such as bribery, tax evasion, theft of state property, cheating on government contracts and stealing of economic information. Under the conditions of a fierce two-line struggle, to continue to allow the five economic sectors (ownership by the whole people, collective ownership, private ownership, state-capitalist economy and capitalist economy) to coexist and develop together without completing the socialist transformation of private ownership of the means of production would have allowed capitalism to develop freely. If this had been the case, China would have taken the capitalist road spontaneously.

Our Party and Comrade Mao Zedong correctly comprehended the law of the historical development of Chinese society. They understood very well the necessity for socialist transformation. Correct principles, policies and measures were taken to carry out the socialist transformation of agriculture, handicrafts and capitalist industry and commerce, and the whole national economy was thus led on to the socialist path. To have completed socialist transformation so smoothly in a big, economically backward, populous country was a great pioneering feat in world history, as well as an important contribution to Marxism-Leninism by our Party and Comrade Mao Zedong. Today, after over thirty years of socialism, it would obviously be very ridiculous to turn around and develop capitalism.

There is another erroneous opinion, which denies the socialist nature of our present society. It claims that a society can be regarded as socialist only when it has attained a high degree of socialization of production and directly owns all the means of production and when commodity production has disappeared and products are distributed directly. This viewpoint disregards our more than thirty years of socialist practice. To judge whether or not a society is socialist, one should see whether it has established the dominant position of socialist public ownership and whether it carries out the principle of "to each according to his work." As for commodity production, the practice of socialism in our country as well as in other countries proves it to be indispensable to socialist society, in which products still cannot be distributed directly but can only be done by means of commodity exchange. Moreover, one should understand that socialist society is a process of constant development and change. There is no doubt that the advantage of the socialist system will be more and more fully displayed as it steadily improves in the course of advancing from its early stage to a mature stage.

Chinese society in the present stage is still not a mature socialist society. However, since it possesses the above-mentioned basic characteristics, it differs fundamentally from the transition period when there existed both socialist and capitalist economic sectors and the individual economy occupied a dominant position in rural China. How can one say ours is not a socialist society?

The socialist road is the only road for China in its historical development. The many problems which arose in the past were not due to the founding of the socialist system, but to the serious mistakes resulting from the failure to recognize and to master the objective laws of socialist society for some time after the basic completion of the socialist transformation of private ownership of the means of production. We should draw serious lessons from all this.

Historical Lessons

One of the serious lessons drawn from the practice of socialism in China is that after the basic completion of the socialist transformation of the private ownership of the means of production, we violated on several occasions some of the principles of scientific socialism. Because we were ideologically unclear about the problems, these "Left" errors became more and more serious, culminating in the mistake of unleashing the "cultural revolution," which inflicted heavy losses on our socialist cause. In carrying forward scientific socialism, it is imperative to make a clean break with these "Left" mistakes. Some manifestations and consequences of the mistakes were:

1. Exaggerating the Class Struggle in Socialist Society. Though class struggle existed only in certain spheres with the establishment of the socialist system and the elimination of the exploiting classes, Chinese society was still considered to be composed of antagonistic classes. The fundamental tasks of the dictatorship of the proletariat were misunderstood and the focus of work was not put on developing the productive forces. Class struggle overshadowed everything and socialist democracy and legality were ignored while emphasis was put one-sidedly on dictatorship and violence. Moreover, the two different types of contradictions, those between the people and the enemy and those among the people, were confused. As a result, the erroneous theory of "continuing the revolution under the dictatorship of the proletariat" was formulated, and the wrong practice of the "cultural revolution" unfolded. The Lin Biao and Jiang Qing counter-revolutionary cliques, taking advantage of the mistake of the "cultural revolution," carried out disruptive activities which had disastrous consequences.

While class struggle was exaggerated, science and technology were looked down upon. Mental work and intellectuals were despised and intellectuals were even regarded as bourgeois elements. An attempt was made to eliminate the differences between mental and manual work by turning mental workers into manual laborers instead of encouraging manual workers to master intellectual work. This greatly hindered the development of science and culture in our country.

2. Overanxious to Transform the Relations of Production. The effect of the relations of production forces was over-estimated, and the law that the relations of production must suit the nature of the productive forces was violated. Political movements and class struggle were used as catalysts to promote changes in economic relations irrespective of the state of the productive forces. It was believed that the higher the level and the larger the scale of collectivization of the means of production were, the more the superiority of the public ownership would be manifested. So there was a rashness to move to large-scale collective ownership, then to the ownership of the means of production by the whole people and finally to communism.

As a result, the peasants' small plots for personal needs, household sidelines, rural fairs and small-scale individual economic activities were called capitalist tails and banned. Furthermore, no distinctions were made between the methods of management and the forms of ownership, and the system of responsibility in production was opposed. The principle of "to each according to his work" was negated and equalitarianism prevailed, wiping out differences in remuneration between those who worked hard and those who did not work. Socialist commodity production was restricted, even banned: the law of value was negated, no business accounting was practiced inside the state economy, no exchange of equal values occurred between state-owned enterprises, and the market was not allowed to play the role as a regulator. Commodity economy was equated with capitalist economy. All this hindered and even disrupted the development of the productive forces.

3. Impatient for Success in Economic Construction. In economic construction, the fundamental economic principles of socialism and the law of planned and proportionate development were violated. The scale of construction was beyond the country's capacity and no importance was attached to overall balance. Because there was impatience for quick results in economic construction, the emphasis was put on opposing "Right" deviation and conservatism and no attention was paid to opposing "Left" tendencies and rash advances. Stress was put only on the political demand for a high-speed economic development but no attention was paid to analyzing whether it was possible economically. Such being the case, high speed, high targets and high accumulation were pursued and large-scale capital construction projects were undertaken in a blind way, thus neglecting

China's real conditions and the people's livelihood. For years, this erroneous idea led to several big rash advances in economic construction which, as a matter of fact, retarded the building of socialism.

The serious mistakes mentioned above, and the ten years of the "cultural revolution" in particular, brought our national economy to the brink of collapse. Incalculable losses in terms of political ideology, culture, education, social morality, etc., were sustained. What is particularly serious, the training and education of a whole generation was neglected. During the decade of the "cultural revolution," institutions of higher learning and secondary technical schools trained several million fewer professional people than they would have done. Spare-time cultural and scientific education of the workers and staff members hardly existed. Illiteracy increased. Social morality degenerated, superstitious activities revived, and many youths became confused ideologically and their mental outlook was affected adversely. All this has seriously hampered the building of our socialist material and intellectual civilization.

The "Left" mistakes, particularly the sabotage of the Lin Biao and Jiang Qing counter-revolutionary cliques, inflicted heavy losses on our country's socialist cause. However, the socialist nature of Chinese society has not been changed at all. Socialism has withstood a severe test. In the end, Lin Biao and the gang of four did not destroy our Party; instead, our Party smashed them. In the few years since the downfall of the gang of four we have quickly restored our national economy which was on the verge of bankruptcy; we have rapidly brought to an end the chaotic and unstable political situation and have embarked on the correct path of building the four modernizations, thus proving the superiority and tremendous vitality of socialism.

The superiority of the socialist system does not manifest itself spontaneously. Socialism provides the possibility for mobilizing the people's initiative and steadily developing socialist economy and culture. To turn its potential into reality, it is not necessary to have certain objective conditions but, more important, to have correct leadership. Since socialism is an unprecedented undertaking, there must be a process in which the masses and their leaders learn to recognize the objective laws governing the development of socialist society. Therefore, both "Left" and Right mistakes can hardly be avoided and this affects the realization of the superiority of socialism. We have gone through twists and turns and committed many mistakes in our efforts to understand socialist revolution and construction. It is only after these mistakes were gradually corrected that we have gained a deep understanding.

The "Left" mistakes in our guiding thought have many causes. Blaming all these mistakes on a single person is not in accord with historical reality, nor is it conducive to summing up our experiences. Comrade Mao Zedong's great achievements are primary, while his shortcomings and mistakes are secondary. We should not, because of the "cultural revolution," negate Comrade Mao Zedong's merits or make no distinction between the mistakes of a proletarian revolutionary and those acts of counter-revolutionary and those acts of counter-revolutionary sabotage undertaken by Lin Biao and the gang of four. Lacking practical experience is one of the chief reasons for committing mistakes. Another is being arrogant after victory and therefore becoming divorced from reality and the masses. We would have committed fewer mistakes and our socialist cause would have advanced further if we had maintained a modest and prudent style of work, guarded against arrogance and rashness, studied conscientiously the theory of scientific socialism, proceeded from China's conditions by seeking truth from facts, paid attention to the opinions of the masses, summed up in good time both positive and negative experiences and carried out socialist construction in an enthusiastic and steady way.

Carrying Out the Line of the Third Plenary Session of the Eleventh Party Central Committee

Since the Third Plenary Session of the Eleventh party Central Committee held in December 1978, the Party Central Committee, following the principles of integrating theory with practice and seeking truth from facts as Marxism-Leninism-Mao Zedong Thought teaches us, has summed up its experiences and corrected its "Left" mistakes. Applying the fundamental principles of scientific socialism to the concrete conditions of our country, it has put forward a correct line, principle and policies, which have brought various areas of our work back to the path of scientific socialism and achieved great successes on all fronts.

In *Our Programme* (1899), Lenin pointed out: Marx's theory "provides only generally guiding principles, which in particular, are applied in England differently than in France, in France differently than in Germany and in Germany differently than in Russia." To adhere to the socialist road, we should neither violate the fundamental principles of scientific socialism, nor can we mechanically copy what is said in books. We must integrate the fundamental principles of Marxism-Leninism with our concrete national conditions and practice.

In our country, particular attention should be paid to these conditions:

Our country's socialist society has emerged from a semi-feudal and semi-colonial society with underdeveloped capitalism. The backward state of our economy, culture and science has still not been basically changed though so many tremendous results have been achieved in our socialist economic and cultural construction that an independent and comparatively comprehensive industrial system and an integrated national economy have been built. The traditional influence of the small production's management style, the force of habits and feudalism are still very extensive and deep-rooted.

China has a vast expanse of land, but is mostly covered with mountains, waters and grasslands. By comparison, its arable land is rather limited, and particularly so when the amount of arable land per person is considered.

China abounds in natural resources; however, they have not been fully explored or effectively utilized.

Of the 1,000 million people in China, 80 percent are peasants, and agriculture, which is operated mainly by hand, still makes up a large proportion of the national economy. Moreover, the natural conditions vary tremendously among different regions and nationalities and the level of their economic development is uneven.

In regard to the question of how to integrate the fundamental principles of scientific socialism with the concrete practice of our country in the course of building socialism, the documents of the Party's Eighth National Congress (1956) and Comrade Mao Zedong's writings such as *On the Ten Major Relationships* (1956) and *On the Correct Handling of Contradictions Among the People* (1957) have brought forward many correct ideas. The line, principles and policies since the Third Plenary Session of the Eleventh Party Central Committee have revived and further developed these thoughts, pointing out how to open up a road of socialist construction that suits our conditions.

1. **Readjusting the National Economy.** Considering the comparatively backward conditions of our country's economy and science, we must, on the one hand, develop the social productive forces as quickly as possible and build a powerful socialist material foundation; on the other hand, we must proceed from what is actually possible, paying attention to practical results and advancing step by step. The first important strategic decision made by the Third Plenary Session of the Eleventh Party Central Committee was to shift the focus of our Party's work to socialist modernization. Simultaneously, in view of the serious imbalance in the proportionate relations of the different sectors of the national economy caused by the long-term influence of the "Left" guiding thought, it was decided to readjust the whole national economy. Fundamentally speaking, readjustment means to readjust the structure of the national economy comprehensively,

reorganize industry rationally and, by integrating readjustment with reorganization, rationalize the economic structure. Only in this way can our socialist modernization cause advance healthily and steadily.

2. Multiple Forms of Public Ownership. In our country, the productive forces have not developed in a balanced way and a modern large-scale industry exists along with a backward agriculture which is operated basically by manual labor. Besides, sectors of industry and communications and transport are still dominated by handicrafts and other small-scale operations. This condition requires us to introduce multiple forms of public ownership. Since the Third Plenary Session, the Party has corrected the mistake of being impatient for transforming the relations of production and the erroneous viewpoint that the higher the level of public ownership is, the better. It has been clearly pointed out that we must adopt many forms of public ownership coupled with certain necessary supplementary forms. Furthermore, on condition that the state economy and collective economy occupy a dominant position, a certain number of urban and rural individual enterprises as well a joint ventures with foreign investment should be permitted.

3. Developing Commodity Economy. Since our commodity economy is underdeveloped and our level of socialized production is not high, it is important to develop our commodity economy in a big way. Some claim that developing the commodity economy will lead to capitalism. This thinking is erroneous. The socialist commodity economy differs fundamentally from the capitalist one in that labor power is no longer a commodity and therefore the relationship of exploitation has been done away with. Under the socialist system, the state firmly controls the economic lifeline and the main economic levers. Under such conditions, the anarchic state of capitalist commodity economy will not appear, to say nothing of the emergence of capitalism. In socialist society, the commodity economy develops in a planned way. As for the system of economic management, the socialist economy combines planning with market regulation and, under the guidance of a unified plan, gives full play to the role of market forces. Only the development of a socialist commodity economy makes it possible to combine the state's material interests with those of collectives and individuals, to mobilize all positive factors, to speed up the accumulation and turnover of funds, to accelerate the expansion of reproduction and the development of the whole social productive forces and thus to ensure that the socialist economy prospers. Since the Third Plenary Session, on the basis of summing up historical experiences, the Party Central Committee has adopted the principle of developing a socialist commodity economy and integrating planning with market regulation. Marked results have been achieved since this principle was put into practice, which proves that it corresponds with the objective laws of the development of a socialist economy.

4. Adaptability and Flexibility in Agricultural Management. Because our country is vast, has a backward economy with work in the collective economy mainly done by hand, and is limited by its natural conditions, greater adaptability and flexibility are needed for managing agricultural production. Since the Third Plenary Session, the Party Central Committee has carried out and readjusted a series of rural economic policies. These include respect for the right of production teams to make their own decisions, the raising of purchasing prices for agricultural and sideline products, the readjustment of the amounts of these products to be delivered and sold to the state and the policies on taxation and loans. The size of private plots has been increased, support has been given to household sideline occupations and rural fairs are no longer banned. The system of responsibility in production, such as fixing output quotas for each special line of production, and basing payment on production (including fixing farm output quotas for each group, or every able-bodied laborer or each household), has been popularized to improve the ways of payment. These policies and measures which have greatly mobilized the peasants' initiative for production has played a positive role in promoting the restoration and development of agricultural production. Simultaneously, we have rid ourselves of the narrow idea of looking at the limited amount of arable land without considering the potential of the other land and just stressing grain crops without seeing the broad prospects for a diversified economy. Efforts have been made to reform the traditional agricultural structure and distribution of production, build up a diversified economy according to the conditions of various localities, develop a socialist rural commodity economy and apply modern science and technology to our country's concrete conditions. The development of the diversified and commodity economy and the application of science and technology in the rural areas will promote an all-round development of our agricultural production, increase social wealth, the peasants' income and the accumulation of funds and help to rationally use the surplus agricultural labor force. This is a strategic measure for bringing about a prosperous rural economy.

Here, I would like to particularly discuss the question of fixing farm output quotas for each household which, as a form of management, suits those scattered, backward and remote mountain villages and some production teams which have, for a long time, failed to run their collective economy well and have had huge difficulties. It is practiced on the basis of the public ownership of land and other chief means of production and is a form of the system of responsibility in production. There is no exploitation, because the buying, selling or leasing of land or the hiring of laborers are banned. It will in the future develop in the direction of socialization as the productive forces are restored and developed and agricultural science and technology (including farm machinery) are applied.

5. Bringing the Role of Small Towns Into Play. We should take the fact that 80 percent of our population reside in rural areas as our starting point while drawing up a long-term plan for developing our economy, politics, culture, education and science. All the major developed countries in the world today have experienced a course of modernization in which a surplus labor force poured into the big cities, resulting in overcrowded metropolitan areas, increased crimes, serious pollution and other social ills. In the process of advancing our country's modernization, the Party Central Committee pointed out, we should try to avoid such problems and gradually bring the role of the country's more than 50,000 small towns into play. With the development of a diversified economy, commodity production and commodity exchanges in the rural areas, these small towns will gradually become rural political, economic and cultural centres. This developmental strategy will help combine our country's human resources with natural resources, and agriculture, industry and commerce with the undertakings of culture, education and science. It is conducive to the rational distribution of our population and economy and to narrowing the gaps between town and countryside and between industry and agriculture.

6. Self-Reliance Supplemented by Necessary Importation. In line with our nation's poor economic foundation and the backward condition of science and technology, we have, since the Third Plenary Session, imported necessary advanced techniques, facilities and foreign funds while persisting in the principle of relying mainly on our own efforts in construction. We have emphasized relying on our own manpower, material resources, financial capacity and natural resources to develop the social productive forces and attached particular importance to realizing modernization by tapping the potential of existing enterprises and reforming them and by making use of the existing machinery, equipment and technical forces. At the same time, facts have proved that supplementing self-reliance with necessary importation can speed up the development of our social productive forces and is indispensable and beneficial to our socialist modernization. Some comrades are worried that introducing foreign funds and setting up joint ventures with foreign investment will lead us off the socialist road. Such a concern is unnecessary. Importing some foreign funds and allowing joint ventures (in the special economic zones there are also a small number of enterprises run totally with foreign funds) is conducive to mastering modern science and technology, learning modern management methods and training managerial, scientific and technical personnel. Socialist construction in a backward country like ours needs such enterprises and they will not lead us to capitalism. The joint ventures serve as a type of aid to our socialist construction;

they are controlled by our country and are organized according to law on the condition that our country's sovereignty will not be endangered. The cost we pay for them is to accept certain degrees of capitalist exploitation which calls up what Lenin said when Russia was carrying out the policy of "concession" during the new economic policy period: "Not only will the payment of a heavier tribute to state capitalism not ruin as, it will lead us to socialism by the surest road" (*The Tax in Kind*, 1921).

7. **Building an Intellectual Civilization and Developing Human Resources.** Our country's backward culture, education, science and technology suffered serious sabotage during the "cultural revolution" which caused a temporary shortage of young people capable of taking over the posts of their elders in national construction. This is out of step with the four modernizations. Without a highly developed culture, education, science and technology, it is impossible to build an advanced socialist material and intellectual civilization. Since the Third Plenary Session, the Party Central Committee, while attaching great important to building a socialist material civilization, has set out to establish a socialist intellectual civilization and put stress on educating and training people. On the one hand, efforts have been made to reopen and develop institutions of higher learning, gradually popularize secondary school education, promote secondary technical school education, professional education and adult education, and reform the present educational system so that the opening of schools and specialties may better serve the needs of economic and social development. On the other hand, it has been pointed out that a socialist intellectual civilization should be built under the guidance of communist ideology. Political and ideological work should be strengthened and improved, especially the ideological education of the youth which is aimed at arming them with the scientific theories of Marxism-Leninism-Mao Zedong Thought and communist morality. To help our young people establish noble communist ideals and moral integrity is an indispensable part of socialist intellectual civilization; it is of decisive significance to the building of material and intellectual socialist civilization and to our country's future.

8. **Improving Democracy and Legality.** During the "cultural revolution," the Party's democratic life and socialist democracy and legality were seriously disrupted. This left us with a great number of forged, falsified and wrongly handled cases, which have been redressed since the Third Plenary Session. At the same time, a great deal of work has been done to achieve a high degrees of socialist democracy. This includes the drawing up of the Guiding Principles for Inner-Party Political Life and a series of laws, and energetic efforts to revive and carry forward the Party's fine traditions and restore and improve socialist democracy and legality.

Since the Third Plenary Session, the people throughout the country, guided by the correct line of the Party Central Committee, have adhered to the four fundamental principles (adherence to Marxism-Leninism-Mao Zedong Thought, the dictatorship of the proletariat, the socialist road and the Party leadership), corrected the "Left" mistakes, overcome the historical disasters caused by the counter-revolutionary sabotage of Lin Biao and the gang of Four and achieved the widely recognized great progress on the economic, political, ideological, cultural, military and diplomatic fronts.

About the socialist society, Marx's following remark deserves conscientious study: "What we have to deal with here is a communist society, not as it has *developed* on its own foundations, but, on the contrary, just as it *emerges* from capitalist society; which is thus in every respect, economically, morally and intellectually, still stamped with the birth marks of the old society from whose womb it emerges" (*Critique of the Gotha Programme*). Marxism never regarded socialist society as a pure society but stated that the "birth marks of the old society" would certainly exist. These old vestiges can only be eliminated step by step on the basis of highly developed productive forces in socialist society. Another noteworthy point is that countries which are relatively less developed economically and culturally will have more of such "birth marks." Trying to eliminate them before conditions are ripe will harm the productive forces. Our practice since the Third Plenary Session has proved, and will continue to prove, that to adapt the relations of production and management system to the present state of our country's productive forces not only helps speed up their development but also will provide conditions for improving our socialist system and advancing it to a higher stage.

*****

DOCUMENT NO. 30

CENTRAL COMMITTEE SESSION ANNOUNCES: PARTY CONGRESS TO OPEN SEPT. 1

(**Beijing Review**, No. 33, August 16, 1982)

The Twelfth National Congress of the Chinese Communist Party will be convened on September 1. This was decided at the Seventh Plenary Session of the Eleventh Party Central Committee.

The plenary session, held on August 6 in Beijing, also examined and adopted a report of the Party Central Committee to the Twelfth Party Congress and the Constitution of the Communist Party of China (revised draft). It unanimously decided to submit the two documents to the Twelfth Party Congress for deliberation.

The Twelfth Party Congress will sum up the rich experience gained since the previous congress held in August 1977, particularly the experience gained since the Third Plenary Session of the Eleventh Party Central Committee held towards the end of 1978. On this basis it will draw up a programme and set the goals for the coming period. The congress will adopt the new Party Constitution, elect a new Party Central Committee, a Central Advisory Commission and a new Central Discipline Inspection Commission.

Attended by 185 members and 112 alternate members of the Party Central Committee and 21 observers, the Seventh Plenary Session of the Eleventh Party Central Committee was presided over by Standing Committee members of the Political Bureau of the Party Central Committee Hu Yaobang, Ye Jianying, Deng Xiaoping, Zhao Ziyang, Li Xiannian, Chen Yun and Hua Guofeng.

A six-day preparatory meeting was held before the plenary session, at which views were fully exchanged and related issues carefully discussed.

Salute Veteran Comrades. The session also discussed and passed letters of respect to Liu Bocheng and Cai Chang, both veteran comrades who have contributed greatly to the cause of the Party.

Liu Bocheng joined the Revolution of 1911 and the war against the Northern warlords in his youth. One of the leaders of the Nanchang Uprising of 1927, he is one of the founders of the Chinese People's Liberation Army and one of its outstanding leaders.

Cai Chang who began her revolutionary career in 1919 is one of the Party's earliest members. She participated in the 25,000-li Long March. She has been an outstanding leader of the Chinese women's movement as well as a noted activist in the international progressive women's movement.

Both Liu Bocheng and Cai Chang have been elected delegates to the National party Congresses and members of the Party Central Committee many times. However, because of their advanced ages and poor health, they will not attend the forthcoming Twelfth Party Congress, nor will they continue to hold Party and government leadership positions. In view of this, the Seventh Plenary Session extended to them cordial regards and great respect on behalf of the entire Party membership.

Fresh Brilliant Chapter. In an editorial on the forthcoming Twelfth Party Congress, *Renmin Ribao*, organ of the Party Central Committee, said: "Five years have elapsed since the convocation of the Eleventh National Congress of the Chinese Communist Party. These five years, especially the last four years since the Third Plenary Session of the Eleventh Party Central Committee, constitute an extremely important period in the history of our Party."

The Third Plenary Session marked a great turning point in the history of our Party since the birth of New China, the editorial said. In the period between the Third and the Sixth Plenary Sessions, the Party fulfilled the historical task of correcting its guiding ideology and reiterated and clarified the Marxist ideological line, political line and organizational line. During this period, it also worked out and implemented a series of correct policies and principles governing both internal and external affairs. As a result, major achievements and measurable progress have been made in various fields of endeavour, the editorial added. History has shown that our Party has great vitality. It is capable of and is taking effective measures to heal the serious wounds inflicted upon it, correct mistakes and open up new avenues for its work.

The Twelfth Party Congress will open up bright and new vistas in China's socialist modernization drive and write a magnificent new page in the history of the Party.

*****

INDEX

bonuses, 419

capital construction, 358–359, 419

consolidation of enterprises, 375–378

danger of departmentalism, decentralism and liberalism, 410–411

development of a commodity economy, 444–445

development of heavy industry, 371

different forms of ownership, 444

distribution of production, 282

distribution of working time, 176

energy and transport promotion, 371–372

financial problems, 379–381, 417–419

immutability of economic laws, 170

increased output vs. overall economic results, 403–407

law of proportionate development, 175–178

long range vs. short range planning, 282–283

low level of management skill, 175

management of, 298–299

need for scientific and general education, 386–389

need for specialization, 177

need for study of, 196–197

need to improve rural development, 368–369

need to learn from capitalist management, 173–174

need to prevent competition among sectors, 411–413

obey the law of value, 178–179

open-door policy, 381–383

plan for local initiative, 176–177

plan for reform, 413–414

problem of afforestation, 368

promote consumer goods, 369–371

reasons for unsatisfactory economic constructions, 365

reliance on importations, 446–447

remuneration based on output, 103–104

reorganization and staffing of enterprises, 414–417

restructuring of, 265, 361–363, 443–444

role of technological transformation, 374–375

rural policies, 285

socialist principles of distribution, 204–205

specialized enterprises, 189–190

stability of, 356

unity of interest among state, enterprise and worker, 181–185

water resources, 367–368

"Outline of Project 571," 134
Ouyang Qin, 114
Ouyang Yi, 122

Pai Hua, 345, 349
Pan Guangdan, 132
Pan Shu, 132
Pan Tianshou, 132
Pan Zili, 114
Peaceful Coexistence, 51
Peaceful evolution, 316–317
P'eng Chen, 17, 20, 63, 111, 114, 116, 120, 123
P'eng Ch'ung, 23
Peng Dehuai. *See* P'eng Te-huai
Peng Jiaqing, 122
P'eng Te-huai, 15, 58, 114, 120
Peng Zhen. *See* Peng Chen
People's communes
    cadres of, 245–246
    capital accumulation, 235
    commercial organizations of, 235–236
    definition and purpose, 225–226
    distribution of income in, 240–242
    education in, 242
    enterprises run by, 234–235
    individual enterprises in, 243
    management of, 226–228, 237–240, 266–267
    members' rights and duties, 244
    organizational structure of, 264–265, 283
    political work of, 246–248
    separation of administration and commune management in, 265–268
    to pursue well rounded agricultural development, 228–230
    workers' welfare, 242–243
People's Daily. *See* Jen-min Jih-pao
People's Liberation Army (PLA), 5, 16, 20, 51, 64, 91
People's Republic of China (PRC)
    appraisal of, 1949–1981, 48–51
    attempted liberalization movement, 14–16
    balance of policies, 24–25
    building socialism, 1956–1966, 56–60
    character of its socialist society, 432–435
    constitution, 11, 55

accusations against, 160–161
indictment of, 110ff
sentence, 166
See also Gang of Four
Wang Jen-chung, 114, 336
Wang Jiaji, 132
Wang Jiaxiang, 114, 117
Wang Jingwei, 44
Wang Jinxiang, 117
Wang Kunlun, 116
Wang Li, 119
Wang Ming, 45, 347
Wang Ping, 122
Wang Pusheng, 143
Wang Qimeo, 123
Wang Renzhong. *See* Wang Jen-chung
Wang Shangrong, 115, 124
Wang Shaoyang, 131
Wang Shitai, 115, 116
Wang Shiying, 116, 117
Wang Shourong, 132
Wang Shuchen, 129
Wang Shunhua, 144
Wang Shusheng, 114
Wang Tianqiang, 132
Wang Tung-hsing, 4, 10, 17
Wang Weigang, 116
Wang Weiguo, 134, 136
Wang Weizhou, 116
Wang Wenlin, 143
Wang Xiaoyu, 130
Wang Xike, 121
Wang Xingyao, 132
Wang Xiuzhen, 139
Wang Yanchun, 122
Wang Yaoqing, 143
Wang Zhao, 122
Wang Zhaohua, 116
Wang Zhen, 98, 114, 115
Wang Zheng, 122
Wang Zhenzhong, 143
Wang Zigang, 117